THE BLUE GUIDES

Austria
Belgium and Luxembourg
China
Cyprus
Czechoslovakia
Denmark
Egypt

FRANCE
France
Paris and Versailles
Burgundy
Normandy
Corsica

GREECE
Greece
Athens
Crete

HOLLAND
Holland
Amsterdam

Hungary

ITALY
Northern Italy
Southern Italy
Florence
Rome and environs
Venice
Tuscany
Umbria
Sicily

Jerusalem
Malta and Gozo

Morocco
Moscow and Leningrad
Portugal

SPAIN
Spain
Barcelona

Switzerland

TURKEY
Turkey: the Aegean
   and Mediterranean Coasts
Istanbul

UK
England
Ireland
Scotland
Wales
London
Museums and Galleries
   of London
Oxford and Cambridge
Gardens of England
Literary Britain and Ireland
Victorian Architecture
   in Britain
Churches and Chapels
   of Northern England
Churches and Chapels
   of Southern England
Channel Islands
USA
New York
Boston and Cambridge

Yugoslavia

Roman copy of Daphnis, from a 2C BC group of Pan and Daphnis attributed to Heliodoros of Rhodes, Musée Royal d'Ârt et d'Histoire, Brussels

BLUE GUIDE

Belgium and Luxembourg

Bernard McDonagh

Maps and plans by John Flower

A & C Black
London

WW Norton
New York

First edition (Belgium and the Western Front) 1920;
Second edition (Belgium and Luxembourg) 1924;
Third edition 1929
Fourth edition 1963
Fifth edition 1977, by John Tomes
Sixth edition 1983, by John Tomes
Seventh edition 1989, by John Tomes
Eighth edition 1993

Published by A & C Black (Publishers) Limited
35 Bedford Row, London WC1R 4JH

A CIP catalogue record of this book
is available from the British Library.

ISBN 0–7136–3732–3

Published in the United States of America by
WW Norton and Company, Inc
500 Fifth Avenue, New York, NY 10110

Published simultaneously in Canada by
Penguin Books Canada Limited
2801 John Street, Markham, Ontario L3R 1B4

ISBN 0–393–30989–4 USA

The author and the publishers have done their best to ensure the accuracy of all the information in Blue Guide Belgium and Luxembourg; however, they can accept no responsibility for any loss, injury or inconvenience sustained by any traveller as a result of information or advice contained in the guide.

Please write in with your comments, suggestions and corrections. Writers of the best letters will be awarded a free Blue Guide of their choice.

For permission to reproduce photographs in the guide, the publishers would like to thank the Institut Royal du Patrimonie Artistique, Brussels (pages 97, 209, 268), A.F. Kersting (pages 195, 289, 354), Ray Roberts (pages 66, 79, 202, 234), Bernard Mc Donagh (pages 2, 158, 377), the Luxembourg Tourist Office (pages 404, 423, 430), the Belgian Tourist Office (page 352), Fédération Touristique du Brabant (page 325), Ralph Broughton (page 347), and Hugo Martens (page 168).

Lecturer, broadcaster, author and former civil servant, **Bernard Mc Donagh** has two consuming passions—travelling and writing. His official duties took him to Kinshasa where he was awarded the Order of Zaire, to Hamburg and Stuttgart where he was British Consul, and to Brussels where he served on several EC committees. In addition to writing this new edition of Blue Guide Belgium and Luxembourg, he is the author of the prize-winning Blue Guide Turkey and a children's book Turkish Village. In 1992 he was given an award by the Turkish Government for his work in making Turkey better known and appreciated abroad.

Dedication. This book is for three great ladies, Molly Skuss, Joyce Moore and Molly Mahony, who have preceded us over the pale stream of Acheron.

Printed in Great Britain by The Bath Press, Avon

PREFACE

I approached the task of producing a new edition of Blue Guide Belgium and Luxembourg with a great deal of pleasure, as I had made many visits to both countries during the last twenty years and felt that I knew them well. However, as my research progressed I was constantly surprised by the richness and diversity of their culture and by the varied forms in which this was expressed. My travels took me to great cathedrals, ancient castles, fortified farms and carefully preserved almshouses. I looked again, perhaps with a fresh eye, at the rich collections in the art galleries of Brussels, Bruges, Ghent and Antwerp and marvelled at a national genius which could produce works as different as those by Hans Memling and Paul Delvaux. I travelled once more with a sense of quickening pleasure through lush farmland of northern Belgium and the rolling hills and wooded valleys of the Ardennes and of Luxembourg. I was frequently delighted by new discoveries like the Gaume and I happily renewed my acquaintance with the ancient winding streets of Bruges. This was an entrancing journey of discovery and rediscovery.

I have written a completely new text for this edition of the Blue Guide. The book has been updated and a great deal of fresh information has been added. The maps and town plans have been amended and there are new illustrations. All this could not have been achieved without a great deal of help. I would like to thank particularly the directors of the Belgian Tourist Office and of the Luxembourg Tourist Office in Great Britain, Pierre Claus and Serge Moes, and their colleagues in Brussels and Luxembourg City. I owe a particular debt of gratitude to Madame Cécile Pierard, Pressconsultant for Flanders who co-ordinated the responses from the regional offices and who provided speedy and full answers to my many questions. To Mmes Elisabeth Puttaert and Tina Vanhoye of Brussels Tourist Office and Jean-Claude Conter at the National Tourist Office in Luxembourg, as well as to the directors and staff of the local tourist offices in Belgium and the Grand-Duchy who spared no pains to show me the beauties of their cities and regions, I offer my sincere thanks. I am also grateful to Monsieur Jean-Charles Balty of the Musée Royal d'Art et d'Histoire in Brussels who provided invaluable information about his museum's collection. I would also like to thank my friend of many years standing Walter de Meester who taught me to know and love his native Bruges.

My journeys were often enlivened and enriched by the kindness and assistance which I received from the citizens of both countries. I recall with particular pleasure my visit to the wonderful church at Trois Vierges in Luxembourg, where Monsieur l'Abbé proudly showed me the treasures there enshrined. This book owes much to *ces amis de voyage*, to those mentioned above and to many others who prefer to remain anonymous.

The assembly of information and the writing of the text were greatly eased by the unstinted help, support and encouragement which I received from my editor, Gemma Davies. The value of the book is substantially enhanced by the work of John Flower who is responsible for all of the town plans and maps. My researches were greatly aided by help received from the librarians and staff of the London Library, Banstead Library, the Central Catholic Library and the Library of the Royal Geographic Society.

I would like to pay a tribute to my predecessors Russell Muirhead and John Tomes whose footsteps I have sometimes followed and sometimes abandoned for paths more enticing to me. Finally, I would like to thank

Robert Moore, Ann and Dennis Franklin, Mike Grisdale, Ralph Broughton, Marjorie Grimes, Riet van Bremen and many other friends who encouraged, advised and entertained me during the year which this book took to write.

For too long Belgium and Luxembourg have been stepping stones to Europe, countries through which one passed quickly on the way to more distant lands. However, the pattern of travelling is changing. Weeks and weekends in places like Bruges, Brussels, Namur and Luxembourg City are now very popular and will attract even more visitors when the Channel Tunnel opens. If this book persuades more travellers to Europe, whatever their method of transport or ultimate destination, to pause and sample the rich variety of Belgium and Luxembourg, it will have fulfilled its purpose.

Now that my labours have finished, may I echo that heartfelt prayer of the anonymous medieval scribe: *Nunc scripsi totum pro Christo da mihi potum.*

A NOTE ON BLUE GUIDES

The Blue Guide series began in 1915 when Muirhead Guide-Books Limited published 'Blue Guide London and its Environs'. Finlay and James Muirhead already had extensive experience of guidebook publishing: before the First World War they had been the editors of the English editions of the German Baedekers, and by 1915 they had acquired the copyright of most of the famous 'Red' Handbooks from John Murray.

An agreement made with the French publishing house Hachette et Cie in 1917 led to the translation of Muirhead's London guide, which became the first 'Guide Bleu'—Hachette had previously published the blue-covered 'Guides Joannes'. Subsequently, Hachette's 'Guide Bleu Paris et ses Environs' was adapted and published in London by Muirhead. The collaboration between the two publishing houses continued until 1933.

In 1933 Ernest Benn Limited took over the Blue Guides, appointing Russell Muirhead, Finlay Muirhead's son, editor in 1934. The Muirhead's connection with the Blue Guides ended in 1963 when Stuart Rossiter, who had been working on the Guides since 1954, became house editor, revising and compiling several of the books himself.

The Blue Guides are now published by A & C Black, who acquired Ernest Benn in 1984, so continuing the tradition of guidebook publishing which began in 1826 with 'Black's Economical Tourist of Scotland'. The Blue Guide series continues to grow: there are now more than 50 titles in print with revised editions appearing regularly and many new Blue Guides in preparation.

'Blue Guides' is a registered trade mark.

CONTENTS

Maps and Plans

NOTES ON USING THE GUIDE

Town and District Names. Many places, especially those near the Language Frontier, have Flemish and French names. Places in the E of the country also have German names. Road signs change, sometimes unrecognisably, as soon as the Language Frontier is crossed.

In general the Blue Guide uses the English versions of place names, where these exist, e.g. Brussels, Antwerp, Ghent, otherwise it employs the local versions. For places near the Language Frontier or in cases where there might be confusion, the alternative versions are given. A list of principal places with the various renderings of their names appears on at the back of the book.

Distances. The introduction to each Route gives its total distance. In both the introduction and the text italicised distances are those between places mentioned in the Route. Other distances, e.g. on diversions, are, with one or two exceptions, given in Roman type. All distances are approximate.

General Index. Routes sometimes cross or run close together. As a result places within easy reach of the Route being followed may be described under another Route. Accordingly, to avoid missing that interesting church, castle or town, it is advisable to consult the General Index from time to time.

Index of Artists. Painters, sculptors, architects, etc. appear in a special index and are not included in the General Index. Their names are given in the customary English versions. Sometimes these may differ from those used in Belgium.

Asterisks. Works of art of special importance, buildings of interest or general attractions are marked by an *.

Opening Times of museums, art galleries, churches, castles, historic sites, etc. are given wherever possible. These have been provided by the authorities responsible and were correct at the time this edition of the Blue Guide was written. However, changes can and do occur, often at very short notice. While these may not affect visitors who do not have a fixed plan or programme, anyone who wishes to visit a particular museum, art gallery, church, etc. or to see a certain painting or other work of art, is advised to check beforehand with the local tourist information office, which will be able to provide up-to-date information.

Particulars given are inclusive, e.g. April–September means 1 April–30 September. Usually the closing time shown is when the building shuts. However, in the case of large buildings or sites last admissions may be a half hour or more before this. In many cases an admission charge is made. This may be reduced for students and senior citizens. Sometimes admission is free on one day each week.

See also Churches, Museums and Art Galleries p62.

Town Plans. Pedestrianised roads are indicated by line shading.

Important parking areas are indicated by the symbol P .

Information Centres are indicated by the symbol 𝒊 .

BACKGROUND INFORMATION

Introduction to Belgium

The visitor to Belgium can enjoy two countries in one. Although constitutionally a single, federal nation, North and South Belgium are very different. North Belgium is Flemish in language, culture and attitude, scenically unremarkable but full of historic cities. The splendid architecture of their buildings, their fine museums and art galleries are legacies from centuries of struggle for independence and a long tradition of fierce civic pride. North Belgium also has an interesting coastline with long sandy beaches and smart resorts. Not far inland are the great battlefields of the First World War.

South Belgium, with its own culture and traditions, is Walloon, French speaking Belgium. It, too, has interesting towns though these may not be quite so striking as those in the North. Walloon Belgium's greatest attraction is its scenery, particularly in the densely forested Ardennes.

The capital of these two very different areas is the bilingual and cosmopolitan city of Brussels, with its splendid public buildings and churches, art galleries and museums. Visitors will enjoy the variety and elegance of its shops and its excellent and varied cuisine. Finally, as the city of the European Community, it is for many the 'capital' of Europe.

Aspects of Belgium

Communities and Languages. The division of Belgium into c 60 per cent Flemish and c 40 per cent French speaking communities is attributed to a number of reasons: the separation in the 3C of the lands colonised by the Germanic Franks and those of the Wala, the Romanised Celts; the Revolt of the Netherlands between 1555 and 1648; and the growth of both Flemish sensibilities and aspirations after the revolution of 1830 which questioned the dominance of French, long the language of the nobility, Flemish and Walloon.

The line between the two communities, which is popularly known as the Language Frontier, was drawn officially in 1962 and has been confirmed by detailed provisions in the new constitution. The different language areas are shown on the map of the Provinces at the back of the book. To the N of the line the language, though called Flemish, is to all intents and purposes Dutch with some local variations and accents. Along the line itself and in the larger towns French is also spoken. However, regional sensitivity is never far below the surface and it is a solecism to assume that French will always be understood. If one does not speak Flemish, then it is both courteous and sensible either to try English, which is widely used and often preferred, or to enquire if French may be spoken. To the S of the line the language is French, though again with local accents and variations, e.g. 'septante' and 'nonante' for 'soixante-dix' and 'quatre-vingt-dix'.

Belgium has also two other language communities. One is the city of Brussels. Officially bilingual with both Flemish and French speaking communes, in practice French predominates at any rate in those districts most visited by tourists. The other community is that of the German-speaking Cantons de l'Est.

The **Royal Family**. For the royal line prior to the accession in 1951 of King Baudouin, see History of Belgium, p 14 et seq. Baudouin, who was born in 1930, married in 1960 the Spanish noblewoman Fabiola de Mora y Aragon, born 1928. The couple are childless. The heir to the throne is the King's brother Prince Albert, Prince de Liège, born 1934. In 1959 he married the Italian Princess Paola Ruffo di Calabria. Albert and Paola have three children, Philippe, born 1960, Astrid, born 1962 and Laurent, born 1963.

National Anthem and Flag. The first French language version of the national anthem was written in August 1830 by the Frenchman L.A. Dechet, 'Jenneval', an actor at the Théâtre de la Monnaie, the birthplace of the revolution of 1830. Fighting with the revolutionaries, Dechet was killed at Lier some six weeks later. François van Campenhout, a violinist at the same theatre, composed the music and named the song 'La Brabançonne' since it was in Brussels in the province of Brabant that the revolution started. For the same reason the national flag uses the colours of Brabant, vertical bands of black, gold and red. In 1860 Charles Rogier rewrote the French words and his is the version in use today. There have been several Flemish texts. The current version received official approval in 1938.

National Constitution. When, in 1970, 1980 and 1988 the Belgian constitution was examined and amended, the federalist trend was accentuated. Belgium is a federation ruled by a constitutional monarch. Below the Crown are the various levels of the federation, each with its defined powers. At the top is a bicameral national government, responsible for matters such as foreign policy, defence and communications, but subject to many checks and balances to ensure fair representation between the nation's communities. Below this level the scene becomes complex. The country is divided into three Communities, Flemish, French and German speaking, and four Regions, Flemish, Walloon, German and Brussels. As an added complication on the Flemish side the Community and Region function as one, while on the French side they function separately. In the regions the principal of 'unilingualism' operates. The regional language is the official language and is used in administration, education, etc.

For some time it seemed that the Provinces would disappear, or at any rate become subordinate to the Regions. Opposition to abolition was, however, both vocal and effective and the Provinces survive, somewhat unhappily, on the sidelines.

Folklore. Folklore, in Flemish Volkskunde, is a word much used in Belgium. It is applied to museums dealing with local customs, crafts and history, whether they are in small villages or in cities such as Ghent or Antwerp. Manneken-Pis in Brussels, Op-Signor in Mechelen, Jean de Nivelles high on his church tower and many others are folklore characters. In puppet theatres such as Toone in Brussels folklore legends are enshrined in the traditional plays.

Folklore is at the roots of the countless processions and festivals, religious and secular, that crowd the Belgian calendar. They range from simple village celebrations to widely known festivals like the carnival at Binche, the Lumeçon at Mons, the Kattestoet at Ypres, the stately pageant of the Golden Tree at Bruges or the aristocratic Ommegang, which is staged in the Grand-Place in Brussels. While most carnivals are held just before Lent, folklore celebrations of varying kinds occur throughout the year. The National Tourist Office publishes an annual Calendar, which lists all the principal folklore events. This also has information about sports meetings, music and art festivals, trade fairs, flower shows, etc.

Carillons, in their various forms, are a feature of many Flemish and some Walloon towns. They originated with the early belfries in which small bells were struck with a hammer to signal the hours. At first there were four bells, known as the 'Quadrilloner', from which the word 'carillon' is derived. Among the oldest belfries are those of Bruges, Ghent and Mechelen.

Carillons of six or eight bells did not appear until the beginning of the 16C. At about the same time the mallet was replaced by the clavier. Oudenaarde in 1510 boasted of having the first keyboard and Mechelen in 1583 claimed to have the first with pedals. Modern times have seen the installation of electric and automatic carillons. There is a carillon school and museum at Mechelen.

Gastronomy. Belgium enjoys a gastronomic reputation second to none, this applying to all regions and to restaurants of all categories; it is rare to be served a poor meal, even rarer to be offered insufficient quantity. For more detail, see p 64.

History of Belgium

Today's independent Kingdom of Belgium dates only from 1831. Thus much of this History is that of the lands and peoples out of which Belgium, as also Holland and the Grand-Duchy of Luxembourg, grew. Constant changes of sovereignty brought corresponding and confusing changes of name. In this History nomenclature has generally been simplified as below.

Netherlands. The combined areas of roughly present-day Belgium and Holland, with also the Grand-Duchy of Luxembourg and parts of northern France. The term is politically valid until the de facto separation of North and South at the end of the 16C.

Spanish Netherlands. The southern part of the Netherlands from its subjection by the Duke of Parma subsequent to the Union of Arras (1579) until the Treaty of Utrecht (1713). **Belgium**. Roughly this same territory from the Treaty of Utrecht to the present day. Over this period Belgium was successively the Austrian Netherlands; briefly the United States of Belgium; again the Austrian Netherlands; incorporated into France; a part of the United Kingdom of the Netherlands; and finally the Kingdom of Belgium.

United Provinces. The northern and Protestant part of the Netherlands, which Parma failed to subdue and which declared its independence under the Union of Utrecht (1579). **Holland** (the Dutch). Roughly this same territory subsequent to the recognition of its independence by the Peace of Münster (1648). *Note*. 1. The name United Provinces in fact continued in use until the republic fell to the French in 1795. 2. Modern Holland is officially the Kingdom of the Netherlands. 'Holland' is simply a popular name deriving from the ancient county, the nucleus from which today's state grew and now forming two of its provinces, and references early in this History to 'Holland' are to this county or province.

Luxembourg. Until 1815 roughly the combined area of today's Grand-Duchy and of the Belgian province of Luxembourg; after 1839 only the Belgian province. **Grand-Duchy of Luxembourg**. The independent Grand-Duchy created in 1815, but whose territories were much changed in 1839. (See also p 407.)

Roman and Frankish Period (BC to AD 843)

Between 57 and 50 BC that part of northern Gaul lying in the basins of the Scheldt and the Meuse was conquered by Julius Caesar. At that time the territory now known as Belgium was inhabited by Gallo-Celtic tribes (Belgae). In 15 BC these conquered lands became the imperial province of Gallia Belgica and the Roman occupation lasted until the 5C. During the 3C, however, as Rome began to weaken, Frankish penetration began (Franks being the generic name for the loose federation of several Germanic tribes), these early Franks being accepted by the Romans as 'foederati', or mercenaries who fought for Rome under their own chiefs. By about 431, under Chlodio, leader of the dominant Salii tribe, Tournai became the capital of the Frankish Merovingian kings, a dynasty named after Meroveus, successor to Chlodio. Meroveus was followed by Childeric I (died 481), who threw off the Roman association, and he was thrown off by Clovis who declared himself Christian, thus gaining Church support and conquering all Gaul except for Burgundy and Provence. Farther north, the eventual withdrawal of the Romans led to the completion of Frankish colonisation of the lower Scheldt and the Lys. The 'Silva Carbonaria', a belt of forest stretching from the Scheldt to the Ardennes, separated these Franks from the Wala (Walloons) or Romanised Celts, thus defining, at least in part, the ethnic and language frontier that persists today. On the death of Clovis in c 511, his realm splintered, and what is now Belgium became a neglected corner.

The Frankish lands developed into two 'kingdoms': Austrasia (capital Metz) in the E, and Neustria (Merovingian) to the S and west. Dagobert, a child who became King of Austrasia in 623, was under the domination of Pepin I of Landen, who was 'Mayor of the Palace', the title enjoyed by the chief court official. In 629 Pepin fell out of favour, returning however on Dagobert's death in 638 and governing Austrasia until his own death the following year. Pepin II (of Heristal), son of a daughter of Pepin of Landen (possibly Begga of Andenne), led Austrasia against Neustria, in 687 winning a battle which marked the beginning of the end for the Merovingian line. The son of Pepin II, Charles Martel, became ruler in effect if not in name of all the Frankish lands. On his death in 741 he was succeeded by his younger son, Pepin III, the Short, who by 751 had deposed the last Merovingian (Childeric III) and had himself crowned King of the Franks. He died in 768. One of his sons was Charlemagne.

Charlemagne reigned from 768 to 814, in 800 being declared by the Pope to be Emperor of the West, at the head of an empire which extended from Denmark to southern Italy and from northern Spain to the Oder. 'Belgium' occupied an important position in this empire and also one adjacent to Charlemagne's favourite residence at Aachen (Aix-la-Chapelle). Charlemagne's reign was one which saw great progress—one aspect being the start of the real use of the waterways, today so important an aspect of Belgium's industrial communications system—but on his death his lands were partitioned and in 843, after bitter fighting between his grandsons, the Treaty of Verdun divided the area of 'Belgium' between Charles the Bald and Lothair. The former, becoming King of West Francia (roughly today's France), received the narrow strip W of the Scheldt (i.e. Flanders);

the latter, with lands along the Rhine and the Rhône (Middle Kingdom), received the remainder, this later becoming the Duchy of Lower Lotharingia (Lorraine). To the E was East Francia out of which would grow Germany.

Feudal and Burgundian Period (843 to 1482)

During the 9C and 10C the Norsemen appeared, raiding and settling, a threat which fostered the growth of defensive feudalism and the emergence in the West of the powerful counts of Flanders. Although nominally vassals of the kings of France, the counts took over more and more land and by the middle of the 11C had become virtually independent.

The first count was Baldwin Iron Arm, who carried off and married a daughter of Charles the Bald, Judith by name, who had already been the wife of two English princes; c 867 he built his great stronghold at Ghent. Baldwin II, child of this marriage, built the walls of Bruges and Ypres and married a daughter of England's Alfred the Great. Matilda, the daughter of Baldwin V (1036–67), shared the English throne with William the Conqueror. Baldwin's son married the widow of the Count of Hainaut, thus becoming ruler of that province, and the son of this marriage, Robert the Frisian, ruled over Holland and Friesland. Count Robert II (1093–1119) was famous for his exploits in the First Crusade, acquiring the title of 'Lance and Sword of Christendom'. Baldwin IX (1172–1206), another Crusader, became, as Baldwin I, the first king of the Latin empire of Constantinople. His pious daughters, the countesses Margaret and Joanna (or Joan), are known for the number of religious houses they founded.

Although Flanders thus became strong and unified, Lotharingia fared differently, breaking up into several minor countships and principalities.

With the wane of feudalism during the 12C and 13C came the rise of the towns, the clothworking Flanders (Flemish) towns of Ghent, Bruges and Ypres attaining an economic prosperity and civic dignity surpassed only by a few Italian cities. With England as their chief wool-supplier, these and many other towns became the principal markets of north-western Europe and maintained an almost complete independence of France.

This autonomy, won and preserved only through great struggle and sacrifice, was the ancestor of today's still fiercely defended local government level of communes. In the North *belfries* and, in the South, *perrons* (usually a decorated column on a platform) now and later became the symbols of civic independence. The former, durable and practical as well as symbolic, served as watch-towers with warning bells, refuges, meeting-places and jails. Perrons, mainly found in Liège, and often destroyed or carried off by new rulers, stood as focal spots for meetings, the reading of proclamations, the exercise of justice, etc.

But the French were determined to reassert their authority and the nobles to regain their privileges. Although during the reign of France's Philip the Fair the towns routed the French nobility at the Battle of the Golden Spurs (near Kortrijk, 1302), by 1322 the francophile Count Louis of Flanders and Nevers had succeeded in reducing Flanders to being virtually a French province. Local rivalries, the jealousies of the guilds (protective associations which may be regarded as the ancestors of the trade unions), the tyranny of the urban oligarchy over the country people and, later, changing trade routes and the emigration of many weavers to England, all combined to bring about a long period of instability leading first to Burgundian supremacy under Philip the Good (1419) and eventually to Habsburg rule (1477). The confusing events, in Flanders and elsewhere, up to the accession of Philip the Good are summarised below.

1338. Jacob van Artevelde of Ghent allied the Flemish towns with England's Edward III during the opening stages of the Hundred Years War.

1345. Death of William II, Count of Hainaut. His lands were divided between his sister, the Empress Margaret, who got Hainaut, and her son William, to whom went the provinces of Holland and Zeeland.

1346. Louis de Male, son of Louis of Nevers, became Count of Flanders. As francophile as his father, much of his countship was a struggle with the towns, in which he largely relied on French backing.

1355. Death of John of Brabant. His daughter Joanna, and her husband, Wenceslas of Luxembourg, became rulers of Brabant and Limburg. In 1356 they were forced to sign the Joyeuse Entrée, a declaration of rights that became a form of charter for Brabant.

1357. Louis de Male invaded Brabant, acquiring Mechelen and Antwerp.

1369. Marriage between Margaret, heiress of Louis de Male, and Philip the Bold of Burgundy.

1382. Philip van Artevelde (son of Jacob) defeated Louis de Male and took Bruges, but later the same year was defeated and killed by the French at Westrozebeke (between Ypres and Roeselare).

1383. The English, with assistance from Ghent, unsuccessfully besieged Ypres. At Louvain the citizens surrendered to Wenceslas; as a result many weavers were forced to emigrate and, with the move of Wenceslas to Vilvoorde, Brussels began to supplant Louvain as capital of Brabant.

1384. Death of Louis de Male. Margaret and Philip the Bold of Burgundy inherited Flanders, Mechelen and Antwerp; also Artois and other territories in France. This year thus marked the end of Flanders as a separate state and the start of the Burgundian period.

1390. Joanna ceded Brabant and Limburg to Philip the Bold.

1404. Philip the Bold was succeeded by John the Fearless, but in Brabant and Limburg by Philip's second son, Antoine.

1411. Antoine acquired Luxembourg by marriage.

1415. Antoine was killed at Agincourt. He was succeeded by John IV of Brabant who married Jacqueline, Countess of Hainaut, Zeeland and Holland.

In 1419 Duke Philip the Good of Burgundy (grandson of Philip the Bold) succeeded to the countship of Flanders. He ruled until 1467 and consolidated Burgundian power. In 1421 he bought Namur. In 1430 he inherited Brabant, Limburg and Antwerp. In 1433 he caused Jacqueline of Hainaut to be deposed and took over Hainaut, Holland and Zeeland. In 1443 he bought Luxembourg. In 1456 he had his nephew, Louis de Bourbon, elected Bishop of Liège, and he also made his bastard son Bishop of Utrecht.

Philip the Good was determined to assert monarchical authority. In 1438 he forced Bruges to surrender many of its privileges, and in 1453, after an unsuccessful revolt, Ghent suffered the same fate. At the same time Philip tried to foster the towns' economic prosperity, amongst other things prohibiting the import of English cloth and encouraging the Antwerp fairs. Two other dates are important. In 1430, in Bruges, he established the Order of the Golden Fleece, partly in compliment to the Flanders wool-weavers and partly in glorification of his own house and court; and in 1465 he summoned representatives of all the provinces (or States) to a States General in Brussels.

Philip was succeeded in 1467 by his son, Charles the Bold. He imposed absolute rule on Liège, acquired Alsace and, by marrying Margaret of York, cemented his alliance with her brother, Edward IV of England. Disappointed in his efforts to be declared a king, he undertook a disastrous campaign in Lorraine and was killed at Nancy in 1477, leaving his lands in turmoil. His successor, his daughter Mary, held virtually a prisoner in Flanders, was forced to sign the Great Privilege, a charter conferring far-reaching rights on the provinces. In the same year she married Maximilian of Austria, the Burgundian federation created by Philip the Good thus passing to the Habsburgs. Mary died in 1482.

The Holy Roman Emperors Maximilian and Charles V (1482 to 1555)

On Mary's death, Maximilian became regent. He made peace with France and subdued the whole of the Netherlands which, on his election as Holy Roman Emperor in 1494, he handed over to his son, Philip the Handsome. Philip married Joanna of Castile, but died in 1506. His Burgundian lands passed to his six-year-old son Charles, for whom his aunt, Margaret of Austria, acted as governor. From 1513 to 1519 England's Henry VIII occupied Tournai in the course of his war with France. In 1515 the States General declared Charles of age, in 1516 he became King of Spain, and in 1519 Emperor (as Charles V, or Charles Quint), thus succeeding to all the Habsburg dominions. Although he relinquished the Austrian territories to his brother, he still held Spain, Sardinia, Naples, Sicily and Milan, Burgundy and the Habsburg lands in Alsace and the Netherlands, which he extended to include Friesland, Utrecht and Groningen. In 1530 Charles appointed his sister, Mary of Hungary, to be regent of the Netherlands, now but a part of a scattered empire and heavily taxed to support the wars of their usually absent ruler. Ghent rebelled in 1540, but Charles personally suppressed the uprising, cancelling the city's privileges and imposing a huge fine. Charles' reign also saw the rapid spread of Protestantism, particularly in the northern Netherlands, despite severe persecution such as under the Edict of Blood which decreed death for all convicted of heresy. Charles abdicated in 1555.

The Revolt of the Netherlands (1555 to 1585. Reign of Philip II of Spain)

Charles V was followed by his son Philip II of Spain, married the previous year to Queen Mary of England. His Catholic zeal, his ruthless persecution of heretics, his introduction into the Netherlands of the Jesuits, and his Spanish garrisons, led to increasing opposition, revolt and the further spread of Protestantism. Allied to this popular opposition, springing from religious and social grievances, was the more selfish opposition of the nobles (some of them 'stadholders', or provincial governors), who were resentful of the increasing centralisation of power into Spanish hands and of the loss of their power of patronage under Philip's plans for the reorganisation of the Church. Philip's reign also saw the separation of the North from the South (i.e. between what would become modern Holland and Belgium) and the emergence of the House of Orange.

Orange, today a town and district on the Rhône in southern France, was an independent principality at the time of Charlemagne. Prince Philibert (1502–30) served Charles V and was rewarded with extensive lands in the Netherlands, lands which became more important to the family than Orange. In 1544 William (the Silent) succeeded to the principality and to the Netherlands territories. He later became leader of the Revolt of the Netherlands and the founder of Holland. Having been seized by Louis XIV in 1672, the principality of Orange was officially transferred to France by the Treaty of Ryswick in 1697, thereafter only the princely title surviving.

Start of the revolt (1558–67). Forced to grant a demand by the States General that all Spanish troops be withdrawn, Philip retired to Spain, leaving Margaret of Parma (natural daughter of Charles V) as governor, with, as chief councillors, Cardinal Granvelle (a French adviser to Philip, made Archbishop of Mechelen) and Berlaymont (a Walloon noble). Opposition hardened, headed by William of Orange, the Inquisition was defied, Protestantism (in particular Calvinism) spread to the nobility, and in 1564 Granvelle was recalled. The following year the League of the Nobility was formed, as both a religious and a political opposition, and petitioned for moderation of the anti-Protestant edicts. Berlaymont rejected the petition, contemptuously referring to the League as 'ces gueux' (those beggars), a taunt which the leaguers accepted as an honorific title. The year 1566 saw the rapid growth of extreme Calvinism, with fanatics rioting and destroying Church property, particularly in Antwerp. But this development, the 'Iconoclastic Fury', split the opposition to Spain, and Margaret, seizing the opportunity to play off the popular party against the aristocratic, regained the support of many of the nobles. William of Orange and Count Egmont (governor of Flanders) attempted to steer a middle course, but failed as the result of a Calvinist uprising in Flanders, and William retired to his estates at Nassau in Germany.

Rule by the Duke of Alva (1568–73). Determined on the absolute suppression of heresy, Philip sent the Duke of Alva and an army of 10,000 to the Netherlands. Alva promptly ushered in a period of savage suppression, setting up the so-called Council of Blood to deal with heretics and insurgents, outlawing William, and executing Egmont, Horn and many other nobles. In Nassau, William attempted to raise an army, but he had no money and in any case gained no support from the towns, all now strongly garrisoned by Alva's troops. But in 1572 the tide began to turn when the Sea Beggars (privateers commissioned by William and hitherto operating from England or East Friesland) captured Brielle at the mouth of the Meuse (Maas). This, and the capture of Flushing (Vlissingen) soon after, gave the rebels footholds in the Netherlands and was the key to the success from now on of the revolt in the North. By the end of the year the rebels controlled most of the province of Holland and William was declared stadholder. Alva, without sea power, could do little in the North, but he put down the simultaneous uprising in the South, retaking Mons which had been seized by William's brother, Louis of Nassau. He then sacked Mechelen, while his son Frederick dealt similarly with Zutphen. But neither Alva nor his son could defeat the now thoroughly aroused northern townspeople. The dykes were cut, Frederick had to withdraw, and Alva, his fleet defeated in the Zuider Zee and his army now unpaid and mutinous, left for Spain.

Separation of North from South (1573–85). Alva was replaced by Luis de Requesens and the fighting continued, with the North determined on religious freedom but the South ready for compromise. Although there were setbacks—amongst these the defeat and death of Louis of Nassau near Nijmegen—the North virtually shook off the Spanish hold and Catholicism was even officially forbidden in the province of Holland. When Requesens died in 1576, William, now stadholder of the combined provinces of Holland and Zeeland, saw his opportunity, advancing into Flanders, occupying Ghent, and starting negotiations with the States General. On 8 November 1576 the Pacification of Ghent was signed, the final impetus to agreement being the arrival of the news of the 'Spanish Fury', the sacking of Antwerp by mutinous Spanish soldiery. The Pacification aimed at securing religious freedom and accepted in principle union between North and South.

The new governor was Philip's bastard brother, Don John of Austria, who, at the time of the signing of the Pacification, was at Luxembourg with a new Spanish army. William persuaded the States General to withhold recognition until Don John accepted the terms of the Pacification. This led to deadlock, until William's hand was strengthened in 1577 by the signing of the Union of Brussels, under which all provinces represented in the States General demanded the departure of foreign troops and the implementation of the Pacification, but at the same time recognised Philip's sovereignty. At this Don John yielded, signing the Perpetual Edict, which accepted most of William's demands. But the unity apparently achieved was shortlived—largely because the growth of Calvinism was alarming the Catholics, and especially the Catholic nobles—and confusion at once followed. Accompanied by Walloon troops Don John withdrew to Namur, which he successfully assaulted. The States General repudiated William; and, secretly helped by southern Catholic nobles, the Archduke Mathias (brother of the emperor, and later emperor himself) arrived in Brussels and in January 1578 declared himself governor.

Philip now sent Alexander Farnese, Duke of Parma, with yet another large army, and helped by this Don John asserted his authority over much of the South. Gembloux, Louvain, Tienen, Bouvignes, Nivelles, Soignies, Binche, Beaumont and Chimay all capitulated to him before his death in 1578. Three months later the last hope for unity between North and South disappeared when the deputies of Hainaut, Artois and Douai signed the Union of Arras (5 January 1579) declaring faith in Catholicism and allegiance to Philip. The North replied with the Union of Utrecht and continued the struggle. But Parma's rear had now been secured by the Union of Arras and between 1580 and 1585 (William of Orange was assassinated in 1584) he made himself master of Tournai, Ypres, Bruges, Ghent and finally Antwerp which, under Marnix van St Aldegonde, capitulated only after a two year siege. Here Parma's progress halted. The United Provinces (as the northern provinces were now termed) were supported by France and England. Philip's resources were weakened by the destruction of the Spanish Armada (1588) and Parma had to move S to fight the French.

The Spanish Netherlands (1579 to 1713)

Although the southern Netherlands (Spanish Netherlands) recognised the Spanish king as their sovereign, there was no longer any question of Spanish domination. There was a Spanish governor in Brussels, but the country was virtually independent, and even if the king did control the army and foreign policy, his hands were tied because only the provinces could levy taxes. On religious matters, though, the king remained supreme and the Spanish Netherlands remained exclusively Catholic.

Parma died in 1592, and Philip, just before his own death in 1598, handed over the whole of the Netherlands to his daughter Isabella (created 'archduke' in her own right) and her husband Archduke Albert, in the hope that as independent sovereigns they might be able to regain the United Provinces. This hope foundered on the insistence that Catholicism was to be the only religion, and after more years of generally indecisive fighting (during which Spain's Admiral Spinola took Ostend, still holding out for the United Provinces) the Twelve Years Truce was agreed in 1609. The 'archdukes' profited by the truce to consolidate Catholicism, in this being much helped by the Jesuits whose influence now became predominant. This was also a period of intellectual and artistic brilliance, with Rubens and Moretus in Antwerp and Justus Lipsius teaching at Louvain.

The Thirty Years War broke out in 1618, and in 1621 Albert and Isabella resumed their campaign against the United Provinces, the fighting dragging on until 1648. The main events, virtually all unfavourable to Spain, are outlined below.

1621. Archduke Albert died. Isabella became governor for Spain's Philip IV.

1629–32. Frederick Henry of Nassau took 's Hertogenbosch, Venlo, Roermond and Maastricht.

1633. Death of Isabella, succeeded as governor by the Infante Ferdinand. France concluded an alliance with the United Provinces.

1635. The United Provinces invaded Brabant, sacking Tienen.

1636–45. Frederick Henry took Breda (1636) and Admiral Tromp destroyed the Spanish fleet (1639). In 1641 Frederick Henry married his son William II to Mary of England (daughter of Charles I), a direct attempt to establish a semi-royal dynasty in the United Provinces. In the South, Arras was taken by the French (1640), who also beat the Spanish at Rocroi (1643). In 1644 the United Provinces captured Hulst, thus gaining control of the whole left bank of the Scheldt estuary. Frederick Henry died in 1647, and was succeeded by William II.

In 1648 Philip IV, compelled by the need to concentrate against France, signed the Peace of Münster. Not only was the independence of the United Provinces recognised, but Philip also gave in to their insistence that the Scheldt be closed. Antwerp was thus ruined, not to recover until the reopening of the estuary in 1795, and commercial prosperity shifted from the South to the North.

Henceforward the story of the Spanish Netherlands became that of Spain's and other countries' successive wars with France. Despite the sacrifices made under the Peace of Münster, Spain was not successful and her influence steadily declined.

Peace of the Pyrenees (1659). France gained most of Artois and several fortresses in the S of the Spanish Netherlands.

War of Devolution (1667–68). Louis XIV ascended the French throne in 1643, coming of age, marrying the Spanish Infanta and assuming power in 1659. It soon became a constant tenet of his foreign policy that the Spanish Netherlands should be subject to France. He used the death of his father-in-law, Philip IV (succeeded by Charles II), as the excuse to claim Flanders for his queen. Turenne conquered Flanders, but the Dutch, fearful of France as a neighbour, organised the Triple Alliance with England and Sweden. Louis partially yielded, but under the Peace of Aix-la-Chapelle nevertheless received Charleroi, Binche, Ath, Tournai and Kortrijk, which Vauban set about fortifying.

Dutch War (1672–78). Knowing that he had to eliminate the Dutch, Louis invaded Holland. But, led by William III, the Dutch cut the dykes, flooding their country, and then formed a coalition which included Spain. Louis had to withdraw, and under the Peace of Nijmegen Spain recovered Kortrijk, Charleroi and Binche, but lost Poperinge, Ypres and a number of places farther south.

Chambres de Réunion (1679–84). Under a cloak of legality Louis unilaterally annexed several places, including Luxembourg, which Vauban at once fortified.

War of the Grand Alliance (1690–97). The Dutch stadholder, William III, became King of England in 1689, England thus turning into an active opponent of France. He formed the Grand Alliance (or League of Augsburg), embracing most of both Protestant and Catholic Europe, and war broke out in 1690. Namur was taken by Louis in 1692, but retaken by William in 1695. By the Peace of Ryswick Spain recovered Mons, Luxembourg and Kortrijk.

War of the Spanish Succession (1702–13). In 1700 Charles II, the last of the Spanish Habsburgs, died. Childless, he willed the crown of Spain and the Spanish Netherlands to Philip of Anjou, grandson of Louis XIV. Quickly seizing his opportunity, Louis forced his grandson to hand the Spanish Netherlands over to France, whereupon, unable to accept such a threat, England and Holland, both led by William III, went to war, thus starting a drawn-out struggle which covered much of Europe.

In the Spanish Netherlands the forces opposing France were commanded by the Duke of Marlborough and Prince Eugene of Savoy. 1702: Marlborough advanced S from Holland, taking the Meuse fortresses, including Liège and Huy. 1704: Marlborough's and Eugene's campaign on the Danube, ending with the destruction of a French army at Blenheim. 1705: the French retook Huy. Marlborough broke through the French lines at Tienen, but could not continue because of lack of Dutch support. 1706: Marlborough's victory at Ramillies (NE of Namur) led to French evacuation of most of the Spanish Netherlands. 1708: the French overran Flanders, taking Ghent and Bruges. Marlborough defeated the French at Oudenaarde, retaking Ghent and Bruges. 1709: Marlborough took Tournai, and then, after near defeat at Malplaquet, Mons.

The Treaty of Utrecht was signed in 1713, France abandoning all claim to the Spanish Netherlands which were placed under the sovereignty of the Emperor Charles VI of Austria.

The Austrian Habsburgs (1713 to 1794)

Belgium, now the Austrian Netherlands, had merely undergone a change of sovereignty, the country remaining as independent under Austria as it had been under Spain since the Union of Arras. Under the Barrier Treaty (1715), though, aimed at discouraging any further French ideas of annexation, Belgium had to accept Dutch garrisons at Namur, Dendermonde, Tournai, Menen and Veurne.

Charles VI died in 1740, leaving no male heir. He had long sought support for his succession by his daughter Maria Theresa, but many of the powers refused to accept her and the **War of the Austrian Succession** broke out. This war came to Belgium in 1744 when the country was invaded by the French under Maurice de Saxe; the Dutch-manned Barrier Treaty forts surrendered, the English were beaten at Fontenoy (near Tournai), and Louis XV occupied Belgium until the war was settled by the Peace of Aix-la-Chapelle (1748), which returned the country to Austria.

Maria Theresa reigned until 1765. Under her enlightened and popular governor, Charles of Lorraine, roads and waterways were built, agriculture modernised, and industry (notably coal and glass) encouraged. Maria Theresa's successor, Joseph II (died 1790), was well-meaning, but autocratic and impatient when faced by stubborn Belgian conservatism. He succeeded in getting rid of the Dutch Barrier Treaty garrisons, but his attempt to open the Scheldt simply by using it nearly led to war (the Dutch fired on his ships), and his plans for internal reforms—logical, humane and modern though they were—merely aroused opposition and bitterness. This was particularly the case with the Edict of Toleration (1781), recognising religious freedom, and the proposals to modernise the country's antiquated administrative system. Encouraged by the revolution in France, there was a local uprising in 1789 which defeated the Austrians at Turnhout. Within weeks the whole country was in revolt (the Brabançon Revolt) and in January 1790 the United States of Belgium was declared. Two Belgian factions now faced one another: the democrats who wanted a revolutionary constitution, and the nobles, supported by the clergy and the majority of the country, who wanted no significant change. Anarchy followed failure to agree, and by the end of the year the Emperor (now Leopold II) subdued the country by force of arms. Wisely, Leopold dropped Joseph's reforms.

In 1792 war broke out between revolutionary France and Austria, the French general Dumouriez winning the battle of Jemappes near Tournai and occupying Belgium. His success was shortlived and a few months later (March 1793) the Austrians defeated him at Neerwinden (Landen). But Austrian days were numbered, and in June 1794 the French under Jourdan defeated them at Fleurus, Belgium again finding herself under French occupation.

Belgium annexed to France (1794 to 1814)

After a little over a year of military occupation Belgium was formally annexed as a part of revolutionary France (October 1795). The measures now pushed through, going far beyond anything proposed by Joseph II and ruthlessly enforced, did at least have the effect of transforming Belgium into a modern state. The Church, hitherto so powerful, was persecuted and its buildings everywhere despoiled. The national administration was centralised and rationalised; ancient privileges were abolished. Conscription was introduced. All this was highly unpopular and led in October 1798 to the Peasants' Revolt which was brutally suppressed. Under Napoleon (after 1799) the process continued, though in more constructive and acceptable form. A modern legal system (Code Napoléon) was established; metric systems were introduced; industry was encouraged and profited from the many markets available within the French empire; the Church and government became reconciled. Most important perhaps was the reopening of the Scheldt and the start of the revival of Antwerp. Here Napoleon also boosted recovery by constructing the docks and naval harbour which he described as 'a pistol aimed at the heart of England'.

But despite all their improvements the French remained unpopular, and the occupation of the country by the allies on Napoleon's fall in 1814 was welcomed with relief.

United Kingdom of the Netherlands (1815 to 1831)

The allies' main objective in 1815 was to establish a deterrent to any future French northward expansion. Therefore, paying scant regard to the wishes of the people—with their differing customs, economic outlook and religion—they amalgamated Belgium and Holland into the United Kingdom of the Netherlands under Prince William of Orange who ascended the throne as William I. (At the same time the allies established the

Grand-Duchy of Luxembourg with William as its first Grand-Duke.) William faced a near-impossible task, not made any easier by his obstinately pro-Dutch character. Nevertheless initially he was not unsuccessful; industry flourished, enjoying Dutch colonial markets, Antwerp prospered, and education advanced as new (lay) schools and universities were founded. But there was much the Belgians would not accept—equality of representation in the States General when Belgium's population was nearly double that of Holland; the wide authority assumed by a Protestant and foreign king; the insistence on Dutch as the official language—nor did the Church willingly adapt to the principle of religious liberty. By 1828 Belgium was approaching revolution, and William's continuing obstinacy and his suppression of the opposition press ensured that it broke out in 1830.

The Revolution. On 25 August Auber's opera 'La Muette de Portici' was played in Brussels, and on hearing the duet 'Amour sacré de la Patrie' the audience left the theatre and the flag of Brabant was hoisted. Similar revolts at once followed in the provinces, and the Belgians were defeated at Hasselt. William sent his elder son to Brussels to negotiate, then, when this failed, his second son Frederick, backed by troops. After some fighting Frederick withdrew, a provisional government was formed, and national independence proclaimed.

Kingdom of Belgium

On 20 January 1831 the London Conference recognised Belgium as an independent and 'perpetually neutral' state. The crown was accepted by Prince Leopold of Saxe-Coburg.

Leopold (1790–1865) was a son of the Duke of Saxe-Coburg-Saalfeld and uncle of Queen Victoria, over whom he long exercised a strong influence. As a youth he saw service in the Russian army, and later he fought in the campaigns of 1813–14, after Napoleon's fall entering Paris with the allied leaders. In 1816 he married Charlotte, only child of the Prince Regent and heiress presumptive to the British throne; she died in childbirth the following year. In 1830 he was offered but declined the throne of Greece. His second marriage (1832) was to Louise-Marie, daughter of King Louis-Philippe of the French. Their daughter, Charlotte, married Maximilian of Austria, who became Emperor of Mexico where he was shot by rebels in 1867.

The Dutch did not easily give way. William invaded within days of Leopold's taking the oath, only retreating when faced by French troops who arrived in response to an appeal by the latter. William next refused to accept the Twenty-Four Articles, setting out the terms of the separation of the two countries, and held on in the citadel of Antwerp, which he only evacuated after assault by the French and a blockade of the Dutch ports. Only in 1839 did William finally accept defeat, the independence and neutrality of Belgium now being guaranteed by the Treaty of London (later to become historic as the 'scrap of paper'), signed by Austria, Great Britain, Prussia, France and Russia. (See also p 409 for the territorial adjustments with the Grand-Duchy of Luxembourg under this treaty.)

The new Belgian constitution ensured maximum rights for the people, the king receiving only minor executive powers. Thanks to this, and to a king who was both cultured and wise, Belgium made great economic progress, keeping clear of the general European revolutionary disturbances of 1848. In 1865 Leopold I was succeeded by his son, Leopold II. A man of strong personality and considerable business acumen, he successfully steered neutral Belgium through the hazards of the Franco-Prussian war (1870) and did much to foster the growth of commerce and transport. Politically the reign saw the official recognition of the Flemish language, with the founding in 1886 of the Flemish Academy and the passing of a law in 1898 establishing Flemish equality with French. In 1893 universal suffrage was introduced, though with qualifications.

Belgian Congo. Leopold II had always been interested in colonial possibilities, in particular in the Congo. In 1878 he formed the Comité des Etudes du Haut Congo, this developing into the International Association of the Congo, and the following year, at Leopold's instigation, H.M. Stanley opened trading stations and made agreements with the chiefs. In 1884–85 the powers recognised the International (but effectively Belgian) Association as an independent state, the Belgian government at the same time authorising Leopold to be sovereign but also declaring that the link between Belgium and the Congo was 'exclusively personal'. The venture brought Leopold great wealth, especially from the Domaine de la Couronne, a vast territory treated as the King's personal property. In 1890, in return for financial investment, the Belgian government was given the right of annexation, a right which it exercised in 1908 under the pressure of serious international charges of gross maladministration (seizure of native land, monopolistic exploitation and even atrocities). The Congo was granted independence in 1962.

Leopold II died in 1909. He was succeeded by his nephew Albert. The main event of his reign was the First World War.

First World War (1914 to 1918)

Opening Phase. In July 1914, with war imminent, the British government formally drew the attention of France and Germany to the neutrality of Belgium guaranteed under the Treaty of London of 1839. Dismissing the treaty as a 'scrap of paper', Germany demanded that Belgium allow her troops free passage. Belgium refused on 3 August and that night Germany invaded, the first units crossing the frontier near Malmédy. Under the undaunted leadership of their King, Belgian resistance was stubborn and heroic, though they could hardly hope to hold the German army. Liège fell on 9 August opening the way to German columns to pour across the plains of Limburg and Brabant. Between 20 and 23 August the French were defeated near Charleroi and the British at Mons, both then falling back into France. Namur, Louvain and Brussels fell by the end of the month, by which time the Germans were in occupation of most of central and southern Belgium. Antwerp had to surrender on 9 October, after which the Belgian army retreated through Flanders. By 15 October an Allied line had been established along the Yser, where the Belgians opened the sluices, creating a vast lake between Nieuwpoort and Diksmuide. In November the Germans took Diksmuide, but this was the limit of their advance and they transferred their main effort towards Ypres, where, despite vast superiority, they were unable to break through the small British army. Both sides dug in and for some three years there was trench warfare from Nieuwpoort to the French frontier on the Lys, and thence to Switzerland. In the small strip of their country still free the Belgians established their headquarters at Veurne, while the King made nearby De Panne his 'capital'.

German Occupation. The many memorials throughout Belgium are testimony enough to the ruthlessness of the enemy and the stubborn heroism of the Belgian people. Among their leaders were men such as Cardinal Mercier, whose pastoral letter 'Patriotism and Endurance' protested against German excesses and defined what should be the people's attitude towards the invader; and the indomitable Burgomaster

Adolphe Max of Brussels who defied the German governor and was deported.

The occupation was administered by German governors, and among the many repressive measures were the merging of executive and judicial powers; the edict that the family was responsible for the actions of its individuals; general property confiscation; mass labour deportation to Germany and the front. German efforts to exploit the differences between Flemings and Walloons met with little success. In the economic field the occupation was disastrous; raw materials were seized, exports ceased, and Belgian factories were stripped of everything which could be of use in Germany. Despite all this, thousands of Belgians escaped and throughout the war the army kept an average strength of 150,000.

Closing Phase. The tide began to turn in June 1917 when British and Commonwealth troops took the ridge at Mesen, 9km S of Ypres, though this was followed by the bloody and inconclusive Third Battle of Ypres which ended in the mud of Passchendaele. In March 1918, with troops freed by the collapse of Russia, the Germans launched their last and nearly successful offensive, but by June American troops and British reinforcements were pouring into France. The Belgian army took Diksmuide in September and by October had liberated West Flanders. On 11 November, Armistice Day, the Canadians had entered Mons while the Belgians had reached beyond Ghent.

Between the Wars (1919 to 1940)

By the Treaty of Versailles Belgium was granted reparations and gained from Germany the eastern territories of Moresnet, Eupen and Malmédy. The neutrality which had proved valueless was abolished and Belgium thus became free to make her own defensive alliances, in 1920 concluding a military convention with France.

Unqualified universal suffrage was introduced soon after the war's end. One effect of this was to sharpen the Flemish question, and in 1921 Flemish was made the official language of that part of the country. The same year also saw the signing of a customs, consular and railway union with the Grand-Duchy of Luxembourg.

1929–31. Like other countries Belgium's economic foundations and political institutions were badly shaken by the Depression, and foreign trade, the country's main livelihood, virtually disappeared.

In 1934 King Albert, the much-loved and respected 'Soldier King', was killed in a climbing accident. He was succeeded by his son, Leopold III, whose reign started with tragedy when the following year his Queen, Astrid of Sweden, was killed in a motor accident while Leopold was driving.

The years 1933–39 were the run-up years to the Second World War. The Nazis supported the Belgian fascists and the Rexists. In 1936, when Germany militarily reoccupied the Rhineland, Leopold, announcing that Belgium's policy was once again one of strict neutrality, renounced all agreements on military aid.

Second World War (1939 to 1945)

Opening Phase. Belgium's reiterated but fragile neutrality lasted only eight months, during which period, despite evidence of German intentions, she refused British and French requests that she should accept their troops or at least hold staff talks. Early on 10 May 1940 Germany attacked Belgium and Holland, in Belgium sweeping past the Liège forts, taking bridges over the Albert Canal, and destroying the 'impregnable' Meuse fort of Eben-Emael. As the Belgians retired to their main line of defence between Louvain and Antwerp, the British and French moved in, the British reinforcing positions between Wavre and Louvain while the French advanced to the line Huy-Tienen. By 13–14 May the French collapsed at Sedan (France), leaving the way open to the sea which the Germans reached near Abbeville by 20 May. Meanwhile in Belgium, despite meeting stubborn resistance, the Germans pressed inexorably forward, superbly prepared and equipped and enjoying an air superiority which they used as ruthlessly against military targets as against the streams of refugees now clogging the roads. Louvain, Brussels and Antwerp all fell and the Allies faced the danger of being surrounded and cut off from the sea by a German pincer movement from Abbeville in the S and Antwerp in the north. An attempt was made to break out of the trap by an offensive against the still thin German line between Sedan and Abbeville, but when this failed a retreat to the coast was the only course open.

It was agreed with King Leopold that his army would cover this retreat. But the enemy broke through the Belgian line either side of Kortrijk and on 28 May Leopold surrendered—an action which only history can judge but which was inevitably contrasted with the behaviour of his father in 1914. The immediate practical result was the disappearance of the Allies' northern flank. The British commander (Gort) at once established his final perimeter on the line Gravelines–Bergues–Veurne–Nieuwpoort in preparation for evacuation, and, after a stand by the British between Ypres and Comines and by an isolated French group near Lille, all the British divisions and many of the French were within this perimeter by 30 May. By 4 June the evacuation from the beaches between Dunkirk in France and De Panne in Belgium had been achieved. The Belgian government escaped first to France and then to England, but the King, considering himself a prisoner-of-war, refused to desert his army.

German Occupation followed substantially the same pattern as that of the First World War, though this time not even a corner of Belgium remained free, nor was it possible to escape over the border into Holland. Resistance again was often heroic, despite such added Nazi refinements as anti-semitism, concentration camps and the Gestapo. The King, a prisoner in his Brussels palace of Laeken, did what he could to help his people, even meeting Hitler at Berchtesgaden and negotiating the return of 50,000 prisoners and some improvement in the allocation of food supplies to Belgium. In 1941 he married Lilian Baels, a commoner who received the title of Princesse de Réthy, and on 7 June 1944 he and his family were deported to Germany.

Closing Phase. The invasion of France started on 6 June 1944 and by the end of August the Allies were on the Belgian and German borders. The liberation of Belgium began at the beginning of September, the forces in the N being largely British and Canadian (under Montgomery), those in the S American (under Bradley). In the N, Brussels was reached on 3 September, followed swiftly by Ghent, Ostend, Bruges and Antwerp. In the S the Americans freed Charleroi, Mons and Namur on 3 September and, by 10 September, Liège and Luxembourg. By the end of the month the Canadians had forced the enemy back into the Breskens corner at the mouth of the Scheldt, while E of Antwerp the British crossed the Antwerp–

Turnhout canal. Soon Belgium was free of the enemy, the front line running along the German frontier from Aachen to Wasserbillig in the Grand-Duchy of Luxembourg at the confluence of the Sûre and Moselle. The Allies now paused to regroup, the plan being to strike into Germany through Aachen in the N and through Alsace in the south. This, though, left the centre very thin, a weakness Hitler was not slow to exploit, on 16 December launching his counter-offensive under Von Rundstedt. For this Battle of the Ardennes (or Battle of the Bulge), see p 303. By the end of January 1945 the Germans were again behind their frontier.

After the Second World War

When the Allies invaded France in June 1944, King Leopold was deported with his family first to Germany and then to Austria. Although freed in May 1945 the King (who soon moved to Switzerland) found that he could not return to Belgium, so high ran feeling about his surrender and, less justifiably, about his relations with the Germans and even about his second marriage. His brother Prince Charles was therefore appointed regent. When in 1950 a referendum on whether he should retain the throne gave Leopold only just over 57 per cent he abdicated in favour of his son Baudouin who ascended the throne in 1951 (see also Royal Family, p 13).

Important post-war events have been the formation of the Benelux Union with Holland and Luxembourg (actually signed in London in 1944 by the governments in exile); the granting of independence to the Congo in 1962; the formal establishment of the 'Language Frontier' in 1962; the growth of Brussels (as home of the EC, NATO and other international bodies) into the 'capital' of Europe; and the continuing and widening tension between the Flemings and the Walloons, culminating in 1980 with the formal change from a centralised constitution to a federal one.

Religious Houses and Begijnhofs

The founding of religious houses (abbeys, monasteries, convents, etc.) and begijnhofs—the former throughout Belgium, the latter mainly in the North—forms a part of the pattern of Belgium's history. Both represent the urge, often on the part of members of noble families and dating from the early Middle Ages, to proclaim their Faith in visible and practical terms. Genuine piety apart, individual motives varied: thanks for the granting of some request, to mark a miracle or great event, or even as a form of religious insurance.

Religious Houses. In the early years of Christianity there were lone hermits, first in the deserts of the East, then in Western Europe. Gradually these holy men banded into communities, compelled by the demands of survival to clear the forest, practise primitive drainage and irrigation. They were, in fact, the pioneers of Belgian agriculture up to about the time of Charlemagne. The monks were also the only literate people in the land, and this automatically gave them power and influence as advisers, teachers and administrators. Abbeys and their rich revenues soon became the reward, not only for genuinely pious monks but also for court favourites who treated them as comfortable and lucrative sinecures. The Norse raids of the 9C and 10C helped to foster the growth of defensive feudalism, many religious houses in the process becoming secular feudal estates. Canons' chapters, also developing at this period, were communities (or colleges, hence collegiate churches) of priests rather than monks. While not fully feudal, the chapters enjoyed important local rights.

The 10C, however, also saw the start of the monastic age proper, impetus being given by the Lateran Synod of 1059 which urged the clergy to live together as communities. The movement reached its peak in the 12C, flourishing in the 13–14C and exercising a considerable influence on Belgium's social, commercial and artistic life. The religious houses, both directly and by example, taught the peasants the techniques of agriculture; they functioned as shrewd and vigorous commercial concerns; they worked the mines, developed forges and became skilled in metalwork; and, through their orders for church furnishings, they were practical patrons of the arts. Many of the monks, too, were artists of genius, responsible for delicate illuminated manuscripts, metalwork, painting and sculpture. But the wars and violent dissensions which for so long plagued Belgium did not spare the religious houses, and some survive now only as ruins. Of the buildings in use today, whether for religious or other purposes, the majority are of the 17–19C, this being due not only to earlier destruction but also to the wealthy abbots of the period. The houses were disestablished and their treasures scattered at the French Revolution. During the 19C many of the great abbey churches were reconsecrated, serving then, as now, as parish churches, often still loosely called 'abbey' although the abbey may have long disappeared. Several abbeys did, however, start up again, and new ones have been founded. Belgium today has many flourishing religious houses.

Augustinians is the name given to various orders which follow the 'Rule of St Augustine'. In fact St Augustine (354–430), a Roman of North Africa and Bishop of Hippo, and not to be confused with the later saint who brought Christianity to England, laid down no rule as such, but left practical advice in letters and sermons. This provided the earliest guidelines for community religious life and was later formulated into a 'rule'. Among Augustinian orders are Augustinian Canons (or Austin Friars, or Canons Regular), Augustinian Hermits (Black Friars) and Premonstratensians (see below).

Benedictines (Black Monks) follow the rule of St Benedict (c 480–c 543). Born in Umbria (Italy) he established no fewer than 12 monasteries in the district around Subiaco, S of Rome. Perhaps his most famous foundation was the monastery of Monte Cassino, between Rome and Naples, from where his rule spread. The rule was not one of great austerity. One feature is that there is no real overall authority, each monastery being independent and monks belonging to their monastery rather than to an order. Another is that the day is divided into fixed periods allotted to worship, labour and study. Education has long been an important Benedictine activity. St Benedict's sister, Scholastica, is the patroness of Benedictine nuns.

Capuchins are an offshoot of the Franciscans, originating c 1520 when the monk Matteo di Bassi became convinced that the Franciscan habit was not truly similar to that worn by St Francis and designed himself a pointed hood (cappuccio). In 1619 the Capuchins were officially granted the status of an independent order.

Carmelites originated by tradition as a Jewish order in pre-Christian times but historically in the 12C when a Crusader from Calabria and ten companions established themselves as hermits on Mount Carmel. In 1220 the Order moved to Cyprus, and then to Sicily, France and elsewhere. The

Order changed from hermit to mendicant in 1247, but in 1562 St Theresa and St John of the Cross founded houses which returned to the original austere and contemplative rule, their adherents becoming known as the Discalced Carmelites because, unlike the others (the Calceated), they went either barefoot or simply with sandals. This division survives today.

Carthusians are an order founded by St Bruno in 1084 at the then desolate spot in France called Chartreuse where Bruno and some companions began to lead a life as hermits. Bruno later founded other monasteries and the Carthusian rule has survived virtually unchanged to the present day. When the Order was able to return to Chartreuse after the French Revolution, practical problems such as the need to pay rent led to the invention and marketing of the now famous liqueur.

Cistercians (Grey or White Monks) were originally Benedictines, but in 1098 the monk Robert of Molesmes, dissatisfied with what he felt to be the laxity of Benedictine life, migrated with twenty followers to Cîteaux, near Dijon, where the Count of Burgundy provided a monastery. In 1112 the energetic and popular St Bernard (1090–1153) joined the community, infusing it with new life. When he died there were 280 Cistercian houses. By the end of the century there were over 500 and the Order enjoyed great influence. The Cistercian rule was a strict adherence to the guidelines laid down by St Benedict. An important feature was the emphasis on manual labour. As a result the Cistercians became renowned as farmers, in Belgium building large farms and granges and being responsible for much of the country's early land clearance. A feature of this labour-intensive rule was the large numbers of lay-brothers.

Dominicans (Friars Preachers) belong to the Order founded by St Dominic (1170–1221) in 1216 at Toulouse. This started from a group of followers who accompanied St Dominic while he was preaching against the heretical Albigenses. St Dominic always travelled in poverty and simplicity, and, from this example, the Order adopted an austere discipline in which the rule of poverty extended beyond the individual friars to the monasteries themselves. The Order was mendicant until the rules were relaxed in the second half of the 15C. Dominican influence soon became, and has remained, worldwide. University theological teaching is one of the Order's main activities. Dominican nuns specialise in teaching, nursing and missionary work.

Franciscans (Friars Minor, Fr. *Frères Mineurs*, Flem. *Minderbroeders*) are members of the Order founded in Assisi in 1209 by St Francis (1181–1226). Devoted to absolute poverty and the service of the poor and the sick, the movement spread quickly. Eventually, in spite of frequent internal divisions, it became worldwide with more members than any of the religious orders. Although a mendicant order, the rule permitted begging only if bread could not be earned by work. The Franciscan nuns are the *Poor Clares* (Grey Sisters, Flem. *Grauwe Zusters*), named for their founder St Clare, also of Assisi, where St Francis received her vows in 1212.

Jesuits are members of the Society of Jesus, founded in Spain in 1540 by St Ignatius Loyola. The spiritual background is purification from worldly standards and identification of the individual mind with God. The Society has always been concerned with preaching, missions, charitable and, above all, educational work. It has produced many scholars and scientists. With its unswerving and often ruthless Catholic attitudes, the Society of Jesus was encouraged to go to the Netherlands by Philip II, there playing its part in sparking the Revolt of the Netherlands. Later its influence became predominant when the 'archdukes' were profiting by the Twelve

Years Truce (1609–21) to consolidate Catholicism in the Spanish Netherlands. Suppressed in 1773 on a number of grounds, but mainly because it
had become too powerful, the Society was restored in 1814.

Premonstratensians, or **Norbertines**, are not monks, but an order of
Augustinian Canons (see above), founded in 1120 by St Norbert at
Prémontré in northern France, his aim being to establish a strict form of
canonical life. Although following the Rule of St Augustine, the Order
added conditions designed to ensure a much greater austerity. Today the
main Premonstratensian abbey is in Belgium at Tongerlo.

Trappists are closely associated with the Cistercians and since 1892 have
officially been called the Reformed Cistercians. In 1664 the abbot of La
Trappe in Normandy, Armand de Rancé, initiated a reform which involved
a way of life far stricter than the Cistercian and even included a vow of
silence. The Order did not spread far and the community was dispersed at
the French Revolution. However, twenty monks settled in Switzerland, and
from here houses were founded in Belgium, England, Ireland, Italy, Spain,
and Canada. La Trappe itself reopened in 1817, and in 1898 the Trappists
recovered Cîteaux, the mother-house (1098) of the Cistercians. There are
now Trappist houses, including some convents, in many parts of the world.
Those in Belgium are famous for the quality of the beer which they produce.

Trinitarians, following an austere version of the Augustinian rule, date
from the founding of a movement in 1198. This sought the release of
Christian slaves held by the Moors and the Saracens, if necessary by the
offering of oneself as a substitute. Over the centuries many thousands of
slaves owed their freedom to the Order.

Begijnhofs (Béguinages) were self-contained lay sisterhoods devoting
themselves largely to charitable work. The word may derive from St Begga,
daughter of Pepin of Landen, but more probably comes from a Liège priest,
Lambert le Bègue who died in 1187. His activities in caring for the bereaved
families of Crusaders led him to encourage associations of widows and
other women who, while enjoying the refuge and companionship of pious
community life, were not bound by vows. Lambert is thought to have
founded the first such community at Liège in c 1189, and the countesses
Margaret and Joanna, daughters of Baldwin I of Constantinople, established others a few years later. The movement soon spread around Europe,
notably in the Rhineland, but later, as it came under the influence of the
various religious orders, fell into disrepute and in Protestant countries was
suppressed at the Reformation. It continued however to flourish in the
Netherlands where most towns of any importance had a begijnhof and it is
virtually only in Flemish Belgium that begijnhofs survive today.

Architecturally two main types developed, one a 'village' of small streets
(e.g. Lier, Louvain), the other surrounding a court or field (e.g. Bruges,
Ghent). There was always a church, other important buildings being the
infirmary and the weaving centre. Although there were community rooms,
most of the women lived in individual houses. Although some begijnhofs
are still occupied by religious and charitable communities, most today serve
other purposes, e.g. almshouses, municipal homes or, as at Louvain, university residences. With their quaint streets and little houses, normally quiet
oases within busy towns, the better preserved merit a visit. Some of the
houses have been preserved as museums of begijnhof life.

ART IN BELGIUM

By Joanna Woodall

Note: Belgium's wealth of paintings and sculpture, from about the 12C to modern times, can be seen throughout the country, though mainly in the North, in numerous churches, museums and galleries. A special index lists most of the artists, including architects.

Art to the end of the 7C: Palaeolithic to Merovingian

Until about the end of the 7C Belgium largely shares her history and her art with much of the rest of northern Europe. Artefacts from the Palaeolithic to the Carolingian period are displayed in the Musée d'Art et d'Histoire in Brussels, while surviving monuments include the ancient Pierre Brunehault standing-stone near Tournai, the Roman wall at Tongeren and the Merovingian chapel in the Collégiale Sainte Gertrude at Nivelles, a product of the great monastic building programme initiated after the conversion of Clovis to Christianity in the 6C.

Architecture, 8–13C: Carolingian and Romanesque

After the Emperor Charlemagne established his court at Aachen, Belgium, and especially the Meuse region, acquired greater importance as 'the outskirts of the capital of the Empire'. The major architectural innovation of the period, the centralised or circular church plan, is epitomised by the Palatine chapel at Aachen, but its many Belgian derivations are now known only through excavations. Although all that can be seen today is a re-erected fragment, excavations during the 1950s revealed that the plan of St Donatian at Bruges was inspired by the circular chapel at Aachen. The traditional basilican or hall church with aisles and apse, which had been used from ancient Christian times, also underwent radical changes during the Carolingian period. The church of St Ursmer at Lobbes is a surviving example of this type of church which in part probably dates from this time.

The Treaty of Verdun (843) divided present-day Belgium politically and culturally at the river Scheldt. Two distinct Romanesque styles emerged: the 'Scaldian style' (from the river Scheldt) to the west, and the 'Mosan style' (from the Meuse) to the east. Since the Meuse region soon came to form part of the Ottonian Empire it is not surprising that Mosan architecture, which centred on Liège and Maastricht (Holland), represents a natural development of Carolingian traditions and is closely connected to contemporary Rhenish architecture. The style is characterised, both in construction and decoration, by simplicity, austerity and strength. Although much altered and restored, the church of St Gertrude at Nivelles remains the most striking example of the Mosan basilica. The rural churches of St Hadelin at Celles and Notre-Dame d'Hastière-Par-Delà typify the style, with their fortress-like west ends (called *westwerk*), characteristic square piers with imposts but no bases, low transepts, flat timberwork ceilings and crypts. The centralised plan also survived and, although no example is fully extant, the rebuilt church of St Jean in Liège reflects an original Romanesque rotunda.

French control of the valley of the Scheldt meant that Scaldian Romanesque, although ultimately deriving from Carolingian precedents, was related to Norman (and consequently sometimes English) developments. On the whole, the Scaldian style is more elaborate than the Mosan, paving the way for the Gothic (the pointed arches in the Scaldian church of St Brice in Tournai are among the first in Belgium). Indeed, while the Mosan style was established in the 11C, the Scaldian did not blossom until the 12C. The oldest surviving monument of the style is probably the church of St Vincent at Soignies (?11C) but its apotheosis is Tournai cathedral (nave 12C), which has been called 'the cradle of Scaldian Gothic art'. Towers above the crossing are characteristic of the style—Tournai has five, but there is usually only one. The nave is often multi-storeyed with complex piers and sometimes alternating supports. Outside, the decoration may become more ornate towards the top, and any *westwerk* is, in contrast to the Mosan practice, pierced by an entrance.

The earliest surviving secular architecture dates from this period—notably the early 13C Koornstapelhuis on the Graslei in Ghent, and parts of the Steen and Gravensteen in Antwerp and Ghent respectively.

Architecture, 13–16C: Gothic

Architecture during this period reveals a gradually increasing tendency towards local interpretations and variations of what were originally northern French innovations. These innovations, such as pointed arches, flying buttresses and lofty piers, have little significance on their own, but they are indicative of a new aspiration to create buildings which minimise their own weight and mass, emphasising rather light and space. In Belgium the result was a number of remarkable achievements in both ecclesiastic and secular architecture which reflect the growing wealth and municipal and regional consciousness of the area. The Belgians were understandably reluctant to abandon this rich and splendid style and it lasted well into the 16C.

Ecclesiastic Building

The first Gothic churches are basically French buildings transplanted onto Flemish soil. Gothic forms were soon incorporated at Tournai (cathedral choir 1243–55) and monks, especially Cistercians, favoured a simple, severe Gothic (e.g. the ruined abbey church of Villers-la-Ville). Regional variations became established during the 13C and three broad distinctions are discernable: Scaldian, Mosan and Brabantine. The two former obviously derive from previous stylistic divisions. Features of Scheldt Gothic, which flourished mainly in the 13C, include foliated capitals, called 'Tournai capitals', polygonal apses, crossing towers flanked by four small stair towers, and chapels placed obliquely between transepts and choir. St Niklaas, Ghent and Onze Lieve Vrouw, Oudenaarde, are outstanding. Churches of the Meuse region, of which Notre-Dame at Huy is quite typical, often have rectilinear apses. Columns tend to be cylindrical at the bottom but polygonal at the top, with banded decoration, and there is often a high gallery above the triforium.

During the 14C Brabantine Gothic gradually became pre-eminent. Louvain was the first major centre, with a number of important buildings (especially the Groot Begijnhof, in part 14C, and St Pieter of 1425). Subsequently the Brabantine Gothic spread throughout the Scheldt valley and it can be broadly equated with the late Gothic or 'Flamboyant' style. The cathedrals of Brussels, Mechelen, Ghent and Antwerp are all, in part at least, interpretations of this Brabantine theme. Splendid western towers epitomise the aims and achievements of ecclesiastical Gothic in Belgium.

Secular Building

Towers are also characteristic of secular architecture of which 'no other country possesses as rich a heritage...from such an early date' (Yarwood, 'Architecture in Europe'). The wealth of such architecture can be directly related to the rise of towns and the increasing influence of their merchant citizens. Civic pride was expressed in the building of elaborate town halls, market and cloth halls and belfries. The earliest surviving buildings come from the Scheldt valley where the cloth halls at Ypres and Bruges date originally from the 13C (Ypres is largely rebuilt, but to the original design). Both these buildings incorporate central belfries, crenelated wings and small corner turrets—features which reappear again and again. A series of superb 15C and 16C town halls bear witness to the sheer exuberance of Belgian secular architecture by this time. The grandeur of Brussels, though somewhat restored, testifies to the growing importance of the city; Louvain is as ornate as a church reliquary, while Oudenaarde (early 16C) is more typical. The stepped gabling which we have seen even in the Romanesque period is characteristic of some guild-halls, such as the Groot Vleeshuis in Ghent (1408) and the Vleeshuis in Antwerp, and private houses, many of which survive in Bruges.

Architecture: 16C

16C architecture in Belgium is characterised by a strange marriage between superficial innovation and a deep underlying conservatism. The style of building which had been developed and enriched in Brabant during the previous two centuries (e.g. the Stadhuis, Louvain, and the church of Notre-Dame du Sablon, Brussels) was both successful and highly popular. During a period when government by foreigners was relatively new and felt by some to be oppressive, this indigenous style was not likely to be discarded lightly. At the same time, however, Habsburg rule meant that the Netherlands were, as never before, at the hub of international trade and politics. As a consequence, the region was open to external artistic influences to an unprecedented degree at precisely the time when Italian art was becoming established as the acme of creative achievement. Patrons anxious to be in the forefront of fashion demanded Italianising buildings and architects were quick to respond by introducing Renaissance motifs, easily accessible by means of engravings. As early as 1515 the decoration of the traditional triumphal arches erected for Charles V's solemn entry into Bruges included classically inspired grotesques and medallions.

But men brought up in the absence of any real classical architecture were understandably slower to assimilate the basic principles of Renaissance proportion and some of their buildings have consequently been described as 'Gothic in fancy dress'. A number of palaces built or renovated during the first half of the 16C, such as Margaret of Austria's residence at Mechelen, the palace of the Prince-Bishops at Liège and Cardinal Granvelle's magnificent palace in Brussels (now destroyed) represent variations on the fertile theme of an amalgamation of contemporary Italian with traditional, native elements. Knowledge of Renaissance architecture increased as the century progressed: visits to Italy by young artists became commonplace and books and engravings of Italian architecture became more accurate and more readily available. *Cornelis Floris*' Stadhuis at Antwerp (1561–66) reveals a sophisticated understanding of Italian principles combined with a conscious determination, interesting in the context of Antwerp's resistance to Philip II, to retain traditional characteristics.

Architecture: 17C

The penchant for traditional structures thinly masked by innovative decoration survived into the 17C. The main developments occurred in ecclesiastical architecture and they should be seen in the context of a counter-reformation promoted by the Spanish 'archdukes' and the Jesuits. St Charolus Borromeüs, the former Jesuit church of Antwerp (begun 1615, designed by the Jesuit *Pieter Huyssens*), has been described as the first baroque church in Belgium. The impressive bell-tower, which was built slightly later, the façade and the interior, decorated by *Rubens*, certainly gave the church a rich baroque flavour, but the destruction of Rubens' work in 1718 revealed that the basic plan remained entirely traditional: a nave with two aisles but no transept. The architect did not consider spatial organisation, in addition to decoration, to be integral to a truly baroque effect. Huyssens and his contemporaries *Jacob Franckaert* and *Wenceslas Coeberger* designed a number of such 'semi-baroque' churches during the first half of the century. They are often attractive and interesting in their varied solutions to the problem of reconciling tradition with fashion. Coeberger's church of Scherpenheuvel, NW of Louvain, is a brave attempt at a centralised plan and Franckaert's façade architecture, as for example in the Begijnhof church in Mechelen, is lively and progressive. However, the outstanding example of a more integrated, although still characteristically Belgian, baroque is the church of St Pieter in Ghent, where the unknown designer has made exciting use of light and space.

The two principal figures of the second half of the century were the Jesuit *Willem Hessius* and *Luc Fayd'herbe*. The former's church of St Michiel in Louvain (begun in 1650), together with the Abbey Church of St Servaas in Grimbergen, illustrate the continuing tendency to produce charming but skin-deep baroque, while the latter's church of Onze Lieve Vrouw van Hanswijk in Mechelen (begun 1663) mistakes the bizarre for the baroque.

In secular architecture baroque ornamentation (often very fine) was generally applied to traditional forms. Rubens' house, although restored, can be fitted into this pattern, while Jordaens' house, also in Antwerp, is somewhat more daring. Even at the very end of the century the guild houses of the Grand-Place in Brussels, rebuilt after the bombardment of 1695, retain their traditional high and narrow format. This was partly, admittedly, for reasons of space, but opportunities for innovation in the composition of the façade, as opposed to its ornamentation, were rarely taken.

Architecture: 18C

The 18C, although a period of stylistic variety, reveals as a whole a gradual weakening of native architectural traditions in the face of foreign influences. The transfer of control of the provinces from the Spanish to the Austrian Habsburgs was significant in this process. The date 1700 for the church of the Minimes in Brussels, where, for the first time, characteristically Belgian features are replaced by an international baroque, seems almost symbolic. But, by contrast with the 17C, the major examples of 18C baroque in Belgium occur in secular building. There was an important difference between the restrained, elegant style of the Meuse district (e.g. *J.A. Anneessens'* wing for the Palace of the Prince-Bishops at Liège), where French influence was skilfully blended with local tradition, and the more flamboyant, partly Austrian-inspired baroque of Flanders. The latter was practised in Antwerp by *J.P. Baurscheit the Younger* and in Ghent by *Bernard de Wilde* (the Hôtel Falignan) and *David 't Kindt*, although these two soon incorporate lighter 'rococo' elements into their façades.

Namur Cathedral, begun in 1751, is another landmark in the internationalisation of architecture in the southern Netherlands. Designed by the Milanese *Gaetano Pizzoni*, who was, significantly, commissioned through the Court at Vienna, the design is completely Italian and a hint of classicism, that international style *par excellence*, is evident in the still basically baroque interior.

Laurent Benoit Dewez (1731–1812), who had received an international training and was the chief architect to the governor, Charles of Lorraine, from 1766–82, was primarily responsible for the establishment of classicism. His château at Seneffe of c 1760, reminiscent of an 18C English country house, is a remarkable achievement. The urban development of Brussels towards the end of the century provided great opportunities for the practitioners of classicism, and the Place des Martyrs (1775, by *Claude Fisco*), the Place and Parc Royale (begun 1775, designed by *Barnabé Guimard*) and the Palais de la Nation (Guimard) are important products of this originally French style.

CASTLES AND CHATEAUX, are found all over Belgium. From feudal times on defence was a powerful building motive, at one end of the scale being great fortresses, serving only secondarily as the homes of their owners, and at the other private manors and farms, used primarily as homes but at the same time fortified in case of trouble. The oldest and most impressive of the great castles is that of the counts of Flanders at Ghent, fragments of which date back to the 9C. Solre-sur-Sambre and Spontin are examples of fortified manors, and fortified farms (château-ferme), many of them most attractive, will be found in many districts, notably in Namur. For the most part the true fortresses of the past survive only as romantic ruins, or as later restorations or rebuildings, often massively impressive. In the 16C, warfare changed and the defensive requirement gave way to the aristocratic urge for palatial, comfortable and elegantly furnished homes; castles became châteaux, these being either new buildings or adaptations of the old around the defensive moat and keep (donjon). A distinctive Belgian style developed; one of mixed brick and stone, of towers of all shapes and sizes, with pepper-pot turrets and often a bulbous crown. This style lasted through until the 18C and, despite the French, baroque and neo-classical influences which then appeared, it remains the basic style of most of the châteaux seen today.

Painting to the end of the 15C

Flemish painting during this period is overwhelmingly religious in content. The development of landscape can, however, be traced in the backgrounds of many works, and during the 15C portraiture became increasingly important. In this century Flemish painting as a whole is characterised by technical excellence, a coherent vision and a wonderfully rich pictorial language. The very nature of these qualities implies that *Jan* and *Hubert van Eyck*, the first 'personalities' in the history of Flemish painting, could not have emerged from an artistic void. Their background is, however, international and knowledge of their antecedents in Belgium is limited, largely because long critical neglect and Belgium's turbulent history and damp climate have dealt harshly with early Flemish painting. Surviving pre-Eyckian work bears witness to the close links between Flanders and the courts of northern France at Paris and Dijon. Outstanding examples of early fresco painting are preserved in the Bijloke Museum in Ghent. The Calvary of the Tanners in the Bruges Cathedral Museum is a rare instance of a 14C panel painting remaining in Belgium.

The true ancestors of the van Eycks seem, however, to have been the miniature painters—at least the bulk of our evidence about the Flemish pictorial tradition before the 15C comes from this type of work. Masterpieces such as *Jacquemart de Hesdin*'s Très Belles Heures du Duc de Berry in the Bibliothèque Royale, Brussels, well repay study. It is worth remembering that the Van Eycks almost certainly originated from the Limburg region in eastern Belgium, which gave its name to the brothers who produced the famous Très Riches Heures at Chantilly.

Jan van Eyck's life is relatively well documented—he was employed by John of Bavaria at The Hague in the early 1420s and by Philip of Burgundy from 1425. From 1430 until his death in 1441 he lived mostly in Bruges where some of his works can still be seen. He signed a number of paintings, an apparently unusual step which may have been prompted by his immediate fame. Hubert is known primarily from an inscription on the back of the brothers' most famous painting, the Adoration of the Mystic Lamb in Ghent Cathedral. The precise contribution of each brother and the meaning of these panels are subjects of endless debate. 15C Flemish painters certainly employed 'disguised symbolism'—the deliberate concealing of usually religious meaning within apparently ordinary elements of the painting—but the extent and nature of the symbolism is hotly debated. The Van Eycks perfected a complex technique of oil painting which still retains its brilliant, transparent effect. Their style is notable for its minute and convincing articulation of surface and space by means of colour and light.

Friedländer has said that 'in the 15C the painter worked modestly, in the spirit of the craftsman, but the artist of genius by his very nature—though not as his aim—produced personal and individual achievements'. Hence we have the apparent paradox of a few individuals standing out against a large crowd of anonymous imitators whose often high quality works can be seen throughout Belgium. They were concerned not with originality but with making a living and they were confirmed in this attitude by the conservatism of most patrons. Among the outstanding figures was the *Master of Flémalle* (probably Robert Campin of Tournai, died 1444), whose work combines intense realism with a concern for decorative values. His influence was widespread, and there are two works attributed to him in the Brussels Fine Arts Museum, but none of his greatest masterpieces remains in Belgium. The brilliant *Roger van der Weyden* (died 1464), who worked in Tournai and Brussels, turned the Van Eycks' technical achievements to the service of his own subjective and dramatic vision. As no one before, he exploited the emotional potential of colours and abstract form. His portraits have a nobility and spirituality which was highly popular with patrons. Again the major works are mainly outside Belgium, but there is an early copy (1440) of his masterpiece, the Deposition, in Louvain and accepted works in the Fine Arts Museums of Antwerp, Brussels and Tournai.

Van der Weyden's influence is evident in the work of *Dirk Bouts* (died 1475) the Haarlem painter who settled in Louvain before 1460. There are major works in the Fine Arts Museum, Brussels ('The Judgement of the Emperor Otto'), Louvain (Church of St Pieter) and Bruges (Cathedral Museum). The isolation of Bouts' elongated and angular figures within his often deep but simplified space and the contrast between his lovely land-scapes and his horrific subjects are emotive and disturbing. The influence of both Van der Weyden and the Van Eycks can be traced in the works of Bouts' contemporary in Bruges, *Petrus Christus* (died 1472). His Lamentation (in the Brussels Museum) is quietly effective. A more original artist, who breaks out of the conventional 'craftsman' mould if only by reason of his ultimate insanity, is *Hugo van der Goes* of Ghent (died 1482). The emotional intensity of his approach is conveyed by a cavalier attitude to space and scale, an ability to intimate movement, a unique palette and, sometimes, an explicit awareness of the viewers' presence. The Death of the Virgin (Groeninge Museum, Bruges) is a masterpiece.

By contrast the technically superb paintings of *Hans Memling* are balanced and rational. The bulk of his work remains in a charming museum in his adopted home of Bruges. Their derivation from Van der Weyden is clear, but they are gentler, more idealised, more homely.

Memling's most important successor was *Gerard David* (died 1523) who came to Bruges from Oudewater in 1484. David's style remains solemn and reticent, but his figures have an animation and suppleness which look towards the 16C. Some of his major works remain in Bruges, for instance the Unjust Judge panels in the Groeninge Museum. A complete contrast to David's gentle approach is the macabre vision of his contemporary *Hieronymous Bosch* (died 1516). Although not strictly a Belgian artist (he spent his life in his home town of 's Hertogenbosch in Holland), Bosch is always linked to the Flemish school and had a profound influence on artists such as Brueghel and Patinir. Bosch's fantastic assemblages of grotesque motifs, all the more horrifying because they derive ultimately from natural phenomena, are not fully understood but they probably relate to popular culture, both secular and religious. Most of Bosch's major works are in Spain—he was a great favourite with Philip II—but there are examples in the Brussels (a fairly orthodox Crucifixion), and Ghent museums.

Painting: 16C

Overall, this period does not achieve the standard of those immediately preceding or succeeding it. It did, however, produce artists of exceptional talent and presents a fascinating record of the development of new genres and of a confrontation between two artistic traditions—the Flemish and the Italian. The term 'Renaissance' is often misleading in a country whose great heritage was not classical art but the still vigorous and highly decorative traditions of the indigenous 'Gothic'. Despite the Italian orientation of most Flemish artists of this period, what seems to have occurred was the assimilation of certain Italian elements and ideals into the native vocabulary of form and style and into the syntax of traditional notions of the role of the artist and the work of art. The result was a distinctive, if sometimes slightly garbled, new language—a prerequisite for the emergence of the 17C masters.

The period sees the rise of Antwerp to economic and artistic pre-eminence. Among the most important artists at the turn of the century was *Quinten Metsys* (died 1530), whose refined and sophisticated sacred works attempted to combine the best of the Flemish tradition with new Italian—chiefly Leonardoesque—ideas, and whose animated portraits and satirical genre scenes were highly influential. Also influenced by Leonardo was *Joos van Cleef*, who astutely adopted many of Metsys' formulae, but whose winsome Madonnas are more frankly charming and decorative. A more vigorous, not to say virile, talent was *Jan Gossaert* (or *Mabuse*) whose visit to Italy in 1508 led to an innovatory concern with the monumental nude in secular, mythological contexts (as exemplified by the Venus and Cupid in Brussels).

The work of these artists is related to 'Antwerp Mannerism', a decorative and anti-naturalistic style produced between c 1515 and 1535 by numerous, often anonymous artists. Incorporating Italian, Dutch and Flemish elements, it is more akin to late Gothic Brabantine architecture than to contemporary Italian art.

Outside Antwerp, *Jan Provoost* was creating lively works in Bruges and in Brussels the painter and designer of tapestry and glass *Bernard van Orley* successfully appropriated Raphaelesque ideas—but it is Raphael at second hand, divorced from nature. The preoccupation with Italy was more comprehensively indulged by a second generation of artists, calling themselves Romanists. Among them were *Michiel Coxie, Pieter Coecke, Lambert Lombard* (died 1566), who was almost a caricature of the Renaissance artist, and Lombard's immensely successful pupil *Frans Floris* (died 1570). Floris reveals a broader knowledge of Italian art than Lombard, in particular familiarity with Venetian and northern Italian techniques. Among Floris' many pupils was *Martin de Vos*, whose work reflects his collaboration with Tintoretto and knowledge of Veronese.

The period sees a gradual but highly significant trend towards secular subject matter. One aspect of this was the establishment of landscape, of which *Joachim Patinir* (died c 1524) was an early practitioner. His airy pictures, with their unnatural 'bird's-eye' view, high horizons and visionary mountains, established a convention which dominated until the end of the century and is reflected in the works of *Herri met de Bles, Bruegel the Elder* and, later, *Gillis van Coninxloo*. It was only finally abandoned by *Paul Bril*. Another flourishing genre was portraiture, and here observation never succumbed to pretension. Until c 1530 extrovert, sometimes rhetorical half-length figures were fashionable; later Lombard, van Heemskerk and Floris created free, direct images. After c 1550 specialist portraitists, aware of, but not dominated by Italy, produced more reticent, often three-quarter length and usually three-quarter view depictions of bourgeois sitters. *Pieter* and *Frans Pourbus the Elder*, *W.* and *Adriaen Key* are fairly typical, while *Antonio Moro*, painter to the Habsburg court, gained international status and helped to formulate the European court portrait. *Frans Pourbus the Younger* was also important.

In the field of genre painting the lead of Quinten Metsys was followed by *Jan Sanders* and the Dutchman *Marius van Reymerswael*. *Pieter Aertsen* and his nephew *Beuckelaer* later developed a novel type of kitchen or peasant scene executed broadly in the style of the 'Romanists'.

The most significant painter of the 16C was, however, *Pieter Bruegel the Elder* (c 1525–69). Painting for a limited circle of intellectual connoisseurs, Bruegel's works (of which there are good examples in Brussels and Antwerp) combine acute observation of peasant physiognomies and customs with Bosch-like fantasy and rich allegorical and symbolic content. His transparent colour, brilliant sense of design and incisive drawing serve an objective yet deeply sympathetic view of humanity. *Pieter Brueghel the Younger* painted attractive copies of his father's work which, however, lack the delicacy and sensitivity of the originals. More significant was the younger son *Jan* (known as 'Velvet') whose small, exquisite genre works and flower paintings were highly prized.

Painting: 17C

The period is dominated by a single figure, *Pieter Paul Rubens* (born 1577) gentleman artist, scholar and diplomat *extraordinaire*. Rubens' significance lies partly in what has been termed his 'creative eclecticism' (Jaffé)—his ability to fuse highly disparate elements into a coherent, attractive and intensely personal idiom. Rubens largely acquired his huge formal vocabulary when, in his twenties, he spent eight years in Italy in the service of the Duke of Mantua and, in 1603, visited Spain. His eager eye assimilated all he saw, from classical antiquity to the Carracci and Caravaggio, and he was at this period perhaps particularly impressed with the 16C Venetians. Rubens' earlier training in Antwerp, especially the time he spent in the studio of Otto van Veen (Venius), was not, however, wasted. Reminiscences of Van Veen and other Flemings often appear in Rubens' works and, at a more fundamental level, the enthusiastic but sometimes awkward re-orientation of Flemish art towards Italy in the 16C was essential to the synthesis achieved by Rubens in the 17C.

Even before Rubens burst upon the Antwerp scene artists such as *A. Janssens* (died 1632) were producing fairly sophisticated interpretations of Italian ideas which reveal knowledge of Caravaggio and the Bolognese school. But Janssens, like so many others, ultimately joined the tide of emulation created by Rubens' enormous success. Two masterpieces, executed soon after his return from Italy and both today in Antwerp Cathedral, heralded Rubens' fame. The Raising of the Cross, rent by a fierce diagonal, is a picture of tremendous, calculated verve and passion which fully merits the label 'baroque', while the Descent from the Cross is a calmer composition of great pathos. Three Adorations of the Magi, also executed in the 1610s (today in the Fine Arts Museums in Brussels and Antwerp and

St Jan, Mechelen) reveal how Rubens could revitalise a traditional Flemish subject and how he continuously developed and refined his ideas. Paintings such as these and Rubens' position as court painter to Albert and Isabella quickly established him as Antwerp's leading artist, with a large and highly efficient workshop. The price of a 'Rubens' varied according to how much of the picture had been executed by the master himself. The small oil sketches by Rubens from which his assistants worked have always been highly valued as 'autograph', but it is worth remembering that they were not primarily intended as independent works of art; their compositions must be visualised on a much larger scale.

Rubens was an artist of many parts: portraitist, landscapist, painter of mythologies, political eulogies and grand religious works, he was ideally suited to serve the 17C Church and State. A large number of his works remain in Belgium and any selection is inevitably a personal one. There are, for instance, the splendid altarpieces from Antwerp churches and, very different in purpose and effect, the series of hunting scenes designed for tapestries to decorate Philip IV's hunting-lodge which are now in the Brussels Museum. Another masterpiece is the utterly confident portrait of Gaspard Gevartius in the Antwerp Fine Arts Museum and, also in Antwerp and in stark contrast, there is the Last Communion of St Francis where all Rubens' skills are marshalled to express a single truth—the mystery of faith.

Although they share a formal idiom and their styles sometimes converge, Rubens and his great contemporaries *Antoon van Dyck* (1599–1641) and *Jacob Jordaens* (1593–1678) are fundamentally different artistic personalities. Van Dyck, who collaborated so closely with Rubens in the late 1610s that connoisseurs find difficulty in separating their work, ultimately developed a more exclusive preoccupation with grace, elegance and emotional sensibility and formulated a different technique and palette. Two works from the series of Mysteries of the Rosary in St Paulus, Antwerp, provide a splendid opportunity to compare the two masters at the moment of their closest collaboration. Although the types and bold movements of the figures in van Dyck's Carrying of the Cross recall Rubens, who is represented by the neighbouring Scourging of Christ, the unstable composition, flickering light, elements of unrestrained pathos and rapid, sketchy technique are van Dyck's own. Van Dyck spent the years from 1621 to 1627 in Italy and after 1632 his career was pursued mostly in England, where he concentrated on portraiture. There are some excellent portraits in Belgium, especially in the Brussels Museum (the sculptor François Duquesnoy—painted in Italy), but the country is particularly rich in Van Dyck's religious works, usually from the period after his return from Italy. A recurrent theme is the Crucifixion (Mechelen cathedral, St Michielskerk, Ghent, Onze Lieve Vrouwe, Dendermonde), a subject which this hypersensitive artist interpreted in terms of despair and pathos. Two Lamentations in the Antwerp Museum also invite a comparison between Van Dyck's earlier and later styles.

Jacob Jordaens was a pupil of *Adam van Noort*, who was also one of Rubens' teachers. He may have co-operated with Van Dyck in the 1610s and from about 1635 on was certainly commissioned to complete works left unfinished by Rubens. Despite these close contacts Jordaens was a highly original artist: the 'Encyclopedia of World Art' characterisation of 17C Flemish painting as deeply affected by the assimilation of Italian art but remaining always 'within the context of Flemish sensibility—naturalistic, sensual, anti-intellectual in a certain sense and devoted to the visual transcription of life perceived as energy and enthusiasm and rendered in the evocative manner of the Flemish tradition' is particularly applicable to him. Jordaens' early style is robust, firm, illusionistic and boldly executed. Complex influences, including Caravaggism (although he never went to Italy), 16C Flemish art and, of course, Rubens combine to produce an entirely personal approach exemplified by the Allegory of Fertility (1620s) in the Brussels Museum. Jordaens' Martyrdom of St Apollonia in St Augustinus, Antwerp (1628), which seems almost to burst with movement and form, can be compared with Van Dyck's St Augustine in the same church, and Jordaens also contributed to the Mysteries of the Rosary series, mentioned above. It seems paradoxical that this painter, famed for his exuberant depictions of revels (including the specifically Flemish theme 'The King Drinks') should have become a Calvinist. His conversion, when aged about fifty, was one cause or consequence of a new moderation and restraint in his religious pictures which, particularly when he relied on the services of his large workshop, lack the energy and verve of earlier works.

The presence of Rubens and his two outstanding followers Van Dyck and Jordaens meant that Antwerp, despite its relative economic decline, remained the centre of Belgian artistic production. The works of innumerable minor Antwerp masters testify to this trio's dominating influence, although painters such as *Gerard Seghers* and *Theodoor Rombouts* were also impressed by Caravaggio and his followers. Some of the more talented artists of the day understandably preferred to work outside Antwerp, but all remained ultimately within Rubens' sphere of influence. In Bruges *Jacob van Oost the Elder* produced sensitive works incorporating Venetian and Dutch elements, while the masterpiece of *Theodoor van Loon* of Brussels was the powerful, Caravaggesque decoration of the church at Scherpenheuvel. *Gaspard de Crayer*, who worked in Brussels and received numerous commissions from Ghent churches (for example St Michiel) profited greatly from the examples of Rubens and Van Dyck but always managed to retain his own identity. In Liège a relatively independent group of artists led by *Gerard Douffet* and including *Bartholomé Flémalle* were influenced by Caravaggism but were also conscious of the impact of Poussin in France.

The 17C saw a proliferation of different genres skilfully practised by numerous artists and often reflecting contemporary Dutch influence. The career of *Adriaen Brouwer*, a painter of landscapes and scenes from everyday life, was short but brilliant. His brushwork is direct and free, his pictures naturalistic yet lyrical. The Fine Arts Museum in Brussels provides a good opportunity to compare Brouwer with his contemporary *David Teniers the Younger* (1610–90). The peasant scenes of the court artist Teniers are also sensitive in treatment, but they are much more detatched and cool in expression. Brouwers and Teniers were the leading figures among the so-called 'kleinmeister', although Belgium's galleries are rich in attractive and amusing scenes of work and play in the 17C by other hands. These two were also, along with Rubens, the major landscapists of the period, but it would be a pity if the greater emotional and formal integration of their landscapes were allowed to obscure the decorative beauty of works by predecessors such as *Joos de Momper* (died 1635), *Kerstiaen de Keuninck* (died c 1632–35) and *Denis van Alsloot* (died c 1628). Later, *Lucas van Uden* and *Jan Wildens* were excellent interpreters of 'the Rubens landscape' and *Jacques d'Arthois* of Brussels managed to combine baroque grandeur with the decorative charm of his fellow citizen Van Alsloot. *Jan Siberechts* (1627–1700/03) was more independent. The best of his pictures achieve a bold and entirely personal monumentality.

In the field of still-life *Frans Snyders* (1579–1657) expanded the tradition of large kitchen and market subjects established by Aertsen and Beuckelaer in the 16C to encompass subjects of hunting and game. *Paul de Vos* (1596–1678) produced pictures which are close in style and theme and equal in quality to those of his brother-in-law Snyders. *Jan Fyt* (1611–61), a pupil of Snyders, preferred to contemplate the trophies of the hunt rather than evoking the frenzy of the hunt itself. His works are striking and decorative, with an impressive feeling for surface textures. The art of flower painting was given its independence at the very beginning of the 17C by Jan Breughel; it achieved greater sophistication in the work of his pupil, the Jesuit *Daniel Seghers* (1590–1661). Both Seghers' paintings and the still-lifes of his influential contemporary *Jan Davidz de Heem* (1616–83/84) have a symbolic as well as a decorative purpose. Among the portraitists *Cornelis de Vos* (brother of Paul) created charming and elegant representations, especially of children and, later in the century, *Gonzales Cognes* achieved great success in Brussels with his fashionable conversation pieces.

Painting: 18C

In the 18C two themes are clear: the continuation and imitation of the ideas and styles of the previous century and the ever-increasing influence of foreign, and especially French, models and ideas. It was natural, for instance, that many artists should hark back to the 'golden age' of religious and history painting in Belgium. The worst productions of this type are merely pallid imitations of Rubens, but the Louvain artist Pieter Verhaghen produced works in the spirit of Jordaens which are, nevertheless, vigorous, attractive and original. On the other hand, a slightly younger artist, *Andreas Cornelis Lens* (1739–1822), reveals a conciousness of French developments in his graceful, classical pictures and *Piat Sauvage*'s sculptural trompe l'oeils in the Cathedral and gallery at Tournai are both fashionably decorative and inspired by Poussin's second seven sacraments series.

The status of genre painting was extremely high during this period—a situation which reflects both contemporary French taste and the brilliant example of the 17C. David Teniers was particularly admired by artists such as *Balthasar van den Bossche* and the talented *Jan Joseph Horemans I.* Despite their aspirations to elegance, Van den Bossche and Horemans adhered firmly to the Flemish tradition. The perspective of other genre artists, such as *Pieter Snayers* and *Pieter van Angelis*, extended to France and Italy, while still others, including *Frans Xaver Henri Verbeek* and *Jacob de Roore* looked north to Holland, and especially to Leiden, for inspiration. The increasing 'internationalisation' of painting during this period can be traced in the development of *Jan Anton Garemijn* of Bruges (1712–99). He began by painting village genre entirely in the tradition of Teniers, later adopted a French-inspired 'rococo' style and finally (c 1790) was influenced by the wave of classicism which was sweeping Europe. The career of *Léonard Defrance* (1735–1805) provides a contrasting example of what is essentially the same process: the weakening of the independent Flemish tradition. The classicism of Defrance's earlier works betrays the proximity of his home to France and his studies in Italy and the south of France. His conversion to the recreation of 17C Leiden genre in 1773 seems to have been partly a result of personal conviction (his works always remain individual) and in part a consequence of his consciousness of a lucrative Parisian market—to which he responded by introducing French elements into his pictures.

In the fields of landscape and flowers the native tradition was also abandoned for French and Dutch models. The landscapist *Karel van Falens*, for example, was inspired by the Dutch painter Wouwerman, while later in the century *Henricus Josephus Antonissen* and *Balthasar Paul Ommeganck* chose Wynants and Berchem as exemplars.

Romanesque Sculpture

The local stone of the low countries is not ideal for sculpture—it is either soft and crumbly sandstone or the exceptionally hard black marble of Tournai. The relative paucity of monumental sculpture of this period and the excellence of work in other media are in part consequences of this problem. There are superb Mosan ivories dating from the 10C and 11C in the treasury of Onze Lieve Vrouw, Tongeren, the Musée Curtius, Liège, and the Musée d'Art et d'Histoire, Brussels (where, indeed, all kinds of Romanesque sculpture can be seen). During the 12C excellent champlevé enamel was produced, also in the Meuse region, and the work of *Godefroid de Huy* was outstanding. His reliquary of Pope Alexander (1145) is in the museum in Brussels. High quality metalwork from this period also survives, for example the wonderful bronze font at St Barthélemy, Liège (1107–18), attributed to *Renier de Huy*. This work has been called 'a Christian resurrection of Classic Hellenism' (Lejeune), so directly do its graceful figures reflect their classical ancestry. It forms a startling contrast with the approximately contemporary (1149) font from St Germanus at Tienen, now in Brussels, where Renier's grace and refinement are countered by primitive vigour and an innate sense of design. At the end of the 12C *Nicolas of Verdun* produced the lovely Reliquary of Notre-Dame at Tournai, and there are many other beautiful but anonymous works of this period, e.g. the Châsse St Hadelin at Visé (12C) and the Châsse St Remaclus at Stavelot (13C). In wood the seated Madonna, known as *Sedes Sapientae*, and the crucifix are the dominant forms. Once again a contrast between a popular and a more aristocratic art is highlighted by the primitive but powerful Virgin from Evegnée, now in the Diocesan Museum, Liège, and the more elegant, gentler image in the Brussels Fine Arts Museum. Simple but eloquent crucifixes survive at Tongeren, Tancremont and Liège.

The architectural division between Mosan and Scaldian styles is also tenable for that monumental sculpture which does survive. In the Meuse region there is the mysterious iconography of the ancient doorways of Sainte Gertrude at Nivelles and the lovely Virgin of Dom Rupert originally from the Abbey of St Laurent, Liège, and now in the Musée Curtius. She is suckling her child—a motif which is to be endlessly repeated in Flemish art. A direct comparison between the Scaldian and Mosan styles is, however, best made by means of the various stone fonts which survive from both regions. By far the richest source for Scaldian architectural sculpture is Tournai cathedral, with its impressive doorways and decorated capitals.

Gothic Sculpture: 13C and 14C

The decisive influence upon Belgian Gothic sculpture was French. This determining factor was common to all the centres—the Meuse, the Scheldt, Brabant—but previous local traditions and the different routes of diffusion of French influence (some French ideas reached the Meuse region via Germany, for instance) produced different results in each area. In Tournai the direct impact of France, and in particular Notre-Dame, Paris, is evident in the reliquary of St Eleutherius of 1247 (Cathedral Treasury) and the Genesis story and Prophets from the Cathedral W façade. But Tournai was by no means merely a provincial outpost of the French style. During the 14C a flourishing school of funerary sculpture developed. Much of the work was for export, but many reliefs can still be seen in the cathedral (e.g. the monument to Jean de Bos) and local churches. Other important works of the Scheldt region are the portal of the hospital of St Jan in Bruges (c 1270), again reminiscent of French prototypes, and the monument of Hugo II, castellan of Ghent, in the Ghent Bijloke Museum.

Reflections of French developments are also to be found in the Meuse region after c 1250, as for instance at the churches in Tongeren and Dinant. The lovely 13C Sedes Sapientae of St Jean, Liège is a good example of Romanesque iconography translated into the Gothic idiom. In the 14C French influence on Mosan sculpture becomes even more marked and it is sometimes difficult to decide the precise origin of isolated works. However, the Porte de Bethléem at Notre-Dame, Huy, is, despite its international character, likely to be local work. Two outstanding Mosan sculptors of the end of the 14C were *Jean Pepin de Huy* and *Jean de Liège*. Both these artists worked mostly for French courts, providing further evidence of the close relationship between these regions. Mosan goldsmiths' work continued to be important, although its quality declined somewhat in relation to the superb production of the Romanesque period. The outstanding name of the 14C was *Hugo d'Oignies*, many of whose exquisite creations are today in the treasury of the convent of Notre-Dame at Namur. There are other important, though anonymous, reliquaries at Stavelot, Amay and the cathedral at Namur.

In sculpture as in architecture the 14C saw the rise of Brabant to pre-eminence. The region was certainly not immune to French influence, as the Black Madonna of Halle clearly illustrates. It was not, however, dominated by France, but rather reacted fruitfully to the stimulus of French influence. *Walter Paris*'s Virgin from Onze Lieve Vrouw ten Poel Kerk, Tienen, of the 1360s, for instance, reveals elements of the new vital realism which was to be most fully developed by Claus Sluter.

Sculpture: late 14C to 1500

A comprehensive history of Belgian sculpture of this period has yet to be written. This is partly because of the complexity of the subject: works ranged from precious metal objects to monumental architectural decoration, and the design and execution of a single item often involved many people. It is also in part a result of the uneven survival of sculpture from this time. Iconoclasm has meant that, until about 1450, so little work remains in Belgium that it is difficult to trace a coherent line of development, while later, although metalwork and monumental sculpture are still relatively rare, there is a proliferation, and ultimately a glut, of small carved altarpieces. These painted wooden retables, produced on a massive scale usually by anonymous craftsmen, largely defy analysis according to the conventional criteria of individual contributions and stylistic progression. What is clear, however, is that the sculpture and sculptors of northern France and the Netherlands exercised international influence and it has been argued that the significance of this sculpture originally rivalled that of Flemish painting of the same period.

Initially, the revolutionary work of the Dutchman *Claus Sluter* was the decisive influence in Belgium. Although Sluter worked principally at the Burgundian court at Dijon, the political union of Flanders and Burgundy (1384) meant that echoes of his realistic, autonomous and vital individuals quickly reverberated throughout Belgium. In addition, Sluter's style may in part originate from the southern Netherlands. Notable works in his idiom are the eight prophets from Brussels Town Hall (now in the Musée Communal), some of the sculpture at the church of Onze Lieve Vrouw at Halle and the Coronation of the Virgin at St Jacques, Liège. The retable of the church of St Salvator, Hakendover, reveals, however, a more conservative approach, perhaps particularly appropriate to small-scale works.

A dominant and fascinating theme throughout the period is the mutual interaction between painting and sculpture. Interesting parallels have been drawn between early 15C alabasters and metal reliefs (of which few remain in Belgium) and contemporary miniature painting. There is also evidence that Robert Campin and Roger van der Weyden (among many other painters) polychromed, if they did not actually design, sculpture. Both artists came from Tournai, a centre of the production of marble reliefs, some of which can still be seen in the cathedral, and it has been suggested that their styles may have been influenced by these reliefs. Certainly Roger's style, in particular, had an enormous impact on sculpture, as is revealed by the characteristic tension between line and volume of the Entombment in St Vincent, Soignies. Some measure of what has been lost from this period is provided by the stone St Adrian in the Musée d'Art et d'Histoire in Brussels, which evokes tantalising thoughts of the brilliant Leyden sculptor *Nicolaus Gerhaerts*; by the restrained and beautiful effigy of Isabella of Bourbon, now in Antwerp cathedral; and by the Paschal candelabrum of 1482–83 cast by *Renier van Thienen*, at Zoutleeuw. On a small scale, the reliquary group of Charles the Bold, made by *Gérard Loyet* of Lille in 1467 (and now in the treasury of St Paul's church, Liège) testifies to the continued vitality and refinement of goldsmiths' work.

Such sculptures contrast sharply in function and style with the innumerable wooden altarpieces produced in the latter half of the century, mostly in Brussels. Crowded, clear-cut and richly decorated, often including genre elements, these works are designed to be appreciated in detail and are, at best, highly expressive and dramatic—still echoing the preoccupations of Roger van der Weyden. Outstanding examples are the *Claudio de Villa* altar (c 1470) in the Musée d'Art et d'Histoire, Brussels, the altar of St Leonard (1479) in the church of St Leonardus at Zoutleeuw, and the altarpiece of the Passion in St Dympna at Geel (c 1480–90).

At the end of the century the emotional grip of the age of Van de Weyden at last relaxes and an unprecedented diversity results. In Brussels the leading master, *Jan Borman the Elder*, produced the St George altar of 1493 (now in the Musée d'Art et d'Histoire, Brussels). A work of superb, if slightly impersonal technique, this retable is notable for the naturalistic elegance of its figures, calm and clear composition and perfection of detail. The choir stalls at St Sulpitius, Diest, are products of similar concerns. In Antwerp the standard of the best craftsmanship was also excellent and here there was a marked tendency towards vivid characterisation and anecdotal detail. Some indication of the richness of this decade can be seen from two almost random examples: the Crucifixion group in St Pieter's Louvain, where traditional forms and emotional values are revitalised and make a stark contrast to the humour of Antwerp, which looks towards the 16C, and the bronze effigy of Mary of Burgundy in Notre-Dame, Bruges, where exquisite decoration and a freer naturalism bear witness to the two decades which divide it from the equally beautiful but more austere effigy of Isabella of Bourbon in Antwerp cathedral.

Sculpture: 16C

In sculpture, as in painting and architecture, the overall impression is of a struggle to assimilate the fundamentally alien concepts of the Italian Renaissance. The attempt certainly produced some approximations to High Renaissance classicism, but it also engendered other fruits which in their decorative extravagance and material richness both perpetuate Flemish traditions and unconciously anticipate some aspects of the 17C baroque.

Mass production of wooden altarpieces reached its apogee at the beginning of the 16C, creating what has been described as an 'embarrassing plenitude' of works (T. Müller). In Brussels *Jan Borman* and his school remained important (e.g. the Auderghem altar in the Musée d'Art et d'Histoire, Brussels), while in Antwerp exaggeration of the local traditions of humour and characterisation led after c 1515 to distortions of form which can be compared to the 'Mannerism' current in painting. The Lamentation altar from Averbode, now in the Vleeshuis, Antwerp, is an example of such work. An apparently new centre of production was Mechelen, where the style was typically more tranquil and subdued (e.g. the St Dympna altarpiece in the church at Geel, by *Jan van Waver*). Fashionable Italianate elements were absorbed into the traditional formats, by the French immigrant *Robert Moreau*, for instance, in his Oplinter altar of c 1530 in the Musée d'Art et d'Histoire in Brussels. The advent of the Reformation, however, destroyed many markets and ultimately reduced the significance of devotional wooden sculpture.

Meanwhile, the inclusion of the Burgundian heritage in Charles V's huge domain meant that the Netherlandish court tended to attract artists from further afield. These men were often imbued with Renaissance ideas and eagerly responded to their patrons' increasing preoccupation with Italy— an attitude neatly symbolised by the presence of Michelangelo's Virgin in the church of Onze Lieve Vrouw in Bruges from 1506. Outstanding among the foreigners was *Conrad Meit* from Worms (died 1550/51) whose marble Virgin and Child in Ste. Gudule, Brussels, reveals a personal but profound understanding of the forms and the concepts of the Renaissance. Another immigrant was *Jean Mone* of Metz. Mone specialised in alabaster work and the translucent surface and inherent delicacy of this medium seem entirely appropriate to a master who tended to concentrate upon the external forms rather than the principles of the Renaissance, and who delighted in the slender decorative motifs of the Italian Quattrocento. His alabaster altar at Onze Lieve Vrouw in Halle, with its lovely, pure details, is like a gorgeous wedding cake. *Jacques du Broeucq* (died 1584) was another important 'Italianist'. His masterpiece, the decoration of the church of St Waudru in Mons, was badly damaged in 1797, but a number of fragments remain. Here Gothic and Renaissance meet: the decoration of traditional church furnishings is conceived in wholly Italian terms.

The most influential of these 'progressive' sculptors, *Cornelis Floris*, was also a distinguished architect. Floris' most important works in Belgium are the tabernacle of St Leonardus in Zoutleeuw (1550–52)—an enormously tall Gothic structure adorned with Italianate motifs—and the much more re-strained tomb of Jan III Mérode at Geel and rood screen in Tournai cathedral. But Floris' influence, like that of his rival *Hans Vredeman de Vries* was exercised chiefly through his engraved designs for decorative ornament (particularly strapwork and grotesques)—designs that were endlessly copied and repeated throughout Belgium and beyond.

The chimneypiece in the Vrije Museum at Bruges epitomises many of the major themes of Flemish 16C sculpture. Commissioned by Margaret of Austria to commemorate the Peace of Cambrai (1529) and largely executed by a foreigner, *Guyot de Beaugrant* of Lorraine, it is a symbol of the new international context of the Netherlandish court. The production of the work by a team of collaborating sculptors to designs by the painter *L. Blondeel* reflects, however, Flemish practice dating at least from the 15C. The lavish decoration and use of contrasting materials have been called a 'Mannerism of abundance' (Vey and Von der Osten), but they can also be seen as a partial translation into Italian of the Flemish 'late Gothic' delight in ornament and rich effects. The work has even been described as 'avant-baroque' (Fierens), partly because of its sheer extravagance, but also because it is an integrated decorative scheme employed to make a political point: the glorification of the House of Habsburg.

Sculpture: 17C and 18C

After the iconoclasm and uncertainty of the second half of the 16C, the establishment of the 'archdukes' Albert and Isabella and the Catholic Church's reassertion of itself in the southern Netherlands were a boon for all artists, but particularly for sculptors, whose work remained to a greater extent than painters' dependent on public and religious commissions. Several excellent artists rose to the challenge of furnishing the new churches and refurbishing the old.

Initially, the most influential figure was, paradoxically, a man who spent his career in Rome and by whose hand only two putti (on the monument of Bishop Triest) are thought to survive in Belgium. This was *François Duquesnoy* (son of Jérôme Duquesnoy the Elder, creator of Manneken-Pis in Brussels), who achieved the remarkable feat of retaining his artistic individuality in Bernini's Rome, and who was the inspiration of his brother *Jérôme II* and of the prolific *Artus Quellin the Elder*. Jérôme the Younger's works (e.g. the rest of Bishop Triest's monument in Ghent and statues in Notre-Dame du Sablon and the cathedral in Brussels) are rather eclectic, but technically accomplished and stylistically up to the minute. Artus Quellin the Elder was more original. A master of the formal repertory of the baroque, Artus nevertheless created personal works which are characterised by a vigorous grasp of observed reality. Although the main commission of his life was for the Town Hall in Amsterdam, good examples of his sculpture remain in Belgium, particularly in Antwerp. Quellin's nephew *Artus the Younger* was also an able sculptor with a fresh approach to the conventions of the baroque style. Rome and François Duquesnoy were the sources of his art, but his later works are themselves innovative: the St Rose of Lima (St Paulus, Antwerp) anticipates the greater refinement and delicacy of the rococo, while the dramatic Creator at Bruges cathedral fully exploits the possibilities of the baroque.

The sculpture of *Luc Fayd'herbe* was sometimes highly successful, sometimes less so. Among the numerous examples of his work which can be seen in Mechelen, for example, there is the monument to Bishop Andreas Cruesen in the cathedral, where the vitality and power of the dead cleric contrasts rather inappropriately with the relatively insipid Christ and Father Time. Meanwhile *Jean del Cour* of Liège (died 1707) produced his interpretation of the baroque in reserved, dignified and highly accomplished works such as the monument of Bishop Allamont in Ghent cathedral (commissioned 1667). Del Çour's figures are aristocratic and sensitive, and his beautiful draperies were a speciality which ultimately became a recognisable mannerism. His most popular and influential work is the Fontaine de la Vièrge in Liège.

In the 18C sculpture, like architecture, loses its recognisably Belgian baroque character and assumes an international, classical aspect. Perhaps the region's transformation from its early 16C position as the economic, political and cultural hub of Charles V's empire to its more peripheral, relatively insignificant 18C role can be seen as having some effect on art. Certainly large commissions declined and a number of sculptors (e.g. *Gabriel Grupello*) went abroad in search of more lucrative markets.

In the first half of the century a series of extraordinary pulpits in wood— the traditional Flemish medium—can be seen as representing a final Flemish flourish in the face of encroaching classicism. Of course such a view is slightly frivolous in its blatant hindsight, but works such as *Hendrik Verbruggen*'s pulpit in Brussels cathedral of 1699 (which set the trend), *M. van der Voort*'s creation in Mechelen cathedral of 1721–23 and *Verhaeghen*'s fantasy in Onze Lieve Vrouw van Hanswijk, also in Mechelen, do incorporate characteristics, such as profuse decoration with little concern for basic structure, vigour and virtuosity in execution and a naturalism which sometimes verges on the anecdotal, which can be associated with previous Flemish sculpture. Love them or loathe them, these pulpits, and other church furnishings in a similar vein, certainly make an impact.

Stone sculpture, which at the turn of the century is still recognisably related to the Quellins and the Duquesnoys (e.g. Grupello's numerous charming works in Brussels), later becomes characterised by a cool classicism. *Laurent Delvaux* (died 1778) and *Pieter Verschaffelt* (died 1793), who had both spent long years in Rome, were fully committed to the new, international style, but earlier artists, such as *M. van der Voort* (died 1737), managed to keep a foot in both the baroque and the classical camps. As we have seen, Van der Voort was responsible for the Mechelen pulpit, but his two earlier monuments in the same cathedral are distinctly classical in feeling. The ultimate triumph of classicism is represented by Delvaux's pupil *G.L. Godecharle*, who, significantly, later studied in Paris. Some of his work is routine, but occasionally, as in the portrait of his wife in Brussels (Musée Communal), he makes a more personal statement.

Art in the 19C and 20C

By *Tania Jones*

In this period the process of 'internationalism' which we have observed in the 18C was completed. After the domination of neo-classicism, individualism reigned, in a country already divided by language, and the art of this time did not have a national identity. This development, which was intimately connected with the enormous social, political and economic changes occurring, meant that Belgium, for the first time politically independent, became, artistically speaking, a province of Europe. There were distinguished Belgian artists throughout this period, eclectic in style, although maintaining their own artistic personalities, who while being participants in broad European movements and ready to absorb strong artistic influences from abroad, were also part of a distinct tradition of Belgian art. They had an eye for detail, an interest in human subjects, and they focused on the depiction of light and colour, which had been the particular characteristics of art in Flanders for centuries. There is an obvious line of descent in emotive works of art from the early primitives and the 17C baroque, to the Romantics, Symbolists, Expressionists, Surrealists of the 19C and early 20C and up to the Social Realists and Hyperrealists of today.

The political annexation of Belgium by France was preceded by an artistic conquest of the country. Thus, by the end of the 18C classicism reigned supreme in all spheres of Belgian art, although many of the artists gained their recognition abroad, for example *Josef Suveé* (1743–1807), *Frans Jozef Kinsoen* (1771–1839) and *Jozef Odevaere* (1775–1830). Although much architecture was destroyed during the French occupation and very little created, classicism remained the dominant style after 1815. Its chief practitioner was the court architect *Charles van der Straeten* (1771–1834), whose masterpiece is the sober Palais Ducale (1876; now the Palais des Académies) in Brussels. The expansion of the universities during this period created opportunities for architects, as for example the division of Louvain University in this century has done for the architect Lucian Kroll and others. Examples of classicist work can be found at Ghent (Louis Roelandt) and Liège (J.N. Chevron).

The outstanding figure among the numerous followers of the French painter Jacques Louis David was *François Joseph Navez* (1787–1869). Navez had trained with David in Paris. He also visited Rome before, in 1830, he became the director of the Brussels Academy and the head of the neo-classical movement there. His best works are portraits: 'The de Hemptinne Family', in the Brussels Museum, approaches the quality of his master. *Mathieu-Ignace van Bree* (1773–1839) was another important link with France: after his training with François-André Vincent, he taught his pupils at the Antwerp Academy, where he became head in 1827, to concentrate simultaneously on the declamatory and the naturalistic aspects of classicism. The result was a type of nationalistic history painting produced by a school of Belgian artists, working mainly in Antwerp, after the country's independence from Holland in 1830. This group, led by *Gustave Wappers* (1807–74), who succeeded Bree at the Antwerp Academy in 1839, *Ferdinand de Braekeleer* (1792–1883) and *Nicaise de Keyser* (1813–87), dominated the scene until sometime after 1850. No longer classicist in style, their works are a glorification of their country in a sort of romantic history painting or patriotic allegory. Wappers' 'Episode during the Belgian Revolt of 1830' (1834; Brussels Museum), de Keyser's 'La Bataille des Eperons d'or' (1836; Brussels Museum), Louis Gallait's 'Les Tétes Coupées' (1857; Tournai Museum), or 'The Plaque at Tournai in 1092' (Tournai Museum) and Emile Wauters' 'The Madness of Hugo van der Goes' (1872; Brussels Museum), are energetic and forceful works, which provide a glamorised view of the past.

Belgian romantic painting consists primarily of historical costume pieces, represented on a grand scale, which sometimes verge on melodrama. The exemplar of this style, and almost a caricature of the 'romantic artist', was *Antoine Wiertz* (1806–65), who trained in Antwerp. His passionate, sometimes hysterical works, reminiscent of Goya, can be seen in the Wiertz Museum in Brussels, which was specially built by the government of the time to house his immense canvases. This period also had a calmer, less grandiose aspect. The important murals painted by *Hendrik Leys* (1815–69) for the Stadhuis in Antwerp look back, nostalgically, to Flemish art before Rubens, in a way which is rather analogous to the Pre-Raphaelites in England. Somewhat later, *Henri de Braekeleer* (1840–88), inspired by the Netherlandish artists of the 17C, produced beautifully painted tranquil interiors and landscapes.

From c 1830 until the end of the 19C architecture in Belgium, as in the rest of Europe, was characterised by eclecticism. The rapid growth of the cities, which demanded massive building programmes, inevitably produced some banal and lifeless work but there were also some remarkable achievements. *Joseph Polaert*'s vast, domed, Palais de Justice (1866–83), which stands on a hill overlooking Brussels, is impressive, while J.F. Cluysenaar's Galeries St Hubert (1846), also in Brussels, are graceful. The Brussels Bourse (1873) by Leon Suys and the Musée de l'Art Ancien (1875–85) by Alphonse Balat, who redesigned the façades and the staircase of the Palais Royal for the King and also designed the botanical hothouses at the Palais Royal at Laeken, are notable buildings, as is also the National Bank in Antwerp (1879) by A. Beyaert.

Just as David's presence in Belgium had a profound impact on painting so for sculpture did the presence of François Rude, the major French sculptor of the early 19C, who lived in exile in Brussels between 1815 and 1827. The influence of French sculpture was continued later in the century by Auguste Rodin, who worked in Brussels, with his master Carrier-Belleuse, on the decoration of the Bourse.

Rude's emphasis on the direct observation of nature undoubtedly influenced the Belgian *Willem Geefs* (1805–85), whose Mausoleum of Frédéric de Mérode in Ste Gudule, Brussels, was regarded by his contemporaries as boldly realistic. In sculpture, as in architecture and painting, eclecticism was a central and often fruitful element. With the growth of the cities sculpture became increasingly important, particularly in public commissions: typical commissions would be for the enrichment of the façades of buildings, sometimes commemorative sometimes decorative in theme, and for statues to be placed at the end of the long avenues. Among notable works of the period are *Eugène Simonis*, equestrian statue 'Godofroid de Bouillon' (1848), Place Royale, Brussels, and Paul de Vigne's 'The Triumph of Art' and Charles van der Stappen's 'The Teaching of Art', grand allegorical figure groups on the façade of the Palais des Beaux Arts (1880s). *Thomas Vinçotte* (1850–1925) received recognition for his pediment group of 'Belgium between Agriculture and Industry' on the Palais de Roi, Brussels, and *Jacques de Lalaing* (1858–1917) was noted for his majestic tomb to the English killed at the battle of Waterloo at Evere cemetery near Brussels.

The Botanical Gardens in Brussels includes works by most of the important Belgian sculptors of the 19C. Among these was *Constantin Meunier* (1831–1905), whose sculptures of heroic workers express a romantic concept of labour which struck a deep chord within newly industrialised Europe. His works reflect a general increase in social awareness, and they still have the power to move. Much of Meunier's material was derived from the mining district of the Borinage, where the deplorable conditions also shocked the Dutch painter van Gogh in his early career. The best collections of Meunier's works are in the Brussels museum and the museum devoted to his work which is also in Brussels and has been restored.

Paul de Vigne's works have an Italianate, almost Donatellesque quality; while the powerful, lusty productions of *Jef Lambeaux* (1852–1908), the Fleming, may inspire thoughts of Rubens or Jordaens, as well as of Giambologna the Renaissance sculptor whose work Lambeaux had seen in Florence and who himself was Flemish. 'The Merry Song' (Antwerp Museum) and the fountain (1887) in the Grote Markt at Antwerp show this strength. Julien Dillens (1849–1904) and Jules Lagae, the latter best known for his 'Expiation' showing pathos in his representations of the struggling prisoners (Ghent Museum), were also Flemish sculptors. Dillens' sculpture is symbolist or even Art Nouveau in style; this affinity was strengthened by his use of ivory which was imported from the Belgian Congo in the 1890s. Others of note are Achille Chainaye, G. Charlier and Victor Rousseau whose small-scale figural sculpture in bronze and marble using classical forms gains a greater sensibility and grace after the influence of Rodin. George Minne, best known for his elongated kneeling figures, especially those in the fountain outside the cathedral of St Bavo in Ghent, was also an illustrator. The use of line developed in his graphic work was important for his work in sculpture, particularly in the creation of emotive subjects. *Rik Wouters* (1882–1916), a painter as well as a sculptor, *Ernest Wijnants* (1878–1964; museum devoted to his work in Mechelen) and *Oscar Jespers* (1887–1970) looked towards modernism by depicting simplified, primitive and almost abstract forms. There is a large collection of late 19C and 20C sculpture at the open air museum at Middelheim, Antwerp.

From 1850 a new impetus can be seen in the paintings of *Florent Willems* (1823–1905) and, particularly, *Alfred Stevens* (1823–1906), a pupil of Navez who later lived almost exclusively in Paris. In their paintings these artists populated interiors with attractive women: 'Women with a Mirror' (Groeninge Museum, Bruges), by Willems, reminds one of a Dutch 17C genre piece like those of Gerard ter Borch. 'Autumn Flowers' (1867; Brussels Museum), is a good example of Stevens' depiction of women in all their finery, contemporary with the mode of the Second Empire in France. Alfred's older brother *Joseph Stevens* (1819–92) and *Jan Stobbaerts* (1838–1914) specialised in painting animals—especially dogs, sometimes satirically, for example Stevens' 'Brussels–the Morning' (1848; Brussels Museum)—and rural life, with a vitality worthy of their Flemish heritage.

The establishment of the Société Libre des Beaux-Arts in 1868 marked the end of the acceptance of the government-sponsored Academies and Salons, held triennially in Ghent, Antwerp and Brussels, and the beginning of avant-gardism in Belgium. Having been inspired by Courbet's 'Stone Breakers', which was exhibited in Belgium in 1851, *Charles de Groux* (1825–70) and Constantin Meunier (already mentioned as a sculptor) were both at the centre of the Realist movement. They were founding members of this group who wished to concentrate on depicting the lives of the poor. *Eugène Laermans* (1864–1940), working almost 30 years later, continued to depict enobled labourers returning from their daily struggle in derelict landscapes analogous to their suffering. A large proportion of the group were landscape painters who wished to paint free from the confines of the studio. Members of the SLBA, including *Louis Dubois* (1830–80), *Alfred Verwee* (1838–95), *Edouard Agneessens* (1842–85), *Felicien Rops* (1833–98), who started as a landscape painter but became most famous for his erotic graphic work (museum devoted to his work in Namur) and *Eugène Smits* (1826–1912), chose to exhibit with French artists to give the group a more European flavour. By the 1870s there was less opposition to Realism, as paintings by these artists were being accepted in the Salons. The success of *Charles Herman*'s painting 'A l'Aube' (1875) was an important turning point in the struggles against neo-classical and romantic painting. His 'realism', like that of Willems and Stevens, was the depiction of the bourgeoisie.

Landscape, which in Belgium as elsewhere in Europe had achieved a position of primary importance around 1865, was well represented by *Théodore Fourmois* (1814–71), *Alphonse Asselbergs* (1839–1916), *Joseph Coosemans* (1828–1904), and *Eugène Huberti* (1819–80), who were friends with the Barbizon painters in France, and by *Hippolyte Boulenger* (1837–74), painter of the Ardennes and the forests of Tervuren. Perhaps the most interesting landscape painters of the late 19C are *Paul-Jean Clays* (1819–1900), *Louis Artan* (1837–90), *Guillaume Vogels* (1836–96), *A.-J. Heymans* (1839–1921) working at Kalmthout, and *Theodoor Baïon* (1840–99) and *Frans Courtens* (1854–1943) working at Dendermonde, who to some extent resisted the seductive appeal of the French Impressionists' style and adopted an atmospheric, translucent style characteristic of Belgian art. An early work by *Emile Claus* (1849–1924), 'The Leie at Astene' (Groeninge Museum, Bruges), marked the transition to yet another kind of impressionism which was called Luminism after the name of the group Vie et Lumière. This group, whose art vibrated with sunlight, was formed by Claus in 1904, with artists like A.-J. Heymans, *George Buysse* (1864–1916) and *Georges Morren* (1868–1941), some 30 years later than the start of Impressionism in France.

The immediate heirs to the Société Libre des Beaux- Arts were the groups La Chrysalide (1875–81) and L'Essor (1876–91), who also organised their own exhibitions. The former comprised artists such as Louis Artan, Guillaume Vogels and others from SLBA; and the latter included the sculptor Julien Dillens, *Jean Delville* (1867–1953), *Léon Frederic* (1856–1940) and *Fernand Khnopff* (1858–1921), who were Symbolists. *Xavier Mellery* (1845–1921), Khnopff's teacher, *William Degouve de Nungues* (1867–1935), *Emile Fabry* (1865–1966) and to some extent *Léon Spilliaert* (1881–1946), who came from Ostend, followed closely in their wake. The ideas of these and future groups were disseminated by the various art journals that came into existence at the same time, initiated by literary as well as professional figures. Their success was partly due to the prevailing atmosphere of liberalism, which kings Leopold I and II upheld. Brussels, which was French-speaking, became the artistic capital of Belgium, international in its outlook and ready to absorb new ideas, while Ghent and Antwerp remained with their Flemish heritage most prominent, only to become important again in the 20C.

Of Belgian painters of this period the most widely known is *James Ensor* (1860–1949). Macabre and fantastic, he is known for his use of skeletons and masks to make social comment in works such as 'The Entry into Brussels 1889'. In the best tradition of Bosch, these pictures still have the capacity to shock, and to fascinate. Even in his early works Ensor is penetrating. The 'Sombre Lady' (Brussels Museum) and the 'Mangeuse d'Huitres' (Antwerp Museum), provoke a response from the viewer.

Although very much an individual Ensor was also a participator. He contributed to both L'Essor and La Chrysalide, and was one of the founding members of the group Les XX (Les Vingt; 1883–94), which was established following the activity of the previously mentioned groups. Les XX, named because of its 20 members and 20 invited exhibitors, and its sucessor La Libre Esthetique (1894–1914), were, again, eclectic in their outlook and recognised the importance of combining all the arts and styles of art. In their exhibitions, held annually, they also had poetry readings and concerts as well as displays of Impressionist, neo-Impressionist, Symbolist, Art Nouveau and decorative works of art from abroad, especially France and England, as well as from Belgium. The Belgian artists were very receptive to these styles. Seurat's famous pointillist painting 'La Grande Jatte', depicting Parisians out on a Sunday afternoon on the Seine, was exhibited at Les XX in 1887 and had the most immediate and profound effect on some of the group's members, especially *Théo van Rysselberghe* (1862–1926), *Georges Lemmen* (1865–1916), *Alfred 'Willy' Finch* (1854–1930), *Anna Boch* (1848–1933) and Henry van der Velde, who all immediately adopted pointillism. Théo van Rysselberghe, however, continued to paint psychological portraiture but using the pointillist technique. In Belgium the approach to pointillism was less scientific then it had been in France but it also became more widespread.

Henri Evenepoel (1872–99) was an individualist. He painted portraits in a style inspired by Manet. Their poster-like quality looks forward to posters of *Jules van Biesbroeck* (1850–1920).

The end of the century saw the emergence of two extremely important architects: *Victor Horta* (1861–1947) and *Henry van de Velde* (1863–1957). Both were seminal figures in the development of Art Nouveau. This style had been imported partly from England with the works of William Morris, Walter Crane and Aubrey Beardsley that had been shown at exhibitions such as La Libre Esthétique. The two-dimensional arabesque lines of Art Nouveau were developed by the architects and designers of Belgium into three dimensions. *Gustave Serrurier-Bovy* (1858–1910), from Liége, designed Art Nouveau furniture. The surviving works of Horta, who used modern materials such as glass and steel to create buildings of an organic and supple grace, are in Brussels. His most famous building, the 'Maison du Peuple' (1896–99) for the Socialist Workers' Party, in Place Emile van de Velde, with its famous wall of glass, was destroyed in the 1960s. His house and studio (1898) is now a museum, and the Hotel Tassel (1892), now used by the Mexican Embassy, was recently restored to its former glory. A more simplified form of Art Nouveau was created by him in the Palais des Beaux Arts in Brussels (1922–29) and also the Museum of Fine Arts, Tournai (1928). Van de Velde, painter, craftsman and influential critic, as well as architect and interior designer, invites comparison with Charles Rennie Mackintosh. Both aimed at creating a total artistic movement. Van de Velde spent many years in Weimar. There he became the director of the Arts and Crafts School, which he designed himself in 1901 and which became in 1919 the first Bauhaus under the direction of Walter Gropius. The concept of unity of the arts, which Les XX had subscribed to, led, eventually, to these achievements. Little of van de Velde's architectural work remains in

Belgium except for 'Bloemenwerf' (1895), his own house in Uccle on the outskirts of Brussels. Façades in the Art Nouveau style remain prominent in the streets of Belgium, particularly in Ghent (Horta's birthplace) and on and around the Avenue Louise in Brussels. *Paul Hankar* (1859–1901) was another architect who had succumbed to the style, although he was less concerned with spatial unity than with decoration. His Ciamberlani house (1897), 40 Boulevard de la Cambre, shows his use of multicoloured brickwork.

One of van de Velde's most famous buildings, although not in the curvilinear style of the fin-de-siècle but in the style of the international modern movement, is the Kröller-Müller Museum in Otterlo, Holland. His influence can be felt in the austerity and refinement of the best early 20C Belgian architecture. *Victor Bourgeois* (1897–1962), who created the Cité Moderne (1922–25), Berchem-Ste Agathe, Brussels, and the studio of Oscar Jespers (1928), used clean white forms. *Louis Herman de Koninck* (1896–1985) was a modernist who after the Bauhaus was forced to close in 1933 taught functionalism at the School of Art and Architecture at Le Cambre, Brussels. This school had been founded in 1926 by Henry van de Velde and is still strong today for visual art and design. De Koninck created his own house in Uccle, where he used his rationalist philosophy of minimum interiors with maximum spatial impact. The work of *Antoine Pompe* (1873–1980), on the other hand, represented a new rationalised way of building in brick, as seen in the Clinic for Dr van Neck (1910), at 55 Rue Wafelaerts, Brussels.

In the early 20C monumental architecture in Belgium became international in character, revealing the influence of contemporary developments in Holland, France and Germany. Amongst the vast quantity of 20C architecture the new universities sited at Louvain-le-Neuve and Sart Tilman near Liège are interesting and original designs. However, architecture after 1945 was not really part of a movement, in fact individualism reigned, unlike in Holland where planning dominated the overall look of the houses and the layout of the cities. For this reason it has been said that Belgium's architecture was a 'spendid and full-blooded chaos', and on the one hand it has been pessimistically interpreted as the 'ugliest country in the world', and on the other as having meaning and freedom admired in the architecture of today. The protagonists of the functionalist movement were, as mentioned above, L.H. de Koninck, Victor Bourgeois and Hoste. The anti-functionalists are Bob van Reeth, Charles Vandenhove, Lucien Kroll—particularly for his Alma metro station, which is Gaudi-like in its biomorphic plasticity—André Loits, Luc Schuiten, Marcel Raymaekers, Jacques Sequaris and Marc Dessauvage. The disparate individualistic styles of these architects, although referring through the use of materials such as brick to the vernacular heritage of building, provide an immensely varied modern geometry within the towns and cities of Belgium and exhibit this country's eclectic tastes.

The marked preference of the early 20C painters and sculptors for surrealism and expressionism can perhaps be interpreted in terms of traditional Flemish tastes for the bizarre, the exuberant and the tactile, as well as the influence of groups like the Symbolists who were exploring the imagination in art. This is first expressed in the religious-pastoral scenes painted by *Jacob Smits* (1856–1928), who was born in Holland and influenced by Rembrandt. The source and centre of Flemish expressionism was the School of Sint Martens-Latem, a village outside Ghent, in which the leading figures were, from the first group established around 1905, sculptor George Minne (1866–1941) and artists Albert Servaes (1883–1966), Valerius de Sadeleer (1867–1941), Gustave van de Woestyne (1881–1947) and Albijn van den Abeele (1835–1918), whose work shows a certain Gothic mysticism. They were influenced by Symbolist painters in Brussels and writers of the time, a few of whom came from Ghent, but they also depicted religious subjects. Minne's sculpture 'Three Marys at the Tomb', Servaes' series of the 'Stations of the Cross' and de Woestyne's 'Crucifixion' are all representative examples. De Saedeleer and Abeele painted landscapes in Flanders with a cold stillness and contemplation about them comparable with Brueghel. From the second group, established around 1909, were Constant Permeke (1886–1952), master of emotional realism, Gustave de Smet (1877–1943) and Frits van den Berghe (1883–1939). Their work shows slight Cubist influence but they are figurative paintings using cubic forms. Flemish expressionism developed independently from that in Germany. It was more humane, evoking pathos by depicting fishermen and peasants in predominantly earthy colours. The Permeke Museum is in Jabbeke and the Gustave and Leon de Smet museums are at Deurle, 3km SE of Sint Marten-Latem.

Meanwhile, Leon de Smet (1881–1966; Gustave's brother), Edgard Tytgat (1879–1957), Jean Brusselmans (1884–1953) from Dilbeek, Hippolyte Daeye (1873–1952), Fernand Schirren (1872–1944), Auguste Oleffe (1867–1931), Louis Thevenet (1874–1930), Willem Paerels (1878–1962), Henri Wolvens (1896–1977) and Rik Wouters (1882–1916) developed their styles. In broad terms these artists are known as Brabant Fauvists because of their use of bold outlines and bright blocks of colour.

René Magritte (1898–1967), one of the most important Surrealist painters, was born and trained in Belgium. His unexpected juxtapostion of motifs, which, while essentially ordinary, are of unnatural scale and remoteness, has been extremely influential. One of his most famous paintings 'The Empire of Lights' (1952; Brussels Museum) is reminiscent of Willem Degouve de Nuncques' 'House of Mystery' (1892; Brussels Museum). After participating in the birth of the movement in Paris, between 1927 and 1930, Magritte returned to Brussels. Although Surrealism has been regarded as French it has an affinity with the peculiar in Belgian painting. In Brussels Magritte painted murals for public buildings, something which Paul Delvaux (1897–), another Belgian Surrealist, also did. From 1935 Delvaux produced obsessional and unforgettable images of sexuality, travel and death. One of his murals can be seen on the exit of the Bourse metro station in Brussels (1978) and there is a museum of his works at Sint Idesbald. Another contributor to the Surrealist movement in Belgium was E.L.T. Mesens who developed the style in collage.

Louis Buisseret (1888–1956), Anto Carte (1886–1954) and Leon Devos (1897–1974) started a group called Nervia in 1928, which was centred around the town of Mons. The idea was to represent Walloon art. The styles of the artists vary but the paintings contain religious, allegorical and genre images in a lyrical almost Graeco-Roman manner. A few of these works can be seen in the museum at Charleroi.

Before the Second World War Belgian art was dominated by the two main movements: Expressionism and Surrealism. The exceptions were Jules Schmalzigaug (1886–1917), who was touched by the Futurist style and whose canvases depicting speed and light are influenced by the Italians Severini and Boccioni, and Marthe Donas, who was a Cubist painter and spent most of her life abroad. Between the wars saw the first experiments in abstraction, with artists like Paul Joostens (1889–1960), Jozef Peeters

(1895–1960), *Michel Seuphor, Karel Maes* and *Joseph Lacasse.* The main protagonist was *Victor Severanckx* (1897–1965). These artists were aware of the developments in Holland through the Belgian George Vantongerloo, who was a friend of Théo van Doesburg.

After 1945 the art world was fragmented. Two major groups having particular connections with Belgium were La Jeune Peinture (1945–50) and Cobra (1948–51). La Jeune Peinture, influenced in part by the lyrical and geometrical abstractions of Victor Severanckx, paved the way for the fully-fledged abstract art of the 1950s and numbered among its adherents Gaston Bertrand, Louis van Lint and Anne Bonnet, Marc Mendelson, Lismonde, Jan Cox and Jo Delahaut. The artists of Cobra, whose name is an acronym of Copenhagen, Brussels and Amsterdam, questioned the distinction between painting and writing and laid great emphasis on spontaneity. The most notable Belgian member of the group was *Pierre Aleckinsky.* Their exhibition at Liège in 1951 had a great influence on future Belgian artists. Prosper de Troyer and Felix de Boeck (museum devoted to his work in Brussels) painted abstractions that were a development from Expressionism without any structured forms. After this it is difficult to mention one name without mentioning many, but perhaps Raoul Ubac, Octave Landuyt and Bram Bogart might be picked out. Pol Mara and Pol Bury were influenced by the Pop or Op art movement. Since the 1960s art has moved back to figuration and a new realism, social or hyperrealism, with artists like Roger Somville, Roger Raveel, Etienne Elias, Raoul de Keyser, Guy Degobert, Marcel Maeyer, Roger Wittevrongel, Marcel Broodthaers and Panamarenko. Here the use of photography becomes important and real objects are exploited to appeal to the imagination. Although in a modern contemporary idiom, the objects and their bizarre juxtapositions have a timelessness and remind us of 'the soul of things' or the expression of 'the invisible through the visible', which was the basis of the art of the Symbolists and Surrealists before them.

Today there are two divided ministries of culture, one for the Flemish, another for the Walloons, and the artistic character of the country is made up of small local communities with a multitude of museums. However, what is certain is that as always Belgium continues actively to contribute to the development of Western art.

PRACTICAL INFORMATION

Tourist Information. The national organisation for tourism in Belgium is located at 61 Grasmarkt (Rue Marché aux Herbes), 1000 Brussels, tel: (02) 5040300. This is composed of two parallel, autonomous bodies, the Office de Promotion du Tourisme de la Communauté Française (OPT) and the Vlaams Commissariaat-Generaal voor Toerisme (VGGT). Brochures published by OPT and VGGT, together with a number of publications produced jointly on subjects of common interest, eg. accommodation, or a calendar of events, may be obtained from the information and enquiry office at 61 Grasmarkt.

Belgian tourist offices abroad represent both communities. The addresses of those in some Western Europe countries and the USA are as follows:
United Kingdom: Premier House, 2 Gayton Road, Harrow, Middx, HA1 2XU, tel: 081-861 3300.
Germany: 47 Berliner Allee, D-4000 Düsseldorf, tel: (0211) 326008.
France: 21 Boulevard des Capucines, 75002 Paris, tel: (1) 4742 4118.
Netherlands: 435 Herengracht, 1017-PR Amsterdam, tel: (020) 6245953.
USA: 745 Fifth Avenue, New York, NY 10151, tel: (212) 7588130.

There is a network of provincial tourist offices in Belgium. These can provide much useful information about their areas. In alphabetical order they are:
Antwerp: 11 Karel Oomsstraat, 2018 Antwerp, tel: (03) 2162810.
Brabant: 61 Grasmarkt, 1000 Brussels, tel: (02) 5040455.
East Flanders: 64 Koningin Maria-Hendrikaplein, 9000 Ghent, tel: (091) 221637.
Hainaut: 31 Rue des Clercs, 7000 Mons, tel: (065) 316101.
Liège: 77 Boulevard de la Sauvenière, 4000 Liège, tel: (041) 224210.
Limburg: 27 Thonissenlaan 27, 3500 Hasselt, tel: (011) 222958.
Luxembourg: 9 Quai de l'Ourthe, 6980 La Roche-en-Ardenne, tel: (084) 411012.
Namur: 3 Rue Notre-Dame, 5000 Namur, tel: (081) 222998.
West Flanders: Kasteel Tillegem, B-8200 Bruges 2, tel: (050) 380296 or 337344.

Many towns and villages in Belgium have their own tourist information offices, though in the smaller places they are usually open during the summer months only. Frequently, these local offices can provide detailed literature and advice which may not be readily available elsewhere.

Sea and Air Services from England, and the Channel Tunnel. Car ferries operated in partnership by P&O European Ferries (Zeebrugge) and the Belgian Regie voor Maritiem Transport (Ostend) sail from Dover to Zeebrugge or Ostend. Crossing times are 3½–4 hours to Ostend and about half an hour longer to Zeebrugge.

P&O European Ferries also operate a service from Felixstowe to Zeebrugge. The crossing time is 5¼ hours on day sailings and c 8 hours at night. Another P&O North Sea Ferries service links Hull and Zeebrugge. Embarkation is at 17.00, disembarkation at c 09.00 the next morning.

Car drivers, for whom the longer cross Channel sea crossings hold few charms, may like to take one of the quicker routes to France and continue by road into Belgium.

Travellers without cars will find the Jetfoil services (small supplementary charge) provided by the Regie voor Maritiem Transport between Dover and

Ostend convenient, quick and comfortable. There are frequent departures (daytime only). The crossing by Jetfoil takes c 1 hour 40 minutes.

Useful addresses: P&O European Ferries, Channel House, Channel View Road, Dover CT17 9TJ, tel: (0304) 203388/081 575 8555. P&O European Ferries, Car Ferry Terminal, 8380 Zeebrugge, tel: (050) 542222. P&O European Ferries, Car Ferry Terminal, Felixstowe IP11 8TB, tel: (0394) 604040. Regie voor Maritiem Transport, 5 Natiënkaai, B-8400 Ostend, tel: (059) 559955. P&O North Sea Ferries, King George Dock, Hedon Road, Hull, HU9 5QA, tel: (0482) 795141; and Leopold II Dam, 8380 Zeebrugge, tel: (050) 543430.

Air Services between London (Heathrow) and Brussels (Zaventem) are provided by British Airways and the Belgian airline SABENA (Société Anonyme Belge d'Eploitation de la Navigation Aérienne). Other operators have flights to Antwerp, Ostend and on to Liège.

Tour Operators. A list of British companies offering inclusive tours to Belgium may be obtained from the Belgian National Tourist Office in London.

The **Channel Tunnel**. Towards the end of 1993 there will be frequent, direct passenger trains services from London to Brussels. Trains will leave Waterloo International every hour. Initially, the journey time will be 3 hours and 10 minutes. This will be reduced by half an hour from 1996, when a new high speed line in Belgium comes into operation. There will be direct services from Scotland, N England and the Midlands.

Flight services from Glasgow, Plymouth and Swansea to Brussels will also be operated. The trains will have sleeper coaches, reclining seats, bar and catering facilities. There will be accommodation for disabled passengers. Customs and Immigration staff will travel on the trains.

Motoring in Belgium. Belgium has an excellent network of motorways and main roads. However, in some towns and rural areas cobbles and rough surfaces may still be encountered. Warning notices are usually posted at the approaches to these.

Belgian traffic laws and signs are generally similar to those found in other Western European countries. Motorways and some major through roads are designated A followed by a national number. Where these roads or sections of them form part of the European system, they will also have an E and a European number. Other major roads have an N (National) designation.

The E sign, often without a place name, is widely used on major highways, so drivers should make map checks to ensure that they are on the correct route to their destination. Maps produced before 1986/7, when the numbering system was changed, should not be used. The following are recommended: Michelin sheets 212, 213 and 214 (1cm: 2km) and sheet 409 (1cm: 3.5km), which covers the whole of Belgium and the Grand-Duchy of Luxembourg.

In Belgium there are two main motoring clubs: The Touring Club Royal de Belgique (TCB), 44 Rue de la Loi, Brussels, tel: (02) 2332211 (affiliated to the British Automobile Assocation). The Royal Automobile Club de Belgique (RACB), 49 Avenue du Globe, Brussels, tel: (02) 3430008 (affiliated to the British Royal Automobile Club). Members of foreign motoring clubs which have reciprocal arrangements with the TCB and the RACB may use their facilities including road patrol breakdown services.

Drivers from Britain and the United States should note that road practices in Belgium differ in some respects from those current in their own countries. Before travelling they are advised to consult their national motoring organisations which can supply specialised publications containing up-to-date, detailed information on laws and practices in Belgium.

The following points should be noted in particular:

Accidents. In the event of an accident of any significance, and always if there has been personal injury, the police should be informed before any vehicle involved is moved. They must also be informed in the case of damage to an unoccupied, stationary vehicle. In the case of minor accidents vehicles must be moved as soon as drivers have exchanged particulars.

For Police, dial 901 (906 in Antwerp, Bruges, Brussels, Charleroi, Ghent or Mechelen).

For Fire or Ambulance, dial 900.

Bicycles. A careful look-out should be maintained for cyclists. Cycle tracks, sometimes marked only by a painted line, may run along one or both sides of the road. Motorists have to be as aware of these as of the road itself. This applies particularly when turning, as bicycles continuing ahead normally have priority.

Insurance is compulsory. Normal British car policies should provide cover for the miniumum legal requirements. However, this does not necessarily mean that full home cover is automatically extended abroad. Motorists should consult their company or broker before travelling. It is advisable to arrange for the issue of a Green Card, which extends the home policy for use abroad during a specified period.

Membership of one of the schemes offered by the motoring associations and others, which cover such matters as breakdown, 'get-you-home', medical expenses, is also recommended.

Licences. A national or international driving licence is required. The minimum age for local validity is 18. Vehicle registration documentation should be carried and vehicles must show appropriate nationality identification, e.g. a GB plate or sticker on vehicles registered in Britain.

Speed Limits. In built-up areas (generally between place name signs) 60 km/h; other roads 90km/h; motorways and some 4-lane roads 120km/h. Note that lower limits are frequently imposed.

Duty-Free Cars. Belgium has a special system, which allows visitors to purchase a European car and take it back to their own country without paying duty. Consult the Yellow Pages in Belgium for details of companies operating this system.

There is also a 'buy back' system. This allows exemption from VAT during the period of your stay. It is a sale financed for a determined time, at the end of which you can return the car or keep it by paying a price fixed in advance.

Traffic Signs. Signs, in Flemish and French, include the following:

Alle Richtingen	= All Directions
Toutes Directions	
Weg Omlegging	= Diversion
Déviation. Route Déviée	
Werk in Uitvoering	= Roadworks
Chantier	
Moeilijke Doorgang	= Difficult road stretch
Passage Difficile	

Uitgezondert Plaatselijk Verkeer	= Entry only for locally
Excepté Circulation Locale	resident or business traffic
Doorgaand Verkeer	= Through traffic
Toutes Directions	
Schijf Verplicht	= Parking disc must be shown
Disque Obligatoire	

A Warning Triangle must be carried by all vehicles. In the event of an accident or breakdown, the triangle must be placed 100 metres behind the vehicle on motorways (30 metres on other roads) and must be clearly visible from a distance of 50 metres.

Travel by Train. Belgium has an extensive and efficient rail network (see the map at the back of the book). A variety of reduced fares available includes tourist-period tickets, weekend tickets, the Benelux pass, group fares, etc. At a number of stations cars and bicycles may be hired, by pre-arrangement. In addition, there are combined train, bus and even boat excursions to many places of interest.

Information: *Belgium*. Any station; or tel: (02) 2192640. *United Kingdom*. Belgian National Railways, Premier House, 10 Greycoat Place, London, SW1P 1SB, tel: 071-233 0360.

Entry Formalities. At present a passport or other internationally recognised identification document must be shown on entry to Belgium. Registration with the police is arranged by hotel, pension or campsite. Visitors, who wish to stay longer than three months, should obtain a permit before entering Belgium.

Foreign Embassies. British Embassy: 28 Rue Joseph II, Brussels; Consular Section, 32 Rue Joseph II, tel: (02) 2179000. American Embassy: Regentlaan 27, 1000 Brussels, tel: (22) 5133830. Canadian Embassy: Tervurenlaan 2, 1040 Brussels, tel: (22) 7356040.

Accommodation. The range of hotels, motels and pensions in Belgium is similar to that found in other Western European countries. A useful list containing up-to-date information on facilities and prices is published annually by the national tourist office in Brussels (address and telephone number given above). All establishments on the list must conform to a legally established standard. The more important and, consequently the more expensive, are placed in one of five Benelux categories. Prices may vary according to the season. The most expensive months are usually July and August. By law the price *per diem* must be displayed in the room.

A useful free nationwide hotel reservation service is operated by BTR (Belgium Tourist Reservations), PO Box 41, 1000 Brussels 23, tel: (from UK 010) 32 2 2305029, (from USA 011) 32 2 2305029.

Camping and Caravanning. Each year the national tourist organisation produces a list of officially approved sites. These are grouped in starred categories. Unofficial sites will also be found throughout Belgium, especially in popular touring districts.

Commonwealth War Graves. More than 204,000 servicemen from the countries of the Commonwealth died in Belgium during the two world wars and are buried or commemorated there. Most of the graves are in war cemeteries in the immediate neighbourhood of the 1914–18 battlefields. The largest, Tyne Cot Cemetery, Passchendaele, 11,900 graves; Lijssenthoek Military Cemetery, 9900 graves; Poelcapelle British Cemetery, 7400 graves; Hooge Crater Cemetery, 5900 graves, are near Ypres.

Other large cemeteries, principally of the 1939–45 war, are at Adegem, Heverlee near Louvain, Schoonselhof at Antwerp, Leopoldsburg, Brussels and Hotton in the Ardennes. In all there are some 175 Commonwealth war cemeteries, but war graves, in large plots or small groups, may also be found in some 460 other burial grounds.

More than 102,000 soldiers, who have no known grave, are commemorated by name on the Menin Gate Memorial at Ypres or on a number of other memorials to the missing at Tyne Cot or on the Ploegsteert Memorial in Berks Cemetery Extension.

The war graves, cemeteries, and memorials are maintained by the Commonwealth War Graves Commission, whose head office is at 2 Marlow Road, Maidenhead, Berks, SL6 7DX, tel: (0628) 34221. The land on which they are situated was generously provided by the Belgian government under the terms of war graves agreements signed after the two world wars.

The Commonwealth war cemeteries vary greatly in size, but in general design they resemble each other. Within an enclosure bounded by a low wall or hedge and planted with trees, flowers and grass plots, the orderly rows of graves are marked by simple headstones of uniform design. These bear the name, rank, unit and date of death of the soldier, his regimental crest, the symbol of his faith and, in many cases, a personal inscription chosen by the next-of-kin.

Officers and men lie side by side as they fought in life. In each cemetery stands a Cross of Sacrifice. In the larger cemeteries there is also an altar-like Stone of Remembrance inscribed with the words 'Their Name liveth for Evermore'.

Relatives and friends, who wish to visit a grave, will find a printed register near the entrance to the cemetery. Those who are uncertain of the location of a grave, cemetery or memorial are advised to contact the Commission's head office in Maidenhead (see above) or its North-West Europe headquarters at 82 Elverdingestraat, Ypres, Belgium, tel: (057) 200118.

The location of First World War cemeteries and memorials in southwestern Belgium and northern France is shown on a special edition of Michelin Map Sheet 51. This may be obtained from the Commission, which also publishes other material of interest and which can supply photographs of war graves for a small fee. The Royal British Legion, 48 Pall Mall, London SW1V 5JG, tel: 071-973 0633 will arrange for poppy wreaths to be laid. There is a small charge for this service.

Churches, Museums and Art Galleries. Most *churches* of interest to tourists are open throughout the day, though some may close between c 12.00 and 14.00. Opening times are usually posted on or near the main door. Apart from attendance for worship, Sundays should be avoided, as visitors are not permitted to walk around while services are being held. Saturday afternoon may also be difficult, as this is a popular time for weddings.

Entry to churches is normally free, but a charge is usually made for visits to the treasury, crypt or tower, or to see important works of art.

Many churches are closed for restoration, a process which may take several years, or because of the difficulty in finding custodians, who are necessary, alas, to prevent theft or vandalism.

There are also churches which are open only for services. In many cases, however, these can be visited by applying to the sacristan or key-holder whose address is often given on the door.

Museums and Art Galleries. Museums abound in Belgium, where the word is interpreted more liberally than in the OED. It can cover almost any building or site where artefacts of historical, archaeological, artistic, folkloric, sociological or craft interest may be seen. As a consequence most small towns and many villages boast of possessing a museum. This is usually devoted to local history, folklore or crafts. While it is only possible to list and describe the most important museums in the Blue Guide, others, often shortlived and with capricious opening times, will be encountered from time to time. The unhurried and inquisitive traveller may find much to interest him in them.

Visitors who wish to see particular artefacts or paintings may find that this is not always possible. From time to time the larger museums and art galleries mount special exhibitions on a selected theme or a certain artist. As a result part of the permanent collection has to be put into store for the duration of the exhibition. Some museums and galleries may be closed, completely or partially, for long periods while the building is being restored or the collection rearranged. In addition, a number have insufficient space to display all their collection at the same time, so artefacts and paintings are rotated. Financial restrictions or the difficulty in recruiting suitable staff may result in some galleries or departments being closed on certain days of the week or even for months at a time.

Sometimes artefacts and paintings are not in the positions mentioned in the Blue Guide, as curators have moved them for artistic or didactic reasons. Accordingly, before visiting a museum or gallery it is advisable to check with the local tourist office regarding opening times, access and any special exhibitions.

Many of the *Castles and Châteaux* of Belgium are romantically sited and are rich in artistic treasures. Details of those worth a detour and a leisurely visit are given in the main text.

Tourist Trains, so called, are to found in many parts of Belgium but especially in the Ardennes. Running along the road, the trains have simple semi-open carriages drawn by an engine, which is often battery-powered. Departing at regular intervals, they offer a pleasant and relaxing way to see the sights.

Banking and Currency. Banking hours are normally between 09.15 and 15.30 from Monday to Friday. However, some banks close for lunch and some remain open until 16.00 on Friday. In the cities there are currency exchanges, which have much longer working hours. In Brussels exchange facilities are available at the Gare du Nord, the Gare du Midi and at Zaventem airport. Cashing Travellers' Cheques can be expensive, as Belgian Banks make a high service charge for each transaction. There is no charge for Thomas Cook or American Express cheques cashed at their own offices. Holders of a UK Bank's Eurocheque card can cash personal cheques up to the current limit at any bank showing the Eurocheque sign. At present Eurocheques accompanied by a Eurocard will be accepted by traders for goods valued at not more than 7000BF.

Credit Cards. Among the credit cards in general use in Belgium are American Express, Diners Club, Visa and J.C.B. (Japanese Credit Card). All these companies have offices in Brussels to which the loss or theft of cards should be reported. The symbols of cards accepted by shops and restaurants are usually displayed at the entrance and by hotels at the entrance and at the reception desk.

The monetary unit is the Belgian franc, which is divided into 100 centimes. However, because of inflation centimes are little used. Banknotes are of 50, 100, 500, 1000 and 5000 francs. Coins are issued in the following denominations: 50 francs, 5 francs and 1 franc (all nickel) and 20 francs and 50 centimes (both copper).

Food and Drink. Belgium is justly famous for the quality of its cuisine—and the size of the portions served in its restaurants. The paintings of Teniers and the Brueghels with their scenes of zestful gourmandising and the lovingly portrayed kitchens and still-life studies of game by Frans Snyders, Paul de Vos, Jan Fyt and others attest to the fact that appreciation of good food and drink has long been a national characteristic. Happily, the tradition continues. Visitors may look forward to some memorable meals.

Belgian food is rich and well flavoured. Much use is made of cream, butter, fat and herbs in its preparation. Throughout the country, but especially in Liège and the surrounding area, soup is a popular dish. A large bowl of one of the speciality soups like chervil is a meal in itself.

In the Ardennes sample the many varieties of pâté, the smoked ham and the game, which includes young boar, venison and hare. Dishes like rabbit are prepared or served with prunes, while beer is often used in cooking braised beef ('Carbonnades flamandes'). Brussels is well known for 'witloof' (chicory). Try 'Witloofs gratinés au four', chicory with ham and cheese. Other Belgian specialities are 'Waterzooi' in which the flavour of the chicken is enhanced by a tangy soup of vegetables and cream and 'Civet de lapin à flamande' stewed rabbit.

Those who like fish will enjoy Ostend oysters, mussels prepared à la marinière or served with a sophisticated sauce, 'anguilles au vert' young eels, tomatoes stuffed with shrimps, pickled herrings or trout from the Ardennes.

For dessert there is a wide choice. 'Herve', that runny cheese, which is completely soft inside and has a very distinctive bouquet, hothouse grapes from Tervuren, one of the many tarts 'au flan', 'au sucre' or 'au riz', 'Gaufre de Bruxelles' waffles or 'Crêpes' pancakes.

For quick snacks there are, in addition to 'Gaufres', delicious 'Frites' (chips). These may be obtained, piping hot in enormous containers and with or without dressing, from vans and stalls in towns and cities all over Belgium.

Belgian cream filled chocolates are famous, almost every city producing its own special variety. These and the many varieties of sweet biscuits and cookies make very acceptable presents or delicious reminders of one's visit.

Beer has been the Belgian national drink since the time of the Gallo-Celtic Belgae. In the Middle Ages the great abbeys encouraged and furthered the art of brewing, notably by the introduction of hops. By the 14C the trade had spread to lay brewers. They were soon organised into guilds, which by the 16C exercised a powerful influence in society. During the 19C the discovery of pasteurisation and other technical processes led to a proliferation of breweries. Today Belgium has about 355 different brands of beer, most of lager type. The national consumption is estimated to be 126 litres per person per annum.

Because of its microclimate more than 3000 vines clothe the hillsides around the litle red-roofed village of Torgny in the Gaume (province of Luxembourg). They produce the delicious 'Clos de la Zolette', which resembles Riesling. To sample this it is necessary to visit the Gaume, as it would appear that the people of the region, very sensibly, consume the greater part of the annual production. They are, however, prepared to share this delightful white wine with visitors!

Medical help. Department of Health pamphlets SA28 and SA30 give details of the medical cover available under reciprocal arrangements between the United Kingdom and Belgium. However, it is important to note that not everyone qualifies and that even those who do should obtain and take with them a Certificate of Entitlement (Form E111).

Visitors may wish to take out private insurance. There are many schemes available from the principal insurance companies, motoring associations and travel agents.

Post. Post Offices are usually open Monday to Friday 09.00 to 16.00 or 17.00. The smaller offices often often close for lunch.

Apart from the office in Avenue Fonsny, Brussels, most post offices are closed on Saturdays, Sundays and public holidays.

Public Holidays
New Year's Day (1 January)
Easter Monday
Labour Day (1 May)
Ascension Day
Whit Monday
National Day (21 July)
Assumption Day (15 August)
All Saints' Day (1 November)
Armistice Day (11 November)
King's Birthday, Fête de la Dynastie (15 November)
Partial holiday, government and official. Christmas Day (25 December).
If one of these falls on a Sunday, the following day becomes the holiday.

Telephone. The cost of calls is given in the kiosks. International calls can only be made from those kiosks which bear symbols (the hats of different countries). In these there are instructions in a number of languages.

Time. Belgium is on Central European time, i.e. Greenwich Mean Time plus one hour in winter and plus two hours in summer (from about early April to the end of September).

Gratuities. In hotels and restaurants service and Value Added Tax are always included in the bill and there is no requirement to leave a tip. However, patrons may like to give a small additional sum as *pourboire*, if the service has been particularly good. In taxis VAT and service are normally included in the amount shown on the meter.

Tips are expected by theatre and cinema usherettes (10 per cent), hairdressers (20 per cent) and public toilet attendants (20 francs, if no fixed amount is indicated). Porters at stations and airports are entitled to an officially determined fee for each item of baggage which they carry.

The Galeries St Hubert, Brussels, opened in 1847, the first shopping galleries in Europe

1

Brussels and Environs

BRUSSELS (French **Bruxelles**, Flemish **Brussel**) has a population of about one million. As well as being the capital of Belgium, it is the capital of the two parts of the Province of Brabant and of each of the new Federal Regions, one of which is Brussels itself.

The city has 19 communes—some Flemish, some Walloon, some mixed— and is officially bilingual with all street names, official notices etc in both French and Flemish. French tends to predominate, particularly in the central area and is also generally understood where Flemish or the mixed Brussels dialect may be the local language.

Two important international bodies are located in Brussels: the European Economic Community (EC or 'Common Market') and the North Atlantic Treaty Organisation (NATO). Each of these has its own diplomatic representation which is quite separate from that accredited to the Belgian Government. The city is also home to a number of other international groups and business organisations and, as a consequence, sometimes regards itself and is regarded by others, as the capital of Europe.

A roughly hexagonal belt of wide boulevards, about 8km in length, marks the boundary of ancient Brussels and encloses the heart of the city. Following the line of the 4C ramparts, the boulevards were constructed between 1818 and 1871. Within this area is the LOWER TOWN, with the Grand-Place and the Place de Brouckère at its centre. Here also are the principal shopping streets of interest to visitors. Along the high ground to the E and S sprawls the UPPER TOWN, where, both within and beyond the ring boulevards, are located the great museums and art galleries, the Palais du Roi with the Parc de Bruxelles, the huge Palais de Justice, many embassies and the headquarters of the EC. On the slope between the upper and lower towns are the Cathedral Saint Michel, the central station and the broad flight of steps, the Mont des Arts, which ascends to the Place Royale.

The buildings in the superb Grand-Place and its adjacent narrow streets are survivals of the past. Other reminders of former times are to be found in the 18C and 19C districts and scattered throughout the city. However, the tendency in the post-war years was to erect massive high-rise blocks, particularly in the central lower town and along the boulevards. Frequently dubbed 'Centres', many of these house restaurants, hotels and large shopping precincts.

Whether this policy has given Brussels an excitingly modern and progressive character or whether it has robbed it of heart and warmth is still being debated by both residents and visitors. The modernist trend was reversed somewhat in the 1980s, when there was a vigorous revival of interest in conservation. This has continued and today the emphasis is more on restoration than destruction and total redevelopment.

Among the principal attractions of Brussels are the magnificent Grand-Place, the cathedral and the richly-ornamented churches, the many museums and art galleries, the superb restaurants (particularly in the two Rues des Bouchers) and the city's excellent shops. These range from large stores in the main streets to smaller specialist shops in the older areas and in the elegant 19C '*galeries*' or within the labyrinthine warrens of the

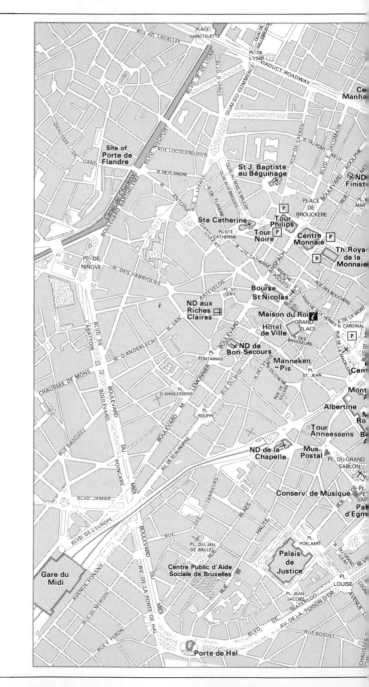

BRUSSELS
Centre
0 metres   400

Gare du Nord
(Railway Mus.)
Ste Marie
Centre Rogier
LACE OGIER
Le Botanique
Porte de Schaerbeek
Cité Administrative
Colonne du Congrès
Tour Madou
PLACE MADOU
Banque Nat.
Cathedral (Ste Gudule)
Mus. Charlier
Palais de la Nation
Parc de Bruxelles
Palais des Beaux Arts
Hot. de Belle-Vue
PLACE DES PALAIS
PLACE ROYALE
St Jacques
Pal. des Académies
Palais Royal
Berlaymont (Common Market
PLACE DU TRONE
Mus. de la Dynastie
Porte de Namur
GAL TOISON D'OR
Luxembourg Sta
Parc Léopold
Mus. Wiertz
Mus. Cam Lemonnier
Inst. des Sciences Naturelles
IXELLES   Mus. des Beaux Arts

RUE ROYALE
BLVD DE BRABANT
RUE ST LAZARE
R. DES CONGRES
DE LA BLANCHISSERIE
BLVD DU JARDIN BOTANIQUE
RUE DU MERIDIEN
CH. DE HAECHT
RUE ROYALE
RUE DE L'ASSOCIATION
RUE DE LIGNE
ND DE BERLAIMONT
RUE DE LA CROIX DE FER
RUE DE LOUVAIN
RUE DES COLONIES
RUE DE LA PRESSE
DE LA LOI
BOULEVARD DU REGENT
RUE DUCALE
AVENUE DES ARTS
RUE JOSEPH II
RUE DE SPA
RUE DES DEUX EGLISES
CHAUSSEE DE LOUVAIN
CHAUSSEE DE LOUVAIN
AVE DESCHANEL
RUE EECKELLERS
AVE DES ARTS
RUE
RUE DE LA LOI
RUE DE TREVES
RUE BELLIARD
RUE MONTOYER
RUE DU LUXEMBOURG
RUE VAUTIER
RAVENSTEIN
R.B.
HORTA
ALBERTIN
R. BREDERONE
DE WATERLOO
AVE STASSART
RUE MARNIX
RUE DE NAMUR
CHAUSSEE
DE WAVRE
RUE DU TRONE
D'IXELLES
RUE DU VIADUC
RUE DU PRINCE ROYALE
CHAUSSEE
RUE DU SCEPTRE
PLACE DE LA NATION

various Centres. The city's clean, efficient and comparatively inexpensive Metro, an object of great civic pride, makes sightseeing a relatively painless operation.

Tourist Information. There are two tourist offices in central Brussels. Immediately N of the Grand-Place at 61 Rue du Marché aux Herbes and on the site of a meat market founded in the 12C there is an office, which not only provides information about Brussels but also about Belgium as a whole and more specifically about the two parts of the Province of Brabant. The multilingual hostesses at this office will also make hotel reservations (tel: 5123030).

Opening hours are: June to September between 09.00 and 20.00 from Monday to Friday and on Saturday and Sunday until 19.00. November to February between 09.00 to 18.00 from Monday to Saturday and on Sunday from 13.00 to 17.00 (NB. It is closed on 25 December and 1 January). March to May and in October between 09.00 and 18.00.

There is no shortage of good accommodation in Brussels. The Hotel Arenberg Stormstraat 15, near the cathedral and the Grand-Place, is comfortable and quiet.

Tourist Information Brussels (TIB) at the Hôtel de Ville in the Grand-Place (tel: 5138940). This office is concerned solely with Brussels. In addition to detailed information about the city, it offers many services. These include qualified tourist guides speaking 14 languages, weekly programmes of cultural events, reservation of tickets for shows and concerts, audio guided tours of the Grand Place, sale of tram, metro, bus and 24 hour tickets, hotel reservations and car hire. Each year the TIB publishes a new edition of its guide (with map) to Brussels.

Opening hours are: April to September between 09.00 and 18.00. October to November: 10.00 to 14.00. NB. The TIB office is closed between December and March.

Public Transport. Moving around Brussels is not difficult. There is a good bus, tram and Metro network, controlled and operated by STIB (Société des Transports Intercommunaux Bruxellois). At the time of writing a single ticket costs 35BF, a card for five journeys 155BF and a card for ten journeys 220BF. There is also a card valid for 24 hours' travel. This costs 140BF and may be used for any number of journeys on the metro and on vehicles of the STIB and on the orange buses of the SNCV (commuter lines) during its period of validity.

A plan of the network and other information may be obtained free of charge from the tourist offices mentioned above or from the Porte de Namur, Rogier and Midi STIB stations.

The Midi Information Centre also provides details of SNCV and SNCB (Belgian Railways) services.

More than 50 modern Belgian artists were commissioned to decorate the metro stations. Their work, which includes mosaics, murals, sculpture, marble and tile designs, can be seen at stations like Parc (Marc Mendelson, Roger Dudant), Bourse (Pol Bury), Porte de Namur (Octave Landuyt), Montgomery (Jo Delahaut, Jean-Michel Folon, Pol Mara), Petillon (Lismonde), Hankar (Roger Somville) and Herrmann-Debroux (Jan Cox, Rik Poot, Roel d'Haese).

A leaflet in Flemish and French, obtainable from the information offices listed above, suggests three metro itineraries, which in effect provide a fascinating tour of the work of some of the best modern Belgian artists. For a more permanent record there is a richly illustrated book which describes the works of art in the metro. This may be purchased from the STIB Offices, 6th Floor, Galeries de la Toison d'Or, 1060 Brussels.

Taxis. Taxis abound in Brussels. Service is included in the price shown on the meter. Taxis, which display a sticker showing a white aeroplane superimposed on an orange background in the top right-hand corner of the windscreen, charge reduced fares for the journey to and from Zaventem airport. Reduced fares may also be charged for outward and return journeys. Ask for details before you start the journey.

Complaints about taxi services may be made to Greater Brussels Taxi Service, Rue Capitaine Crespel 35, 1050 Brussels. They should, if possible, include the registration number of the vehicle, its make and colour.

Parking. The private motorist will find several convenient parking facilities in the city centre. There is a comprehensive list of these in the TIB guide (see above). Charges are calculated on a reducing scale.

Parking meters take 5BF and 20BF coins. Their use is obligatory at certain times in a number of areas of the city.

Airport. Brussels' airport is at Zaventem , 14km to the NE of the city. There is a special train service between the Gare du Nord (at 43, 18 and 00 minutes past the hour), the Gare Centrale (at 55, 39 and 14 minutes past the hour) and the Gare du Midi (at 51 minutes past every hour) and the airport. The journey takes about 20 minutes from the Gare du Nord. At present the first train outwards leaves at 05.39 (Gare Centrale), 05.43 (Gare du Nord) and 05.51 (Gare du Midi). The last train leaves at 23.14 (Gare Centrale), 23.18 (Gare du Nord) and 22.51 (Gare du Midi). Inward services operate between 06.00 and 23.45. It is advisable to check departure times and frequency of service in both directions, as these may change.

Tickets for the train service to and from the airport are sold at railway stations and at the Tourist Information Office in the airport baggage hall. NB. A substantial supplement is charged on tickets purchased on the train.

Some taxis based at the airport charge higher rates than those operating in the city. However, taxis, which display a sticker showing a white aeroplane superimposed on an orange background in the top right-hand corner of the windscreen, will charge reduced fares for the journey to and from Zaventem.

There is a Tourist Information Office in the baggage hall and a Post Office, a Telephone, Telegram, and Telex Office and several banks at the airport. Religious services are held in the Catholic Chapel, the Protestant Chapel, the Synagogue and the Mosque at Zaventem.

Railway Stations. *Gare du Nord* to the N of Place Rogier.

Gare Centrale at the Carrefour de l'Europe (Boulevard de l'Impératrice) above the Grand-Place.

Gare du Midi off the SW ring boulevard.

Post Offices. The principal offices are:
Brussels X (Gare du Midi), 48A Avenue Fonsny. This office is open every day of the year round the clock, except for money orders, when the usual opening hours apply. Centre Monnaie (Gare Centrale), Centre de Communication Nord (Gare du Nord), 80 Rue du Progrès, Bourse, Palais de Justice, 1 Boulevard Charlemagne.

Most post offices are open from Monday to Friday between 09.00 and 17.00. However, some close later on Friday evening. All offices, apart from Brussels X and a few which open on Saturday morning, are closed at weekends and on public hoildays.

Note that certain transactions can only be carried out at specified hours.

Telephone, Telegram, Telex. *Telephone*. Telephone boxes showing international flags accept international calls and telegrams. Have a sufficient number of 5BF or 20BF coins or a Telecard with you.

To reach a number in the UK dial 00 + 44 + the area code; for the USA dial 00 + 1 + the area code.

Some RTT offices are: (Régale des Télégraphis et Téléphones) Gare du Midi, Avenue Fonsny. 17 Boulevard de l'Impératice. 23A Rue de Brabant (near the Gare du Nord). Place de Luxembourg. Zaventem Airport.

Telegrams. Dial 1325 for general service and service outside Europe or use one of the RTT offices listed above.

Telex. RTT, 13 Boulevard de l'Impératrice. For information telephone 5134490. Open daily 07.00 to 22.00.

Money Exchange. Normal banking hours are Monday to Friday from 09.15 to 15.30, but some branches also open on Saturday morning.

Outside these hours money can be changed at various exchange offices in the city. Many near the Grand-Place are open until 19.00 or even later.

There are also exchange offices at the three main stations. Those at the Gare du Midi and the Gare du Nord are open every day including Sundays and public holidays between 07.00 to 23.00. At the Gare Centrale the office is open from 08.00 to 21.00 including Sundays and public holidays. It is advisable to check opening times, as these may vary.

Religious Services. Times of services are usually given on a noticeboard outside churches. Bruxelles Accueil, Rue de Tabora 6, 1000 Brussels, tel: 5112715, 5118178 can supply the times of Catholic, Orthodox, Anglican and Protestant services in foreign languages. The office is open from Monday to Saturday between 10.00 and 14.00. It is closed on Sunday.

Communaute Israelite de Belgique is at Avenue de Kersbeek 96, 1190 Brussels, tel: 3766672.

Centre Islamique et Culturel de Belgique-Mosquee is at 14 Parc de Cinquantenaire, 1040 Brussels, tel: 7352173.

Tours. A number of agencies arrange tours in the city and its environs including Laeken, the Atomium and Waterloo. Among these are Sightseeing Line, TIB office (every day in English, French, Dutch, German, Italian, Spanish and Japanese), Panorama Tours, 105 Rue du Marchè-aux-Herbes, bte 20., De Boeck's Sightseeing Tours, 8 Rue de la Colline. For a full list consult the TIB office (see above).

There are also agencies, which arrange tours throughout Belgium.

Newspapers, Books, Television and Radio. In addition to Belgian *newspapers* in French, Flemish and German, British and American papers are sold widely in Brussels. There is also a local English language newspaper, 'The Bulletin', which is addressed mainly to members of the international community living in Brussels.

Books. There are several shops which specialise in foreign language books. These include: W.H. Smith, 71–75 Boulevard Adophe Max., The Strathmore Bookshop, 131 Rue Saint Lambert, The House of Paperbacks, 813 Chaussée de Waterloo, Gutenberg Buchhandel, 37 Place de la Vielle Halle-aux-Blés.

Television and Radio. As well as the national television and radio channels, which provide a wide range of programmes in French and Flemish, the cable network offers 15 programmes from Great Britain, France, Germany, Italy, etc. Many hotels subscribe to the cable service and make it available to their clients in the public rooms and in most bedrooms.

Theatres and Cinemas. More than 30 *theatres* in Brussels present plays, both classic and modern, in French and Flemish. These range from the *Théâtre Royal de la Monnaie*, Place de la Monnaie, the historic opera house, to the *Toone*, Petite Rue des Bouchers, a puppet theatre.

Cinemas. Cinemas in the city centre and environs, many of them with several auditoria, offer the latest films in French and Flemish. For programme details see the daily papers. It is well worth making a visit to Kinepolis, Bruparck, Plateau du Heysel. This has 24 cinemas, one of which has a screen 600 m sq.

Brussels By Night. Brussels, like most large cities, has an extensive and varied night life. Because many nocturnal establishments enjoy a somewhat ephemeral existence it is impossible to provide a definitive or comprehensive list. The current TIB guide has details of many of the cocktail bars, café-theatre, café-concert, piano bars, late night restaurants and bistros, discothèques, jazz and cabaret shows in Brussels. However, to avoid a wasted journey, it is advisable to telephone before making a visit to any of these.

Floodlighting. The following are some of the areas and buildings which are floodlit at night: until 02.00, the Grand-Place; until 00.30, the baroque Eglise Saint Jean Baptiste au Béguinage, the Eglise Sainte Catherine, the Bourse, the Cathédrale Saint Michel and most of the area from the Parc de Bruxelles to the Place Royale and the Palais de Justice. Note in particular Notre-Dame du Sablon.

Red Light Districts. City Centre: Rue du Colombier, Rue du Pont-Neuf, Rue du Cirque, Boulevard Jacqmain, Rue de Malines.

Nord District: Rue du Marché, Rue du Progrès, Rue d'Aerschot, Rue du Pont, Rue Verte, Rue Linné, Rue des Plantes.

Parliament District: Rue du Nord, Rue de l'Association, Rue Croix de Fer, Rue de l'Enseignement, Rue du Moniteur.

Up Town: Rue de Stassart, Rue des Chevaliers, Rue des Drapiers, Rue de la Grosse Tour, Rue de la Concorde.

Emergency Aid Telephone Numbers
Accidents 100
Police 101
Gendarmerie 101

Fire Brigade 100
Standby doctors 4791818 and 6488000
Standby dentists 4261026 and 4285888
Ambulance 6491122

Lost Property

On aircraft. Office in arrival hall at airport, tel: 7236011.

Airport. Office of Airways Management (RVA), in the visitors' hall on the first floor, weekdays only, tel: 7223940.

Metro, buses or trams. Lost Property Office, 15 Avenue de la Toison d'Or, tel: 5152394, Hours: 09.30 to 12.30.

On trains. Lost Property Office, Gare du Quartier Lèopold, tel: 2186050. Enquiries after one week.

On the street. Nearest police station or Central Police Station, 30 Rue du Marchè-au Charbon, (Grand-Place), tel: 5179611.

In a taxi. Nearest police station to point of departure.

Markets. Brussels is fortunate in possessing a large number of interesting markets, where the visitor may pass many pleasant hours in search of bargains. The following are a few selected from the long list in the TIB guide:

Antiques and Second Hand Goods: Place du Grand Sablon, Saturday, 09.00 to 18.00, Sunday, 09.00 to 14.00. Place du Jeu de Balle, daily, 07.00 to 14.00.

Birds: Grand-Place, Sunday, 07.00 to 14.00.

Flowers: Grand-Place, daily, 08.00 to 18.00.

Flea Market: Place du Jeu de Balle, daily, 07.00 to 14.00.

Fruit and Vegetable: Place Sainte Catherine, daily, 07.00 to 17.00.

Domestic Animals: Place Saint-Denis, Forest, second Monday of October from 09.00 to 18.00.

Paintings and Engravings: Place des Ecoles, Berchem-Saint Agathe, Friday from 15.00 to 19.00; Place Saint-Denis, Forest, second Monday in October from 09.00 to 18.00.

History. Excavations conducted by Belgian archaeologists have shown that the site of Brussels was occupied in neolithic times. In the early centuries of the Christian era the river Senne, which today is canalised and covered along its course through the city, formed an extensive area of marsh. After the withdrawal of the Romans, this provided a place of refuge for the Gallo-Roman inhabitants from the attacks of the Franks. It is possible that the city's name is derived from this early settlement, as Bruocsella (Broekzele) means village of the marsh.

There is a shadowy connection with Saint Géry (6C) who is said to have founded a chapel on one of the islands (today's Place Saint Géry). The first recorded mention of Brussels is in a document of 966. In time the village grew, largely because it provided an easy river crossing on the trade route between Cologne, Ghent and Bruges. (This route can still be traced in the succession of streets following the course of the ancient Steenweg, see p 75).

In 977 the settlement fell to the dukes of Lower Lotharingia, who built a castle on an island in the Senne. This had a chapel dedicated to St Géry. In 1041 the ducal residence was moved to higher ground, to the Coudenberg. The new castle, which occupied a part of what is now the Parc de Bruxelles, later became the chief palace of the Netherlands. Six years later a church dedicated to St Michael was built in the settlement.

In the early 12C the first fortified wall was built. Fragments of this still survive in the form of three small towers, Noire, Villers and Anneessens. As the village grew into a town the merchants established a market, which later became the Grand-Place. The growing power of the bourgeoisie was confirmed by the Charter of Cortenberg granted in 1312. This charter was confirmed in 1356 on the occasion of the 'Joyeuse Entrée' of Wenceslas of Luxembourg and Joanna of Brabant, the rulers of the dukedom of Brabant in which Brussels lay.

New walls enclosing a wider area were raised between 1357 and 1383. Strengthened in the 16C, these defences remained standing until the 19C, when, apart from the Porte de Hal, they were demolished to construct the ring boulevards.

The whole of the Middle Ages is marked by civil disturbance. Conflict between the common people and their rulers was frequent; in this the weavers were among the most turbulent and unruly.

As Brussels prospered, acquiring a trade in luxury articles such as lace, tapestry, jewellery and ecclesiastical furnishings like retables, work was started in 1402 on the Hôtel de Ville. With the extinction of the House of Leuven, the way was open for the ambitious House of Burgundy. Three Burgundian dukes ruled Brabant in succession. They favoured Brussels and the city became a centre of ostentatious luxury, where artists and craftsmen found ready employment.

The hazards of politics and a series of dynastic marriages brought the Netherlands under the rule of the Habsburgs. The seat of government was transferred in 1531 from Mechelen to Brussels. There in 1568 the patriot leaders, the Counts of Egmont and Horn, were executed in the Grand-Place.

Under the enlightened rule of Archduke Albert and Isabella (1598–1621) the Spanish yoke was milder and the arts flourished, but disaster came with the War of the Grand Alliance. In 1695 Louis XIV's Marshal Villeroi bombarded the city for 36 hours, destroying 16 churches and nearly 4000 houses. Much of this damage occurred in and around the Grand-Place.

In 1706, during the War of the Spanish Succession, Brussels opened its gates to Marlborough, but when this war ended in 1713 with the Treaty of Utrecht Belgium was awarded to the Habsburgs. Six years later the leader of the city guilds, Frans Anneessens, was beheaded in the Grand-Place for defending the privileges of Brussels against the demands of its Austrian rulers. In 1731 the Coudenberg palace burnt down.

Although occupied by the French under Marshal Saxe in 1746 during the War of the Austrian Succession, Belgium was soon restored to Austria. Under the rule of the cultured Charles of Lorraine, appointed governor by his sister-in-law Maria Theresa, Brussels enjoyed a period of peace and prosperity. Charles wanted to make Brussels a northern Vienna and during the second half of the 18C the Palais du Roi was built, partly on the site of the old Coudenberg palace. The Palais de la Nation and the Place Royale were constructed at the same time and the gates of the city wall were demolished.

After the French Revolution, the status of Brussels diminished. It became the capital of the French department of the Dyle. The city walls were demolished and a start was made on the construction of the great boulevards, which replaced them. Saved in 1815 from a further period of French occupation by the Battle of Waterloo, which was fought only 20km from the city, Brussels alternated with The Hague as the royal residence of King William I. Finally, Belgium, an unwilling partner in the United Kingdom of the Netherlands, revolted against the Dutch in 1830. The revolution began in Brussels' Théâtre de la Monnaie on 24 August of that year.

After Belgium had gained her independence the transformation of Brussels into a modern city began. Indeed the 19C was marked by a spate of frantic activity. Large areas of rotting slums were cleared and replaced by fine new streets. In 1834 Brussels Free University was founded. In 1835 continental Europe's first passenger train service (between Brussels and Mechelen) was inaugurated. In 1846 the Galeries Saint Hubert were opened. Between 1866 and 1883 the Palais de Justice was built and in 1871 sanitation and public health were improved, when the Senne was covered over. In the same year work on the ring boulevards was completed. This opened the way for the spread of the Upper Town, particularly in the direction of the Parc du Cinquantenaire and along the Avenue Louise. The development work was due largely to the drive of Burgomaster Anspach and the effect of the great Jubilee Exhibition of 1880 in the Parc du Cinquantenaire.

At the start of the First World War Brussels was left undefended. The German army entered the city on 20 August 1914. The passive resistance of the people was encouraged by their burgomaster, Adolphe Max. He refused to co-operate with the invaders and, as a result, was deported. During the war an underground newspaper 'La Libre Belgique' was produced in the capital.

In 1915 the English nurse Edith Cavell was condemned to death and shot in Brussels for helping fugitive soldiers to escape to neutral Holland. In the following year the Belgian heroine Gabrielle Petit was executed by the invaders for her resistance activities.

Occupied again by the Germans during the Second World War the citizens repeated their open and underground resistance. During the years of occupation, from May

1940 to September 1944, much help was given by the people of Brussels to Allied airmen and resistance fighters.

The post-war years were marked by a vigorous modernisation of the city. Impetus for this was provided by the World Fair of 1958 whose symbol, the Atomium, still dominates the north-western outskirts of the city. At this time, too, the ring boulevards were given a system of tunnels which has been copied by many other cities.

Brussels became the headquarters of the EEC in 1959 and of NATO in 1967. It began to be regarded as the capital of Europe. Modernisation, albeit now strongly tempered with conservation, has continued. Notable features of the last two decades are the highly efficient and very decorative Metro and the ambitious outer ring motorway. There have been administrative changes, too. During the 1980s, because of Belgium's new federal constitution, Brussels has become the 'capital' of each of the new Regions, of which the city itself is one.

Routes from Brussels. *Ostend*, see Route 8; *Ronse, Oudenaarde* and *Kortrijk (Courtrai)*, see Route 12; *Mechelen* and *Antwerp*, see Route 15; *Louvain (Leuven)* and *Liège*, see Route 21; *Tournai*, see Route 22; *Mons*, see Route 23; *Charleroi*, see Route 24; *Namur*, see Route 27.

A. The Lower Town

The Lower Town has two centres, 400m apart, the relatively modern Place de Brouckère and the ancient Grand Place. The main streets of the Lower Town are the Boulevards Anspach and Adolphe Max, which run roughly S and N out of the Place de Brouckère and the Rue Neuve, which is parallel to the Boulevard Adolphe Max. All of these streets date from the second half of the 19C, when the Senne was covered over and the great slum clearance made.

From at least as early as the 10C, Brussels' main artery was the Steenweg, a part of the trade route which linked the Rhine with Ghent and Bruges. It is not difficult to follow the course of this ancient way.

On reaching Brussels from the E, the Steenweg divided. One section entered the city at the Porte de Schaerbeek, then continued past the cathedral to the Rue de la Montagne; the other came through the Porte de Namur and descended the Mont des Arts to the Rue de la Madeleine.

The two sections met in the Lower Town at the E end of the Rue du Marché aux Herbes, which at that time bordered a rivulet that rose in the Coudenberg and joined the Senne somewhere near the modern Bourse. Flanked by stalls and markets, the Steenweg crossed the Senne near the town wharf, which continued to function here until the 16C. It then followed the line of the Rue Sainte Catherine and the Rue de Flandre to the Porte de Flandre.

The Grand-Place

The **··GRAND-PLACE** (Grote Markt) is, perhaps, the most beautiful of Europe's many historic city squares. Its magnificent Gothic Hôtel de Ville, much restored Maison du Roi and elaborately decorated guild houses encapsulate in a charming way the history of Brussels.

Under the towering, gilded turrets and pinnacles of its great buildings life in the square, from which motor traffic is usually excluded, is a leisurely affair. Here the summer visitor may shop without haste, enjoy a meal at an umbrella-shaded table or spend an agreeable hour over a glass of wine or beer, while, as daylight fades and dies, the floodlit façades of the Hôtel de Ville and Maison du Roi change imperceptibly from rose to gold. Winter pleasures in the Grand-Place are equally beguiling. Then, in the cafés and restaurants the splendours of Belgian cuisine are enjoyed in dining rooms, where great, roaring fires keep the biting cold at bay.

Colour and animation are provided by the daily flower market, while on Sunday morning the Grand-Place resounds to the song of the cage-birds, which are being bought and sold. Among the many ceremonies held here, perhaps the most interesting is the 'Ommegang'. This historic pageant, which takes place on the first Thursday of July, can trace its origins directly to 1549 and indirectly to 1348.

The site, originally a part of the Senne marsh, was drained in the 12C and named the Nedermerct, Lower Market. It acquired its modern name, Grand-Place, in 1380. During the 15C splendid tournaments were staged here. In 1438 Philip the Good fought in the lists. On 5 June 1568 Counts Egmont and Horn were beheaded in the Grand-Place by order of the Duke of Alva. He watched the executions from the Maison du Roi. Villeroi bombarded the square in 1695, causing immense damage. This was made good within less than four years, an achievement which, even today, is a source of civic pride. In 1719 another patriot, Frans Anneessens, was executed by the Austrians in the Grand-Place.

The * *Hôtel de Ville with its Gothic façade, is one of the noblest buildings in Belgium. Occupying most of the SW side of the Grand-Place, it is open from Tuesday to Friday between 09.30 and 17.00 and on Sunday and some holidays between 10.00 and 16.00. There are daily guided tours. The last tour starts 30 minutes before closing time. No visits are permitted during meetings of or receptions by the City Council. It is closed on 1 January, 1 May, 1 and 11 November and 25 December.

A fragment of the porch of a stone building erected on this site c 1353 is incorporated in the base of the tower of the Hôtel de Ville. The present building was started in 1402. The earliest part, the eastern wing, is by Jacob van Thienen. In 1455 Jan van Ruysbroeck completed the tower. A marvel of lightness 96m high, this is topped by a figure of St Michael, the work of Martin van Rode, 1455. Later restored, it serves as a weathervane. The first .stone of the west wing, which was built c 1444–80, was laid by the future Charles the Bold, then the nine-year-old heir to the dukedom of Burgundy. This wing is shorter than the other because the unknown architect was told that he must not encroach upon the Rue Tête d'Or.

The statues, which represent prominent local personalities from the 14C onwards, are of the 19C. Fragments of older sculpture can be seen in the Musée Communal in the Maison du Roi. The courtyard, with its fountains representing the rivers Meuse and Scheldt and the rear portion on the site of the cloth hall, which was destroyed in 1695, date from 1705–17. The Salle du Conseil Communal, once the council room of the States of Brabant, has 18C tapestries, after designs by Abraham Janssens. The painting on the ceiling of the Gods on Olympus is by the same artist. In the next room, the Salle Maximilienne, there are portraits above the chimneypiece by André Cluysenaer of Maximilian of Austria and Mary of Burgundy. On the walls hang 18C Brussels tapestries.

In the Portrait Gallery there are full-length representations of Charles V, Philip the Handsome, Philip IV, Albert and Isabella, Charles II and Philip II. All are by Louis Grangé, 1718. The Antechamber contains interesting views of old Brussels by the late 19C painter J.B. van Moer. The Salle Gothique has fine woodcarving and 19C Mechelen tapestries of figures representative of the guilds. On the Escalier des Lions there are two paintings by Emile Wauters: John of Brabant granting a charter in 1421, and Mary of

Burgundy swearing in 1477 to protect the liberties of Brussels. The escutcheons of the guilds are reproduced on the ceiling of the Salle des Mariages, while on the Escalier d'Honneur there are busts of burgomasters, allegorical wallpaintings by Jacques de Lalaing and, at the foot, a fountain with a figure of St Michael by Charles van der Stappen, 1890.

Across the Grand-Place from the Hôtel de Ville stands the **Maison du Roi**. In the 14C or perhaps earlier a wooden building on the site served as the bread market. Later this was replaced by a stone building. When in the 16C the Duke of Brabant used it to house various officials, the name was changed from Broodhuis, Bread House, to Maison du Duc. Charles V ordered a complete rebuilding, which was carried out by Antoon and Rombout Keldermans, Hendrik van Pede and others. His new house was given the name Maison du Roi, although, in fact, it has never been a royal residence. Much damaged by the bombardment of 1695, it was restored in 1763 but thereafter neglected. The Maison du Roi was virtually demolished and rebuilt in the 1870s by Victor Jamaer. He based his work on old engravings and on van Pede's town hall at Oudenaarde, but added the galleries on the façade and the tower.

The Maison du Roi now houses the **Musée Communal**. This is open on Monday, Tuesday, Wednesday, Friday from 10.00 to 12.30, 13.30 to 17.00, on Thursday from 10.00 to 17.00, on Saturday, Sunday and some holidays from 10.00 to 13.00. It closes at 16.00 from October to March and is closed on 1 January, 1 May, 1 and 11 November and 25 December.

Paintings, plans, furniture and sculpture are used with great effect in the museum to give an interesting account of the city's past. Many visitors, attracted by its bucolic humour, seek out the *Marriage Procession by Pieter Brueghel the Elder, which is normally hung in the first room to the right of the entrance. On the top floor the bizarre wardrobe of the Manneken-Pis, which contains a selection of the 400 suits donated to the statue since Louis XV made one of the first contributions in 1747, also draws large crowds.

However, there are other exhibits which should not be missed. In the rooms to the right of the entrance are 15C and 16C retables, 16C and 17C tapestries, including one based on a cartoon by Rubens, and porcelain and silver of the 18C and 19C are displayed. In the rooms to the left of the entrance look for the stone and wood sculpture, especially the 14C and 15C stonework from the Hôtel de Ville, Notre-Dame du Sablon and Notre-Dame de la Chapelle. A reminder of the city's more recent history is provided by a statue of St John Nepomuk. Dating from 1725, this stood on the last bridge over the Senne, which was demolished in 1868.

In a large upstairs room there is usually a display of plans and models of the city at various periods. There are also illustrations for some spectacular late 19C schemes to link the lower and upper districts by an aerial gallery (1898) or a soaring funicular (1890). Flanking the stairs to the second floor, where there is a fine hall devoted to the story of the people of Brussels and the room with the costumes of the Manneken-Pis, a stained-glass window glitters with the arms of the far-flung possessions of Charles V.

The ***Guild Houses** were used as official and social meeting-places by the various city guilds. Their names, acquired over the centuries, generally refer to some decorative architectural feature. Our visit proceeds in a clockwise direction from the Rue de la Tête d'Or.

No. 7, the *Maison du Renard* (the fox), was the House of the Haberdashers. A 14C wooden structure, which later became the property of the guild, was replaced by the present stone building in the 17C. The bas-reliefs by Marcus de Vos and Jan van Delen represent trade activities. The statue on the top is of St Nicolas, patron saint of merchants. No. 6, the *Maison du Cornet* (horn), the House of the Boatmen, is a rebuilding of 1697 by Antoon Pastorana. The gable takes the form of the stern of a 17C ship. No. 5 is the *Maison de la Louve* (she-wolf). This, the House of the Archers, which was completed in 1691 to plans by Pieter Herbosch, was virtually untouched by the bombardment of the city four years later. No. 4, the *Maison du Sac* (sack), the House of the Joiners and Coopers, dates from 1644. Its gable was rebuilt by Pastorana in 1697. The guild moved to this site in the 15C, their earlier house having been razed to make way for the new Hôtel de Ville. No. 3 was the House of the Tallow Merchants. The guild bought the site in 1439. The stone house built in 1644 was damaged in the bombardment and restored in 1697 by Jan Cosyns. The house is known as the *Maison de la Brouette* (wheelbarrow). A statue of the guild's patron, St Gilles, stands in the gable. Nos 1 and 2, the *Maison du Roi d'Espagne* (King of Spain), named after a statue of Charles II, was the House of the Bakers. A bronze bust of their patron, St Aubert, decorates the façade. The building, attributed to Jan Cosyns, dates from 1697.

Six simpler houses, not all belonging to guilds, stand to the W of the Maison du Roi. These are No. 39 *L'Ane* (donkey); No. 38 *Sainte Barbe*, also known as *La Ronce Couronnée* (the crowned blackberry bush); No. 37 *Le Chêne* (oak), the House of the Hosiery Makers; No. 36 *Le Petit Renard* (small fox); No. 35 *Le Paon* (peacock), always privately owned; No. 34 *Le Heaume* (helmet).

To the E of the Maison du Roi is No. 28 *Ammanskamerke* (magistrate's room). Nos 26 and 27 are the *Maison du Pigeon*, also known as the *Maison des Peintres* (painters). Their house was destroyed in 1695, and the site was sold by the painters' guild to the architect Pierre Simon who probably put up the present building. Victor Hugo lived here in 1852. *La Maison des Tailleurs* (tailors) occupies Nos 24 and 25. Originally there were two separate houses. No. 24 *La Maison de la Taupe* (the mole) was owned by the de Mol family and No. 25 was called *La Chaloupe d'Or* (golden boat). After 1695 the houses were made into one for the tailors and given a single façade by Willem de Bruyn. No. 23 *L'Ange* (angel) was also rebuilt by de Bruyn, who gave it Ionic and Corinthian columns. Nos 22 and 21 join to form the *Maison Joseph et Anne*. No. 20 is *Le Cerf* (stag).

The E side of the square is occupied by the *Maison des Ducs de Brabant*, a mansion with a pilastered front, a rounded pediment, three pairs of steps and the busts of the dukes from which it derives its name. The building, by Willem de Bruyn, was divided at an early stage into six houses. From N to S these are *La Bourse; La Colline* (hill), the home of the Guild of Masons; *Le Pot d'Etain* (pewter pot), which belonged to the Guild of Cabinet Makers; *Le Moulin à Vent* (windmill), which belonged to the millers; *La Fortune*, which belonged to the tanners and *L'Hermitage*, which was used at different times by the wine and vegetable merchants.

Five fine houses stand E of the Hôtel de Ville. Nos 12 and 11, the *Maison du Mont-Thabor* (1699) and *La Rose* (1702), were both private houses. The latter was owned by the van der Rosen family. No. 10 is *L'Arbre d'Or* (golden tree), better known as the Brewers' House and still in use as such; a part is arranged as a 17C brasserie. It contains a small museum. This is open from Monday to Friday, 10.00 to 12.00, 14.00 to 17.00; on Saturday from April to September 10.00 to 12.00; closed 1 January and 25 December. The house of 1698, surmounted by a statue of Charles of Lorraine, is a rebuilding by de Bruyn. The *Maison du Cygne* at No. 9 was rebuilt in 1698 by C. van

The house of the Taylors' Guild, La Chaloupe d'Or (Golden Boat), 1695, Brussels

Nerven for Pieter Fariseau, a founder of the Brussels opera. In 1720 Le Cygne became the house of the butchers' guild, and later still, in 1885, the Belgian Labour party was founded here.

No. 8, *L'Etoile* (star), is one of the oldest in origin and, historically, most interesting houses in the Grand-Place. Its name goes back to the 13C. Destroyed in 1695 it was rebuilt, only to be demolished in 1850 to ease access to the Grand-Place. However in 1897 Charles Buls, the burgomaster, had the house rebuilt over a pedestrian arcade.

Look in the arcade for the memorial to the 14C Brussels alderman Everard 't Serclaes. He was the leader of the guilds in their struggle against the francophile Count of Flanders, Louis de Male. Attacked by the count's allies from Gaasbeek in 1388, he died in L'Etoile. There is a tradition that good fortune will come to those who stroke the arm of his effigy. Another memorial honours Charles Buls, who died in 1914. In addition to restoring L'Etoile, he did much else to preserve old Brussels.

Around the Grand-Place

From the Grand-Place it is only a step by way of the picturesque, narrow streets, many of whose names recall past markets and trades, to the shops of the elegant arcades (galeries).

To the NORTH, across the Rue du Marché aux Herbes, are the Petite Rue des Bouchers and the Rue des Bouchers, whose names recall the meat hall, which once occupied the site of the nearby Tourist Information Office. These two streets form an animated and picturesque quarter largely given over to restaurants.

Off the Petite Rue des Bouchers is the *Toone Puppet Theatre*, which continues a tradition dating from the time when Spain ruled the Netherlands (1579–1713). Incensed by open criticism and insults from the stage, the Spanish authorities closed all the theatres. When this happened, puppets took over and proved to be a popular and effective method of reviling the foreign rulers, and one which could not be suppressed easily.

The present theatre was founded in 1835 by Antoine Toone. Its plays are a strange mixture based on various classics: Hamlet, Carmen, the Passion, etc. Performed in the Brussels dialect, they are filled with popular local and topical allusions. The puppet theatre's past is recorded in a small museum, which is open during intervals in the performances.

The Rue des Bouchers divides the **Galeries Saint Hubert** into the Galerie de la Reine and the Galerie du Roi. Housing some excellent shops, these light and attractive structures, which were built by J.P. Cluysenaer in 1846, were the first of their kind in Europe.

From the SOUTH of the Grand-Place follow the Rue Charles Buls, by the side of the Hôtel de Ville, to the Rue des Brasseurs. There in July 1873 the 19-year-old poet Rimbaud was shot and wounded by his companion Verlaine, when he threatened to terminate their relationship. Verlaine was imprisoned for six months at Mons for attempted murder.

At 6 Rue de la Violette, the next street to the SE, is the **Musée de Costume et Dentelle**. This is open on Monday, Tuesday, Wednesday and Friday from 10.00 to 12.30, 13.30 to 17.00, on Thursday from 10.00 to 17.00, on Saturday, Sunday and some holidays from 14.00 to 16.00. It closes at 16.00 from October to March and is closed on 1 January, 1 May, 1 and 11 November, 25 December. The museum has displays of lace, and clothes from the 17C to the present day. The exhibits are changed from time to time.

From the Rue Charles Buls continue to the Rue de l'Etuve. This crosses the Rue de Lombard, where at No. 30A there are the fascinating three-dimensional displays of the **Musée de l'Holographie**. Open Tuesday to Sunday from 11.00 to 18.00.

Return to the Rue de l'Etuve. On the corner where it meets the Rue du Chêne is the fountain of **Manneken-Pis**, a bronze statuette of a nude child urinating. Designed in 1619 by the elder Jérôme Duquesnoy, the statuette was stolen in 1817. Later found smashed, the fragments were assembled to form the mould from which the present figure was produced. The

Manneken-Pis or Petit Julien, as he is sometimes called, soon became part of the folklore of Brussels, capturing the affection of burghers and common people alike. He is famous for his elaborate wardrobe. The first contribution to this was made in 1698 by the Elector of Bavaria. Another early benefactor was Louis XV, who in 1747 gave a costume and conferred a decoration on the Manneken in compensation for the ill-treatment which he had suffered at the hands of Louis' soldiers. The costumes, which now number about 400, are kept in the Musée Communal (see above).

From the Manneken-Pis the Rue du Chêne ascends in a SE direction to to the Provincial Government Buildings. Here take the Rue de Villers on the right to the **Tour de Villers**, one of the few surviving fragments of the city's 12C walls. Return to the Rue du Chêne and continue to the Place Saint Jean. There a memorial honours Gabrielle Petit, who was shot by the Germans in 1916. Endowed with a photographic memory she was active in the resistance movement. When condemned to death she was told that if she appealed she would almost certainly be reprieved. This she refused to do, proudly replying that she would show her captors how a Belgian woman could die.

Return to the Grand-Place and take the Rue au Beurre from the NW corner to the **Eglise Saint Nicolas**. Open 09.00 to 18.30, closed on most holidays. Appropriately for a commercial district the church is dedicated to the patron saint of merchants and traders and, as was the custom in medieval times, small shops still crowd its exterior. Built on the site of an ancient church, the present building dates from the 14–15C, the choir is from 1381. However, there was a major reconstruction in 1955 and the façade is effectively of that date. Among the paintings in the church are works by Bernard van Orley and Antoon Sallaert as well as one attributed to Rubens. Note also the Vladimir Ikon (1131) and the striking modern blue window over the W porch.

Parts of the Lower Town

The busy PLACE DE BROUCKERE, with its many pavement cafés, is the modern centre of the Lower Town. It is named after Charles de Brouckère (1796–1860) who headed various ministries, founded the Banque de Belgique and was burgomaster of Brussels from 1848–60. The districts to the South, West and North of the Place de Brouckère are described below.

SOUTH OF PLACE DE BROUCKERE. The S of the Place de Brouckère is overlooked by two large modern buildings. To the W there is the *Tour Philips* and to the E the soaring, winged **Centre Monnaie**. Named after the mint which once stood here, this houses the city administration, the main post office, shops, a Metro station and an underground car park. Immediately to the E of the Centre Monnaie, across an open area reserved for pedestrians, stands the **Théâtre Royal de la Monnaie**. Mainly used for performances of opera and ballet, the present building is by Joseph Poelaert. It replaces the theatre, destroyed by fire in 1855, where the signal for the revolution of 1830 was given during a performance of Auber's 'La Muette de Portici'. On hearing the words of the duet 'Amour sacré de la Patrie, Rends-nous l'audace et la fierté', the audience rushed into the street and hoisted the old flag of Brabant on the Hôtel de Ville.

In June 1815 the diarist Fanny d'Arblay (née Burney, 1752–1840) lodged for some time in a house in the Rue d'Assaut, a short distance to the E of the theatre. Convinced, as were most of her friends, by the ever louder sound of the guns at Waterloo that Napoleon would soon enter the city, she had tried, without success, to find a barge which would take her to Antwerp. Later, hearing cries of 'Bonaparte est pris! Le voilà', she saw from her window 'a general in the splendid uniform of France', a prisoner tied to his 'noble war-horse'. This was Count Lobau.

In the **Centre Anspach**, immediately to the SW of the Centre Monnaie, is the *Musée de Cire* (waxworks museum). Here hundreds of wax figures grouped in tableaux recall, with the aid of appropriate sound effects, events in the history of Belgium. The museum is open daily from 10.00 to 18.00, closed on 1 January, 25 December.

Boulevard Anspach, named after the 19C burgomaster who did so much for the modernisation of Brussels, leads S to the **Bourse**. Designed by the younger Suys, this was completed in 1873. The site was previously occupied by a convent. In the concourse of the Bourse Metro station a large work by Paul Delvaux recalls past forms of municipal transport.

From the 17C church of **Notre-Dame de Bon Secours**, by Jan Cortvriendt, follow the Boulevard Anspach to the Place Fontainas and thence by its continuation, the Boulevard M. Lemonnier, to the Place d'Anneessens, where there is a statue of the patriot by Vinçotte. Roughly opposite, the Rue de Tournai leads to the Place Rouppe. This is named after N.J. Rouppe (1769–1839), who is remembered for his opposition to the French during the annexation, as a leader of the revolution of 1830 and as the first post-revolution burgomaster of Brussels. The bus (W) for Waterloo starts from this square.

The Boulevard M. Lemonnier from Place Fontainas and the Avenue de Stalingrad from Place Roupe pass through a rather dreary district before reaching the Boulevard du Midi, which is almost 1km away. On the other side of this, the western ring boulevard, is the Gare du Midi.

WEST OF PLACE DE BROUCKERE. Some of the older parts of Brussels lie to the W and SW of the Place de Brouckère. For a long time drab and run-down, this district is being improved gradually. About 300m NW of the Place de Brouckère, across the Rue de Laeken, is the church of **Saint Jean Baptiste au Béguinage**, which was built in 1657–76 by Luc Fayd'herbe. This is open on Tuesday, Thursday, Friday and Saturday between 09.00 and 17.00 and on Sunday from 10.00 to 17.00. The baroque façade (floodlit), one of the finest in Belgium, has three gables. Inside there are works by Theodoor van Loon and a Crucifixion by de Crayer. The béguinage had disappeared by the mid 19C.

About 200m to the S by way of the Rue du Cyprès and the Place du Samedi is the Place Sainte Catherine, where there is a fruit and vegetable market. The church of **Sainte Catherine**, built in 1854 by Joseph Poelaert, is a large building in a mixture of styles. The belfry of its 17C predecessor stands on the S side. Just E of the church is the little *Tour Noire*, a survival from the 12C town walls.

Two parallel streets running northwards from the church, the Quai au Bois à Brûler and the Quai aux Briques, were once busy quays on either side of a waterway. Flanked by small houses, which date mainly from the 19C, and separated by an open space with water and fountains, today they form a quiet oasis. The noise and bustle, the overpowering modernity of the Place de Brouckère seem very far away. The area's restaurants, many of which specialise in seafood, will tempt the gourmet. This is a place where the visitor may pause, rest and enjoy a good meal in surroundings filled with reminders of a more gracious, a more elegant, age.

At the N end of the Quai aux Briques is the *Cheval Marin*, a fine building which dates from 1680. Much restored it is now a restaurant. From the Quai aux Briques several alleys lead to the Rue de Flandre. Once a section of the old Steenweg (see above), its only building of note is No. 46, the *Maison de la Bellone*. A patrician house of the late 17C, once the headquarters of the Ommegang, it is now used for exhibitions, mainly concerning the entertainment arts. The house owes its name to the figure above the door of Bellona, the Roman goddess of war.

At its N end the Rue de Flandre ends at the Canal de Charleroi. Of the Porte de Flandre, which once stood here, not a trace remains.

From Rue de Flandre retrace your steps to the Place Sainte Catherine. The route of the Steenweg continues along the Rue Sainte Catherine and the Marché aux Poulets. This crosses the Boulevard Anspach near the site of the old Senne wharf.

Take the Rue des Poissoniers, a turning to the right from the Rue Sainte Catherine, and then the short Pont de la Carpe to the **Place Saint Géry**. This is generally accepted as the site of the island on which Saint Géry built his chapel in the 6C. The Dukes of Lower Lorraine had a residence and chapel here in 979. These were replaced by a church in the 16C, which in turn was demolished in 1798. In 1881 the *Marché Saint Géry* was established here. A plaque at the E end of the market suggests how the island may have looked.

Just S of Place Saint Géry is the church of **Notre-Dame aux Riches Claires**, a good Flemish Renaissance work by Luc Fayd'herbe. Dating from 1665, it was enlarged in the 19C. Open from 08.00 to 18.00; closed Sunday afternoon and all holidays.

NORTH FROM PLACE DE BROUCKERE. Two important parallel shopping streets run NE, the broad Boulevard Adolphe Max and the more interesting, narrow, crowded Rue Neuve. About half-way along the Rue Neuve, a turning to the right leads to the quiet **Place des Martyrs**, a dignified square surrounded by uniform buildings, the work of Claude Fisco, which date from 1775. In the centre of the square there is a monument above the graves of the patriots who fell in the revolution of 1830. There are also memorials to Count Frédéric de Mérode, who perished in the same cause, and to the author of the words of the 'Brabançonne', the Belgian national anthem.

Further along the Rue Neuve is the little church of **Notre-Dame de Finistère** which dates from 1708. It has a baroque interior and a much venerated figure of Notre-Dame du Bon Succès, brought here from Aberdeen in 1625. There is a reminder in the name of the adjacent Rue du Pont Neuf of the course of the Senne. The last street to the E of the Rue Neuve is the Rue de la Blanchisserie, off which the Rue des Cendres bears N. In a house within the angle of these two streets the Duchess of Richmond, Charlotte Gordon, wife of the 4th Duke, held her famous ball on 15 June 1815, just before the Battle of Waterloo. It is difficult to picture this brilliant occasion in today's setting of rather mean back streets. Here Wellington, on hearing that the French were already at Quatre-Bras, calmly finished his supper before asking his host 'Have you a good map in the house?'.

City 2 at the N end of Rue Neuve is one of Brussels many shopping centres.

Boulevard Adolphe Max and Rue Neuve both end at the northern ring boulevard opposite Place Rogier. Beyond Place Rogier is the Gare du Nord, with the museum of the Belgian railways. These places are described in C, the Ring Boulevards.

B. The Upper Town

> This section describes the Upper Town within the ring boulevards. For the
> boulevards themselves, and the Upper Town beyond them, see Sections C.
> and D.

E of the Grand-Place the Rue du Marché aux Herbes ends at the apex of a
large triangular open space which reaches upwards from the Lower to the
Upper Town. The sloping sides of the triangle are formed by the Rue de la
Madeleine and the Rue de la Montagne. Both of these streets are lined with
old or restored houses. The base of the triangle is provided by the Boulevard
de l'Impératrice. This wide street is burdened with several rather characterless buildings—the telephone exchange, the air terminal and the Gare
Centrale. To the left of these rise the great towers of the Cathedral of
St Gudule.

The square, which faces the air terminal and the Gare Centrale, is known
as the Carrefour de l'Europe.

> Formerly thickly covered by small houses, this part of Brussels was transformed by the
> 'Jonction' scheme for linking the Gare du Nord via a Gare Centrale to the Gare du
> Midi. Involving a series of tunnels and cuttings, the scheme was started in 1911, and
> only completed with the opening of the Gare Centrale in 1952.

Cross the Boulevard de l'Impératrice at the point where it is joined by the
Rue de la Montagne. This will bring you to the parvis of the cathedral.

The Gothic *Cathedral of **Saint Michel**, usually known as **Sainte Gudule**,
is the national church of Belgium. It is open daily from 07.00 to 19.00, 18.00
in winter.

> From Carolingian times or earlier a succession of chapels or churches stood on this
> site. One of the earliest was dedicated to St Gudule, a maiden of the Pepin family. She
> persisted in her pious practices in spite of the pranks played upon her by the devil. He
> amused himself by blowing out her candle whenever she crossed the marsh to pray.
> In 1047 her body was brought to a church dedicated to St Michael, which stood on the
> site at that time. This appears to have been burnt down in 1072. The Rheno-Mosan
> foundations, now exposed in the nave, may belong to this or, perhaps, to a later
> building. By the 12C the church on the site was dedicated to both St Gudule and
> St Michael.
>
> Construction of the present building began with work on the choir in the early 13C
> and continued into the 15C. There was a good deal of later rebuilding. The towers
> date from the 15C and are, in part, the work of Jan van Ruysbroeck. The glittering
> religious ceremonies of the Order of the Golden Fleece were held in St Gudule, notably
> by Philip the Good and Charles the Bold.
>
> The body of St Gudule disappeared during the troubles which beset the cathedral
> during the 16C. The building suffered again at the time of the French Revolution.
> Napoleon, wishing perhaps to make amends, gave the first donation towards its
> restoration. A new carillon of 49 bells was installed in 1975.

The NAVE is from the 14C and 15C, the S side being the older. The statues
of the Apostles on the piers date from 1634–54 and are by Luc Fayd'herbe
(James the Greater and Simon), Jan van Mildert (Philip, Andrew, Peter),
Jérôme Duquesnoy the Younger (Paul, Thomas, Thadaeus, Bartholomew),
and Tobias de Lelis (Matthew, James the Less, John). The pulpit (1699) was
made by Hendrik Verbruggen for the Jesuit church at Louvain and transferred here in 1776, when the Order was suppressed. The great W window,
which dates from 1528, depicts the Last Judgement and is the work of an
unknown Antwerp master. Note   the foundations of a Rheno-Mosan
church.

The TRANSEPTS, which date from the late 13C and early 14C (S) and the late 14C (N), contain two triptychs painted by Michiel Coxie, when aged 89 and 92. The windows, from designs by Bernard van Orley, represent (S) Louis of Hungary and his wife Mary, sister of Charles V, with their patron saints, and (N) Charles V and his wife Isabella of Portugal.

In the CHOIR (1215–65, triforium 1273) lie, amongst others, Duke John II of Brabant, d. 1312, and his wife Margaret of York, d. 1322, the daughter of King Edward I of England. The windows above the high altar are a glorification of the Habsburg dynasty. The three in the centre, by Nicolas Rombouts, depict Maximilian of Austria and Mary of Burgundy, flanked by their son Philip the Handsome and his wife Joanna of Castile on the left and their grandsons Charles V and Ferdinand of Austria on the right. The outer window on the left is by Jan Ofhuys and shows Philip III of Spain and his wife Margaret of Austria, while that on the right by Nicolas Mertens shows Philibert of Savoy and Margaret of Austria, aunt of Charles V. Immediately behind the high altar, which dates from 1887, are (N) the mausoleum of the Dukes of Brabant, surmounted by a lion in gilt copper cast in 1610 from a design of Jean de Montfort and (S) the Mausoleum of Archduke Ernst of Austria, d. 1595. Both are by Robert de Nole from designs by Josse de Beckberghe.

Off the early 13C AMBULATORY is the apsidal chapel. Built in 1282, this was reconstructed in 1675 by Leo van Heil. Its main feature is an alabaster retable of 1538 by Jean Mone, which was originally in the Abbaye de la Cambre. On the N side of the ambulatory there is a memorial, erected in 1957, to the painter Roger van der Weyden, who is buried in the cathedral.

The two large chapels on either side of the choir date from the 16C and 17C. They replaced the seven chapels and the chapter-room, which formerly surrounded the ambulatory.

The CHAPELLE DE NOTRE-DAME DE LA DELIVERANCE (S), which dates from 1649–55, was built from drawings by Jérôme Duquesnoy the Younger. The windows, executed by Jan de la Baer of Antwerp from designs by Theodoor van Thulden, depict, on the upper level, scenes from the life of the Virgin and, below, the donors. Also in this chapel are the tomb of Count Frédéric de Mérode by Charles Fraikin and a retable of 1666 by Jan Voorspoel with a painting of the Assumption by J.B. de Champaigne.

The CHAPELLE DU SAINT SACREMENT DE MIRACLE (N), built in 1534–39, owes its construction to a 14C legend concerning the Host. The story, widespread at the time, has been disproved by historical research and was officially declared to be unfounded in 1968.

It was said that in 1369 a Jew living in Enghien arranged for the theft of a consecrated Host. Soon after, he was murdered and his wife fled to Brussels, bringing the Host with her. On Good Friday in the synagogue in Brussels the assembled Jews stabbed the Host with their daggers, whereupon blood spurted forth. In great fear they ordered a woman to get rid of the Host, but instead she returned it to the church where it became a precious relic under the protection of the cathedral. By the 16C the veneration of the relic had grown to such an extent that it was decided to build this chapel.

The first three of the chapel's windows, proceeding from W to E, were executed by Jan Haeck from designs by Bernard van Orley and, centre window, by Michiel Coxie. Incidents from the legend are depicted on the upper sections, while below there are representations of the donors— John III of Portugal and Catherine of Aragon, Louis II and Mary of Hungary, Francis I of France and Eleanor of Austria. All three ladies were sisters of Charles V. The donors of the next window were Ferdinand, brother of

Charles V, and Anna of Poland. The window above the altar, which shows the Adoration of the Sacrament, was made in 1848 by J.B. Capronnier. This is a good copy in the earlier style of a window by Bernard van Orley, which was destroyed in 1772. Behind the altar, which dates from 1849, a piece of the beam, in which the Host was hidden during the turbulent years of the 16C, may be seen. In the crypt lie the Archduke Albert, the Archduchess Isabella, Charles of Lorraine and other dignitaries.

The **Palais de la Nation** in the Rue de la Loi is easily reached from the cathedral. It may be visited between 10.00 and 16.00, when Parliament is not sitting, but is closed on holidays and on Saturday and Sunday from November to March.

Built in 1783 for the States of Brabant from plans by the French architect Barnabé Guimard, it has a sculptured pediment by Gilles Godecharle. Between 1815 and 1830 it alternated with the Binnenhof at The Hague as the seat of the States General of the United Kingdom of the Netherlands. During that period one wing was the residence of the Crown Prince of the Netherlands, later William III of Holland, who was born here in 1817. Since 1830 it has been the meeting-place of the Belgian Parliament. Edith Cavell was tried here in 1915.

The adjacent Parc de Bruxelles and the other buildings around it are described below.

From the cathedral the **Colonne du Congrès**, 300m to the NE, may be reached by following the Rue de Ligne. The column, 47m high, designed by Joseph Poelaert, is surmounted by a statue of Leopold I, the work of Willem Geefs. It was erected between 1850–59 to commemorate the National Congress of 1831, which proclaimed the constitution after the revolution. Bronze figures at the angles represent Freedom of the Press and Education, both by Jan Geefs, of Association, by Charles Fraikin, and of Religion by Eugène Simonis. The two lions are also by Simonis. Unknown soldiers of the First and Second World Wars are buried at the foot of the column, where an eternal flame burns.

To the N of the column is the *Cité Administrative*, which houses government departments.

From the cathedral follow the Boulevard de l'Impératrice in a S direction to the **Gare Centrale**. Constructed in 1952 this has an interesting wall-painting by J. Hayez inside above the main entrance. Outside, reliefs either side of the entrance recall the old quarters of the city, which were demolished as part of the 'Jonction' scheme (see above).

Below the station to the W, in the Rue de la Madeleine, is the church of **La Madeleine**, a 15C Gothic building restored in 1958. It has acquired the baroque façade of the Chapelle Sainte Anne, which was in the nearby Rue de la Montagne.

From the Gare Centrale there is a choice of ascents to the level of the Place Royale.

VIA THE GALERIE RAVENSTEIN. Behind the station is the spacious **Galerie Ravenstein** with a rotunda, restaurants and cafés. This may be reached either by a subway or by an entrance off the Rue Cantersteen. The arcade ends at the Rue Ravenstein, which will be of interest to readers of Charlotte Brontë. The Rue Baron Horta, which ascends out of Rue Ravenstein, replaced the Escallier Belliard, where the Pensionnat Heger once stood. Charlotte was there in 1842 and 1843, first as a pupil then as a teacher, and there suffered an unrequited passion for Monsieur Heger. Her stay provided the background for 'Villette' and 'The Professor'.

The **Palais des Beaux Arts**, by Victor Horta, which is used for various cultural purposes, stands within the angle of Rue Ravenstein and Rue Baron Horta. The building was restricted to one storey in order not to obstruct the view from the royal palace above.

The *Musée du Cinéma* in the Rue Baron Horta has a permanent exhibition on the history of the cinema before the development of cinemascope. It may be visited between 17.30 and 22.30 or by appointment. There are two projections of silent films, with piano accompaniment, each day.

In the Rue Ravenstein, formerly Rue Isabelle, Charlotte Brontë's 'Rue Fossette', is the picturesque 15C *Hôtel Ravenstein*. The last survivor of the Burgundian period patrician mansions of Brussels, this now houses learned societies.

VIA THE MONT DES ARTS. The rising ground to the S of the Gare Centrale is the **Mont des Arts** or the **Albertine**. This focus for cultural, educational and conference interests was conceived in 1934 as a memorial to King Albert. It was completed between 1954 and 1965, apart from the Musées Royaux des Beaux Arts, which were finished in the mid 1980s. A street on the left ascends through an arch formed by a conference building, Dynastie. On the upper side of the arch are a clock and a carillon, 1964, and a number of small figures who are identified below. On top an elegant gentleman strikes the hour with his stick. In the centre, starting from a statue of the King, a broad sweep of steps rises through gardens, once the steep Rue Montagne de la Cour, to the *Palais des Congrès*.

The **Bibliothèque Royale Albert I** occupies the western side of the complex. It has five principal departments or, as they are frequently called, museums. All are closed on Sunday, holidays and during the last week of August. Entrance is free, except to the Museum and Historical department.

The *Musée du Livre*, open Monday, Wednesday and Saturday, 14.00 to 17.00, has a selection of manuscripts, printed matter and bindings, which provide a panoramic view of the history of books from ancient times to the present day. There are also reproductions of the studies in which notable Belgian men of letters worked. The *Musée de l'Imprimerie*, open Monday to Saturday from 09.00 to 17.00, is devoted to typography, lithography and bookbinding, the emphasis being on the 19C and early 20C. The *Archives and Literature Museum*, open Monday to Friday, 09.00 to 12.00 and 14.00 to 17.00, houses documents, recordings, and video and audio tapes relating mainly to Belgian literature and theatre in French. There are frequent audio-video projections, screenings of video cassettes etc. The *Chalcography Department* is open Monday to Friday from 09.00 to 12.45 and 14.00 to 16.45. It has a collection of some 5000 engraved wood and copper plates. Finally, there is the Library's Museum and Historical Section, which is open, on payment, to approved researchers only.

Incorporated in the E wall of the library is the early 16C Gothic *Chapelle Saint Georges* or *Chapelle de Nassau*. This can be seen on request, or during the exhibitions which are held there from time to time. Like the Bibliothèque Royale, it is closed on Sunday, on holidays and during the last week of August. The chapel is the only surviving part of a mansion which was replaced by the splendid Hôtel de Nassau (p 100). The latter is depicted in a bas-relief by G. Dobbels, 1969 on the outside wall. Note the chapel's stepped windows. These are a reminder of the steepness of the Rue Montagne de la Cour beside which it stood.

The steps of the Mont des Arts end at the Rue Coudenberg, opposite the Hôtel Ravenstein (see above). From here continue by the short surviving stretch of the Rue Montagne de la Cour to the Place Royale. On the right, filling the angle with the Rue de la Régence, are the **Musées Royaux des Beaux Arts**, which are devoted to Ancient and Modern Art. These and the Apartments of Charles of Lorraine are described in Section E.

The PLACE ROYALE, built during 1772–85 from designs by Barnabé Guimard, forms a neo-classical ensemble inspired by Charles of Lorraine. His statue stood in the square until the time of the French Revolution. The present statue, by Eugène Simonis, 1848, is of Godfrey de Bouillon raising the standard for the First Crusade.

The church on the SE side of the square, **Saint Jacques sur Coudenberg**, 1776–85, stands on the site of the chapel of the duke's chaplains. The interior contains sculptures by Laurent Delvaux, 1696–1778, and Gilles Godecharle, 1750–1835.

By the side of the church is the Rue de Namur, a part of the ancient Steenweg. Take the first turning on the left from the Rue de Namur into the Rue Bréderode, for the **Musée de la Dynastie**. Here is recorded the story of the Belgian royal family from 1830 until the present day. The museum is open Wednesday to Saturday from 14.00 to 17.00 and Tuesday to Saturday from 11.00 to 17.00, when the Palais Royal is open. It is closed on 1 January, 21 July and 25 December.

The PARC DE BRUXELLES, immediately NE of the Place Royale, was laid out in its present French formal style in 1835. Much of the Coudenberg Palace, which was burnt in 1731, stood here. In 1830 the park was the scene of some of the earliest and fiercest fighting of the revolution. Among the sculptures in the park are a Diana by Gabriel Grupello and a monument by Vinçotte to the sculptor Godecharle.

The Palais de la Nation, on the N side of the park, is described on p 86.

The Rue Ducale, along the E side, has a line of once aristocratic mansions. No. 51 was occupied by Byron in 1816. According to the commemorative plaque, he left England which had failed to recognise his genius.

The *Palais des Académies*, at the S end of the Rue Ducale, was built in 1823 for the Crown Prince of Orange. In 1876 it became the seat of the Académie Royale de Belgique.

The **Palais Royal**, open in summer, is sited to the S of the Parc de Bruxelles. It occupies the position of the Coudenberg Palace which burned down in 1731. The Coudenberg was the residence of the Dukes of Brabant and later rulers like Philip the Good and Charles V, who signed his abdication here in 1555. The present palace, built between 1740 and 1827, was transformed in 1904–12 from plans by Jean Maquet. The pediment sculpture of Belgium between Agriculture and Industry is the work of Vinçotte. The palace is the sovereign's official town residence.

The pavilion at the W end of the palace is the **Hôtel de Bellevue**. Absorbed into the Royal Palace during the reign of Leopold II, it was the residence of Leopold III and Queen Astrid, when they were Duke and Duchess of Brabant. Today a museum, a department of the Musée d'Art et d'Histoire, it has displays, in period rooms, of 18C and 19C furniture, glassware, porcelain, etc. Much of the collection belonged to the royal family. It is open daily, except Friday, from 10.00 to 17.00, closed 1 January, Easter Monday, Whit Monday, 1 May, 21 July, 1 and 11 November and 25 December and on election days.

From the Place Royale it is a short walk along the Rue de la Régence, by the entrance to the Musée d'Art Ancien, which is described in Section E., to the church of **Notre-Dame du Sablon**. This is open Monday to Friday between 07.30 and 18.30, Saturday, Sunday and holidays between 09.00 and 19.00.

In 1304 the Guild of Crossbowmen built a chapel here. In 1348 a pious woman of Antwerp, who prayed regularly before a neglected statue of the Madonna, had a vision. She was told by the Virgin to take the statue to Brussels. Installed in the Sablon chapel, the statue was so venerated that the crossbowmen decided to build a new church. This in time developed into the present building. During the times of religious strife the statue was destroyed by the Calvinists. In the 17C this part of Brussels became the aristocratic quarter, as can be seen by the memorials in the church. In 1615 the governor Isabella succeeded in shooting down the guild's target bird on the church, a feat which caused much acclaim.

The lavishly decorated Gothic church, largely of the 15C–16C, has a good W portal. The two great piers, which support the crossing, date from c 1400 and are the oldest part of the interior. The choir was built about ten years later. Note particularly the beautiful slim choir lancets. At the W end of the S aisle there is the curious skeletal monument of Claude Bouton, chamberlain to Charles V, who died in 1556. In the S transept there is a triptych by Michiel Coxie. On either side of the choir are the baroque funerary chapels of the Tour et Taxis family, that on the left contains sculptures by Jérôme Duquesnoy the Younger and Gabriel Grupello.

The church stands above the PLACE DU GRAND SABLON, whose name reminds us that this was once a sandy patch amid the marshes. Today, the sloping square, surrounded by old or restored houses, is known for its antiques shops. On Saturday and Sunday a market for antiques and books is held here.

A fountain by Jacques Bergé, 1775, records the gratitude of Thomas Bruce, 3rd Earl of Elgin, 2nd Earl of Ailesbury and friend of James II, to Brussels. A Jacobite exile, he lived here from 1696 to 1741.

The **Musée Postal**, at No. 40, records the history of the Belgian postal service. On display are large collections of Belgian and foreign stamps and much interesting telecommunications equipment. Open Tuesday to Saturday from 10.00 to 16.00, Sunday and holidays from 10.00 to 12.30, closed 1 January and 25 December.

Across the Rue de la Régence rises the PLACE DU PETIT SABLON. In a formal garden laid out in 1890 there are ten statues of 16C dignitaries, a fountain-group of Counts Egmont and Horn and, on the fine wrought-iron balustrade, 48 statuettes representing the medieval guilds.

The building overlooking the garden is the **Palais d'Egmont**, also known as the **Palais d'Arenberg**, from the name of the family which owned it in the 18C. It was built c 1548 for Françoise of Luxembourg, mother of the Count Egmont executed by the Dukes of Alva. Here Voltaire met and quarrelled with J.B. Rousseau in 1722. The palace was rebuilt in 1750 and again after a fire in 1891. Sold to the state in 1964, it is now used by the Ministry of Foreign Affairs. It was here that Great Britain, Ireland and Denmark signed the agreements on 22 January 1972 under which they became members of the EEC. The best view of the palace is from the garden, entered from the ring Boulevard de Waterloo or from the Rue du Grand Cerf. In the garden there is a replica of Frampton's 'Peter Pan'.

The **Conservatoire de Musique**, on the corner of the Rue de la Régence and the Place du Petit Sablon, was built by J.P. Cluysenaer in 1876 on the site of the Tour et Taxis mansion, where in 1516 the Prince de Taxis founded the first international postal system. The building houses the **Musée Instrumental**, a unique collection of more than 500 musical instruments from all over the world and from the Bronze Age onwards. It is open on Tuesday, Thursday and Saturday from 14.30 to 16.30, on Wednesday from 16.00 to 18.00 and on Sunday from 10.30 to 12.30. It is closed on holidays.

The immense Graeco-Roman-style **Palais de Justice** was built by Joseph Poelaert between 1866 and 1883. It stands on a raised plateau dominating a large part of Brussels, the site of the medieval Galgenberg, the gallows hill. The dome, over 100m in height, was rebuilt after fire damage in 1944. Around its colonnade are figures representing Justice, Law, Mercy and Strength. The portico, flanked by Doric colonnades, leads to two open vestibules between which a stairway ascends to the great hall, which occupies the centre of the building. On the right of the stairs are statues of Demosthenes and Lycurgus, on the left of Ulpian and Cicero. It is open daily from 09.00 to 12.00 and 14.00 to 16.00, closed Saturday and Sunday and on public holidays.

The large open space in front of the Palais de Justice is the PLACE POELAERT. A road tunnel descends from here to the Place Louise. On the terrace there is a monument to the Belgian infantry, while on the other side, in the Rue des Quatre-Bras, a memorial, unveiled by the Prince of Wales in 1923, records Britain's gratitude for help received from Belgium during the First World War.

The terrace, which has an orientation table and telescopes, commands a fine view of the Lower Town. The tower to the right belongs to the church of the Minimes, 1700–15. The now vanished convent of the Minimes stood partly on the site of the house of the anatomist Andreas Vesalius, who was born in Brussels in 1514.

The QUARTIER DES MAROLLES, which lies below and to the W of the Palais de Justice, is a cheerful, densely populated district. This is still the home, though decreasingly, of the true natives of Brussels, who speak a mixed dialect. Close to the S end of the quarter's main street, the Rue Haute, is the Porte de Hal. This is described in section C.

The **Centre Public d'Aide Sociale de Bruxelles** in the Saint-Pierre Hospital, 298A Rue Haute, houses art treasures from charitable institutions of the *ancien régime*, notably gold and silverware, furniture, and paintings from the 15C to the 18C. It is open on Wednesday from 14.00 to 17.00.

132 Rue Haute was the home of the artist Pieter Brueghel the Elder, who was so respected that he was exempted from having to provide billets for Spanish troops. He was buried in the church of Notre-Dame de la Chapelle (see below). His great grandson, the painter David Teniers, died here.

The Place du Jeu de Balle, off the parallel Rue Blaes, is the home of the daily Vieux Marché, the flea market. To the N and E is the church of **Notre-Dame de la Chapelle**. This was always a people's rather than a nobles' church. A chapel founded here in 1134 was replaced by the present part Romanesque and part Gothic structure, which was erected between 1210 and the end of the century. The nave and aisles were destroyed by fire in 1405 and later reconstructed. The tower, badly damaged by the French bombardment of 1695, was rebuilt by Antoon Pastorana in 1708. The bas-relief of the Trinity in the tympanum of the main portal is by Constantin Meunier, 1831–1905. The tomb of Pieter Brueghel the Elder is in the third chapel off the S aisle. The memorial was erected by his son, Pieter Breughel, and bore a painting by Rubens. This is now in a private collection. Notice also the pulpit, 1721, by Pierre Plumier, who carved the Spinola family memorial in the Chapelle du Saint Sacrement. In the same chapel there is a monument, 1834, to the patriot Frans Anneessens, who is buried in the church. The 19C choir stalls retain their original stone seats.

A remnant of the 12C fortifications, the **Tour Anneessens** or **Tour d'Angle** stands just E of Notre-Dame de la Chapelle. Once attached to the Steen-poort, the tower survived as a prison and it was here that Frans Anneessens was held in 1719 prior to his execution.

C. The Ring Boulevards

The ring boulevards were constructed between 1818 and 1871 along the line of the city's 14C walls. Since then they have been turned into very wide, multi-lane, fast motor roads, which pass at intervals through tunnels. On several stretches there are, above the tunnels, central roads in each direction with smaller roads at the sides. The latter are often described as 'avenues' and bear names that differ from their companion boulevards. The ring is interrupted by a number of 'places' e.g. Madou, Louise, but these are more busy traffic intersections than conventional squares. In general they correspond to the old gates and still mark the city's main entrances and exits. The ring measures c 8km. Its main functions are to provide a fast and efficient road for those who wish to bypass the city, a number of convenient points of entrance to and egress from the centre and easy access to the Gare du Midi.

The section of the ring road between the Porte de Hal, the Place Sainctelette and the Place Rogier boasts few attractions.

The places of interest between the Place Rogier and the Place Louise are described below. These may be reached by extending the routes described in sections A. and B. or by travelling to the appropriate Metro station. Shoppers will find the boutiques at the Place Louise and in the nearby Avenue de la Toison d'Or irrestibile, if somewhat expensive.

PLACE ROGIER, at the end of Boulevard Adolphe Max and half-way along the northern ring, is named after Charles Rogier. He was a leader of the 1830 revolution and later the minister primarily responsible for starting Belgium's railways and for negotiating freedom of navigation on the Scheldt. On the edge of a district of redevelopment, especially to the NW, the square is dominated by two 'centres', *Rogier* and **Manhattan**, where there is an entrance to the Metro station. To the W a viaduct carries a main road, which passes the prominent Basilique Nationale to join the Ostend and ring motorways.

Near the **Gare du Nord**, behind the Centre Rogier, at 76 Rue du Progrès, is the **Musée des Chemins-de-Fer Belges**. This is open from Monday to Friday and on the first Saturday of the month between 09.00 to 16.30. It is closed on Sunday and public holidays. Documents, models and uniforms trace the development and activities of Belgian Railways from 5 May 1835, when continental Europe's first passenger train service began. On that day three trains took 900 excited travellers from the Allée Verte station to Mechelen. The third was pulled by the engine 'L'Eléphant' which is exhibited in the museum. This historic event is recorded in a large painting. Upstairs there are displays of prints, photographs, etc. Note the attractive aquarelles by James Thiriar, which show 19C railway workers in the uniforms of the time.

The *Hôtel Liégois* in the Rue du Progrès was Verlaine's usual haunt on his numerous visits to Brussels. The drunken brawl and his attempt on Rimbaud's life took place not here, but in the Hôtel de Courtrai near the Grand-Place (see above).

Le Botanique (Metro), now a cultural centre, occupies the high ground to the E of the Place Rogier. The sculpture in the grounds includes works by Constantin Meunier. At the Porte de Schaerbeek the Rue Royale crosses the ring boulevard. To the E of Le Botanique is the Jesuit church. At the N end of the Rue Royale is the church of **Sainte Marie**, an octagonal building in Byzantine style built in 1844 by Hendrik van Overstraeten.

BRUSSELS
& Environs

0 kilometres   2

A12
Antwerp

Grand Palais

Brussels
International
Trade Markt

Parc du Centenaire

Atomium

Pa
Chin

Parc de
Laeken

Japona

E40
Ostend

Palais
Royal

ND de Laeken

JETTE

SO
DE TRO

GROOT
BIJGAARDEN

Koekelberg

Bas. Nationale
du Sacré-Coeur

BOULEVARD LEOPOLD

MOLENBEEK

See large scale
map

Cath

GRAND
PLACE

N8
Oudenaarde

CHAUSSEE   DE   NINOVE

Canal de Charleroi

CHAUSSEE DE MONS

Mont
des
Arts

Gare
du Midi

ANDERLECHT

St Pierre et St Guidon

Maison d'Erasme

ST-GILLES

BARRIERE

Ste Trinite

M
H

WATE

FOREST

Cavell
Inst

St Denis

CHAUSSEE   D'ALSEMBERG

UCCLE

N

D des Affligés

Mons
N6

DROGENBOS
E19 Mons & Charleroi

Beersel

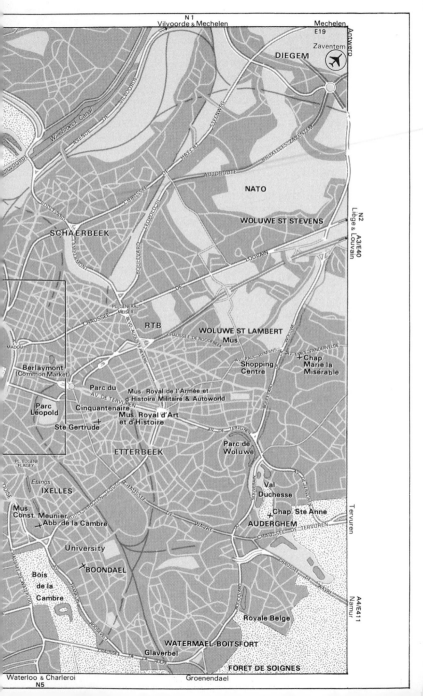

Zaventem

DIEGEM

NATO

WOLUWE ST STEVENS

N2
A3/E40
Liège & Louvain

SCHAERBEEK

Willebroeck Canal

AVENUE DE VILVOORDE

CHAUSSEE DE HAECHT

STEENWEG

BRUXELLES-ZAVENTEM

AUTOROUTE

BOULEVARD

WILVOORDE

CHAUSSEE DE VILVOORDE

CHAUSSEE DE LEOPOLD III

BOULEVARD LAMBERMONT

DE

LOUVAIN

PL. GENERAL
MEISER

CHAUSSEE DE LOUIS SCHMIDT

RTB

CHAUSSEE DE ROODEBEEK

WOLUWE ST LAMBERT
Mus.

AV. PAUL HYMANS

AV. EMILE VANDERVELDE

PL.
MADOU

Chap.
Marie la
Misérable

Berlaymont
(Common Market)

Shopping
Centre

Parc du

AV. DE TERVUEREN

Mus. Royal de l'Armée et
d'Histoire Militaire & Autoworld

BOULEVARD

Parc
Léopold

Cinquantenaire

Ste Gertrude

Mus. Royal d'Art
et d'Histoire

AV. DE TERVUEREN

Parc de
Woluwe

PL. EUGENE
FLAGEY

ETTERBEEK

Etangs

IXELLES

Mus.
Const. Meunier

Abb. de la Cambre

CHAUSSEE D'IXELLES

FORET DE SOIGNES

CHAUSSEE

DE

WAVRE

Val
Duchesse

Chap. Ste Anne

AUDERGHEM

AV. DE TERVUEREN

Tervuren

CHAUSSEE DE TERVUEREN

University

AV. FRANKLIN ROOSEVELT

BOONDAEL

Bois
de la
Cambre

CHAUSSEE DE WATERLOO

AV. DE LA COURONNE

CHAUSSEE DE WAVRE

BOULEVARD

A4/E411
Namur

Royale Belge

WATERMAEL-BOITSFORT

Glaverbel

CHAUSSEE DE LA HULPE

At the top of the rise the ring curves S to the PLACE MADOU (Metro). Here the Chaussée de Louvain leads E, reaching after 2km Place Général Meiser (p 108). From the SE corner of the Place Madou follow the Avenue des Arts to No. 16, the **Hôtel Charlier**. Open Monday to Friday from 13.00 to 17.00, this private mansion was converted in 1890 into a museum. It contains the collections of the sculptor Guillaume Charlier—furniture, 19C silver, pictures by Constantin Meunier, James Ensor, Jacob Smits, Mme Fantin Latour and Henri de Braekeleer, as well as sculpture by Charlier himself.

Continuing in a S direction you cross the Rue de la Loi (one-way E–W), at the far end of which are the headquarters of the EC and the Parc du Cinquantenaire (see Section D.). Both may be reached by Metro from here. About 300m along the ring is the parallel Rue Belliard, the main W–E artery. Having passed the Parc Léopold (see Section D.), at the Parc du Cinquantenaire this joins the Avenue de Tervuren to become the city's finest exit and entrance road.

At the PLACE DU TRONE (Metro Luxembourg), where a statue of Leopold II stands near a side entrance to the royal palace, the ring bears SW and soon reaches the the the PORTE DE NAMUR (Metro). At 150 Chaussée de Wavre is the *Musée Camille Lemonnier*, where the literary life of this Belgian writer, 1844 to 1913, is evoked in documents and books. The museum is open on Wednesday between 13.00 and 15.00 and, by appointment only, from Tuesday to Thursday from 09.00 to 12.00 and 14.00 to 17.00. It is closed on public holidays and in July and August.

From the Porte de Namur to the PLACE LOUISE (Metro), the centre of the ring is occupied by the Boulevard de Waterloo, while on the outer side is the Avenue de la Toison d'Or. For an interesting diversion, which will take you to some elegant shops, enter the long **Galerie de la Toison d'Or**, which extends some 200m eastwards across the Rue de Stassart to the Chaussée d'Ixelles. Continue your walk by way of the **Galerie d'Ixelles** and, having crossed the Chaussée de Wavre, return through the **Galerie de la Porte de Namur** to the Porte de Namur. These arcades, with the shops in the northern part of the Avenue Louise, and its adoining **Galerie Louise**, form a very attractive shopping district.

On the N side of the ring there is an entrance to the garden of the **Palais d'Egmont**. Further W on this side, in the Place Jean Jacobs, a memorial honours the victims of the wreck in 1908 of the first Belgian training ship.

The **Porte de Hal**, at the point where the ring turns N, is all that remains of the city's 14C defences. Because it was used as a prison, it escaped the fate of the other gates, which were destroyed in the early 19C. The Chaussée de Waterloo, to the S of the gate, leads to the battlefield. On the N side of the boulevard is the Rue Haute (p 90).

From the Porte de Hal the ring, now the Boulevard du Midi, continues in a northerly direction. Between mid July and mid August the central parking area in front of the Gare du Midi is taken over by a fairground, which with its roundabouts, roller-coasters, ebullient atmosphere and abundant local colour is well worth a visit. Having passed the **Gare du Midi**, at 1.5km from the Porte de Hal the ring reaches the Porte d'Anderlecht, where it becomes the Boulevard de l'Abattoir. From the Place de Ninove, it follows the course of the Canal de Charleroi for 1km to the PLACE SAINCTELETTE, a busy intersection below the viaduct from the Place Rogier.

The Quai de Willebroeck, NE of the nearby Place de l'Yser, soon becomes the Allée Verte, a fashionable residential district in the 18C. In the 19C continental Europe's first railway station for passenger services was sited here.

D. Parc du Cinquantenaire and Parc Léopold

The Parc du Cinquantenaire, at the E end of the Rue de la Loi, and the Parc Léopold, to the S of the parallel Rue Belliard, are about 1km from the eastern edge of the ring boulevard. The parks are important for their museums: the Musée Royal de l'Armée et d'Histoire Militaire, the Musée Royal d'Art et d'Histoire, and Autoworld in the Cinquantenaire, and adjoining the Parc Léopold: the Musée Wiertz and the Institut des Sciences Naturelles.

The Berlaymont, headquarters of the EC, is just W of the Parc du Cinquantenaire.

Motorists should note that the Rue de la Loi is one-way from the Cinquantenaire to the ring. To reach the parks from the W it is necessary to take the Rue Belliard. By far the easiest way to get to them is by Metro.

Parc du Cinquantenaire

The rather characterless Parc du Cinquantenaire was laid out for the exhibition of 1880, which celebrated the 50th anniversary of the founding of the modern state of Belgium. Beneath the park runs the road tunnel which links the Rue de la Loi and the Rue Belliard with the Avenue de Tervuren. The Brussels mosque is in the NW corner. A short way to the S there is a memorial, 1921, by Vinçotte to Belgium's explorers and missionaries. The dominant feature of the park is the **Palais du Cinquantenaire**. Originally the main building of the exhibition, it has been enlarged to house the museums. Semicircular colonnaded wings lead up to a triumphal arch by Charles Girault with a quadriga by Vinçotte. On either side there are figures representing the provinces of Belgium, the two provinces of Flanders being treated as one.

The **Musée Royal de l'Armée et d'Histoire Militaire** is open from Tuesday to Sunday, 09.00 to 12.00, 13.00 to 16.45. It is closed on Monday, 1 January, 1 May, 1 November, 25 December and on election days. Occupying the N wing of the Palais du Cinquantenaire, the museum has three main sections. The first is devoted to the history of the Belgian army from 1789 to the present day. Somewhat overcrowded, it has collections of weapons, uniforms, medals and equipment, portraits of military figures and a number of theatrical battle pictures. Waterloo is not forgotten. In a large hall beyond there is a display of armoured vehicles, artillery, etc. The Air Section has a fine collection of both civil and military aircraft and their associated air and ground equipment.

The **Autoworld Automobile Museum** is open daily between 10.00 and 18.00 from April to October and until 17.00 during the rest of the year. It is closed on 1 January and 25 December. The museum, which occupies a part of the S wing of the palace, is a must for the veteran car enthusiast. The ground floor, which is concerned with the period from about 1885 onwards, contains the de Pauw Collection and a section concernng the development of tyres. The upper floor houses the Mahy and other collections and is used also for temporary exhibitions.

The remainder of the S wing of the palace is devoted to the ****Musée Royal d'Art et d'Histoire**. The entrance is on the W side. The museum is open from Tuesday to Friday between 09.30 and 17.00 and on Saturday, Sunday and some public holidays from 10.00 to 17.00. It is closed on 1 January, 1 May, 1 and 11 November, 25 December. Visitors who are interested in a particular exhibit or department are advised to check with the TIB office or the museum (tel: 733 96 10) before making a visit, as departments may be closed on certain days. Information about special exhibitions may be obtained from the same sources.

The museum has educational and information departments, a reference library, a collection of more than 70,000 transparencies which may be borrowed, a casts and moulds workshop, a photographic service and a café.

Special arrangements are made for handicapped visitors. There are, from time to time, exhibitions for the blind, with documentation in Braille, on the chronological study of materials and of the techniques relating to them. The exhibits used are those that can be appreciated by touch. Enquiries about these special services should be made to the museum beforehand.

The museum is divided into the following departments: the Ancient World: the Near East and Iran, Egypt, Greece, Rome, Islam and Eastern Christian Art.

Non-European Civilisations: Far East, Pre-Columbian America, Polynesia and Micronesia, India and SE Asia.

There are also sections dealing with the Archaeology of Belgium, Folklore, Carriages and the Decorative Arts in Europe. In addition the museum has two dependencies: the Chinese Pavilion and Japanese Tower, Avenue van Praet, Laeken (see Section F.) and the Hôtel de Bellevue Museum, Place des Palais (see Section B.).

THE ANCIENT WORLD. *Near East and Iran*. The artefacts in this section come from an area which extends from the Mediterranean to the Zagros Mountains and from the Caspian Sea to the Arabian Gulf. They date from the prehistoric period to pre-Islamic times and are arranged in geographical and chronological order. Note in particular the Anatolian stone axes and black pottery of Yortan, the cylinder seals, pottery, figurines and the neo-Sumerian relief of Gilgamesh from Mesopotamia, the Babylonian astrological tables, the bronzes of Luristan, the reliefs from Palmyra and the gilded statuettes of the gods from Phoenicia.

Egypt. More than 9000 objects trace the history of Egypt from the earliest times to the period of the Roman conquest. They include prehistoric vases, the stele of Den, the reconstructed mastaba of Neferirtenef, an archaic female statue known as 'La Dame de Bruxelles', Middle Empire reliefs, models and the bust of an unidentified pharaoh, a limestone relief of Queen Tiy, sarcophagi, coffins, mummies, figurines and scarabs from various periods, a colossal diorite head believed to be that of Ptolemy VIII from Nubia, a basalt statue of the vizir Bakenrenef, the bas-relief of Petamenope, the head of Ptolemy VIII (?) and many funerary portraits on wood and cloth from the Ptolemaic and Roman periods.

Greece. The museum's collection of Greek artefacts, arranged by style and area, is presented chronologically. Of particular interest are the Cycladic idols and a Mycenaean gold cup. Vases from the Archaic, Geometric, Orientalising and Classical periods include an archaic (late 6C BC) black figure Attic amphora: the departure of the warriors, an archaic red figure amphora: the archer, a 6C BC red figure stamnos signed by Smikros: banqueting scene and a late 5C BC kantharos signed by Douris: Hercules and the Amazons. There are also several fine terracottas from Tanagra.

Rome. This section includes works from Etruria, North Africa, Syria and Asia Minor. There is also an excellent model of the city of Rome in the 4C AD. Note particularly the Etruscan bronze candelabra and tripods, the busts from the Republican and Imperial periods, especially those of Augustus and

*4C AD mosaic of the hunt from the house Au Triclinos Apamaea,
Syria, in the Musée Royal d'Art et d'Histoire, Brussels*

Drusus (?), of Tyche and Septimius Severus, a wallpainting from Boscoreale
and the uninhibited, lustful reliefs from Dionysian sarcophagi.

From 1930 to 1938 Belgian archaeologists worked at the ruins of the
ancient city of Apamaea ad Orontem in Syria. Some of their discoveries,
including a reconstruction of the 2C AD Grand Colonnade and several
splendid mosaics, are displayed in the museum. Note especially the mosaic
of Therapenides on the subject of neoplatonism, the geometric mosaics

from the synagogues and, from the house of the governor of Syria, a large 4C AD mosaic depicting the perils and the pleasures of the chase.

Among a large group of Roman copies of Greek sculptures are: the Venus of Cnidus by Praxiteles, a Bacchus (style of the Westmacott Ephebe) by Polycleitus, a pensive Daphnis, from the group Pan and Daphnis sometimes attributed to Heliodorus of Rhodes and, from a famous Hellenistic group, an exultant Satyr full of fierce, pagan joy.

Islam. In this room are exhibited ceramics and textiles from Central Asia, India, North Africa, Syria, Turkey, Spain, Sicily and Iran. These include vessels and wall tiles from Iznik and Kadjar, elaborately decorated with floral and geometric patterns and representations of the human figure. The textiles, some richly embroidered, others recording ancient legends, are mainly from Iran and Turkey.

Eastern Christian Art. Opened in 1979 this is a collection of objects from the world of the Orthodox Church. The earliest date from the Byzantine period, the latest from 19C Greece and the Balkans. They include icons, ceramics, church furniture and vestments. There is also a small display of church objects from Ethiopia.

NON-EUROPEAN CIVILISATIONS. The civilisation of *China* is represented by a rich collection of artefacts from every dynasty. Of special interest are the magnificent 19C wooden statue of the Bodhisatva, the 7C and 8C stone heads from Tianlongshan, the bronzes, carved ivories, mirrors, ceramics, ritual vases, costumes and examples of delicate calligraphy.

There are also temporary exhibitions of objects from Japan and Korea.

Pre-Columbian America. In this gallery more than 15,000 artefacts are used to illustrate the history and folklore of the cultures of the American continent. Terracotta figurines, mosaics, stelae, vases, gold and silver statuettes, textiles, cult masks, musical instruments, tools and feather headdresses provide a fascinating record of the many civilisations, which flourished between Alaska and Tierra del Fuego.

Polynesia and Micronesia. The Galerie Mercator houses a magnificent collection of archaeological and ethnographical artefacts from New Zealand, the Fiji Islands and Easter Island. Arranged according to function—weaving, stone and wood working, fishing, farming, house building, furniture making and warfare—they also include material collected by the 1934/35 Franco-Belgian expedition to Easter Island. The display is dominated by the andesite statue of Pou Hakanononga, the God of Tuna Fishing.

The collections from *India and SE Asia* are shown in six rooms devoted to the following subjects and countries: Hinduism–Jainism, Arts of the Himalyas, Buddhisim–Lamaism, Vietnam, Thailand and Indonesia. Masques, theatre marionettes, lamps, statues, temple columns, reliefs, bronzes, paintings and ceramics are combined in a dazzling display.

The section on the *Archaeology of Belgium* traces, with reference where appropriate to sites in other European countries, the various cultures which the land of Belgium has known. Objects from the Palaeolithic, Neolithic, Bronze and Iron Ages and the Gallo-Roman period illustrate various stages of development. Note particularly the Bronze Age spear imported from Britain, the gold filigree decoration from a la Tène drinking horn, the Roman period processional standard surmounted by a figure of Serapis and the bronze and silver gilt Merovingian buckles.

The *Folklore* collection reflects various aspects of life in earlier times— marionettes from the Toone Theatre (see Section A.), an ancient pharmacy, pipes, decorative collars associated with the Guilds. There is also a room devoted to toys—dolls, dolls' houses, miniature shops, clothes and utensils, toy soldiers, miniature cars and model railways. The collection made by M. Schombroodt of amateur cinematograph cameras and projectors claims to have an example of every model sold between 1922 and 1987.

The collection of *Carriages* has examples of most vehicles used in the 17C, 18C and 19C. Pride of place goes to a superb Louis XVIII Coupé de Gala with painted panels in the style of Boucher. Prints, lithographs and models complete this magnificent display of ancient methods of transport.

Decorative Arts in Europe. It is claimed that the galleries in this part of the collection contain a representative selection of European works of art from the Middle Ages to the 20C.

In the room devoted to Mosan (Meuse) Art there is a vast variety of religious objects. Note the portable altar from the Abbey of Stavelot, a polychrome wooden statue of the Virgin and Child (a Sedes Sapientiae), reliquaries of the Holy Cross, ivories and sculptures.

Among the stone sculptures there are baptismal fonts (Mosan) and funerary monuments. Examples of stained-glass from the Middle Ages and the Renaissance include fragments from the Cathedral of Brussels and a 13C Annunciation. The history of the patriarchs is recorded in ten tapestries made in Brussels in 1534 after the designs of Barnard van Orly. Among the religious metal works are lecterns, thuribles, crosses, statuettes, fonts and a wide range of domestic utensils in silver and pewter. The scientific instruments include clocks, astrolabes and orreries. Note the medieval wooden religious figures and the fine 15C and 16C retables. There are displays of lace, ceramics, textiles (Oriental, Egyptian, Persian, Byzantine, French, English, etc.) and domestic furniture. The cradle of Charles V is given a prominent place.

There is a rich display of *Art Nouveau and Art Deco* objects, including works in silver by Philippe and Marcel Wolfers and Henry van de Velde, ceramics by Paul Gauguin, Gallé, Lachenal and textiles by Morris, Liberty and the Wiener Werkstätte.

The **European Community** occupies the huge four-winged *Berlaymont* building, by L. de Vestel, J. Gilson and A. and J. Polak, on the W edge of the Parc du Cinquantenaire. Named after a monastery, which once occupied this site, it stands on the Rond Point Schuman. This commemorates the Frenchman Robert Schuman, promoter of the 1951 plan to pool Europe's steel and coal resources, out of which the EC grew. The founder members, which signed the Treaty of Rome in 1957, were Belgium, France, Germany, Italy, Holland and Luxembourg. The United Kingdom, Ireland and Denmark acceded in 1972, Greece in 1981 and Spain and Portugal in 1985.

In the church of **Saint Gertrude**, off the Place van Meyel 200m S of the Musée d'Art et d'Histoire, there is a beautiful late 15C *statue of St Gertrude which was found in the loft in 1935.

Parc Léopold

The Parc Léopold is an attractive steep-sided park, with a small lake at the foot of the hill. At the top is the Institut des Sciences Naturelles. This may be entered from the park or from the nearby Rue Vautier, where the Musée Wiertz is situated.

The **Institut des Sciences Naturelles** is open daily between 09.30 and 16.45. It is closed on Monday, 1 January, 25 December and election days. It has displays of minerals, insects and fossils but is, perhaps, best known for its palaentological collections. These include a famous *series of 250-

million-year-old fossil iguanodons, which were discovered in 1875 at Bernissart in Hainaut. Note also a mammoth from Lier, skeletons of Stone Age miners and a collection of prehistoric tools.

The **Musée Wiertz** is open from Tuesday to Sunday between 10.00 and 12.00 and 13.00 and 17.00; from November to March it closes at 16.00. It is closed on Monday, on 1 January, 1 May, 1 and 11 November and 25 December. The museum was formerly a studio built by the government for the romantic painter Antoine Joseph Wiertz, 1806–65. He was pre-occupied by the macabre and some of the large canvases in the museum are gruesome in the extreme. Their subjects include Hunger, Madness and Crime, Vision of an Executed Criminal and Premature Burial. Inevitably, the collection is dominated by these paintings, which Wiertz refused to sell, but the visitor is advised not to miss the smaller and more conventional pictures in the main hall and the side rooms.

E. Musées Royaux des Beaux Arts

The Musées Royaux des Beaux Arts, two separate but linked galleries for ancient and modern art, form the upper part of the Mont des Arts or Albertine complex. A long-term programme of modernisation and extensions, which was completed by the mid 1980s, has embraced part of the 18C buildings, by Jan Folte, which extend down the narrow Rue du Musée. Known collectively as the *Ancienne Cour*, they occupy much of the site of the former Hôtel de Nassau.

The Duvenvoorde mansion here, c 1344, passed by marriage to the Nassau family in 1404. At the close of the 15C Englebert of Nassau rebuilt the house and its Chapelle Saint Georges. The chapel is now incorporated in the Bibliothèque Royale Albert I and is usually known as the Chapelle de Nassau. Destroyed and rebuilt, the mansion became the property of William III of England. Marlborough lived here in 1706. After the Coudenberg palace was burnt down in 1731, the Hôtel de Nassau became the residence of the Austrian governors. After 1756 it was almost entirely rebuilt by Charles of Lorraine. Here in 1763 the eight-year-old Mozart performed before the governor. Charles of Lorraine's apartments, with a monumental staircase and sculpture by Laurent Delvaux, have been restored and are shown to groups on request (tel: 519 53 57).

The two galleries have separate entrances, but are linked internally by escalator. The *Musée d'Art Ancien* is open from Tuesday to Sunday between 10.00 and 12.00 and 13.00 and 17.00. The *Musée d'Art Moderne* is open from Tuesday to Sunday between 10.00 and 13.00 and 14.00 to 17.00. Both are closed on Monday, 1 January, 1 May, 1 and 11 November, 25 December and election days.

The ****Musée d'Art Ancien** occupies a neo-classical building, 1875–85, by Alphonse Balat. This was modernised inside and a long extension was constructed at the rear. The four pillars at the entrance support statues by Guillaume de Groot of Painting, Sculpture, Architecture and Music. Above the door are busts of Rubens, Giambologna and van Ruysbroeck, while on either side are allegorical reliefs, some by Thomas de Vinçotte, and groups by Charles van der Stappen, on the left, and Paul de Vigne, on the right.

The Old Masters collection dates from the later years of the 18C, when a number of inferior works of art, which had been left behind by the French, were exhibited in a part of the former Court. In 1801 the Musée du Département de la Dyle was established by Napoleon. Later it received two consignments of paintings from the Louvre. These included a number of French and Italian paintings and four altarpieces by Rubens. The first curator, G.J.J. Bosschaert, 1737–1815, made strenuous efforts to get back those works of art which had been carried off to France and, after the fall of Napoleon, he recovered three more altarpieces by Rubens. In 1873 forty paintings from the collection of Duke Englebert of Arenberg were purchased by the museum. In the years that followed it received many gifts. These included paintings by van Dyck, sketches by Rubens, Brueghel the Elder's Winter Landscape and a magnificent collection of 4250 drawings by Rembrandt and other Dutch masters.

At present the museum has about 1200 paintings. These date from the 14C to the 18C. Most European schools are represented, often by works of the first quality. However, its great glory is the collection of Flemish pictures.

Because of the number of paintings involved, it is only possible to mention the most important works here. However, the museum publishes a detailed catalogue and a picture book in English. These will be of interest to those visitors who have both the time and the stamina to examine the collection in detail.

To assist the public the museum authorities have marked out three routes. The Blue Route: paintings of the 15C and 16C in Rooms 10 to 34 on the first floor; the Brown Route: paintings of the 17C and 18C in Rooms 50 to 62 on the second floor; the Yellow Route: paintings of the 19C in Rooms 69 to 91.

THE BLUE ROUTE. From the large rectangular hall, where sculpture is usually displayed, go to Room 10 on the first floor and then follow the blue arrows.

Early Netherlands Master: Retable of the Life of the Virgin, dated to the late 14C and one of the oldest works in the museum. Despite the fact that it has been damaged, especially on the right, this is a vibrant and moving work. *Petrus Christus*: Pietà. *Roger van der Weyden*: Pietà, and circle of van der Weyden: Sforza Triptych. *Master of the Aix Annunciation*: the prophet Jeremiah, with Noli Me Tangere on the reverse.

Master of Flémalle: Annunciation in a Flemish interior. Mass of St Gregory. *Master of the Legend of St Catherine*: Nativity, a part of a triptych. *Roger van der Weyden*: *Man with an Arrow. Recent research suggests that the portrait is of Anthony of Burgundy. As he wears the collar of the Golden Fleece, it can be dated to 1456 when Anthony was elected a chevalier of the order. Portrait of Laurent Froimont, a nobleman. This is part of a diptych. *Hugo van der Goes*: St Anne, Virgin and Child, with a Franciscan donor.

Dirk Bouts: *Judgement of the Emperor Otto. Two fascinating paintings. One shows the Punishment of the Innocent Count, the other the Ordeal by Fire. Bouts died while working on the former which was very likely completed by his sons. The Emperor Otto executed a nobleman, who was falsely accused by the Empress. Appealing to God to prove her husband's innocence, the widow successfully underwent the ordeal by fire, whereupon Otto sent the Empress to the stake. The pictures were commissioned for the town hall of Louvain.

Master of 1473: Triptych of Jan de Witte, a leading citizen of Bruges, and his wife, probably commissioned to celebrate their marriage. *Hans Memling*: Martyrdom of St Sebastian, painted c 1470 for the archers' guild of Bruges. Portraits of Willem Moreel, burgomaster of Bruges, and of his wife (c 1478), painted for the hospital of which Moreel was a governor. A later (1484) portrait of Moreel and his wife hangs in the Groeninge museum in Bruges. *Jean Hey*: Ecce Homo (1494). This artist was active in the Val de Loire but, an inscription on the reverse, *per m. Jo. hey. teutoni. cu*, suggests that he came from the S Netherlands.

There are also interesting works by the *Master of the Legend of St Barbara*: Scenes from her life. The *Master of the Legend of the Madeleine*, the *Master of the Vue de Sainte Gudule*, and the *Master of the Life of Joseph*: portraits of Philip the Handsome and Joanna the Mad.

From 15C foreign artists there are works by *Master of the Holy Kindred*: A Striking Calvary set in a contemporary landscape. *Master of the Kaufbeuren Sacristy Cupboard*: An inventive temptation of St Anthony. *Carlo Crivelli*: Virgin and Child Enthroned. Central panel of a large altarpiece. A second panel depicting St Francis of Assisi is also in the museum.

Works by 16C artists include: *Albert Bouts*: Triptych of the Assumption: *Hieronymus Bosch*: Crucifixion with donor, a restrained work. The town in the background is believed to be 's Hertogenbosch, where Bosch was born. *The Temptation of St Anthony. An early copy of the painting now in Lisbon. A work full of strange and disturbing images. *Lucas Cranach the Elder*: Adam and Eve, Venus and Cupid. Two paintings full of barely submerged sensuality.

Gerard David: *Virgin and Child, à la Soupe au Lait, a tranquil, delightful picture. *Quinten Metsys*: Triptych of the Life of Holy Kindred. Dated and signed 1509, this was commissioned for the Chapel of the Holy Kindred in the church of Sint Pieter at Louvain. *Anon. (Netherlands School)*: *Child with a dead Bird, a masterly insight into a child's emotion. *Jan Gossaert (Mabuse)*: Venus and Cupid. Gossaert studied in Italy and this is one of the earliest Netherlands pictures with a mythological subject. *Two portraits of Donors, wings of a triptych whose centre is lost. This is far removed from the conventional representations of donors. The man's eyes are defiant and challenging, while the woman's expression is proud and disdainful. There is little sense of prayer or meditation in the picture. *Lucas van Leyden*: Temptation of St Anthony, painted when the artist was aged between 17 and 22. (There is a dispute about his date of birth.) In addition to the usual demons it has some interesting new ones—frogs and a chained pig. *Bernard van Orley*: Portrait of the physician, George de Zelle, who lived in the Place Saint Géry, and a triptych The Virtue of Patience. This is based on a poem by Margaret of Austria. Closed it shows the story of Lazarus, open it depicts the trials of Job. *Pieter Huys*: Last Judgement (1554). Reminiscent of Bosch it places a strong emphasis on the tortures of the damned, who flaunt their vices, while awaiting punishment. *Pieter Aertsen*: The Cook (1559), portrait of a robust lady who practices her metier with gusto.

**Room 31 is devoted to *Pieter Brueghel the Elder*. The museum authorities provide a useful leaflet in English, which gives an outline of the artist's life and comments on the pictures. Those normally on show are the Fall of the Rebel Angels, the Adoration of the Magi and the Census at Bethlehem. The biblical subjects are very firmly placed in an uncompromisingly Flemish setting and may be seen as the artist's comments on contemporary society and politics. Man Yawning. Perhaps a representation of sloth from a lost series of paintings on the Seven Deadly Sins. Landscape with the Fall of Icarus. This is a poignant representation of the indifference which we show to the suffering and tragedy of others. The shepherd guards his flock, the fisherman casts his line, the peasant ploughs his land, the ships sail by while Icarus, ignored and abandoned, drowns in a placid sea.

Among the 16C works by artists from the northern part of the Netherlands, mainly Antwerp, are *Antonio Moro*: Portrait of Hubert Goltzius (1576), painter, engraver and antiquary. *Pieter Pourbus*: Portrait of Jacob van der Gheenste (1583), an alderman of Bruges. *Martin de Vos*: St Paul at Ephesus (1568), a picture full of swirling movement. *Frans Pourbus the*

Elder: the Marriage of Hoefnagel, a painter and humanist who was a friend of the artist. The work gives a charming, if somewhat stilted representation of a Protestant family occasion. Both painter and subjects were members of the Antwerp Protestant community. *Paul Bril* an evocative Harbour Scene. *Jacob Grimmer*: Landscape with Castle.

The Blue Route also takes in Rooms 37 to 45 where the DELPORTE BEQUEST is displayed. The collections of Dr Franz Delporte, who died in 1973, include paintings, sculpture, ceramics and objets d'art from the 13C–18C. Among the paintings are works by *Abel Grimmer, Adriaen Key, Joachim Patinir, Pieter Brueghel the Younger, Marten van Heemskerk* and *Pieter Brueghel the Elder*: *Winter landscape with Skaters. As well as the European works of art, there are ceramics and objets d'art from Persia, Egypt, Mexico, China, Japan and West Africa.

THE BROWN ROUTE, Room 50 to Room 62, covers the 17C and 18C. Undoubtedly, the greatest attraction in this part of the museum is the famous *collection of paintings by *Pieter Paul Rubens*, which range from huge canvases to small works and include portraits and sketches. Generally they are displayed in Rooms 52 and 62.

Among the large canvases are: The Coronation of Mary. Pietà with St Francis. The Intercession of Mary and St Francis. The Ascent to Calvary. Dating from 1636–37, this large, crowded scene was painted for the abbey of Afflighem towards the end of the artist's life, when he suffered from rheumatism in his right hand. The Martyrdom of St Livinius, another great dramatic work of the same period, was commissioned for the Jesuit church in Ghent. Adoration of the Magi, painted for the church of the Capucines at Tournai.

Smaller works include: The Woman taken in Adultery. Studies of a Negro's Head, a masterpiece of observant portraiture. The same model was used by Rubens in the Adoration of the Magi and also by van Dyck. Madonna with Forget-me-nots. Landscape with the hunt of Atalanta, a picture which influenced both Gainsborough and Constable. The Martyrdom of St Ursula (sketch). This vigorous, almost theatrical, portrayal of the story of the massacre of the saint and of the 11,000 virgins, who accompanied her may be compared with earlier, more traditional versions of the legend, notably Memling's painted reliquary of 1489 at Bruges.

Among the portrait subjects are: the Archduke Ernst, Governor of the Netherlands. Peter Pecquius, man of letters and chancellor of Brabant. Hélène Fourment, the artist's second wife. The Archdukes Albert and Isabella, painted for one of the triumphal arches erected when the Infante Ferdinand made his entry into Antwerp in 1635.

In other rooms on this route there are works by the following artists (names in alphabetical order): *Adriaen Brouwer*: Drinkers at a Table. The Flute Player. *Jan Both*: Italian Landscape at Dusk. *Antoon van Dyck*: several portraits, including A Genoese Lady and her Daughter. Jean Charles della Faille (c 1629). Della Faille was a distinguished Jesuit and professor of mathematics at Madrid. Rinaldo and Armida, sketch copy of the artist's painting now in Baltimore. St Francis. St Felix. Martyrdom of St Peter. *Jan Fyt*: Cock and Turkey. The Dog Cart. *Jan van Goyen*: View of Dordrecht, a work vividly conveying a feeling of wind and cold. River Mouth. *Frans Hals*: Portraits. *group of children, a part of a large picture of a family in a garden.

Meindert Hobbema: Landscapes. *Jacob Jordaens*: *Allegory of Fertility (c 1625), held to be among the finest of this artist's works, Pan and Syrinx. Satyr and Peasant. *The King Drinks. *Nicolas Maes*: *Old Woman Dreaming, a touching study of old age. *Rembrandt*: Portrait of N. van Bambeeck.

Dead Woman. *Jan van Ruisdael* and *Salomon van Ruysdael*: Landscapes.
Frans Snyders: Fish Market. Dogs fighting over a Bone. Oysters and Fish.
Deer Hunt. *Jan Steen*: The Rhetoroticians. *David Teniers the Younger*: Card
Players. Flemish Fair, a scene of rustic jollity. The château in the back-
ground was rented by Teniers. *Village Doctor. *Lucas van Uden*: On the
way to the Market, an interesting representation of contemporary life.
Cornelis de Vos: Portrait of the Artist and his Family (1621).

In Room 50 there are paintings by Spanish artists. These include works
by *Ribera*: Apollo flaying Marsyas; and *Murillo*.

Rooms 50 and 51 have paintings by a number of Italian artists. *Francesco
Guardi*: The Doge In St Mark's. *Tiepolo*; *Il Guercino*: Donor presented to
the Virgin. *Tintoretto*.

In Room 61 paintings by French artists include *Philippe de Champaigne*:
Presentation in the Temple. *Claude Lorrain*: *Aeneas hunting the stag on
the coast of Libya. In this late work diffused lighting, mysterious shadows
and sombre colours lead us gently into the world of myth. *Nicolas de
Largillière*: Portrait of a Man.

Rooms 55 and 56 house the Della Faille Bequest.

In the **YELLOW CIRCUIT**, Rooms 69 to 91, works of the 19C are displayed. In principle the rooms and pictures should be as described below.

Rooms 69 to 71, which are detached from the remainder, are devoted to
neo-classicism and Romanticism. *Jacques Louis David* is represented by
The Assassination of Marat, a stark, rather unattractive work, and by a
warm, sensual rendering of Mars disarmed by Venus. Note the prudishly
tactical ingenuity employed by the painter in the latter. Among the works
by David's most famous Belgian pupil, *François Joseph Navez*, are a sombre
depiction of Agar and Ishmael in the Desert and a number of portraits. *Louis
Gallait* has several groups and portraits. Note especially his charming
depiction of *Simonne Bucheron, aged three.

The Yellow Route continues with Realism as the main theme of Rooms 72
to 80. By *Charles de Groux* there are The Pilgrimage of St Guido, The
Gleaners, and Benedicite, by *Louis Dubois*, Roulette and The Storks and
by *François Lamorinière*, The Pond at Putte.

Here too is *Emile Wauters'* haunting depiction of Hugo van der Goes at
the Convent after he had gone mad. This has been described by one critic
as a fascinating glimpse of the past through the rose-tinted spectacles of
the 19C. By *Louis Artan* there are several typical sea scenes including
L'Epave (The Wreck), by *Edouard Agneessens*, *At the Theatre and *Sleep-
ing Adolescent, and by *Joseph Stevens*, Marchè aux Chiens.

One room is devoted almost entirely to pictures by *Alfred Stevens*.
Compare the sense of elegant despair in his picture, The Widow and her
Children, with the unrelieved hopelessness of the poor, which is so power-
fully conveyed by the canvases of *Eugène Laermans*.

In Room 79 the pictures and sculptures of *Constantin Meunier*, one of
the most prolific and best known 19C artists, record the dignity and the
pathos of manual labour. (See also Constantin Meunier Museum p 110.) In
the next room there are several interesting interiors by *Henri de Braekeleer*
and a number of portraits by *Jacob Smits*. Note particularly the deeply
sobering Father of the Condemned.

Symbolism follows with *Léon Frederic's* huge, astonishing triptych The
Cascade, The Stream, The Lake, pictures filled with a teeming mass of pink,
nude children. The same artist's *The Ages of the Peasant traces its theme
from the Little Girls to The Aged through a series of five groups.

Other artists represented are *Fernand Khnopff*: Memories, and Lawn

Tennis; *Jean Delville*: The Treasures of Satan; *Jan Verhas*: School Procession, 1878, a delightful study of the faces, characters and attitudes of a procession of small girls.

Luminism is represented largely by *Frans Courtens* and by the typical gentle landscapes of *Emile Claus*. Room 88 is devoted to the work of *Henri Evenepoel*. The room beyond is largely given over to the first artists of Sint Martens-Latem. These include *Albert Servaes*: a gloomy Pietà and Peasants in the Fields; *Gustave van de Woestyne*: Sunday Afternoon, a study of rural sensuality, and a Crucifixion with a grotesque grimacing Christ; and drawings and sculptures by *George Minne*.

The Yellow Route continues with works by *Renoir*, *Boudin*, *Sisley*, *Gauguin*, *Seurat*, *Fantin-Latour* and *Monet*. It ends with the Hess Vandenbroek Bequest in Room 91.

The main entrance to the **Musée d'Art Moderne** is on the W side of the Place Royale, but it may also be reached from the Musée d'Art Ancien by a passage lined with busts by *Gilles Godecharle* of Homer, Racine, Milton, Washington, Fénélon, Schiller, Wieland and Seneca.

An imaginative architectural achievement, the galleries descend through eight subterranean, semicircular levels. Within these there are 1200 arches sheltering more than 11,000 modern works of art. Mostly Belgian, they include paintings, sculpture, collages and assemblages in wood, metal, plastic and other materials. Although the levels are reasonably clearly defined and signposted, they tend to merge both thematically and physically and it is easy to stray from one to another.

While visitors with specialist understanding and taste will head for their chosen subjects, others will be content to descend from level to level, admiring, hating, scoffing at or just being baffled by the exhibits. It is unlikely they will be bored.

LEVEL 1 is devoted to Contemporary Tendencies (temporary exhibitions).

LEVELS 2 and 3 are reception areas.

LEVEL 4 has works by James Ensor, Leon Spillaert, neo-Impressionism, Nabis and Fauvism. Note particularly *Théo Rysselberghe*'s exuberant Arabian Fantasia. This contrasts interestingly with his reflective Portrait of Madame Charles Maus, charming The Promenade, and Woman Reading to a Small Girl. *Rik Wouters* is represented by The Flautist, Lady with a Yellow Neckband and the sculpture Domestic Cares. Visitors are drawn to *Jan Cox*'s wild and garish Fight for the Body of Patroclus, Battle of the Gods and Finis. In addition to *Ensor* and *Spillaert* there are pictures by *Pierre Bonnard*: Nu à Contre-jour; *Kess van Dongen*: Portrait of Louis Barthou and *Raoul Dufy*: View of Marseille. *Ossip Zadkine* has three very different sculptures: a symbolic City Destroyed (Rotterdam, see 'Blue Guide Holland'), a towering Diana in wood and a sober bust of André Gide.

LEVEL 5 is devoted to the Nervia group and Expressionism (first part). The most interesting works are by the important Flemish expressionist *Constant Permeke*. These include Spring, The Betrothed, Golden Landscape, a number of nudes and a sculpture of Niobe. Here also are seven pictures by *Jean van den Eeckhoudt*. Of particular interest is the sensitive Self-portrait of the Artist and his Wife.

LEVEL 6 is the realm of Expressionism (second part), Cubism, Neo-Plasticism and Surrealism. *Gustave de Smet* is represented by a number of portraits and groups, *Frits van den Berghe* by Man in the Clouds and Sunday and *Salvador Dali* by The Temptation of St Anthony. Many visitors are drawn to the enigmatic works of *Paul Delvaux*: the poignant Crucifixion, the eerily fantastic La Voix Publique, a Pygmalion redolent of female sensuality and male impotence and the uncomfortably spectral Evening Train.

LEVEL 7. Realism, Animism, Jeune Peinture Belge, 1945–48. Among the most interesting works are:*Isidore Opsomer*: Portrait of Camille Huysmans, *Jan Cox*: Self-portrait, and paintings by *Leon de Smet, Henri Wolvens* and *Ossip Zadkine*.

LEVEL 8 is for Cobra, Surrealism after 1940, Lyric Abstract, Geometric Abstract and New Figuration. These five themes offer a bewildering choice of medium, colour and design. Note especially *Francis Bacon*'s Pope with Owls, a Self-portrait by *Jan Cox* and, dominating one section, *Octave Landuyt*'s desperate L'Englouti.

F. Outer City and Suburbs

Northern Districts

LAEKEN, with its striking church, royal palace and the Atomium, is the northern district likely to be of greatest interest to the visitor. There are good services by underground, bus and tram.

From the Lower Town Laeken may be reached by several roads which converge at Square Jules de Trooz. This is sited on the Charleroi to Antwerp canal which, with its basins, serves as the port of Brussels.

Dedicated in 1870, the **Eglise Notre-Dame de Laeken** by the architect Joseph Poelaert was erected in memory of Louise-Marie, the first Queen of the Belgians. In the royal crypt rest Leopold I, Leopold II, Albert I and Queen Astrid. Outside, on the N, are a monument to Marshal Foch and a memorial erected in 1927 to a French Unknown Soldier. In the cemetery stands the choir of the earlier 17C church.

From the church the Avenue du Parc Royal skirts the Domaine Royal surrounding the **Palais Royal**, which is clearly visible from the road. There is no admittance to the palace but the hothouses (*Serres Royales*) are sometimes open, usually in May.

The governors Maria Christina of Austria and Albert of Saxe-Teschen had this palace built in 1782–84 by the architects Louis Montoyer and Antoine Payen on the site of an old manor. It was restored in 1802 by Napoleon, who signed the order for the advance of his armies into Russia here. The palace was largely rebuilt in 1890 after a disastrous fire.

In the public PARC DE LAEKEN, opposite the palace entrance and stretching away towards the Atomium, are the neo-Gothic *Monument Leopold I* (1881) and the *Villa Belvédère*, residence of the heir to the throne. At the busy traffic junction where the Avenue du Parc Royal ends stands the *Fontaine de Neptune*, a replica of the 16C fountain by Giambologna in Bologna's Piazza Nettuno.

The **Pavillon Chinois**, on the opposite side of the road to the right, was built for Leopold II in 1906–10. It now houses a valuable collection of Chinese porcelain. At the time of writing the Pavilion is closed for restoration. Check with the TIB for its reopening date and visiting hours. The *Tour Japonaise*, opposite, was bought by Leopold II at the Paris exhibition of 1900.

Constantin Meunier, "Monument au Travail"

The **Atomium** by Eugène Waterkeyn, an aluminium structure 120m high, dominates the PARC DES EXPOSITIONS. Constructed for the 1958 International Exhibition, it represents the atom in the form of a metal crystalline molecule enlarged 165 billion times. A fast lift takes visitors to the top and escalators link the spheres. In three of these there are exhibitions on the history of medicine, the laboratory, genetics, virology, immunology, etc. The Atomium is open in summer from 09.45 to 18.30 and in winter from 09.30 to 18.00.

At a nearby roundabout the memorial to Burgomaster Adolphe Max is inscribed with his calm, defiant words to the Germans, who occupied Brussels in 1914.

To the N of the Atomium, within the PARC DES EXPOSITIONS, is the large **Brussels International Trade Markt**, by John Portman 1975. A little further N the even larger **Palais du Centenaire**, built in 1935 to celebrate the centenary of Belgian independence, was a major feature of the exhibitions of 1935 and 1958.

Cinephiles will wish to visit **Kinepolis** in the Bruparck. This has 24 cinemas, one of which has a screen 600 m sq. For details of programmes in French telephone 479 23 23, for programmes in Dutch 479 60 60 and for programmes on Imax (the large screen) 479 79 69.

A short distance SW of the Atomium is the **National Planetarium**. For opening times and schedules of programmes with English commentary ask the TIB.

In the commune of JETTE, to the SW of the Atomium, the 18C abbot's palace at 14 Rue Jean Tiebackx is all that survives of the Abbey of Dieleghem, a Premonstratensian house founded in 1100. The palace now houses two museums, the *Musée Communal* and the *Musée Nationale de la Figurine Historique*. With the aid of hundreds of statuettes and dioramas the latter traces the history of civilisation. Both museums are open from Tuesday to Friday and on the first weekend of the month between 10.00 and 12.00 and 14.00 and 16.00.

The NE commune of EVERE is the home of NATO, the **North Atlantic Treaty Organisation**. The headquarters of NATO moved from Paris to a site beside the road to Zaventem airport in 1967.

Further to the N at DIEGEM the **Eglise Sainte Catherine** has a striking 'wedding cake' tower, which dates from 1654. At the shrine of St Cornelius in the church there is a painting of the saint by Jan van Houbraken (1643). Below the church is the small, 15C, restored *Châtelet* of the former manor house.

In the village of ZAVENTEM, which gives its name to Brussels' airport, the church contains a painting of St Martin by van Dyck. It is said that, while on his way to Rome, the painter stayed in the Café van Dyck (1624), which is in the square adjoining the church. There he fell in love with one of his host's daughters, but his request for her hand was refused. The church also has a work by Gaspard de Crayer .

Eastern Districts

The Chaussée de Louvain leaves the ring boulevard at Place Madou and after 2km reaches Place Général Meiser in the commune of SCHAERBEEK. This is an important road junction for the motorist. The main approaches to the airport and to the Mechelen and Antwerp motorway are to the NE, while the start of the motorway to Louvain, Liège and Germany is c 400m to the SE.

Just S of Place Général Meiser are the tower and buildings of the Belgian radio and television service (RTB). They occupy the site of former military rifle ranges. In the Place des Carabiniers, between the buildings and Boulevard Auguste Reyers, the *Monument des Fusillés* commemorates Nurse Cavell and other patriots who were shot here by the Germans.

The smart residential commune of WOLUWE SAINT LAMBERT has an excellent **Shopping Centre** in the area between Avenue Paul Hymans and the main N–S Boulevard de la Woluwe.

Just E of the Shopping Centre along Avenue Emile Vandervelde is the mournfully named *Chapelle Marie la Misérable*. This honours a pious girl of the 13C who refused the advances of a nobleman. In revenge he hid a valuable cup in her hovel and accused her of stealing it. As a result she was condemned to death and buried alive. Later a number of miracles took place at her grave. The chapel was built and her body was placed under the altar. The chapel is open every day from 07.30 to 17.30.

The Boulevard de la Woluwe joins the Avenue de Tervuren at the **Parc de Woluwe**, a pleasant oasis of hills, trees and lakes.

AUDERGHEM, to the S, is reached by the Boulevard du Souverain. To the E of the boulevard is the estate of **Val Duchesse**, site of the first Dominican community in the Netherlands (13C). The Romanesque *Chapelle Sainte Anne* (12C, restored) in the Avenue Valduchesse is open from 14.00 to 17.00 every Wednesday from July to September and on 26 July, the saint's feast day.

Farther to the SE between the Chaussée de Tervuren and the Chaussée de Wavre some of the 14C buildings of the *Abbaye du Rouge Cloître* survive. They include the S wing, now a restaurant, and parts of the farm. Here, too, is an Information Centre for the Forêt de Soignes. This is open on Tuesday, Wednesday, Thursday, Saturday and Sunday from 10.00 to 12.00 and 14.00 to 17.00. It is closed during July and on all holidays.

Southern Districts

The description that follows covers the Abbaye de la Cambre, the Bois de la Cambre, the Forêt de Soignes and the districts of Ixelles, Uccle, Forest and Drogenbos.

To the E of the elegant AVENUE LOUISE, which links the ring boulevard with the Bois de la Cambre, is the **Abbaye de la Cambre (Camera S. Mariae)**. Composed mainly of 18C buildings, which form two quadrangles, it was founded by a Brussels noblewoman named Gisèle in 1201, who gave it to the Cistercian order. The church dates in part from the 14C, with a N transept added in the 15C. It contains the shrine of St Boniface of Lausanne, who died in 1265. A pupil of the nuns, he retired from his see at Lausanne to end his days as chaplain at La Cambre. A painting by Albert Bouts hangs in the nave. The cloister of the 13C and 14C, destroyed in 1581 during the Wars of Religion, was rebuilt in 1598 and restored between 1922 and 1934. It has modern windows with the arms of the abbesses, including Mary Scott of Buccleuch, Scotland, and murals of 1957 by Irene van den Linden, which tell the story of St Adelaide. A nun of La Cambre, St Adelaide was blind and endured uncomplainingly the pains of leprosy and paralysis. Segregated from her community, she offered her sufferings for the souls in purgatory and saw in visions their release to paradise.

The **Bois de la Cambre** is immediately S of the abbey. Once part of the Forêt de Soignes, it was acquired by the city in 1862 and landscaped to form a particularly attractive park. It has a number of restaurants.

The FORET DE SOIGNES, a survival of the ancient Silva Carbonaria, spreads in a wide arc to the SE of Brussels. Under its magnificent beech trees there are cycle, walking and horse riding tracks. Within the confines of the forest are the *Geographical Arboretum of Tervuren* with forest flora from the old and new continents and the Groenendaal Arboretum. The latter houses some 400 forest species in an 18C farm building, which once belonged to a former Augustinian priory (see below). It is open during May, June, September and October from 13.30 to 17.30.

Separating the forest from the Bois de la Cambre is the Chaussée de la Hulpe, which curves SW to meet the main Tervuren to Waterloo road at a major intersection. Just S of the junction a side road, the Avenue Dubois, leads through the forest to the *Château de Groenendael*. Now a restaurant, this 18C priory was the successor to an Augustinian foundation of c 1340. At the priory fishponds a bench with a medallion memorial commemorates the mystic and first prior, Jan van Ruysbroeck (1293–1381). He was the author of The Book of Supreme Truth, The Adornment of the Spiritual Marriage and The Sparkling Stone, works which had a profound effect on later mystical writers.

The **Musée des Beaux Arts** (1892), 71 Rue Jean de Volsem, is in that part of the commune of IXELLES which lies to the E of Avenue Louise. Its collection includes objets d'art, sculpture and paintings dating from the 16C to the 20C. There are works by de Braekeleer, van Rysselberghe, Jacob Smits, Delacroix, Courbet and Joshua Reynolds. Among the interesting collection of posters from many countries is an almost complete set signed by Toulouse-Lautrec. The museum is open from Tuesday to Friday between 13.00 and 19.30 and on Saturday and Sunday from 10.00 to 17.00. It is closed on Monday and public holidays.

To the S of the Place Eugène Flagey, by the ponds known as Etangs d'Ixelles, there is a memorial to Charles de Coster (1827–79), author of a well-known modern version of the legend of Till Eulenspiegel. From the ponds it is an easy walk to the Abbaye de la Cambre (see above).

Visitors interested in police work may like to visit the *Centre d'Histoire et de Traditions de la Gendarmerie* at 98 Rue Juliette Wytmans. Located to the E of the ponds it traces the history of the gendarmerie through uniforms, weapons and documents from the *Ancien régime* to the present day. The museum is open on working days from 09.00 to 12.00 and 14.00 to 17.00.

The **Université Libre de Bruxelles (ULB)**, Avenue Franklin Roosevelt and Boulevard General Jacques, on the E side of the Bois de la Cambre opened its doors to students in 1834 in the Ancienne Cour (p 100). Its founder, Theodoor Verhaeghen, is commemorated by a fine statue.

Four museums are associated with the university:

The *Musée de l'Histoire de l'Art et Archéologie*, Building D, 9th Floor, 30 Avenue Antoine Depage, has full-size replicas of Greek and Roman sculpture from the archaic period to the time of the Roman Empire, annotated documents on the restoration of medieval paintings, and information on and material from the university's archaeological department's excavations. It may be visited during the academic year on request (tel: 642 24 19 and 642 27 14).

The *Musée de Minéralogie*, 30 Avenue Antoine Depage has over 1000 samples from all over the world. It is open from Monday to Friday between 09.00 and 12.00 and from 14.00 to 16.00, closed Saturday and Sunday, public holidays and from 1 July to 31 August.

Museum of Scientific Instruments, 50 Avenue Franklin Roosevelt. Information from Professor G. Sylin, tel: 642 22 11.

Museum of Zoology, 50 Avenue Franklin Roosevelt (tel: 650 36 78). The museum is open during the academic year from 09.00 to 17.00. It is closed on Saturday, Sunday, public holidays, second week of Easter and from 15 July to 15 August.

About half-way down the W side of Avenue Louise take the Rue du Bailli to the **Eglise de la Sainte Trinité**. This incorporates the baroque façade of the Augustinian church (Jacob Franckaert, 1642), which was formerly in the Place de Brouckère.

A short distance to the SW, at 25 Rue Americaine, is the **Musée Horta**. Occupying the house of Victor Horta, one of the most famous architects of the 'Art Nouveau' style, it contains a large collection of documents and photographs. It is open from Tuesday to Sunday between 14.00 and 17.30 and closed on Monday and public holidays.

The *Musée Constantin Meunier** is at 59 Rue de l'Abbaye, a turning to the W at the S end of the Avenue Louise. The artist's home has a rich collection of his work—some 170 sculptures and 120 paintings and drawings. It is open from Tuesday to Sunday between 10.00 and 12.00 and from 13.00 to 17.00, closed on Monday, 1 January, 1 May, 1 and 11 November, 25 December and election days.

To the W of the Bois de la Cambre in the commune of UCCLE the **Musée David et Alice van Buuren**, 41 Avenue Leo Errera, contains a magnificent private collection of paintings, drawings, sculpture and Delftware from the 16C to the 20C. Apart from a fine version of the Fall of Icarus by Brueghel the Elder there are works by Fantin-Latour, Patinir, Ensor, Permeke, Rik Wouters and van de Woestyne. The museum is open on Monday from 14.00 to 16.00 and on other days by appointment for groups (minimum 15 persons). It is closed on Sundays and public holidays.

A short way to the E of the museum in the Rue Edith Cavell is the *Institut Edith Cavell*.

Nurse Edith Cavell (1865–1915) was head of a large school for nurses which she had founded with Marie Depage, who was drowned when the *Lusitania* was torpedoed by a German U boat. When war broke out in 1914 Nurse Cavell actively helped fugitive soldiers to escape to Holland. Arrested, she was held at the prison of Saint Gilles (c 1 km to the N) before being tried in the Palais de la Nation, sentenced to death and shot on 12 October 1915. Her calm words, 'Patriotism is not enough', are inscribed on her memorial in London's St Martin's Place. The Institute bears a memorial to its founders and an adjacent street is named after Marie Depage.

In the Rue de Stalle, in the SW part of the commune is the little *Chapelle Notre-Dame des Affligés*. Also known as Notre-Dame du Bon Secours or simply as the Chapelle de Stalle, it dates from the 14C and 15C.

In the commune of FOREST, to the NW of Uccle, is the *Abbaye Saint Denis*. Established in 1238 as a retreat for noblewomen, it later became a Benedictine foundation. The present buildings, a reconstruction of the 18C, are used for cultural purposes. The adjacent mainly 13C early Gothic church has a Romanesque 12C chapel, which contains the tomb of St Alène. She was a noble lady whose conversion to Christianity enraged her father and he cut off her arm. However, the severed limb worked so many miracles that eventually he too was converted.

At DROGENBOS, to the SW of Forest, the **Museum Felix de Boeck** at 222 Grote Baan has about 60 canvases by this artist, who was born in 1898. His work represents many of the artistic trends of this century.

Western Districts

In ANDERLECHT to the E of the railway line there are two museums.

The **Musée Gueuze** at 56 Rue Gheude, just S of the Chausée de Mons, is concerned with the traditional methods of brewing typical Brussels beers like Lambic, Gueuze, Kriek and Faro. It is open from Monday to Friday between 09.00 and 16.30 and on Saturday from 10.00 to 18.00 in winter and 10.00 to 13.00 in summer.

About 600m to the SW, at 14 Rue van Lint, the *Musée de la Résistance* recalls the great courage and many forms of opposition used by the gallant members of the Belgian resistance movement during the two World Wars. The museum is open from Monday to Thursday between 09.00 and 16.00.

To the W of the railway, there are three buildings of particular interest around the Place de la Vaillance.

The ***Maison d'Erasme**, dating from 1515, was not in fact the home of Desiderius Erasmus, but the guest house of the chapter of Anderlecht. Erasmus stayed there c 1520, when visiting his friend Canon Wijkman. The rooms have been arranged in the style of the 16C and contain documents on Erasmus's life and works. There is also a small collection of excellent 15C and 16C paintings. These include works by Roger van der Weyden, Dirk Bouts, Hugo van der Goes, Cornelis Metsys and a *triptych of the Epiphany by Hieronymus Bosch. The house is open every day, except Tuesday and Friday, from 10.00 to 12.00 and from 14.00 to 17.00.

Desiderius Erasmus (1466–1536), born in Rotterdam or perhaps Gouda, was a Renaissance humanist and theologian with a passion for learning. His attitude was one of reason and common sense applied to human affairs. He rejected the pedantic attitude of the schoolmen, exposed the abuses of the church and engaged in controversy with Luther, von Hutten and the scholastic theologians of the Sorbonne. Attacked by those on both sides of the religious argument, he was unjustly accused of being lukewarm to Catholicism and even of being sympathetic towards Luther. He enjoyed a succession of generous patrons and spent long periods in England where he was an intimate of Thomas More. In 1516 he came to Belgium as adviser to the young Charles V. Later he lived at Louvain where he helped found the Collegium Trilingue. At this time he was at the peak of his fame and conducted witty and erudite correspondence with admirers all over Europe. In 1521, with the increasing hysteria about Lutheranism, he left Louvain. After six years in Freiburg, he settled at Basle in Switzerland. His considerable literary output included an annotated edition of the New Testament, his Enchiridion Militis Christiani and his satirical Encomium Moriae. He also left a considerable amount of correspondence. More than 3000 letters, including several written from this house, provide a unique picture of his times.

Nearby is the remarkable Collegiate **Eglise Saint Pierre et Saint Guidon**. One of the most interesting churches in Brabant, the date of its foundation is not known, but it was certainly before the 11C. The present church was built between 1470 and 1515 by Jan van Ruysbroeck and Hendrik de Mol. The tower, designed in 1517 by Mathias Keldermans, was never finished, but a spire was added in 1898. There are some restored 15C wallpaintings inside. The Romanesque crypt, one of the oldest in Belgium, contains the 11C–12C tomb of St Guidon or St Guy. A native of Brabant, he was known as the 'Poor Man of Anderlecht'. At one time sacrist of Notre-Dame de Laeken, he spent seven years as a pilgrim in the Holy Land. After his return to Brussels, he was admitted to the public hospital at Anderlecht, where he died. The church is open from Monday to Saturday between 09.00 and 12.00 and from 14.30 to 18.00 (December, January and February until 17.00) and on Sunday and Holy days from 09.00 to 12.00 and 16.00 to 19.00. Visits are not permitted during services.

Four 17C habitations in the recently restored small *Béguinage* to the N of the church are open to visitors. Founded in 1252 by the Dean and Chapter of Anderlecht, it was occupied by nuns until the 18C. It is open daily, except Tuesday and Friday, from 10.00 to 12.00 and from 14.00 to 17.00.

From the ridge of MOLENBEEK-SAINT-JEAN to the N of Anderlecht Villeroi bombarded Brussels in 1695.

Karreveld, in the N part of the commune, is a fortified farm whose origins reach back to the 13C. The present buildings date from the 16C and 17C.

Further N in the commune of KOEKELBERG is the vast **Basilique Nationale du Sacré-Coeur**. Begun in 1905 to a grandiose design of P. Langerock—he envisaged six towers, each 90m in height—it was completed in 1970 to a more modest plan by A. van Huffel and P. Rome. The basilica is dedicated to the Sacred Heart of Jesus and is a national memorial to those who gave their lives for their country. The interior with its rich marble and stained-glass is very impressive. The basilica is open daily from 08.00 to 19.00 in summer and from 08.00 to 17.00 in winter. Visits to the gallery may be made, on request, from 09.00 to 17.00.

G.   Waterloo and Tervuren

Waterloo

The battlefield of Waterloo is 20km S of Brussels on the Charleroi road (N5). The town of Waterloo is 3km N of the battlefield. Public transport services, Route W, leave about every half-hour from Place Rouppe. In summer many agencies run coach excursions. The main points of interest can also be reached by car.

At the battlefield, apart from obvious features such as the motorway, there have been two major changes to the landscape since 1815, both of them along the line held by Wellington. The first is the *Butte du Lion*, which was built in 1824. This, and the area occupied by the buildings below it, was open farmland. Secondly, at the time of the battle the road now leading from N5 to the Butte was a narrow sunken lane.

It is also worth remembering that the valley was planted with rye. This crop, which was allowed to grow much higher in the 19C, gave good cover at least at the start of the battle.

The Butte offers a good general view of the battlefield. Most of the places mentioned in the description of the battle can be readily identified from it. However, it should not be forgotten that the ridges and folds, so vital to the soldiers, cannot be appreciated from this height.

Visitors are likely to be surprised by the small size of the stage on which one of the most decisive events of Europe's history took place and on which some 140,000 men fought and 39,000 died.

Before the Battle (see also Routes 24 and 27). On 1 March 1815 Napoleon landed in France after his escape from Elba and rapidly reassembled his troops. Only two armies, which were both in Belgium, posed a threat to him: Blücher's Prussians and Welling-ton's mixed force of British, Belgians, Dutch and Germans. Napoleon, determined to separate his opponents, crossed the frontier near Charleroi on 15 June and the next day mauled Blücher at Ligny. Wellington stood at Quatre-Bras. Blücher fell back towards Wavre, forcing Wellington to retire to the area just S of Waterloo which he had already chosen for his defence of Brussels. Early in the morning of 18 June Wellington received an assurance from Blücher that he would join him as soon as he could. In the event he was not able to do this until the evening, so the French attack had to be met by Wellington alone.

The Battle. Napoleon had about 72,000 men and 246 guns. Wellington, who had about 68,000 men, 24,000 of them British, and 150 guns, was apprehensive about both the steadfastness and the loyalty of some of the non-British contingents. The two armies were drawn up only some 1500m apart. The French faced N with the farm of La Belle Alliance as their centre. Wellington occupied the ridge to the N; his centre was roughly where the Butte du Lion stands today.

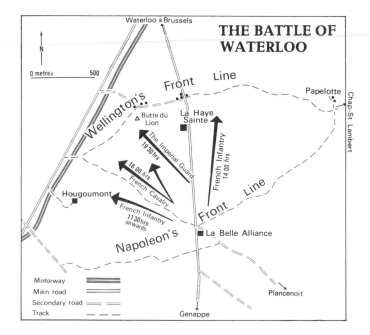

Throughout the night of 17–18 June it had rained heavily. The sodden ground favoured the defenders, as the attacking French had to advance uphill over mud, even though Napoleon had postponed his main attack from dawn until early afternoon in the hope that the ground would dry. The fighting divides itself into four distinct phases. The times given are approximate.

Phase 1. 11.30. The French attack on Hougoumont, which was vital for the defence of Wellington's right. The attack failed and did not force Wellington to divert reinforcements for its defence. Hougoumont continued under fierce attack throughout the day.

13.00. The Prussians reached the area of Chapelle St Lambert, 6km NE of La Belle Alliance, and Napoleon detached Lobau to meet this threat.

Phase 2. 14.00. After a half-hour artillery barrage, the French infantry attacked Wellington's left (E of today's N5). The Scots infantry charged and engaged the French hand-to-hand. Soon after the British cavalry charged through the infantry and the French broke. The cavalry continued too far and were driven back by French cavalry.

Phase 3. 16.00. Led by Marshal Ney, the French cavalry attacked Wellington's centre (towards and just W of the Butte), but failed to break Wellington's infantry squares and were driven back down the slope by Allied cavalry. Further French cavalry waves met the same fate.

16.30. In the SE the Prussians forced Lobau back through Plancenoit, but failed to hold the village when Lobau was reinforced by Napoleon's Young Guard.

Phase 4. 18.00. The French stormed and took La Haye Sainte, but only after the Hanoverians had run out of ammunition. Only 41 out of 350 defenders survived.

19.30. The French Imperial Guard attacked Wellington's centre, struggling up the slope, which had been churned to mud by the earlier cavalry assaults. Met by devastating fire from Allied infantry, who remained lying down and were hidden until the last moment, the Guard broke and fled for the first time in its history.

To the SE the Prussians finally defeated Lobau. At about *21.15* Wellington and Blücher met at La Belle Alliance.

After the Battle. Wellington handed over the pursuit to the Prussians. Napoleon, fleeing in his coach, reached Genappe, where he just had time to change to a horse. At 05.00 he reached Charleroi. Thence he fled to Paris, a second abdication, fruitless negotiations for sanctuary in America or England, and finally exile and death on St Helena.

The town of **Waterloo** was Wellington's headquarters, and here he spent the night of 17–18 June before riding forward to the battle area. The house which he occupied in 1815 was an inn and thus an obvious choice. It is now the *Musée Wellington.* From April to mid November it is open daily from 09.30 to 18.30 and from mid November to March daily from 10.30 to 17.00. It is closed on 25 December and 1 January.

A circuit signposted in green is concerned with local history. Room 14, probably the best starting point, is an imaginatively arranged small hall in which a series of clear illuminated plans, together with tableaux, trace with the aid of an English text the various phases of the battle. A circuit, signposted in red, takes us on a tour through several rooms which have small souvenirs and many contemporary, or nearly contemporary, pictures. In Room 4 where Alexander Gordon, Wellington's aide-de-camp from Peninsular days, died his bed and rather bulky correspondence box are kept. Room 6, with a fine copy of Lawrence's famous portrait, is the Duke's Room. Rooms 7, 8 and 10 are devoted to the Netherlands, the Prussians and the French. There are several souvenirs of Napoleon. Room 11 explains the various measures being taken to conserve the battlefield area. There is also a monument commemorating the amputated leg of Lord Uxbridge, commander of the British Cavalry.

Opposite the museum is the church. Only the late-17C round portion was in existence in 1815. Both church and graveyard are full of memorials.

The battlefield is reached at the crossroads of the N5 and N27 sometimes called '**Waterloo-Gordon**' because of the memorial to Sir Alexander Gordon, Wellington's aide-de-camp who was killed in the battle. The top of the mound on which this stands marks the original height of the ridge before the earth was removed to build the Butte du Lion. There are also memorials to the Belgians and Hanoverians here. In the SW angle a tree marks the position of Wellington's command-post. This replaces the original, which was pillaged by souvenir hunters in the years after the battle.

The road to the E marks the line of Wellington's left flank, while that to the W leads along his centre to the **Butte du Lion**, built by the government of the United Netherlands in 1826 on the spot where the Prince of Orange was wounded.

At the foot of the mound there are car parks, cafés and souvenir shops. Here also are the *Panorama de la Bataille*, open daily from 09.30 to 18.00, 18.30 on Sunday and holidays, and the *Musée de Cires* with wax figures of important people associated with the battle, which is open daily from Easter to October 09.00 to 18.30 and during the winter daily 10.15 to 16.45.

A reception and information centre, open every day of the year, was inaugurated in May 1990 by the non-profit-making association 'Bataille de Waterloo 1815'. As well as providing access to the mound, the centre has a working model which re-enacts the main phases of the battle and a film, 'Waterloo 1815'. The 10 m sq model employs special scenic and audiovisual effects including a video-laser, which is projected on to a curved screen to explain the sequence of events. In addition, visitors may use computer terminals to examine photographs and descriptions of more than 40 historic sites connected with the battle. This information is available in English, French, Dutch and German. Tours of the battlefield and educational visits are arranged by the centre and members of the staff are available to answer questions. There is a comprehensive stock of relevant literature in various languages. A wide range of events, including mock battles and exhibitions, is held at the centre.

The Butte du Lion may be visited from 09.30 to 18.30 (April to October) and 10.30 to 16.00 (November to March).

The road continues W along the ridge, which was the target of the French cavalry and Imperial Guard attacks, and along which Wellington rode to and fro during the day of the battle, until it reaches the N27.

A short distance S is the farm of *Hougoumont*. This is signposted 'Goumont' across a motorway bridge. At the time of the battle it was a fortified farm immediately N of a wood. Most of the building was burnt down during the fighting and the wood has disappeared.

The main road S from 'Waterloo-Gordon' passes the farm of *La Haye Sainte*, rebuilt after the battle and little changed since. In the second attack the French crept along the wall beside the road and seized the barrels of the defenders' rifles poking out of loopholes.

La Belle Alliance, also little changed since 1815, is 1km farther south. Here, on the morning of the battle, in a scene of splendour and enthusiasm, Napoleon reviewed his troops. Here in the evening Wellington met Blücher.

From La Belle Alliance a road bears SE for Plancenoit. This passes at 400m *Napoleon's Viewpoint*, which he occupied from mid afternoon onwards. After another 500m it reaches the *Prussian Monument*.

On the main road, just S of La Belle Alliance, are (E) a monument to Victor Hugo and (W) the *French Monument* of 1905, a wounded eagle in bronze by Jean Gérôme. Napoleon's headquarters was at the *Ferme du Caillou*, about 2km S of La Belle Alliance. Here before the battle he breakfasted off crested silver plate and confidently asserted that the fighting would amount to no more than a cannonade and a cavalry charge, after which he would lead the Imperial Guard against the English. The 1757 farm is now a museum exhibiting weapons, paintings, etchings and plans, the table on which Napoleon spread his maps and his bed. It is open from April to October: Tuesday–Sunday 10.00 to 18.30. November to March: Tuesday–Sunday 13.30 to 17.00. It is closed in January.

Tervuren

Tervuren, 13km from central Brussels, is reached by the Avenue de Tervuren, which passes underneath the Parc du Cinquantenaire. Shortly after it reaches the Square Montgomery with a statue of the Field Marshal.

On the right side of Avenue de Tervuren is No. 281, the Stoclet house, a striking building clad in white marble framed by gilded mouldings. A precursor of Art Deco, this is the work (1911) of the Austrian architect Joseph Hoffman,

At No. 364 the *Musée du Transport Urbain Bruxellois* traces the history of public transport from horse-drawn vehicles to electric trams. It is open from the first Saturday in April to the first Sunday in October on Saturday, Sunday and public holidays from 13.30 to 19.00. There are rides in vintage tram cars between Woluwe and Tervuren between 14.00 and 18.00. Every Sunday from May to October a special tourist tram makes the journey Woluwe–Brussels–Woluwe. At the time of writing the fare for this excursion was 300BF or 600BF with lunch.

Pleasantly sited at the NE corner of the Forêt de Soignes, Tervuren is the home of the *****Musée Royal de l'Afrique Centrale**. Located to the E of the town on the Louvain road, this fine museum, which is also a distinguished scientific institution, started as an African outstation of the Brussels Universal Exhibition of 1898. The following year it became the Musée du Congo. The present building, by Charles Girault, was opened in 1910. In 1960, the year of the Congo's independence, the museum formally extended its scope to cover the whole of Africa and, in some fields, areas beyond. It is open daily from 09.00 to 17.30 in summer and from 10.00 to 16.30 in winter.

In 19 exhibition rooms, arranged around a central court, there are displays on the following subjects: ROOM 1. *Agriculture, Mining, Wood.* Note the large collection of commercial wood. ROOM 2. *African Mountain Scenery.* Good dioramas of the various levels of Ruwenzori. ROOM 3. The *Memorial Hall.* ROOM 4. *History: Europe and Central Africa.* Souvenirs of the great explorers. ROOM 5. *Jewellery and Ornaments.* ROOM 6. *Ethnography and Art outside Central Africa.* Exhibits generally in a cultural context with the emphasis on Black Africa. ROOM 7. *Sculpture, Central Africa.* Of particular interest for its representation of the various ethnic groups. ROOM 8. *Temporary Exhibitions.* ROOM 9. *Ethnography of Central Africa.* Exhibits from a vast area including Zaire, northern Angola, Rwanda and Burundi. ROOM 10. The *Rotunda.* Views of the park. Some of the statues are from the 1897 Exhibition.

ROOM 11. *Comparative Ethnography.* Material culture such as food production and handwork and social and spiritual culture as evidenced in social structure, religion and custom. ROOM 12. Large *Zoological Dioramas* of the northern savannah, equatorial forest and southern savannah, showing typical mammals and birds. ROOM 13. *Insects.* ROOM 14. *Fishes and Reptiles.* ROOM 15. *Birds.* Shown systematically and in natural settings. ROOM 17. *Mammals.* Displayed in some excellent dioramas. ROOM 18. *Prehistory and Archaeology.* Material from recent museum excavations. ROOM 19. *Geology and Mineralogy.*

At a roundabout near the entrance to Tervuren are the remains of the early 19C *château*, which was destroyed by fire in 1879. This had replaced a castle, which from the 13C had been a hunting-lodge of the rulers of Brabant. Charles of Lorraine died here in 1780. The castle chapel of Saint Hubert (by Wenceslas Coeberger, 1617) survives and is said to occupy the place where the saint died in 727. It is just inside the park behind the town. St Hubert was a courtier of Pepin of Heristal. Converted while hunting, he succeeded St Lambert as bishop of Maastricht. The patron saint of hunters, his emblem is a stag bearing a crucifix between its horns. As well as the chapel the park has a fine French formal garden.

In the town the ducal *Eglise Saint Jean* (13–15C) contains a reconstructed choir-gallery of 1517 attributed to Mathias Keldermans.

Take the Jezus Eiklaan to an *Arboretum*, which was laid out in 1902 on land to the S of Tervuren given by Leopold II.

Duisburg, 3km E of Tervuren, is the centre of a grape-growing district and is surrounded by hothouses. The church has a 13C nave and choir.

NORTH BELGIUM

Provinces of West and East Flanders, Antwerp, northern Brabant and Limburg

The people, language and culture of North Belgium are Flemish. Of Frankish origin, their history stretches back to the time of the powerful counts of Flanders. Nominally the vassals of the kings of France, the counts had become virtually independent by the 11C. In the course of time they extended their rule to Antwerp, Brabant and Limburg. However, the towns of Flanders, grown rich from the cloth trade, struggled continually for their freedom. In 1384 Flanders was inherited by Margaret and Philip the Bold of Burgundy. That marked its end as a separate state, but not as an ethnic and cultural entity. The vigorous civic pride of the Flemish people led to the construction of the splendid religious and secular buildings that are such a feature of northern Belgium, while their generous patronage of the arts is evidenced by the magnificent paintings and sculptures which fill the museums and art galleries of Flanders.

Vistors to North Belgium fall into two groups: those who want a holiday by the sea, and those who are attracted by the beautiful, historic towns of *Antwerp, Bruges* and *Ghent*. Famous for the charm of their old buildings and winding canals, the museums, galleries and churches of all three are filled with superb art treasures. They are a perfect setting for the works of the great Flemish Masters.

The smaller towns of Flanders should not be forgotten. Many have an interesting market place, fine old buildings and a museum of some distinction. Visitors will enjoy places like *Oudenaarde*, with its spacious Grote Markt and elegant town hall, *Kortrijk*, where ancient buildings stand cheek by jowl with chic modern shops, *Mechelen*, with its great cathedral tower, *Louvain*, for notable Gothic architecture, a historic university and an excellent museum, *Lier*, famed for its elaborate astronomical clocks, *Diest*, whose museum is housed in medieval cellars and *Tongeren*, the oldest town in Belgium where there is an imaginatively arranged Gallo-Roman museum.

The First World War BATTLEFIELDS of *Yser* and *Ypres* attract many visitors. Described in Routes 4, 5, 6 and 7, this region with its war cemeteries, memorials and campaign museums is full of names that recall deeds of bravery and unselfish sacrifice.

First World War. After the fall of Antwerp on 9 October 1914 the Belgian army, supported by a Royal Navy flotilla, retreated through Flanders. A front, protected by the sea at Nieuwpoort, was eventually established along the *Yser*. Here heavy fighting between 18 and 30 October ended when the Belgians opened the sluices and flooded the area between the river and the railway. Until 1918 the front was stabilised from *Nieuwpoort* southwards behind the flooded zone to about *Boezinge*, then round the notorious salient of *Ypres*. This corner of Belgium was totally devastated. After the war much of the rebuilding was in the old style. Ypres, with its great Cloth Hall, is the outstanding example of this restoration.

In the **Second World War** the Germans again quickly forced their way to the sea. This time there was no Allied stand and between 27 May and 4 June 1940 the great evacuation took place from the beaches between *De Panne* and *Dunkirk* in France. Compared with the First World War, damage to the area was negligible. Again much of the rebuilding was in the old style.

COAST AND POLDERS. The **coast**, which stretches for c 60km from the French to the Dutch frontiers, has a string of resorts which are usually

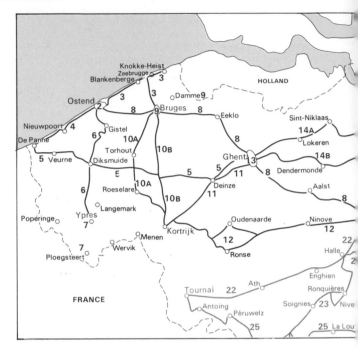

backed by sand dunes. Many are virtually joined to each another and, superficially, look like their neighbours. A perimeter of villas and other buildings in the dunes encloses a town centre ending in a seafront esplanade. Inland from some of the resorts there is a parent village or small town, the 'dorp'. The dunes, while still a distinctive part of the landscape, are rapidly being built over. The resorts, with magnificent sands and casinos, which are cultural and entertainment centres as well as gambling rooms, have facilities to suit most tastes. Lively and overcrowded in summer, many are bleak and deserted out of season.

Ostend, the principal town, is half-way along the coast. *Zeebrugge*, with its historic mole, is a little to the east. A tram service covers the whole stretch from De Panne to Knokke in about 2 hours. En route, however, because of the dunes and high buildings not much is seen of the sea.

Behind the coastal strip are the **Polders**, a reclaimed plain drained by canals and protected by dykes. The scattered villages may be picked out by the church steeples. In between the plain is dotted with large farms. The most attractive polder district is between Bruges and Holland. Here the canals are lined with trees. Many cottages have been restored and converted into restaurants and the area has acquired a certain gastronomic reputation.

The name FLEMISH ARDENNES has been given to a small range of hills running through *Ronse*. From a number of high points there are extensive views over the Flanders plain and into Hainaut and northern France. To the E the country is gently undulating.

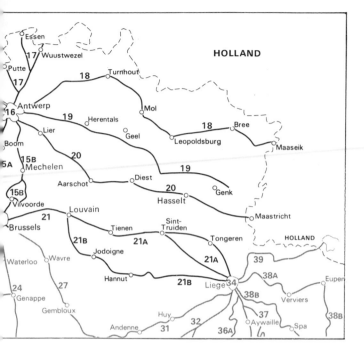

Sint Niklaas is the principal town of WAASLAND, a district bounded by the Ghent-Terneuzen canal on the W, by the Dutch frontier on the N, and by the river Scheldt on the S and east. Basically composed of sand and clay, the addition of richer soil and the application of scientific farming have turned it into a land of exceptional fertility. The poplars bordering the roads and the many irrigation ditches are a distinctive feature of Waasland.

The KEMPEN, a large district covering more than half of the provinces of Antwerp and Limburg, occupies the NE corner of Belgium. Starting just E of Antwerp, and bordered on the N by Holland, it stretches E to the Maas (Meuse) and S to the road through Aarschot and Hasselt. The *Albert Canal*, with the E313 motorway parallel to its S side, cuts W–E through the centre. There are large areas of heath, moor, dunes and pines. However, motorways, spreading towns and industry are combining to change hitherto remote and unspoilt landscapes. An impression of the old Kempen villages and farms may be obtained from a visit to the *Bokrijk* estate and open air museum between Hasselt and Genk. The Kempen contains a number of large recreational parks and some districts are signposted for walking. There are several historic and thriving abbeys, notably *Averbode, Postel*, in typical Kempen landscape, and *Tongerlo*, with its special 'theatre', where there is a famous copy of Da Vinci's Last Supper by one of his pupils. The district is described in Routes 18 and 19, while Route 20, skirting the southern edge, links interesting towns such as *Lier, Aarschot* and *Diest*.

2

Ostend

OSTEND (Oostende; population 69,000) is Belgium's principal coast town.
As well as being a popular resort, offering plenty of entertainment, it is a
thermal spa and conference centre. It has some 8km of good beaches and
an important and busy harbour, which services cargo and fishing boats,
yachts and the cross channel ferries to Dover.

Ostend has excellent restaurants, a lively night life and is an interesting
place to visit at any time of the year. After Brussels (Zaventem) its airport
is the busiest in Belgium. International trains leave at frequent intervals for
all parts of Europe and the E40 motorway leads to the heart of the Continent.

Centre. Wapenplein.

Tourist Information Office. Wapenplein, tel: 701199. Open Easter and Whitsun and
from late June to mid September daily from 09.00 to 19.00. During other periods,
Monday to Friday from 08.00 to 12.00 and 13.45 to 17.45, Saturday from 09.00 to 12.00
and 14.00 to 17.00.

In July and August an Information Office at the station is open daily from 10.00 to
12.30 and from 14.00 to 18.00.

Station. On E side of the town adjoining the ferryboat and jetfoil quays.

Post Office. Hendrik Serruyslaan.

Airport. *Middelkerke*, 3km west.

Beaches. There are five official beaches. *Kleinstrand* (small beach) is by the harbour
entrance, *Grootstrand* (large beach) stretches from the Casino to the Thermen,
Mariakerke extends from the Thermen to Dorpstraat and *Raversijde* continues to the
west. The fifth beach, *Oosterstrand*, is to the E of the harbour entrance. Access to all
beaches is free although a charge is made for some sections, e.g. the Lido. There are
beach huts, booths for storing personal belongings and free showers on some of the
beaches. In July and August at the Dolfijnen (Dolphins) club near the Lido children
up to 12 are admitted and play under the supervision of trained staff. Bathing is only
permitted in marked and guarded areas in the beaches mentioned above. The flag
signals, Green = Safe, Yellow = Dangerous, Red = Bathing forbidden, should be noted
and obeyed.

History. An 11C fishing village known as Oostende-ter-Streepe, 'the E end of the strip',
was given a charter as a town by Margaret of Constantinople in 1267. From this time
onwards the port grew in importance, becoming one of the main departure points for
the crusades. Until Zeebrugge began to be developed in the 19C, it was the only
significant harbour along the coast. In 1273 the Ostend Company was formed for the
purpose of trading with the Indies. Although under pressure from England and
Holland its charter was later revoked, it none the less opened the way to greater
prosperity. During the Revolt of the Netherlands Ostend supported the United
Provinces. It was taken by the Spanish commander Spinola in 1604, though only after
a bitter siege which lasted three years.

Increasingly Ostend became the port for sailings between England and the Continent. The town first became a royal residence in 1834 and four years later Leopold I
inaugurated the Ostend–Brussels railway. The first Casino-Kursaal was opened in
1852 and after the dismantling of the fortifications in 1860–70 the town began to spread
along the coast and inland.

From 7–13 October 1914 the Belgian government was in Ostend. The Germans
marched in on 15 October and from then on Ostend was a destroyer and submarine
base. An attempt was made to block the harbours of Ostend and Zeebrugge on the
night of 22–23 April 1918. This failed, but the crews volunteered for a second attack,

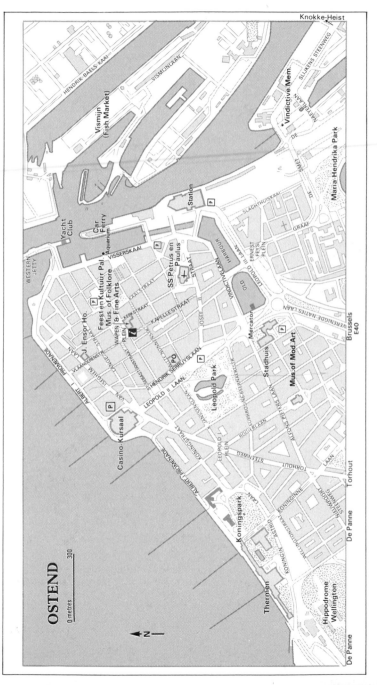

Knokke-Heist

OSTEND

0 metres 300

N

Vismijn (Fish Market)

Vindictive Mem.

Maria-Hendrika Park

Station

Yacht Club

Car Ferry

Aquarium

VISSERSKAAI

WESTERN JETTY

SLACHTHUISKAAI

SS Petrus en Paulus

HARBOUR

Feesten Kultuur Pal. Mus. of Folklore & Fine Arts

J. Ensor Ho.

KAPELLESTRAAT

Mercator

Stadhuis

Mus. of Mod. Art

Leopold Park

ALBERT I PROMENADE

HENDRIK SERRUYSLAAN

LEOPOLD II LAAN

Brussels E40

WERENIGDE NATIES LAAN

Casino Kursaal

Torhout

Koningspark

De Panne

Thermen

Hippodrome Wellington

De Panne

which was successfully carried out on 9–10 May. The *Vindictive*, which had been used the previous month at Zeebrugge, was sunk across the port entrance. The Germans evacuated Ostend on 17 October 1918 after blowing up the station and harbour facilities. During the Second World War, Ostend served as a German coastal fortress. The town suffered considerably from air attacks. It was liberated by the Canadians on 9 September 1944.

In 1933 the Palais des Thermes was opened and in 1953 the Casino-Kursaal. The motorway to Brussels was completed in 1958 and work on the extension of the airport has continued since 1976.

The town may be divided into two parts. To the E of the the harbour, Vindictivelaan, Hendrik Serruyslaan and the shore is the animated 'popular' quarter'. The area to the W of the broad, garden-lined Leopold II Laan is more spacious and elegant in character.

The **Sint Petrus en Pauluskerk** (1905–07) is across the Visserskaai from the station. In a chapel behind the high altar is the tomb, by Fraikin, of Queen Louise-Marie, the first Queen of the Belgians. She died in Ostend in 1850. At the rear of the church is the quaintly named *Peperbus* or Peppermill. This was the tower of the old church which was almost completely destroyed by fire in 1896. Note the interesting *Calvary and Purgatory*, which date from 1764, on the ground floor.

Running N from here, between the town and the Montgomerydok, is Visserskaai, a wide thoroughfare with many restaurants. On its E side, the former shrimp market now houses the **North Sea Aquarium**. This has displays of North Sea flora and fauna including fish, molluscs, crustacea shells and algae in their natural environment. It is open daily from April to September between 10.00 and 12.00 and from 14.00 to 17.00. During the other months it is open on Saturday and Sunday at the same times.

To the W of the station Vindictivelaan skirts the old harbour. Here the *Mercator*, a three-masted merchant fleet training ship built in 1932, is moored. Taken out of service in 1960, the ship is now a museum displaying material largely collected during its voyages to 54 different countries. It is open as follows: in January, February, November and December on Sunday and holidays from 10.00 to 12.00 and 13.00 to 16.00 (but closed on 1 January and 25 December), in March and October on Saturday and Sunday from 10.00 to 12.00 and 13.00 to 17.00, during April and May on Saturday, Sunday and holidays from 09.00 to 12.00 and 13.00 to 18.00, at Easter and from June to September daily from 09.00 to 12.00 and 13.00 to 18.00.

Kapellestraat, which is for pedestrians only and is one of the liveliest streets in Ostend, connects Vindictivelaan with the WAPENPLEIN, the town centre. On the S side of this square is the **Feest en Kultuur Paleis**. Completed in 1958, it occupies the site of the town hall and museum which were destroyed by bombing during the last war. Note the large clock with signs of the zodiac. Concerts are given from time to time and a melody is played automatically each half-hour on the building's carillon (1965) of 49 bells.

The Feest en Kultuur Paleis houses the *Tourist Information Office* and two museums. The **Museum voor Schone Kunsten** has an interesting collection of paintings, sketches and engravings by James Ensor, paintings by Léon Spilliaert, Jan de Clerck, Constant Permeke and other 19C and 20C artists associated with Ostend, examples of Flemish Impressionism and Expressionism and works by contemporary artists from many European countries. These replace more than 400 paintings which were destroyed by fire in 1940. The museum is open daily, except Tuesday, from 10.00 to 12.00 and 14.00 to 17.00. It is closed on 1 January, 1 May, during October and on

25 December. The **Folklore Museum De Plate**, devoted to local history and customs, has artefacts from the prehistoric and Roman periods which were found in the Ostend area, costumes, interiors including a fisherman's home and an old tobacco shop, and sections on wooden shipbuilding, the Ostend–Dover ferry and fishing vessels. It is open daily (except Tuesday) during the Easter holidays and at Whitsun weekend and in July and August from 10.00 to 12.00 to 15.00 to 17.00 and during other months on Saturday from 10.00 to 12.00 to 15.00 to 17.00.

There are two other museums in this part of the town. At 41 Sebastiaan-straat (W out of Wapenplein) the **Museum voor Religieuze Kunst** occupies a former chapel. The varied and interesting collection of religious pictures and sculpture covers the period from Impressionism to the present day and includes works by James Ensor. There are special exhibitions in spring and summer. It is open as follows: from Easter to May, July to September and at Christmas every day except Tuesday and Wednesday from 15.00 to 18.00.

The **James Ensorhuis** is at 27 Vlaanderenstraat, which runs N out of Wapenplein. It was the home of this artist (1860–1949), born here of an English father and an Ostend mother. The shop, where Ensor's aunt and uncle sold shells and curios, has been reconstructed on the ground floor. The first floor is devoted to documentation, while the second floor recreates the painter's studio. There are no original works on view. The house is open daily, except Tuesday, at Easter, Whitsun and from 1 June to 30 September from 10.00 to 12.00 and 14.00 to 17.00.

Vlaanderenstraat continues to the Albert I Promenade. To the E is the monument (1953) to seamen who lost their lives during the war. Just beyond is the North Sea Yacht Club at the landward end of the western jetty. The jetty, the embarkation point for sea excursions, is much favoured by visitors for pre and post prandial strolls.

The **Casino-Kursaal** (1953), Ostend's principal entertainment centre, may be reached by walking W along the Albert I Promenade. The successor to the first casino of 1852, it offers a varied programme of opera, ballet, concerts and light entertainment. It has an excellent restaurant, a night club and gaming rooms, one of which is decorated with murals by Paul Delvaux.

Farther W are the **Koningspark**, the gardens of the former royal residence, the **Thermen**, with Turkish baths, a medical centre and a hotel and the **Hippodrome Wellington**, a popular venue for flat racing and trotting.

To the W of the racecourse is the suburb of MARIAKERKE. Here in the hamlet of Dorpstraat is the **Onze Lieve Vrouw ter Duinen Kerk**, the church of Our Lady of the Dunes. This Gothic church, dating from the second half of the 14C, has early baroque furniture and decoration. In the tiny churchyard is the simple tomb of James Ensor.

From the Casino-Kursaal it is a short walk S along the broad Leopold II Laan to Leopold Park. Two ha. (five acres) in area this has an elaborate floral clock, sculptures, a 19C bandstand and a small lake. Opposite the floral clock in Hendrik Serruyslaan, is the **Post Office**, which was begun in 1939 and completed after the war. It has a large and striking sculpture by Joseph Cantré.

The **Stadhuis** (Victor Bourgeois, 1956–60), at the end of Leopold II Laan faces the old harbour. This is the successor of the 17C town hall in the Wapenplein, which was destroyed by bombing in 1940. Ostend's arms, carved by A. Michiels, are on the S façade. The interior has pictures by Alice Frey.

The **Provincial Museum of Modern Art**, at 11 Romestraat two blocks W of the Stadhuis, uses paintings, sculpture, graphics, film and video to provide a comprehensive survey of Belgian modern art. It is open daily, except Tuesday, from 10.00 to 18.00.

To the S of the Stadhuis is the **Maria Hendrika Park** (18 ha) (45 acres). This has fish ponds, boating and an outdoor swimming pool. Its 'Mirror Lake', which is 400m in circumference, is popular with joggers.

In a small garden below the Blankenberge road where it divides to cross the inner docks, is the *Vindictive Memorial*. This incorporates the bows of the ship and the masts of HMS *Thetis* and *Iphigenia*. Approximately 1km farther the road crosses more docks. Immediately afterwards a road bears NW for the *Vissersdok*, where the fish market is located.

For Ostend to Blankenberge and Knokke-Heist, see Route 3; for Nieuwpoort and De Panne, see Route 4; for Ypres, see Route 6; for Bruges, Ghent and Brussels, see Route 8.

3

Ostend to Knokke-Heist

Total distance 32km.—*20km* **Blankenberge**—*4km* **Zeebrugge**—*8km* **Knokke-Heist.** For most of the way the main road runs through the dunes and built up areas, so little is seen of the sea. From Ostend the tram takes c 26 minutes to Blankenberge, 45 minutes to Zeebrugge and 70 minutes to Knokke.

Ostend, see Route 2. From the sunken garden of the *Vindictive* memorial the road crosses the top of the fish docks and then continues parallel with the coast to *Bredene*, a village lying behind the dunes.

11km **De Haan** is small resort nestling in the midst of tree-covered dunes. According to an ancient legend it obtained its name one stormy night when some local fishermen, who were unwittingly steering for the shore, were saved from danger by hearing a cock crow in the village.

9km **Blankenberge**, population 15,000. At the W end of this pleasant resort is the picturesque harbour, which was constructed between 1862 and 1876. The Tourist Information Office is in Koning Leopold III Plein by the station. Also near the station are the modern *Stadhuis*, the fifth in Blankenberge's history, and the *Sint Antoonskerk*. Dating from 1335–58 but much restored, the church has some interesting 17C and 18C paintings. These include a Temptation of St Anthony by Jan Maes, Storm and Sea attributed to Jacob van Oost the Younger and Flight into Egypt believed to be the work of David Vinckeboons.

Kerkstraat runs NW from the station passing the *Oude Stadhuis* of 1680, the fourth in the series, to reach the shore near the *Casino*. To the E is the pier where *Aquarama* shows local and tropical fish, fluorescent minerals, shells and ship models. This is open daily from Easter to mid September between 10.00 and 19.00, 22.00 in July and August.

Approximately *4km* **Zeebrugge** is a huge artificial port, which is still being enlarged. It began behind the mole built by Baron de Maere between 1895 and 1907, at the same time as the Boudewijn Kanaal linking Zeebrugge with Bruges was constructed. From the crossroads the road S leads to Bruges (see below). Opposite is the short approach to the small resort district, the base of the original mole and the W side of the harbour with the ferry services to England. The windmills around the quays generate sufficient power to operate many of the port installations.

The mole will long be associated with the heroic St George's Day raid of 1918.

Zeebrugge and its canal were an important German submarine base. An attack, under Vice Admiral Roger Keyes, was launched on the night of 22–23 April 1918 to block the entrance. The task force consisted of the old cruiser *Vindictive*, two Liverpool ferries, *Daffodil* and *Iris II*, the submarine *C3* and several smokescreen and rescue craft. Under heavy fire *C3* rammed the wooden viaduct, which formed the first part of the mole, and was blown up. Her crew escaped by collapsible boat. *Thetis* ran aground just clear of the mole but *Intrepid* and *Iphigenia* were sunk across the channel and their crews rescued by launches. *Vindictive* and the landing party returned to Dover. Although not as decisive as had been hoped, the partial closing of the port reduced German submarine operations at a crucial time in the war. The simultaneous attack on Ostend and the later operation there by *Vindictive* are described in Route 2.

During the Second World War Zeebrugge was blocked in May 1940 and blown up by the Germans in 1944. The port was finally reopened in 1957 when *Thetis*, the last of the 1918 blockships, was removed.

Dwarfed by more recent developments in the port, Baron de Maere's mole has largely lost its identity. The 1918 raid is commemorated by the *St George*'s Day Memorial, which replaces one destroyed by the Germans during World War II. It has been placed at the E end of Zeedijk, the promenade in Zeebrugge's resort quarter. This is effectively the base of the mole, the first section of which is marked by a path also named for St George's Day. The memorial, in part a bas-relief of the plan of the raid, incorporates a plaque honouring the part played by the submarine *C3*.

A huge area of the port of Zeebrugge, which is still being developed, extends S. The town lies on either side of the road heading E. To the N are the fishing port and market. There are boat tours of the port (duration 1½ hours) at Easter and daily mid June to mid September at 11.00 and 14.30.

ZEEBRUGGE TO BRUGES (13km). The main road to Bruges is not very interesting. A more pleasant route is by the minor road to the E of the Boudewijn Kanaal. This may be reached from 4km *Lissewege*, a little polder village whose name is believed to be derived from the Celtic 'Liswege', house of Liso.

It is worth climbing the 265 steps to the top of the huge brick tower of Lissewege's restored 13C church for the fine view across the polders. An ancient legend is sometimes invoked to explain the presence of such a large building in a village which had fewer than 300 souls. According to this the church was built to house a much revered image of the Madonna. Found in a local stream, the Lisput, the image returned to the stream every time it was removed. So the villagers built a chapel and later this church over the Lisput, which still flows underneath. In the centre of the principal nave there is a cover which provides access to the stream.

The pulpit, organ case and rood loft are the work of Walram Romboudt (1652), a local craftsman. Among the paintings are a Visitation by Jacob van Oost the Elder (1652) and Pilgrims honouring St James of Compostela by Jan Maes (1665). The church possesses a fine cope with 14C orphreys, a red 14C chasuble and dalmatic and a violet chasuble with 16C orphreys, a monstrance of 1619 and a chalice and a ciborium of 1620, the work of the Bruges goldsmith Melchior van Blootacker. Note the 17C funerary monuments set in the walls just inside the entrance with their clear portrayal of the clothing of the period.

Just S of Lissewege, between the main road and the canal, is the site of the abbey of *Ter Doest*. Founded in 1106 by Lambert de Lissewege near the chapel sheltering the miraculous Madonna, it was ruled by 38 abbots between 1174 and 1569. In 1571 the abbey was pillaged and burned by religious fanatics. Only the great *barn of c 1250 remains. (For entry to the barn, apply to the restaurant nearby.) Below the immense roof of some 38,000 tiles the interior, 58m by 24m, is divided into three sections by two rows of oak piers resting on stone bases.

The small baroque chapel at the entrance to the estate dates from 1687. It was built by Abbot Martin a Colle of the abbey of Dunes at Bruges to commemorate his success in a law suit at the tribunal of Louis XIV.

Dudzele, 3km S of Lissewege and across the canal, preserves the Romanesque tower of its former 12C church.

Beyond Zeebrugge the road having crossed the Schipdonk and Leopold canals, which drain the polders bordering the Dutch frontier, reaches *8km* **Knokke-Heist** (population 30,000. Tourist Information: Lichttorenplein, Knokke). This is the collective name given to the 7km-long string of beach resorts of Heist, Duinbergen, Albertstrand, Knokke and Het Zoute.

Each resort has its own character. Heist is relaxed, a family place; Duinbergen is quiet and residential; Albertstrand is lively with a casino and night life. Knokke at the centre is the busy heart of the strip, while Het Zoute is residential, full of elegant houses.

Knokke-Heist claims to be more than a summer resort. It has theatre and ballet performances, film galas and exhibitions. There are the annual firework and flower festivals and the World Cartoon Exhibition, which has been held here each year since 1962. The casino at Albertstrand, the main centre for cultural and entertainment activities, has some interesting art of its own. Outside there is a statue, the Poet, by Ossip Zadkine and inside murals and paintings by René Magritte, Paul Delvaux and others.

Until it silted up towards the end of the 15C, **Het Zwin**, the estuary 3km E of Het Zoute, brought prosperity to Sluis in Holland, to Damme and to Bruges. In 1340 the fleet of Edward III of England, commanded by the king in person, sailed up the estuary. With his Flemish allies Edward inflicted great destruction on the French fleet which was assembled in the roadstead in preparation for an invasion of England. Some idea of the size of the estuary can be gained from the fact that the English are said to have had 250 sail and the French 200.

Today most of the reclaimed land is cultivated, but 150 ha. of dune and marsh near the sea, including 25 ha. on the Dutch side of the border, have been preserved as a nature reserve and bird sanctuary. Over half of this area is open to the public. Among the birds that may be seen are oyster catchers, avocets, storks, greylag geese, golden orioles and collared doves. The reserve is open daily from 09.00 to 19.00. From November to April it is closed on Wednesday. In summer there is a bus service from Knokke and Het Zoute.

4

Ostend to De Panne

Total distance 29km.—*8km* **Middelkerke**—*8km* **Nieuwpoort**—*9km*
Koksijde-Bad—*4km* **De Panne**—As far as Nieuwpoort there is a choice
between the N34 close to the shore or the older N318 which keeps parallel
about 1km inland. From Ostend the tram, mostly running inland, takes
35 minutes to Nieuwpoort or 70 minutes to De Panne.

Ostend see Route 2.—*3km* **Mariakerke** see p 123.—*Ostend Airport* is on
the N318 between Mariakerke and (*5km*) **Middelkerke**. This village has a
casino and a modern church which incorporates an early Gothic belfry once
used as a lighthouse.

During the First World War *4km* **Westende** was just within range of the
Allied guns behind the Yser (Ijzer). From here westwards there was
devastation.

2km **Lombardsijde**, on the right bank of the Yser near its mouth, changed
hands in October and November 1914. Thereafter what remained was
virtually the German front line for four years. The Allied sentry in the dunes
to the W of the village was known as 'l'homme de l'extrême gauche', the
first man along a front which stretched from the Belgian coast to Switzerland.

Lombardsijde is of ancient origin. Some authorities link its name with the Lombards
who inhabited the lower Elbe. It is said that they established a harbour on the estuary
of the Yser, which was formerly much wider. The river silted up about the 12C, leaving
Lombardsijde high and dry and Nieuwpoort, the 'Novus Portus' of its charter, took its
place.

Just before Nieuwpoort, at the Yser bridge, three waterways meet the
estuary in a group of six sluices arranged in an arc. Three allow access to
canals and three are for the flow of excess water. Here there is a group of
memorials. Perhaps the most striking is the *Koning Albert Monument* of
1938. A rotunda designed by Julien de Ridder with an equestrian statue by
Karel Aubroeck, its interior is encircled by some resounding French verse
by Maurice Gauchez and some lines in Flemish by Auguste van
Cauwelaert. Albert's queen, Elisabeth, who died in 1968, is commemorated
by a tablet. Steps lead to the top gallery, where there are orientation tables.

Nearby, guarded by defiant lions, is the quietly moving British memorial.
This lists, by unit, the 566 men who were lost at the Antwerp fighting of
1914 and along this coast during the following years. Just across the canals
are a French monument and, on the right among the trees, the Yser
Memorial by the sculptor Pierre Braecke.

Battle of the Yser (see also Route 5). By October 1914 an Allied line had been
established across the NW corner of Belgium, from the coast up the Yser to Ypres. The
Belgians held the northern 35km between Nieuwpoort and Steenstraat on the Yser–
Ypres canal.

The Battle of the Yser was fought at the same time as the opening phase of the First
Battle of Ypres. Despite heavy attacks, the Belgians resisted for two days. On the night
of 21–22 October the Germans managed to get a force across the Yser at Tervate and
reinforced their position the following night in the face of gallant Belgian counter-
attacks. On 24 October a major German offensive broke through the front at this point,
only to find that the Belgians, supported now by a French division, had retired and

were strongly deployed along the embankment of the Nieuwpoort–Diksmuide railway.

Checked, the Germans turned their attention to Diksmuide. Having burned the town, they attacked through the rubble at midnight 24–25 October. This attack and another the following night were repulsed. Exhausted and running out of ammunition, the Belgians decided to use the sea. To safeguard their positions, they blocked all the culverts along the railway. Then on 27, 28 and 29 October they opened the Veurne canal sluices at high tide. The result was disappointing. It became clear that the sluices of the Noordvaart, the N canal, must also be opened, despite the fact that they lay in No Man's Land. The daring operation on the night of 29 October was successful. The sea water poured in and made large lagoons in the flat meadows between the river and the railway. Three German divisions which had taken Ramskapelle and Pervijze were forced into hasty retreat. The Battle of the Yser was won. A front was established which would not change significantly for nearly four years.

To the SE at 3km the N367 crosses the Yser by the *Uniebrug*. Nearby the figure of a soldier, indifferent to the roar of passing traffic, keeps lone watch. On the right a tablet records the gallant action here of the Belgian 14th Régiment de Ligne between 22 and 24 August 1914. In defending the last free part of its country, the regiment lost 900 of its soldiers.

Ramskapelle, 2km S of Nieuwpoort, was a key place along the railway which ran immediately to the E. The rails have been lifted, but a low embankment marks the position of the historic line and shows the culverts, once so heroically blocked, and vestiges of concrete defences. After the area to the E had been successfully flooded during the night of 29 October 1914, a Belgian and a French regiment retook Ramskapelle by bayonet charge. This exploit is commemorated by a joint memorial on the village churchyard wall. For *Pervijze*, 4km S of Ramskapelle, see Route 5.

From the Koning Albert Monument the road crosses the Yser. On the left is a memorial to the Resistance and, farther along the waterfront, the national memorial to Belgium's fishermen (1958).

2km **Nieuwpoort**, population 8000. This small town and port on the left bank of the Yser estuary is the centre of a municipality, which includes *Nieuwpoort aan Zee* with its large marina and the inland village of *Ramskapelle*.

History. The 'Novus Portus', which received its charter in 1163, suffered much from war. It was besieged nine times between the 13C and the 18C. On 2 July 1600 the Dutch, under Maurice of Nassau, defeated a Spanish army commanded by Archduke Albert on the sands to the NW of Nieuwpoort. An English contingent, led by Sir Francis and Sir Horace Vere, fought on the Dutch side. The town was fortified until 1862. Throughout the First World War Nieuwpoort remained in Allied hands, but the little that survived the Yser battle and the bombardments of the following years was destroyed in the fighting of 1918.

Boat Excursions. Two interesting excursions may be made during the summer months, one to Diksmuide, the other to Veurne. Apply to the Tourist Information Office.

In the Grote Markt in the town centre there are a several interesting buildings. The *Onze Lieve Vrouwkerk* was dedicated in 1163. Destroyed several times, it has been rebuilt largely in the original style. After a succession of towers, it was given a detached *belfry* in 1539. Razed in 1914, this was replaced in 1952 and now houses a chromatic carillon of 67 bells. There are concerts from mid June to mid September on Wednesday and Saturday at 20.30 and on Friday at 11.15. From mid September to mid June they are on Sunday and Friday at 11.15.

Immediately to the E are the *Stadhuis*, a neo-Renaissance building of 1922, and the *Halle*, a rebuilding also of 1922 in the style of its corn exchange predecessor of c 1280. The town's two museums are located here, one of ornithology and the other of local history. They are open at Easter and in July and August every day except Sunday from 09.30 to 12.00 and from 14.00 to 17.30.

In the eastern part of the town, to the S of the sluices, is the *Laurentius-toren*, known also as the 'Duivelstoren' because it was here that a witch came to meet the devil. First built c 1281 as part of the Sint Laurentius church, the tower was later incorporated into a fortress built by Philip the Bold. It continued to be part of the ramparts until they were demolished in 1862. During the First World War the tower was used as an observation post and, as a result, was largely destroyed.

Beyond *Nieuwpoort aan Zee* the road skirts the shore to reach (*6km*) **Oostduinkerke-Bad** (population 15,000). The Tourist Information Office is in Astrid Plein. A resort with a magnificent beach, it is famed for its shrimps. These are caught by fishermen who ride out on horseback and sweep the breakers with nets spread out on either side.

Leopold II Laan leads S to the inland village, passing at 1.5km the modern *Sint Niklaaskerk* by J. Gilson, 1955 with a huge crucifix by Arnost Gause.

Some 500m farther on, to the E in P. Schmitzstraat, is the *Nationaal Visserijmuseum* with ship models, fishing equipment, a reconstruction of a fisherman's home and café, and paintings and carvings of fishing subjects. The museum is open daily from 10.00 to 12.00 and from 14.00 to 18.00. It is closed on 1 January, 1 November and 25 December.

3km **Koksijde-Bad**, population 15,500. Tourist Information: Gemeente-huis. This resort claims to have the highest dune, the 33m *Hoge Blekker*, on the Belgian coast. It is sited to the SW of *Doornpanne*, the dunes' nature reserve, which lies to the E of the town.

From the town centre Jaak van Buggenhoutlaan leads past the modern *Onze Lieve Vrouw ten Duinenkerk*, J. Landsoght 1964, to the site of the abbey of Ter Duinen. Well signposted from the main coastal road is the interesting *Scientific and Cultural Centre of the Abbey of the Dunes and of the Westhoek*. The exhibits in the Centre may be divided into four groups: artefacts discovered during the 1949 excavations at the abbey, archaeologi-cal material from the region dating from the Iron Age, the Roman Period and the Middle Ages; flora and fauna from the beach, dunes, sea and polders; exhibits illustrating daily life during the Middle Ages. There is also an arboretum, which covers six ha., and a garden of medicinal plants. The Centre is open at Easter and from July to September daily between 10.00 and 18.00; other months from 09.00 to 12.30 and 13.30 to 17.00. It is closed in January.

The Cistercian abbey of Ter Duinen was founded in 1108, rebuilt after a flood in 1237 and destroyed by the Protestant 'Sea Beggars' in 1566. In 1597 some of the monks re-established themselves at their grange of *Ten Bogaerde*. Located 1.5km to the S, the present buildings date mainly from 1612, though part of the 12–13C barn survives. The abbey was transferred to Bruges in 1627 and suppressed in 1796.

Near the museum is a windmill of 1773, which was built at Veurne and brought here in 1954. Beside J. van Buggenhoutlaan a chapel of 1819 marks the grave of Blessed Idesbald van der Gracht, the third abbot of Ter Duinen, who died in 1167. Born in Flanders, Idesbald spent his youth in the service of the count of Flanders. Canon of Veurne in 1135, he resigned to become a Cistercian at Ter Duinen (see also p 177).

In **Sint Idesbald**, the W extension of Koksijde-Bad, admirers of Paul Delvaux should follow the signposts on the main coastal road to the *Musée Paul Delvaux*, 42 Kabouterweg. Delvaux produced much of his work in

Koksijde, so it is appropriate that the museum should be sited here.

The large and well-displayed collection covers a long and stylistically varied period of the artist's life. It includes the Bride's Dress (1969); *La Petite Mariée (1976); On the Way to Rome (1979); The Dioscuri (1982); View of the Quartier Léopold station, Brussels (1922), a conventional if slightly impressionistic picture; The Red Chair (1936), a less ethereal model than found in later paintings; the Dream of Constantine (1955), somewhat removed from his usual style; *The Sabbath (1962), notable for its lighting and draped cloth; and *The Procession (1963), a passing train contrasts strikingly with nine nudes proceeding tranquilly through a grove.

The museum is open daily, except Monday, from 10.30 to 18.30 from April to June and in September, in July and August every day, from October to December on Saturday and Sunday from 11.00 to 17.00. It is closed from January to March and on some holidays.

4km **De Panne**, population 9500. Tourist Information: Gemeentehuis, Zeelaan. The resort gets its name from the slight depression, 'panne', of dunes and woods in which it lies. Here in 1831 King Leopold I set foot on Belgian soil for the first time, an event commemorated by a memorial at the W of Zeedijk. From 1914 to 1918 De Panne was effectively the capital of the small section of Belgium which remained unconquered. King Albert and Queen Elisabeth lived at the Villa Maskens at the N end of the promenade. The Queen worked as a nurse in a field hospital, which had been set up at Hôtel de l'Océan. In May 1940 the retreating British army reached the sea at De Panne and were evacuated from the beaches between here and Dunkirk in France. There is a memorial to the evacuation on Leopold I Esplanade.

The frontier with France is 2km to the W. The land in between is a dunes nature reserve of 340 ha., with signposted paths, known as the *Westhoek*. A useful guide to its flora may be obtained from the Tourist Information Office.

Just S of De Panne, on the road to Adinkerke, is *Meli* a recreational park with many attractions for children. This is open daily April to September from 09.30. For De Panne to Diksmuide and Ghent, see Route 5.

5

De Panne to Ghent

Total distance 86km.—*6km* **Veurne**—*17km* **Diksmuide**—*34km* **Tielt**—*13km* **Deinze**—*4km* **Ooidonk**—*12km* **Ghent**.

De Panne, see Route 4.

6km **Veurne (Furnes)** population 11,500. Tourist Information Office: Grote Markt. Veurne is an agricultural centre at the junction of several canals. These form a moat which follows the course of the old ramparts. In the large, attractive Grote Markt there are several interesting Flemish and Spanish style buildings.

Veurne began as a fortified settlement, created at the time of the 9C and 10C Norse raids. The town's ramparts were not demolished until 1771. During the First World War Veurne, 9km behind the Yser front, was the Belgian military headquarters. It suffered much from intermittent bombardment during the First World War and from the fighting which took place there in May 1940.

The 'Boete Processie', the Penitents' Procession, is held in Veurne on the last Sunday in July. Begun as a 12C ceremony in honour of a relic of the True Cross (see below), the procession in its present form dates from 1644.

The most interesting buildings in Veurne are grouped around the Grote Markt. Note the neat row of 17C gabled houses on the N side.

From Easter to September there are guided tours of the *Stadhuis*, a mixed Gothic and Renaissance building of 1596–1612 by Lieven Lucas at the NW corner of the square. This has a loggia by Jérôme Stalpaert in front and an octagonal turret behind. There are some paintings, sculpture and tapestries of note. The Stadhuis communicates with the more severe *Gerechtshof*, built in 1613–18 mainly by Sylvanus Boullain. Note the interesting chimneypiece by Stalpaert in the hall. It was in these buildings that King Albert had his headquarters in 1914.

Behind is the *belfry* of 1628. Its campanile was restored after the last war.

According to an ancient tradition the *Sint Walburgakerk*, at the back of the Gerechtshof, stands on the site of a temple dedicated to Wotan. The choir of 1230–80 was rebuilt after a fire in 1353. The transepts, begun c 1300, were completed together with the short nave in 1902–04. The ruined 14C tower in the park was never finished. The choir stalls of 1596 are by Osmaer van Ommen, the pulpit of 1727 by Hendrik Pulincx. There is a Descent from the Cross attributed to Pieter Pourbus. In the sacristy is the 16C reliquary of the True Cross.

In 1099 Count Robert II of Flanders, on his way home from Jerusalem, was caught in a gale. He vowed that, if saved, he would offer the relic of the True Cross, which he was carrying, to the first church he saw. This was Sint Walburgakerk. The gift was duly made and a brotherhood was founded to honour the relic with an annual procession.

On the W side of the Grote Markt the house next to the Stadhuis dates from 1624. On the S side the *Hoge Wacht*, once the house of the night watch, was enlarged in 1636 and made into a main guard headquarters.

Leave the square by the Ooststraat. On one side is the graceful façade of the former *Vleeshuis*, the meat hall of 1615. This is now the public library and cultural centre. On the other is the *Spaans Paviljoen*, c 1450 enlarged 1528–30, which served as the town hall until 1586. Later it was occupied by officers of the Spanish garrison. Today it is used by the magistracy.

The *Sint Niklaaskerk*, in the Appelmarkt off the SE corner of the Grote Markt, is a late 15C hall-church with a choir of 1773. The massive brick tower is much older, it dates from the 13C. This houses a huge bell of 1379. Known as *t' Bomtje*, it is one of the oldest bells in Belgium. In the well lit modernised interior there is a triptych of 1534 ascribed variously to Pieter Coecke and Bernard van Orley.

No visitor to Veurne should fail to visit the *Bakery Museum* at 2 Albert I Laan where there are demonstrations of the preparation of bread, cakes, confectionery, etc. It is open between April and September from Monday to Thursday from 10.00 to 12.00 and 14.00 to 18.00; in July and August during the same hours on Friday; on Saturday, Sunday and holidays from 14.00 to 18.00; from October to March from Monday to Thursday and on Sunday between 14.00 to 17.00.

The château of **Beauvoorde**, 7km S of Veurne, was rebuilt c 1591–1617, probably by Boullain, on the site of an old castle by then in ruins. It has some good chimneypieces, including one attributed to Stalpaert, paintings, ceramics, glass and silverware. The château is open daily, except Monday, between June and September 14.00 to 17.00.

Houtem, 3km W of Beauvoorde, was King Albert's headquarters from 1915 to 1918. N from here stretches the polder of *De Moeren*, which was drained in 1627 by Wenceslas Coeberger using windmills.

Lo, population 2000. This small town, 12km SE of Veurne, was once important because of its Augustinian abbey which was founded in the 12C and suppressed at the time of the French Revolution. All that remains of the abbey is an attractive *dovecot* of 1710 behind the present church. This 19–20C successor to the abbey church has baroque stalls and a pulpit of 1626 by Urbain Taillebert.

The *Westpoort*, with two pepperpot turrets, dates back to the 14C. Tradition holds that Julius Caesar tethered his horse to the ancient yew here. The *Stadhuis* is a restoration of a 16C building. Nearby is the restored 15–16C convent of the Grauwe Zusters, the Grey Sisters or Poor Clares.

9km Pervijze, taken by the Germans on 28 October 1914, was almost immediately evacuated when the Belgians flooded the area. A tower to the SW of the central crossroads served as an observation post from 1914 to 1918. Today the tower may seem of little importance, but, if viewed from the S, its tactical value is evident.

At *3km* a minor road signposted OLV Hoekje and Dodengang forks E. Almost immediately after a smaller road heading N for *OLV Hoekje* marks an exposed and remote part of the Belgian front. Flat, bleak, bare, this area has a number of poignant reminders of 1914–18. They include a bunker, some regimental memorial stones around a monument, and a plaque honouring a Franciscan friar turned artillery officer. He set up his observation post in the ruin of an old chapel. Just beyond the chapel, a bald inscription on a demarcation stone records the dramatic fact that the invaders were halted here. Inside the chapel there is some vivid stained-glass with war scenes and a number of fast deteriorating wartime pictures and maps.

The *Dodengang*, Boyau de la Mort, Trench of Death, may be reached by returning S and bearing E along the minor road off the N35. Near the entrance there are some interesting 1914–18 photographs. The upper floor of the entrance building affords an overall view and some tactical appreciation of a section of a 1914–18 trench complex. However, this quite extensive system along the Yser, with its neat concrete sandbags and immaculate duckboards, is altogether too clean and tidy to be entirely convincing. It may be visited daily from 09.00 to 17.00 in April and September, until 18.00 in May and 19.00 in July and August; from 1 to 15 October on Sunday from 09.00 to 17.00.

Return to the N35 and continue to the bridge over the Yser at c *4km*. To the right are the ruins of the *Ijzertoren*, a Flemish nationalist monument erected in 1930 as a war memorial and a dramatic cry for peace. Blown up in 1946 by an unknown hand, it was replaced by a new tower, which was built close to the remains of the original. The vertical lettering AVV stands for All for Flanders, the horizontal VVK means Flanders for the King. In front are the Heroes' Gate and the Paxpoort, the Peace Gate, which were constructed from the ruins of the original tower. In the crypt there are memorials to Flemish patriots. The exhibits in the museum are on Flemish patriotism and the fighting which took place around Diksmuide. A lift speeds the visitor to the top of the tower. Below are spread the dunes, the polders, the rich farmland, the dark woods of Flanders, while far away in the distance the towers and steeples of Nieuwpoort, Veurne, Ypres and Bruges float, insubstantial, ethereal, unreal, as though painted by a Memling or a van der Weyden.

The tower is open daily in March, April, October and November from 09.00 to 17.00, in May, June and September from 09.00 to 19.00, and in July and August from 08.00 to 20.00.

At *1km* is **Diksmuide**, population 15,000. The Tourist Information Office is in the Grote Markt.

In the 9C and 10C fortifications protected a settlement here against the Norse raiders. By the middle of the 16C Diksmuide, now a small town, was garrisoned by the Spanish. In 1680 it was one of several places arbitrarily annexed by Louis XIV. During the First World War Diksmuide bore the brunt of the German attacks at the time of the battle of the Yser. Thereafter it became part of the front line and was so devastated that it was identified by a board bearing its name. It has been rebuilt, largely in the old style.

The spacious Grote Markt has a number of houses which recall the old pre World War I Diksmuide. Above them rises the tower of the *Sint Niklaaskerk*. A 14C foundation, it was rebuilt in the 17C and again after both World Wars.

The *Musée Municipal*, 55 Wilgendijk, has a collection of paintings, folklore objects, militaria etc. It is open daily from 09.00 (10.00 on Sunday) to 12.00 and from 14.00 to 17.00 from Easter to September.

The *Begijnhof* was founded during the 13C and functioned as such until the First World War. It has been rebuilt. The approach alley from the canal bridge bears the name of St Thomas. This recalls a tradition that Thomas à Becket once stayed there.

At *20km Lichtervelde* the Sint Jacobskerk has a late Romanesque font.

14km **Tielt**, population 19,000. The Tourist Information Office is in the Stadhuis. Tielt has long associations with textiles and shoemaking. It was the birthplace of Olivier le Daim, an itinerant barber who achieved great power as confidant of France's Louis XI. This could not save him, however. One year after the King's death in 1484 he was hanged. During the First World War the town was for a time the German headquarters on the Flanders front. Here on 1 November 1914 the Kaiser narrowly escaped death from a bombing attack by British aircraft.

Two of Tielt's most interesting structures are in the Markt—the *belfry* of 1275, with a spire of 1620, and the largely early 17C *Halle*, the trades hall. The coats of arms below the windows are of various local lords. A plaque on the S façade commemorates the Peasants' Revolt of 1798. Also of interest are the *Stadhuis*, essentially 19C, but with a wing along Tramstraat, part of which belonged to a 13C convent hospice, the 1937 *Onze Lieve Vrouwkerk*, which is best known for its sculpture and bronze Stations of the Cross, the *Sint Pieterskerk*, founded in the 11C, with a tower of 1646 and interesting church furnishings, which include a rococo-style pulpit of 1857, the 17C *Stockt Chapel* whose stained-glass windows depict the sufferings of the plague, and the *Minderbroederskerk*, with splendid baroque altars and the 17C cloisters of its monastery.

Meulebeke, 5km S of Tielt, was the birthplace of Karel van Mander (1548–1606), the Flemish painter of portraits. He is, perhaps, best known for his 'Schilderbouck', a collection of short biographies of painters from the Netherlands. This is a key source book for the history of art in the Low Countries. It earned van Mander the title of the 'Flemish Vasari'. In the *Ancienne Gare*, open on request, there is a collection of World War I memorabilia.

At *6km Aarsele* there are a Romanesque church and a restored windmill. Just beyond is the border between W and E Flanders.

7km to the E on the river Lys (Leie) is **Deinze**, population 25,000. The town has an interesting late 13C/early 14C church. It was the birthplace of

St Poppo of Stavelot, one of the great monastic figures of the 11C. As a young man he followed a military career and led a loose and dissolute life for a number of years. After his return from a pilgrimage to Rome and Jerusalem, St Poppo became a Benedictine monk. He helped to produce a revival of monastic discipline and became one of the most trusted advisers of the emperor St Henry. He was superior-general of some of the largest and most ancient monasteries in Lotharingia and neighbouring areas.

At Nos 3–5 L. Matthyslaan is the modern *Museum van Deinze en De Leiestreek*. It has two distinct parts. The first is an art gallery with works of all kinds by most of the artists associated with the Leie or Lys district. Among these are Emile Claus, George Minne, Constant Permeke, A. Servaes and Leon and Gustave de Smet. Do not miss La Récolte des Betteraves by Emile Claus, a gift to the museum from his wife. The other part of the museum is devoted to the archaeology, history and folklore of Deinze and its environs. It includes objects from the prehistoric and Roman periods, Flemish pottery and furniture. The museum is open on Monday and from Wednesday to Friday between 14.00 and 17.30 and on Saturday, Sunday and holidays from 10.00 to 12.00 and 14.00 to 17.00.

There is a choice of roads from Deinze. The road S of the Lys through Deurle is described in Route 11. This Route continues N of the river. After *4km* it reaches the Château of **Ooidonk** which is located just S of the village of Bachte-Maria-Leerne. In wooded parkland it stands at the end of a long avenue of copper beeches. This elaborate moated château began as a 13C fortress. Burnt by the citizens of Ghent in 1501, because the owner supported Philip the Handsome, and again in 1578 by Ghent Calvinists, the castle was rebuilt at the end of the 16C by Philippe de Montmorency as a residence. The corner towers are the only significant survival from the 13C fortress. The interior, mainly 19C, has some good furniture, porcelain, Beauvais tapestries, and an interesting collection of royal portraits. It is open on Ascension Day, Whit Sunday and Whit Monday and from July to mid September on Sunday and holidays from 14.00 to 1800. The park is open daily.

Continue for *8km* to **Drongen**. The Abbey of Drongen was founded by Premonstratensians in 1138 on an earlier Benedictine site. Erasmus was a frequent visitor. Dissolved by the French at the end of the 18C, the buildings were used soon afterwards by Lieven Bauwens, an enterprising tanner turned businessman, to house Belgium's first cotton-mill. He smuggled machinery and men from England to set it up and work in it.

The abbey returned to church ownership later and has been occupied since 1837 by the Jesuits. The buildings extant, the tower, the church, the cloister and the abbot's lodging are mainly from the 17C and 18C. The church of 1736 has a Pietà of the school of Roger van der Weyden. It is dedicated to St Gerulph, who died c 746. He was a Flemish youth who was heir to a vast estate. He was killed, on his way home after receiving confirmation, by a relative who hoped to inherit his wealth. Gerulph pardoned his murderer as he lay dying.

For *4km* Ghent, see Route 13.

6

Ostend to Ypres

Total distance 45km.—*9km* **Gistel**—*6km Sint Pieters Kapelle—10km*
Diksmuide—*15km Boezinge—5km* **Ypres**—Between Sint Pieters Kapelle
and Boezinge the road follows the line of the 1914–18 front, and from
Boezinge to Ypres the base of the Ypres salient (Route 7B).

Leave **Ostend** (see Route 2) by the Torhoutsesteenweg. At 5km the road
crosses the Ostend–Nieuwpoort canal.

Continue in an easterly direction along the S bank of the canal for an
interesting diversion to 7km **Oudenburg**. At one time on an arm of the sea,
this village occupies the site of a prosperous medieval port. The remains of
a large Roman coastal fortress and necropolis have been found at Oudenburg. Today little is visible above ground. The considerable finds, which
include fibulae, pottery, glass, coins, spearheads, combs and a fine ivory
plaque bearing a representation of the *magister militum* Stilicho, are
preserved in the *Musée Communal*, 25 Markstraat. This museum is open
only on request.

There are some 17C buildings of a Benedictine abbey founded in 1084
by St Arnulf of Soissons. Born in Flanders, Arnulf served in the armies of
Robert and Henry I of France. He became a Benedictine and lived as a
recluse for a number of years. In 1082 he was appointed bishop of Soissons.
Later he retired to Oudenburg, where he died in 1087.

Return to the main road and continue in a SE direction crossing the E–W
arm of the E40 motorway. At *9km* is **Gistel**, population 6000. This is an
ancient place, whose name may be derived from the stables, the stallingen,
of the counts of Flanders. In the church, which dates from c 1500, is the
shrine of St Godeleva (Godliva). Married at a young age to Bertulf of Gistel,
Godeleva was ill treated by him for a number of years before being
strangled on his orders. The abbey of *Ten Putte*, 3km to the W, is a 19C
foundation, which occupies the site of a Benedictine convent established
soon after the saint's death, reputedly on the position of the castle where
she was murdered. The *Musée St Godelieve* at the abbey has an interesting
historical and iconographical collection. It is open daily from Easter to the
end of September from 10.00 to 12.00 and from 13.30 to 18.00.

This Route now bears SW on the N367 across a district called *Moere Blote*,
marshland largely drained between 1620 and 1623 by Wenceslas
Coeberger. At *6km* Sint Pieters Kapelle it turns S on the N369 for *5km*
Keiem. Much of the country to the W of the road between Sint Pieters
Kapelle and Keiem was flooded in 1914–18. The outposts of the opposing
armies were 3km apart in places and patrolling was carried out in boats.
Tervate, 3km W of Keiem, is the place where the Germans first got across
the Yser in strength. At *5km* is **Diksmuide**, see Route 5.

Just beyond Woumen is the lake of *Blankaart*. Today this a nature reserve,
but during the First World War it was part of the Yser front flooding. At
13km the N369 crosses the Ypres–Yser canal near the hamlet of Steenstraat.
For this and for the road to *2km Boezinge* and *5km* **Ypres** see Routes 7B,
Northern Salient and 7A.

7

Ypres and the Salient

A. Ypres

YPRES is the English and French name for the Flemish town of **Ieper**, population 34,500. It is strategically located at the S end of the canal from the Yser and is c 12km from the French border. From the 13C to the 15C it was an important place, ranking first among the ancient cloth-working towns of Flanders. It was rich and this wealth was reflected in a profusion of fine buildings.

Today Ypres is known to many as a place where some of the fiercest fighting of the 1914–18 war took place. The town, at the base of the notorious Ypres Salient, was reduced to ruins. Immediately behind the front line, the routes through it were shelled continuously long after the buildings had disappeared. The junction of the Grote Markt with the Menen road became known as 'the most dangerous corner in Europe'. However, the lines of the cobbled streets survived and the town was rebuilt after the war to its former plan. Many of the buildings, notably the great cloth hall and the cathedral, are faithful copies of their predecessors. Within and around Ypres many memorials and military cemeteries remind us that over half a million men from both sides of the conflict perished here.

Tourist Information. Stadhuis, Grote Markt.

Hotels. Ypres has some very good hotels. A list may be obtained from the Tourist Information Office. The comfortable, pleasant Hotel Ariane is recommended.

Post Office. Rijselstraat.

World War I. Ypres is an excellent centre for visiting places connected with the 1914 to 1918 war.

Commonwealth War Graves Commission. 82 Elverdingestraat. There are some 40 British military cemeteries within 3km of the Grote Markt and 130 others around the Salient. At the Commission maps can be consulted and directions obtained. Many cemeteries may be reached by bus. The office is open from Monday to Friday between 08.30 and 12.30 and from 13.30 to 17.00 or 16.30 on Friday.

Coat of Arms. In gules a cross of vair, in which the bells in the vertical bar stand upright and those in the fess are directed horizontally to the sides; with argent chief in which there is a gules cross patée. Above the shield, a golden mural crown; and at the left of it, a statant lion in or, acting as a supporter, with an argent cannonbarrel on its dexter shoulder. Under the champain, the British Military Cross and the French Croix de Guerre, suspended from their ribbons.

English Church. The memorial church of St George is at the corner of Elverdingestraat, just NW of the cathedral.

Festival. 'Kattestoet'. The procession of cats, giants, etc. is held every two years on the second Sunday in May (see below). It will take place next in 1993.

History. In the 10C Ypres occupied the place where the Paris to Bruges trade route crossed the river Ieperlee. In those days the river was navigable. It is now canalised underground. The town became a powerful centre, deriving great wealth from its weaving and sharing with Bruges and Ghent the effective control of Flanders. Circa 1260–1304, when the Cloth Hall was built, it boasted a population of some 40,000.

Cloth from Ypres was in great demand throughout Europe. It was sold as far away as Novgorod.

The first of the Flemish 'Chambers of Rhetoric' was founded here in the 14C and called 'Alpha en Omega'. These literary societies played an important part in the life in the Burgundian dominion up to the 17C.

The prosperity of Ypres began to wane towards the end of the 14C. In 1383 the English, aided by 20,000 troops from Ghent, besieged the town (see the picture in the cathedral). Ypres held out, but the surrounding district was ravaged and the weavers were forced to leave. They took their lucrative industry with them. Chaucer's description of the skill of the Wife of Bath as surpassing that of the weavers of 'Ipres and Gaunt' dates from about this time. The dispersion of the weavers marked the beginning of a period of decline. Rivalries between the towns and the rigid traditionalism of their guilds hastened the recession and by the close of the 16C the population had dwindled to 5000.

In strategic terms Ypres remained important. It was taken and sacked by the Duke of Parma in 1584 and throughout the next century was fought over continually by France and Spain. In 1678, under the Peace of Nijmegen, Ypres became French and Vauban strengthened the defences. However, peace did not last long and, after surviving the War of the Grand Alliance (1690–97), Ypres changed hands several times during the War of the Spanish Succession, 1702–13, during the War of the Austrian Succession, 1744–48, and during the war of 1792 beween revolutionary France and Austria. It became a French town again in 1794. In 1815 Ypres was incorporated in the kingdom of the Netherlands by the Congress of Vienna.

On 13 October 1914 Ypres was occupied by German cavalry. They withdrew the next day, when the British Expeditionary Force arrived. A description of the Salient of which Ypres became the pivot is given in Route 7B. On 1 May 1920 the town was awarded the British Military Cross.

During the Second World War Ypres escaped direct attack, other than from the air.

Along the N side of the Grote Markt stretches the famous ***Cloth Hall**, the Lakenhalle. Long the most splendid Gothic public building in Belgium, this was a proud monument to the wealth and power of the medieval guilds. Built c 1260–1304 along the river Ieperlee, which in those days was busy with shipping, the hall was a combined market, warehouse and covered quay. During the winter months, when wool was stored on the upper floor, cats were used to control the mice. In spring the cats, no longer needed, were thrown down to the people below. This custom, which symbolised the killing of evil spirits, continued until 1817 as part of the 'Kattestoet' festival. It is still celebrated every two years on the second Sunday in May, but the cats are now cloth replicas. The next celebration will be in 1993.

After surviving centuries of siege and warfare, the hall was completely destroyed, largely by an artillery barrage, on 22 November 1914. It was rebuilt to its original design in 1933–34. However, it was not until 1967, and after another war, that King Baudouin performed the opening ceremony.

The façade, 125m long, is crowned by a superb square belfry 70m high. The present spire with its helmet and dragon of 1692 is an exact copy of the original. It has a carillon of 49 bells which cover four octaves. There are carillon concerts every Sunday, except the first and second Sundays of August, from June to September between 21.00 and 22.00. The best place to hear a concert is the inner courtyard of the Cloth Hall.

From the upper gallery of the belfry there is a superb view of the town and surrounding countryside.

The lower courses of the Cloth Hall incorporate part of the original 13C building. Above the 'Donkerpoort' are the municipal coat of arms and a statue of Our Lady of Thuyne, the protectress of Ypres since the siege by the English in 1383. On the right-hand side of the passage are statues of Earl Baldwin IX of Flanders and his consort, Mary of Champagne, who laid the first stone in 1200. The statues on the left are of King Albert and Queen Elisabeth, in whose reign the rebuilding was started. On the right of the entrance a tablet commemorates the French victims of 1914–18.

The *Nieuwwerk*, which houses a part of the town hall, adjoins the Cloth Hall on its E side. This elegant Renaissance building was constructed above a vaulted gallery between 1619 and 1624. Destroyed by bombardment in 1914, it was reconstructed in 1962 by P.A. Pauwels, who took his inspiration from the Cloth Hall. Above the large window are the arms of Philip IV of Spain. In the niches are statuettes of Our Lady of Thuyne and figures representing justice and prudence. The Council Chamber, with a fine stained-glass window by Arno Brys, may be visited on work days between 08.00 and 12.00, if not in use.

In the gallery are the *Tourist Information Office* and the **Ypres Salient Museum**. The Museum has a comprehensive collection of wartime memorabilia which has been arranged with verve and imagination. It compares very favourably with some of the rather opportunist displays around the Salient. The material, Allied and German, includes: pictures and photographs, civil and military; a section devoted to war cemeteries; some excellent dioramas of the conditions in 1917 at Passchendaele, Menin Gate, Lille Gate; a large *model of the devastated town and another of an aerodrome of 1917–18; trench signs and examples of trench art; official proclamations; instructive maps; a reconstruction of a section of a trench; and many personal mementoes.

The museum is open daily from 1 April to 15 November from 09.30 to 12.00 and from 13.30 to 17.30 and on request for groups outside of these periods.

Behind the Cloth Hall is **Sint Maartens Kathedraal**, a reconstruction of the original 13C Gothic building which was destroyed in 1914. (Note that though a spire is shown on early plans, the original church did not have one.) The first church on this site was erected c 1073. Part of an early cloister survives on the N side of the cathedral against the reconstructed domestic buildings of the 12C abbey.

Most of the works of art in the cathedral were lost in 1914. A Flemish diptych of 1525 with scenes of the Passion survives on the W wall, where there is also a memorial to Abbé Camille Delaere, 1860–1930. He was a parish priest who, though always under fire, gallantly ministered to the wounded in 1914. The rose window above the S door, a memorial to King Albert, was presented in 1935 by the British Army and the Royal Air Force. There is an explanation of the design and motives near the entry to the S transept. The S transept contains the reconstructed tomb of George Chamberlain, who was born in Ghent of English parents. He was Bishop of Ypres between 1628 and 1634. Here too is a memorial to all the French soldiers who fell in Belgium during the Great War.

The British Empire Memorial is in the N transept. Of standard design, it is one of a number in churches along the 1914–18 front line. It commemorates the one million dead of the Empire 'many of whom rest in Belgium'.

In the E chapel hangs a graphic picture of the 1383 siege of Ypres by the English and their allies from Ghent. Here also are three alabaster effigies of 17C bishops and the black marble tomb of Guillaume de Saillant, chancellor of Ypres, 1552. Count Robert de Béthune, who died in 1322, and Bishop Jansenius (Cornelis Jansen, 1585–1638), are buried in the chapel. Jansenius was the theologian and author of a four-volume study, *Augustinus*, who gave his name to Jansenism.

This was a movement in the Catholic Church which was based on Jansenius' reading of the teachings of St Augustine against the Pelagians. Pelagius held that in spite of the sin of Adam, man was free to do good and could obtain salvation by his own merits. To counter this heresy, Augustine had emphasised the limitations of man and Jansenius carried this teaching to extreme lengths. He stated that man could only be saved by the grace of Christ which was given to a small number of the elect only. This belief in predestination soon brought Jansenism into conflict with the Holy See. It was condemned by Pope Urban VIII in the bull *In Eminenti* in 1642. The Jesuits were among its most vocal opponents.

Jansenius himself kept clear of serious trouble. He became professor of theology at Bayonne, Bishop of Louvain in 1630 and in 1636 Bishop of Ypres. Two years later he died of the plague. He left a statement in which he accepted the judgement of the Church on his teachings.

Supported by Pascal and the Port Royalists the controversy provoked by Jansenius continued in France for many years after his death. It also led to the formation of a small breakaway sect in the Netherlands which promulgated his views.

The cathedral may always be visited, except before and during services.

Outside the NE corner of the cathedral a Celtic cross, the *Munster Memorial* with inscriptions in Irish, English, French and Flemish, honours the Irish soldiers killed in the First World War.

To the NW, at the corner of Elverdingestraat, is **Saint George's English Memorial Church**, by Reginald Blomfield, 1929. The armoured figure on the font cover is a memorial to Field Marshal the Earl of Ypres, Sir John French, 1852–1925, commander of the British Expeditionary Force in 1914–15. Virtually everything in the church commemorates a unit or individual soldier. For details refer to the notices on either wall just inside the entrance. The church is open every day. A service is held on Sunday at 18.00.

Just beyond the W end of the Grote Markt on the corner of Boterstraat are the *Gedenkteken*, the memorial to the people of Ypres of both wars. In Boomgardstraat is the reconstructed *Vleeshuis*. The ground floor was built in 1275, the brick upper floor in 1530. It is now a youth centre. Take the parallel Rijselstraat, Rue de Lille, from the Grote Markt, to No. 38, the **Belle Godshuis**. This almshouse was founded c 1276, but rebuilt in the 16C and 17C. It bears a plaque to its physician founder Jean Yperman. The house is now a museum. It has an interesting collection of paintings, including a Madonna with Donors of 1420, 17C vestments, 17C and 18C silver, furniture, city seals, lace, etc. It is open from October to May from Monday to Friday between 10.00 and 12.00 and 14.00 to 16.00, from June to September from Tuesday to Sunday between 10.00 and 13.00 and 15.00 and 18.00.

Farther S, on the left, at 2 Merghelynckstraat is the **Hôtel-Musée Merghelynck**, a reconstruction of a patrician home of 1774. The French-style façade illustrates the architectural changes which took place between the reigns of Louis XV and Louis XVI. In more than a dozen period rooms and annexes there is a splendid collection of 18C works of art—paintings, silver, clocks and furniture. Do not miss Rubens' Vanity of Riches which was painted at the request of Bishop Jansenius (see above). Part of the collection was saved from the destruction inflicted on Ypres during the 1914–1918 war. The museum is open daily from 10.00 to 12.00 and from 14.00 to 17.00. It is closed on Sunday, on holidays and from 15 to 31 July.

Beyond, on the left, the *Sint Pieterskerk* has traces of Romanesque building in the lower course of its W tower. Off to the right in Ieperleestraat is the *Municipal Museum*. This occupies an almshouse of 1277. It has a collection of photographs and drawings about the history of Ypres, 19C painting, the Cloth Hall and the religious life of the town. It is open daily, except Monday, from 1 April to 31 October from 09.30 to 12.00 and from 13.30 to 17.30.

Rijselstraat ends at the **Rijselpoort**, the Lille Gate, with Ramparts Cemetery, two pre-Vauban flanking bastions, and vaulted chambers on either side. The chamber on the E was a 17C guardroom. Those on the W, used for water control, are at the point where the Ieperlee starts its underground course through the town. Less exposed than the Menin Gate, the Lille Gate was the favoured exit to the front.

The E side of the Grote Markt is occupied by the *Gerechtshof*, the Law Courts. They are built on the site of a 12C almshouse which was still standing in 1914.

S of the Grote Markt in St Jacobstraat a convent founded in 1665 and occupied mainly by Irish nuns was destroyed during the bombardment of 1914. Among its treasures was the flag carried at the battle of Fontenoy in Hainaut in 1745 by the Irish Brigade, that famous band of exiles who served in the French Army. At Fontenoy the Duke of Cumberland who later acquired the sobriquet 'Butcher of Culloden', and his army of British, Austrian, Hanoverian and Dutch soldiers, were defeated by the French under Marshal Saxe. The charge of the Irish Brigade was irresistible and ensured the French victory. The nuns found a new home in Kylemore, Connemara.

From the Law Courts take the Menenstraat to the **Menin Gate**, one of the main entries to the town and successor to earlier gates in the ramparts—the Antwerp Gate and, after a visit by Napoleon in 1804, the Napoleon Gate. In its present form it was opened by Field Marshal Plumer in July 1927 as a memorial to the armies of the British Empire and to those of their dead, who have no known grave. The gate stands on the site of the chief and very dangerous approach to the Salient battlefields from the town. The memorial, by Sir Reginald Blomfield, takes the form of a gateway with three entrances. Above the main archway is a brooding lion by Sir W. Reid Dick. The names of nearly 55,000 men, who fell within the Salient and were listed as missing, are inscribed on the walls and beside the steps and galleries, which lead to the adjoining ramparts.

Every evening at 20.00 the traffic is halted briefly at the Menin Gate and the Last Post is sounded. This simple but very moving ceremony was started by the Chief of Police in 1928 and, apart from 1939–45, has been carried out ever since.

Remains of the **ramparts**, with a moat below, of ancient origin but largely the work of Vauban in the 17C, line the E side of the town. They were used very much by British artillery observers. The paths along the top still command a view of the arc of ridges, from left to right, Pilkem, Zonnebeke and Mesen, or Messines, where the Germans were established after the Second Battle.

The vaulted rooms under the ramparts resisted the heaviest bombardments. They contained bedrooms, a signals headquarters, a hospital and a cinema. Some of the casemates may be visited, but only if accompanied by a city guide.

For Ypres to Ostend, see Route 6.

B. The Salient and the Battles of Ypres

The 'Salient' was the name given during the First World War to the arc of the Allied front to the E of Ypres. The scene of some of the costliest fighting of the war in terms of manpower losses, it produced few results.

The Salient was established by the first battle of Ypres in 1914, much reduced by the second battle in 1915, and modestly enlarged by the third battle in 1917. The key tactical feature was the range of low ridges, from Pilkem in the N to Mesen (Messines) in the S. Holding these from 1915 to 1917, the Germans were able to keep much of the Allied forward and rear areas under observation.

This is a flat and not particularly exciting land of isolated farms and neat villages. Apart from having better roads, a motorway and cars, instead of horsecarts, it has changed little since the beginning of the century. In such bucolic surroundings it is not always easy to picture the utter devastation and desolation that marked the years from 1914 to 1918.

The horrors of hell so graphically depicted in the paintings of Bosch and Brueghel were outmatched by what happened in the Salient. Here a pile of rubble marked the site of a village, there a broken cross and ruined walls the remains of a desecrated church. Beyond, the flooded, stinking trenches, crowned with entanglements of rusty wire, meandered through a nightmarish landscape of tortured trees. In this place, thousands of young men, deafened by constant shelling, died horribly, not a few drowning in the sea of mud which surrounded them.

There are some relics of those terrible times. Now and again the visitor will encounter battered concrete bunkers, eroded and overgrown trenches, tangles of barbed wire and areas pockmarked with mine craters. These and the many crowded cemeteries, the monuments, modest and grandiose, Allied and German and the old photographs in the local museums will help him to understand what happened in the Salient.

There are also more dangerous reminders—stacks of shells or other war material at the road side or at the base of a memorial or signpost. They have not been placed there for souvenir hunters, but are awaiting collection by the Belgian bomb disposal units, so that they may be destroyed safely.

Explosive becomes progressively less stable with age. It is extremely dangerous to touch almost any kind of wartime débris. It is also dangerous, particularly in the woods, to stray off the regular paths.

The Battles of Ypres

In October 1914 the Allies aimed to strike at the German communications across Flanders. At the same time the Germans mounted an offensive. The two attacks met and became the **First Battle of Ypres**, which raged from 19 October–22 November. The Allied strength was about one-third that of the Germans.

During the course of the battle the British lost Zandvoorde and Hollebeke and were forced back to the Mesen–Wijtschate ridge. Geluveld was lost. On 1 November Mesen and on 2 November the Wijtschate ridge were captured by the Germans. This was a disaster for the Allies, as it gave the Germans a view over Ypres and its surroundings.

By 2 November the Allied line, from N to S, was manned as follows: from the canal at Steenstraat round Langemark to Zonnebeke, by the French, from Zonnebeke along the E of Polygon Wood to Hill 60 and the railway, by the British, from the railway to W of Mesen, by the French, and from there to the Lys at Frelinghien, by the British. Subsequently there were only minor changes and by 22 November open combat had given way to trench warfare.

Although there were withdrawals by the Allies, Ypres was saved and a salient established that lasted until April 1915. Until the end of October, during the first part of the Battle of Ypres, the Battle of the Yser (Route 4) was being fought to the N.

Second Battle of Ypres. 22 April–25 May 1915. Concentrating now against Russia, the Germans were on the defensive in the W, but wished nevertheless to try out their new weapon, gas. On meteorological advice the Ypres front was chosen for the test.

On the British front the Canadian 1st Division held the section next to the French. At 17.00 on 22 April a yellowish cloud of chlorine gas, released from cylinders, drifted towards the French positions. Forced to retreat behind the canal, they left the entire British flank exposed. The Germans took Langemark and the Pilkem ridge and crossed the canal at Steenstraat.

At 04.00 on 24 April there was a second gas attack, this time against the Canadians. After two days fierce fighting, in which Graventafel and Sint Juliaan were lost, the British were left holding an untenable long narrow strip pointing towards Passchendaele (now Passendale).

May saw a two-stage withdrawal. When the battle closed on 25 May, the base of the Allied salient had been shortened from 13km to 8km, and its maximum depth from 9km to a mere 4km. The Salient now ran from S of Boezinge, S of Wieltje, through Hooge and Sanctuary Wood to NW of Hill 60 and then followed the original line W of Mesen to the Lys.

The **Third Battle of Ypres** in 1917 was intended to open the way for an offensive against the German positions along the coast. It may be divided into two phases. The first was the *Battle of Mesen* on 7 June. Its objective was to secure the German salient along the Mesen–Wijtschate ridge. A fierce artillery barrage, the use of mines and the gallantry of the Australian, New Zealand, Irish and London regiments brought success. By evening the whole ridge was in British hands.

The *Main Offensive* opened on 22 July with a ten-day artillery barrage by 2300 guns. On 31 July, in heavy rain, the infantry attacked along a 24km front. On the left Bikschote, Sint Juliaan and the Pilkem ridge were all taken, but in the central section by the Menen road there was no progress.

A second attack on 16 August had much the same result. The left passed the ruins of Langemark, but the centre achieved nothing. Fresh offensives, always in heavy rain, between 30 September and 4 October gave the British, largely Australian and New Zealand divisions, the main ridge from Geluveld by way of Polygon Wood to Broodseinde. This was far from being enough. The 'forest' of Houthulst with the high ground behind had to be won, if the coastal campaign was to be possible. Several attacks were made. All foundered in the mud. However, on 4 November the Canadians fought their way across the morass to the site of Passendale village.

Thus ended the tragic and barren Third Battle of Ypres, generally considered to have been doomed from the start by the combination of German preparedness and their use of mustard gas. Another factor was the all pervasive mud. This had been made worse than usual by the continuous rain and heavy bombardment. As a result much of the battlefield was an impassable quagmire.

Battle of the Lys. 1918. On 9 April the Germans made their last drive to end the war. The main weight of the attack fell along the Lys and against the Salient. By 30 April, when the battle ended, all the Allied gains of 1917 had been lost. S of Ypres the Allied line no longer reached the Lys but ran through Voormezele, Vierstraat, and Loker. However, all was regained in the final victorious Allied offensive of August to October.

The Northern Salient

This is a tour of c 27km, much of it across the country which suffered the first German gas attack in April 1915.

Leave Ypres by the N369. After Dudhallow Cemetery you pass the *Essex Farm Cemetery*, marked by the tall obelisk of the 49th Division Memorial. In the grass bank to the left just behind the Cross of Sacrifice are some British dugouts. In surprisingly good condition, they demonstrate how even a modest feature like this bank could provide a good defence.

It was at a dressing station here that John McCrae, an officer with the Royal Canadian Medical Corps, wrote his poem 'In Flanders Fields'.

'In Flanders fields the poppies blow
Between the crosses, row on row
That mark our place; and in the sky
The larks, still bravely singing, fly
Scarce heard amid the guns below.

We are the Dead. Short days ago
We lived, felt dawn, saw sunsets glow,
Loved and were loved, and now we lie
In Flanders fields.....'

At 5km from central Ypres **Boezinge**, now bypassed, long marked the northern point of the British sector. This joined with the French on the N side of the village. After the Second Battle the village was at the NW corner of the much reduced Salient. The war is commemorated in Boezinge by a bunker with a German mortar on top.

At 1km to the E along the Langemark road, beyond the railway crossing, there is a memorial of a very different kind. Honouring the French 87th and 45th divisions, it is made up of a calvary, a dolmen and a small menhir, all of which were brought from Brittany. An orientation table and map recall that during the late afternoon of 22 April 1915 the men of these divisions faced the first German gas attack. The concrete posts surrounding the site represent the early wooden ones to which the barbed wire was attached before the provision of iron screw-pickets.

In April 1915 **Steenstraat**, 3km N of Boezinge, was near the end of the French line. Here the Germans, profiting from the surprise achieved by their gas attack, held a bridgehead on the W side of the canal for three weeks from 22 April to 15 May.

On the left just after the N369 bends to the right at Lizerne, is a memorial generally known as the *Cross of Reconciliation*. Slim and effectively simple, the dark aluminium cross replaces a French monument of 1929. This was destroyed by the Germans in 1942, because they objected to being described on it as 'barbarians'. The Franco-Belgian replacement commemorates, in a less controversially worded inscription, the first gas victims. During the 1915 fighting the Belgian and French lines ran close to one another in this area. This is recalled by a number of Belgian memorials, both to units and to individuals.

Now leave the N369 for a minor road which heads SE through Bikschote for Langemark. In the area to the SW, between this road and the canal, there are bunkers of all sizes. A network of smaller roads facilitates exploration.

Langemark was attacked as early as October 1914. German student battalions played a large part in what was expected to be a walkover. However, it was not taken by the Germans until April 1915, when their gas clouds blew towards the French and Canadians defender. Retaken by the British 20th Light Division on 16 August 1917, what little remained of the town was lost again in April 1918. Regained the following September, it was by then just a heap of rubble.

DIVERSIONS FROM LANGEMARK. The road due N soon passes a large German war cemetery. In a special room the names of those students who lost their lives in the abortive and costly assault of October 1914 are recorded.

Cross the Sint Jansbeek. Immediately over this stream turn left to the British *34th Division Royal Artillery and Royal Engineers Memorial*. This stands in front of a German bunker and commemorates those 'who fought near this spot, October–November 1917'. Taken in September 1918, the bunker served for a time as a British advanced dressing station.

Continuing N through Velhoek after 5km the road passes the SW edge of *Houthulst Forest*, a place once surprisingly described by Napoleon as the 'key to the Netherlands'. A century later the Germans also considered the forest to be of great importance. Having overcome stubborn Belgian and French resistance by October 1914, they used it for the next four years as a main rear concentration zone for the Salient campaigns. There is a Belgian cemetery and several memorials.

Poelkapelle, 2km E of Langemark, was in German hands for most of the war. Here is the memorial to Georges Guynemer, 1894–1917, the best known and most dashing of France's air heroes. Credited with 54 victories, he was shot down near here on 11 September 1917. Guynemer's squadron was known as 'The Storks' and the poignant memorial of 1923, with a portrait-plaque, shows a crippled bird retracing the airman's last flight.

On the SW side of Langemark, to the right just before the Steenbeek, stands the *20th Light Division Monument*. This rather unattractive grey cenotaph, in its drab modern setting, commemorates those who freed the ruins of Langemark in August 1917.

After crossing the Steenbeek the road passes *Cement House Cemetery*, so called from a bunker in the nearby farm. The crossroads beyond were one of the most heavily bombarded spots in the area.

A left turn at Groenestraat, followed almost at once by a right fork, will take you past *Goumier Farm*, part of which was fortified by the Germans. After changing hands frequently, Goumier was taken by 38th Welsh Division in July 1917. This is commemorated by a plaque. From here minor roads lead S to Ypres and NW to Boezinge.

After 2km the road SE out of Langemark reaches a crossroads with the N313. This is known as Vancouver Corner. Beside it is the impressive *Canadian Memorial*, a lofty shaft of granite, which merges into the bust of a Canadian soldier, whose head is lowered and whose hands rest on reversed arms. Surrounded by a sombre garden in which clipped trees and low bushes represent shells and craters, this is a memorial to the 18,000 Canadians on the British left who suffered the first German gas attacks on 22 and 24 April 1915; 2000 lost their lives.

Continue SW on the N313 through Sint Juliaan to the Seaforth Cemetery.

Beside and to the N of this is a German bunker known as *Cheddar Villa.* Today peacefully incorporated in a farm, the bunker was captured in July 1917. A month later it was the target of German shelling. Direct hits killed or wounded most of the members of a platoon of the 1st Buckinghamshire, who were sheltering there.

Beyond, at *Wieltje*, in the shadow of the motorway and close to Oxford Road Cemetery, stands a dignified obelisk, the monument of the 50th Northumberland Division. This also honours the same division's fallen of 1939–45. After passing two more cemeteries, Wieltje Farm and White House, you arrive back at Ypres.

The Central Salient

This is a circuit of some 30km, through places which recall the desperate rallies that saved the wavering British line during the Second Battle, the costly Third Battle with its tally of heroic deeds in the mud, the retreat almost to the gates of Ypres in Spring 1918 and the final victorious push in September of that year. The battlefields are particularly associated with Canadian, Australian and New Zealand arms. We return to Ypres by the N8, the notorious Menin Road, the W section of which was a main link between Ypres and the front.

Leave Ypres by the Menin Gate and take a left fork for the village of *Potijze*. To the N there are four British cemeteries. To the S, down the road signposted Menen and Zillebeke, is a blockhouse half hidden by a farm building. This is Hussar Farm, a valuable Allied observation point for four years, which was under constant enemy bombardment.

Beyond Potijze, the French flag flies over the great cemetery of *Saint Charles de Potyze*. Its monument, particularly striking in sombre stone, is a Crucifixion and grieving women.

A little farther is the British Aeroplane Cemetery.

Zonnebeke is a prosperous little place, where neat houses line the main road. It was among the most contested places along the curve of the Salient. At the beginning of the war Zonnebeke was chosen by the Germans as the base from which the Kaiser would make his triumphal entry into Ypres on 1 November 1914. However, the village was defended stubbornly until May 1915. In an aerial photograph of October 1917 it appears as an eerie mass of grey rubble in a nightmare landscape of muddy craters and shattered trees. Recaptured by the Allies in September 1917, it was lost in April 1918, but retaken the following September.

The hamlet of *Broodseinde* straddles a crossroads on the tactically important ridge of the same name. The interesting geometrical monument in brick commemorates the French soldiers who gave their lives in the defence of the crest. A short way down the Beselare road is the memorial of the British 7th Division which fought here in 1914 and 1917.

From Broodseinde bear N along the N303 to *Tyne Cot Cemetery, which is on the left side of the road. It was given its name by the soldiers of the 50th Northumbrian Division, who thought that an old barn there, which survived in the defensive complex they were attacking, looked like typical Tyneside cottages. The complex was eventually taken by the 2nd Australian Division on 4 October 1917. It was lost again in April 1918 and retaken the following September. While in Allied hands the largest of the bunkers was used as a forward dressing station. Those who died were buried nearby.

Designed by Herbert Baker, this is the largest British war cemetery in the world. It has nearly 12,000 graves and a memorial to about 35,000 missing. From the entrance the path ascends the gentle green slope between the massed graves to the Cross of Sacrifice, which is flanked by blockhouses on the mound. Below, and forming the mound, is part of the large bunker which was the objective of the 2nd Australian Division. Note the plaque which commemorates this attack. Later the bunker became the forward dressing station mentioned above. It is said that George V suggested that it be preserved and the Cross sited above it.

Between the Cross and the Stone of Remembrance, the scattered graves of October 1917 to April 1918 remain in their original positions. The great wall of the Memorial to the Missing records in a central apse the names of the New Zealand missing of Broodseinde and Passendale in October 1917.

The New Zealand soldiers who lost their lives in the Battle of Broodseinde on 4 October 1917, are also remembered on another memorial c 2km NW on the site of 's Graventafel crossroads, which the New Zealand Division assaulted and won.

From Tyne Cot the view northwards is across a tranquil landscape. In 1917 it was a scene of bloody carnage, as the Canadians fought their way in torrential rain through a sea of mud up the valley of the Strombeek towards Passendale.

Continue N on the N303. On the right along a grassy path there is a cairn monument to the 85th Canadian Infantry Battalion, Nova Scotia Highlanders, who fought here in 1917.

Passendale, perhaps better known as Passchendaele, is a name frequently used to describe the main offensive of the Third Battle of Ypres which ended with the capture of this ridge. It is a name, too, which has become synonymous with heroism, superhuman effort and tactical futility.

Held by the Germans from early in the war, the rubble, all that remained of Passchendaele, was taken by the Canadians on 6 November 1917. There have been many vivid descriptions of the contrast between the bloodied morass of water and mud on the western slope, up which they had fought, and the unsullied green fields which stretched away eastwards.

The principal monument here is the Canadian *Crest Farm Memorial*. It is sited just W of the small town, above the shallow valley where those who are commemorated suffered as much from the quagmire as from the shot and shell of the enemy.

In the town a window in the N transept of the church remembers the 66th Division. Tablets on the Stadhuis recall the Belgian Grenadiers and Carabiniers, who in September 1918 took Passendale after its reoccupation by the Germans during their desperate last fling in April 1918.

Two other tablets remind us that Passendale suffered in World War II. It was defended in 1940 by the Belgian 43rd Régiment de Ligne and liberated in 1944 by the 1st Polish Armoured Division.

In 1382 *Westrozebeke*, 4km to the N, was the scene of a very different kind of battle. Charles VI of France defeated the Flemish weavers here and killed their leader, Philip van Artevelde. The battle, which is described by Froissart, was fought on the spur of Goudberg to the S of the village. This high ground also marked the limit of the 1917 Allied advance.

We now turn S through Broodseinde and pass the 7th Division Monument to reach at Molenaarshoek, 1.5km S of Broodseinde, a minor road which bears SW. This will take us in an anticlockwise direction round the once notorious **Polygon Wood**, until 1914 the home of the Belgian army's Polygon riding school. All or parts of the wood changed hands several times between 1914 and 1918. As a result it became a lethal wilderness of pockmarked ground and shattered tree stumps. Today, replanted and carefully tended as a State forest, with the A19 motorway sweeping past its SW flank, the wood is a very different place. However, there are British and German bunkers, partially eroded shell craters, a number of memorials and two cemeteries to remind us of the past.

To the N of the circuit road *Polygon Wood Cemetery*, largely filled with New Zealand dead, lies behind a polygonal wall. Opposite, the *Buttes New British Cemetery* is approached through a glade. It is so called because until 1870 this was a Belgian army firing range. Its butts are marked today by a large mound surmounted by a memorial to the 5th Australian Division, which retook the wood in September 1917. Below are the serried ranks of graves and beyond is the New Zealand Memorial Pavilion, where the names of all the New Zealand missing, who fell in this sector between September 1917 and May 1918, are listed.

Rounding the wood the minor road crosses the motorway near Black Watch Corner, so called because the Royal Highlanders and Cameron Highlanders defied the Prussian Guard here in November 1914. It joins the Menen–Ypres road 2km W of **Geluveld**, which was lost, retaken and lost on 31 October 1914 during the First Battle of Ypres. The 2nd Welsh Regiment and 1st South Wales Borderers were driven from their trenches and forced back to the château. Brigadier General FitzClarence, later awarded the VC, with the 2nd Worcestershire Regiment, to which he had attached all the cooks, orderlies and others he could muster, relieved the Welsh and drove the enemy back. In this way he forced a delay, which is generally considered to have prevented a breakthrough to Ypres and even to the Channel ports.

Zandvoorde, 2km S of Geluveld, is closely associated with the Household Cavalry. On 26 October 1914 they charged to hold this position. Then, reinforced by other units, they dug in and held on until overwhelmed. The tall, graceful monument, which may be reached by a footpath off Komenstraat on the SE edge of the village, commemorates the 1st and 2nd Lifeguards and the Royal Horse Guards. Its simple inscription states that they 'died fighting in France and Flanders in 1914, many of them in defence of the ridge on which this cross stands'.

Menen, 3km E of Geluveld and just over the border from France, is an industrial town on the Lys. It was fortified by Vauban in 1685. The church at *Dadizele*, 6km N of Menen on the road to Roeselare, was built to house a miraculous statue of the Virgin which has been venerated since the 14C.

Returning towards Ypres from Geluveld the road passes a memorial on the right to the 2nd Worcestershire Regiment. Immediately afterwards it reaches the intersection once known as *Clapham Junction*. Here, on either side of the road, are two similar obelisk memorials. The memorial on the S is to 18th Division, engaged here in 1917. The other is to the Gloucestershire Regiment. One of its battalions fought around Geluveld in 1914 and another at Clapham Junction the following year.

Just beyond Clapham Junction is the *Bellewaerde Park*, a recreation centre and animal park. This has a safari train, monorail, cowboy village, Mexican village, wild-water river and many other amusements. Visitors buy a day ticket which provides unlimited admission to all the attractions. The park is open from Easter to the end of September.

Bellewaerde Park is spread over the area where the King's Royal Rifle Corps fought. Their memorial stands beside the coach park. Here, too, is

Hooge Crater Cemetery to the S. The Stone of Remembrance stands within a symbolic crater. The actual crater from which the cemetery takes its name was the result of a British mine exploded in July 1915. This is on private ground opposite.

Also roughly opposite is *Hooge Château*, a name notorious in the Salient story. On 31 October 1914 the château was the headquarters of the 1st and 2nd Divisions. Most of the staffs of these divisions were killed or gravely wounded by shelling at the crucial time of the fighting at Geluveld. The château was taken by the Germans after a gas attack in May 1915. Here two months later they used their new flame-thrower weapon, liquid fire, for the first time.

To the S, beyond Hooge and just before Birr Crossroads Cemetery is reached, a road, Canadalaan or Maple Avenue, turns back SE to pass *Sanctuary Wood Cemetery*. Here is the grave of Lieutenant Gilbert Talbot MC, after whom Talbot House at Poperinge is named (see below). The road continues to *Sanctuary Wood Trenches Museum* where scarred and long dead tree stumps, scattered débris and trenches mock its placid name. In the museum there are some remarkable bioscope photographs. These, the many pictures of devastated Ypres and of the wood, make it clear that if ever a sanctuary existed here, it was not for long. It probably derives its name from the brief period in October 1914, when orders were given by a brigade commander that some stragglers collected here were not to be sent back into the line immediately. However, the wood soon became a part of the front line. It was fought over by both sides, notably by the Canadians from April to August 1916. Their memorial is on Hill 62, or Mount Sorrel, just beyond the museum.

Rather more than 1 km W of its junction with Canadalaan, the N8 reaches the crossroads for Zillebeke to the S and Potijze to the N. This exposed spot of infamous reputation was known as *Hellfire Corner*. Today a scene of rural peace, typical of modern Flanders, it is difficult to see it as the centre of a flat expanse of devastation. The roads were lined with canvas screens, which may have been moderately successful in thwarting enemy observers, but did nothing to deter the gunners, who knew that there would always be a target behind them. In 1918 the Germans reached this spot, less than 1 km from Ypres.

The Southern Salient

This is a tour of some 40 km which includes the notorious Hill 60, the Messines or Mesen Ridge, dramatic scene of the opening phase of the Third Battle, Ploegsteert or 'Plugstreet' Wood, and the French area around Kemmelberg.

Leave Ypres by the Rijselstraat, which soon becomes the N365. This exit was less exposed than the Menen road and consequently was a more favoured approach to the front. Nevertheless the road crossing just beyond the first railway line soon earned itself the name of Shrapnel Corner. Just beyond this point the N365 continues in a southerly direction, but we turn E, cross another railway line and make a sharp turn to the SE. We pass the *Railway Dugout Burial Ground* or Transport Farm, where there are still traces of concrete in the embankment.

Zillebeke lake, just to the N, has a long history. Excavated some time before 1300 as a reservoir, it was for centuries a peaceful place. All this changed in 1914. The area around the lake became a morass, as artillery and other units dug into its banks. Today it is peaceful once more. A centre for angling and sailing, it supplies Ypres with water. Visitors have to search hard to find any traces of the war.

Continue to the SE and recross the railway tracks. After c 2km a sign indicates a turn to the left back across the railway to **Hill 60**. Before the war this was known as 'Côte des Amants', the Lovers' Knoll. However, from 1914 to 1918 this man-made hill, the spoil from the laying of the railway during the 19C, had, after Passendale, the most notorious name in the Salient. Fought over bitterly, the hill and the surrounding area changed hands six times between 1914 and 1918. Shelled unceasingly, drenched in gas, its mixed sand and clay was subjected to mining warfare on a massive scale. It very soon lost all resemblance to its original shape.

In 1930 Hill 60 was given to the Imperial War Graves Commission as a gift to the nations of the British Empire. Since then this unique memorial has been left, as far as is possible, in a natural state.

There are two monuments beside the parking area. One is to the 14th Light Division, the other to the 1st Australian Tunnelling Company which took over responsibility for the mine shafts in November 1916. The two mines here were the most northerly pair of the series stretching from the Messines Ridge. Their detonation on 7 June 1917 marked the opening of the Third Battle of Ypres. The bullet scars on the memorial bear witness to the fact that Hill 60 was fought over again in the Second World War.

To the left is the modern entrance with, beside it, a stone outlining the story of Hill 60. We may wander at will around this cratered place, but of course will see only what is on the surface. Below ground the war was waged as viciously as above. It is a salutary thought that beneath our feet is a tortuous labyrinth of collapsed tunnels and mineshafts, where countless Allied and German dead rest forever in catacombs made by their own hands.

The blockhouse, German in origin, was used by both sides. The memorial to Queen Victoria's Rifles, who fought here in 1915, was badly damaged in the fighting of 1940. Rebuilt, it now commemorates the victims of 1939 to 1945 also.

Beside the road, just beyond the Hill 60 entrance, there is a café which incorporates the *Hill 60 Museum*. The photographs in the museum are perhaps its most interesting feature.

We now return over the railway line and bear right and then left for *Sint Eloi* on the N365, passing en route the adjoining Chester Farm and Spoilbank cemeteries.

Wijtschate, 2km farther S and on the Messines Ridge, which overlooked Ypres and was therefore tactically vital, changed hands several times in bitter fighting. Signalling the start of the Third Battle of Ypres in June 1917, the German trenches here were blown apart by huge mines. The reverberations were felt as far away as London.

A glimpse from the German point of view of the days before the mines were exploded is offered by a museum 2km N of Wijtschate along a minor road which runs roughly parallel to the N365. Called variously the *Museum of Peace*, Bois 40 or, in German terminology, Croonaert, the museum has indoor and outdoor sections. The trenches and bunkers formed the advanced part of the German line from 1915–17. In them, it appears, Corporal Adolf Hitler was wounded in 1917. At any rate Hitler visited the area in 1940; see the photograph in the museum.

Perhaps the most interesting feature is a German mine shaft, 30m to 40m deep. There is no entry, but with care it is possible to peer into the flooded depths. The pond at the museum entrance marks the position of a German mine crater which was probably set and exploded from the shaft in the museum. A few metres away, beside Croonaert Chapel Cemetery, a French memorial recalls the fighting here in 1914.

At *Spanbroekmolen*, 2km SW of Wijtschate, off the Kemmel road (note the memorial to the 16th Irish Division en route) there is the crater of one of the largest of the 19 mines exploded at 03.10 on 7 June 1917. This had a charge of 91,000 lbs of ammonal laid at the end of a tunnel 517m long. Known as Lone Tree Crater, the site was acquired in 1930 by Lord Wakefield for Toc H. Now a pond c 25m deep, it is known as the Pool of Peace and preserved as a shrine, although for all its superficial tranquillity it can never shed its sinister associations.

Mesen (**Messines**) is 2km S of Wijtschate. On the left just outside this small town is the *London Scottish Memorial*. It records that near here on Hallow E'en 1914 the regiment went into action. By doing so, it earned the distinction of being the first Territorial Army battalion to engage the enemy. Its gallant, though doomed, charge attempted to relieve the cavalry which had held out against overwhelming odds for over 48 hours.

Mesen was taken in 1917, following the detonation of the mines, by the New Zealand Division which is commemorated in two places here. The *New Zealand Memorial to the Missing* is at Mesen Ridge Cemetery, immediately W of the town beside the Wulvergem road. *New Zealand Park* is just to the S of Mesen. Here there are two German bunkers close to the white obelisk divisional memorial, which records the capture of the ridge and an advance of 2000 yards to the division's objective beyond Mesen. The town is twinned with Featherston, New Zealand.

In the modest museum in the town hall, some emphasis is placed on the New Zealand Division and its exploits. The crypt of the church, all that survived the early fighting, is said to have sheltered Hitler.

Ploegsteert nicknamed 'Plugstreet' by the soldiers, 4km S of Mesen, is best known for its wood. Today thickly grown and private property, this still stretches across the northern high ground. Descending through the wood, the N365 passes the rotunda of the Ploegsteert Memorial to the Missing on the right and, opposite, Hyde Park Corner Cemetery. Until April 1918 *Ploegsteert Wood* was never fully taken by the Germans. For much of the war it was considered to be a relatively quiet area.

Turn E in the village and follow the roads, which encircle the wood, to visit the cemeteries. Perhaps the most interesting is Prowse Point which lies beyond the wood's northern edge and to the W of the village of Saint Yvon. It is named after Major, later Brigadier, Prowse who fought here with the Hampshire Regiment and Somerset Light Infantry in October 1914. Many of the graves are of members of the 2nd Dublin Fusiliers and 1st Royal Warwickshire, who defended this sector in the following month. The water below the Cross is part of the front line. Note the concrete shelter.

The road NE out of Ploegsteert, which starts the circuit of the wood, reaches *Comines* (Komen), at 10km. This is the principal town of an enclave of the province of Hainaut. It stands on the Lys, which forms the border with France. French Comines is across the river.

Comines was the birthplace of Philippe de Comines, c 1445–1509, the French statesman, biographer and historian. He entered the Burgundian court in 1463, but joined the service of Louis XI in 1472. Richly rewarded, he became one Louis' closest advisers. After Louis' death he fell from grace, lost many of his possessions and was imprisoned for eight months in an iron cage. He later regained favour and accompanied Charles VIII to Italy, where he met Machiavelli. His *Mémoirs* are considered to be the first French *essai* in history as distinct from chronicle.

W out of Ploegsteert and then N will bring you at 6km to *Nieuwekerke*, an important road junction. This was lost in 1918, but only after a party of the Worcestershire Regiment had held out for some time in the town hall, while the Germans occupied the rest of the town. **Kemmelberg**, 159m, 4km farther to the N, was long an invaluable buttress of the Allied position. Its loss by the French in April 1918 gravely endangered Allied communications, especially along the important Ypres–Poperinge road. The hill was retaken on 31 August by the British 34th Division.

The visitor who comes from Nieuwekerke, Dranouter and the W sees the *Ossuaire Français*, an obelisk surmounted by a cock. This covers the remains of 5294 men killed near here. Only 57 were identified and not all of these with certainty.

Beyond, at the top of a steep cobbled approach, stands the French monument to all who died in Belgium, and especially to those who lost their lives here in 1918. An unattractive column bearing a characterless Winged Victory, the monument was unveiled by General Pétain in 1932. Later it was damaged by lightning and the laurel-crowned helmet, which had crowned it, has never been replaced.

Farther along the road there is a look-out tower which is open from April to September. This is a rebuilding, which does not follow the design of the original. The woodland of Kemmelberg is still in part trenched and pockmarked, but the ground here is soft and erosion is steadily levelling and softening the marks of the past.

At the close of the 1918 German Spring offensive, the Allied line in this area ran from Vierstraat, 4km NE, to Loker, 3km W, which was twice lost and retaken by the French, thence to Méteren in France, 8km SW of Loker. The hills along the border, *Rodeberg* (Mont Rouge) and *Zwarteberg* (Mont Noir) form a small chain which became vital for Allied observation after the loss of Kemmelberg.

Kemmel is 8km from Ypres. At 2km, just before Vierstraat, the road passes an American memorial. A simple white stone honours 'the services of American Troops who fought in this vicinity 18 August–4 September 1918'.

Circa 1km to the W, on the road to Ypres, is the lake of *Dikkebus*. Access is from the N375. This was produced by the damming of the 'Kleine Kemmelbeek' in 1320. Water from the lake passed to the town through oak pipes. It still supplies Ypres with water, though now by way of a filtration and pumping station. On the bank is the Vauban Tower of 1684. This is used to regulate the water supply by means of a sluice gate. The lake, which has an area of 36 ha., is a popular place of recreation with facilities for rowing and angling.

Poperinge

Poperinge, 12km W of Ypres, may be reached by either the N308, the old road, or by the faster N38. Through this back area five million British and other troops marched, first to run the gauntlet at Ypres and then to take their places around the Salient. One million returned wounded. About 300,000 died.

Known simply as 'Pop' to the British soldiers, Poperinge is a pleasant, rather sedate town with a population of c 20,000, the centre of a district where hops have been grown since about 1400. It has some very good hotels and is an excellent centre for visiting places connected with the Great War. Poperinge is twinned with Hythe in Kent.

Once a cloth town, Poperinge was unable to compete with Ypres and in the early 15C turned to hops. It is mentioned several times in English literature. Chaucer, c 1345–1400, says that the hero of the 'Rime of Sir Thopas' was born 'in Flaundres, al beyonde the sea, at Popering, in the place'. Mercutio in Shakespeare's 'Romeo and Juliet', 1594, refers to the 'poperin pear', a variety which came to England from this district, while Sebastian, in 'The Atheist's Tragedy' by Cyril Tourneur, c 1575–1626, describes a 'poppring pear tree'.

In 1436 Philip the Good was helped by the men of Poperinge when he attacked Calais, which was held by the English. In revenge the English besieged Poperinge, burning down the Sint Bertinuskerk and killing 2500 of the inhabitants. Lancelot Blondeel, the painter, was born here in 1496.

Occupied by the Germans in August 1914, it was retaken in October. Poperinge was shelled from time to time during the 1914 to 1918 war and bombed in May 1940. Fortunately the principal buildings suffered little damage.

The *Sint Bertinuskerk* is dedicated to a Benedictine abbot who died c 700. Sited in the Botermarkt, the main square, it is an outstanding example of the Flemish hall-church. Dating from the 15C, it replaced the church burnt down by the English in 1436. The interior has some good woodwork, including an 18C pulpit brought from the Dominican church in Bruges, two baroque confessionals and an 18C rood-screen.

The town has two other interesting churches. Both date from c 1290 but have later alterations and additions. The church of *Onze Lieve Vrouw*, in Kasselstraat, has a tower of c 1400, a 16C portal and splendid choir stalls of 1752 by E. Wallijn. The church of *Sint Jan*, in Bruggestraat, also has woodwork by Wallijn. It houses a miraculous figure of Our Lady of St John.

In Gasthuisstraat, so called from an ancient hospice founded here in 1312, is *Talbot House*. This was popularly known as 'Toc H' from the army signallers' alphabet of the First World War. It was named after Gilbert Talbot, who was killed at Hooge on 30 July 1915. He was the younger brother of the senior chaplain of the 16th Division. The house, placed in the charge of the Revd P.B. Clayton, served as club and home, 'Everyman's Club', to half a million officers and men from December 1915 until the end of the war.

The Revd P.B. Clayton CH, MC, 1885–1972, founded Toc H, a world-wide active Christian voluntary movement for people of all ages. Talbot House, bought by Lord Wakefield for Toc H in 1929, now serves as a centre of European reconciliation. Visitors are welcome and limited self-catering accommodation is available. The house has many interesting features. Much of its contents were saved during the Second World War by local people who hid them in their homes.

Skindles, a short distance along the street, was originally an 18C patrician home. During the First World War it was, in turn, the advanced head-quarters of Sir Douglas Haig and a British officers' club.

The *Nationaal Hopmusem* at 71 Gasthuisstraat occupies the former municipal weighhouse which dates from 1866. The weighbridge, which was in use from 1866 to 1966, forms part of the museum. All aspects of the growing of hops and their use are explained. The visit ends with a taste of the regional brew. The museum is open in May, June and September on Sunday and public holidays from 14.30 to 17.30, and in July and August daily at the same times.

The huge war cemetery of *Lijssenthoek*, 3km SW, has some 9900 Commonwealth graves, mostly of men who died of their wounds in the nearby casualty clearing stations.

8

Ostend to Brussels

Total distance 116km.—*15km* **Jabbeke**—*10km* **Bruges**—*24km* **Eeklo**—*18km* **Ghent**—*26km* **Aalst**—*23km* **Brussels**. For Jabbeke, take the E40 motorway; from Bruges to Brussels follow the N9.

At *15km* **Jabbeke** the *Constant Permeke Museum*, 341 Gistelsesteenweg, has been established in a house built by the artist in 1929. Permeke, 1886–1952, was a painter, sculptor and one of the leaders of the Flemish Expressionist movement.

The house, which he called 'Les Quatre Vents', because the façades look to the four cardinal points, contained a large studio. In addition to 80 canvases and sketches, the museum possesses almost all of Permeke's sculptures. Among the paintings, note especially 'Au Sujet de Permeke', 'La Moisson', 'Paysage Breton', 'L'Adieu' and 'Le Pain Quotidien' and among the sculptures, 'Niobé', 'Le Semeur' and 'Marie Lou'. The museum is open daily, except Monday, from April to October between 10.00 and 12.30 and from 13.30 to 18.00, 17.00 from November to March.

Klein Strand, a popular recreational area just NW of Jabbeke, has a beach and lake where water skiing displays are given in summer.

For *10km* Bruges, see Route 9.

Leave Bruges by the Kruispoort. At *4km Male* the abbey of Trudo occupies the site and part of a castle which belonged to the counts of Flanders. The 14–15C keep has been restored.

The border with East Flanders is crossed before 8km Maldegem.

9km **Eeklo** (population 19,000), is an important agricultural and textiles centre. It is the principal town of the MEETJESLAND, the land of little meadows. The Tourist Information Office is in the fine Markt Plein. Note the early 17C *Stadhuis* with belfry. Karel Ledeganck, 1805–47, a leading Flemish poet, was born in Eeklo.

The town's museum, the Musée de la Forêt et du Folklore 'Het Leen', is in the provincial park 2km to the S. Its collection is concerned mainly with folklore, natural history and trade. The museum is open daily, except Monday morning, from 10.00 to 12.00 and 14.00 to 16.00 between Easter and September.

Kaprijke, 4km to the NE, has an attractive 17–18C town hall. From here the road N traverses polder country en route to 6km **Watervliet**, which is near the Dutch border. Here the 15C church was restored in 1893, when the tower was built, and again in 1973 to make good war damage. It has an altar from the workshop of Luc Fayd'herbe, a pulpit and other woodwork by Hendrik Pulincx and a 15C Descent from the Cross which is ascribed to Quinten Metsys.

For *18km* **Ghent**, see Route 13. After leaving Ghent you cross the Scheldt at *8km Melle*. There are begonia gardens and a horticultural college on the N bank.

At *18km* is **Aalst** (population 78,000), on the canalised river Dender. The Tourist Information Office is in the Grote Markt. Today a textiles and brewing town, Aalst was from the 13C a seat of the court of the counts of Flanders and an assembly-place of the States-General until the end of the 15C. It suffered bombardment during the First and bombing during the Second World War.

The centre and the most attractive part of the town is the irregular GROTE MARKT. Here there is a statue by Jan Geefs, 1856, of Dirk Martens, c 1450–1534, a humanist and the first Belgian printer. He produced his work, 'Speculum Conversionis Peccatorum', at Aalst in 1473.

At the NW corner of the square stands the *Schepenhuis*, the former town hall. Of the original building of c 1225 only the left and rear façades and something of the lower part survive. Most of what is visible today dates from the early 15C. The *belfry*, completed in 1466, has statues of a knight and a citizen, symbols of power and freedom. Concerts are given on the carillon of 52 bells during the summer. The Flamboyant Gothic corner gallery of 1474 was used for the making of proclamations. Its 19C statues represent Justice; Charles V; Dirk, the last lord of Aalst, 1166; Pieter Coecke, 1502–50, who lived here and was one of the apostles of Renaissance art and Cornelis de Schrijver, 1482–1588, secretary of Antwerp.

The *Stadhuis* by Louis Roelandt, 1831, preserves in its courtyard the façade of the Landhuis of 1646, seat of the States of Flanders when Aalst was the provincial capital.

The arcaded building on the left, now a restaurant, was originally the *Vleeshuis*. Later it became the meeting-place of the Barbaristes, the literary guild of St Barbara. Burnt in 1743, it was rebuilt five years later.

The *Sint Maartenskerk*, just E of the Grote Markt, is a large Gothic building of 1480–1638. In the main it follows the designs of Jan van der Wouwe and Herman and Domien Waghemakere, father and son, who built the cathedral at Antwerp. However, because of the wars of the 16C the church was never finished. A baroque portal was added in 1730.

Do not miss the celebrated painting by Rubens in the S transept of *St Roch receiving from Christ the gift of healing the plague-stricken. This saint, 1350–80, was a native of Montpellier in France. He devoted his life to tending victims of the plague. He is often depicted with a dog licking a plague spot on his leg. Rubens' large and highly decorative composition is in a contemporary carved wood frame, which also encloses some minor works from the painter's studio. Carried off to Paris in 1794, the picture was returned in 1816, largely through the efforts of the Duc de Berri, who had been a refugee in Aalst.

In the next chapel there is a picture of St Simon Stock by Gaspard de Crayer. Simon Stock, among the first English members of the Carmelites, became in 1247 the sixth general of the order. He was largely instrumental in establishing Carmelite houses in many European university cities— Cambridge in 1248, Oxford in 1253 and Paris in 1260. His relics are kept at the Carmelite Priory at Aylesford in Kent.

The fine marble *tabernacle of 1605 is by Jérôme Duquesnoy the Elder. Some of the guild chapels have vault paintings. The oldest and best dates from 1497. Restored in 1947 it is in the E chapel. In the chapel of the Sacré-Coeur is the tomb of Dirk Martens the printer (see above). This bears an epitaph by Erasmus. In the first ambulatory chapel on the right there is an Adoration of the Shepherds by Otto Venius.

Just to the E of the church at 13 Oude Vismarkt are the 15–17C buildings of the former hospital of *Onze Lieve Vrouw*. The restored courtyard and surrounding rooms provide an attractive setting for the *Museum Oud Hospitaal*. This has an interesting collection of objects from Aalst and its environs including some material from the Roman period. It is open from Monday to Thursday between 10.00 and 12.00 and from 14.00 to 17.00, on Saturday from 14.00 to 17.00 and on Sunday from 10.30 to 12.00 and 14.00 to 18.00.

From the church follow Pontstraat in a SE direction. Off the left side is the *Begijnhof* with a chapel of 1787. This has been converted into a group of small houses, more or less on the lines of the original foundation.

At *Moorsel*, 4km to the E, there are a 13–14C church and, beside the road, a moated château built in 1646.

5km from Aalst you reach *Hekelgem* and cross the border into Brabant. This town of 11,000 inhabitants was once famous for its 'Zandtapijts', sand carpets or sand pictures.

The art of Zandtapijts, once widespread in Flemish villages, demands many weeks of meticulous work and is now rarely seen. The 'carpet' is built up on a board divided into squares. On this the artist first produces his outlines and then lays down the chosen sand colours. Pictures may be originals or copies of famous works.

The *abbey of Afflighem* is on the N edge of Hekelgem. Founded in the 11C, it was almost completely destroyed in 1796. All that survive are one wall of the church nave and some 17C buildings. These include the entrance lodge. Since the site was reoccupied by the Benedictines in 1869, there has been extensive rebuilding. The large church was completed in 1972. At Afflighem lie Godfrey of Louvain and his daughter Adeliza, who died in 1151. She was the second queen of Henry I of England.

For *18km* Brussels, see Route 1.

9

Bruges and Damme

BRUGES is the English and French name for the Flemish town of **Brugge**, population 119,000, the capital of the province of West Flanders. Almost entirely surrounded by waterways, which follow the line of the old fortifications, the town is linked to its port at Zeebrugge, to Ostend and Ghent and, via Damme, to Sluis in Holland by canals.

The beauty of its buildings and their setting along the many small, picturesque canals which meander under the bridges that give the town its name, its rich historical and commercial background and its wealth of art treasures combine to make Bruges one of Belgium's most popular tourist centres.

However, Bruges is not only a tourist town. Since the opening of the canal to Zeebrugge and the development of the port at the turn of the 19–20C, it has regained much of its medieval prosperity and become of increasing industrial importance. Industry, however, is confined to the perimeter and is not allowed to intrude into the historic part of the town.

Centre. Markt.

Tourist Information. *Bruges* at the Stadhuis 12 Burg, tel: 050-448111. Open between April and September from Monday to Friday 09.30 to 18.30, Saturday, Sunday, public holidays, 10.00 to 12.00 and 14.00 to 18.30; October to March from Monday to Saturday 09.30 to 12.45 and 14.00 to 17.45.

Provincial Tourist Board for West Flanders: Kasteel Tillegem, 8200 Brugge, tel: 050-380296, located to the SW between Bruges and the motorway.

Post Office. Markt.

Station. On the S edge of the town, 1.5km from the centre. There is a taxi rank and frequent bus services to the Markt and places in the surrounding area.

How to see the Town. *On Foot*. Most places of interest to visitors are within walking distance of the Markt. The Tourist Office outline guide and map suggest several walking itineraries, most of which are based on specific themes. In July and August there are daily guided walks. These usually leave the Tourist Information Office in the Burg at 15.00.

Horse-drawn Carriage: March to November daily between 10.00 and 18.00. Departures, on demand, are from the Burg or on Wednesday morning from the Markt. Duration of tour 35 minutes.

Bicycle Hire: Rent-A-Bicycle 'T Koffieboontje, 4 Hallestraat and Eric Popelier, 14 Hallestraat.

Canal Boats: There are several embarkation points. March to November daily from 10.00 to 18.00; duration of tour 35 minutes. Bookings may be made at the Tourist Information Office or directly with the companies.

There are also boat excursions to Damme from April to September daily, and to Ghent. Apply to the Tourist Information Office for details.

Coach and *Minibus*. Information and bookings through Tourist Information.

Museum Tickets. A combined ticket for the Groeninge, Gruuthuse, Memling and Brangwyn museums saves money.

Lace. Bruges has long been known for the quality of its lace, which reached the apogee of its fame in the 17C. Today lacemakers are rarely seen on the doorsteps of their houses. However, Bruges still produces excellent hand and machine made lace. This can bought from many shops in the town centre. The best-known Bruges designs are the flower pattern, rose lace and the witch-stitch. Visitors with a particular interest in lace should visit the Gruuthuse Museum and the Kant Centrum, the Lace Centre.

History. Bruges developed under the protection of a castle built in 865 by Baldwin Iron Arm, the first Count of Flanders, mainly for defence against the attacks of Norse raiders. Thereafter the settlement prospered rapidly because of its proximity to the estuary, Het Zwin (see Route 3), which at that time penetrated as far as Damme and was connected to Bruges by the Reie. In the 13C Bruges was further enriched by the manufacture of cloth. Its annual fair was one of the most important in Flanders.

Dissentions between the francophile counts, set on protecting their privileges, and the merchants gave Philip the Fair of France a pretext for intervening in the affairs of Bruges. He made a triumphal entry in 1301. The luxury displayed by the wives of the burghers on that occasion excited the envy of Philip's consort, Joanna of Navarre.

French rule proved to be oppressive and in the following year the citizens, headed by Pieter de Coninck and Jan Breydel, rose in revolt. On 18 May 1302 they massacred the French, putting to death all those unable to pronounce correctly the shibboleth 'Schild en Vriend', shield and friend. This event became known as the 'Bruges Matins'. Six weeks later Bruges played a prominent part in the defeat of the French at the Battle of the Golden Spurs near Kortrijk, when large numbers of the French nobility were slain.

During the 14C and 15C, the period of Burgundian rule, despite having to surrender many of its privileges to Philip the Good, Bruges reached its greatest level of prosperity. It became the chief market of the Hanseatic League, an association of cities, mainly in N Germany, which flourished from the 14C to the 17C. The league's principal aims were the suppression of piracy and the arrangement of commercial treaties. As well as being a famous banking centre, Bruges traded in fabrics from Italy and the East, furs from Russia and the Balkans, metals from Hungary, Poland and Bohemia, wool, cheese and coal from the British Isles, fruit from Spain, Arabian spices and Rhenish wines. It is recorded that as many as 150 vessels entered the port in a single day and that the population grew to over 80,000.

The town's tapestry manufacturers became world-famous. Great artists like Jan van Eyck and Hans Memling found patrons among its rich citizens. In 1430 Philip the Good established his famous Order of the Golden Fleece here, partly as a compliment to the skill of the Flemish weavers. Bruges was the meeting-place of the first States General of the Netherlands held in 1464.

After the death of Philip in Bruges in 1467, there began a period of slow decline in the fortunes of the town. Among the factors contributing to this were the silting of Het Zwin, a general recession in the cloth industry, changing trade routes and the transfer from Burgundian to Habsburg sovereignty. As retaliation against infringements of its privileges, Bruges somewhat unwisely held its ruler, the Archduke Maximilian, prisoner for three months in 1488. One unfortunate result was that from then onwards Maximilian favoured Antwerp. That town rapidly outstripped Bruges and became the official Hanseatic emporium in 1545. Bruges acquired the sobriquet 'Bruges-la-Morte'.

From the 16C to the 18C it suffered frequent attacks and was besieged often. It did not begin to recover its prosperity until the digging of the Boudewijn Kanaal and the development of the port of Zeebrugge in the period 1895 to 1907.

Prominent Natives and Foreigners. Bruges, 'Brugges', is mentioned frequently by Chaucer and other early English writers. Later Wordsworth wrote of its quiet streets and Longfellow of its towering belfry. Life in 15C Bruges is described vividly by the modern Scottish author, Dorothy Dunnett.

Caxton, c 1422–91, while living in Bruges, was acting 'governor of the English nation', i.e. head of the Merchant Adventurers in the Low Countries from 1462–70. Here he 'practised and learnt at great charge and dispense' the art of printing. Later, in partnership with the Bruges printer Collaert Mansion, he set up a press and produced his 'Recuyell of the Historyes of Troye', the first printed book in English.

The exiled Charles II established his court in Bruges in 1656 and was elected by the burghers 'King of the Archers' Guild of St Sebastian'. In the same year he founded the Royal Regiment of Guards, thus making Bruges the birthplace of the Grenadier Guards.

Simon Stevinus, 1548–1620, mathematician and physicist, writer on fortifications, book-keeping and decimals, inventor of a carriage propelled by sails, and expert in the use of sluices for war purposes, was born here. So was Frans Gomeer, or Gomarus, 1563–1641, rigid Calvinist theologian and opponent of Arminius.

Bruges also attracted great artists. Jan van Eyck lived in what is now Gouden Handstraat and died here in 1441. Hans Memling occupied a house in the present Sint Jorisstraat, the extension of Vlamingstraat and Frans Pourbus the Younger lived in the parallel Jan Miraelstraat. Gerard David died in Bruges in 1523.

For Damme, see Section C. below. For Bruges to Ostend, Ghent and Brussels, see Route 8, to Zeebrugge, see Route 3, to Kortrijk, see Route 10.

A. Central and Southern Bruges

The geographical and social centre of the town is the MARKT, a typical Flemish square of irregular shape. With several 17C houses, it is dominated on the S by the ancient Halle and Belfry. In the centre stands a monument by Paul de Vigne, 1887, to Jan Breydel and Pieter de Coninck, the leaders of the 'Bruges Matins' uprising of 1302. On the E are the 19C buildings of the **Provinciaal Hof**, seat of the provincial government and of the **Post Office**. The N side is lined with restaurants and cafés, many with outside terraces. Sint Amandstraat, leading off the W side, has on one corner the *Huis Bouchoute*, a tall square house of the late 15C, which in 1656–57 was the residence in exile of Charles II of England. On the other side of the street the Craenenburg, where Maximilian was held by the burghers for three months in 1488, once stood.

The 13C **Halle**, a quadrilateral block built around a central courtyard, has been restored several times, mainly in the 16C and 17C. The building long served as the main market. Until the late 18C there was a canal up to this corner of the Markt. Until 1769 laws were promulgated from the balcony above the entrance.

The Belfry, Bruges

The *Belfry, one of the finest structures of its kind, is the most prominent architectural feature in Bruges. Since the 13C a symbol of civic power and pride, it is visible for many miles across the polders. Replacing a wooden tower which was burnt down in 1240, it is 83m in height and leans 1.19m to the SE. The two lower storeys date from 1282–96 and the octagonal upper portion from 1482–87.

The Belfry may be climbed from April to September daily between 09.30 and 12.30, 13.30 and 18.00, from October to March daily from 09.30 to 12.30 and 14.00 to 17.00. There are 366 steps to the top. The first halt is at the Treasure Room. Usually this may be viewed only through the door grille. The town charters were once kept here. The fine vaulting dates from 1285, and the equally fine wrought-iron, the work of Nicolaas Grootwerc, from 1300. At the 172nd step you will cross a room which affords a view upwards. At the 220th step there is a landing with a board on which visitors, who cannot resist the urge, are invited to write their names instead of elsewhere. At step 333 the carillon with its huge drum and the works of the clock of

1748 by Antonius de Hondt is reached. The clock chimes every quarter-hour. In good weather there is a magnificent panoramic view from the top of the tower. Incised arrows indicate the direction of places which can be seen.

On the S side of Oude Burg behind the Halle an archway provides access to the small Karthuizerinnenstraat, named after the Carthusian nuns whose chapel of 1632 was much restored in 1927. Here is a War Memorial Chapel, set up by the town in honour of the fallen of both World Wars. In the crypt-like interior there are an effigy of a soldier in white marble, and the ashes of victims who perished in Dachau concentration camp.

Wollestraat, beside the Halle, is the shortest way from the Markt to the canal, the boat embarkation stages and the Groeninge, Brangwyn and Gruuthuse museums (see below). No. 28 Wollestraat is the house *In de Grote Mortier*, 1634, decorated with damaged carvings of the relief of Bruges from a siege of 1631.

Beside the Post Office, Breidelstraat leads to the BURG. This square occupies the site of the original 9C fortress, in whose shadow Bruges developed. On the left, on entering the square, stands the **Landshuis**, a late Renaissance building of 1664 by F. van Hillewerve. This was formerly occupied by the Provost of the church of Sint Donatian, the patron saint of Bruges. A Roman, who became Bishop of Rheims, Donatian died in 390. His relics were brought to Bruges in the 9C. The church, which dated from the 10C, stood in the adjacent garden. It became a cathedral in 1559 and was demolished by the French in 1799. A fragment of the choir with a small reproduction of the apse has been re-erected here. A statue of the painter Jan van Eyck, who was buried in the church, stands nearby.

Opposite, forming a splendid group, are from right to left the Basilica of the Holy Blood, the Town Hall, the former Recorder's House, and the old Law Courts building where the Tourist Office is now located.

The **Heilig Bloedbasiliek**, the Basilica of the Holy Blood, derives its name from a precious relic, some drops of the blood of Christ, which is enshrined here. The building has two storeys. Below is a chapel of the 12C. Above this, a 15C or 16C chapel, which is reached by a staircase of 1523, houses the relic of the holy blood. According to an ancient tradition this was given by the Patriarch of Jerusalem to Dirk of Alsace, Count of Flanders in 1147, during the Second Crusade. It was a reward for the bravery the Count had shown in battles against the Saracens. The coagulated blood, in a rock-crystal phial which dates from the 11C or 12C, has been preserved intact since its arrival in Bruges. The first reference to the relic is in a document dated 1256. However, some historians suggest a different provenance. They are of the opinion that the relic came from Constantinople and that it was part of the treasure stolen by the Crusaders after they had attacked and captured that city in 1204. An account by a French knight, Robert of Clari, who was present at the siege and who witnessed the subsequent looting, states that a number of sacred relics were found by the Crusaders in the chapel of the Bucoleon, the imperial palace of the Byzantine emperors. These included two large sections of the True Cross, the lance and nails which had pierced the side, hands and feet of Christ and 'a crystal phial which contained a good quantity of his blood'.

Baldwin of Flanders, who was chosen to be the new emperor of Byzantium, presumably had the pick of the ill-gotten gains which he would have sent for safe keeping to his daughters Margaret and Joanna who ruled in Flanders during his absence. These pious ladies, famous for the number of religious and charitable foundations which they established during their reign, would have had no difficulty in finding suitable locations for their new treasures.

Supporters of this theory point out that the style in which the rock crystal phial is cut suggests that it was produced in Constantinople. However, because of the centuries which separate us from the events and the paucity of reliable information about the relic it is unlikely that we will ever discover how the relic of the holy blood came to Bruges.

The Lower Chapel was built to house a relic of St Basil the Great. This was brought from the Holy Land c 1099 by Count Robert II of Flanders, who also brought the relic of the True Cross now at Veurne. St Basil, c 330–79, was Metropolitan of Caesarea in Cappadocia. He preached and wrote against the Arians and Macedonians and saved Cappadocia for the Catholic faith. In the Eastern Church Basil is revered as the first of the three Holy Hierarchs, in the West as one of the four Great Doctors.

The chapel, rebuilt in 1134 by Count Thierry of Alsace, was restored in the 19C. It is a dark, crypt-like Romanesque structure, one of the purest of its kind in Flanders. It has a 13C or 14C figure of the Virgin, protected by part of its original iron enclosure and an altarpiece of 1530. There is also a (?) 12C bas-relief of the baptism of Christ or, perhaps, of St Basil.

The relic of the Holy Blood is kept in the Upper Chapel. Originally Romanesque, this is 15–16C Gothic in style with many alterations, the latest made in 1934. The stained-glass windows of 1847 have portraits, based on 15C originals, of the dukes of Burgundy. The pulpit of 1728 by Hendrik Pulincx, representing the terrestrial globe, is carved from one piece of oak.

The sacred relic is in a silver reliquary presented by Albert and Isabella in 1611. It is venerated every Friday between 08.30 and 11.45 and from 15.00 to 16.00. There is a religio-historical Procession of the Holy Blood on the first Monday after 2 May through the old part of the inner town.

The **Museum of the Holy Blood**. This is a small, single-room museum where church treasures and pictures are exhibited. On the entrance wall hangs a Flemish tapestry of 1637 depicting the Translation of the body of St Augustine. In a case below there are 15C chasubles and a number of manuscripts. Along the left side of the room, on either side of a reliquary of the Holy Blood of 1614–17, are two very fine shutters of a triptych depicting Members of the Brotherhood of the Holy Blood by Pieter Pourbus, 1556. The reliquary is an exquisite work in gold, silver and precious stones by Jan Crabbe of Bruges. Note also a triptych of the Crucifixion attributed to van Dyck, a 15C Life of St Barbara by the Master of the St Barbara Legend, and several pictures within an illustrated frame of the Life of the Virgin by an unknown artist of c 1500. On the opposite wall are a triptych of the Descent from the Cross, 1620, by the Master of the Holy Blood and an Adoration of the Magi by van Dyck.

The museum is open daily, except on Wednesday afternoon, between April and September from 09.30 to 12.00 and 14.00 to 18.00 and between October and March from 10.00 to 12.00 and 14.00 to 16.00. It is closed on 1 January, 1 November, 25 December.

The **Stadhuis**, which dates from 1376–1420, is the oldest Gothic town hall in Belgium. It provided a magnificent setting for the first meeting of the States General of the Netherlands, which took place here in 1464. The façade has three graceful octagonal turrets. In the niches between the windows are statues of the counts and countesses of Flanders. These replace effigies destroyed by the French in 1792.

The entrance hall has a joisted ceiling resting on four stone pillars. Off this is a broad passage where large 19C canvases, the Death of Mary of Burgundy by Camille van Camp, 1878, and Rubens at the deathbed of Brueghel by Bruno van Hollebeke, are hung.

The great *Gothic Hall, scene of the meeting of the first States General, is on the first floor. The superb wood ceiling, with a double row of six hanging painted arches, dates from 1385–1402. The 12 vault-keys have scenes from the New Testament and the 16 corbels represent the months and the elements. Around the walls are 12 paintings by Albert and Julien Devriendt, 1895, which illustrate the history of Bruges in a vivid and animated fashion. The Maritime Hall, opening off the Gothic Hall, is devoted to the harbour of Bruges and the Boudewijn canal to Zeebrugge.

The Stadhuis is open daily from 09.30 to 17.00 from April to September and from 09.30 to 12.30 and 14.00 to 17.00 from October to March. It is closed 1 January and on Ascension Day afternoon.

To the left of the Stadhuis stands the **Oude Griffie**, the former Recorder's House. Now used as part of the Law Courts, it is a richly decorated Renaissance building of 1537 by Christian Sixdeniers, with sculptures by Willem Aerts.

The **Gerechtshof**, the former Law Courts, now houses the Tourist Office. It was built in 1722 on the site of the palace of the Brugse Vrije, the Liberty of Bruges, an independent jurisdiction whose writ stretched as far as Dunkirk, but did not include the town of Bruges. Fragments of the 15C palace survive. These include a part of the Schepenzaal, the hall in which the magistrates of the Liberty held their courts. This now houses the **Brugse Vrije Museum**. Note the splendid Renaissance *chimneypiece in black marble, with oak carvings, executed in 1529 by various artists working under the direction of Lancelot Blondeel. The wooden statues by Guyot de Beaugrant are, centre, Charles V, right, Maximilian of Austria and Mary of Burgundy and, left, Ferdinand of Aragon and Isabella of Castile. The princes wear the insignia of the Golden Fleece and the composition may be regarded as a glorification of the Order.

The museum is open daily, except Monday, from April to September between 10.00 to 12.30 and 14.00 to 17.00, and from October to March on Saturday and Sunday from 14.00 to 16.00.

The road under the arch of the Oude Griffie passes the site of the old south gate, which is marked by a plaque. It then crosses the main canal, which runs through central Bruges. On the left in Groene Rei, the extension of Steenhouwersdijk, is *De Pelicaan*, a picturesque ancient almshouse which overlooks a quiet stretch of canal. Ahead and to the left is the *Vismarkt*, the fish market, with its Doric colonnade of 1821. Beyond in the Braambergstraat are several 17C façades. To the right, where the canal turns sharply, is an attractive little square, the Huidevettersplaats. Canal boat tours start from here. At Nos 11 and 12, the *Huidevettershuis*, 1630 and 1716, was the guild house of the tanners. Note the descriptive stonework above the windows.

Following the canal, continue along Rozenhoedkaai to the bridge at the foot of Wollestraat. The statue on the parapet is of St John Nepomuk. A native of Nepomuk in Bohemia, he became canon of Prague and chaplain to Queen Sophie, the second wife of the dissolute Wenceslas IV. According to tradition he was thrown into the Moldau and drowned in 1383 or 1393, because he refused to reveal to the king details of the queen's confession.

From 1578 to 1583 the Holy Blood was hidden from the Protestant iconoclasts in the turreted house of c 1480 in the angle of the quay. The road now becomes a pleasant promenade by the canal. Here, on Dyver, the footsore traveller may rest for a quiet hour on a tree-shaded bench. Hopefully, his lazy contemplation of the unhurried, unending procession of boats will refresh and strengthen him for the next cultural encounter.

BRUGES
Centre
0 metres   200

N

St Jacob

Theatre
BEURS

Prinsenhof

MUNT
PLEIN

Munt Poort

MARKT

Belfry

St Salvator
Cathedral

Gruuthuse
Museum

Orged
Mus.

T. ZAND

Onze Lieve Vrouw

St Jans Hosp.
(Memling Mus.)

Begijnhof

Lock
Ho.

Minnewater

GENTHOF
OENSDAGMARKT
St Anna
PEPERSTRAAT

huis
N VAN
KPLAATS
SPINOLARE
orters Loge
ENGELSESTRAAT
KONINGSTRAAT
St Walburga

JAN STRAAT
MOLENMEERS

ST. WALBURGASTRAAT
RIDDERSTRAAT
BOOMGARDSTR
VERBRAND NIEUWLAND

TWIJNSTRAAT
HILIPSTOCKSTR
LANGESTRAAT

HOOGSTRAAT
De Pelicaan
GROENE REI

ndshuis
PREDIKHERENSTRAAT
ELSTRAAT
BURG
Gerechtshof
STEENHOUWERSDIJK
WITTE
COUPURE

Stadhuis
Oude
eilig
Griffie
WAALSESTRAAT
ZWART
LEERROUWERS
loedbazilïek
Fish
Mkt
BRAAMBERGSTRAAT
KRUITENBERGSTR
LEERROUWERS STRAAT
HUIDEVETTERS
PLAATS

LLESTRAAT
ROZENHOEDKAAI
WAALSESTRAAT

War
emorial
Chap
EEKHOUTSTRAAT
JOZEF SUVEESTR
GEVANGSTR PARK
WINGFIBROTGESTRAAT
ENGEL STRAAT

DYVER
Koningin
SCHAARSTRAAT
COUPURE

EEKHOUTPOORT
Astrid

angwyn Mus.
Park

Groeninge
Mus.
GARENMARKT
CAPAARDSTRAAT

FACIUSBRUG

GROENINGE
GENTWEG
NIEUWE
GENTWEG
WILLEMIJNENDREEF

NIEUWE
GENTWEG
WERKHUISSTRAAT
GENTPOORTSTRAAT

OUDE
GENTWEG
Gentpoort

TELLINESTRAAT
OUDE GENTWEG

Acad. of Fine Arts
VISSPANSTRAAT
BOUDEWIJN RAVESTRAAT
GENTPOORTVEST

On Saturday and Sunday afternoons from March to October a lively flea market is held by the water's edge. At No. 2 Dyver the Brugse Boekhandel, perhaps the best bookshop in Bruges, has a large selection of publications in several languages including English. Farther along the quay on the left and close to each other are the Groeninge, Brangwyn and Gruuthuse museums. A combined ticket, which saves money, will admit the visitor to all three museums and to the Memling museum.

The **··Groeninge Museum**, reached through an archway, occupies the site of the ancient abbey of Eekhout. In a neighbourhood which has been called 'Groeninge' since the 13C, it was built between 1929 and 1930 to bring under one roof a number of collections which belong to the town. These include its greatest glory, an outstanding group of Flemish Primitive paintings. There are, in addition, some fine works of the 16C, 17C and 18C, and a representative selection of paintings of the 19C and 20C.

The collections have outgrown the exhibition space available, so some pictures are shown in rotation. The following account deals with a representative selection and offers a more or less chronological tour through the 15 rooms of the museum. Room numbers indicate probable locations. For a more detailed account of the collection visitors are referred to the handsomely illustrated catalogue in English published in the series Musea Nostra. This may be obtained in the museum.

The Groeninge Museum is open daily from April to September between 09.30 and 17.00, from October to March, daily except Tuesday, from 09.30 to 12.30, 14.00 to 17.00. It is closed 1 January and Ascension Day afternoon.

Our visit begins with *Jan van Eyck's* ··Madonna with St Donatian, St George and the donor, Canon van der Paele, 1436, which was commissioned for the cathedral of St Donatian. ·The Portrait of Margareta van Eyck, 1439, the artist's wife, bears the painter's comment *'als ich can'*, the best I can do. *Roger van der Weyden*: Philip the Good and St Luke painting the Virgin, both 15C copies. *Hugo van der Goes*: ·Death of the Virgin. The muted colours resemble stained-glass.

Master of the Legend of St Ursula: The Story of St Ursula, eight panels of a polyptych from the convent of the Black Sisters in Bruges. The legend of St Ursula and her 11,000 virgin companions, all of whom were believed to have been martyred in various ingenious ways by Maximian at Cologne, was very popular in the Middle Ages and became part of the Golden Legend. The cult was suppressed by the Church in 1969.

Master of the Strauss Madonna: Crucifixion, the work of a Bavarian painter who was inspired by van Eyck and other Flemish artists. *Master of the Court Portraits*: the Portrait of Lodewijk of Gruuthuse is in its original frame which bears the sitter's motto, 'Plus est en Vous' (see below). *Master of the Lucy Legend*: St Nicholas. Note the skilful and detailed rendering of the richly decorated cope.

Hans Memling: the Annunciation, two *grisailles* exterior panels of triptych from the Abbey of the Dunes; ·triptych of SS Christopher, Maurus and Giles, with the donors Willem Moreel, burgomaster of Bruges, and his wife, Barbara van Vlaenderberg, 1484. Memling's earlier, 1478, portrait of Moreel and his wife is in the Musée d'Art Ancien in Brussels.

Gerard David (R4), ·Triptych, 1508, the Baptism of Christ, and on the wings the donor Jean des Trompes, his son and St John the Evangelist, the donor's first wife, Elisabeth van der Meersch, her four daughters and St Elizabeth of Hungary. On the back of the wings are a Virgin and Child, and a portrait of the donor's second wife with her daughter and St Mary Magdalene. This is one of the finest paintings of the last great master of

The Annunciation by Petrus Christus, 1452, the Groeninge Museum, Bruges (Hugo Martens)

the Bruges school. Two panels, 1498, illustrating the story of the Unjust Judge told by Herodotus.

In 1488 Bruges held its ruler, Archduke Maximilian, prisoner. This action was opposed by Pieter Lanchals, Maximilian's treasurer, who was executed by the townspeople for his pains. By way of atonement, the magistrates of Bruges commissioned these panels in 1498. The first shows the corrupt judge, Sisamnes, who had been bribed to deliver an unjust judgement, being sentenced by Cambyses to death by flaying. The second depicts the execution of the sentence in all its gruesome detail. In the background the skin of Sisamnes hangs over the judicial seat, which is now occupied by his son.

R5. *Hieronymus Bosch*: *Last Judgement has a combination of motifs illustrating man's ability to bring hell into the world even before the last judgement; *Ambrosius Benson*: Rest on the Flight to Egypt; 16C *Anonymous Bruges Master*: two panels of the Legend of St George with much emphasis on torture; *Abel Grimmer*: the Carrying of the Cross with its animated procession of figures in a beautifully painted landscape; *Adriaen Isenbrant*: triptych with Madonna and Child, St John and St Jerome; *Jan Provoost*: Last Judgement, with the resurrection of the dead, a graphic Crucifixion and a terrifying Death and the Miser; *School of Bernard van Orley*: Legend of St Roch; *Lancelot Blondeel*: St Luke painting Our Lady. The central figures are surrounded by a painted frame so elaborate that it borders on the grotesque.

In Rooms 6 and 7 there is a change of emphasis. Religious subjects begin to give way to portraits, land and seascapes and historical themes. *Frans Pourbus the Younger*: Portrait of Petrus Ricardus, Portraits of Albert and Isabella. *Marcus Gheeraerts*: Portrait of Lady Anne Rushout. *Pieter Pourbus*: several portraits and a Last Judgement with the separation of the saved from the damned. (Compare this with Jan Provoost's treatment of the same subject.) *Hendrik van Minderhout*: two large harbour scenes. *Jacob van Oost the Elder*: A Bruges Family. *Jan van Goyen*: river scenes. *Adriaen Key*: Portrait of a Man; *after Pieter Brueghel the Elder*: the Preaching of John the Baptist. *After Pieter Brueghel the Younger*: one of several versions of The Peasant Lawyer.

In Room 9 we move into the 18C. *Jan Garemijn's* astonishing Digging of the Ghent Canal with its swarm of ant-like workers is irresistible. In Room 10, by way of contrast, hang *F.J. Kinsoen's* perceptive female portraits and moving Belisarius at his Wife's Death Bed. In Room 11, an even more startling contrast is provided by *Jean Delville's* huge, ghostly L'Homme-Dieu. Some relief is offered by the homely realism of *Leon Frederic's* depiction of washerwomen in La Buée and by the sensitive Life's Sunset and portraits of *Edmond van Hove*.

Room 12 has a number of 19C and early 20C landscapes by *Emile Claus* and others. In Room 15 hangs the grotesque, yet strikingly effective, Last Supper by *G. van Woestyne*. Here, too, are *Leon de Smet's* Lady with a Fan, *Constant Permeke's* Flemish Farm and The Angelus. A bronze sculpture group by *George Minne*, Three Holy Women by the Tomb, conjures up a different mood. *René Magritte* is represented by L'Attentat and *Paul Delvaux* by Le Lever and the ethereal *Sérénité*. Finally, do not miss the attractive Nude with Conch by *Jan Brusselmans* and two striking paintings by *Frits van den Berghe*, The Cowherd and The Lovers in the Village.

A tree-shaded path to the W of the museum leads to a picturesque small bridge, the *Bonifaciusbrug*, so named because there were relics of this saint in the nearby church of Onze Lieve Vrouw. By the bridge there is a bust of Juan Luis Vives, c 1540, the Spanish scholar and friend of Erasmus. Vives, 1492–1540, edited St Augustine's *Civitatis Dei* and dedicated it to Henry VIII. He was tutor to Princess Mary, taught at Oxford and became fellow of Corpus Christi. He was imprisoned for his opposition to Henry's divorce from Catherine of Aragon. After his release he left England for Bruges, where he introduced a system of public assistance.

The **Brangwyn Museum** has a fine collection of the paintings, drawings and etchings of Frank Brangwyn, 1867–1956. Born in Bruges, he presented these works to the town of his birth. There are also collections of *Views of old Bruges and of pewter, brass and porcelain. The carriages and sleighs near the entrance arch are a part of the Gruuthuse museum collection.

The museum is open daily, except Tuesday, between October and March from 09.30 to 12.30 and 14.00 to 17.00, from April to September from 09.30 to 17.00. It is closed on 1 January and on Ascension Day afternoon

The **Gruuthuse Museum**, which occupies an elegant patrician mansion, is open at the same times as the Brangwyn Museum. Its name comes from 'gruit', a mixture of herbs and flowers which was added to barley to improve the flavour of the beer. At one time gruit was stored in a building on or near this site. Although the wing overlooking the canal dates from 1420, the main part of the mansion was built c 1465–70 by Louis de Bruges, lord of Gruuthuse and lieutenant-general for Charles the Bold of Holland, Zeeland and Friesland. His portrait is in the Groeninge museum. In 1470–71 Louis succoured England's fugitive Edward IV and his brother Richard. On regaining his throne, the grateful Edward conferred the earldom of Winchester on Louis. The title was renounced by his son, John, in 1500.

Louis' coat of arms with the motto 'Plus est en Vous' surmounts the entrance arch. Entering the huge courtyard, with its original paving stones, we may pause for a moment to admire the turrets, ornamental chimneys and elaborately decorated windows of the mansion's towering façade. From the entrance hall we pass into the first of 32 rooms, in which more than 2300 objects are displayed. Because of its size and the richness of its collection, visitors are advised to make a quick tour and then return to examine in more detail the objects which interest them particularly. A detailed guide to the museum is available from the ticket office.

In the great hall is the celebrated polychrome terracotta bust of Charles V by the German sculptor, Konrad Meit. Dating from c 1520, this is crowned with a large flat hat of oak. Charles is portrayed as a rather solemn 20-year-old with a long, pointed chin and a Roman nose. Wearing the insignia of the Order of the Golden Fleece, he stares over the viewer's left shoulder in a disconcerting manner.

Before leaving this room note the fine chimneypiece and the windows which are decorated with the arms of the guilds.

Continue to the kitchen, which is equipped with all the cooking utensils required to prepare large and elaborate meals. In the rooms that follow there are displays of tapestries, furniture, coins and medals, musical instruments, silver, ceramics, lace and arms.

Do not miss the two works attributed to Peter Pourbus in Room 7, the picture of the Battle of 's Hertogenbosch by S. Vranckx in Room 8 and a spinet of 1591 in Room 11.

In the oratory, which overlooks the choir of the church of Onze Lieve Vrouw, the lords of the Gruuthuse worshipped. In Rooms 18–20 there is a fine •collection of old Flemish lace, lace-making tools and pattern blocks. Note the magnificent altar cloth which was the property of Charles V. In Room 22 there are arms and weapons and a secondhand guillotine which was bought in Hazebrouck in N France. After being tested on a blameless sheep, the guillotine, now sharpened to a keen edge, was used to despatch two criminals a few days later.

In the little square opposite the museum and the church of Onze Lieve Vrouw there is a statue of the Flemish poet Guido Gezelle, 1830–99, for 28 years curé in Courtrai. He was also chaplain to the nuns of the English convent in Carmersstraat, which was founded in 1629.

The early Gothic **Onze Lieve Vrouwekerk** traces its origins to a chapel of the 10C. This or a successor was burnt down in 1116. Of the next church there are no traces, but the building started c 1220 survives as the central part of the present structure. Outer aisles were added in the 14C (N) and

15C (S). Its outstanding feature is the 13C tower, at 122m the highest in Belgium. The spire has been rebuilt several times. The pinnacles at the angles were added in 1872. Note the graceful N portal of 1465, known as 'Paradis', a corruption of the French 'parvis', a small square in front of a church. The alley round the N end of the church leads to the Bonifaciusbrug (see above).

Onze Lieve Vrouwekerk is open between April and September from 10.00 to 11.30 and from 14.30 to 17.00, from October to March from 10.00 to 11.30 and from 15.00 to 16.30. On Sunday and Holydays it is closed in the morning. Visits are not allowed just before and just after services.

This church is particularly rich in paintings and other works of art. In the NAVE there are statues of the Apostles, 1618, and a baroque pulpit of 1722 based on a sketch by Jan Garemijn. At the W end of the SOUTH AISLE hangs an *Adoration of the Magi, a masterpiece of 1630 by Gerard Seghers. Lower down, on the second pillar, there is a Virgin, Child and St Joseph by de Crayer.

In the chapel at the E end of the S aisle, in the centre of the 18C altar, is the white marble ***Virgin and Child** by Michelangelo. Commissioned in 1505 by Jan van Moescroen, a merchant of Bruges, it was given to the church in 1514 or 1517. It was stolen by the French in 1794 and again by the Germans in 1944. Michelangelo's sketch for the head of the Virgin is in the Victoria and Albert Museum in London. The tomb, 1560, with black marble statues, in the right-hand corner of the chapel, is of the Sire de Haveskerke and his two wives. The painting, 1628, of Christ at the House of Simon the Pharisee is by Frans Francken the Younger.

There is a fee for entry to most of the CHOIR AND AMBULATORY. The choir is separated from the nave by a black and white marble rood-screen of 1722. The high-altar and stalls date from 1770–79. Above the stalls are the painted armorial bearings of the Knights of the Golden Fleece. This commemorates their eleventh chapter held here in 1468. In the choir are the *Mausolea of Charles the Bold, died 1477, and of his daughter Mary of Burgundy, 1457–82. That of Charles the Bold was erected in 1559–62 from the designs of Cornelis Floris of Antwerp. The mausoleum of Mary of Burgundy, the finer of the two, is the work of Pieter de Beckere of Brussels and dates from 1495–1502. Both mausolea bear magnificent heraldic decoration.

Charles the Bold was killed in battle at Nancy where he was later buried. In 1550 Charles V ordered that the remains be brought to Bruges, an order which was so opposed by the authorities in Nancy that some doubt exists as to whether the body removed was Charles's or that of one of his knights. The transfer took several years. En route the body rested for three years in Luxembourg. By the time the remains eventually reached Bruges Charles V had abdicated and it was Philip II who ordered the construction of the mausoleum.

About Mary, however, there is no doubt. Her tomb is in the centre rear of a group below the mausolea. However, the coffin, with a box containing the heart of her son Philip the Handsome on top, is a 19C replacement. When masonry collapsed during restoration work, it exposed the original coffin which was then broken up and plundered by workmen. The other three tombs are those of canons of the late 13C and early 14C.

Also in the choir hangs a large triptych of the Crucifixion and Passion, begun by Bernard van Orley, completed by Marcus Gheeraerts in 1561 and restored by Frans Pourbus the Younger in 1589.

In the SOUTH AMBULATORY there is a painting by Caravaggio, the

Disciples at Emmaus. Compare this with Caravaggio's treatment of the same subject in the National Gallery in London. There are two works by Jacob van Oost the Elder and two wings of a triptych with portraits of the donors by Pieter Pourbus. At the E end hang the centre panel of a triptych by Gerard David c 1520, and side panels with donors and children by Pieter Pourbus, c 1573. The Lanchals Chapel, off this ambulatory, contains a monument to Pieter Lanchals (p 165) and some c 14C tombs. Note also a Last Supper by Pieter Pourbus (1562), a *Madonna of the Seven Sorrows (1518) by Adriaen Isenbrant, rich in fascinating detail, and a Crucifixion (1626) by Antoon van Dyck.

Behind the high-altar there is a reliquary of St Anthony, a saint much invoked against plague, especially that scourge of the Middle Ages, the Black Death.

In the NORTH AMBULATORY the Gothic oratory of 1474 of the Gruuthuse family communicates with their mansion. Pictures include large paintings by de Crayer, Jacob van Oost the Elder, Louis de Deyster and, at the E end, a triptych of 1574, the Adoration of the Shepherds, by Pieter Pourbus.

Sint Jans Hospitaal with the *** *Memling Museum** is immediately SW of the Onze Lieve Vrouwekerk.

The hospital and museum are open daily between April and September from 09.30 to 17.00 and between October and March daily, except Wednesday, from 09.30 to 12.00 and from 14.00 to 17.00. They are closed on 1 January and Ascension Day afternoon.

The tympanum of the old main porch has 13C reliefs of Death and of the Coronation of the Virgin.

On the right, just inside the entrance, a corridor leads to the 15C Dispensary. In use until 1971, this now contains old equipment, including a number of attractive pharmacy jars. A painting shows the dispensary being used at the beginning of the 19C. The room beyond, used for meetings of the hospital board, contains two fine chests with carvings of hospital scenes, a 14C Christmas cradle, and a collection of Delft tiles depicting a series of children's games.

Opposite the dispensary is the entrance to the Hall, which is closed from time to time for temporary exhibitions, and to the Chapel. The 13–14C Hall, together with the adjoining smaller room, now the museum entrance, once formed one huge hospital ward. A picture by Jan Beerblock, 1778, shows it in use. At the end of the main hall there is a copy of the 13C reliefs above the outer porch.

The Chapel, which dates from the 15C, has good woodwork and marble decoration. It now houses the *** *Memling Museum**. The principal works are his altarpiece, the Mystic Marriage of St Catherine, and the Reliquary of St Ursula.

The large winged *** ***Altarpiece*, dedicated to the patron saints of the hospital, St John the Baptist and St John the Evangelist, was painted for the chapel. The middle panel depicts the Mystic Marriage of St Catherine. On the inner wings are the Beheading of St John the Baptist and the Vision of St John the Evangelist at Patmos. On the outer shutters are the donors and their patron saints. The signature 'Opus Johannis Memling, 1479' was added at a later date.

The *** ***Reliquary of St Ursula*, 1489, in carved wood in the shape of a Gothic chapel, is decorated by Memling's finest, if smallest, paintings. It is exhibited on a revolving pedestal. A magnifying glass is provided on request. This engaging legend of Early Christian times is represented with the freshness and precision of a contemporary event. The participants wear the clothes of Memling's time and the buildings of Cologne are faithfully reproduced. On one end is the Virgin with two nuns. On the other St Ursula shelters ten maidens beneath her cloak. The top is adorned by six medallions, possibly the work of a pupil. The story of St Ursula and the 11,000 virgins is depicted on the sides.

Several versions of this apocryphal story existed in the Middle Ages (see above). In this one Ursula, daughter of a Christian king of Britain or perhaps Brittany (the reference is to 'in partibus Britanniae'), was asked in marriage by the son of a pagan king. She consented, on condition that he should embrace Christianity and send 11,000 virgins with her on a three year pilgrimage to Rome. The reference to 'thousand' may be due to a misreading of an early manuscript, but it has added much to the charm of the tale.

Memling's reliquary depicts the following incidents: first: Arrival in Cologne. The picture shows the cathedral, the church of St Martin and the Bayenturm. Second: Entry into Basel, where the party disembarks in order to cross the Alps. Third: Ursula is welcomed in Rome by the Pope. She receives the Sacrament and her companions are baptised. Fourth: The party, accompanied by the Pope, who has been told in a vision to travel with them, re-embarks at Basel. Fifth: Returning to Cologne, the virgins are massacred by the pagans. Sixth: The pagan prince, moved by Ursula's beauty, offers to spare her life if she will marry him. She refuses with an expressive gesture and is killed by an arrow.

The cult of St Ursula was removed from the Calendar in 1969 and is no longer celebrated.

Other works by Memling are exhibited in the museum. They include a triptych, the *Adoration of the Magi (1479), with the donor Jan Floreins and his (?) brother on the left. The inner wings show the Nativity and the Presentation in the Temple, the outer shutters St John the Baptist and St Veronica. A diptych, the Virgin with an Apple. The *Portrait of the donor Martin van Nieuwenhove at the age of twenty-three, 1487, is considered to be one of Memling's finest portraits. Another triptych, a Pietà of 1480, has St Barbara and the donor, Brother Adriaan Reyns, with St Adrian on the inside leaves and the empress Helena and St Mary of Egypt on the outside. The so-called Sibylla Zambetha or Persian Sibyl, 1480, marred by restorers, is a portrait of Maria Moreel, daughter of the burgomaster of Bruges.

A short diversion by way of St Kaolins and Wijngaardstraat takes us to the Begijnhof which is c 800m S of Sint Jans Hospitaal. In St Katelijnestraat, on the right down an alley, Nos 8–18 are old almshouses. Part of No. 84, the *Academy of Fine Arts*, occupies the site of a former orphanage. To the E of St Katelijnestraat in Nieuwe Gentweg there are more old almshouses, *Meulenaer*, 1613, and *St Joseph's*, 1567.

We now come to one of the most attractive parts of Bruges. The ***Begijnhof**, the adjacent Wijngaardplaats and the Minnewater form a pleasant oasis which merits a leisurely exploration. The old stone buildings, the ancient trees and the still waters of the canal have an air of tranquil beauty which is difficult to resist.

A begijnhof founded here c 1235 received a charter from Margaret of Constantinople ten years later. In 1299 Philip IV of France absolved it from dependence on the city magistrates and allowed it to use the title 'Béguinage princier de la Vigne'. The 'Vigne' is believed to refer to the vineyard which had occupied the site of the original enclosure. In the 16C the begijnhof served from time to time as a place of refuge. In 1584 during one such occupation peasants accidentally burnt the church. This was rebuilt in 1605. Today the buildings are occupied by Benedictine nuns.

The gateway dates from 1776. The buildings, 15C and later, surround a large courtyard shaded by trees. A house to the left of the entrance serves as a museum. Here the simple arrangements and furniture of the original lay community are preserved. In the first bay on the N side of the church is a Romanesque doorway, a relic of its predecessor.

The **Minnewater**, just S of the Begijnhof and now a quiet lake, was the busy inner dock of the harbour during the Middle Ages. The *Lock House* at the N end, built in the 15C, was restored in 1893. At the S stands the *Poedertoren*, the powder magazine. This dates from 1398 and is a relic of the old fortifications.

The course of the old fortifications is followed by a ring road. Of the original seven gates, four remain. These are the *Gentpoort*, 1km NE of the Minnewater, the *Smeden-poort*, on the SW edge of the town by the start of the N367, the *Ezelpoort* or Oostendepoort, NW where the N9 leaves the town, and the *Kruispoort*, to the E.

The railway station is c 500m W of the Minnewater.

From the Minnewater we return to Sint Jans Hospitaal and continue along Heilige Geeststraat for c 300m to the **Kathedraal Sint Salvator**. This Gothic building, essentially of the late 13C, replaced a Romanesque church established here in the 9C. The base of the W tower incorporates some early 13C brickwork. The Romanesque-style upper part dates from 1844–71. The W part of the choir and part of the transepts are from the end of the 13C. The nave and S transept were rebuilt after a fire in 1358. The ambulatory and apsidal chapels are the work, 1480–1530, of Jan van der Poele. In the garden the statues of St Peter and St Paul are by Pieter Pepers, 1765.

The former cathedral of Bruges, dedicated to St Donatian, was demolished by the French in 1799 and the bishopric of Bruges was abolished by Napoleon in 1802. When the bishopric was restored in 1834, this church was chosen to be the new cathedral and received many of the treasures which had belonged to its predecessor.

Our visit begins in the NAVE. The pulpit of 1778–85 is the work of Hendrik Pulincx. The baroque 17C rood-screen of bronze, wood and marble at the W end is crowned by a figure of the Creator of 1682 by Quellin the Younger. Until 1935 the screen stood at the entrance to the choir (see picture in the cathedral museum). In the S aisle hangs a Resurrection by P. Claessins (1585). In the N aisle, in the baptistry, a picture by Hendrik van Minderhout of c 1672 shows a scene from the Battle of Lepanto. In 1571 a Christian fleet under the command of Don John of Austria defeated the Turks decisively, so ending the threat of Ottoman naval supremacy in the Mediterranean.

Off the NORTH TRANSEPT is the Chapel of the Shoemakers. This has a screen of 1430 and a 14C crucifix from the Abbey of Eeckhoutte. The emblem of the guild, a boot surmounted by a crown, may be seen on the altar, on the chairs and on the doors.

In the SOUTH TRANSEPT there is an Adoration of the Shepherds by Jacob van Oost the Elder and a Gobelins tapestry. The handsome bench with carved horses and a bust of St Eloi was once the property of the Guild of Waggoners.

In the 13C CHOIR the misericords on the stalls of 1430 are in the form of small carvings of crafts, proverbs and scenes of everyday life in Flanders. The armorial bearings above the stalls are those of the 13th chapter of the Order of the Golden Fleece held in 1478. The two episcopal tombs on either side of the high altar are by Hendrik Pulincx, 1749–58. The painting of the Resurrection on the altar is by Abraham Janssens. The brass lectern in the form of an eagle dates from 1605. The tapestries, copies of paintings by Jan van Orley, are six out of a collecton of eight. They were made in Brussels in 1731.

Off the AMBULATORY there are five chapels. The first chapel from the right is dedicated to Our Lady of Loretto. A pious story about her is depicted in three paintings. Over the altar a retable of c 1500 shows the family tree of St Anne.

The second chapel is dedicated to Our Lady of Seven Sorrows. The 17C statue of the Mater Dolorosa holds a red plague staff. The staff was donated by a Father Melchior in gratitude for having been spared from the plague. The funeral brass in the floor commemorates members of the Confraternity of Our Lady of the Seven Sorrows.

In the centre chapel, which is dedicated to the Blessed Sacrament, there is a statue of the Blessed Virgin by Pieter Pepers, 1776, also two paintings by Jacob van Oost the Elder of SS Peter and John and some fine 19C stained-glass.

The fourth chapel, which is dedicated to the Holy Cross, has a 15C retable with scenes from the Passion.

In the last chapel, formerly dedicated to St Barbara, the central stained-glass window was made in 1903 from glass salvaged from a window of 1531, which was destroyed by Protestant iconoclasts. The alabaster mausoleum of 1549 is of Jean Carondelet, Archbishop of Palermo and Provost of the Canons of St Donatian's Cathedral.

Just beyond, and not part of the ambulatory proper, are two small chapels. One was the guild chapel of the coachbuilders. Their wheel emblem is incorporated in the Renaissance period door. The other has a memorial stone of 1942 in the floor of Charles the Good, Count of Flanders, who was murdered in St Donatian's Cathedral in 1127.

The CATHEDRAL MUSEUM, built as an annexe in 1912, houses some objects which always belonged to St Salvator's and others which came from St Donatian's.

The museum is open from April to June and in September: Monday to Saturday between 14.00 and 17.00. In July and August: Monday to Saturday from 10.00 to 12.00 and 14.00 to 17.00. From October to March: Monday and Tuesday, Thursday to Saturday 14.00 to 17.00. It is closed during these months on Wednesday, Sunday and public holidays.

In the Gallery there is a group of six funerary *brasses of 1387–1555. Among those commemorated are Jacob Schelewarts, priest of St Salvator, d. 1483, who taught theology at the University of Paris and Adriaan Bave, d. 1555, who was burgomaster of Bruges.

Rooms One, Two and Three are little more than recesses off the gallery. In Room One there is a *triptych by Dirk Bouts and Hugo van der Goes. This depicts the Martyrdom of St Hippolytus. The right and centre panels, both by Dirk Bouts, show the Emperor Decius, notorious for his persecution of Christians, trying to persuade the saint to deny his faith and Hippolytus about to be torn apart by four horses. The donors in the left panel are by van der Goes. Hippolytus, a priest in Rome, was an important ecclesiastical writer. Martyred in 235, it would seem that he did not die by the method shown in the picture. There are many apocryphal stories about his life and death.

Room Two has vestments dating from the 15C, reliquaries and a 17C crozier which belonged to the 32nd Abbot of Eeckhoutte Abbey. In Room Three are the silver shrine of St Donatian, made in 1843 with 12C and 13C silver and ornamentation, and a 13C crozier-head in Limoges enamel. This shows St Martial, died c 250, first bishop of Limoges, receiving the heart of St Valeria, a saint whose existence is now questioned. According to a legend popular in the Middle Ages she was converted by St Martial and later beheaded for her faith. There is also a triptych of the Presentation in the Temple by Adriaen Isenbrant.

In Room Four there are tombstones of 1380 which were found under the floor of the church, a painting of the Crucifixion by an unknown Flemish master of c 1500, and a rare 6C ivory crozier.

Room Five has more 14C tombstones from the cathedral and a reliquary of St Eloi by Jan Crabbe of c 1616. Eloi or Eligius, 588–660, was a skilled metalworker of Limoges. Ordained in 640, he later became bishop and spent the rest of his life evangelising Flanders. He was one of the most popular saints in the Middle Ages. Also in this room are a painting of the Virgin between St Luke and St Eloi by Lancelot Blondeel, 1545, and a late 14C altarpiece, a Calvary, of the Tanners' Guild. This is one of the oldest paintings in Bruges.

In Room Six there are church vestments and an early 16C woodcarving showing the consecration of a bishop. An interesting painting of the interior of St Salvator's in the 17C, by Cornelis Verhouven, shows the rood-screen in its original position.

In Room Seven, where the Canons of the cathedral meet, there is a cloth antependium of 1642 from Eeckhoutte Abbey. This shows the Blessed Virgin surrounded by the Doctors of the Church. There are also a triptych of the Last Supper by Pieter Pourbus, 1599, and another triptych by Anthony Claessins of the Descent from the Cross.

On leaving the cathedral take Zuidzandstraat which runs in a SW direction. This has some old, if restored, façades, notably No. 41 of 1570, No. 40 of 1630 with interesting stone carving, and No. 18 of 1703. This street ends at 'T ZAND, an open space with a large underground car park. 'T Zand was the site of a railway station which was dismantled and then rebuilt at Ronse. The present station, of 1931, is to the S, and may be reached by Koning Albertlaan, a wide boulevard with well-kept gardens. Note the fine equestrian statue of King Albert I.

Just W of 'T Zand is the *Orgel Museum* where music boxes, street organs, etc. are exhibited. The entrance is at 3 Zwijnstraat. The museum is open daily from Easter to early or mid November between 10.00 and 18.00.

Return to the cathedral and follow Steenstraat, in a NE direction, to SIMON STEVINPLAATS where there is a statue of the Flemish mathematician, geographer and town-planner Simon Stevinus, 1548–1620. This polymath is credited with having invented the decimal point. Between the square and the Markt there are a number of interesting façades. Note especially No. 90 of 1570, No. 40, the guild house of the shoemakers of 1527, No. 25, the guild house of the masons of 1621, and No. 28, 'De Lam' of 1654.

An alternative, if slightly longer, route to the Markt is by Kemelstraat NW out of Simon Stevinplaats. This crosses Zilverstraat where No. 38, dating from 1468, was the house of Juan Vasquez, secretary of Isabella of Portugal, the third wife of Philip the Good. The street parallel to Zilverstraat on the NE is Noordzandstraat. From the W side, roughly opposite the Hôtel du Sablon, a narrow approach leads to the picturesque *Prinsenhof*. This marks the courtyard of the 15C palace in which Philip the Handsome was born in 1478.

Return to Noordzandstraat and continue to Geldmuntstraat, off the W side of which the vaulted *Muntpoort*, rebuilt 1961, leads to Muntplaats, the site of the Bruges mint. Here a gabled front bears a bust of Marc Houterman,

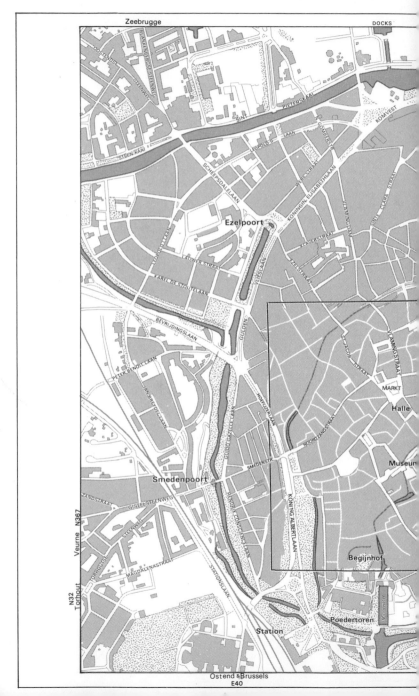

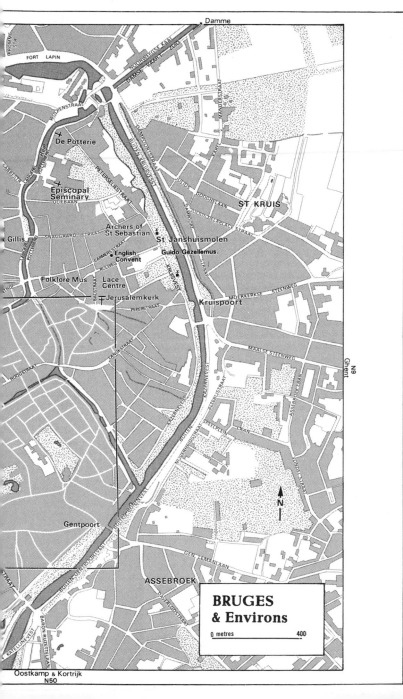

Damme

KROMME VTH

FORT LAPIN

WUOPENSTRAAT

NOORWEEGSE KAAI

DAMSE VAART ZUID

KARELVANDERSTRAAT

De Potterie

DAMPOORTSTRAAT

PETERSELIESTRAAT

Episcopal
Seminary

GIELEBAAN

ST KRUIS

JUTLDS DOOGHELAAN

JULIUS DELAPLACE STRAAT

SNAGGAARD STRAAT

Gillis

Archers of
St Sebastian

St Janshuismolen

English
Convent

CARMERSTRAAT

ROLWEG

Guido Gezellemus.

Folklore Mus.

Lace
Centre

Jerusalemkerk

BALSTRAAT

KRUISVEST

MOERKERKSE STEENWEG

Kruispoort

PEPERSTRAAT

MAALSE STEENWEG

LANGESTRAAT

N9
Ghent

HOOGSTRAAT

KAZERNEVEST

RUTTEN

ASSEBROEKLAAN

SPEELKLEIN

KAZERNEVEST

NIJVERHEIDSSTRAAT

LONDESTRAAT

N
↑

Gentpoort

BUITENBOEVERIES

GEN. LEMANLAAN

ASSEBROEK

BUITENGENTPOORTVEST

RIVIEROOGSTRAAT

BRUGES
& Environs

0 metres   400

KAELELINEVEST

BARON RUZETTELAAN

Oostkamp & Kortrijk
N50

1537–77, who was organist at St Peter's in Rome. Geldmuntstraat ends at the attractive small Eiermarkt, adjoining the Markt. In the Eiermarkt and the Markt there are many restaurants and cafés which offer rest and refreshment.

B. Northern and Eastern Bruges

This circuit, which starts in the Markt and returns to it, covers some 6km. It is possible to use a car from Jan van Eyckplaats onwards.

Leave the Markt by the Sint Jacobstraat, which skirts the Eiermarkt, and continue to the **Sint Jacobskerk**. The base of the tower, the N transept and the NE chapel, which was once the choir, date from c 1240. The rest of the church was built between 1459 and 1478. The pulpit of 1690 is by Bonaventure de Lannoy. There are paintings by L. Blondeel of SS. Cosmas and Damian, 1523, Albert Cornelis of the Coronation of the Virgin, 1520, van Oost the Elder of the Presentation of the Virgin, 1665 and works by Pieter Pourbus and Louis de Deyster.

Roughly opposite the church, take the narrow arched Boterhuis to Naaldenstraat. By the junction there is a house with a graceful 15C brick turret. Farther along Naaldenstraat, **Hof Bladelin**, with its turret and spire, was the home of Pieter Bladelin, died 1472, the treasurer of the Order of the Golden Fleece. Later the house became the residence of Tomaso Portinari, fl. c 1480, a Florentine banker and agent for the Medici. Where Naaldenstraat joins Grauwwerkersstraat turn sharp right. At the N junction of Grauwwerkersstraat and Vlamingstraat, the house called *Ter Beurze*, which dates from 1493 and is now a bank, was the mansion of the van der Beurze family. They welcomed merchants of all nations who came to their house to exchange goods and money. Versions of the van der Beurze name are used in many languages to describe a place of commercial or financial exchange. At the S junction of Vlamingstraat and Grauwwerkersstraat is the *Natiehuis van Genua* of 1399, altered 1720. Sometimes called the Saaihalle, this was the headquarters of the Genoese merchants in Bruges.

A short distance S along Vlamingstraat is a square in the centre of which stands the municipal theatre, the **Schouwburg**.

Opposite Ter Beurze, Academiestraat leads NE to JAN VAN EYCKPLAATS. This is at the head of a canal arm which formerly continued to the Markt. Largely ignored by visitors, the square is the centre of one of the most characteristic and lively 'popular' quarters of Bruges. The statue of van Eyck is by Henri Pickery, 1878. The **Poorters Loge**, on the S side, was originally the meeting-place of the merchants who lived inside the walls. Regarded as privileged, they were distinguished from those who resided outside the walls and were under the jurisdiction of the Brugse Vrije. The original 14C building, apart from the tall, slender turret, was destroyed by fire in 1755. It was at one time the meeting-place of an exclusive society known as the White Bear. The bear of 1417 in a niche on the turret, 'Beertje van de Loge', is affectionately regarded as being the oldest citizen of Bruges.

On the N side of the square are, left, the *Pynderhuis*, Guildhouse of Free Porters, of 1470 and, right, the *Tolhuis*, the customs house of 1477, which was rebuilt 1878, and is now the municipal library. It has a valuable collection of manuscripts and incunabula. The tall house, *Roode Steen* on the E at the corner of Spiegelrei and Genthof, is a restored late 16C mansion.

Woensdagmarkt, a short way along Genthof, was formerly Hans Memlingplaats. It still has a statue of the painter, by Henri Pickery, 1871. The tall 15C turret is a relic of the House of the Smyrna Merchants.

Just beyond is Oosterlingenplaats, which was named after the consular house here of the Easterlings, the Hanseatic Merchants. The **Sint Gilliskerk**, a hall-church c 200m N beyond the canal, was founded in 1277 by Walter de Marvis, bishop of Tournai and enlarged during the 15C. It has works by Jacob van Oost the Elder, Louis de Deyster and a polyptych by Pourbus the Elder. Note also the 18C paintings by Jan Garemijn on the work of the Trinitarian brothers, who ransomed Christian slaves. Many painters, including Memling, Provoost, Blondeel and probably Pourbus the Elder, were buried in the churchyard of Sint Gillis. Collaert Mansionstraat, to the E of the church, is named after Caxton's partner. Jan van Eyck lived in Gouden Handstraat, a short way to the S.

The Reie waterway, c 100m E of Sint Gillis, is flanked by the Langerei to the W and Potterierei to the E. On the Potterierei c 500m N of the bridge is the **Groot Seminarie**, the Episcopal Seminary. This occupies the buildings of the former abbey of Ter Duinen, transferred here in 1627 from its original site at Koksijde and suppressed in 1796. During the time of the French Revolution the buildings were used as a military hospital, as a school and as an army depot. The cloister, with interesting mural paintings, dates from c 1630. The church, which bears the name of the abbey, is a rebuilding of the 18C.

Just beyond the seminary is **De Potterie**, a hospice founded in 1276 for aged women. The name may derive from the chapel, which belonged to the Potters Guild, or the hospice may be built on land which at one time belonged to the guild. The worthy charitable tradition continues. Old people are still cared for here by the OCMW, a welfare institution.

The three gables are, from N to S, the front of the hospital of 1529, that of the early church of 1359, and that of a chapel of Onze Lieve Vrouw which was added in 1623.

Visitors are admitted to the chapel and a small museum from April to September daily between 09.30 and 12.00 and from 12.45 to 17.00, from October to March daily from 09.30 to 12.30 and from 14.00 to 17.00. The chapel and musuem are closed on Wednesday and from 6 January to 6 February.

Between the two aisles of the chapel tapestries are hung from Easter to October. These include a late 15C Our Lady adoring the Child Jesus, a 16C Our Lady and two saints, and a *series of three late 16C tapestries depicting miracles worked by Our Lady in the hospital. These stories also appear in the stained-glass opposite.

On the right-hand altar is a miraculous statue of the early 14C of Our Lady. In the side-chapel in the modern tomb of St Idesbald, who died 1167 and was originally buried at Ter Duinen. In the left aisle the rood-screen dates from 1644. The statues are later. Behind the screen is an Adoration of the Magi by J. van Oost the Elder. On either side of the altar are the tombs of two burgomasters. Nicholas Despars, on the left, died in 1597 and Jan de Beer, on the right, died in 1608.

The museum has a number of pictures. These include a triptych of the Descent from the Cross, 1520, a portrait of a sister of the Hospice de la Madeleine, 1575, and some pen and ink drawings attributed to Jan van Eyck. There are also a 16C leper's clapper in carved wood, a coloured relief of the Agony in the Garden and illuminated missals.

From De Potterie, follow Peterseliestraat, which bears SE, and after c 600m becomes Kruisvest. Here stands **Sint Janshuysmolen**, which dates from 1770 and is one of three windmills along this stretch of canal. It may be visited at Easter and daily between May and September from 10.00 to 12.00 and 13.00 to 18.00.

From the windmill go to the Carmersstraat. On the corner with Kruisvest is the **Schuttersgilde Sint Sebastiaan**, the Guild House, of 1565, of the Archers of St Sebastian. During his exile Charles II of England was a regular visitor at the guild and an enthusiastic user of the bow. Members of the guild still practice here. There are some interesting paintings by van Dyck and van Oost, a collection of gold and silverwork and records that go back to 1416. There is also a portrait by van Boeckhorst of Henry, Duke of Gloucester, the brother of Charles II. The guild house may be visited on Monday, Wednesday, Friday, Saturday 10.00 to 12.00 and 14.00 to 17.00.

A little way along Carmersstraat a domed chapel of 1736 belongs to the Convent of the Regular Canonnesses of St Augustine. Better known as the **English Convent**, this was founded in 1629. It has a relic of St Thomas More, the humanist and scholar. Two English monarchs were entertained by the sisters, Charles II during his exile and Queen Victoria during a visit to Bruges in 1843. It is reported that she expressed satisfaction at the warmth of her reception. Modern visitors may emulate royalty. The convent chapel is open to visitors.

The building at the corner of Rolweg, which also runs W from the windmill, is the **Guido Gezellemuseum**. The birthplace of the Flemish poet, 1830–99, it contains documents and memorabilia. Gezelle was chaplain to the English Convent and Vice-Rector of the Seminarium Anglo-Belgicum which trained English seminarists in Bruges. He translated Longfellow's 'Song of Hiawatha' into Flemish. The museum is open daily from 09.30 to 12.00 and 14.00 to 18.00; from October to March it is closed on Tuesday and on other days from 17.00.

Two blocks S, near the corner of Stijn Streuvelsstraat, is the **Schuttersgilde Sint Joris**, the Guild House of St George. This has an interesting display of crossbows and ancient archives. It is open daily, except Wednesday, between 10.00 and 12.00 and from 14.00 to 18.00.

The **Kruispoort**, a short way S along Kruisvest, is a gate of 1402. One of the oldest structures in Bruges, it has been much altered.

From the Kruispoort, Peperstraat leads W to the privately owned **Jeruzalem kerk**. This started out as the chapel of the Adorne family of Genoa, one of several foreign merchant families which settled in Bruges during the 13C. The chapel was replaced c 1427 by the present church, which was built by the brothers Pieter and Jacob Adorne after their return from a pilgrimage to Jerusalem. It follows, in general, the plan of the Church of the Holy Sepulchre. The Jeruzalemkerk still belongs to descendants of the family. Of particular interest is the black marble tomb of Anselm Adorne who died in 1483, and of his wife, Margaretha van der Banck, who died in 1463. Note the dog and the lion at their feet, symbols of fidelity and strength. The son of Pieter Adorne, Anselm became burgomaster of Bruges. He was also consul for Scotland. On a visit to that country he was foully done to death. The 15C and 16C stained-glass is some of the finest in Bruges. The choir may be reached by stairs. In a crypt near the altar there is a copy of Christ's Tomb.

To visit the Jeruzalemkerk ring the bell at the gate on the right. The church is cared for by the nuns who live in the former Adorne mansion which adjoins the church.

From the church walk N along Balstraat. On the W side is the **Museum voor Volkskunde** with interiors, costumes and domestic objects. It is open daily, except Tuesday, from October to March, between 09.30 and 12.00 and from 14.00 to 18.00. It closes at 17.00 from October to March.

Opposite is the **Kant Centrum**, the Lace Centre, where the ancient craft of making bobbin lace is taught and demonstrated. It is open from Monday to Saturday between 10.00 and 12.00 and from 14.00 to 18.00 (17.00 on Saturday) and on Sunday and public holidays from 14.00 to 17.00.

A short distance to the W of the Jeruzalemkerk is the **Sint Annakerk**. Founded in 1496, it was demolished in 1581 by the dreaded Protestant Beggars and rebuilt between 1607 and 1621. The spire was added in 1624. Guido Gezelle was baptised in this church. The interior is in a rich baroque style, with fine wooden panelling, 17C stalls, confessionals and pulpit. The rood-screen of 1628, in marble and porphyry, is by Jan van Mildert. There are paintings by Louis de Deyster, Jacob van Oost the Elder, and a huge Last Judgement by Jan Baptist Herregoudts.

The **Sint Walburgakerk** c 300m to the W of St Anna is, rather confusingly, in Sint Maartensplaats. It was built in 1619–40 by Pieter Huyssens for the Jesuits and was the first church to be dedicated to St Francis Xavier. His statue is on the imposing façade. Sint Walburgakerk became the parish church after the suppression of the Jesuits in 1779. Note the marble communion-rail by H. Verbruggen of 1695, the pulpit of 1667 by Artus Quellin the Younger, a marble retable of 1643 and a painting by Joseph Benoît Suvee (1783).

From the church it is a short walk back to the Markt. The most attractive route is via Koningstraat to Spinolarei, then along the water's edge to Jan van Eyckplaats.

The **Docks** are at the N edge of the town by the start of the Boudewijn canal.

On the S outskirts of Bruges is the **Boudewijn Park**. It is located to the E of Koning Albertlaan in the direction of the Ostend to Brussels motorway. A favourite recreation area, it has among its many attractions a Dolphinarium and an astronomical clock. The park is open daily from Easter to September between 10.30 and 18.00.

C. Damme

Damme (population 10,000; Tourist Information in the Stadhuis) is a delightful old town in typical polder country. Only 7km from Bruges, it is sited near the point where the tree-lined canal from Bruges to Sluis, in Holland, crosses the adjoining Schipdonk and Leopold canals. Well known for its small, comfortable hotels and good restaurants, Damme is quiet and uncrowded, a conveniently situated alternative centre to Bruges with which it is connected by boat during the holiday season.

Damme was founded in the 12C by Philip of Alsace, Count of Flanders, on the estuary, Het Zwin (see Route 3). The new town was to serve as the port of Bruges. In 1213 it was pillaged by Philip Augustus, Philip II of France, during his war against Count Ferdinand of Flanders. However, Ferdinand's English allies burnt most of Philip's fleet in Damme harbour. The port, with a population that grew to 10,000, became sufficiently important to have its own maritime law, the 'Zeerecht van Damme'. Two dynastic marriages took place here—in 1430 Philip the Good married Isabella of Portugal and in 1468 Charles the Bold married Margaret of York, sister of England's Edward IV. With the silting of Het Zwin during the 15C, the fortunes of the town declined and Damme lost its importance. The town was taken by Marlborough in 1706 and its fortifications were dismantled.

Damme is associated with Jacob van Maerlant, c 1235–1300, who lived, died and is buried here. The 'father of Flemish poetry', he was also one of the most learned scholars of his time, being best known for his verse translations and French and Latin originals like the 'Spiegel Historiae', a history of the world. Local tradition, originating perhaps from the title of Maerlant's book, asserts that Till Eulenspiegel, the 14C peasant clown and practical joker, also lived and died in Damme. In fact he was a German folklore figure from the area around Hanover. However, his putative connection with Damme was reinforced by the publication of 'The Legend of Tyll Owlglass' by Charles de Coster in 1867.

The *Stadhuis* was built between 1464 and 1468 on the site of a trade hall of 1241. Already Damme was losing its importance and the building had to be financed by a special tax levied on the barrels of herrings discharged here. The ground floor was used as a market—the four shutters were for small shops. Statues on the façade, on either side of the double stairway, commemorate historical figures connected with the town. On the left are Philip of Alsace, the founder of Damme, the countesses Joanna and Margaret of Constantinople, the latter bearing a model of the hospital which she is said to have established. On the right, Charles the Bold is shown giving a wedding ring to a rather bashful Margaret of York. The turret rising from the centre of the steeply pitched roof houses a carillon of 25 bells. Two are dated 1392 and 1398. There is a clock of 1459. The interior has a monumental chimneypiece, tiling, and some very curious woodcarving. Note in particular the scene of a man and woman together in a bath. A statue of 1860 of Jacob van Maerlant stands in front of the Stadhuis.

The Stadhuis may be visited daily from July to September between 09.00 and 12.00 and from 14.00 to 18.00.

A short distance to the NE is the *Huis Sint Jan*, a patrician house of 1468. On 3 July 1468 Charles the Bold and Margaret of York were married here. Bishop Beauchamp of Salisbury blessed the union.

In Kerkstraat the *Museum Sint Janshospitaal* houses a collection of furniture, liturgical objects, ceramics and gravestones. The hospital was founded c 1249, it is said by Margaret of Constantinople.

It is open between April and October on Monday from 14.00 to 17.30, from Tuesday to Saturday from 10.00 to 12.00 and from 14.00 to 18.00, on Sunday and public holidays from 11.00 to 12.00 and from 14.00 to 18.00; between November and March daily from 14.00 to 17.00.

A short way to the S is the *Onze Lieve Vrouwekerk*. This has a high square tower of c 1210–30, separated from the 14C body of the church by two ruined bays with a triplet triforium. The transepts were demolished in 1725 and the central nave abandoned. The lower part of the rood-loft, of 1555, serves as a vestibule. There are baroque confessionals from the cathedral of St Donatian in Bruges, 14C statues of the Apostles and an Assumption by Jan Maes. The 1636 altar of the Holy Cross has a cross brought up from the sea by fishermen. Jacob van Maerlant was probably buried below the tower. His gravestone was sold during the 19C and replaced by a plaque. A popular tradition holds that Till Eulenspiegel also lies here. There is a small statue of the rustic clown in the garden.

Tower ascent daily from April to September between 10.00 and 12.00 and from 14.30 to 17.30. Apply to 37 Kerkstraat.

10

Bruges to Kortrijk (Courtrai)

A. Via Torhout and Roeselare

Total distance 49km.—*19km* **Torhout**—*12km* **Roeselare**—*18km* **Kortrijk**.

Leave **Bruges** (see Route 9) by the Smedenpoort. Soon after, the N32 passes through the woods of *Tillegem*. Once the estate of a château, this is now a provincial recreational park. The large moated château, which was founded in the 9C, rebuilt in the 13C and much altered at the end of the 19C, now houses the West Flanders tourism offices, Westtoerisme.

Just beyond the Ostend–Brussels motorway, the Benedictine abbey of *Zeven-Kerken*, or *Sint Andries*, lies half hidden in woods at the end of a long avenue. Founded c 1100 at St Andries in the suburbs of Bruges, it was destroyed in 1793 during the French Revolution and rebuilt here in the Byzantine style in 1899–1902. Benedictine sisters occupy a nearby convent.

The château at *Loppem*, 2km to the E, is an outstanding example of Flemish neo-Gothic. First designs were by Edward Welby Pugin, but it was built between 1858 and 1863 in the Flemish Gothic style to new plans drawn up by Baron Jean Béthune. It is open daily, except Monday and Friday, between April and October from 10.00 to 12.00 and 14.00 to 18.00.

The church at *Zedelgem*, *10km* from Bruges to the W of the road, has a 12C font of Tournai marble.

9km **Torhout**, population 17,000. Tourist Information Ravenhof. An industrial and agricultural centre, Torhout is the 'capital' of the Flemish HOUTLAND, the Wooded Land. Destroyed in both World Wars, the *Sint Pieterskerk* has been rebuilt to the original Romanesque plan. It has a Martyrdom of St Sebastian by van Dyck. The *Stadhuis* of 1713 houses the local museum, where multicoloured pottery of a type associated with this district for several centuries is exhibited. It is open on weekdays from 10.00 to 12.00 and from 14.00 to 17.00.

At **Wijnendale**, 3km NW of Torhout, part of the historic, but much restored, 12C château has been arranged as a museum with tableaux illustrating its history. Here in 1292 the Count of Flanders Guy de Dampierre, son of Margaret of Constantinople, received an embassy from Edward I of England asking for the hand of his daughter for Edward's son. Largely because of this request Guy's suzerain, Philip the Fair, who wished the future Edward II to marry his own daughter, had Guy imprisoned in France and forced him to cede Flanders. It was while hunting in the park that Mary of Burgundy had her fatal fall from her horse (see the picture of this event in the Stadhuis at Bruges). In 1940 the château was the scene of the final meeting between Leopold III and his prime minister, Pierlot. The decision to surrender was made here and the armistice with Germany was signed here. The château is open from mid May to mid September on Tuesday, Wednesday and Sunday from 14.00 to 18.00.

At *7km Gits* a road forks SW for 20km Ypres passing *Westrozebeke* en route (p 146).

At *5km* you reach **Roeselare**, population 52,000. Tourist Information in the Stadhuis. During the First World War this was the headquarters of the

German forces facing the Ypres Salient. The *Sint Michielskerk*, 1497–1504, has some interesting woodwork, including an elaborately carved 18C pulpit from the Carmelite church in Bruges. The pictures include a 'Scourging of Christ' by Abraham Janssens, 1575–1632. The torturers are in the dress of the artist's time.

Just S of the town, near the road, stands the very attractive red-brick *Château of Rumbeke*. This dates mainly from the 16C. Some parts are earlier. The park, laid out in 1770 by F. Simoneau, is now a provincial recreational estate, Sterrebos, but the château is open only to groups. Across the road from the château stands a monument to men of the 1st Grenadier Guards, who fell near here on 17 May 1940.

8km Izegem, population 26,000. This town has been for centuries an important centre for two industries—brush making and footwear. Both have museums; brushes at 2 Wolvenstraat and footwear at 9 Wijngaardstraat. They are open on Saturday from 10.00 to 12.00.

For *10km* **Kortrijk** (Courtrai), see Route 11.

B. Via Oostkamp

Total distance 37km.—*5km Oostkamp—23km Ingelmunster—9km* **Kortrijk**.

For **Bruges**, see Route 9. The N50 crosses the Bruges–Ghent canal and at *5km* reaches *Oostkamp*. Here there is an octagonal 12C church tower, and a castle where Louis de Gruuthuse entertained the exiled Edward IV of England. The road then crosses the Ostend–Brussels motorway. The Diksmuide–Tielt road (Route 5) is met just E of *15km* Koolskamp. About 3km to the S is the shoe-making town of *Ardooie* (population 8000), the birthplace of Victor Roelens, 1856–1947, first Bishop of the Congo.

8km Ingelmunster (population 10,000) has an 18C château, which replaced the castle where Philip the Fair of France received the keys of Bruges in 1301 (p 156). A battle near here in 1580, following the signing of the Union of Arras, was one of Parma's first successes against the Protestants.

9km **Kortrijk** (Courtrai), see Route 11.

11

Kortrijk (Courtrai) to Ghent

Total distance 37km.—*4km* **Harelbeke**—*19km Petegem* (**Deinze**)—*5km* **Deurle**—*9km* **Ghent**.

KORTRIJK (Courtrai, population 77,000. Tourist Information: Schouwburgplein) is a pleasant and lively commercial town on the Lys (the Leie) which combines the old with the new very successfully. Modern pedestrian shopping streets co-exist happily with ancient buildings. Though mostly Flemish-speaking, Kortrijk is only 7km from the frontier with France. Mouscron or Moeskroen, in the NW bulge of the province of Hainaut, is only 14km from Lille in France.

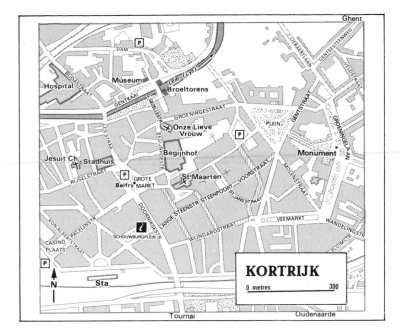

Kortrijk was known to the Romans as *Cortoriacum* or *Curtracum*. It was established as a town, possibly during the 7C, but was later destroyed by the Norsemen and then rebuilt in the 10C by Baldwin III . Outside its walls the weavers of Ghent and Bruges routed the French knights under Robert of Artois at the Battle of the Golden Spurs on 11 July 1302. This was one of the first defeats inflicted by a trained infantry of yeomen and burghers on elite mounted knights. Charles VI wreaked a savage revenge in 1382 by burning the town after his victory at Westrozebeke over Philip van Artevelde. A century later Charles VIII came to the aid of the Flemish in their struggle against Maximilian and occupied Kortrijk between 1488 and 1492.

The Lys, a chalk-free river especially suitable for flax-retting, ensured Kortrijk's prosperity as a manufacturing centre of linen. By the 15C the population of the town and district had risen to around 200,000. Kortrijk was taken by the French in 1793 and became the chief town of the department of the Lys.

Captured by the Germans in 1914, Kortrijk became a main base behind the Ypres front. Between 1940 and 1945 the town suffered severely from aerial bombardment, but after the war restoration work was undertaken very quickly. The painter Roelant Savery, 1576–1639, was born here. He moved later to Utrecht.

The centre of the town is the irregularly shaped GROTE MARKT. Most places of interest lie to the E and N. The pedestrian-only shopping streets are to the SE of the Markt. In the middle stands the 14–15C **Belfry**, all that remains of the cloth hall which was damaged irreparably by bombing in 1944 and later demolished.

The **Stadhuis** in the NW corner of the Grote Markt dates from 1519 but has been repeatedly enlarged and restored. The last restoration was by J. Vierin and his son Luc in 1959–62. The statues of the counts of Flanders on the façade are modern. In the Schepenzaal on the ground floor modern stained-glass windows and frescoes depict events in the town's history. There is also a fine 16C chimneypiece with the arms of Ghent and Bruges, figures of Albert and Isabella, etc. Upstairs in the Council Chamber a more elaborate *chimneypiece of 1527 has three rows of statuettes. Those above represent the Virtues, those in the middle the Vices, and those below the punishments and torments of Hell. Enigmatically, it also has figures on brackets of Charles V, Isabella and a personification of Justice.

The Stadhuis may be visited Monday to Friday between 14.00 and 17.00.

Just to the W of the Stadhuis is the *Jesuit Church of St Michael* of 1607–11. On the S side, in a modern Romanesque chapel, there is an early 13C ivory statuette of Our Lady of Groeninge. Made in Arras, this was presented by Countess Beatrice de Dampierre in 1285 to the Abbey of Groeninge in Groeningestraat, Kortrijk. A convent of the Poor Clares now occupies part of the original abbey building.

Parts of the **Sint Maartenskerk**, to the SE of the Grote Markt, date from the 13C. This church was largely rebuilt in the 15C and suffered further restoration in the 19C. It has a richly carved and gilded stone tabernacle of 1585 by Hendrik Maes and a triptych of 1587 by Bernard de Ryckere.

To the SE of the church the long pedestrian precinct of Lange Steenstraat, Steenpoort and Voorstraat runs from SW to NE. At the junction of Steenpoort and Voorstraat, take Sint Jansstraat and continue in a SE direction. At the corner with Potterijstraat is the *Bagghaertshof*, a group of old almshouses with a small courtyard and a chapel of 1638.

The **Begijnhof**, immediately N of the church of Sint Maarten, was founded in 1238 by Joanna of Constantinople. She is commemorated by a statue of 1891. The Begijnhof has been destroyed many times and most of the small houses extant are from the 17C. The side wall of the 18C chapel on Begijnhofstraat dates from the 15C. There is a small museum in one of the houses.

The **Onze Lieve Vrouwekerk**, mainly of the 13C, was partly rebuilt in the 18C and again after war damage of 1944. The W exterior, with arches along the pavement, is unusual. The church generally has a fortified appearance. There is an alabaster *statue of St Catherine of 1374–84 ascribed to André Beauneveu of Valenciennes in the Chapel of the Counts. Founded by Louis de Male c 1365, restored in 1963, this has an interesting collection of portraits of all the counts of Flanders and of some of their wives. In the N transept the *Raising of the Cross of 1631 by van Dyck was one of the artist's last paintings before his departure to England. In the adjoining chapel there is an Adoration of the Shepherds by Louis de Deyster. Another of his works hangs in the S transept. One of the chancel lecterns dates from 1695 and is by Ignace de Cock, who is better known as a bell-founder, the other of 1711 is by Jan Lepies.

From the church take the Guido Gezellestraat to the river. The bridge here is flanked by the squat, massive **Broeltorens**, impressive survivals of Kortrijk's ancient fortifications. The S tower dates from the 12C, the N from the 15C.

Across the bridge, on the left, in an 18C mansion is the **Stedelijk Museum**. It has an important collection of local lace and damask, ceramic, pewter, copper and bronze objects, period furniture, coins, prehistoric and Roman artefacts and paintings by Roelant Savery and others.

The museum is open daily, except Monday, from 10.00 to 12.00 and 14.00 to 17.00.

Circa 400m W of the museum is the *Onze Lieve Vrouwhospitaal*. Founded by Margaret of Constantinople in 1219, it was almost entirely rebuilt in the 16–17C. It has a baroque-style chapel. In a courtyard there are some 13C fragments.

The place where the BATTLE OF THE GOLDEN SPURS took place is commemorated by a monument in Groeningelaan, 700m to the E of the Grote Markt. The battle was fought on 11 July 1302 between Flemish weavers and burghers under Pieter de Coninck, already famed as a leader of the Bruges Matins, and an army of French knights led by Robert of Artois. The Flemish army was drawn up facing a stream, now the Groeningelaan. Their left was protected by the Lys and their right by a marsh. The French knights, contemptuous of their low-born opponents, made two frontal attacks across the stream. Each was repelled by the Flemish pikemen, the French losing 63 nobles, including Robert of Artois, and 700 knights. It is said that after the battle 700 pairs of golden spurs were collected and displayed in the church of Onze Lieve Vrouw. The battle, the first occasion on which ordinary citizens defeated mail-clad knights, is important in medieval military and social history as it marked the beginning of the end for chivalry.

Kortrijk's long association with flax is recorded in the *Nationaal Vlasmuseum* at 4 E. Sabbelaan in the SE outskirts of the town beyond the motorway ring. Here, in a restored 19C flax farmhouse, the story of flax from cultivation to weaving is told through a series of tableaux in period-furnished rooms.

The museum is open from Monday to Friday between March and November from 09.30 to 12.30 and from 13.30 to 18.00.

Leave Kortrijk by the Gentsesteenweg. At the edge of the town on the N side of the road there is a memorial in the form of a moose to Newfoundlanders who fell in Belgium in 1914–18. At *4km* **Harelbeke**, in a flax- and tobacco-growing district, there is an 18C neo-classical church. The detached 11C Romanesque tower, part of the earlier church, was badly damaged in 1940. It was restored in 1954 and later given a 50 bell carillon.

Opposite the old town hall of 1764, a statue commemorates the composer, Pierre Benoît, 1834–1901. Born here he attempted to establish a distinctive Flemish style in music.

At Harelbeke, Route 12 bears SE for Deerlijk and Kerkhove. This Route continues to *11km* Petegem which straddles the Lys. From here there is a choice of roads. For the road N of the river, Deinze, and the château of Ooidonk, see Route 5. We continue S of the river to *5km* **Deurle**, a scattered village in woods beside the Lys. Deurle has become an elegant residential and gastronomic centre. Because it was popular with the painters of two successive schools who settled around the village of Sint Martens-Latem, 3km to the NE, it is also important for the arts. The first school, the Symbolists of c 1905, included George Minne and Gustave van de Woestyne, the second, the Expressionists of c 1910, Constant Permeke, Gustave de Smet and Frits van den Berghe. At Deurle, works by these and other artists are exhibited in several museums.

The *Museum Gust de Smet* is open daily, except Monday, between March and November from 10.00 to 12.00 and from 14.00 to 18.00 (16.00 during the first half of March). At 1 Gust de Smetlaan, it is the house which the artist built in 1935 and in which he lived until his death here in 1943. Virtually unchanged, it contains many of de Smet's works.

The *Museum Leon de Smet*, at 18 Museumlaan, exhibits works by this artist, together with memorabilia and documentation. It is open on Sunday from 10.00 to 12.00 and from 14.00 to 18.00 and on Tuesday, Wednesday, Thursday and Saturday from 14.00 to 18.00.

The purpose-built *Museum Mevrouw J. Dhondt-Dhaenens* was the gift, with their private collection, of Jules and Irma Dhondt-Dhaenens. Virtually every 19C Flemish artist is represented here. This museum is open between March and November from Wednesday to Friday from 14.00 to 17.00, 18.00

between May and September and on Saturday, Sunday and public holidays from 10.00 to 12.00 and from 14.00 to 17.00.

At Sint Martens-Latem the *Museum Minne-Gevaert*, at 45 Kapitteldreef, contains works by George Minne in a house built in 1922 by his son-in-law. It is open from Wednesday to Sunday between 15.00 and 18.00.

At *5km* is **Sint Denijs-Westrem**, with Ghent's airport just N of the Ostend–Brussels motorway. At *Afsnee*, to the W of the airport, is the interesting small church of Sint Jan. Successor to a foundation of 945 or earlier, it has an early 13C octagonal tower. For *4km* **Ghent**, see Route 13.

12

Kortrijk (Courtrai) via Oudenaarde and Ronse to Brussels

Total distance 81km.—*4km* **Harelbeke**—*15km Kerkhove*—*9km* **Oudenaarde** or **Ronse**—*13km* **Brakel**—*8km Ophasselt* (with diversions N to **Zottegem** and S to **Geraardsbergen**)—*10km* **Ninove**—*22km* **Brussels**.

For **Kortrijk** and *4km* **Harelbeke**, see Route 11. At Harelbeke this Route bears SE to *2km Deerlijk* where the church contains an early 16C altarpiece with scenes from the life of St Columba.

At *13km Kerkhove* we reach the river Scheldt (the Escau). Here you can choose between two roads, northwards through *9km* Oudenaarde or southwards through *9km* Ronse. The two roads are approximately the same length and meet at Brakel. Oudenaarde and Ronse, 10km apart, are in the province of East Flanders. Linked by the N60, both merit a visit.

Oudenaarde, in French **Audenarde** (population 28,000. Tourist Information in the Stadhuis), is a busy textile manufacturing and brewing town on the Scheldt. However, it is not this industrial activity which will attract the attention of visitors. The huge Grote Markt, the town's many elegant old buildings and the open areas by the river will convey an impression of antique spaciousness, of calm and dignity which will linger in the memory.

The name, Oudenaarde, means 'old anchorage ' or 'old landing place'. Situated by the river on a trade route, it is likely that there was a settlement here before Roman times. Proof of Roman occupation is provided by the discovery of coins and artefacts. According to medieval accounts St Amandus brought the Christian message to Pamele, the district E of the river, in 613. Under the terms of the Treaty of Verdun of 843 the river formed the boundary between the land of Lothair, Germany, and of Charles the Bald, France.

In the early 11C the area fell to the counts of Flanders. Sheltered by the *Turris Aldenardensis* of Baldwin IV a town began to grow and prosper. Around 1030 the first meeting of the States of Flanders was held here. A charter granted by Philip of Alsace in 1193 gave an impetus to trade, especially in cloth. By the 15C Oudenaarde was famous for its tapestry, a craft which reached its zenith in the 16C only to die out completely in the 17C.

The town has had a turbulent history. From 1325 to 1382 it suffered during the revolt of the Flemish communes. From 1527 to 1584 it was fought over during the religious disturbances. Then followed the revolt against the Spaniards in the 16C, the wars of Louis XIV from 1658 to 1684, the Wars of the Spanish Succession, the wars of Louis XV in 1745 and the two World Wars. All left their mark on Oudenaarde.

Governor of the Netherlands from 1560–67, Margaret of Parma, illegitimate daughter of Charles V and his mistress Joanna van der Gheynst, was born here in 1522. The painter Adriaen Brouwer was also born in Oudenaarde in 1605. In 1708, during the War of the Spanish Succession, Marlborough defeated the French at the Battle of Oudenaarde to the N and NW of the town. In 1745, during the War of the Austrian Succession, the French took the town and dismantled its fortifications.

In the centre of Oudenaarde is the large GROTE MARKT. Our visit begins here. At the N end is the strikingly beautiful ****Stadhuis**, which replaced a Romanesque building burnt by a carnival mob in 1525. It was built c 1525–36 by the Brussels architect Hendrik van Pede in Flamboyant Gothic style. The sculptured façade is supported by an arcade with a projecting porch. In the centre rises a tower with a cupola in the shape of a crown. Above this stands the gilded figure of Hanske de Krijge, Little John the Warrior, waving a banner bearing the town's arms. The fountain in front was presented by Louis XIV in 1675. At the rear is the rectangular Romanesque *Halle*, 13C with 17C alterations.

The main feature of the interior of the Stadhuis is the carving by Paul van der Schelden. Note particularly the chimneypieces and a magnificent *oak doorway of 1531 with 28 panels. Reproductions of this doorway are exhibited in the Louvre in Paris and in the Victoria and Albert Museum in London. In the Stadhuis and Halle there are archives dating from 1200, tapestries, paintings including the Five Senses attributed to Adriaen Brouwer, material relating to the guilds, archaeological finds from the area, seals, coins and weapons. There are guided tours of the Stadhuis daily, except Friday afternoon, from April to October at 09.00, 10.00, 11.00, 14.00, 15.00 and 16.00. There is no 09.00 tour on Saturday, Sunday and public holidays. The tour lasts one hour.

In the *Liedtskasteel* of 1883, in the park of the same name, some 300m to the NE, there is a general regional museum. This is open from Monday to Friday between 09.00 and 12.00 and from 14.00 to 17.00, on Sunday from 14.00 to 18.00.

From the Hoogstraat walk in a northerly direction to the Tacambaroplein. Here a monument of 1867 commemorates volunteers from Oudenaarde who fell in Mexico fighting for the ill-fated Emperor Maximilian, the son-in-law of Leopold I. Also in this square are an American war memorial, a local war memorial and a monument to the deportees of the First World War.

The *Sint Walburgakerk* is off the SW corner of the Grote Markt. St Walburga, c 710–79, was the sister of SS Willibald and Winebald. A nun of Dorset, she went to Germany at the invitation of St Boniface and became abbess of Heidenheim. Her relics are preserved at Eichstätt.

The choir of Sint Walburgakerk dates from the 12–14C. The nave, by Jan van Ruysbroeck, and the apse are from the 15–16C. The spire was burnt in 1804. Since then the tower has ended in its bell-shaped lantern.

The interior has tapestries from Oudenaarde, a triptych of the Trinity by a local artist, Simon de Paepe, screens by Luc Fayd'herbe, and in the choir a monument to four Catholic priests, who were murdered in 1572 by Protestant fanatics (see below).

To the N of the church the *Hospital* of Onze Lieve Vrouw was founded in the 12C. The present buildings date mainly from the 17C and 18C, but preserve a 13–14C chapel.

To the S of the church are the *Boudewijnstoren*, a relic of the 11–13C fortifications and possibly of the early castle, and the early 16C *Huis van Margareta van Parma* where, it is believed, she was born.

From the SW of the Grote Markt follow the Burgstraat, and its continuation the Kasteelstraat, to the river. At their meeting point is the mellow 17C portal of the Begijnhof, founded during the 13C. The Scheldt bridge is 150m to the NE. To the left across the bridge, the Bourgondiestraat recalls the Burgundian castle built in 1385 by Philip the Bold, which stood here. Louis XI of France took refuge in the castle during his exile c 1460. In 1572 Protestants threw four Catholic priests from the castle windows into the Scheldt, where they drowned. They are commemorated by a monument in the church of Sint Walburga (see above).

The *Huis de Lalaing* of c 1717 at 9 Bourgondiestraat close to the law courts, has a tapestry centre which undertakes restoration work and displays the products of local artists. It is open from Monday to Friday from 09.00 to 16.00.

To the SW stands the *Onze Lieve Vrouwekerk* of Pamele, the ancient name of this district. A Scheldt Gothic building it was started in 1234 and largely completed in only four years. The church was founded, and for the most part, designed by the monk, Arnulf de Binche. The first master-builder in Belgium to be known by name, he is commemorated by a plaque bearing an inscription in Latin on the outside wall of the choir. The N transept dates from the 14C and there are two chapels of the 16C. Inside the church some of the pillars and walls have taken alarming angles. There are paintings by Simon de Paepe and a magnificent triptych by Jan Snellinck. Note also the tombs of two lords of Pamele and of their wives, 1504 and 1616.

The NE suburb of **Ename**, an early fortress of the German emperors and until the 11C a prosperous trading centre, was taken by Count Baldwin IV in 1002. When its castle was demolished by Baldwin V in 1047, much of Ename's trading activity ceased. Its people moved to Oudenaarde and found shelter under the *Turris Aldernardensis*.

Ronse, in French **Renaix**, population 25,000. The Tourist Information Office in the Stadhuis, Grote Markt. A pleasant town best known for its textile industry, Ronse lies along the line of hills sometimes known as the Flemish Ardennes. The road from Kerkhove and the Scheldt passes between two of the high points, *Kluisberg* to the S, 140m, and *Hotondberg* to the N, 150m. Hotondberg has a useful orientation table. The *Mont de l'Enclus*, also to the S, 141m, offers an extensive view over the countryside. Ronse is just inside East Flanders, but the Hainaut province border is barely 1km away and the town is bilingual.

In the MARKT stands an *Obelisk*, erected in 1815 and originally surmounted by the initial W for William I of the United Kingdom of the Netherlands. The W, removed during the revolution of 1830 is now kept in the Stedelijk Museum (see below). It has been replaced by the Habsburg eagle and the arms of the town.

The *Stadhuis* by Frank Blockx, also in the Markt, is a 1953 reconstruction in the 16C Spanish style. From the N of the Markt take the Hospitaalstraat and continue into Priesterstraat.

At the end of this street is the *Sint Hermeskerk*, a late Gothic building of the 15–16C with a high W tower. Hermes was a Roman martyr of c 117. An exorcist, he is believed to have suffered under Aurelian. About 855 his relics were given by Pope Leo IV to Lothair of Lower Lotharingia. He donated them to Ronse where they attracted many pilgrims and were thought to provide a cure for lunacy. The richly embroidered 17C reliquary of the saint takes the form of an equestrian figure leading a chained demon. It is kept in the S choir chapel, where a life-size statue repeats the motif. The iron rings on an old bench in a niche opposite the altar were used to secure the demented, while awaiting exorcism. The church has a large Romanesque crypt dating from 1089. Restored in 1267, enlarged and again restored in 1518, this is still used for worship. The crypt is open daily from Tuesday to Friday between 10.00 and 12.00 and from 14.00 to 17.00.

Outside the church, beside the N wall, is a section of the foundations of the church of *Sint Pieter*. Built c 1100, enlarged in 1510, this was demolished in 1843. Hedges trace out the lines of the cloister.

In the nearby Bruul Park are the town's two museums. The *Stedelijk Museum* is in the late 18C houses formerly occupied by the canons. It has period rooms with pictures by local artists, memorabilia of distinguished citizens of Ronse and its environs, material relating to the guilds, prehistoric objects, archaeological material, a folklore section, inn life, and objects connected with old crafts such as weaving, basket making, clogs, shuttle making and printing. The museum is open daily from Tuesday to Friday from 10.00 to 12.00 and from 14.00 to 17.00 and on Sundays and public holidays from 10.00 to 12.00 and from 15.00 to 18.00. It is closed on Monday. The *Textiel Museum* has the same opening hours. It offers an interesting survey of the local textiles industry from 1800 to 1950.

The *railway station* to the S of the town was originally at Bruges. It was transferred, by rail of course, brick by brick and rebuilt here. In front stands the figure of 'Bonmos', symbol of the local 'Fools' Monday' carnival, which is now held on the Saturday after the Epiphany.

At *13km* Brakel the roads from Oudenaarde and Ronse meet. Continue to *8km* Ophasselt where interesting excursions may be made to the N and S. NORTH. **Zottegem**, 7km NW of Ophasselt, is an industrial town of 25,000 inhabitants, which was once a fief of the counts of Egmont. In the vault below the church are buried Lamoral, the patriot victim of Alva, his wife and his two sons. The family château is largely a rebuilding of the 19C.

The château of *Leeuwergem* accepts visits by groups only and then by appointment. Approximately 2km NE of Zottegem, it was built in 1724 on the site of a 12C castle.

SOUTH. **Geraardsbergen** (**Grammont**, population 30,000. Tourist Information Office in the Stadhuis) is 5km S of Ophasselt. A small town of considerable antiquity, it lies below the *Oudeberg*, 113m, whose steep slope, the 'Mur de Grammont', is well known in cycle-racing circles.

The *Stadhuis*, 14C in origin, dates mainly from the 18C. Outside are the 15C *Marbol*, the 15C market cross and a copy of the *Manneken-Pis*, presented by Brussels in 1745.

The 15C, much-altered *Sint Bartholomeuskerk* has a chapel, dedicated to Our Lady of the Market, attached to it. Formerly a separate building, the lower part of the chapel dates from the 13C. In the church there is marble work of 1770 by Pieter Pepers, a painting, the Martyrdom of St Bartholomew, by De Crayer, and 18C confessionals and pulpit.

Signs from the Markt point N to the former abbey of *Sint Adriaan* on the slope of the Oudeberg. The grounds have been converted into public gardens and a children's playground. The buildings contain a museum where artefacts from the area and portraits of the abbots are displayed. It is open between Easter and October from Monday to Friday between 09.30 and 11.30 and from 13.30 to 16.30 and on Saturday, Sunday and public holidays from 14.00 to 18.00.

10km from Ophasselt is **Ninove**, population 33,000. Here the *Onze Lieve Vrouwekerk* is all that survives of the abbey of SS Cornelius and Cyprian. Founded in 1137, disestablished in 1796, its domestic buildings were demolished in 1822. Constructed in the baroque style, the church dates from 1660–1723 and is famous for the richness of its interior. The tower was added in 1844. The furnishings are by three of the best 18C sculptors, Theodoor Verhaeghen, J.B. van der Haeghen and Jacques Bergé. The choir stalls date from the mid 17C.

In Vestbaan, c 200m SE of the church, is the *Koepoort*, the town's only surviving 14C gate.

You cross into the province of Brabant to reach at *6km* the village of *Onze Lieve Vrouw Lombeek*. On the S of the road is the 13–14C church with its superb *retable of the Virgin of 1512–16, a masterpiece of Brabant carving, and a 15C rood.

At *6km* **Schepdaal** the *Musée du Tram*, also known as the *Musée Vicinal*, records the story of the tramways and light railways of Belgium. Located in a typical country tram depot of 1888, the museum has around 30 vehicles. It is open between April and October on Sunday and public holidays from 14.00 to 18.00, and in July and August on Saturday at the same hours.

The château of **Gaasbeek** is 5km to the S. The first building on this site was erected in the 13C. It was destroyed by the citizens of Brussels after the murder of Everard 't Serclaes in 1387. Rebuilt, the castle was converted into a château in 1545. There were further additions and restorations during the 18C and 19C. In 1921 Gaasbeek became state property and a museum. It has some notable tapestries from Brussels of the 16C and 17C, from Tournai of the 15C and from England of the 17C. There is also a fine collection of furniture, ceramics of the 15C and 16C and a large number of valuable objets d'art. Among the pictures are a Tower of Babel by Martin van Valekenborgh, which once belonged to Rubens, and a portrait of the Countess of Dorset by van Dyck. It is open from April to October daily, except Monday and Friday, from 10.00 to 17.00. In July and August it is also open on Monday.

10km **Brussels**, see Route 1.

13

Ghent

GHENT (population 235,000), is the English name for the Flemish town of **Gent** (in French *Gand*), the capital of the province of East Flanders. The principal seat of the counts of Flanders, its medieval quarters, its massive castle and its splendid cathedral are redolent of history. It has fine museums and possesses one of the great masterpieces of Flemish painting, the 'Adoration of the Mystic Lamb' by Jan van Eyck.

Ghent is a place of waterways. In the centre are the rivers Lieve and Lys, (Leie) and to the S the Scheldt. They and their islands add not a little to the attractive appearance of the town. Although a major industrial centre served by one of Europe's largest inland ports, it is, not surprisingly, also a leading tourist town.

Ghent, surrounded as it is by nurseries devoted mainly to azaleas, rhododendrons and begonias, claims for itself the title, 'City of Flowers'. The internationally known 'Floralies' pageant is staged here every five years. It will be held next in 1995.

Centre. Sint Baafskathedraal—Koornmarkt.

Tourist Information Offices. *Ghent*: Stadhuis, in the crypt, from April to October daily from 09.30 to 18.30. From November to March daily from 09.30 to 16.30. *Province of East Flanders* at 64 Koningin Maria Hendrikaplein, opposite Sint Pieters station, Monday to Friday from 08.30 to 12.00 and from 13.15 to 16.45.

Post Office. Koornmarkt.

Transport. *Sint Pieters*, in the SW of the town c 2.5km from the centre, is for all mainline services. Public transport, which connects it with the centre, passes near to Bijloke and Fine Arts (Schone Kunsten) museums. *Dampoort*, in the N of the town c 1.5km from the centre, is for local services to Eeklo, Zelzate, Antwerp.

How to See Ghent and Environs. *On Foot*. Guided walks. From April to June and August to September on Saturday, Sunday and public holidays at 14.30 from the Tourist Information Office. Duration at least two hours.

Horse-drawn Carriage. From April to October from Sint Baafsplein. Standard tour c 35 minutes.

Public Transport. Free with a Tourist Card.

Boat. Inner town waterways tours from Koornlei and Graslei. Frequent departures from about Easter to October, duration c 35 minutes. There are also excursions on the Lys from Recollettenlei from May to September, duration five hours, and to Bruges from Recollettenlei in July and August, duration 11 hours including two hours in Bruges.

Private Car. Not really practical, though it is worth noting that there is parking at both the Museum voor Schone Kunsten, Fine Arts and the Bijloke Museum.

Horticulture. The principal horticultural districts are *De Pinte* 8km to the SW, *Merelbeke* 5km to the S, *Lochristi* 8km to the NE, and *Laarne*, with its château 8km to the SE. Note, begonias are at their best from July to September.

History. The abbeys of St Baaf and St Pieter, founded by St Amand in the 7C, probably formed the nucleus of the first settlement. This grew into a riverside village which clustered around the castle built by Baldwin Iron Arm c 867 at the confluence of the Lieve and Lys for defence against marauding Norsemen. During the 11C and 12C the town was fortified and enlarged. In the 13C much land was reclaimed and the Ghent to Bruges canal was constructed, as Dante relates in the Inferno (XV. 4-6):

'Quale i Fiamminghi tra Guizzante e Bruggia
temendo il fiotto che 'nver lor s'avventa,
fanno lo schermo perché 'l mar si fuggia.

The cloth industry became important at an early date. By the end of the 13C Ghent was larger than Paris. At that time relations between the nobles, who were generally loyal to the French king, and the wealthy and ambitious burghers came to a head. Revolutions and insurrections were frequent.

The town had been granted charters by the counts of Flanders c 1180 and 1191. Around 1212 the Council of Thirty-nine affirmed and maintained the rights of the citizens against their rulers. It introduced the election of magistrates. Up to that time they had been nominated. However, prosperity brought an increasing assertion of independence and in 1302 a contingent from Ghent, led by Jan Borluut, contributed to the defeat of the aristocracy at the Battle of the Golden Spurs.

In 1338, at the start of the Hundred Years War, the count sided with France against England, thus endangering the cloth trade. Jacob van Artevelde, 1287–1345, a noble who supported the merchants, made himself master of the town and entered into an alliance with Edward III of England. Edward's third son, John of Gaunt (Ghent), was born in the abbey of Sint Baaf in 1340. Both Ghent and the wool-growers of England prospered. In 1345 van Artevelde was murdered by guildsmen who mistrusted his ambition. His son Philip, 1340–82, took his father's place in 1381 and inflicted a severe defeat on the pro-French Count Louis de Male. However, the following year Charles VI of France came to his vassal's assistance. He crushed the rebels at the Battle of Westrozebeke, where van Artevelde was killed. Two years later in 1384 Louis de Male died. Because of the marriage between his daughter and heiress and Philip of

Burgundy, Flanders ceased to exist as a separate state and the period of Burgundian rule began.

The townspeople soon revolted against their Burgundian overlords. After five years of struggle from 1448 to 1453 they were subdued and subjected by Philip the Good to a humiliating limitation of privileges. Undaunted, on the death of Philip's son Charles the Bold in 1477, the citizens held Charles' daughter Mary a virtual prisoner. They forced her to sign the Great Privilege which gave them a more liberal constitution. On Mary's death, Flanders passed to her husband, Maximilian of Austria. He subdued the town. The birth of his grandson, Charles V, Charles Quint, in Ghent in 1500 helped to improve the loyalty of the townspeople.

By this time the cloth industry had been ruined by English competition. However, helped by the growing prosperity of Antwerp, Ghent found a new source of wealth in the export of grain from France via the Lys and Scheldt. The boatmen replaced the clothworkers as the leading guild. A canal to Terneuzen (in Holland) was dug in 1547. Thanks to this forwarding and carrying trade and to a revival of the tapestry industry, Ghent continued to flourish in the 16C, at a time when Bruges and Ypres were already in decay.

Ghent supported Charles V, at the beginning of his reign, but later refused to pay taxes for his military adventures in France. Charles' reaction in 1540 was swift and effective. He crushed the rising, abolished the town's privileges, filled in the moat, and built a new citadel on the site of the abbey of Sint Baaf at the town's expense.

During the years that followed Ghent, like the other towns in Flanders, was racked by the religious disturbances. In 1561 the bishopric was established by Philip II. The excesses by the Calvinist iconoclasts, which followed in 1566, were soon punished with great ferocity by the Duke of Alva. In 1576, on the death of Requesens, Alva's successor as governor, William of Orange marched into Flanders and occupied Ghent. The Pacification of Ghent, which attempted to secure religious freedom and the withdrawal of the Spanish soldiery from the Netherlands, was signed in November of that year. A brief period of domination by the Calvinists was ended by the Duke of Parma, Philip II's governor, in 1585. He retook Ghent and most of what makes up present-day Belgium. The Catholic faith was restored. However, the United Provinces were able to close the Scheldt and, in consequence, Ghent went into commercial decline.

In 1814 the treaty which ended the war of 1812–14 between England and America was signed in Ghent. In 1815 the fugitive Louis XVIII, accompanied by Chateaubriand and other royalists, took refuge here during Napoleon's Hundred Days. The town shared in the industrial growth of the 19C. It dates its modern prosperity from the introduction of cotton-spinning in 1799. This it owes to Lieven Bauwens, 1769–1822, a local tanner turned businessman. He smuggled machinery and workmen out of England and set up the first Belgian cotton-mill in the buildings of the recently dissolved abbey of Drongen. A great boost to prosperity was given in 1822–27, when the 16C canal to Terneuzen (in Holland) on the Scheldt estuary was replaced by a larger canal capable of taking sea-going vessels. This provided Ghent with a fine new maritime port.

Natives and Visitors. For British readers perhaps the best known native of Ghent is John of Gaunt, i.e. John of Ghent. The theologian Henry of Ghent, Doctor Solemnis, c 1217–93, and the painter Justus van Gent were born here. The brothers Jan and Hubert van Eyck were probably the greatest of the many painters who worked in Ghent. Other distinguished natives were Lucas de Heere, 1534–84, painter and poet, the Latinist Daniel Heinsius, 1580–1655, one of the leading scholars of the Dutch Renaissance, and Maurice Maeterlinck, 1862–1949, author and winner in 1911 of the Nobel prize for literature.

Two saints are associated with Ghent. St Amand, c 584–c 675, born near Nantes, founded monasteries in Carinthia, Navarre and Flanders. He died a nonagenarian at Elnon near Tournai. St Baaf or Bavo or Bavon, died c 655, was a native of Brabant. Converted by St Amand, he founded the abbey of St Peter on his estate at Ghent.

Ghent is described in four parts: A. Central Ghent, which includes the Cathedral, the Belfry, the Castle of the Counts and the medieval district;

B. Southern Ghent, with the Bijloke and Schone Kunsten (Fine Arts), museums; C. Eastern Ghent, with the Klein Begijnhof and the ruined Abbey of Sint Baaf; and D. the Port of Ghent and the Terneuzen canal.

A. Central Ghent

The circuit described below covers a distance of rather more than 2km, or 4km if the extension N and W of 's Gravensteen is included.

**Sint Baafskathedraal, one of the most splendid churches in Belgium, is justly celebrated for its many works of art. These include the famous van Eyck 'Adoration of the Mystic Lamb'.

The *Cathedral*, the *'Mystic Lamb'* and the *Crypt* may be visited at the following times: from April to September, Monday to Saturday from 09.30 to 12.00 and from 14.00 to 18.00, Sunday and Holy days from 13.00 to 18.00. From October to March, Monday to Saturday from 10.30 to 12.00 and from 14.30 to 16.00, Sunday and Holy days from 14.00 to 17.00. There is fee for the 'Mystic Lamb' and the Crypt.

It is known that a chapel dedicated to St John the Baptist stood here in 941. During the 12C the chapel was replaced by a Romanesque church. Towards the end of the 13C this in turn began to give way to the present Gothic church. Only the central part of the Romanesque crypt survived. The choir dates mainly from c 1290–1310. The transepts, nave and aisles, started during the 15C, were completed c 1550. The W tower, 82m high, rose between c 1460 and 1554.

The seventh chapter of the Order of the Golden Fleece was held here in 1445 by Philip the Good, and the twenty-third by Philip II in 1559. Charles V was baptised here in 1500. In 1540, as part of his reprisals for the town's revolt, Charles demolished much of the abbey of St Baaf to make way for a fortress. The abbey chapter then transferred to this church and its dedication to St John was changed to St Baaf. In 1561 Philip II created a bishopric in Ghent. The Calvinist iconoclasts did much damage to the cathedral in 1566 and again in 1576. After their second outburst Sint Baafskathedraal was used for Protestant worship for nearly ten years. In 1585 it was restored to Catholic hands by the Duke of Parma.

The beautifully proportioned interior is remarkable for the richness and variety of its decoration. Particularly noticeable is the difference between the 13–14C choir, with its grey-blue Tournai stone, and the 16C white stone in the remainder of the building.

In the NAVE the carved oak and marble pulpit of 1745 is by Laurent Delvaux. In the aisles there are paintings by Gaspard de Crayer and Abraham Janssens. In the N transept hang works by Theodoor Rombouts and Michiel Coxie.

The CHOIR is embellished with sumptuous marble screens, the gift of Bishop Triest, who died in 1657. He did much to restore the church after the destruction wreaked by the iconoclasts. His tomb, by Duquesnoy the Younger, on the N side, is the finest of the four episcopal monuments that flank the high-altar. The tomb of Bishop Allamont, who died in 1673, is by Jean del Cour. In front are four copper candlesticks by Benedetto da Rovezzano. They bear the arms of England's Henry VIII, for whose tomb at Windsor they were originally made, and of Bishop Triest, who presented them to the church after they had been sold by Cromwell. On the altar the statue of St Baaf of 1719 is by Hendrik Verbruggen.

A visit to the AMBULATORY and its chapels begins in the S transept where the hatchments of the Knights of the Golden Fleece are displayed. Many of the chapels contain fine works of art.

FIRST CHAPEL: *Christ among the doctors, a masterpiece by Frans Pourbus the Elder. This has portraits of Charles V, Philip II, the Duke of Alva, Viglius ab Aytta, the chief secretary of Charles V and Philip II, and of Bishop Jansenius, the first bishop of Ghent, who died in 1576. On the wings are the Circumcision and the Baptism of Christ, and on the outside another portrait of Viglius, who died in 1577. His tomb is opposite.

SECOND CHAPEL: Martyrdom of St Barbara by Gaspard de Crayer.

FOURTH CHAPEL: Tombs of bishops.

SIXTH CHAPEL: it was to this chapel in 1422 that Joos Vydt, a patrician of Ghent, presented the painting The Adoration of the Mystic Lamb, which he had commissioned from the van Eyck brothers. For reasons of space and security the masterpiece is displayed in a special room at the W end of the N aisle (see below).

SEVENTH CHAPEL: bronze doors of 1633 and a Pietà by Gerard Honthorst.

NINTH CHAPEL: Glorification of the Virgin by Niklaas de Liemakere.

TENTH CHAPEL: *St Baaf entering the Abbey of St Amand or The Conversion of St Baaf by Rubens (1624). The saint has distributed his belongings to the poor. His wife and two followers are on the left. The bearded head is a portrait of Rubens. Also in this chapel are the Raising of Lazarus, by Otto Venius, and the alabaster tomb of Bishop Damant who died in 1609.

ELEVENTH CHAPEL: Martyrdom of St Livinius, by Gerard Seghers.

LAST CHAPEL: The Seven Works of Mercy, by Michiel Coxie.

The large CRYPT was begun c 1150 and extended laterally when the present choir was built c 1300. The crown of five chapels to the E was added c 1400. The mural paintings, which were discovered in 1936, date from 1480–1540. Of the 26 bishops of Ghent, 21 are buried here. The chapels house the tombs of several patrician families. The oldest, that of Margaret de Gistel, who died in 1431, is in the SE chapel.

Part of the Treasury is displayed in the crypt during the summer. This includes the 1616 shrine of St Macarius by Hugo de la Vigne and a reliquary of the Crown of Thorns which may have belonged to Mary Queen of Scots. Among the vestments is the 16C English Ornement de St Liéin. The documents, illuminated manuscripts, books and incunabula include a 10C Evangelistary, rolls of the abbots of St Baaf and a work on natural history with wonderful medieval monsters. Among the pictures there are triptychs by Frans Francken the Elder–Calvary, Via Dolorosa and Descent from the Cross–and Justus van Gent; also the Story of St Andrew in a series of 14 paintings by Frans Pourbus the Elder.

The **ADORATION OF THE MYSTIC LAMB**, one of the great masterpieces of the Early Flemish School, is famed for its spirituality, the delicacy of its crowded detail and its glowing, luminous colours.

The polyptych, which is 3.65m high and 4.87m wide, has more than 250 figures in 20 paintings. Commissioned by Joos Vydt, a patrician of Ghent, and his wife, Isabella Borluut, it was presented to the church of St John and placed in one of the ambulatory chapels in 1432 (see above). The orthodox view is that it was designed and partly painted by Hubert van Eyck and finished by his brother Jan van Eyck. However, this has been questioned. There is some doubt as to whether Hubert van Eyck ever existed. No paintings signed by him are known.

The work has survived many adventures and has suffered many vicissitudes. Philip II coveted it. In 1566 it narrowly escaped destruction by the fanatical Calvinist iconoclasts. During the 18C, the prudish Joseph II taking exception to the naked state of Adam and Eve, placed the panels portraying them in the museum in Brussels and

The carved oak and marble pulpit of Sint Baafskathedraal, Ghent, by Laurent Delvaux, 1745

substituted clothed versions. These may be seen at the W end of the nave. During the French Revolution the picture was stolen by the French and taken to Paris. It was returned in 1815. The outer wings were then sold to the Berlin Museum. Their place was taken by 16C copies by Michiel Coxie. The wings were restored in 1919 under the terms of the Treaty of Versailles. In 1934 the panel showing the Just Judges was stolen. It has never been found. In 1941 it was replaced by an excellent copy made by Jef Vanderveken. To ensure that his work should not be taken to be part of the original, this artist included the features of Leopold III. Soon afterwards the painting was stolen again, this time by the German invaders, and placed in an Austrian salt mine. Returned after the cessation of hostilities, it was replaced in its chapel, where it remained until moved to its present position.

The subject of the picture is the Mystic Lamb of God, who redeemed the world from sin. Adored by angels, the Lamb stands on an altar, blood flowing from its side into a chalice. A dove, representing the Holy Spirit, links the Lamb to the figure of Christ above. In the foreground is the Fountain of Life. Patriarchs and prophets kneel on the left, apostles and confessors on the right. In the background there are processions of bishops, popes and virgins. Across the left-hand panels ride judges and soldiers, the defenders of the faith. On the opposite panel pilgrims and hermits come to adore the Lamb.

In the centre of the upper register Christ Triumphant is seated in majesty. He is flanked by Our Lady and St John the Baptist. Angels sing his praises. On either side Adam and Eve stand, a dejected pair, trying ineffectually to conceal their nakedness. Above them there are monochrome representations of the murder of Abel and the sacrifice of Isaac.

The landscape, which provides the background to the figures, is clear and accurate. Botanists have identified more than 40 of the plants, including the lesser celandine, saxifrage and swallow-wort, which appear in it. On the wings are the towers and pinnacles of the New Jerusalem, accurate representations, it is said, of the skylines of Bruges, Utrecht, Cologne and Maastricht.

On the back of the hinged panels, visible when the retable is closed, are portrayals, mostly in monochrome, of the donors kneeling in prayer, of the prophets Micah and Zachariah, of the sibyls of Cumae and Eritrea, of the Annunciation, and of St John the Baptist and St John the Divine.

Just E of the cathedral, beside an arm of the Scheldt, stands the **Gerard Duivelsteen**. Dating from 1245, with a fine Romanesque undercroft, this is a good example of one of the private fortresses built by the nobility in the 13C. Later the building was used as an armoury, a school, a seminary, a mental hospital, a prison, an orphanage, a fire station and, recently, an archive. Enquire at the Tourist Information Office for the opening times.

Nearby there are monuments to Jan and Hubert van Eyck, by George Verbanck, 1913, and to Lieven Bauwens, by P.P. de Vigne-Quyo, 1885.

The open space immediately to the W of the cathedral, the SINT BAAFS-PLEIN, has a statue by Isidoor de Rudder of Jan Frans Willems, 1793–1846, father of the Flemish nationalist movement. To the N the little Biezer-kapelstraat leads to some attractive old houses (see p 197). Also on the N stands the *Nederlandse Schouwburg*, the Netherlands Theatre, built in Renaissance style in 1899.

The W side of the square is occupied by the Lakenhalle and the Belfry. Although they now stand clear of other buildings, this has only been so for the last hundred years. For centuries they were surrounded by crowded narrow streets.

The **Lakenhalle**, the Cloth Hall, dates from 1425. Its vaulted undercroft is used today as a restaurant. In the large hall on the first floor there are audio-visual presentations on Ghent and its past. Lasting about 20 minutes they are given in four languages, Flemish, French, English and German in that order throughout the day.

The **Belfort**, the Belfry, was built between 1321 and 1380, but has been modified several times. The spire, restored to its original form in 1913, is topped by a dragon in gilded copper. Legend would have us believe that this was taken by the men of Ghent from Bruges, that city having obtained it from the followers of Baldwin who brought it back from Constantinople during the Fourth Crusade. The truth is more prosaic. It was made in Ghent in 1378.

Built on to the Belfry is the former lock-up and gaoler's house, 't Kindt of 1741, popularly known as the 'Mammelokker', from the suckling on the stone relief on the façade. The vaulted ground-floor room was called the 'Secret', as from 1402 to 1550 it housed the iron chest in which the charters of the privileges of Ghent were kept. Today the sole survivor of the four stone armed figures of 1338 that once stood at the belfry's corners is displayed here. In other rooms there are exhibits about the belfry and its history.

Above are the 52 bells, 37 of which were cast in 1660 by Pieter Hemony of Zutphen. Most of the others date from the 18C, but the largest, 6050kg and made in 1948, replaces one called 'Roelant', cast in 1318, and its successor 'Triomfante' by Hemony. The original 'Roelant' was once taken down by order of Charles V after being convicted of 'having played a very turbulent part with its tongue' during the uprising against him. 'Triomfante' cracked in 1914 and now stands in the Burgemeester Braunplein, immediately W of the belfry.

There are only guided visits to the Belfry. The times are: 16 November to March: daily from 10.30 to 16.30. From April to 15 November: daily from 10.00 to 18.00.

Near the belfry there is a fountain with kneeling figures, 'Youth', 1892, by George Minne.

The **Stadhuis** occupies the corner of Botermarkt and Hoogstraat 100m N of the Belfry. It came to this site in 1321 when the aldermen had to move from their previous meeting-place, which was razed to make way for the Belfry. Of the 14C building all that survives are two vaulted rooms in the basement.

The present building has two distinct parts. The N front, facing the Hoogpoort, is a fine example of Flamboyant Gothic. Dating from 1518–c 1560 it is by Rombout Keldermans and Domien de Waghemakere. The E façade of c 1581, in a more sober style, reflects the Calvinist regime of that period. The parts facing the Stadhuissteeg and the Poeljemarkt were added during the 17C and 18C.

Inside there are several fine halls. The *Pacificatiezaal* has painted arms of the governors of Flanders and a curious 'maze' paving. Here the Pacification of Ghent, a treaty between Catholics and Protestants, was signed in 1576. The *Trouwzaal*, the Marriage Room, was formerly the chapel. In the *Troonzaal*, the Throne Room, hang a number of historical pictures. These include the Abdication of Charles V by de Crayer and William the Silent defending the Catholics brought before the Calvinist magistrates by M. van Bree. The *Collaciezaal*, or Armoury, of 1482 was first the meeting-place of the 'Collace', the representatives of the tradesmen. Later it was used for the storage of weapons. The last chapter of the Order of the Golden Fleece was held here in 1559.

There are guided visits only to the Stadhuis. These take place between April and October every afternoon from Monday to Friday.

There are several attractive old houses near the Stadhuis. In Hoogpoort, No. 33, which dates from the 15C, was the *Goldsmiths' Hall*. Across Botermarkt on the corner with Nederpolder, is *Sint Jorishof* of 1477, now a hotel. Once the home of the Guild of Crossbowmen, it was here that Mary of Burgundy was compelled to sign the Great Privilege. Beyond, in Neder-polder, there are two fine 15C gabled houses on the right, *Grote Moor* and *Zwarte Moor*. Then there is a group of three houses, which once belonged to the van der Sikkelen family. These are *Grote Sikkel* with a 14C double gable, now the Academy of Music. On the other side of Biezerkapelstraat,

Rabot & Donkere Poort

PRINSENHOF

ABRAHAMSTRAAT

Archives

GAWAD

Discalced
Carmelites

's Gravensteen

Mus. Volkskunde

OUDBURG

ZUIVELBR

KANON

RECKELINKESTR

ST.
VEERLEPLEIN

P

KRAANLEI

Leie

LANGE MUNT

ONDER

BURGSTRAAT

Vismarkt

Mus. Sierkunst

Groot
Vleeshuis

HOOGPOO

DRABSTRAAT

GRASBRUG

RAMEN

POEL

KORENLEI

GRASLEI

KORENMARKT

DONKERSTEEG

HOOGSTRAAT

ST MICHIELSSTRAAT

RAVENSTEIN

PO

KLEINE TURKIJE

GOUDEN
LEEUWPLEIN

St Niklaas

BURGEME
BRAUNF

OUDE HOUTLEI

INGELANDGAT

ST MICHIELSBRUG

St Michiel

CATALONIESTRAAT

PREDIKHERENLEI

VELDSTRAAT

ST NIKLAASTRAAT

BENNESTEEG

Het Pand

ZWARTZUSTERSSTRAAT

ONDERBERGEN

HOORNSTRAAT

VOLDERSTRAAT

University
Aula

PUSSEMIER STR

Lys

KORTE MEER

POSTEERNESTRAAT

Hot. Vander Haeghen

P

STRAAT

VELDSTRAAT

Hot. d'Hane
Steenhuyse

VANDEVELDESTR

GEBR

ST MARTENS

ZONNESTRAAT

KOUTER P

ZANDPOORTSTRAAT

RECOLLETTENLEI

Leie

Gerechtshof
(Law Courts)

SCHOUWBURGSTRAAT

Opera

PEKELHARING

KETELVEST

PEINSTRAAT

NEDERKOUTER

SAVAANSTRAAT

Citadel Park

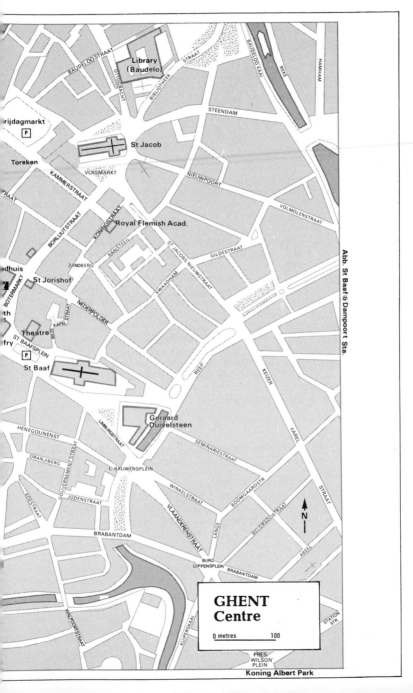

Library (Baudelo)

rijdagmarkt

P

Toreken

St Jacob

Kammerstraat

Baudeloostraat

Ottogracht

Bibliotheek

Straat

Baudeloo Kaai

Reke

Hamham

Steendam

Vlasmarkt

Nieuwpoort

Volmolenstraat

Royal Flemish Acad.

Koningsstraat

Raalsteeg

St Jacobs Nieuwstraat

Gildestraat

Zandberg

Kwaadham

Borluutstraat

Botermarkt

dhuis

St Jorishof

Nederpolder

Biezekapelstraat

Kapel

Theatre

St Baafsplein

fry

P

St Baaf

Reep

Keizer

Karel

Abb. St Baaf & Dampoort Sta.

Geraard Duivelsteen

Limburgstraat

Seminariestraat

Henegounenst.

Oranjiberg

Gouvernementstraat

L. Bauwensplein

Winkelstraat

Boomgaardstr.

Belgradostraat

Straat

Jodenstraat

Jolstraat

Brabantdam

Vlaanderenstraat

Lange

Abeel

N

GHENT Centre

0 metres   100

Burg. Lippensplein

Brabantdam

Kuipersstraat

Waldpoortstraat

Station Str.

Pres. Wilson Plein

Koning Albert Park

there is *Kleine Sikkel*, a Romanesque building of the 13C with the family arms above the old door. In a little courtyard off Biezerkapelstraat, the 14–15C *Achter Sikkel* forms the rear part of Grote Sikkel. Opposite the Kleine Sikkel stands the 18C *Hôtel van der Meersch*, with a 16C corner wing.

ZANDBERG, just N of Nederpolder, is a pleasant square surrounded by 18C houses. In its centre there is a pump of 1810.

The **Sint Niklaaskerk**, just W of the belfry, is the Scheldt Gothic successor of an 11C Romanesque church which stood here until c 1200. Only the base of the tower and the nave walls of the present church date from the early 13C. The baroque W porch is of 1681. The transepts and the W part of the choir were built after 1230. The tower, which was Ghent's first belfry, was completed c 1300. The apse is of 1432.

Albrecht Dürer lodged in 1521 at the 12–16C *Rode Hoed*. Once the house of the grocers' guild, this is in Kleine Turkije, to the N of the church. The house *De Fonteyne*, of 1539, at the corner of Gouden Leeuwplein has a fine Renaissance façade, the oldest of its kind in Ghent. It was the home of a chamber of rhetoric.

For Ghent S of Sint Niklaas, see B.

The W front of Sint Niklaas faces the KORENMARKT, a large and lively square. This was the medieval corn market. It remains in many respects the centre of Ghent. There are some Renaissance houses on the W side. Others were demolished in 1906 to make room for the imposing *Post Office*. On the E side is the *Borluutsteen*, the 13–15C mansion of the family, which gave Ghent its leader at the Battle of the Golden Spurs.

South-west of the Korenmarkt, the Lys is crossed by the ***Sint Michiels-brug**. This offers Ghent's most famous view (see below). To the S is the **Sint Michielskerk**, which was begun in the Flamboyant Gothic style in 1440 and completed, less its tower, in 1648. Since the 15C no fewer than six plans for a lofty tower were prepared. All were rejected for various reasons and the tower remains unfinished. Inside the church there is a Crucifixion by van Dyck, and works by Gaspard de Crayer, Otto Venius and Jean-Baptiste de Champaigne.

For Het Pand, immediately to the S of the church, see B; see p 203 for the Dominican Friary, c 350m W.

There is a fine view from from Sint Michielsbrug of the old port of Ghent, which lies to the N. To the right superb old houses, some of which belonged to the guilds, line the Graslei. The houses along the Korenlei, to the left, date mainly from the 17–19C.

The view across the water from the Korenlei is particularly striking. As you walk along, note particularly the *Huis der Onvrije Schippers* of 1740, with its distinctive gilded boat. No. 24 in the Korenlei, now restored to a 17C appearance, was originally a Romanesque building of c 1200.

Return to the bridge and cross over to the ***Graslei**. Walking from S to N, you will see the following houses. The *Gildehuis der Vrije Schippers*, built between 1500 and 1531 by C. van den Berghe. The *Gildehuis der Graanmeters* of 1698, the second House of the Grain Weighers. The tiny *Tolhuisje* of 1682, the customs house. The *Spijker* or *Koornstapelhuis*, a public warehouse used for the storage of grain taken as customs duty payment in kind. A plain Romanesque building of c 1200, this is the oldest house along Graslei. The 16C *Korenmetershuis*, the first House of the Grain Weighers. The *Gildehuis van de Metsers* of 1526, the House of the Masons.

To the S of the junction of the Lieve and Lys, across the Grasbrug, the

Korenlei ends. A short distance to the NE is the distinctive **Groot Vleeshuis** of 1406–10, the medieval meat market with its many small gables. Against the S side of the building are the little annexes where offal was distributed to the poor.

The **Museum voor Sierkunst**, Decorative Arts Museum, at 5 Jan Brey-delstraat occupies a mansion of 1754, which belonged to the de Coninck family. It has good collections of period furniture, ceramics, woodcarving, etc. The museum is open daily, except Monday, from 09.00 to 12.30 and from 13.30 to 17.30. It is closed on 1 and 2 January, 25 and 26 December.

Approximately 100m farther on, near the junction of Burgstraat and Gawad, there are some 16–17C house-fronts. Note especially the *Huis der Gekroonde Hoofden*, House of the Crowned Heads, with heads of the counts of Flanders down to Philip II.

Turn into Reckelingestraat and continue to SINT VEERLEPLEIN. At the S side is the portal of the **Vismarkt**, the Fish Market. Built by Artus Quellin the Younger in 1689, it was destroyed by fire in 1872. A rebuilt and enlarged market absorbed the site of the 15C Hospice Wenemaer. Early frontages of the fish and meat markets, bearing appropriate tile pictures, are round the corner in Reckelingestraat. The house on the left of the fish market occupies one of the transepts of a former church, partially demolished in 1578. This was dedicated to St Veerle, an 8C virgin martyr of Ghent. Around the square, especially in the SE corner near Kraanlei, there are some old houses with interesting carving. Until the late 18C public executions were frequently held in Sint Veerleplein.

To understand the early history of Ghent it is essential to pay a visit to ***'s Gravensteen**, the Castle of the Counts.

This magnificent feudal fortress is open daily from 09.00 to 19.00, or 17.00 from October to March. It is closed on 1 and 2 January and 25 and 26 December. The rooms devoted to a display of the instruments of torture are accompanied by horrific and detailed illustrations. The most important parts of the castle are identified by notices in English.

It was here, at the confluence of the Lieve and the Lys, that c 867 Baldwin Iron Arm built his castle. Parts of this structure survive in the cellars of the keep. Baldwin's castle was for defence against the Norsemen. Its successor, begun in 1180 by Philip of Alsace, was for the express purpose of overawing the unruly citizens of the town. It did not succeed. In 1302, at the time of the Battle of the Golden Spurs, the castle was stormed by the burghers of Ghent and, in 1338, by Jacob van Artevelde. From 1349 until the end of the 18C it was used for special ceremonies, as a prison, mint and law court. From 1797 to 1887 it housed a factory. Major restoration was carried out between 1894 and 1913.

From the gatehouse ascend to a walkway along the outer wall. Crossing over the gatehouse, note the holes down which boiling oil could be poured on the heads of attackers. Continue along a further stretch of wall, which has toilets perched high above the water, to the Count's Residence N of the keep. On the ground floor the vaulted Audience Chamber was for some 300 years the meeting-place of the Council of Flanders. Above are a group of rooms, once used by the counts and their families. Today they contain instruments of torture. Beyond is the Upper Hall, where the torture theme continues. A winding stair will take you to the roof, which commands fine views over the town. You then descend to the Upper Hall and then continue down to the Great Hall, scene in 1445 of a banquet of the Order of the Golden Fleece presided over by Philip the Good.

The cellars are also worth a visit. In one, below the keep, there are parts of the 9C castle and two grim oubliettes. Another was used as a stable until the 14C and then as a torture chamber. A third housed the refuse dump and cesspit. This was uncomfortably close to the well, which supplied the castle with fresh water.

NORTH AND WEST OF 'S GRAVENSTEEN. A leisurely walk of c 2km will take you through the historic, and often picturesque, district N and W of 's Gravensteen. Geldmuntstraat recalls by its name the mint of the counts of Flanders which was established here during the 14C. Continue N by Sint Margrietstraat. On the W side, where it meets Academiestraat, stands the **Sint Stephanuskerk**. This was founded in 1606 and rebuilt in 1838 after a fire. It has a good baroque door. Inside there are altar paintings by Gaspard de Crayer. The baroque furnishings were formerly in the nearby *Carmelite Church*. Built between the 14C and 16C, this lies within the angle of Lange Steenstraat and Vrouwebroerstraat. Now deconsecrated, the former church belongs to the town and the rest of the complex to the provincial government. An octagonal tower of the Carmelite house founded in 1285 survives in a corner of the first courtyard.

At 1 Academiestraat are the mainly 17C buildings of the *Augustinian Monastery* founded in 1296. Academiestraat leads to Sint Antoniuskaai along the N bank of the Lieve. Here, among other old houses, is **Sint Antoniushof Godshuis**, a building of 1641 which was once the house of the

Medieval guild houses along the Graslei quay, Ghent

shooting guild of St Anthony. In 1805 it became an almshouse. Note the display of cartridges and crossed arquebuses.

We cross the river at the next bridge which offers a good view of the area. To the NW is the **Rabot**, a fortified sluice of 1491. The **Donkere Poort**, the Dark Gate, just across the bridge, is a vaulted archway between two turrets. This is a relic of the palace, the Prinsenhof of 1353, in which Charles V was born in 1500. A plaque on the inner side shows the palace as it was in the 16C. The Prinsenhof is also recalled by the name of the street, which leads us in a SE direction from here. At the far end we turn right into Abrahamstraat. At 13 are the *City Archives*, housed since 1932 in the *Mons Pietatis*, the former public pawnshop. Founded in 1621, this was built by Wenceslas Coeberger. Note the inscription about lending to the poor. By the corner with Abrahamstraat, at No. 13 Gawad is the *Museum of Industrial Archaeology and Textiles*, which is open from Monday to Friday from 09.00 to 12.30 and 13.30 to 16.30. Arrangements can be made here for an industrial-archaeological tour through Ghent.

We continue S and turn right into Burgstraat. A short distance to the W, on the right at No. 46, are the mainly 17C buildings of the *Friary of the Discalced Carmelites*. The church of 1712 has three baroque altars. In the garden there is a fragment of the Prinsenhof palace.

To the W of Burgstraat is SINT ELISABETHPLEIN. Off this square is the Sint Elisabeth Begijnhof which was founded in the 13C. Some 16C and 17C houses survive. The begijnhof's 16C portal was removed during the 19C and now forms the entrance to the Bijloke Museum (see below). The body of the church dates from the 15C, the transepts from two centuries later.

If you walk eastwards along Burgstraat, you will return to 's Gravensteen. If, however, you wish to see another religious house, follow Peperstraat S from Sint Elisabethplein to the *Dominican Friary* at 41 Hoogstraat. Once a medieval leper house, it was rebuilt in the 17C as a convent and school. In 1845 it was given to the Dominicans.

In Kraanlei, beside the Leie, to the NE of Sint Veerleplein, there are some picturesque and elegant houses. No. 65, the *****Museum voor Volkskunde**, Folklore, occupies some beautifully restored 14C almshouses.

These almshouses, the Hospitaal der Kindren Alyns, owed their existence to a quarrel between two Ghent families, the Ryms and the Alyns. This culminated in the assassination by the Ryms of the two leading Alyns. The Ryms were sentenced in 1354 to have their houses razed and in 1362 were ordered to provide an annuity for a hospice. In a gesture of reconciliation and goodwill, the surviving Alyns offered their house in the Kraanlei. A chapel was built in 1363. More houses were added in 1519 by Lieven van Pottelsberghe, the guardian at that time. (His portrait hangs in the Museum of Fine Arts.) A new chapel was built between 1543 and 1547. After their acquisition in 1940 by the town of Ghent, the almshouses were restored as a home for the Folklore Museum.

The museum attempts to recall the life of the people of Ghent, particularly that of its craftsmen, during the 19C. There are games and toys, including a hobby-horse made by the sculptor Laurent Delvaux for his grandchildren. A grocer's shop. A cooper's workshop. A cobbler at work, with an interesting water-filled glass bowl for concentrating light. A puppet theatre, with a show, usually on Saturday afternoon. An inn of c 1900. A clog-maker. Fashion and clothing. Printing. A baker. A barber's saloon of c 1900. An exhibition on lighting. A chemist and apothecary's laboratory. Lace. A typical room of one of the occupants of the almshouses.

The chapel of the almshouses may also be visited. In the adjoining sacristy a graphic painting shows the Ryms murdering the Alyns.

The museum is open daily from April to October from 09.00 to 12.30 and from 13.30 to 17.30, from November to March daily, except Monday, from 10.00 to 12.00 and from 13.30 to 17.00. It is closed on 1 January and 25 December. There is a short guide to the collection in English.

Just beyond the museum two 17C carved fronts are worth noting. No. 77 has the Seven Acts of Charity or the three Theological and Four Cardinal Virtues. No. 79 the five senses, a flying deer, the virtues, a flute player, etc.

Cross the Zuivelbrug to Groot Kanonplein. Here stands the 15C iron mortar known as '*Dulle Griet*', Mad Meg. This was used by Ghent in an attack on Oudenaarde.

The nearby VRIJDAGMARKT was once the focus of the town's political and civic life. Here the medieval guilds met, talked and frequently brawled. Today it is the scene of a busy Friday market. There is a bronze statue by de Vigne-Quyo of 1863 of Jacob van Artevelde, whose uprising of 1338 may have started here. At the SE corner the *Toreken* of 1460, with a slim turret, was the House of the Tanners.

The **Sint Jacobskerk** was begun in the 12C. The two Romanesque W towers belong to that period. The lower part of the steeple, above the crossing, was finished between the 13C and 15C.

We leave the Vrijdagmarkt by Kammerstraat. The painter de Crayer died in 1669 at No. 18. In Koningstraat, a short distance to the SE, the 1746 façade of the *Royal Flemish Academy* is by 't Kindt.

Just N of the church of Sint Jacob are the 17C buildings of the former Cistercian abbey of *Baudelo*. Originally only a refuge, in the 17C it became a full abbey. It now houses a school and library. It is said that Mozart played on the Hemony carillon in the turret. Some 600m to the NW across the river is FRATERSPLEIN. Here there is a statue of Pieter van Gent, 1486–1572, known for his educational work in Mexico. The statue, erected in 1976, is a copy of one in Mexico City. On the N side of the square is the convent of *Sint Jan de Deo*, formerly a Carthusian foundation. It houses the *Museum Meerhem*, open Sunday from 14.00 to 17.00, which has documentation on local history reaching back over five centuries.

From the church of Sint Jacob take the Borluutstraat to the Stadhuis, a distance of c 300m.

B.   Southern Ghent

Southern Ghent is visited mainly for the Bijloke or Archaeological Museum and the Museum voor Schone Kunsten, or Fine Arts. The Bijloke Museum is a short distance to the NW of CITADEL PARK. The Fine Arts Museum is at the park's E corner. This area can be reached by public transport from the Korenmarkt. Visitors who prefer to walk should proceed S along Veldstraat and its continuations to the junction of Kortrijk-sepoortstraat and Ijserlaan with Burgemeester K. de Kerchovelaan, a distance of c 1.5km. A quieter route for pedestrians starts at Sint Michielsbrug. Follow the E bank of the river, Predikherenlei, in a S direction. Most of the housefronts here date from the 16C to 19C. Across the river is **Het Pand**, the site of an ancient hospice where the Dominicans built a friary in the 13–14C. The buildings now form a part of Ghent university. Cross to the W bank S of Het Pand and continue over the *Coupure* canal. After passing a number of scientific institutions connected with the university, you will reach the Bijloke Museum.

Veldstraat leads S out of the Korenmarkt. The shop on the corner of Volderstraat was formerly the *Hôtel Schamp*. John Quincy Adams and his staff resided here during the negotiations that culminated with the signing of the Treaty of Ghent in 1814. This ended the war between England and the United States of America. A plaque commemorates the event. On the same side of the street, the former *Hôtel d' Hane-Steenhuyse*, an 18C mansion with a rococo façade, was the residence of Louis XVIII of France during Napoleon's Hundred Days. The house is now used for exhibitions on urban renovation and expansion. Opposite at No. 82 is the **Hôtel Vander Haeghen**, another 18C mansion. This serves as a centre for various exhibi-tions and houses documentation and other material on Maurice Maeterlinck, 1862–1949, winner of the Nobel prize for literature in 1911, and a collection of the graphic work of the Ghent artist Victor Stuyvaert, 1897–1924.

The *Aula* or Assembly Hall of the University of Ghent, which was founded in 1816 by King William of the Netherlands, is 100m E along Volderstraat. It occupies a porticoed building of 1826 by Louis Roelandt. The university has been wholly Flemish since 1930. Adjacent is the 1642 gateway of the former Jesuit college.

The university's **Museum Wetenschap en Techniek**, Science and Technology, at 9 Korte Meer is open on Monday and Wednesday from 14.00 to 17.00. It has exhibits illustrating the work of various early scientists and inventors.

Korte Meer continues S into the large, tree-lined open space known as the KOUTER, the ploughed field. From earliest times this has been a popular venue for political demonstrations, archery contests, military parades and markets. A flower market has been held here since 1772.

The **Koninklijke Opera**, to the SW in Schouwburgstraat, was built by Louis Roelandt between 1836 and 1848. There are performances from October to mid June. No. 29, the *Handelsbeurs*, the commercial exchange occupies the former Guard House of 1738. On the N side, the 18C *Hôtel Falignan* by Bernard de Wilde is now a club.

To the W the *Gerechtshof*, the Law Courts, by Louis Roelandt, 1836–46, stands at the junction of Schouwburgstraat and Veldstraat. In front there is a statue by Julien Dillens, 1886, of Hippolyte Metdepenningen, 1799–1881, a prominent lawyer and political figure.

From Veldstraat continue in a S direction to Nederkouter and the Kortrijksepoortstraat. At the crossroads the Bijloke Museum is on the right and the Museum voor Schone Kunsten 500m farther S on the left. Approximately 900m along the Kortrijksesteenweg is **Sint Pieters Station**. In a garden by the corner of Bijlokekaai, a statue by G. de Vreeze, 1952, commemorates Jan Palfijn, 1650–1730, a surgeon credited with the invention of the forceps.

The *****Bijloke Museum**, which, rather misleadingly, is also called the Archaeological Museum, occupies the very attractive 14–17C domestic buildings of the abbey of Bijloke.

The museum is open daily, except Monday, from 09.00 to 12.30 and from 13.30 to 17.30. It is closed on 1 and 2 January and 25 and 26 December.

The abbey was founded on this site as a hospice and hospital in 1228 by a group of nuns who came from the Cistercian convent of Nieuwenbosse, 3km SE of Ghent. It suffered severely during the religious troubles of the 16C. In 1579, during the years of Calvinist domination, the construction of new ramparts led to the demolition of many of the abbey buildings. The refectory and dormitory survived. The nuns returned in 1585 when the Duke of Parma reoccupied Ghent. Much rebuilding was undertaken in the 17C. Expelled again in 1797, the nuns returned in 1801. Since then they have occupied buildings which date mainly from the 17C. The hospital survived the various troubles. Today a 13C ward forms part of the municipal hospital and is staffed by nuns.

The museum houses a variety of material relating to the history of Flanders and of Ghent. Entrance is through the 1660 portal of the former Sint Elisabeth Begijnhof. This was removed from its original position and set up here c 1874. Immediately to the right are two rooms and a passage. The 17C Room of the Governors of the Poor House has a chimneypiece and panelling by Norbert Sauvage. Over the chimneypiece hangs an allegorical representation by Joos van Cleef of the founding of the Poor House. In the

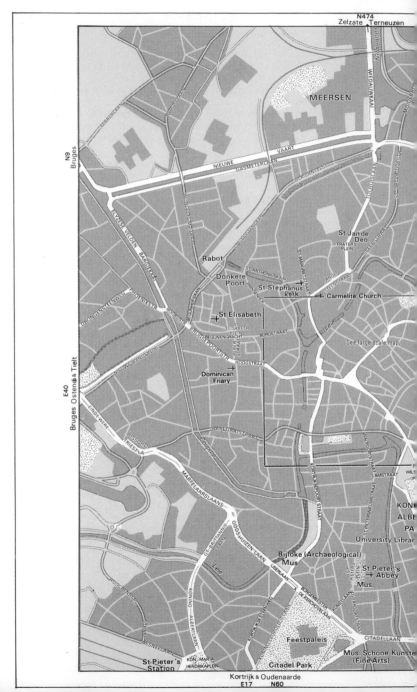

GHENT
& Environs

0 metres   600

passage there are some interesting plans of 1518 for the Stadhuis and 17C woodcarvings of the Four Seasons by Laurent van der Meulen. These are reminiscent of the work of Grinling Gibbons. The second room, the Room of the Abbots of Baudelo, has some late 17C and early 18C Brussels tapestries.

We now cross the COURTYARD. The buildings from left to right are the 17C House of the Abbess, the 14C refectory and dormitory, and part of an 18C façade from Veldstraat. An entrance from the courtyard leads to a corridor. In a room off the corridor there is a collection of woodcarving from old Ghent houses which have been demolished. Stairs ascend from the cloister to the *REFECTORY. This is a superbly proportioned hall with a high wooden vault. In the centre is the *monument of Hugo II, castellan of Ghent, who died in 1232. This was found in 1948 in the ruins of the abbey of Nieuwenbosse. On a wall by the entrance there is a 14C *mural of the Last Supper, with the Coronation of the Virgin above. On the fireplace wall there are representations of St John the Baptist and St Christopher. The other exhibits include Rhenish engraved copper grave-plates dated to the late 12C, which were found in the Scheldt.

In the UPPER CLOISTER there is a variety of exhibits. These include medieval ceramics, Delft tile walls from old houses in Ghent, porcelain and glass, costumes of the 18C and 19C, weapons and armour, brass, pewter and ironwork, a collection of intricate locks and keys and the large *brass of Leonard Betten, Abbot of Sint Truiden, who died in 1667.

The DORMITORY, another fine hall, which opens off the SE corner of the upper cloister, is largely devoted to the guilds. Its centre-piece is a model ship carried by the Free Boatmen in the procession of 1767.

On the S side of the LOWER CLOISTER is the 16C lavatorium. On the W side a fascinating Panorama of Ghent in 1534 is sometimes hung. The stucco ceiling of 1715 in the large hall was moved from the refectory when that room was restored to its original state. Off the N side there are three large rooms with gilt hangings. All are concerned mainly with the shooting guilds. In the first there are guild chairs and historical pictures, in the second a small cannon and a painting of a meeting of the Guild of St Anthony, in the third there are more guild chairs. On the E side there is a painting, the Coronation of Christ, by Dirk Bouts.

From the SW corner of the cloister a passage leads to the 17C HOUSE OF THE ABBESS. This has a series of rooms containing furnishings from old Ghent houses, abbeys and hospices. The kitchen has an interesting collection of historical cooking utensils. In the last room there is a fine chimney-piece by Norbert Sauvage and a painting showing aldermen meting out justice.

Leaving the Bijloke Museum we take Ijserlaan to Karel de Kerchovelaan, which flanks the N side of Citadel Park (see below). Karel de Kerchove was burgomaster of Ghent between 1857 and 1881, a time when a great deal of modernisation took place. He is commemorated by this street and by a fountain of 1898, the work of Hippolyte Leroy, at its NW end.

At the SE end of Karel de Kerchovelaan, on the right just inside the park, is the ***Museum voor Schone Kunsten**. This occupies a building of 1902, which has two series of rooms numbered 1 to 15 and lettered A to L. Its range extends from the Flemish Primitives to modern works. Paintings of the 19C and 20C start in Room 13 and continue through to Room L.

The museum is open daily, except Monday, from 09.00 to 12.30 and from 13.30 to 17.30. It is closed on 1 and 2 January, 25 and 26 December.

In most of the rooms covering the earlier periods there are excellent

The Carrying of the Cross by Hieronymus Bosch, Museum voor Schone Kunsten, Ghent

multilingual guide boards. The following is a representative selection of the works on show in the museum.

In the large hall just inside the entrance there are some fine Brussels tapestries. One 17C group from the Abbey of St Peter in Ghent tells the Story of Darius. An 18C group from the Château of Oudburg portrays the Glorification of the Gods.

ROOM 1 is devoted to 15C painting from Ghent. Note particularly the Pietà from the school of Hugo van der Goes and the Ecce Homo by a follower of the Master of Flemalle. There is also an exquisite 13C French Sedes Sapientiae.

In ROOM 2 there are two fine paintings by *Hieronymus Bosch*: *The Carrying of the Cross, one of the artist's last works, and St Jerome at Prayer. Note also *Adriaen Isenbrant's* gentle rendering of the Madonna and Child, *Christian Engerbrechtsz's* Pietà, from the destroyed Dominican church in Ghent, and *Gheeraert Hoorenbaut's* *Triptych of St Anne with the portraits of the donors, Lieven van Pottelsberghe and his wife. Circa 1515 Lieven van Pottelsberghe became guardian of the Hospitaal der Kindren Alyns, now the Folklore Museum (see above).

ROOM 3 has some fine medieval sculptures, including two 14C bas-reliefs, the Baptism of Christ and the Coronation of Mary, both work of the Nottingham school. Do not miss the striking 14C Italian Coronation of Mary and a beautiful antiphonary of 1498.

In ROOM 4 there are works by *Frans Pourbus the Elder: Portrait of a Young*

Woman, the artist's last known signed and dated work, *Marten van-Heemskerk*: Calvary and *Frans Francken the Younger*: another Calvary, a work in an unusual dark and restrained style with the emphasis on human sorrow rather than historical drama.

ROOM 5 has some very large canvases. These include the Rest on the Flight to Egypt by *Jacob Jordaens*, the Judgement of Solomon and other works by *Gaspard de Crayer*, the *Crown of Thorns and the Annunciation by *Jan Janssens* and the *Stigmata of St Francis of Assisi by *P.P. Rubens*.

ROOMS 6 and 7 are devoted mainly to 17C Flemish and Dutch painting. Of particular interest are *Theodoor Rombouts*'s Allegory of the Five Senses, *Philippe de Champaigne*'s Portrait of Pierre Camus, *Jacob Jordaens* two studies for a head, *Gaspard de Crayer*'s Head of a Young Man, *P.P. Rubens'* The Scourging of Christ, a sketch for the painting now hanging in Antwerp's Sint Paulus church, and *Antoon van Dyck*'s: Jupiter and Antiope.

In ROOM 8 your eyes are drawn to *The Village Lawyer by *Pieter Brueghel the Younger*, an original work by an artist better known for the copies which he made of his father's paintings. This is a fascinating scene of contemporary bureaucracy. Note also the landscapes by *Roelant Savery*, and the Scourges of Mankind by *Kerstiaen de Keuninck*, an artist who was unknown until 1902, when this work was discovered in the museum's storeroom.

In ROOM 9 there are marine paintings by *Willem van de Velde the Younger*. Other works of interest are by *Paul de Vos*, Buffalo attacked by Dogs, and *Andries van Eertvelt* , Ships in Distress, a rather theatrical storm at sea.

In ROOMS 10 and 11 there are portraits, landscapes and still life paintings by *P. de Keyser*, *Willem Claesz Heda*, *Jan de Bray*, *Frans Hals*, *Aelbert Cuyp*, *Govert Flinck*, *Nicolas Maes* and *Jan van Goyen*.

ROOM 12 has paintings by foreign artists, including *Tintoretto*'s Portrait of a Sculptor and *Alessandro Magnasco*'s, Monks at Prayer.

In ROOM 13 our tour of the gallery reaches the 19C and 20C. Works from these centuries are also shown in ROOMS 14 and 15 and in ROOMS A to L. Pictures tend to be moved around in these rooms and are often displaced to provide space for temporary exhibitions. The following is a brief selection from the many works usually on display. *Henri Evenepoel*: *The Spaniard in Paris; *Emile Claus*: Winter Scene and Cows swimming across the Lys; *Jan Verhas*: *The Master-Painter, a delicious study of childen around a table; *H. Remaeker*: The Painter; *Gustave de Smet*: Village Fair; *Edgard Tytgat*: The Painter's Studio (1934); *Jan Brusselmans*: Nude; *Rik Wouters*: Woman Seated (1915); *Gustave van der Woestyne*: Young Peasant Woman (1913); *James Ensor*: several typical works; *Théodore Rysselberghe*: *The Poet E. Verhaeren reading to his Friends.

Sculptures. *George Minne*: Boy kneeling; Man weeping over his dead Dog; Kneeling Man and Woman; *Constantin Meunier*: The Prodigal Son.

The Department of Contemporary Art concentrates on visual art forms of the 20C. The emphasis is on the period after 1945, on movements such as Jeune Peinture Belge, Cobra, Lyric Abstract, Pop Art, Minimal Art and Conceptual Art.

The CITADEL PARK was laid out in 1871 on the site of a fort raised by the Duke of Wellington. Oswald de Kerchove, 1844–1906, son of the Karel de Kerchove mentioned above, was a distinguished botanist and horticulturalist who played a leading part in establishing the 'Floralies'. He is commemorated by a statue by G. van den Meersche, 1923. There are two other memorials of interest, both in the E part of the park. One by Yvonne Serruys,

1926, near the large lake, honours Emile Claus, the painter and leader of Flemish Impressionism, the other by Jules van Biesbroeck, 1926, close to the Museum voor Schone Kunsten, is to Edmond van Beveren, 1852–94, who was prominent in the Ghent Socialist movement.

The university's **Botanic Garden**, with over 7500 species, is located to the SE of Citadel Park. It is open from Monday to Thursday from 14.00 to 17.00 and on Saturday, Sunday and public holidays from 09.00 to 12.00.

From the N side of Citadel Park we follow Kunstlaan or Overpoortstraat for c 400m to the large, open SINT PIETERSPLEIN, which is bounded on the E by the buildings of the former abbey of **Sint Pieter**. Founded by St Amand in the 7C, the abbey suffered many vicissitudes during the centuries that followed. A rebuilding started in 1584 was not completed until the 18C. Fortunately, it was not destroyed during the French Revolution, but was used as public offices. Today the N wing, which includes the chapter house, has been converted into an *Arts and Culture Centre*. The former hospital and reception wing house the **Schoolmuseum Michiel Thiery**, an institution of wide scope which makes lavish use of models. Its exhibits, which embrace natural history, geography, the evolution of man and the history of the computer, attract large numbers of schoolchildren and many adults. A daily audio-visual presentation on Ghent and the Emperor Charles V provides a useful introduction to a fascinating period in the history of the town. The museum is open daily from 09.00 to 12.15 and from 13.30 to 17.15. It is closed on Friday afternoon and on public holidays.

Beyond the courtyard some of the old abbey buildings have been partly excavated. The **Sint Pieterskerk** of 1629–1719, designed by Pieter Huyssens with a fine dome, is in the Renaissance style. It has a wrought-iron choir screen of 1748 by Maniet, paintings by Niklaas de Liemakere and Theodoor van Thulden, and the porphyry cenotaph of Isabel of Austria, 1501–26, sister of Charles V and queen of Christian II of Denmark. Her remains were removed to Odense in Denmark in 1883.

From the abbey we take Sint Pieternieuwstraat and walk in a N direction and, passing the library and various scientific departments of the university en route, continue by Walpoortstraat and its successors to the town centre. Near the beginning of Walpoortstraat, Lamstraat on the right crosses an arm of the Scheldt to President Wilsonplein (see C. below).

C. Eastern Ghent

The principal places of interest in Eastern Ghent are the Klein Begijnhof and the Abbey of Sint Baaf. The circuit described below is c 3km and will not tax the energetic. It may also be done by car. Parking is usually possible near both main sites.

Leave the cathedral by Limburgstraat and proceed in a SE direction. Passing the Geraard Duivelsteen, the van Eyck and Lieven Bauwens monuments, continue along the broad Vlaanderenstraat to President Wilsonplein.

Here the long, narrow KONING ALBERT PARK extends to the SE. At this end there is an exhibition building and, in the park, an equestrian memorial of 1937 to King Albert. The pedestal is by J.A. de Bondt, the statue by Domien Ingels. In a triangular garden near the park's SW corner is the Congo Star, 1936, or the Memorial of the Colonials.

Leave the park on the E side by Twee Bruggenstraat, then turn right into Lange Violettenstraat. The **Klein Begijnhof** is a little way down on the left. It was founded in 1234 by the sisters Margaret and Joanna of Constantinople. The present buildings, which date from 17–19C, surround a quiet enclosure, where cattle or sheep may be found grazing peacefully. The baroque style church dates from 1658–1720; the façade belongs to the later period. It has an interesting polyptych, the Fountain of Life, by Lucas Hoorenbaut, and altarpieces by de Crayer and Niklaas de Liemakere. Liemakere's work, the Presentation in the Temple, is one of his most charming paintings.

Take the Twee Bruggenstraat to the Nieuwe Bosbrug and the Lousbergs-brug, two bridges over parallel channels of the Leie. Then turn left and follow the Lousbergskaai for c 500m. The ruined **Abdij Sint Baaf** is on the right. This is open daily except Monday, 09.00 to 12.30, 13.30 to 17.30. It is closed 1 and 2 January and 25 and 26 December.

This Benedictine abbey was founded by St Amand in the 7C. Laid waste by the Vikings in the 9C, it was rebuilt by the Count of Flanders a century later. The abbey flourished greatly, especially during the 12C and 13C. In 1340, at the time of Jacob van Artevelde's alliance with England, Edward III visited Ghent. His queen, Philippa of Hainaut, gave birth to their third son, John of Gaunt, in the abbey. In 1369 the wedding of Philip the Bold of Burgundy to Margaret, heiress of Louis de Male, took place here. This alliance had momentous consequences, as it presaged the coming of Burgundian rule to Flanders. In 1540, after he had crushed the revolt of the people of Ghent, Charles V built a fortress here. He destroyed the abbey church and used the domestic buildings as barracks and armouries. This fortress was demolished during the 19C. The abbey remains then became the *Museum voor Stenen Voorwerpen*, the Lapidary Museum.

The E wall of the Gothic cloister, partly restored, has vaulting of 1495. On the left is the small, altered, octagonal 12C *Lavatorium*. The 13C chapter-house has Romanesque bays. Notice the two curiously shaped ancient tombs, one with a head-rest. Beyond is the old refectory which dates from 12C or earlier. From the 13C onwards this was used as a store. In the N side of the cloister, steps ascend to the large 13C refectory which has a 16C wooden ceiling and round-headed windows. From 1589 to the end of the 18C this great hall served as the abbey chapel and from 1834 to 1882 as the local parish church. It now houses a lapidary collection which includes a Romanesque font, a 12C double-tympanum from the destroyed abbey church, and a number of ancient tombstones including one said to be that of Hubert van Eyck.

Dampoort Station, 400m NE of the abbey is at the S end of Achterdok (see D.). The neo-Gothic **Groot Begijnhof**, c 400m E of the station, was built in 1872 as an extension of the Sint Elisabeth Begijnhof. It has two gateways. The one on the Ghent side has a statue of its patron saint, the other bears the arms of the Arenberg family which bought the land. A museum, at No. 64, offers an interesting survey of begijnhof life. The Groot Begijnhof is open from April to October on Wednesday, Thursday, Saturday and Sunday and on public holidays between 10.00 and 11.00 and 14.00 and 18.00.

From the Abdij Sint Baaf the cathedral is c 700m to the W.

D.   The Port of Ghent and the Terneuzen Canal

Ghent has long been a port. At first it was connected to the sea by the 13C canal to Bruges, which in turn was linked to Het Zwin. From 1547 its citizens used the new canal to the Scheldt estuary at Terneuzen, which is now in Holland. In early times the port was spread along the waterways in the town, notably on the Graslei and the Korenlei. The Scheldt was closed by the United Provinces from 1648 to 1795, but in 1827 the Terneuzen canal, 30km long, was opened to sea-going vessels. This turned Ghent into a major port. In 1968 a new lock at Terneuzen opened the canal to ships of 60,000 tons deadweight and there are plans now to include a facility for vessels of 125,000 tons. Much of the port area is served by public roads which offer excellent views of the ships and barges. The land on both sides of the canal is rapidly being developed into a vast industrial zone. A drive along the road which follows the W bank is recommended.

The southern arm of the port, *Achterdok* and *Handelsdok* is close to Dampoort Station. From here we travel on the W side of the basin for 1.5km to Muidebrug, where the main port area with the Grootdok and its three arms and, beyond, the Sifferdok for larger ships, is located.

A diversion eastwards to the suburb of **Oostakker** brings us to the *Basiliek Onze Lieve Vrouw van Lourdes*. Dedicated in 1877, it was built to plans by Baron Jean Béthune, who was also responsible for much of the painted decoration of the interior. In the gardens nearby there is a grotto of Our Lady of Lourdes.

On Gefusilleerdenstraat, between Oostakker and the main road to Antwerp, the *Monument der Onthoofden* honours 56 members of the Resistance who were executed by the Germans here. Dedicated in 1951, the site has memorial crosses and bronze statues by George Vindevogel representing the shot, the beheaded, the hanged and the political prisoners.

From Muidebrug, Sassekaai bears briefly S to Neuseplein. Just beyond, we cross a canal by Nieuwe Tolhuisbrug. At Wiedauwkaai we pass the *Tolhuis*, the Customs, on the right, then head N beside *Voorhaven*. At the end of Voorhaven, c 3km from Nieuwe Tolhuisbrug, is the entrance to *Grootdok*, where the canal starts officially. To the W in **Wondelgem** the church is an imposing baroque structure of 1687.

We leave the water briefly before crossing the *Ringvaart*, the ring canal. The entrance to *Sifferdok* is some 500m farther on. The road continues as Wondelgemkaai and Langerbruggekaai. Across the water, 2.5km from the Ringvaart, is the *Petroleumdok*, surrounded by oil tanks. After a further 3.5km we reach the site of the projected *Kluizendok*. This, 400m wide, will extend nearly 2km NW towards Ertvelde. Across the canal, the *Rodenhuizedok*, 1km in length, is the planned starting-point for the projected 125,000 tonnes canal, which will loop E of Wachtebeke and Zelzate. Continue beside the canal, passing *Rieme*, where a memorial marks the execution site of a group of Resistance fighters. **Zelzate**, 19km from Ghent-Dampoort, is a modern industrial town of 13,000 inhabitants on the Dutch border. For **Terneuzen**, on the Scheldt 15km farther on, and for the Dutch district of Zeeland Flanders, see 'Blue Guide Holland'.

From Ghent to *De Panne*, see Route 5, to *Bruges* and *Ostend*, and to *Brussels*, see Route 8, to *Kortrijk*, see Route 11, to *Antwerp*, see Route 14.

14

Ghent to Antwerp

A.   Via Sint Niklaas and Temse

Total distance 58km.—*20km* **Lokeren**—*13km* **Sint Niklaas**—*7km* **Temse**—
18km **Antwerp**.

This road traverses the WAASLAND, one of the most productive agricultural districts of Europe. Until about the 12C this was a virtually
uninhabitable tract of swamp and undrained forest. The development of
the district started when it came under the rule of the counts of Flanders.
Gradually the hermit settlements developed into religious communities,
whose members cleared the land and built the first dykes. Peat-cutting
grew as an industry. A network of small waterways was dug to serve both
for drainage and for transporting the peat. Sheep were introduced to meet
the wool demands of Ghent. Villages and towns sprang up. Although the
reclaimed land was largely of sand and clay, it has been made
increasingly fertile by the addition of rich soil and the spread of scientific
farming skills.

We leave **Ghent** (Route 13) by the N70, which takes us through the suburb
of *Sint Amandsberg*. Here are the Groot Begijnhof, and suburb of
Oostakker 3km to the N. (For these, see also Route 13.)

At *9km* is *Lochristi*, a flower-growing centre, which concentrates mainly
on begonias.

5km on, Zeveneken is 4km S of *Domein Puyenbroeck* , a provincial park
in typical Waasland scenery which offers swimming, boating, riding, a
zoological garden and a mill museum. It is open daily from 09.00. Closed
on 1 January, Easter Sunday, 1 November, 25 December. The mill is open
daily from May to September from 10.00 to 12.00 and 13.00 to 18.00. During
March, April and October it is open on Sunday from 14.00 to 17.00.

6km **Lokeren** (population 33,000. Tourist Information Office at 1 Toren-
straat), is a pleasant town on the small river Durme. After Sint Niklaas it is
the most important centre in the Waasland. There are several 17–18C
buildings, including the town hall, and a local museum at 3 Grote Kaai. In
the church of 1721, which is dedicated to Sint Laurentius, there is a pulpit
of 1736 by Theodoor Verhaeghen. At *Daknam*, 2km to the NW, the church
dates from the 11C and 12C.

13km **Sint Niklaas** (population 68,000. Tourist Information Office at 45
Grote Markt) is the chief town of the Waasland. It has the largest market
square in Belgium. More than 3 ha. in area, this was given by Margaret of
Constantinople, Countess of Flanders, to the parish of St Niklaas in 1248.

The *Sint Niklaaskerk*, dedicated to St Nicholas of Myra in S Turkey, dates
in part from 1262 but is mainly 16C and 17C. The side altars in the baroque
style are from 1664. They are the work of Hubert and Norbert van den
Enden of Antwerp. Above the high altar of 1836 is the Descent from the
Cross by Pieter Thys and next to it are the monumental statues of SS Peter
and Paul by Luc Fayd'herbe. Note also the pulpit of 1706 and the confessionals of 1707–10. There is a church museum. This is open only to
groups and by prior arrangement.

On the other side of the square is the *Stadhuis*, with a tower and carillon. A pleasingly proportioned 19C rebuilding of its 17C predecessor, it has some interesting paintings, including Jozef Odevaere's Taking the Oath by William I. There are frequent carillon concerts.

The neo-Byzantine church of Our Lady of Succour of the Christians, behind the Stadhuis, was built in 1844. It is crowned by a 6m-tall statue of Our Lady. The work of a local sculptor, Fr. van Havermaet , the statue was brazed in copper and gold-plated.

To the SE of the Grote Markt in the municipal park is the *Walburghof*. This was built in 1550 on the orders of William van Waelwijck.

The *Stedelijk Museum* at 49 Zamanstraat, 400m NE of the Grote Markt, has an interesting collection devoted to local archaeology, history and art. There are objects from the prehistoric, Roman and Frankish periods, a Folklore Department, some fine Flemish and Dutch paintings of the 17C, 18C and 19C, a picture attributed to P.P. Rubens and an excellent selection of works by the Belgian School of Painting of 1850–1900. In the Mercator Collection there are 40 atlases, a terrestrial globe of 1541 and a celestial globe of 1551 made for his patrons by the Waasland geographer, who was born at Rupelmonde in 1512 (see below).

The museum is open between April and September from Tuesday to Saturday from 14.00 to 17.00 and on Sunday from 10.00 to 17.00.

The direct road to Antwerp, the N70, continues NE through *Beveren* where the 15C church contains baroque furnishings, gold- and silverware. A more interesting road bears SE for *7km* **Temse** (population 23,000), an industrial and shipbuilding town on the Scheldt. Temse has long been associated with St Amelberga, the niece of Pepin of Landen, who died c 772. According to an ancient legend she escaped from an importunate suitor by crossing the river on the back of a giant sturgeon. St Amelberga is commemorated by a procession on Whit Tuesday. The town has two small museums. The Municipal Museum at 16 Kasteelstraat is open on Saturday from 14.00 to 19.00 and on Sunday from 10.00 to 12.00 and 14.00 to 19.00. The Museum of Heraldry at 74 Kasteelstraat is open on Saturday from 14.00 to 18.00 and on Sunday from 10.00 to 12.00 and from 14.00 to 18.00.

South of the Temse bridge, in the province of Antwerp, there is a strange lost district of marshland enclosed by the Scheldt and the Oude Scheldt, a channel abandoned by the river during the 13C. The regional museum, the *Zilverreiger*, in the picturesque village of **Weert**, is open daily, except Monday, Easter to October from 14.00 to 18.00.

Bornem (population 11,000), is a centre of asparagus growing and basket weaving. A monument commemorates the Peasants' Revolt of 1798, a Catholic uprising against the anti-clerical French. The church has a 12C choir and tower-base and the 10–11C crypt of a Benedictine priory church.

At *5km* is **Rupelmonde** opposite the confluence of the Rupel and the Scheldt. The cartographer, Gerhard Kremer, better known as Mercator, 1512–94, was born here at 54 Kloosterstraat. His statue of 1871 stands in the square. By the waterfront, which preserves something of the atmosphere of a fishing village, there is a ruined tower, all that remains of the powerful castle which in the 13C protected an important regional market.

The church at *2km Bazel* stands within a pleasant close which has some interesting old façades. The best view of the nearby château, now a restaurant, is from the back across the lake and moat.

3km Kruibeke has a church of c 1300, which is exceptionally rich in baroque woodwork of 1711–45 by members of the Kerrickx family.

Just to the N, the road enters the province of Antwerp. Looping around one of the city's great outer forts, it joins the motorway to cross the Scheldt by the J.F. Kennedytunnel.

For **Antwerp**, 8km from Kruibeke, see Route 16.

B. Via Dendermonde

Total distance 69km.—12km **Laarne**—20km **Dendermonde**—10km **Sint Amands**—10km **Fort Breendonk**—17km **Antwerp**.

Leave **Ghent** (see Route 13) by the Dendermondse Steenweg in the S part of the suburb of Sint Amandsberg.

At 12km **Laarne** there is a moated *château. Only the cellars, and perhaps the chapel, belong to the original 12C castle. The present building dates mainly from the 13–14C, with 16–17C additions and alterations. It possesses some outstanding 16C Brussels tapestries which depict the domestic life of a noble household. It also has a notable collection of 15–18C silver. The château is open daily, except Monday, from 10.00 to 12.00 and 14.00 to 18.00. It is closed from 24 December to 31 January.

7km Overmere was the scene of the first incident of the Peasants' Revolt of 1798 against the anti-clerical policy of the occupying French. This is commemorated by a monument. The Boerenkrijkmuseum at 2 Baron Tibbautstraat is open on demand only. Donkmeer, a short distance to the E, is the largest lake in Flanders. An abandoned arm of the Scheldt, the lake was formed during the 16C by the flooding of peat diggings. Its attractions include boating, fishing, an animal park and a duck decoy.

At 13km is **Dendermonde**, population 42,000. The Tourist Information Office is in the Stadhuis. This busy, picturesque place at the confluence of the Dender and the Scheldt has barge traffic passing virtually through the centre of the town. There are two fine works by Antoon van Dyck in the church.

Dendermonde's strategic situation ensured that it had a turbulent history. Incorporated in the county of Flanders in the 13C, it was the first town to be taken by Maximilian in 1484, when he subdued the Netherlands. Louis XIV was forced to withdraw in 1667, when the inhabitants flooded the whole district. Marlborough took the town in 1706. It was occupied by the Dutch under the Barrier Treaty of 1713. In 1914 Dendermonde was largely destroyed by the Germans, who looted and burned it.

The Stadhuis is on the E side of the Grote Markt. Built in the 14C and 16C, it was formerly the cloth hall. All that survived the 1914–18 war were the belfry and the outer walls. It was restored to its original appearance between 1921 and 1926.

On the N is the Vleeshalle of 1460, with an octagonal turret. It now houses the Oudheidkundig Museum, which has a collection of historical objects from the area. The museum is open from April to October on Wednesday from 14.00 to 18.00, and on Saturday, Sunday and public holidays from 10.00 to 12.00 and 14.00 to 18.00. Just off the square stands the huge Justitiepaleis of 1924.

Beyond the Dender, off Brusselsestraat, is the Begijnhof. Reached by a narrow street, this forms a triangle largely enclosed by 17C houses. Founded in 1233, the community settled here in 1288. The church was rebuilt in the 1920s on the original foundations.

Farther on, near the station, there are two gateways of the 17C ramparts.

Behind the Vleeshalle take the wide Kerkstraat W to the *Onze Lieve Vrouwekerk*, with its distinctive octagonal central tower. Successor to an earlier church and chapel, the present Gothic church dates mainly from the 14–15C. The tower was badly damaged when Dendermonde was attacked by Ghent in 1379. It is said that six cartloads of stones were removed by the defenders and used as ammunition. Rebuilding was not completed until c 1468, when Margaret of York, wife of Charles the Bold, visited the town.

The church has two major works by van Dyck, a *Crucifixion, which hangs in the baptistry and the *Adoration of the Shepherds, which is in the N aisle. Also in the baptistry is a 12C font in Tournai marble. This bears a representation of the Last Supper. In the N ambulatory there is a picture by de Crayer, which shows a donor in prayer before the Virgin. The N transept and choir have early 15C murals.

At *10km* **Sint Amands**, population 7000, is a small, straggling town in the province of Antwerp, 2km to the N of the road. On a pleasant, open area beside the Scheldt there is a tomb-memorial of the poet Emile Verhaeren, who died in 1916. He was born in 1855 at No. 69 in the street which bears his name. Near the memorial stands a modern sculpture, the Ferryman, by M. Macken.

There is a mill museum at 7 Emile Verhaerenstraat and the Verhaeren Museum at 22 Kade. The latter is open between March and June and mid September to October on Saturday and Sunday from 12.00 to 19.00, from July to mid September daily, except Monday and Friday, from 12.00 to 19.00.

10km **Fort Breendonk**. The fort and the road from there to *17km* **Antwerp** is described in Route 15A.

15

Brussels to Antwerp

The fastest approach to Antwerp is by the motorway, A1/E1. This skirts the W side of Mechelen; see Route 15B below.

A. Via Boom

Total distance 45km.—*11km* **Meise** (for **Grimbergen**)—*15km* **Fort Breendonk**—*4km* **Boom**—*15km* **Antwerp**.

There are several exit roads from central **Brussels** (see Route 1). The easiest are through Laeken or along the NE flank of the Domaine Royal. These meet at the Pavillon Chinois and, passing the Atomium on the left, cross the outer ring motorway.

At *11km* **Meise**, immediately W of the road, is the *Plantentuin*, the national botanic gardens famed for their superb trees and beautiful stretches of green. The Palais des Plantes of 1966 has several large hot-houses, including one devoted to tropical water plants. The 18C Orangery now serves as a restaurant and lakeside café. The gardens are within the estate of Bouchout, whose 13C castle was much altered during the 17C. It became the residence of the widowed Empress Charlotte of Mexico, who never fully recovered her reason after her many ordeals. She died here in 1927.

The gardens are open daily from 09.00 to sunset, the Palais des Plantes from Monday to Thursday from 13.00 to 16.00, and on Sunday and Public holidays from Easter to October between 14.00 and 18.00. The castle is not open to visitors.

At **Grimbergen**, 3km SE of Meise, there is the huge baroque **Abbey Church of Sint Servaas*. The abbey, founded here in 1128, was destroyed in 1579. After the return of the monks in the following century, Brother Gilbert van Zinnik began work on the present church. The towering high altar of 1701 is by Frans Langhermans. The monument of Philippe-François, lord of Grimbergen, who died in 1704, is the work of Theodoor Verhaeghen. The four confessionals and the transept altars are by Hendrik Verbruggen. The pulpit may be by Verhaeghen or Verbruggen. The sacristy is a rococo achievement of 1763. Between it and the church some Romanesque arches have survived.

On the NW edge of Grimbergen, beside the Meise road, an unusual monument honours Frans Hemerijckx, 1902–69, who worked among lepers.

At *Wolvertem*, *2km* from Meise, there is a church with interesting baroque confessionals. A pulpit in similar style has a vivid representation of the story of St Hubert. A courtier of Pepin of Heristal, this saint was converted while hunting. A stag at bay turned to him bearing an image of Christ crucified between its antlers.

Beyond Londerzeel the road crosses into the province of Antwerp. After *13km* we reach **Fort Breendonk**, where this route joins with Route 14B from Ghent and Dendermonde. The fort, built between 1906 and 1914 as an outlying defence of Antwerp, was used by the Germans during the Second World War as a concentration and reprisals camp. Today it is maintained as a memorial museum which preserves the cells, torture room and execution site. The 1954 monument to the resistance movement at the entrance is by S. Jankevitsj.

The fort is open daily between April and September from 09.00 to 17.00, from October to March daily from 10.00 to 16.00. It is closed on 1 January and 25 December.

At **Willebroek**, just E of the fort, the church has a 12C Romanesque tower. The inn at the bridge, Het Gulden Vlies, was the meeting-place in 1567 of William the Silent and Count Egmont.

This small town straddles the canal of the same name which links Brussels with the river Rupel. First authorised by Mary of Burgundy in 1477, the project was bitterly opposed by Mechelen, which would have been by-passed, thus losing toll rights. The canal was not opened until 1561.

At *4km* we cross the Brussels–Scheldt canal and the river Rupel, by bridge or tunnel, and arrive in **Boom**. This town of 15,000 inhabitants is the most important brickmaking centre in Belgium. Its museum at 196 Noeveren is open from Monday to Friday between 09.00 and 17.00.

At Boom you have a choice. You can continue N on the main road to *15km* **Antwerp** (see Route 16) or take the busy, industrialised road via Hemiksem, which is closer to the Scheldt.

At *Hemiksem* something survives, mainly from the 18C, of the former abbey of Sint Bernard. Founded in 1246, it gave hospitality in 1338 to Edward III of England, who was allied to Jacob van Artevelde (see above).

The monks of Sint Bernard founded the local brick industry in the 13C.

From Hemiksem you approach Antwerp through the industrial suburb of *Hoboken*. Its town hall occupies a mansion of 1745 built by the younger Baurscheit.

B. Via Mechelen

The quickest road to Mechelen and Antwerp is the motorway. As there are several places of interest between Brussels and Mechelen, the Route follows national and minor roads over this stretch. Beyond Mechelen it is assumed that most visitors will wish to take the motorway. Attention is, however, drawn to points of interest on either side.

Total distance 46km.—*12km* **Vilvoorde**—*12km* **Mechelen**—*22km* **Antwerp**.

From **Brussels** (see Route 1) there is a choice of roads to Vilvoorde. One, not without industrial interest, follows the N side of the canal and basins, which extend NE from Place Sainctelette. Starting as the Avenue du Port, it becomes the Chaussée de Vilvoorde, Vilvoordsesteenweg, which skirts the SE side of the Domaine Royal. It then passes below the outer ring motorway and crosses the canal into Vilvoorde.

Alternatively, you may take the airport and motorway road from Place Général Meiser, branching off to visit such places as *Evere, Diegem* and *Zaventem*, all of which are described in Route 1F.

12km **Vilvoorde**, population 32,000, is an industrial town on the Willebroek canal. Its 14–15C church has an unusually broad yet well-proportioned interior. The baroque choir stalls of 1663, amongst the best in Belgium, are from the former abbey of Groenendael. The pulpit of 1665 by Artus Quellin the Younger came from the church of Sint Joris in Antwerp. Among the church's many pictures are works attributed to P.J. Verhaghen and Michiel Coxie.

William Tyndale, who was strongly influenced by Luther, translated the New Testament into English. In 1531 he published the Pentateuch in Antwerp. This contained many marginal glosses, in which he violently attacked the Pope and the bishops. He managed to evade the agents of Henry VIII, who for many years had tried to capture him. In 1534 he published a revised version of his translation of the New Testament. Denounced to the authorities as a heretic, he was arrested in Antwerp in 1535 and imprisoned in the castle of Vilvoorde. Tried there in 1536, he was sentenced to death. On 6 October that year he was strangled and his body was burned in the castle.

Antonie van Straelen, 1521–68, the burgomaster of Antwerp who supported William of Orange, was also executed there. The castle was torn down later to make way for a gaol.

The direct road to 12km Mechelen, the N1, continues N out of Vilvoorde.

However, our Route will take us by minor roads to a number of interesting places E of the motorway. From Zaventem bear NE for a crossroads at **Steenokkerzeel**. Here is the château of *Ham*. Badly damaged in 1942 and shorn of its turrets, this was once the home of Charles de Lannoy. He received the surrender of Francis I of France after the battle of Pavia on 24 February 1525. Francis, imprisoned for a year, was obliged by Charles V to cede Artois, Burgundy, all his Italian possesions and Flanders.

Proceeding N from the crossroads, you soon reach **Perk**, the home of Hélène Fourment, Rubens' second wife, and of David Teniers the Younger who bought the house in 1663. The attractive *Gemeentehuis* of 1652 appears in some of his paintings. On the SE side of the village stands the large, turreted 17–19C *Château Ribaucourt*.

Elewijt, 4km N, is 2km E of *Het Steen* or *Rubenssteen*, which is clearly visible from the road. First mentioned in 1304, this château was bought by Rubens in 1635 and sold on the death of Hélène Fourment in 1681. It was much restored in 1875 and 1918.

At *Hofstade*, 4km N of Elewijt, there is a recreation park whose attractions include swimming and boating. **Planckendael**, a short distance to the N of Hofstade and reached from the Leuven–Mechelen road, is the breeding park of the Antwerp zoo. It has many animals and birds in a beautiful, open setting. The park may be visited during the summer between 08.30 and 18.30 and in the winter from 10.00 to 17.00.

At *12km* from Vilvoorde is **MECHELEN**, in French *Malines*, population 76,000. In the province of Antwerp and strongly Flemish in character, Mechelen is an attractive, ancient town on the rivers Dijle and Nete. Famous for the massive tower of its cathedral, nearly 100m in height, for its tapestries, for its carillon school and carillon concerts, the richness and variety of its architecture and its art treasures attract many visitors.

The inhabitants of Mechelen have been known as 'Maneblussers' or Moondousers since 1687. In that year a citizen returning home after an evening's carousal mistook the ruddy glow of the moon on the cathedral tower for a fire and roused the whole town to put it out!

The Cardinal-Archbishop of Mechelen is Primate of Belgium. The town has been the ecclesiastical capital since the mid 16C.

The **Tourist Information Office** is in the Stadhuis, Grote Markt.

History. In the early centuries a settlement grew up among the marshes beside the Dijle. In 756 St Rombout, who probably came from Ireland, founded an abbey here and converted the people to Christianity. In some accounts he is described as the bishop of Dublin and son of the king of the Scots, i.e. the Irish. He was martyred in 775 for having reproached two men about the wickedness of their lives. His body was fished out of the river and a church was built over the place of his burial.

At the beginning of the 11C the settlement became a fief of the prince-bishops of Liège, but in 1213 this sovereignty was delegated to the locally powerful Berthout family. Despite disputes over ownership the settlement grew into a town. Its citizens were granted charters in 1301 and 1305 and enjoyed a large measure of freedom until c 1333, when Mechelen was acquired by Louis de Male, Count of Flanders. After his death it passed, with the rest of Flanders, to the dukes of Burgundy.

Much of the town was destroyed in a fire of 1342. In 1452 work started on the great tower of the cathedral. In 1473 Charles the Bold founded the Grand Council as sovereign tribunal for the Netherlands, with its seat at Mechelen. After the death of Charles, his widow Margaret of York, sister of Edward IV of England, settled here.

In 1506, Margaret of Austria was appointed governor of the Netherlands, as regent for the infant Charles V. She chose Mechelen as her capital. Her court attracted some of the best intellects and the most talented artists of the day. Among them were the painters Jan Mostaert, Jan Gossaert, Bernard van Orley and Albrecht Dürer, the humanist Hieronymus van Busleyden and the architect Rombout Keldermans. This period of intellectual brilliance ended with Margaret's death in 1530, when the capital was transferred to Brussels.

Nevertheless Mechelen, formerly in the diocese of Cambrai, was made an archbishpric in 1559. Antoine Perrenot de Granvelle, 1517–86, Philip II's French adviser, was the first holder of the see. Archbishop Granvelle was created Primate of Belgium, a title held ever since by his successors. A brief interlude of Calvinist domination was ended by the capture and sack of the town by the duke of Alva in

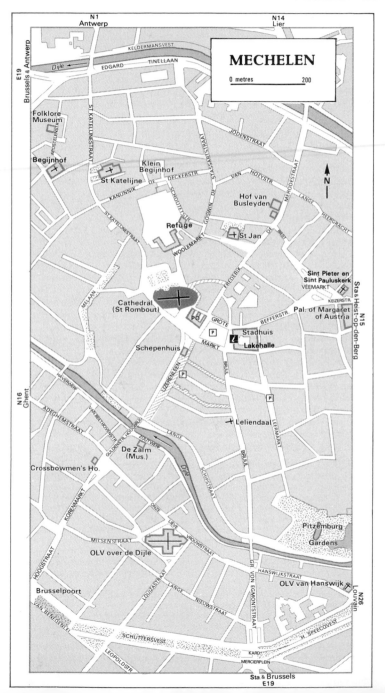

MECHELEN

0 metres   200

N1
Antwerp

N14
Lier

E19
Brussels & Antwerp

KELDERMANSVEST

Dijle

EDGARD — TINELLAAN

JODENSTRAAT

Folklore
Museum

Begijnhof

ST KATELIJNESTRAAT

APOSTELENSTR

Klein
Begijnhof

St Katelijne

DE DECKERSTR

VAN HOEYSTR

MERODESTRAAT

N

Hof van
Busleyden

KANUNNIK

SCHOUTETSTR

GOSWIN DE STASSARTSTRAAT

LANGE HEERGRACHT

ST KATELIJNESTRAAT

Refuge

WOOLEMARKT

St Jan

DE BEST

MELAAN

Cathedral
(St Rombout)

FREDERIK

Sint Pieter en
Sint Pauluskerk

VEEMARKT

KEIZERSTR

Sta & Heist-op-den-Berg

N15

PO

GROTE

Stadhuis

Pal. of Margaret
of Austria

Schepenhuis

MARKT

BEFFERSTR

Lakehalle

N16
Ghent

HAVERWERF

VAN BEETHOVENSTR

IJZERENLEEN

BRUL

Leliendaal

LEERMARKT

ADEGHEMSTRAAT

GULDENSTR KOOLBRUG

ZOUTWERK

LANGE

De Zalm
(Mus.)

Dijle

SCHIPSTRAAT

BRUL

Crossbowmen's Ho.

ONZE

LIEVE

Pitzemburg
Gardens

HOOGSTRAAT

KOREMARKT

MILSENSTRAAT

VROUWSTRAAT

OLV over de Dijle

GR VON EGMONTSTRAAT

HANSWIJKSTRAAT

OLV van Hanswijk

N26
Louvain

Brusselpoort

JAN BENEDENLEI

LOUIZASTRAAT

LANGE

NIEUWSTRAAT

H. SPEECQVEST

SCHUTTERSVEST

LEOPOLDSTR

KARD
MERCIERPLEIN

Sta & Brussels
E19

1572. However, Mechelen soon recovered and during the 17–18C became famous for its lace and its baroque style woodwork, and during the 19C for its tapestry.

In 1914 the town was bombarded three times before being occupied. The resistance of the Belgian people to the German invaders was much encouraged by Cardinal Mercier's famous pastoral letter 'Patriotism and Endurance'. At the close of the Second World War much damage was caused by bombing and by German V weapons.

Mechelen was the birthplace of the painters Michiel Coxie, 1499, and Frans Hals, 1580, the sculptor John van Nost or van Ost, fl. 1686–1729, and of Beethoven's grandfather, 1712–73.

Our tour of Mechelen starts in the GROTE MARKT and continues in a roughly clockwise direction around the district to the N of the square, a circuit of some 2.5km. You can then visit the area S of the Grote Markt.

In the centre of the Grote Markt there is a statue, erected in 1849, of Margaret of Austria. This is surrounded by a paved circle equal in size to the clock dial once on the cathedral tower. The **Stadhuis** on the E side of the square is made up of two very different parts. On the right is the former Lakenhalle. Begun in 1320 and modelled on the Cloth Hall at Bruges, it was badly damaged by the great fire of 1342. The tower was never completed. The octagonal turrets date from the 16C. In 1526 the N wing was demolished to make way for a new building which Charles V intended to be used as the meeting-place of the Grand Council. Designed by Rombout Keldermans, work on this building started in 1530. It ceased in 1534, a casualty of the death of Margaret of Austria and the move of the court to Brussels. The site was used for various purposes from time to time, but more often than not was neglected. A fake façade was set up for formal occasions. Only in 1911 did the town take over the site and complete the building to Keldermans' original plans. In a niche, and looking a trifle grim, sits Charles V. An arch in the Lakenhalle leads to a courtyard where there is a modern sculpture, 'Mother', by Ernest Wijnants.

On the W side of the square the *Post Office* occupies an 18C house on 13C foundations. Until 1911 this was the town hall. A short distance to the S is the **Schepenhuis**. A building of 1374, this was the seat of the Grand Council from 1474 to 1618. Later it served as town hall, theatre and museum. It housed the town archives until 1991.

The best known feature of *****Sint Romboutskathedraal** may be its great tower, but it would be a pity not to visit the beautifully proportioned interior where there are some fine furnishings and a number of excellent paintings.

Around 1217 work started on the draining of the marsh by the Dijle and the construction of a church. Parts of this survive in the crossing and transepts, the central nave and the lower courses of the choir. Dedicated in 1312, it was badly damaged by the fire of 1342. Rebuilding included the construction of the triforium and the enlargement of the choir with its ambulatory and chapels. The chapels off the N aisle date from 1498–1502. The church was completed during the 16C.

The TOWER was started in 1452. It was probably designed by Wouter Coolman, who died in 1468. However, some authorities believe that the plans were prepared by Jan Keldermans, who died in 1445. The original proposal for a height, with a spire, of 167m was abandoned. There is a model of this plan in the cathedral and there are designs in the Hof van Busleyden (see below). Under the direction of the Keldermans family, it reached its present height of 97m in 1546.

The tower may be climbed. The 514 steps pass the two carillons. Both have 49 bells. One was installed in 1981. The bells in the other date from the 15C onwards. Carillon concerts are given from June to mid September on Monday between 20.30 to 21.30. There is a guided visit to the tower at 19.00.

The cathedral is 99.5m long and 30m wide. The height of the central nave, transept and choir is 28m. The statues of the Apostles in the nave date from the 17C. In front of the Chapel of the Blessed Sacrement in the N aisle there is a *baroque-style Communion Bench in white marble. Attributed to Artus Quellin the Younger, who died in 1700, this came from the ancient chapel of Laliëndael. In the chapel is a painting by Michiel Coxie of 1580 of the Circumcision of Christ and the tomb of 1837, by Louis Jehotte, of Archbishop de Méan, who died in 1831. He guided the church in Belgium during the dangerous times of the French Revolution. Note also the chapel's fine vault.

In the Chapel of Our Lady of the Miracle there is an ancient image of the Blessed Virgin, which has been venerated in the cathedral since the beginning of the 16C. There is also a statue of 1688 by a local sculptor, Niklaas van der Veken, of Christ Suffering.

The Chapel of Cardinal Mercier is at the E end of the N aisle. Cardinal Mercier, who died in 1926, won world-wide fame for his courageous stand against the Germans during the First World War. His *Appeal to All Christian People* led to the Malines Conversations of 1921–26, which aimed at bringing about the union of the Roman Catholic and Anglican Churches. A plaque in the chapel, presented by representatives of the Church of England in 1966, honours Cardinal Mercier and those who took part with him in the Malines Conversations.

The bronze figure of the cardinal on the marble tomb was designed by a Capuchin friar, R.P. Ephrem. The stained glass windows recall various incidents in the life of Cardinal Mercier.

In the N transept the altar of Our Lady by Frans Langhermans, 1699, has a painting of the Adoration of the Shepherds by *Jan Erasmus Quellin.* Opposite is an interesting picture of the interior of the cathedral in 1755.

In the S transept the altar of 1700 dedicated to St Anne was made by Jan van der Steen for the masons' guild. It is surmounted by a **Crucifixion** by *Antoon van Dyck*, of 1627. Originally in the church of the Friars Minor of Mechelen, it is regarded as one of the artist's finest achievements. The decorated blind arches behind the altar are some of the oldest parts of the cathedral.

The eight statues on the walls and columns of the transept are by Luc Fayd'herbe, Theodoor Verhaeghen and Pieter Valckx. They represent the following saints: Mark, Luke, Ambrose, Augustine, Charles, Gregory, Jerome and Joseph.

In the choir the spectacular high altar, by Luc Fayd'herbe, is dominated by a huge statue of St Rombout. The relics of the saint are in a reliquary protected by a grill decorated with arabesques.

There is a Mater Dolorosa by Luc Fayd'herbe above a door near the N entry to the ambulatory. In the ambulatory is the tomb of the Berthout family, lords of Mechelen during the 13–14C. Opposite is a triptych, the Martyrdom of St George, by *Coxie.*

There are nine chapels in the ambulatory. In a clockwise direction:

The first chapel has a triptych of 1607 by *Jean le Sayve the Elder* with scenes and figures from the Old Testament—David the Conqueror of Goliath, the Sacrifice of Abraham and Judith leaving the Tent of Holofernes. There is also a Virgin and Child surrounded by Saints of 1649 by *Gaspard de Crayer.*

The second chapel has funerary monuments and grave slabs from the 17–19C.

The third chapel is dedicated to St John Berchmans. It has the gravestone of Igramus van Achelen, president of the Grand Council, who died in 1604.

The fourth chapel is dedicated to St Joseph. It has the gravestone of

Arnould de Mérode, who died in 1553, and of his wife, Catherine de Gottignies.

The fifth chapel is the Chapel of the Blessed Sacrament. Its stained glass windows commemorate the first Eucharistic Congress, which was held in Mechelen in 1930.

The sixth chapel is dedicated to St Engelbert in memory of Cardinal Engelbert Sterckx, who died in 1867.

The seventh chapel is dedicated to the priests from the dioceses of Mechelen, who fell during the First World War. It has a picture by *de Crayer* of St Francis in prayer before the Madonna.

The eighth chapel is the Chapel of the Relics. It has a reliquary of the Martyrs of Gorcum or Gorinchem, near Dordrecht in Holland. They were 19 monks, priests and laity killed by Calvinists in 1572. The martyrs were canonised in 1867. There are also the hatchments of the Knights of the Golden Fleece, who were present at the chapter held in the cathedral in 1491. Note, too, the tombstone of Jacques Godin, who died in 1559. He was lawyer to the Grand Council.

The ninth chapel has a picture of 1632 by *Abraham Janssens* of St Luke painting the Virgin.

There is a triptych by *Coxie* showing the martyrdom of St Sebastian on the sacristy wall. In the baptistry there is painting by *Jean le Sayve the Elder* of the Baptism of Christ.

At 5 Minderbroedersgang, immediately W of the cathedral, the *Ernest Wijnants Museum* exhibits works by this sculptor. It is open from Easter to the first Sunday in October on Saturday, Sunday and public holidays from 10.00 to 12.00 and from 14.00 to 17.00. It is also open on Monday in July and August.

Follow Sint Katelijnestraat in a NW direction for c 400m to Sint Katelijnekerk. We enter this mid 14C church by a 15C portal. Its *Confessionals of 1700 are by Niklaas van der Veken. At the entrance to the choir there is a statue of 1716 of St Catherine by Piérard de Lyon. The stalls have 18C reliefs by Pieter Valckx. Note the exquisitely carved faces.

The baroque **Begijnhofkerk** is almost opposite on the left. It was built between 1629 and 1647 by Jacob Franckaert. Outside there are two statues by Luc Fayd'herbe: St Catherine, above the porch and God the Father, at the top of the façade. Inside there are sculpture and paintings by Fayd'herbe, Jan van der Steen, Jerome Duquesnoy the Younger, de Crayer, Jan Erasmus Quellin and Cornelis Cels.

The quaint KLEIN BEGIJNHOF with small houses picturesquely sited in ancient alleyways, is just E of the church of Sint Katelijne.

The story of the Mechelen Begijnhof is little documented and rather confused. It seems to have been formed during the 13C and to have become an autonomous parish to the N of the town c 1295. Some of the older members, however, chose to settle in the area known since 1562 as the Klein Begijnhof. The main Begijnhof was frequently attacked and pillaged, notably by the Calvinists in 1580–85. As a result a new close was obtained within the town in 1595. This, known as the Groot Begijnhof, had the familiar plan of small houses and narrow streets. It is sited to the W of the Begijnhof church.

Immediately to the S of the Klein Begijnhof, between Kanunnik de Deckerstraat and Schoutetstraat, are the *Refuge of the Abbey of Tongerlo* of 1483, and the *Refuge of the Abbey of St Truiden* of c 1500. The latter has a particularly attractive setting by a pool, all that remains of a covered branch of the Dijle. It is best seen from Wollemarkt, the SW extension of Goswin de Stassartstraat.

Opposite, the little Klapgat leads to the 15C **Sint Janskerk**. This has a *triptych of 1619 by *Rubens*. The artist's first wife was the model for the Virgin Mary in the centre panel, which shows the Adoration of the Magi. The benches and organ case at the W end of the church were carved by Pieter Valckx; the pulpit and two benches by the transept pillars are by Theodoor Verhaeghen and pupils. There is a painting of the Disciples at Emmaus by *G.J. Herreyns*.

To the NE of the church and next door to one another are the Carillon School and the Hof van Busleyden.

Students come from all over the world to the *Carillon School*, the *Koninklijke Beiaardschool 'Jef Denyn'*. This is named after Mechelen's distinguished master-carilloneur, 1862–1941, on whose sixtieth birthday the school was founded.

The **Carillon Museum**, with bells, carillons and documentation, is on the S side of the main entrance to the Hof van Busleyden. It is usually open at the same times as the Hof van Busleyden (see below).

The **Hof van Busleyden** of 1503–17, was the home of the humanist, Hieronymus van Busleyden, c 1470–1517. It now houses the municipal museum. Few collections are lucky enough to be housed in such a fine setting. This old and very beautiful mansion deserves a visit for its own sake. It is open daily, except Tuesday, from 10.00 to 12.00 and from 14.00 to 17.00.

Hieronymus van Busleyden, a member of a noble Luxembourg family, studied at Louvain and Bologna and became a Doctor of Law. He so impressed Philip the Handsome that he was appointed counsellor to the Grand Council. A friend of Thomas More and Erasmus, he helped the latter found his *Collegium Trilingue* for the study of Latin, Greek and Hebrew at Louvain. Van Busleyden was a member of the brilliant and scholarly circle that formed around Margaret of Austria. He died on the way to Spain while on a mission for Charles V.

The Hof van Busleyden was probably designed by Antoon Keldermans and built by his son Rombout. In 1619 Wenceslas Coeberger opened a municipal pawnshop here and the building continued to be in part used for this purpose until the First World War.

The **Municipal Museum** has a valuable collection of objects connected with the history of Mechelen and the surrounding area. There are also a number of good pictures.

In the Entrance Hall is the mascot of Mechelen, 'Op Signoor'. Its name derives from 'señor', which was applied at one time, in mockery, to the citizens of Antwerp. This woodcarving of 1647 by *Valentyn van Lanscroon* played an important part in the town's annual processions. After being kidnapped by the students of Antwerp in 1949, it was placed in the museum for safety.

In Rooms 1 and 2 Gallo-Roman objects are exhibited. In Room 6 there is an interesting plan of Mechelen in 1574. In Room 8 there are pictures of the Great Council in session and of its chairman. In Room 9 are the 'Poupées de Malines', 16C handmade, wooden dolls. Room 10 is devoted to the Habsburg family. Note the statue of Margaret of Austria and the two fine terrestrial globes. In Room 11, once van Busleyden's dining room, there are murals attributed variously to *Bernard van Orley* and *Michiel Coxie*.

Upstairs in Room 12, on the left, there are sculptures by *Fayd'herbe*. Rooms 14 and 16 contain Loius XV furniture. In Room 17 there is the former reliquary of St Rombout and sculptures by a number of local craftsmen. Rooms 23 and 24 are concerned with the halberdiers and arquebusiers with individual and group pictures. Rooms 20 to 27 contain the works of 20C artists and sculptors. These include *Weynants, Servaes* and *Wouters*.

Across from the Carillon School, the street known as Biest leads to the triangular VEEMARKT and the Sint Pieter en Sint Pauluskerk. Built between 1670 and 1677 in a style popularised by the Jesuits, the church has paintings by *Jan Erasmus Quellin* and others depicting the life of St Francis Xavier and a pulpit of 1700 by Hendrik Verbruggen which symbolises the saint's missionary work.

The **Palace of Margaret of Austria** is roughly opposite on Keizerstraat. The seat of the Grand Council between 1618 and 1794, it now houses the law courts. The Renaissance front, among the first of its kind in the Netherlands, is by Guyot de Beaugrant. The oldest part of the building, in the courtyard, dates from 1507–17. This is by Rombout Keldermans.

The **Schouwburg**, the municipal theatre, opposite, is sometimes known as the Keizershof. For a time in the 15C it was the palace of Margaret of York.

Circa 300m to the NE, by way of Keizerstraat, and near the Nekkerspoel station, is the *Centrum voor Speelgoed en Volkskunde*, the Toy Museum, which sees life through the eyes of children. It is open daily, except Monday, from 14.00 to 17.00.

From the Schouwburg it is a short walk of c 350m to the Grote Markt by way of Befferstraat.

SOUTHERN MECHELEN. This circuit, excluding the diversion to the Brusselpoort, covers c 2.5km. Leave the Grote Markt by Ijzerenleen and proceed in a SW direction. The name Ijzerenleen comes from the iron railings of 1531, which here bordered a canal. This was covered over during the 17C. Ijzerenleen ends at the **Hoogbrug**. Dating from 1298, it replaced the town's first bridge which was made of wood. Rebuilt in 1595 the Hoogbrug has irregular arches and traces of its guard towers.

On Haverwerf, Oats Wharf, across the river to the right and beyond a brewery, there are three 16–17C façades, one of which is of wood. Van Beethovenstraat, which bisects the brewery, is named after the composer's grandfather, 1712–73, who was born here.
From the Hoogbrug take Guldenstraat to Korenmarkt, where the *House of the Crossbowmen* is on the right and continue to the end of Hoogstraat. Circa 500m from the Hoogbrug is the stout **Brusselpoort**, the only one of Mechelen's original 12 gates to survive. Built c 1300 the gate had parts added to it in the 17C.

To the left across the Hoogbrug on the picturesque Zoutwerf, the Salt Wharf, is **De Zalm**, the Salmon, a house with a façade of 1530. Built for the Guild of Fishmongers, it is now a small museum. A number of rooms are devoted to lace. Upstairs there is some interesting metalwork, including several intricate old locks. It is open daily, except Friday, from 10.00 to 12.00 and 14.00 to 17.00.

Circa 250m to the S is the church of **Onze Lieve Vrouw over de Dijle**. The nave and tower were built during the 15C. The church was completed in the 17C by Jacob Franckaert, who was working at the same time on the Begijnhof church. Damaged by artillery fire in 1914, by air raids in 1944 and by a V weapon in 1945, the church was restored by J. Lauwers between 1962 and 1968. In the S transept hangs the *Miraculous draught of Fishes, a triptych painted by *Rubens* in 1618 for the Guild of Fishmongers. Above the high altar there is a Last Supper by *Jan Erasmus Quellin*.

From the church follow Onze Lieve Vrouwstraat in a SE direction to a small open space known as VIJFHOEK.

To the S, Graaf van Egmontstraat leads to Kardinaal Mercierplein and to the station.
   To return to the Grote Markt from here, cross the river and follow Bruul for c 600m.
You pass, en route, the 1662 Jesuit church of **Leliendaal**, by Luc Fayd'herbe.

Take Hanswijkstraat, E from Vijfhoek, to the basilica of **Onze Lieve. Vrouw van Hanswijk**. Built between 1663 and 1678 to plans by Fayd'herbe, it has statues and reliefs by him. The pulpit is the work of Verhaeghen. Just beyond the church there is an old fulling mill beside the river.
   We cross the river to the **Kruidtuin**, or Pitzemburg Garden, where there is a statue of the botanist Rembrecht Dodoens, 1517–85, who was a native of Mechelen. From the NW corner of the garden a short walk of c 400m along the Leermarkt will bring you to the Grote Markt.
   Mechelen to **Antwerp** (Route 16) by motorway is a journey of 22km. Travellers who are not in a hurry, and who have their own transport, may like to visit the following places which lie to the W and E of the motorway.

WEST OF THE MOTORWAY. **Heindonk**, S of the Rupel, has a town hall of 1550. **Rumst**, within the N angle of the confluence of the Rupel and the Nete, is an important horticultural centre. At **Reet**, 3km NW of Rumst, the church has a 15C tower. The Hof van Reet is a château of the 17C.

EAST OF THE MOTORWAY. **Duffel**, on the Nete, was famous during the 16C for its manufacture of woollen garments. It is alleged to have given its name to the 'duffle coat'. The town was the birthplace of Kilianus (Cornelis Kiel), 1528–1607, founder of Dutch philology and associate of Christopher Plantin. The castle of Ter Elst dates from the 16C.
   Kontich traces its origins to Gallo-Roman times. There is a 'fountain' from this period in the municipal park. The *Sint Maartenskerk* has a 12C Romanesque tower. There is a small museum at 32 Molenstraat.
   At **Hove**, 3km NE of Kontich, the *Urania Observatory* is open on Tuesday and Friday at 20.00. At **Edegem** there is a Grotto of Our Lady of Lourdes. The château of Ter Linden dates from 1760.

16

Antwerp

ANTWERP (Flemish **Antwerpen**, French *Anvers*; population 500,000), is the principal city of Flemish Belgium and capital of the province of the same name. Not only is it the locus of a rapidly expanding industrial complex and an international port, it is also one of the most important tourist centres in Belgium. Its plenitude of historic buildings, its ancient cathedral filled with religious works by Rubens and other masters, its many and varied churches, its museums and galleries crammed with art treasures, bring visitors from all over the world to Antwerp. However, the attractions of the city are not only cultural. There is also Flemish *cuisine*. A leisurely stroll through the streets of the old quarter or a walk along the busy waterfront may well end in one of the many lively cafés or restaurants which abound.
   Antwerp, on the right bank of the Scheldt, is one of Europe's leading ports. As it is some 90km from the sea, vessels travel through Dutch waters for the greater part of their passage to the city. The international boundary is a short distance beyond the limits of the port area. For centuries this has had a decisive influence on Antwerp's fortunes.

The heart of Antwerp lies within a semicircle of boulevards, the Italielei, Frankrijlei and Britselei. Nearly 4km long, they were laid out in 1859 along the course of the former ramparts. An outer ring of fortifications about 30km in circumference, which replaced the earlier walls, proved ineffective in 1914. Though something may still be seen of the great star-shaped forts, these defences are being swamped by the ceaseless spread of the modern city.

LEFT BANK. The land enclosed by the abrupt curve of the Scheldt, once the site of a great moated redoubt but now largely covered by modern residential and office development, is of little interest to visitors. By the exit from the Sint Annatunnel there is a garden with anchors, buoys and other maritime *objets trouvés*. Farther N, beyond the yacht basin, is *Sint Annastrand* a popular waterside area and beach.

Industrialisation of the left bank of the Scheldt is increasing rapidly.

In 1584 at *Kallo*, 8km from Antwerp's Waaslandtunnel, the duke of Parma built a long barrage into the river in order to block the port, which at that time was under siege. The star-shaped fort to the N marks the NW limit of the fortifications built during the 19C and 20C.

Doel, a polder village 8km farther N and close to the Dutch border, has a picturesque port and an old stone windmill. To the N there is a nuclear power station.

City Centre. The central axis extends from the Grote Markt by way of the Meir and other streets to the Centraal Station.

Tourist Information Offices. *City*: 15 Grote Markt from Monday to Saturday between 09.00 and 18.00. On Sunday and public holidays from 09.00 to 17.00. Tel: 232 01 03. *Province of Antwerp*: 11 Karl Oomsstraat.

How to See the City. Many places of interest to visitors are reasonably close to the Grote Markt. However, Antwerp is a large city, so a good deal of walking must be expected.

Guides. The Tourist Information Office will arrange individual guided visits. These include some of the museums, the city, and the port. Minimum length 2 hours.

Coach. Coach tours normally depart from the Grote Markt. Information from the Tourist Office.

Public Transport. A very efficient tram system, which in part becomes a Metro. Map from Tourist Information Office.

Horse-drawn Carriage. From the Grote Markt, Easter to September from about 12.00 to 18.00.

Boat. See Boat Excursions below.

Private Car. Antwerp is reasonably well provided with parking facilities. With someone to navigate it is practicable to use a car, at least for sites outside the immediate centre.

Railway Stations. *Centraal*, E of the ring boulevards, for most main line services; *Berchem*, to the S, for many international expresses.

Airport. 5km from the centre.

Scheldt Tunnels. In the S the *J.F. Kennedytunnel* is for the A14/E17 motorway to Ghent. The 500m long *Sint Annatunnel*, a short distance upstream from the Steen, is for pedestrians and cyclists. *Waaslandtunnel*, entrance in Tunnelplaats, off Italielei, is for motor traffic only. A fourth tunnel is reserved for the Metro.

Post Office. The main office is at 42 Groenplaats. There are many others, including 12 Pelikaanstraat near the Centraal Station. Most offices are open from Monday to Friday from 09.00 to 17.00.

Telephone. The main office, 1 Jezusstraat is open daily from 08.00 to 20.00; also at Centraal Station, Monday to Friday, from 09.00 to 17.00.

Diamonds. Lodewijk van Bercken, a native of Bruges who lived in Antwerp, developed the art of diamond polishing in 1476. Since his time diamonds have become an important industry both in Antwerp province and in the city. Something of the background of this industry may be seen at the Provinciaal Diamantmuseum at 31–33 Lange Herentalsestraat.

Boat Excursions. Operated by Flandria on Steenplein, tel: 233 74 22. The principal excursions are: the local Scheldt cruise, duration 50 minutes, an extended Scheldt cruise, duration 1½ hours, and the round of the port cruise, duration 2½ hours. Day excusions may include Ostend and, in Holland, Flushing (Vlissingen), Zierikzee, Middelburg, Veere, Willemstad and Rotterdam.

History. Legend associates the origin of the city with the activities of a giant named Druon Antigonus. It is said that he exacted tribute from ships passing up and down the Scheldt, cutting off the hands of all who failed to pay. This explains the severed hands on the armorial bearings of the city and also, perhaps, the origin of the city's name—from 'hand werp', meaning 'hand throw'. Antigonus was finally vanquished by Silvius Brabo, a youthful relative of Julius Caesar. He became the first duke of Brabant, taking the title of his dukedom from his own name.

However, a more likely if less colourful explanation of the city's name is that it comes from 'Aen de werpen', which means 'at the cast' (of the anchor) or simply 'at the wharf'.

Putting legend aside, it is known that there was a settlement here in the 2C. The first church is said to have been built by St Amand in 660. Benedictine monks from Ireland commenced the draining of the polders.

In the 9C, the Norsemen destroyed a fortress here. The first town walls date from the 11C, when the counts of Ardennes and Bouillon were the margraves of Antwerp. Godfrey de Bouillon, c 1061–1100, one of the principal commanders and later the leader of the First Crusade, was so styled.

In the 13C the town passed to the dukes of Brabant, one of whom, John II, who died in 1312, was married to Margaret, daughter of Edward I of England. In 1338–40, when Jacob van Artevelde of Ghent made an alliance between the Flemish towns and England, Edward III held court at the abbey of St Bernard, near Hemiksem. His second son Lionel, later the Duke of Clarence, was born there. In 1357 Louis de Male invaded Brabant and regained Antwerp for the counts of Flanders. With the rest of Flanders, the town passed to Burgundy in 1384.

In the 15C Antwerp rose rapidly in importance, at the expense of Bruges, then in full decline. While Het Zwin was silting up, the Scheldt had been widened considerably by flooding in Zeeland. Antwerp became the chief port of the Netherlands and by the beginning of the 16C a thousand foreign business houses were established here.

The Antwerp Guild of St Luke, founded in 1454 by Philip the Good for the encouragement of painting, may be regarded as a foundation of the Flemish School. The guild was host to Albrecht Dürer during his stay in Antwerp, 1520–21.

The prosperity of Antwerp waned during the reign of Philip II. The city was rent by religious dissensions. In 1566 the cathedral was pillaged by the Calvinists during the religious disturbances and many of its priceless treasures were destroyed by their iconoclastic vandalism. Ten years later came the 'Spanish fury', when Antwerp was sacked by Alva's mutinous soldiery. The following year, 1577, with William of Orange in Flanders, Antwerp threw off the Spanish yoke and for eight years the open practise of Catholicism was forbidden. But 1580 saw the beginning of the duke of Parma's campaign of reconquest for Spain. In 1585, after withstanding a year's siege under Marnix van St Aldegonde, the city capitulated, giving Parma his last real success. This meant that Antwerp was destined to belong to Belgium rather than Holland, while from now on the United Provinces, an ever-present threat to the vital Scheldt, ruled most of the lands to the north.

The reign of Archduke Albert and his wife Isabella, who made their state entry on 20 December 1599, inaugurated a brief interlude of peace, when Antwerp regained something of its pristine glory. With Rubens as their leader, the painters of this period included David Teniers the Elder, David Teniers the Younger and Jacob Jordaens. A literary circle, revolving round Balthasar Moretus, included G.C. Gevaerts, or Gevartius, poet and secretary of the city, and also the poetesses Anna and Maria Visscher. Jean de Bolland (Bollandus; 1596–1665), the learned Jesuit died here.

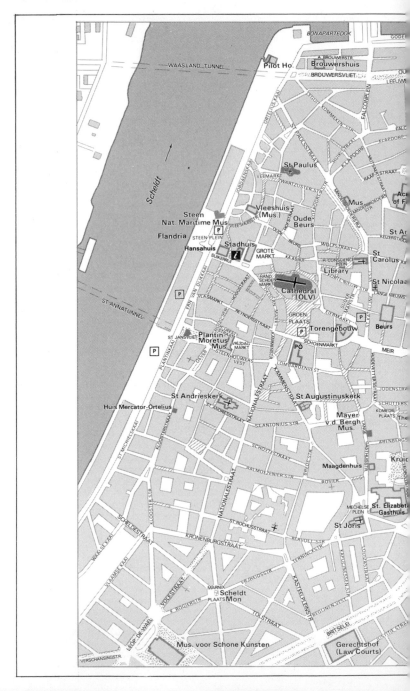

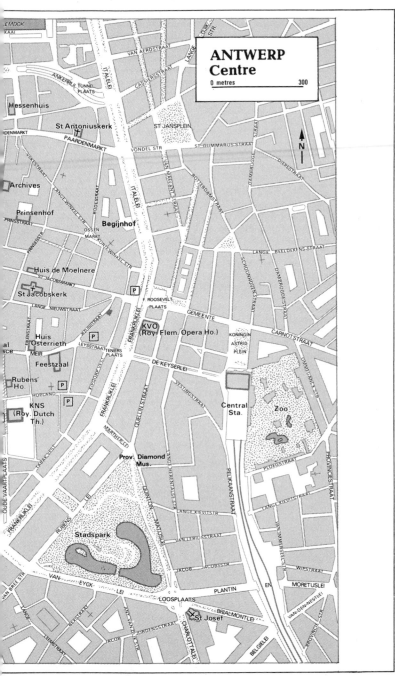

ANTWERP
Centre

0 metres — 300

EMDOK
KAAI

ANKERRUI TUNNEL
PLAATS

VAN AERDSTRAAT

CASSIERSSTRAAT

LANGE

DIJK STR

ST JANSPLEIN

Hessenhuis

St Antoniuskerk

IDENMARKT

PAARDENMARKT

VONDEL STR

ST GUMMARUS-STRAAT

N

DAMBRUGGESTRAAT

DIEPESTRAAT

Archives

LANGE WINKEL STR

RODESTRAAT

ROTTERDAMSTRAAT

Prinsenhof

PRINSSTRAAT

Begijnhof

OSSEN
MARKT

KORTE WINKEL STR

VAN WESENBEKE STRAAT

LANGE BEELDEKENS STRAAT

SCHIJNPOORTSTRAAT

Huis de Moelnere

ST JACOBSMARKT

St Jacobskerk

LANGE NIEUWSTRAAT

KRUISSTRAAT

P

F. ROOSEVELT
PLAATS

GEMEENTE

DAMBRUGGESTRAAT

CARNOTSTRAAT

Huis
Osterrieth

MEIR

LEYSSTRAAT

P

TENIERS
PLAATS

KVO
(Roy. Flem. Opera Ho.)

KONINGIN
ASTRID
PLEIN

Feestzaal

DE KEYSERLEI

Rubens'
Ho.

HOPLAND

P

P

FRANKRIJKLEI

QUELLINSTRAAT

VESTINGSTRAAT

Central
Sta.

Zoo

KNS
(Roy. Dutch
Th.)

MEISTRAAT

MAERTHELEI

Prov. Diamond
Mus.

LANGE HERENTALSE STR

PELIKAANSTRAAT

PLOEGSTRAAT

PROVINCIESTRAAT

OUDE VAARTPLAATS

TABAKSVEST

LEI

QUINTEN MATSIJS

LANGE KIEVITSTR

LANGE KIEVITSTRAAT

RUBENS

VAN LERIUSSTRAAT

VAN IMMERSEEL STR

Stadspark

JACOB JACOBSSTR

VAN BREE STR

VAN
EYCK
LEI

PLANTIN

EN

MORETUSLEI

LOOSPLAATS

BRIALMONTLEI

VAN DEN NESTLEI

WIPSTRAAT

LANGE

LEENSTRAAT

BEXSTRAAT

JACOB

VAN DIJCK STR

JORDAENSSTRAAT

CHARLOTTELEI

St Josef

BELGIELEI

PROVINCIELEI

BROUWERS STR

The Thirty Years War finished in 1648 with the signing of the Peace of Münster, under whose terms Spain had to agree to the closing of the Scheldt. Antwerp was ruined. Not until 1795, when the estuary was reopened, did it begin to recover its prosperity.

By the close of the 18C the city, now ruled by the French, had a population of only 40,000. It had reached the lowest point of its fortunes. It owed its revival to Napoleon, who not only reopened the Scheldt but also constructed docks and a naval harbour, to make 'a pistol aimed at the heart of England'.

The United Kingdom of the Netherlands, 1815–30, was ended by the Belgian revolution. Antwerp suffered considerably from a bombardment by the Dutch in 1830. A garrison of Dutch soldiers in the citadel was forced to surrender in 1832 by Marshal Gérard, who led a French force assisting the first Belgian king, Leopold I.

Antwerp's present prosperity and the growth of its port date from 1862, when the right to levy dues on Scheldt shipping, granted to Holland in 1839, was redeemed by Belgium's payment of 36 million fr.

Antwerp played an important part at the beginning of the First World War. The government arrived from Brussels on 17 August 1914 followed soon after by the German invaders, who besieged the city on 28 September. The forts, vaunted as the last word in modern defence, were quickly silenced. On 4 October the British First Lord of the Admiralty, Winston Churchill, arrived with Royal Marines and Royal Navy reinforcements, but two days later the Germans pushed forward to bombardment range of the city. The government sailed for Ostend, and Antwerp surrendered on 10 October. Many of the population fled to Holland and some 2500 British troops were forced across the border into internment. During the Second World War Antwerp was abandoned at an early stage of hostilities. In the final days of the war it suffered severely from V1 and V2 attacks.

Routes from Antwerp. To Holland, see Route 17, to Turnhout and Maaseik, see Route 18, to Genk, see Route 19, to Hasselt and Maastricht, see Route 20, to Ghent, see Route 14 and to Brussels, see Route 15.

The description of Antwerp is in four parts: A. The centre. B. The area South-West of the Centre. C. The area South-East of the Centre; and D. The Docks and Beyond, the Havenroute. Three of the principal museums have their own sections: E. Plantin-Moretus, F. Rubens' House, and G. Schone Kunsten.

A. Central Antwerp

Many of the places of interest to visitors to Antwerp are in the GROTE MARKT or within easy walking distance of it. These include the Stadhuis, the Cathedral, the Volkskunde Museum (folklore and ethnology), the Plantin-Moretus Museum (printing, art treasures), the waterfront with the Steen fort, which houses the Maritime Museum, and the Vleeshuis, the ancient Butchers' Hall with its museum of applied art. A little farther afield are the Sint Pauluskerk and the Brouwershuis, Rubens' House and the Mayer van den Bergh and Maagdenhuis collections.

In the centre of the GROTE MARKT is the **Brabo Fountain**, of 1887, by Jef Lambeaux. Silvius Brabo, the eponymous first duke of Brabant is shown throwing the hand of the giant, Antigonus, into the Scheldt (see above).

Around the square there are a number of old or restored houses. Many of these are now restaurants or cafés. On the N side are No. 3 *In den Engel* of 1579, No. 5, the *Coopers' House* of 1579, Nos 7 and 9, the *Oude* and the *Jonge Handboog* of 1582 and c 1500, which belonged to two guilds of crossbowmen, and No. 17, the *Mercers' House* of c 1515.

On the SE side No. 38 was the *Drapers' House* of 1615, and No. 40 the *Carpenters' House*. On both there are carvings relating to their trades.

The **Stadhuis**, which occupies the W side of the Grote Markt, was built in Renaissance style between 1561 and 1565 by Cornelis Floris, possibly working to plans by the Florentine Nicolo Scarini. Ten years later, during the 'Spanish Fury', the building was in part destroyed by rioting Spanish soldiers, largely because it contained the city's armoury. It was rebuilt immediately afterwards.

The Stadhuis is open from Monday to Wednesday between 09.00 and 15.00, on Thursday from 14.00 to 15.00, on Friday from 09.00 to 15.00 and on Saturday from 12.00 to 16.00. It is closed during official receptions.

In the centre of the long façade there is a crowned figure of the Blessed Virgin holding the Child in her arms. Below are the arms of the duchy of Brabant, to the left, of the margravate of Antwerp, to the right, and in the centre of Philip II of Spain. There are also the figures of Justitia (Justice) and Prudentia (Wisdom).

Inside, a stairway ascends to the landing. This part of the building was covered during the 19C. Previously it was an open courtyard where the city artillery was kept. Paintings here of 1899 show historic events from the first half of the 16C history of Antwerp. Those on one side are concerned with the economic prosperity of the city, those on the other with the arts.

The Grote Leyszaal contains four large historical paintings by Hendrik Leys, who died in 1869 before completing the planned six. Other pictures of 1855 by the same artist, which were once in his house, now hang in the Kleine Leyszaal.

In the Trouwzaal, the Wedding Room, the 16C chimneypiece has two caryatids by Cornelis Floris. The murals, by Victor Lagye, 1886, depict Belgian wedding ceremonies throughout the centuries. In the Militia Room, where young men formerly drew lots for conscription in the army, there is a picture of the town hall of 1406. The Raadzaal, the Council Chamber, has ceiling panels by Jacob de Roore. Painted c 1715 they offer an allegorical reaction to the Barrier Treaty, which was designed to discourage any further attempts at annexation by the French. They suggest the benefits that will come to Antwerp if the Scheldt is reopened. The Burgemeesterzaal, arranged in the style of 1885, has a 16C chimneypiece attributed to Pieter Coecke.

Behind the Stadhuis is the short Gildekamerstraat. In 1954 this was rebuilt in the old style. Note especially No. 4, which perhaps originally was by Cornelis Floris. Nos 2–4 house the **Volkskundemuseum** devoted to Antwerp and the surrounding area with particular reference to archaeology, customs, crafts and the guilds. It is open daily, except Monday, from 10.00 to 17.00. It is closed on 1 and 2 January, 1 May, Ascension Day, 1 November, 25 and 26 December. Note. On those Mondays which are public holidays, the museum is open.

At the S end of the Stadhuis stands Constantin Meunier's figure, 'The Docker'. From here take the short Suikerrui to the Scheldt. At No. 19 is the Ethnographic Museum with its interesting display of objects from many countries. On the corner of the quay is the **Hansahuis**, decorated with female figures by Jef Lambeaux, 1852–1908.

S of Suikerrui, 11–13 Hoogstraat occupy the site of the birthplace in 1593 of the painter Jacob Jordaens. Nearby at No. 4 Reyndersstraat is the house he built in 1641 and in which he lived until his death in 1678.

Parallel to Reyndersstraat, Heilig Geeststraat leads into the VRIJDAGMARKT, where

The Brabo Fountain, of 1887, by Jef Lambeaux, Antwerp

an interesting second-hand market is held on Wednesday and Friday mornings. On the W side of the square is the *** *Plantin-Moretus Museum**. This is described in Section E. The adjacent *Prentenkabinet*, Print Room, contains a valuable collection of prints and engravings, especially by Antwerp masters. Admission is normally restricted to those who wish to study the collection.

The **Sint Annatunnel** beneath the Scheldt, built in 1933 for cyclists and pedestrians, starts from Sint Jansvliet, an open space just W of the Vrijdagmarkt.

The QUAYS, started by Napoleon, were completed between 1880 and 1885. Today used less and less, as the main port downstream expands, they stretch for some 5km from SW of the J.F. Kennedytunnel to beyond the Waaslandtunnel. They took the place of the crowded, untidy old waterfront. To build them the river bank was straightened, some 800 houses were demolished, and a pier which carried the town crane was removed. Near the foot of Suikerrui are the Steen fortress and the wharf used by the 'Flandria' excursion boats. From here in either direction there are open warehouses, which have fine ironwork pediments and which carry pedestrian terraces.

The foundations of the **Steen** date from the 9C. A fortress was built here to defend the frontier established by the Treaty of Verdun between the territories of Charles the Bold and Lothair, the grandsons of Charlemagne. The oldest section of visible wall dates from c 1250. Later in the 13C the building served as a prison. Restored in 1520, during the rule of Charles V, by Domien de Waghemakere and Rombout Keldermans, the Steen was rebuilt in 1890. Further work was done on it in 1953. The present structure represents only the gatehouse and front buildings of the castle.

At the entrance stands the figure by A. Poels, 1963, known as 'Lange Wapper'. In medieval times the canal from Herentals, which was used for bringing clean water to the breweries, ran under a bridge. The brewers constructed a large wooden fork with a long beam, a wapper, on the bridge to raise the barrels of water. When this landmark, known as the 'Lange Wapper', disappeared, popular imagination replaced it with a similarly shaped folklore figure, who was notorious for his strange gifts and pranks. One of these was the ability to grow at will and peer in through windows.

Today the Steen houses the **National Maritime Museum**, which is open daily from 10.00 to 17.00. It is closed on 1 and 2 January, 1 May, 1 November and 25 December.

The museum is arranged in a series of small rooms linked by narrow passages and steep stairs. Especially interesting is its collection of model ships. There are twelve sections:

1. The Waterfront, arts and crafts. 2. The Waterfront, ship models. 3. The Waterfront, religion and superstition. Note the votive ship of c 1757 and a graveslab bearing the representation of a caravel. 4. The Waterfront, the people.

5. Inland navigation, with two attractive and interesting pictures of old Antwerp by Jan Ruyten. 6. Fishing, with models explaining methods of netting. 7. A room with a variety of ship models. 8. Shipbuilding, with a particularly good diorama of an Antwerp shipyard of c 1850.

9. History of shipping from early times to the close of the 18C. This section and No. 10 contain some of the finest and largest models: also fragments of a 2C boat found in 1899 during the digging of the Bruges–Zeebrugge canal. Pictures by Willem van de Velde the Younger , including Salute to an Amsterdam ship. 10. History of shipping in the 19C and 20C. The models range from Napoleon's state barge to modern ships. 11. New acquisitions. 12. Council chamber, with paintings by Bonaventure Peeters and J.B. de Bonnecroy which vividly recall old Antwerp and its waterfront.

Behind the Steen in an open-air section of the museum there is a lighter, the 'Lauranda', 1928, which may be visited. This is sometimes used for exhibitions. In a large shed there are barges, lighters and other craft. A plaque honours the 1st Canadian Army which, with British and Polish units, liberated the Scheldt estuary in autumn 1944 and reopened the port of Antwerp.

Across the road from the Steen the short Vleeshuisstraat leads, through a cut in the old wall, to the *Vleeshuis. This large gabled and turreted building was erected by Herman de Waghemakere in 1503 for the Butchers' Guild. Today it houses a museum with a rich and varied collection of exhibits.

The museum is open daily, except Monday, from 10.00 to 17.00. It is closed 1 and 2 January, 1 May, 1 November and 25 December. Open on Easter Monday, Whit Monday and the Monday following the second Sunday in August. Apart from the collection, the building is well worth visiting for its magnificent interior. The Ground Floor Hall, vaulted in brick from a central row of six columns, was used for the sale of meat until the middle of the 19C. It now has exhibits of metalwork, arms and armour, 16–18C sculpture and woodcarving, notably an oak pulpit and a Brabant altarpiece of 1514, an embroidered cope of 1525, several fine chests and 16C murals from an old Antwerp house.

A long, steep spiral staircase leads to the First Floor. At the top there is a small picture-tiled kitchen with a huge pump and, around the corner, a small room with leather wall hangings. Gilt-leather and tapestries cover the walls of the Council Chamber of the Butchers. In this room there are musical instruments, objects of gold and silver, and some jewellery and furniture, including a 14C chest.

A picture on this floor by an anonymous artist depicts the so-called Spanish Fury of 1576. Believed by some to be the work of an eye-witness, it is filled with lurid detail. In the bottom left corner there is a nauseating scene of incipient rape.

Another steep stairway leads to the Second Floor. Here there is a small Egyptian section and the main collection of musical instruments.

Our visit to the Vleeshuis ends in the spacious, brick-vaulted Basement, where a Lapidarium houses old stonework from churches and other buildings in Antwerp.

The Burchtgracht, running N from the Vleeshuis, was once the moat of the 'burcht' or castle, the Steen.

The area in the immediate neighbourhood of the Vleeshuis has been redeveloped, with considerable imagination, in the old style. To the E, beyond a small housing complex, is a street named Oude Beurs, the Old Exchange. At the W end, behind a modern building, which incorporates a baroque portal, there is a house with a turret known as *De Spieghel*. Before being tried as a heretic and executed at Vilvoorde (see above), William Tyndale, the translator of the New Testament into English, lived as a refugee from 1534–35 in Oude Beurs.

No. 15, in the adjacent Hofstraat, is the actual Oude Beurs, the Old Exchange, of 1515. The painter Adam van Noort lived in a house which once stood on the opposite side of the street.

To the North of the Steen and Vleeshuis

A short walk of c 200m from the Vleeshuis brings you to the church of Sint Paulus, noted for the works by Rubens and other 17C masters. Circa 300m farther N is the Brouwershuis, which supplied Antwerp's breweries with clean water.

The *Sint Pauluskerk stands on the site of a church built for the Dominicans in 1276. The present church, one of the last in the Gothic style, was begun in 1517, though not consecrated until 1571. Seven years later the Dominicans were expelled by the Calvinists. Most of the transepts and choir were torn down. Their stones were used to ballast the fireships which were sent in 1584 against Parma's barrage on the Scheldt at Kallo. After their return to Antwerp the Dominicans commenced work on the church. The rebuilding was completed by 1639. In 1679 the tower was destroyed by fire and then rebuilt in the baroque style. Badly damaged by Dutch bombardment in 1830, the church suffered further destruction by fire in 1968.

From May to September the Sint Pauluskerk is open daily, except Sunday and Monday, from 14.00 to 17.00. Entrance in the Veemarkt. From October to April daily from 09.00 to 12.00. Entrance at 20 Sint Paulustraat.

A requirement of baroque art that all the iconography of a building should come together under one heading is met in this church. Its theme is the Church of Christ as an instrument of salvation. The choir represents the Church Glorious, the central nave, the transepts and the side aisles the Church Militant, and the Calvary in the friars' cemetery the Church Suffering.

On entering, the visitor's attention is captured immediately by the glowing richness of a row of paintings along the wall of the N aisle. Depicting the Fifteen Mysteries of the Rosary, all were produced between 1617 and 1619. Among the artists are Frans Francken the Younger, who painted the Visitation, Cornelis de Vos, the Nativity and Presentation in the Temple, David Teniers the Elder, Gethsemane, Antoon van Dyck, the Carrying of the Cross, Jacob Jordaens, the Crucifixion and Pieter Paul Rubens, the Scourging at the Pillar. A sketch for the Rubens' painting may be seen in the Museum Voor Schone Kunsten in Ghent.

The statues of the apostles in the Central Nave are attributed to Michiel van der Voort and the organ carving to Pieter Verbruggen the Elder. The low relief of the 'Soeten Naem', the Sweet Name of Jesus, of 1644 is the work of Artus Quellin the Elder.

The five confessionals in the S aisle are attributed to Pieter Verbruggen the Elder.

In SOUTH TRANSEPT the two altars of 1654 and probably the communion bench of 1655, are the work of Verbruggen. The Disputation on the Nature of the Holy Sacrament, above one altar, painted by Rubens c 1609 was superbly restored in 1973. The Pietà of c 1651 above the other altar is by Gaspard de Crayer. The 17C Road to Emmaus is by Erasmus Quellin.

In the NORTH TRANSEPT is Rubens' magnificent Adoration of the Shepherds, painted c 1609. Badly damaged by the fire in 1968 it was restored and returned to the church in 1972. Other paintings include Our Lady and St Dominic by Gaspard de Crayer and a copy of Caravaggio's Madonna of the Rosary by B. de Quertemont. The original, removed by the Emperor Joseph II in 1781, is now in Vienna's Kunsthistorisches Museum. Note also the 17C marble figure of St Rose of Lima, one of the most beautiful productions of the Flemish baroque, by Artus Quellin the Younger.

In the CHOIR the high altar is in part the work of Pieter Verbruggen the Elder. At one time the altar was surmounted by Rubens' Vision of St Dominic. This is now in the Musée des Beaux Arts at Lyon. It has been replaced by the Descent from the Cross by Cornelis Cels, 1807. The stalls, which bear the arms of donors, are attributed to Verbruggen. Of the eight statues of Dominican saints, four—Catherine of Siena, Raymond of Pennafort, Vincent Ferrer, Anthony of Florence—are the work of Verbruggen, Hyacinthus is by Artus Quellin the Elder and Peter of Verona by J.P. Baurscheit the Elder.

The CHAPEL OF LEPANTO, which, unfortunately, is not always open, gets its name from four paintings by Jan Peeters, 1668, of the Battle of Lepanto.

In the Gulf of Patras in 1571, the fleet of the Christian League, which was made up of ships contributed by the Pope, Venice and Spain under the command of Don John of Austria, defeated the Ottoman Turks and released some 15,000 Christian slaves. This was the last major sea battle in which ships propelled by oars were used by both sides. Lepanto has always been of special significance to the Dominicans, as the Christian fleet sailed under the protection of Our Lady of the Rosary and all its chaplains were Dominican friars. The battle and Don John of Austria, the natural son of Charles V, are celebrated in the splendid martial rhythms of Chesterton's poem 'Lepanto':

> ...'But Don John of Austria is riding to the sea.
> Don John calling through the blast and the eclipse
> Crying with the trumpet, with the trumpet of his lips,
> Trumpeth that sayeth ha!
> Domino Gloria
> Don John of Austria
> Is shouting to the ships.'

Another picture in this chapel, Christ Mocked, is attributed to Otto Venius, 1558–1629.

In the grounds of the church the CALVARY of 1697–1747 has a grotto and 36 statues which commemorate the suffering of Christ, the story of Mary Magdalene and of some of the penitents who stayed in the Holy Land. It was erected by the Society of the Pilgrims of Jerusalem, which was associated with the church. Their aim was to encourage pilgrimages to Palestine. The statues are the work of well-known local sculptors.

From the Sint Pauluskerk we walk the short distance N to the **Brouwershuis** at 20 Adriaan Brouwerstraat, a road branching E off the quay just before the docks and 500m from the Steen. Formerly the Waterhuis, it was built in 1554 by Gilbert van Schoonbeke as part of a system for supplying Antwerp's breweries with clean water brought by barge along canals from Herentals, 28km to the E.

Until the late 19C the street at the back, Brouwersvliet, was a canal lined with breweries. The clean water, discharged into a cistern from the barges, was raised by a bucket-chain, at first powered by horses and later by an engine. The stable is on the ground floor beyond the hall. The bucket-chain is behind a trap-door in the wall by the entrance to the court where the mechanism may be seen. The cistern, from which the water was raised, is below. An attractively carved stairs leads to a landing where there is a painting of Vulcan's Forge by the Venetian Antonio Pellegrini and a tile-picture of 1680, which was brought here in 1932. Off the landing are the Laboratory and the Council Room, the latter has a fireplace of c 1660 and Mechelen leather hangings. Note the overmantel, with the Four Seasons, by Pellegrini and the 16C chandelier, an excellent specimen of Antwerp glasswork. Above a cabinet of 1625 are the brewers' insignia in carved wood.

The Brouwershuis is open daily, except Monday, from 10.00 to 17.00. It is closed 1 and 2 January, 1 May, 1 November and 25 December. Note. It is open on Easter Monday, Whit Monday and the Monday following the second Sunday in August.

Off the SE corner of the Grote Markt and below the W face of the cathedral is the small, attractive HANDSCHOENMARKT. Now lined with cafés and restaurants, this was once the glove market. It is surrounded by old houses.

No. 13 was the birthplace in 1610 of the painter David Teniers the Younger. The stone well, with a graceful ironwork canopy, is ascribed to Quinten Metsys, c 1495. It is said that Metsys started life as a smith, but exchanged the anvil for the brush because of his passion for a painter's daughter. Hence the inscription on a tablet beside the cathedral door 'Connubialis Amor de Mulcibre fecit Apellem', 'Connubial love turned Mulciber (Vulcan) into Apelles' or 'Twas love connubial taught the smith to paint'. The figure with a glove on the well canopy is Silvius Brabo (see above). At the SW corner of the cathedral there is a lively monument by Jef Lambeaux to Pieter Appelmans, who with others planned and built the cathedral.

The ****Cathedral**, Onze Lieve Vrouw, the largest Gothic church in Belgium, is hemmed in by buildings and, unfortunately, cannot be seen as a whole. Among its many treasures are paintings by Rubens and other 16C and 17C masters.

Major restoration work started in 1965 and probably will not be completed until the end of the century. Much of the exterior, including the tower, has been finished. The nave may be visited, though it will be some time before visitors may see the choir and its ambulatory chapels. Some of the paintings are also being restored. Where possible the major works are exhibited in the nave and in an Art Room, which unfortunately may not always be open.

The cathedral may be visited from Monday to Friday between 10.00 and 18.00, on Saturday from 12.00 to 15.00, Sunday and holidays, 13.00 to 16.00.

History. An ancient chapel was replaced during the 12C by a Romanesque church, parts of which are being revealed by the restoration work. The present cathedral was built between 1352 and c 1525. The first part to be completed was the choir which seems to have been finished early in the 15C. The main cathedral plan can probably be ascribed to Jan Appelmans, whose son Pieter (died 1434), took over the direction of the construction. By 1425 work had begun on a new W front. The Romanesque nave was demolished and work started on the Gothic nave, much of this was undertaken by Herman de Waghemakere. The superb tower, 123m high, erected in 1431 as far as the gallery beneath the clock, was completed c 1521 by Domien de Waghemakere.

In 1519 Charles V commissioned a new choir, as large as the existing church, and laid the foundation stone in 1521. However, the project was abandoned in 1533. In that year the church was badly damaged by fire. In 1566 it was pillaged by the Calvinist iconoclasts. In 1794 most of the art treasures, including paintings, stained-glass and the choir stalls, were removed by the French, who closed the building. Reopened for worship in 1802, some of its treasures were returned and additional material donated by other churches.

The Bells. Besides its carillon of 49 bells, the cathedral has a number of other bells. The largest dates from 1507 and is named 'Carolus', after Charles V, who stood sponsor at its 'baptism'.

PAINTINGS. *Rubens*: 1. ****The Raising of the Cross. This triptych, painted in 1610, was the artist's first major work after his return from Italy. The central panel shows the Nailing to the Cross, the right shutter a group of Roman soldiers with the two thieves in the background, and the left shutter the disciples and the holy women. Note the superbly portrayed old woman in the centre. On the outside of the shutters are, left, St Eligius and St Walburga and, right, St Catherine and St Amand. Originally there was also an upper panel with God the Father and two Angels, and a predella. Rubens appears to have taken the idea for this work from Tintoretto's great Calvary in the Scuola di San Rocco at Venice.

2. ****Descent from the Cross, a triptych painted in 1611–14 for the altar of the Guild of Arquebusiers. The central panel is perfect in composition, and in its restrained style, reflects the lessons the artist had learnt during his

stay in Italy. Van Dyck is said to have contributed to this work as restorer of damage it suffered in Rubens' studio. To him are attributed the cheek and chin of the Virgin and the arm of St Mary Magdalene. On the inside of the shutters are the Visitation and the Presentation in the Temple, on the outside, St Christopher and the Hermit.

3. On the high altar is *The Assumption which was painted in 1626. This is one of the finest of the six versions of this subject painted by Rubens.

4. The Resurrection, with John the Baptist and St Catherine on the wings.
Paintings by other artists include:

Jacob de Backer: A Triptych of the Last Judgement, with Christopher Plantin, his son and St Christopher on the left wing, and his wife, his daughters and St John on the right. Normally this hangs above the tomb of Christopher Plantin in the fourth choir ambulatory chapel.

Ambroos Francken: The Descent of the Holy Spirit. Attributed to *Frans Francken the Elder*: The Fifteen Wounds; Jesus in the Temple Confronts the Doctors, with, it is said, Portraits of Luther, Calvin and others as the doctors. *G.J. Herreyns*: Portraits of Christopher Plantin and Jan Moretus; Men of Emmaus.

Leonardo da Vinci (?): Head of Christ, painted on marble. *Adam van Noort*: The Miraculous Draught of Fishes. *Cornelis Schut*: The Ascension. *Otto Venius*: Last Supper; The Entombment; The Raising of Lazarus. *Cornelis de Vos*: Triptych: A Pietà with donors. *Martin de Vos*: The Marriage Feast at Cana; A Pietà.

OTHER WORKS OF ART. NAVE. The nave has seven aisles, separated by six rows of pillars. These rise, without capitals, to the vault, which dates from 1614.

For ease of identification, some works of particular interest are listed below under four sectors:

In the SW. *Artus Quellin the Younger*: carved memorial of Bishop Capello, 1676. Marble statue of Jonathan, 1650–60. Marble of Our Lady of the Immaculate Conception. *Abraham van Diepenbeek*: The Four Almoners, 1635. This is a fragment from a window destroyed in 1794. *J.B. Capronnier*: Stained glass of SS Peter and Paul, 1867.

In the NW. *Artus Quellin the Younger*: statue of Gideon; *Pieter Scheemaeckers*: memorial to the Tuerlinckx family.

In the NE. *Artus Quellin the Younger*: altar of Our Lady. Pietà.

In the SE. *Hendrik Verbruggen*: white marble communion rail of 1687; *M. van der Voort*: pulpit of 1713, made for the abbey of Hemiksem. *Nicholas Rombouts*: glass, The Last Supper, 1503.

The CHOIR AMBULATORY CHAPELS, which may be closed because of the reconstruction work, are described from S to N. Some of the objects mentioned are temporarily in the nave.

Second chapel: Monument of the printer Jan Moretus, who died in 1601, and of his wife.

Third chapel: tomb of Bishop Capello, who died in 1676, by *Artus Quellin the Younger*.

Fourth chapel: tomb of Christopher Plantin, who died in 1589.

Sixth chapel: A polychrome Mater Dolorosa by *Artus Quellin the Younger*. The sculpture of Christ in the Tomb, in a niche on the left, dates from the 15C. This chapel, at the back of the high altar, contains the tomb of Isabella of Bourbon, who died in 1465. She was the second wife of Charles the Bold.

Ninth chapel: Here, and beyond, the statues on the confessionals are by *Hendrik Verbruggen*.

On the left of the outer altar in the last chapel, which is dedicated to

St Anthony, there is an interesting window of 1503. This shows the kneeling figures of Henry VII of England and his wife. It was erected to commemorate the commercial treaty between Henry and Philip the Fair. The altarpiece of St Michael and the Dragon, on a gold background, is 15C Spanish.

Immediately to the S of the cathedral is the GROENPLAATS , once the town graveyard. This is now a spacious open area reserved for pedestrians with, in the centre, a bronze statue of Rubens, by Willem Geefs, 1843. The Post Office is on the S side, and below the square there is an underground station and concourse.

The Fine Arts museum and a number of other places of interest to visitors lie to the S of the Groenplaats on either side of Nationalestraat and its continuation, Volkstraat. From Groenplaats to the museum is rather more than 1km. This part of the city is described under B. South-West of the Centre.

Take the Schoenmarkt, once the shoe market, E out of Groenplaats and, passing on the right the former provincial government buildings, once the 18C episcopal palace, continue to the *Torengebouw* of 1930, Europe's first 'skyscraper'. This stands at the W end of the MEIR, at one time a swamp but now a wide and busy, main thoroughfare.

The description of Central Antwerp that follows is divided into three parts: along the Meir, and South and North of the Meir.

Along the Meir

The short Twaalfmaandenstraat, Twelve Months Street, where Plantin printed his first book in 1555, leads to the **Beurs**. This was rebuilt between 1868 and 1872 by J. Schadde in the style of its predecessor, which was designed by Domien de Waghemakere in 1531 and later destroyed by fire. De Waghemakere's building served as a model for other European exchanges, including Gresham's in London. The large hall has a ceiling decorated with the arms of the seafaring nations.

The Beurs may be visited from Monday to Friday between 07.30 and 17.00.

Farther E along the Meir, c 250m from the Torengebouw, is the former **Royal Palace**. Occupying the corner of the Meir and Wapper, this 18C rococo-style building, once the van Susteren mansion, is now an international cultural centre.

Wapper is a pleasant, open pedestrian area with a fountain and benches. On the E side stands the ****Rubens House** (see F. below).

We continue our walk along the Meir to No. 85, the *Huis Osterrieth*, another rococo-style patrician mansion. Like the former Royal Palace it is the work of J.P. Baurscheit the Younger. Opposite is the *Feestzaal* of 1907 by A. van Mechelen.

A monument to Lodewijk van Bercken, by F. Joris, 1906, stands at the junction of Jezusstraat and Leysstraat. In 1476 van Bercken established the diamond polishing industry in Antwerp.

At the end of the Leysstraat is Teniersplaats, which is bounded on the E by a section of the ring boulevard, here called the Frankrijklei. Across the boulevard stands the **KVO**, the **Royal Flemish Opera** , which was built by van Mechelen in 1907. At Franklin Rooseveltplaats to the N of the opera there is a busy bus terminal. From Teniersplaats the broad De Keyserlei continues to the main railway station and to the zoo (see C. South-East of the Centre).

South of the Meir

From the W end of the Meir follow the Huidevettersstraat, the Tanners Street, in a S direction for c 250m to Lange Gasthuisstraat. At No. 19 is the *Mayer van den Bergh Museum. This holds an eclectic collection of objects many from the medieval, late Gothic and Renaissance periods.

The museum is open daily, except Monday, from 10.00 to 17.00. It is closed on 1 and 2 January, 1 May, 1 November and 25 December. It is open on Easter Monday, Whit Monday, and the Monday following the second Sunday in August.

Emil Mayer, 1824–79, was born in Cologne. He settled in Antwerp in 1849, became a wealthy businessman and, in 1857, married Henriette van den Bergh, the daughter of a prosperous local family. Their son, Fritz Mayer van den Bergh, 1858–1901, devoted his life to the study and collection of art treasures. He acquired not only the works of great masters but also those by lesser known artists which appealed to his taste. Henriette Mayer van den Bergh provided constant artistic and financial support and, when her son was killed accidentally in 1901, she established this museum in his memory. Although 16C in appearance, the building incorporates the most modern display methods known at that time. On Henriette's death in 1920, administration of the museum passed to a trust.

In the large and diverse collection there are paintings, furniture, metal-work, sculpture, tapestries, ceramics and objets d'art. No more than an indication of the museum's wealth can be given here. It rivals the best private collections in London or Paris.

Most of the rooms have fine furniture and chimneypieces. Small 15C and 16C stained-glass panels and medallions have been placed in some of the windows.

Among the many outstanding pictures, perhaps the most important is Pieter Brueghel the Elder's 'Dulle Griet' in Room 9.

GROUND FLOOR PASSAGE. 16C and 17C tapestries from Bruges and Oudenaarde. Portrait of Henriette Mayer van den Bergh.

ROOM 1. 17C portrait groups by *Jan Rotius, Christiaen van Couwenbergh* and *Jan Mytens*.

ROOM 2. Small works by *Jan Brueghel, Hans Bol, Frans Hals* and *Gillis van Coninxloo*. Also paintings by *Daniel Seghers, Adriaen van Ostade, Jacob Jordaens, David Teniers the Younger* and *Gérard de Lairesse*.

ROOM 3. Two stone columns with female figures, early examples of French 12C Gothic sculpture; a Mechelen portable altar of c 1500; a polychromed stone Virgin and Child of c 1380.

ROOM 4. A *Calvary Triptych by *Quinten Metsys*; a 15C embroidery with St Mary Magdalene.

STAIRS. 16C and 17C tapestries from Oudenaarde and Bruges; portrait of Fritz Mayer van den Bergh.

ROOM 5. The theme is Still life, with works by *Willem Heda, Roelof Koets* and others.

ROOM 6. An outstandingly important *polychromed wood sculpture of St John resting his head on the breast of Christ by *Heinrich of Constance*, c 1300. Also in this room are three small panels of a polyptych, (the remainder are in Baltimore, USA), dating from c 1400 and one of the earliest examples of Netherlands panel painting. A carved late 15C retable from Brabant; *small ivories with the Baptism of Jesus, 8–9C, Miracles of Jesus, 9–10C, Birth of Jesus, 11C.

ROOM 7 is mainly devoted to Renaissance works. Peasant Interior by

Pieter Aertsen, 1556. Landscape by *Herri met de Bles*, 1550. Triptych by *Ambrosius Benson*. Adoration by *Adriaen Isenbrant*. St Christopher by *Jan Mostaert* .

ROOM 8. Small 13C to 15C sculptures arranged chronologically in a row of cases. Against the balustrade, a case with portrait medallions, including one of Christina Metsys by *Quinten Metsys*. This is one of the earliest examples from the Netherlands of this kind of work, a small retable, c 1490, of the Passion.

In ROOM 9 hangs what is generally accepted to be the museum's most important painting, •••Dulle Griet or Mad Meg by **Pieter Brueghel the Elder**. It was bought by Mayer van den Bergh in 1894 for 394 marks at an auction in Cologne. Previous owners included the Emperor Rudolph II.

Painted at a time when Brueghel was strongly influenced by Bosch—the picture is full of his motifs—it shows Dulle Griet striding resolutely towards the mouth of hell. Various interpretations have been placed on the painting. Dulle Griet is a witch or sorceress. She is a Flemish folklore figure used to scare the children. She personifies the inherent wickedness of the female sex, which is always ready to embrace the devil and his works. The figure behind Dulle Griet, who is ladling coins out of his distended anus, suggests to some critics that the picture is an allegory of avarice. The presence of so many symbols relating to alchemy convinces others that it is concerned with that pseudo-science. E. Michel in *Bruegel*, Paris 1931, is of the opinion that it refers to the wars and civil disturbances which devastated the Low Countries in the 16C. Critics may dispute the meaning of this picture. Few will question its stature as a work of art.

Also by Brueghel the Elder there are The Twelve Proverbs, painted on wooden plates. By *Pieter Brueghel the Younger* there is a copy of his father's Census at Bethlehem.

ROOM 10 is the Library. There are Portraits by *Adriaen Key*, 1589, *Jan Rotius*, 1659, and *Jan Mytens*, 1658; a collection of plaquettes by the German *Peter Flötner* c 1535.

ROOMS 11 and 12 were designed to display 18C panelling from a house in Tournai. There is also porcelain and there are portraits by the 18C French artists *Nicolas de Largillière* and *Louis Tocqué*.

At 33 Lange Gasthuisstraat is the **Maagdenhuis**, which was formerly an orphanage for girls. The entrance and chapel date from 1564. The rest of the building was completed in 1636. The first residents are recalled by some delightful carvings above the entrance and in the pleasant courtyard there is a 17C wooden figure of one of the orphans, 'Houten Klara'.

The building now houses a fine collection of 16C and 17C paintings and an archive which holds material concerning the orphanage. It is open on Monday and from Wednesday to Friday between 10.00 and 17.00, and on Saturday and Sunday from 13.00 to 17.00. It is closed on Tuesday and on public holidays.

A concise, illustrated catalogue of the collection in English is on sale. All the exhibits are clearly numbered or lettered. The following is a short selection of those on show: in the former CHAPEL, to the right of the entrance, 46 and 47: Porridge bowls, Antwerp and possibly Frisian, 16C and 17C; 50: Bull of Pope Honorious III, 1226; 51 to 53: seals; No. 51 is the oldest known seal of Antwerp, 1232; 49: certificate of Election of Charles V as Holy Roman Emperor, 1519, with five of the original seven seals; 26: Panel of the Last Supper by Lambert Lombard, 16C; 24: The Last Supper by Pieter Pourbus.

Note also the following interesting items in a cabinet: A. caps and coats worn by the orphans in 1860; C. 19C orphans' tokens for bread and peat; D. the token of a child, reclaimed by its mother in 1811; F, collar, shawl and caps of 1860.

From the Chapel we move to the ROOMS on the left of the entrance. Some interesting items listed in the catalogue are:

1. An Orphan Girl at Work and 2. Portrait of an Old Lady before a Crucifix by Cornelius de Vos. 4. The Multiplication of Jacob's Flocks by David Teniers the Younger. 6. and 7. Polychrome, 16C wooden statues of SS Barbara and Anna. 12. Descent from the Cross by Jacob Jordaens. 16. St Hieronymus by A. van Dyck. 18. 15C Triptych of the Virgin with Saints by Gerard van der Meire. 22. The Mass of St Gregory by an Unknown Master of the late 15C. 26. The Last Supper by Lambert Lombard. 31. Mary Magdalen by Jan Massys. 36. The Adoration of the Shepherds by Jan van Scorel. 38. The Men of Emmaus by Theodor Rombouts. 43. St Philip baptising the Eunuch of the Queen of Sheba by Michiel van Coxcyen. 57. The Wedding at Cana by Frans Francken the Elder. 58. The Holy Family by Pieter van Avont. 74. Chasuble with scenes of the Passion, mid-16C, 93. and 94. Pilgrims Visiting a Dilapidated Temple and the Holy Family, with Angels, in Dilapidated Temple, both by Hendrik Peres. 143. Invocation of Christ in Favour of Poor Families by P.P. Rubens. 145. The Passion by Hieronymus Cock, 148. Triptych of Calvary by the 16C Master of the Antwerp Crucifixion, 149. *Last Judgement, the Seven Works of Mercy and the Seven Deadly Sins by an Unknown Antwerp Master of the late 15C. Note how the presence of Christ identifies the Mercies, that of the Devil the Sins.

On leaving the Maagdenhuis continue down Lange Gasthuisstraat to the Sint Elisabeth Gasthuis. This hospital is the oldest foundation of its kind in Antwerp. Established c 1204 within the city walls, by 1238 it needed to expand and moved to a site in a meadow outside the walls, which is still known as Gasthuisstraat.

Your Maagdenhuis ticket will admit you to the hospital's chapel. There is a comprehensive guide in English which indentifies the chapel's features and contents. The nave dates from the 15C. Note particularly the altar surround by Artus Quellin the Younger and the pulpit by Erasmus Quellin.

In Mechelseplein, at the end of Gasthuisstraat, is the **Sint Joriskerk** of 1853. This incorporates parts of the 14C church, in which Jan Brueghel and Jan and Pieter Appelmans were buried.

From the church, take Sint Jorispoort to the Leopoldplaats, where there is a statue of Leopold I by Willem Geefs, 1867. Continue by Leopoldstraat, passing en route the small **Kruidtuin**, the Botanic Garden, to the Komedieplaats. In this square is the **KNS**, the **Royal Dutch Theatre**, which was built by Bruno Bourla in 1834. Rubens' House and the Meir are c 150m to the N.

North of the Meir

In the district N of the Meir and W of Italielei, which measures c 1km by 1km, there are some fine old houses and a number of churches. It may be explored by several routes. The one outlined below, which starts from Hendrik Conscienceplein, c 150m NW of the Beurs, covers most places of interest.

HENDRIK CONSCIENCEPLEIN, a quiet small 17C square reserved for pedestrians, is named after the prolific Flemish novelist, 1812–83, who is best known for his historical work 'The Lion of Flanders'. His statue by F. Joris, 1883, stands in the square.

On the E side of the square is the church of **Sint Carolus Borromeus**. This baroque style building was erected between 1615 and 1625 by the Jesuit architect Pieter Huyssens. St Charles Borremeo was one of the great figures of the Counter-Reformation. Zealous, selfless, holy during his lifetime (1538–84), he was canonised in 1610.

The superb W front is said to have been designed by Rubens. He also painted the ceiling of the nave and aisles. In 1718 the church was struck by lightning and set alight. All that survived the fire were the choir, two chapels, the portal and the tower. Reconstruction by Jan Baurscheit the Elder began in the following year. He and Michiel van der Voort were responsible for much of the interior woodwork. The Lady Chapel, which survived the fire, is lined with the coloured marble that was a feature of the earlier building.

The church is open on Monday and from Wednesday to Friday from 07.30 to 13.00 and from 07.30 to 12.00 and 15.00 to 18.15 on Saturday. It is closed on Tuesday.

The S side of the square is occupied by the 17C former Jesuit House. This is now a municipal library

From Hendrik Conscienceplein three parallel streets, with several connecting streets, run in an easterly direction. Nos 9 and 10 in the KEIZER-STRAAT, the northernmost of the three, are the 17C *Huis Delbeke* and the 16C patrician **Huis Rockox**. Between 1603 and 1640 the Huis Rockox was the home of Nicolaas Rockox, burgomaster of Antwerp and friend of Rubens. His portrait is on a triptych by Rubens in the Museum voor Schone Kunsten. The Huis Rockox, with its works by Rubens, tapestries and fine furniture, is open daily, except Monday, from 10.00 to 17.00. It is closed 1 and 2 January, 1 May, 1 November and 25 December. It is open on Easter Monday, Whit Monday and the Monday following the second Sunday in August.

Farther along the street, on the N side, is the 16C *Sint Annakapel*. It has a baroque-style doorway of 1624.

KIPDORP, the central of the three parallel streets, runs into Sint Jacobs-markt. Near the junction is Sint Jacobskerk (see below).

At the W end of the third street, LANGE NIEUWSTRAAT, is the 15C *Sint Nicolaaskapel* (no admission). No. 43 once belonged to Sir Thomas Gresham, an English merchant who lived in Antwerp between c 1555 and 1567. He acted as financial agent for four Tudor sovereigns. By clever, if somewhat dubious means, he raised the value of the pound sterling on the Antwerp exchange. As a result England's debts were paid off.

No. 31 is the so-called **Chapelle de Bourgogne**, the Burgundian Chapel (no admission). This was built in 1496 by Domien de Waghemakere for Jan van Immerseel, margrave of Antwerp. Its name is derived from four historic Burgundian marriages which form the subjects of some fine murals.

*Sint Jacobskerk was begun in 1491 by Herman de Waghemakere and continued after 1503 by Domien de Waghemakere. It was not completed until 1656. Favoured by the patrician families of Antwerp,who had their burial vaults, private chapels and altars here, it was richly endowed with paintings and sculptures.

After a serious fire in 1967 the paintings were removed to the Museum voor Schone Kunsten for safekeeping and restoration. Now the church has been fully repaired and its important paintings, church plate, vestments and statues have been returned. Perhaps its greatest attraction is the Rubens' Chapel.

The church is open between April and October from Monday to Saturday from 14.00 to 17.00 and from November to March from 09.00 to 12.00. Entry is from Lange Nieuwstraat.

We begin our visit in the SOUTH TRANSEPT and proceed in an anti-clock-wise direction.

Among the paintings in the S transept there are works by *Gaspard de Crayer*, *Bernard van Orley* and *Jan Metsys*. The most interesting feature in this part of the church is the richly carved marble communion rail of 1696 by *Hendrik Verbruggen* and *Willem Kerrickx* in the Chapel of the Blessed Sacrament. The altar of 1670 is by Pieter Verbruggen the Elder.

In the CHOIR the 17C stalls, which bear the arms of benefactors, are by *Artus Quellin the Elder*, *Artus Quellin the Younger* and their pupils, the brothers *Herry*. The magnificent high altar of 1685 with a figure of St James was the gift of the prosperous art dealer Hendrik Hillewerve. It was the work of *Artus Quellin the Younger* with decorative detail by *Willem Kerrickx*.

Seven chapels radiate from the AMBULATORY:

The first, Trinity, was once the chapel of the doctors. Here hang a Trinity by *Hendrik van Balen*, based on a similar work by Rubens, and a St Peter by *Jacob Jordaens*.

The second chapel is dedicated to St Ivo, 1253–1303, a priest from Brittany who is the patron of lawyers. Opposite the altar are two wings of a triptych by *Otto Venius*. The centre panel is in the chapel of St Job off the S nave aisle.

The third chapel, Resurrection, was associated with the powerful merchant family of Le Candele-Vincque.

The fourth chapel, directly behind the high altar, is the Rubens' Chapel. Here the artist and his family are buried. The altar is the work of *Cornelis van Mildert*. The figures of the Mater Dolorosa and attendant angels are by *Luc Fayd'herbe*.

The most striking feature in the chapel is the **Painting of Our Lady, the Christ Child and Saints, one of *Rubens'* greatest works, which was painted by him for this position. It is generally accepted that St George is a self-portrait, that Our Lady has the features of the artist's first wife, the Christ Child those of his son, Mary Magdalene those of his second wife and St Jerome those of his father.

On the artist's tombstone in the chapel pavement are his armorial bearings. The Latin inscription gives a summary of Rubens' life and records restoration work of 1775.

The fifth chapel is dedicated to St Charles Borromeo, 1538–84. It is interesting that this cardinal-archbishop of Milan and uncompromising leader of the Counter-Reformation, should have been portrayed in 1655 by the Protestant *Jacob Jordaens*. The picture shows the saint pleading with the Blessed Virgin on behalf of those stricken by the plague in Milan in 1576. This chapel was the gift of Jacob Antoon Carenna, whose gravestone is on the floor outside.

The sixth chapel is dedicated to St Peter and St Paul.

The seventh chapel, the Visitation, was a gift of 1640 by Bento Rodriguez, consul of Portugal, and others. The altar painting is by *Viktor Wolfvoet*. He has given Mary the features of Rubens' second wife.

Nearby are 17C confessionals and a painting of the Virgin and Child surrounded by Flowers by *Ambroos Brueghel*, the son of Jan, and an Adoration of the Shepherds by *Hendrik van Balen*.

NORTH TRANSEPT. At the entrance to the ambulatory the marble statues of the Apostles John and Paul are by *Michiel van der Voort*. He also sculpted the epitaph in the Chapel of Our Lady to the nobleman Michiel Peeters and his wife. Also in this chapel are an altar by *S. van den Eynde*, 1664, a polychrome Pietà by *Artus Quellin the Elder*, to the left of the altar, and a St Joseph and the Infant Jesus on the right central pillar. The stalls are by *Artus Quellin the Younger*. The memorial to Jan de Gaverelle (1579–1645), admiral, statesman and priest is also by him. The stained-glass window of the Annunciation and the Visitation are by *Jan de la Baer*.

High above the church's N door hang three paintings, the Annunciation by *Gerard van Honthorst*, Jesus in the Temple by *Robert van Audenaerde* and the Adoration of the Magi by *Gerard Seghers*.

On the W wall of the transept there are an Ascension of the Virgin by *Pieter Thys* and an Adoration of the Shepherds by *Erasmus Quellin*.

NAVE. NORTH AISLE. There are six chapels off the N Aisle:

The first, the Holy Cross, sometimes called the Robyns Chapel after its founder, has the last work of *Wenceslas Coeberger*, *Constantine the Great kneeling before the Cross held by St Helena. The features are those of Joos Robyns and of his wife.

The second chapel, All Saints or St Hubert, belonged in succession to the peat and the coal carriers. The latter dedicated an altar here in 1520. There is a triptych of 1608 by *Ambroos Francken*. The 16C window of the Last Supper is the oldest in the church.

In the third chapel, St Dympna, rest members of the Rockox family. They are portrayed on the panels of a triptych by *Jan Sanders* , which is opposite the altar.

The fourth chapel, the Three Kings, was the chapel of the woodworkers. There is an altar-triptych by *Hendrik van Balen* of the Adoration of the Magi. He also painted the two small panels immediately below.

In the fifth chapel, the Holy Name, the philanthropist Cornelis Lantschot, who died in 1656, is commemorated with a gravestone, a carved wall-epitaph by *S. van den Eynde* and a portrait by *Abraham van Diepenbeek*.

In the sixth chapel, St Gertrude, there is a macabre memorial by *Pieter Scheemaeckers* showing the last hours of Francesco Marcos del Pico, Spanish governor of Antwerp, who died in 1693. Note also the bronze balusters. One was donated by Rubens.

NAVE. SOUTH AISLE. There are also six chapels off the S aisle:

The first from the W end, is dedicated to Our Lady. It has a painting of St George and the Dragon by *van Dyck*.

In the nave close to this chapel is the tomb of *Hendrik van Balen* and of his wife. At the foot of a pillar, forming part of a stone memorial, hangs a Resurrection by this artist. The portraits above are also by van Balen.

The second chapel is dedicated to St Anthony, portrayed here by *Martin de Vos*, who used his wife as a model for the demonic temptress. Here also hangs a Madonna by *Guido Reni*.

The third chapel is dedicated to St Roch, who c 1337 gave his life caring for the plague-stricken in Italy. The altar with its figure of the saint, one of the finest pieces of sculptures in the church, is by *Artus Quellin the Elder*. The altar picture of the saint is a self-portrait by *Erasmus Quellin*.

The fourth chapel belonged to the Guild of Musicians. St Job, to whom the chapel is dedicated, was their patron. The altar picture by *Otto Venius* is the central piece of a triptych, whose wings are in the chapel of St Ivo off the choir ambulatory.

In the fifth chapel, dedicated to St Ann, the altar painting is by *Frans Floris*.

In the sixth chapel, dedicated to John the Baptist, there is an altar painting by *Michiel Coxie*, a triptych of which the central panel showing the Martyrdom of St James is by *Martin de Vos*.

To the N of the church, in Sint Jacobsmarkt, the Royal Academy of Music once occupied the 16C *Huis de Moelnere*.

A short distance to the NE former is the small OSSENMARKT. Nearby at 39 Rodestraat is the doorway to the 15–16C **Begijnhof**.

From Ossenmarkt we take Pieter van Hobokenstraat to Prinsstraat. No. 13 is the dignified **Prinsenhof** or **Huis van Liere**, a large 16C building with a 17C façade. Charles V lived here in 1520. It was occupied by English merchants from 1558 until the closing of the Scheldt in 1648. The Prinsenhof belonged to the Jesuits until 1773. Purchased by the order in 1929, it now houses faculties of the St Ignatius University.

From here we head N along Venusstraat, passing en route the *Archives* at No. 11. They are housed in a rebuilt 17C building, which was formerly the municipal pawnshop.

At the E end of the PAARDENMARKT, once site of the horse market, there were two 16C charitable institutions opposite the 19C **Sint Antoniuskerk**. No. 92 was an asylum and No. 94 an orphanage.

The parallel street N of Paardenmarkt is Falconrui. At the E end, in Hessenplein, is the **Hessenhuis**. Built in 1562 by Cornelis Floris, this was once the house of the German merchants. 47 Falconrui, with a good doorway, was the 17C Lantschot Hospice; No. 33 was the 16C van der Biest Hospice. At the W end of the street is the *International Seamen's House*.

From here we follow Mutsaertstraat in a SE direction to Raapstraat. No. 27, the 16C **Huis de Raap**, has one of the oldest façades in Antwerp. At the S end of Mutsaertstraat the **Academie voor Schone Kunsten**, the Academy of Fine Arts, occupies part of a 15C, former Franciscan house. To the W at 22 Minderbroedersstraat is the **Museum voor het Vlaamse Cultuurleven**, Flemish Culture, which has a large collection of documents, books and pictures.

B.   South-West of the Centre

The principal place of interest is the Museum voor Schone Kunsten, the Fine Arts Gallery, which is c 1.5km S of the Grote Markt. For a description of the gallery, see Section G.

Leave the Groenplaats by Nationalestraat and take a left fork into Kammenstraat and to the 17C baroque-style **Sint Augustinuskerk**. Some of this church's more important paintings may be seen in the Museum voor Schone Kunsten.

In Sint Andriesstraat, off the W side of Nationalestraat, is the **Sint Andrieskerk**. Built between 1514 and 1529 and enlarged during the 18C, the church has pictures by Gerard Seghers, Erasmus Quellin and Otto Venius. It is open to groups only. Prior arrangement necessary.

To the W of the church at 11–17 Kloosterstraat is the *Huis Mercator-Ortelius*, erected in 1619 but rebuilt later. Rubens lived in this street c 1610–17. He lodged with the Brant family, one of whom, Isabella, became his first wife. Ortelius, the geographer, who died in 1592, lived at No. 43.

Farther S, a turning to the E from Nationalestraat takes us to Sint Rochusstraat where the 17C, former Capuchin Chapel is located.

To the SE of the junction of Nationalestraat and Volkstraat, in the MARNIX-

PLAATS, is the towering, elaborate **Scheldt Monument** by J.J. Winders, 1883. This celebrates the redemption by Belgium in 1862 of Holland's right to levy dues on Scheldt shipping.

Continue along Volkstraat to LEOPOLD DE WAELPLAATS, which is named after the burgomaster of 1876, who negotiated the purchase of the Plantin-Moretus Museum. Here is the ****Museum voor Schone Kunsten**, which is described in Section G.

Opposite the museum, Verschansingstraat leads SW to GILLISPLAATS and the **Waterpoort**. This 1883 reconstruction of a gateway set up in 1624 in honour of Philip IV has a representation of the Scheldt and the arms of Spain by H. van den Eynde. Originally positioned farther N, at the foot of Vlasmarkt, the gate was moved to its present site when the Sint Anna tunnel was built.

At the rear of the Museum voor Schone Kunsten is Amerikalei, a section of the ring boulevards. To the NE, where the boulevard becomes Britselei, the *Gerechtshof*, Law Courts, was built by L. and F. Baekelmans between 1871 and 1877. Farther N, where Britselei becomes Frankrijklei, the *National Bank* of 1879 is by H. Beyaert.

C.   South-East of the Centre

This circuit starts at the Centraal Station. The principal places of interest are the Zoo to the W of the station, the Provincial Diamond Centre and the Ridder Smidt van Gelder Museum, which is c 1km to the S.

There are good public transport services to Middelheim Park with its open-air Museum of Modern Sculpture. This is c 4km S of the Centraal Station.

The **Centraal Station** of 1905, by L. Delacenserie, is c 400m E of the ring boulevard, the Frankrijklei, its high neo-Renaissance façade forming one side of KONINGIN ASTRIDPLEIN. The station is linked with the city centre by the De Keyserlei, which crosses the busy Frankrijklei to reach the E end of the Meir. The area to the N and W of the station is filled with hotels, cafés, restaurants and bars.

The **Zoo** (Dierentuin), one of the best in Europe, has a dolphinarium, a planetarium, a museum of natural history, an aquarium, a 'nocturama' for animals which prefer darkness and a 'baby zoo' with small domesticated animals and a children's playground.

It is open daily from 08.30, but has seasonal closing times. These are generally 18.30 in summer and 17.00 in winter.

The Zoo's breeding park at Planckendael near Mechelen is described in Route 15B.

There are a number of ways of getting to the Stadspark from the Centraal Station. We are going via Lange Herentalsestraat so that we may visit the Provincial Diamond Museum en route.

In the **Provinciaal Diamantmuseum** at 31–33 Lange Herentalsestraat the exhibits cover all aspects of the diamond industry including the mining of the stones and their cutting and polishing. The geological structure of the mines, the history of the industry in Antwerp, the tools and the methods employed to produce gem stones and industrial diamonds are also covered. Explanations are provided in English. The museum is open daily from 10.00 to 17.00. Demonstrations on request on Saturday between 14.00 and 1700. It is closed on 1 and 2 January and 25 and 26 December.

The triangular **Stadspark**, c 400m SW of the station, was laid out on the

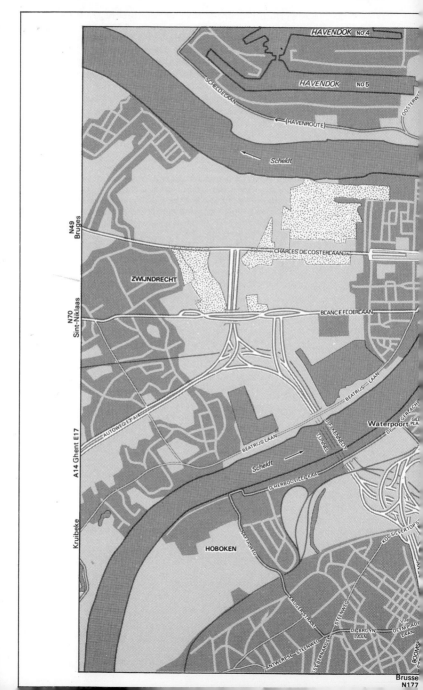

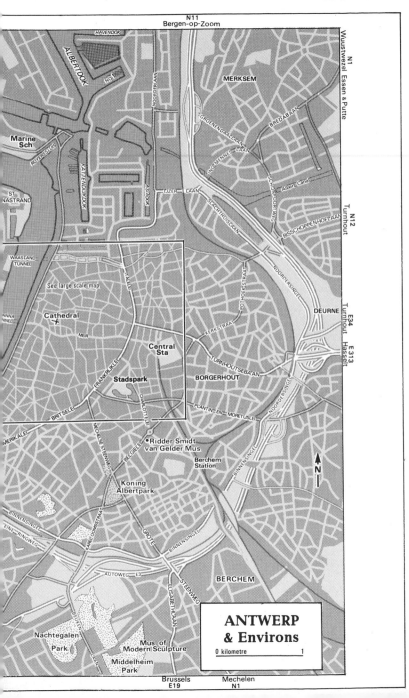

ANTWERP & Environs

0 kilometre   1

site of a bastion of the old fortifications. The moat has been converted into
an ornamental lake. Sculpture in the park includes a war memorial by
E. Deckers, 1935, Mother and Child by George Minne, 1938, in memory of
Queen Astrid, and a fountain-figure by Slojadinovic , 1954.

Leave the park at its SE corner. Loosplaats, named after a burgomaster
of 1848–62, leads to Charlottalei. A further 350m brings us to the *Ridder
Smidt van Gelder Museum at 91 Belgielei. The museum houses the
exquisite collection made by the Chevalier Pieter Smidt van Gelder, 1878–
1956. Together with his 18C mansion, he presented this to the city in 1949.
It includes furniture, tapestry, porcelain, jewellery, objets d'art and many
fine paintings. Among the artists represented are Joachim Patenir,
Giovanni Paolo Panini, van Ruysdael, Jan van Goyen, Pieter Claes, van de
Velde, van Vliet, Abel Grimmer, Lucas van Uden, Jan van Oosten, Pieter
Wouwerman and Jan ten Compe. One of the charms of the museum is that
the collection is presented informally, almost casually, as the personal
treasure of a wealthy connoisseur. Behind the house there is an attractive
garden.

The museum is open daily, except Monday, from 10.00 to 17.00. It is closed
on 1 and 2 January, 1 May, 1 November and 25 December. It is open on
Easter Monday, Whit Monday, and the Monday following the second
Sunday in August.

On leaving the museum we follow Belgielei in a SW direction to the
Koning Albertpark. Once the site of the gallows and known as the
Galgenveld, the park was laid out by the Marquis d'Herbouville, prefect
of Antwerp under Napoleon.

Near the SW corner, at 22 Koningin Elisabethlei, is the high-rise block
housing the Antwerp provincial administration. The Provincial Tourist
Office is at 11 Karel Oomsstraat, a short way to the S across the intersection
of the main roads.

SE of the park, in the suburb of BERCHEM, is the railway station for
international destinations. To the SW is Jan van Rijswijklaan, the road to
Boom and Brussels. After some 2km a Cromwell tank commemorates the
liberation of Antwerp.

S of the Koning Albertpark, Karel Oomsstraat crosses the railway and
motorway and becomes Beukenlaan. This traverses Nachtegalenpark,
Nightingale Park, which was laid out in the 18C by the Frenchman Barnabé
Guimard. A pleasance of some 120 hectares, it embraces three estates:
Vogelenzang, Birds' Song, with an aviary, animal enclosure and an edu-
cational garden, Den Brandt, with its 18C mansion, and Middelheim.

Since 1950 a part of Middelheim has been arranged as a Museum of
Modern Sculpture. The exhibits appear to have been placed at random on
the green, tree-shaded lawns. Among the artists represented are Rodin, Rik
Wouters, Ossip Zadkine, Meunier and Henry Moore.

The exhibition may be visited daily from 10.00. The closing times, which
vary according to the time of the year, are: November to mid February 17.00,
mid February to mid March and October 18.00, mid March to mid April and
September 19.00, mid April to the end of May and in August 20.00, June
and July 21.00.

D. The Docks and Beyond

A visit to the vast, and still expanding, dock area is not only interesting, but is essential to any proper understanding of Antwerp's commercial status. There are boat excursions by the 'Flandria' and bus tours, but these normally go only as far as van Cauwelaertsluis and Leopolddok. The car circuit HAVENROUTE, outlined below, is marked by hexagonal signs. It starts at the Steen and covers a distance of some 60km. There are two shorter tours: one using the Frans Tijmanstunnel is c 35km, the other of c 12km cuts across the base of Nos 5 and 4 Havendoks and Leopolddok.

From the Steen follow the quays N as far as the *Pilot House* of 1894. Serving both the Belgian and the Dutch pilotage services, this is roughly opposite the Brouwershuis. From here the Havenroute continues N passing *Bonapartedok* to the right. Bonapartedok and *Willemdok*, which is immediately to the E, were constructed on Napoleon's orders between 1804 and 1813. They are Antwerp's oldest docks.

Kattendijkdok, N of Willemdok, which contains municipal drydocks, dates from 1860–81. It is the largest of the 19C docks. The route now crosses two locks, *Kattendijksluis* and *Royerssluis*. The latter, constructed in 1907, is the first large sea lock.

Bearing left we pass the **Hogere Zeevaartschool**, the High Merchant Marine School, and continue along the stretch known as Noord Kasteel. This was the site of one of the city's former northern fortresses. Here we may follow Scheldelaan past petro-chemical installations or take an inland road along the S side of *Havendok No. 5*.

Just before the petro-chemical installations, a diversion N by Oosterweelsteenweg will take us past the ends of Havendoks Nos 5 and 4 and the Leopolddok to the last section of the complete Havenroute circuit.

Pylons carry electricity cables across the river. On the far bank is a huge industrial complex made up of firms like Polysar, Union Carbide and BP Chemicals.

Following a bend in the river, the Havenroute now bears NE, passing on the right the small *Industriedok*, used for ship repairs, and on the left the Esso installations.

The **Petroleumbrug** separates Marshalldok on the left, from a large stretch of water on the right. Off this open several docks. These include *Hansadok*, which can take the biggest ships, and *Kanaaldok*, which extends some 9km to the NW.

Marshalldok, built with Marshall Aid funds in 1951, is surrounded by petro-chemical installations. On its NW side is SIBP, Société Industrielle Belge des Pétroles, Belgium's largest refinery.

Beyond Petroleumbrug, on the right, there are large jetties for supertankers. Soon afterwards the Havenroute crosses the parallel and adjacent **van Cauwelaertsluis**, 1928, and **Boudewijnsluis**, 1955. The latter, until the opening of the Zandvlietsluis (see below), was Antwerp's largest lock. From here there is a good view E across the main complex of docks with, from N to S, Churchilldok, Havendok No. 6 and Hansadok. Facing the administrative buildings stands the figure of the Universal Worker by F. Libonati, 1962.

Beyond the locks the road curves NW to skirt the huge Bayer Chemicals plant and reach a road junction by a windmill. Dating from 1745, the windmill once stood farther E on land now submerged by Kanaaldok. To the right the **Frans Tijsmanstunnel** and the **Lillobrug** cross Kanaaldok, offering a short cut to the last part of the Havenroute.

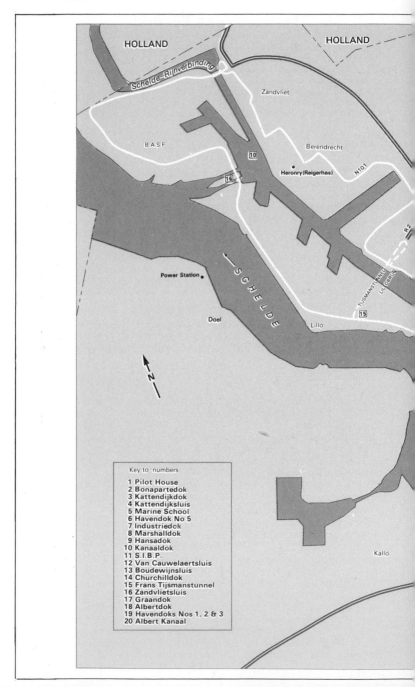

Key to numbers

1 Pilot House
2 Bonapartedok
3 Kattendijkdok
4 Kattendijksluis
5 Marine School
6 Havendok No 5
7 Industriedck
8 Marshalldok
9 Hansadok
10 Kanaaldok
11 S.I.B.P.
12 Van Cauwelaertsluis
13 Boudewijnsluis
14 Churchilldok
15 Frans Tijsmanstunnel
16 Zandvlietsluis
17 Graandok
18 Albertdok
19 Havendoks Nos 1, 2 & 3
20 Albert Kanaal

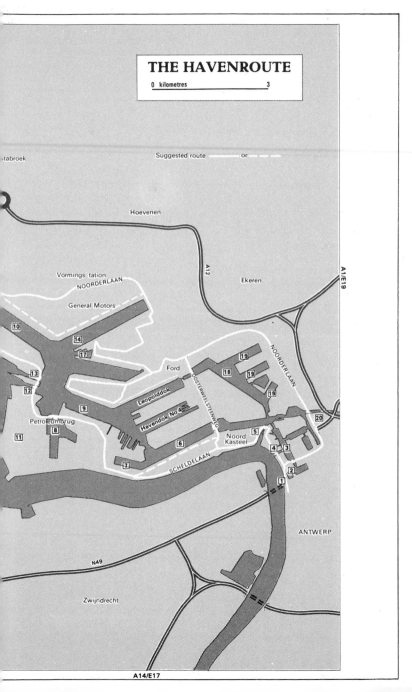

THE HAVENROUTE

0 kilometres _____ 3

Suggested route _____ or __ __ __

-tabroek

Hoevenen

A12

Ekeren

A1/E19

Vormings tation
NOORDERLAAN

General Motors

10

14

17

NOORDERLAAN

Ford

13

12

Leopolddok

OOSTERWEELSTEENWEG

18

19

19

19

9

Havendok No 4

6

20

Petroleumbrug

8

Noord
Kasteel

5

11

4 3

7

SCHELDELAAN

2

1

ANTWERP

N49

Zwijndrecht

A14/E17

Lillo, to the left beside the Scheldt, is all that is left of a much larger village, which stretched across to the area now occupied by the Kanaaldok. A picturesque spot, it has a *Polder Museum* devoted to the life and folklore of the now fast-disappearing Antwerp polders. This is open from April to September on Sunday and public holidays from 14.00 to 18.00.

The Havenroute continues N past more petro-chemical installations to **Zandvlietsluis** with a figure by Ossip Zadkine. Opened in 1967, this lock, 500m long and 57m wide, allows access to the port by ships of up to 100,000 dwt. We may cross the lock by the great drawbridge or by going over the gates. The road now passes BASF, Badische Anilin und Sodafabrik, and continues to within a few metres of the Dutch border. For a short distance it runs beside the Scheldt–Rhine canal, 1975, which shortens the distance between Antwerp and the Rhine by some 40km.

Crossing the entrance to the Kanaaldok, we bear S through **Zandvliet** and **Berendrecht**. Although now incorporated into the administrative district of Antwerp both try to remain quiet polder villages. They provide a pleasant contrast to the surrounding industrial development which threatens to engulf them. Between Berendrecht, whose name derives from the Latin 'Ursipraedium', the land of the bear, and Kanaldok there is a heronry at Reigersbos. Every year a large colony of blue herons nests here in the trees, blithely ignoring the noise and bustle of the port. The heronry may visited from mid February to the end of June.

Continue in a S direction, crossing a development area to an intersection at the E end of the Tijsmanstunnel, which links up with the motorway back to the city. The Havenroute turns right from the tunnel approach and continues under the road to the bridge. We pass a German Second World War concrete landing-ship, Quay 526, which has been turned into a church and a bar.

Shortly after we have a choice. We may take Noorderlaan, which runs between the Antwerp North marshalling yards, Vormingstation and the General Motors complex, or follow a road to the W and S of General Motors. Until 1962 the land occupied by General Motors was the polder village of Oorderen.

We now make a diversion to the areas separating Churchilldok, Havendok No. 6 and Hansadok. *Churchilldok*, to the S of General Motors, was opened in 1967 for container traffic. The church tower here is all that remains of the village of Wilmarsdonk which was evacuated in 1962. The small *Graandok*, between the entrances of Churchilldok and *Havendok No. 6* (1964), is used by barges and coasters. They carry the grain offloaded from seagoing vessels, which have berthed at the special pier equipped with grain elevators at the rear of Graandok.

The Havenroute skirts the SW side of Havendok No. 6, then rounds the tip of the promontory. Note the view across to van Cauwelaertsluis and Boudewijnsluis. It continues along the NE side of Hansadok, where the great loading bridges are used in the handling of ores.

We rejoin Noorderlaan, near the **Nieuw Entrepotcomplex**, the bonded warehouses and Ford Tractors and continue in an E direction with *Albert-dok* to the right. From W to E the principal activities here are timber, fruit and nitrates. Between Havendoks *Nos 3* and *2* is the network of pipes for potassium. The road now curves S, crosses the *Albert Kanaal* and reaches the city at Noorderplaats.

E.   Plantin-Moretus Museum

The ****Plantin-Moretus Museum**, 25 Vrijdagmarkt, occupies the house and workshops of the famous printer Christopher Plantin and his successors. With much of the old equipment still in situ, it provides a unique picture of the domestic and business environment of a rich master-printer of the 16C. The museum has many art treasures, including several works by Rubens. All the exhibits are labelled and explained in English and there is an excellent descriptive catalogue in English.

The museum is open daily from 10.00 to 17.00. It is closed on 1 and 2 January, 1 May, 1 November and 25 December.

The Family. *Christopher Plantin*, 1514–89, was born in France at St Avertin near Tours. While apprenticed to the printer Robert Macé in Caen, Normandy, he married Jeanne Rivière. In 1549 he left France and came to Antwerp. He became a citizen and a member of the Guild of St Luke in 1550. At first he worked as a bookbinder and enjoyed considerable success at this trade. While crossing the Meir one evening in 1555 he was assaulted by some drunkards, who mistook him for a man who had insulted them. He received a serious sword wound in his shoulder and was obliged to give up manual work. Taking up printing he soon published his first work 'La Institutione di una fanciulla nata nobilmente', a guide for the education of young ladies of good family.

Plantin made his name four years later with his sumptuous book on the funeral ceremonies of Charles V. In 1572 he produced, in eight folios, the famous 'Biblia Polyglotta', an edition of the bible in Latin, Greek, Hebrew, Chaldean and Syriac, with detailed appendices on the grammars and vocabularies of the languages, and studies on the customs and way of life of peoples in the Near East in biblical times.

In 1570 he received the title of Prototypus Regis from Philip II. His good relations with the Spanish monarchy earned him the monopoly of printing missals, breviaries, antiphonaries and other liturgical books for Spain and the Spanish empire. During the Calvinist years he continued to practise his faith, but managed to maintain good relations with the Protestants. He received a visit from William of Orange and became official printer to the States-General and the city of Antwerp.

From 1583–85 financial difficulties and other problems forced Plantin to live in Leyden and Cologne. However, he was not happy in those cities and returned to Antwerp, after the city had been taken by the Duke of Parma. He continued his printing business there until his death on 1 July 1589.

After Plantin's death the business passed to his son-in-law Jan Moerentorf or *Moretus*. He proved as professional as Plantin and his publications were much in demand. Jan Moretus died in 1610 and was succeeded by his son *Balthasar*, who ran the business until his death in 1641. In many ways the most brilliant member of the family, Balthasar was in touch with all the principal scholars and artists of his day. He was an intimate friend of Rubens, who designed illustrations and title pages for many of his books.

The firm continued to produce books until the middle of the 19C. However, it was kept going largely for sentimental reasons. The family's wealth was safely placed in land and investments. In 1876, when Edward Joannes Hyacinth Moretus-Plantin ceased to be master of the firm, the *Officina Plantiniana* was handed over to the city and turned into a museum.

The Building. In 1576 Christopher Plantin moved to this house and gave it the name, the Golden Compasses, which had also been borne by his previous residence. The compasses, and the star of Moretus, may be seen in various places in the building. At that time the house faced Hoogstraat and was backed by a large garden. The only access to Vrijdagmarkt was by a narrow passage. Plantin made many changes. He constructed houses along Heilig Geeststraat and, in 1579, a printing workshop in the S part of the garden, where it still stands. He also obtained permission to cover a part of the canal which ran along the S side of his property. There he built the small Renaissance-style house which, after three centuries as a store, is now occupied by the caretaker of the museum.

Balthasar made many improvements. In particular, he is responsible for the delightful appearance of the inner court. In the 18C several small houses, which stood immediately E of the Plantin-Moretus house, were acquired by the family and demolished. The existing façade took their place and the Plantin-Moretus house, no longer relying on the narrow passage, finally faced Vrijdagmarkt. The bas-relief above the door, by *Artus Quellin the Elder*, was originally on the Hoogstraat façade. In 1945 considerable damage was caused to the building by a German V weapon which exploded in Vrijdagmarkt.

The Museum. Over the centuries the family collected art treasures of many kinds, including several works by Rubens, a result of the friendship between the artist and Balthasar. When printing ceased in 1867, the city of Antwerp decided to acquire the property and its contents. With some government help and thanks to the generous attitude of Edward Moretus-Plantin, this aim was achieved in 1876. The museum opened its doors to the public the following year.

Successive curators have added to the collections. Although they suffered some damage from Allied air attacks and a German V raid during the the Second World War, they are extraordinarily rich. Three libraries contain more than 20,000 volumes. As well as the publications of the Plantin-Moretus family, there are many works by other Antwerp firms and foreign printers. There are about 150 incunabala, including the only copy in Belgium of the 36–line Gutenberg Bible.

In addition to an extensive archive relating to the printing house, there is a fine collection of manuscripts, drawings and paintings. There are c 15,000 woodblocks, 3000 copperplates and a variety of printing tools. A small, but excellent, collection of china and pottery made by various members of the family is also on display.

ENTRANCE. Near the entrance stand busts of Edward Moretus-Plantin and Burgomaster de Wael, who together negotiated the sale of 1876. Off the vestibule an 18C room has been arranged as a memorial to the poet Emile Verhaeren.

ROOM 1. Rare 16C Flemish tapestries which relate the story of Queen of the Massagetes, who defeated and slew Cyrus the Great. Note the compasses of the Plantins woven into the tapestries. Over the chimneypiece is an old copy of Rubens' Lion Hunt. The original is in the Munich Alte Pinakothek.

ROOM 2. Portraits of the Plantin family and their friends. Ten are by *Rubens* and two, Balthasar and Gevartius, by *T.W. Bosschaert*. Two 17C cabinets. Silver-gilt clock, in the shape of a bell-tower, traditionally a gift to the family by the Archdukes Albert and Isabella.

ROOM 3. Paintings by *Seghers, L. van Noort, Erasmus Quellin* and *van Helmont*.

The cases contain rare manuscripts from the 9C to the 16C. These include the 15C *Chronicle of Froissart, an early 15C Bible of King Wenceslas of Bohemia, Sedulius' Carmen Paschale, 9C, with Prosperus' Epigrammata, Boethius' De Consolatione, 9C, a 16C German illustrated manual on firearms, and 15C and 16C Books of Hours in Flemish and in Latin.

Under the windows there is a selection of the drawings, title-pages and vignettes by masters who worked for the Plantin firm—Martin de Vos, Adam van Noort, van der Horst, Jan de Cock, Richard van Orley, Pieter de Joode and others.

One side of the COURTYARD is covered by a vine planted in 1640. From here you can see the S and W façades, the oldest parts of the Plantin house. A 17C pump of bluestone occupies the centre of the gallery. The marble busts of Plantin, Jan Moretus the Younger and Justus Lipsius are copies, the originals are in the museum. The bust of Jan Moretus the Elder is an original of 1621 by *Hans van Mildert*.

THE SHOP. Room 4 faced Heilig Geeststraat, from where it was entered by a small flight of steps. It contains the index of forbidden books, published by Plantin in 1569, and also the price-list of school books and prayer books, as authorised by the city authorities. On the counter stands the money-balance, essential in an age when coin clipping and debasing of the coinage were frequent occurrences.

OFFICE. Room 5. Above the door, a portrait of Jan Moretus. Cashier's desk and seat.

DRAWING ROOM, Room 6. 17C tapestries from Oudenaarde. Typical 17C patrician furniture. Portraits of Christopher Plantin and his wife.

ROOM 7. Here are illustrated the processes involved in the making of a book—from manuscript to printed copy—and the development of books from c 1450 to the 20C.

ROOM 8 is the kitchen. At one time this room was used for weighing paper.

The PROOF READERS' ROOM, Room 9 dates from 1637. The doorway was carved by *Paul Dirickx*. The picture, The Proof Reader, is probably by *Pieter van der Borcht*. It is generally thought to represent Cornelis Kiel, Kilianus, the founder of Dutch philology.

OFFICE, Room 10. The oldest part of the house begins here, the part known to Plantin. With its desk, safe, money-balance and barred windows, this is clearly a place where business was conducted. The walls are hung with gilded Mechelen leather. The painting of Christ and the woman of Samaria is by *Erasmus Quellin*.

The JUSTUS LIPSIUS ROOM, Room 11. Here Lipsius, the great Flemish humanist and intimate friend of the family, was accustomed to work. It is hung with rare, gilt, 16C Spanish leather. The picture of Lipsius and his pupils is a copy of a work by *Rubens*. The original is in the Palazzo Pitti in Florence. One of the pupils is Rubens' brother and Rubens himself may be seen in the background. The portrait of Seneca, who was much admired by Lipsius, is by *Rubens*.

ROOM 12 contains books, documents and memorabilia relating to Lipsius. The portraits are of scholars and humanists, contemporaries of Lipsius. The bust is by *Hans van Mildert*, 1621. There is a copy in the courtyard (see above).

There is a bust of Plantin, also by *van Mildert*, in the passage which leads to the TYPE ROOM, Room 13. Here there are shelves full of different kinds of type. Stocks of spare letters, in their original packing, are on the lower shelves. The 18C wooden statues over the fireplace represent Honour, Courage and Orthodoxy.

The PRINTING ROOM, Room 14, has been arranged as it was in 1576. Of the seven presses, five date from the 17C and 18C. They are ready for use. On one of them Plantin's sonnet 'Le bonheur de ce monde' is still printed. The presses against the back wall, under a 17C statue of Our Lady of Loreto, are older. They may date from Plantin's time. Note the type, cast in the time of Plantin and his successors, which awaits the compositors hand to set it in the galleys.

The next two rooms, on the first floor, are in the 18C front of the house. On the landing is a Louis XV-style clock and a painting by *Sporckmans* of the Carmelite Order confirmed by the Pope. Until 1769 this was in the Antwerp church of the Discalced Carmelites.

ROOM 15 contains a bas-relief in leather depicting Christ before Caiaphas, probably by *Justin Mathieu*, 1796–1864, and a case with specimens of Plantin's productions. There is also a portrait of Plantin, by an unknown 16C master. This was used by Rubens when painting the portrait in Room 2.

ROOM 16. Cases illustrating Plantin's life and work. The *Biblia Polyglotta, the famous multilingual Bible, was without doubt his greatest production. This eight folio book has been described as the most important work ever produced by a single printer in the Netherlands. Philip II, the king of Spain, was an enthusiastic supporter of the project. He provided financial aid and sent his chaplain, the humanist Arias Montanus, to be scientific director of the project. Printing was started in 1568 and the book was completed in 1572. It is in five languages, Latin, Greek, Hebrew, Syriac and Chaldean (Aramaic) and has Greek, Syriac and Chaldean grammars and glossaries. There are studies of Hebrew customs, and descriptions of ancient measures and clothing in the Near East in biblical times. A dozen copies of the Bible were printed on vellum for Philip II.

The pictures in Room 16 include a Landscape by *L. van Uden* , Balthasar Moretus on his deathbed by *T.W. Bosschaert* and portraits of later members of the family. There is also an 18C Boulle cabinet and a clock.

The rest of the museum is in the 17C part of the house.

In the SMALL LIBRARY, Room 17, and the MORETUS ROOM, Room 18, there are works printed by Plantin's successors, a number of forgeries and the first known representation of a potato plant. This dates from 1588. The bust, 1644, of Jan Moretus the Younger, once in the courtyard, is by *Artus Quellin*.

The RUBENS' ROOM, Room 19, has sketches and engravings by *Rubens*, who worked for Plantin as an illustrator. There are also a number of portraits, probably by the artist's studio. Note the receipts signed by Rubens. The chimneypiece and doorway are by *Paul Dirickx*, 1622 and 1640.

ROOM 20. Books by other Antwerp printers. Portraits of local and foreign scholars whose works were published in Antwerp.

The DRAWING ROOM, Room 21 is hung with rare French gilt leather. The chimneypiece of 1638 is by *Dirickx* and the 17C landscape above it by *Pieter Verdussen*. There is a harpsichord of 1734 by J.J. Coenen. This is a rather unusual instrument as it combines a clavecin and a virginal. The painting inside the cover shows St Cecilia playing an organ—an adaptation of Rubens' picture of the saint playing a harpsichord.

In ROOM 22 there are the licences granted to the Plantin press by Belgian and foreign sovereigns and various other records concerning the printing-house.

The GEOGRAPHY ROOM, Room 23 recalls the great contribution made by the Netherlands to this science from the 16C to the 18C. There are 16C atlases by *Gemma-Frisius, Mercator*, and *Ortelius*. Note also a great plan of Antwerp of 1565 by *Virgilius Boloniensis* and *Cornelis Grapheus*, a map of Flanders by *Mercator* and 17C terrestrial and celestial globes by *A.F. van Langeren*.

ROOM 24 is concerned with printing outside Antwerp. The display is arranged chronologically and by countries. Undoubtedly the most important exhibit is the 36–line *Gutenberg Bible. The large copper engraving of the Triumphal Entry of Charles V and Pope Clement VII in Bologna on 24 February 1530 is by *Niklaas Hogenberg* .

In ROOM 25 there is a portrait of Edward Moretus by *Joseph Delin* (1879).

ROOM 26, hung with Mechelen gilt leather, is a typical rich man's 17C bedroom.

ILLUSTRATIONS ROOM, Room 27. Here are exhibited the best of the c 15,000 woodcuts and 3000 copperplates in the collection. At first Plantin mainly used woodblocks, later changing to copperplate. He was a pioneer in this technique.

From the Alcove, ROOM 28, we return to Room 25 and take the stairs to the TYPE FOUNDRY, Rooms 29 and 30. The first is a workroom with a bench, anvil, vices, files and other tools. These are scattered around the room in a haphazard fashion, as though the workmen had put them down a moment before our entry.

Print types were cast in the foundry. Punches, matrices and moulds were required for this operation. Because of the risk of fire from the smelting furnaces the floor of the foundry was made of stone. Note the large collection of stamps and matrices which Plantin bought from the best specialist makers. They were mainly French.

We return downstairs to the LIBRARY (Rooms 31 and 32), which was established by Balthasar the Elder in 1640. It contains only some of the 30,000 books in the museum. The larger room was used as a private chapel. Here members of the family and the workmen heard Mass each day before beginning work. The painting of the Crucifixion, attributed to *Pieter Thys*, served as an altarpiece. The altar has disappeared.

The MAX HORN ROOM, Room 33, contains the rare bindings and valuable books bequeathed by the bibliophile Max Horn, 1882–1953. The treasure of the collection is in Case No. 1. This is a 13C volume with the oldest known panel-stamp. It was made for, or perhaps by, Wouter van Duffel an Antwerp priest. Here, too, is a huge coloured woodcut on vellum, another version of Charles V and Pope Clement VII at Bologna. This is by the Liège artist *Robert Péril*.

F. The Rubens House

The ****Rubens House**, 9–11 Wapper, a large patrician mansion which includes a studio, was built for the artist between 1610 and 1617 shortly after his first marriage. He paid 10,000 florins, an immense sum at that time, for the land on which it stands. In 1620 Woverius, the humanist and town clerk of Antwerp, expressing the pride of his fellow citizens, wrote that it, and the house of Balthasar Moretus, '…will evoke the astonishment and admiration of visitors.'

Today it is visited as a house of the period, for its association with Rubens and for its many paintings by him and other artists. The house is open daily from 10.00 to 17.00. It is closed on 1 and 2 January, 1 May, 1 November and 25 December.

In this house happiness and sadness entered the artist's life. His son was born here in 1618. His daughter died here in 1624. Her death was followed two years later by that of his first wife, Isabella Brant, who perished probably from the plague. In 1630 he brought his second wife, Hélène Fourment, here.

The house soon became a meeting-place for the noble and cultivated society of Flanders. Among the many distinguished visitors were Isabella, the daughter of Philip II, who bore the personal title of Archduke, Marie de Medicis and George Villiers, Duke of Buckingham. Artists like van Dyck, Snyders, Luc Fayd'herbe came here and, from time to time, worked in the studio.

Rubens died in 1640. From 1649 to 1660 the house was occupied by William Cavendish, later Duke of Newcastle, who fled from England a short time before Charles I was beheaded. He established a riding school in the garden, which was attended by Charles II.

Under later owners the mansion fell into disrepair and its contents were dispersed. Efforts to secure it for the city started as early as 1762. They were successful in 1937.

Although little of the original structure remained beyond the framework, the building was skilfully restored by E. van Averbeke and furnished in the style of Rubens' time. It was opened as a museum in 1946.

The Flemish patrician house is on the left, the Italianate baroque studio on the right. At present visitors enter through the studio. On the façade of this building there are busts of a faun, a satyr, Pan and Silenus, Plato, Socrates, Seneca, Sophocles and Marcus Aurelius. The gods, Mars, Juno, Jupiter and Vesta are represented as herms and caryatids. The friezes show Iphigenia sacrificed by Agamemnon, the Coronation of Alexander the Great, the toilet of Venus, the Judgement of Paris and a drunken Hercules.

The ticket desk is in an ANTECHAMBER, which has fine gilt leather wall hangings.

In the adjoining GREAT STUDIO there are works by Rubens and other artists. These include Neptune and Amphitrite by *Jordaens*, Landscape with Figures by *Jan Wildens*, Portrait of Jean le Mire the Fourth Bishop of Antwerp by *Venius*, and Cimon and Pero, Adam and Eve, the Ethiopian Magus all by *Rubens*. Note the special, high, narrow door through which large canvases were taken out of the house.

From here, visitors cross the entrance court, separated from the garden by a baroque portico, which appears in various paintings by Rubens, van Dyck and others. It has survived virtually intact, but the statues on top are modern replacements by Edward Deckers, 1939, of earlier figures of Mercury and Minerva.

Above the keystones of the side arches there are two quotations in cartouches from Juvenal's Satires. These remind us of Rubens' humanism and stoicism and emphasise his interest in classical art and literature:

Permittes ipsis expendere numinibus, quid
Conveniat nobis, rebusque sit utile nostris,
Carior est illis homo quam sibi.

(Leave it to the gods to give what is fit and useful for us;
man is dearer to them, than to himself.)

Orandum est ut sit mens sana in corpore sano
Fortem posce animum et mortis terrore carentem
Nesciat irasci, cupiat nihil.

(One must pray for a healthy mind in a healthy body, for a courageous soul,
which is not afraid of death, which is free of wrath and desires nothing.)

The rooms are described below in the order in which they are normally visited. However, this, and the arrangement of the pictures and other exhibits, may change. The exhibits generally belong to the period of Rubens' life, but, with a few exceptions, were not part of his own collection.

In the PARLOUR visitors waited before being shown in to meet the master. Among the paintings are a Presentation in the Temple by *Jordaens* and an Adoration of the Magi by *van Noort* . The portrait of Jan Wildens is an old copy of the van Dyck original now in Vienna. The print by Harrewijn after a drawing of Jan de Croes of the house was used, with others, by the restorers between 1938 and 1946.

We pass into the tiled KITCHEN with its pot hangers, ointment jars and plate-racks. The folding table is believed to be early 17C Dutch.

Next is the SERVING ROOM. Dishes brought from the kitchen were placed here before being taken into the dining room. Note the linen press in the centre of the room.

According to his nephew, Rubens was abstemious at table. He ate little during the day, in case his work was affected. At five o' clock it was his custom to take a little excercise on horseback. Then he returned home to dine quietly with friends.

In the DINING ROOM there are several interesting paintings. The most important is a *self-portrait by *Rubens*, which dates, probably, from 1625–28. The flower-study is by the Jesuit painter, *Daniel Seghers*. Rubens was on friendly terms with the Jesuits of Antwerp. He designed ornaments and provided pictures for their church. The still-life is by *Frans Snyders*.

Over the entrance to the ART GALLERY there is a 17C stauette of the Madonna in stone. In this gallery Rubens displayed the best pictures in his large personal collection. At the time of his death, when it was dispersed, there were some 300 paintings in the collection.

Today the room is used once again as a picture gallery. The pictures include works by *Aertgen van Leyden*: Christmas Night. *Lucas van Uden*: Landscape with a Rainbow. *Rubens*: sketches in oils for the Adoration of the Shepherds, and the Martyrdom of St Adrianus. *Frans Francken the Younger*: Corner of a studio, 1618. Attributed to *Hendrik van Balen*: The Israelites in the Desert.

One of the most interesting pictures in the house is by *Willem van Haecht*: The Gallery of Cornelis van der Geest. This records a visit by the Archdukes Albert and Isabella to the collection, among the most distinguished of its time, of Cornelis van der Geest. A wealthy merchant and friend of Rubens, van der Geest is shown discussing a picture by Quinten Metsys with his visitors. Works by Rubens and Dürer are also included in the painting.

Among other items of interest are a small ivory group of Adam and Eve made in 1627 by *Jörg Petel* which may have belonged to Rubens, and a book, 'Palazzi di Genova', which was published by the artist in 1622. This contains plans and elevations of a number of Genoese palaces. It was intended for the use of architects.

Rubens was a numismatist, so it is appropriate that there should be a small collection of Greek, Roman, Byzantine and Celtic coins here.

We now enter the small, apsidal Sculpture Gallery, a reminder that Rubens owned a much-admired collection of ancient statues, which he acquired during his stay in Italy.

Among the sculptures on show are busts of a satyr and of Pan, which are attributed to *Luc Fayd'herbe*. The bust formerly believed to be of Seneca is now thought to be of either the Alexandrian grammarian and poet Philetas of Cos, born c 330 BC, or of Aristophanes, c 444 BC–c 380 BC, the author of many witty comedies. This may have been one of the pieces brought back from Italy by Rubens.

Upstairs in the LARGE BEDROOM, the room in which Rubens died, hangs a portrait of Burgemeester Nicolaas Rockox, the 17C Antwerp Maecenas and friend of Rubens. This is attributed to *Otto Venius*. There is also a Martyrdom of St Marcus and St Marcellinus by *Veronese* . The rock-crystal necklace in a gold setting is thought to have belonged to Hélène Fourment. The gold chain with a medallion of Christian IV of Denmark was a present to Rubens, possibly from Golnitzius, the king's secretary, who visited the painter c 1625. Note also the 17C ebony cabinet with ivory and tortoise-shell decoration.

In the SMALL BEDROOM the portrait of Hélène Fourment is attributed to *Jan van Boeckhorst*.

The LINEN ROOM contains an early 17C five-door Antwerp cupboard.

In the CORNER BEDROOM is Rubens' official chair as Dean of the Guild of

St Luke. His name, Pet. Paul Rubens 1633, in gilt lettering is on the back. The coat of arms below belongs to the chamber of rhetoric, 'De Violieren', which was closely associated with the Guild.

LIVING ROOM. In this room, where the family met in the evening, there are several paintings. These include *Adam van Noort* : Sermon of John the Baptist. *Pieter Snayers*: View of Antwerp and *Jacob Claesz*: Portraits, 1530, of Rubens' grandparents.

From the LANDING we have a good view of a 17C Brussels tapestry which tells the story of the Death of Achilles, who could only be wounded mortally in the heel. Note also a Descent from the Cross by *Jordaens*.

As the PUPILS' STUDIO is used for special exhibitions, it may not always be open. There is an excellent view of the garden and courtyard from the windows.

From the landing we descend by the finely carved staircase, a reconstruction of the 1617 original, past a gallery overlooking the Great Studio to the starting point of our tour.

Prints of 17C gardens and a picture by Rubens, the Walk in the Garden, now in the Alte Pinakothek in Munich, were used by the modern restorers of the GARDEN to ensure authenticity. The pavilion was designed by Rubens as a temple where the protectors of the land would be honoured. It contains a statue of Hercules, the guardian of the soil. This is attributed to *Luc Fayd'herbe*. The hero is flanked by Bacchus, who holds a bunch of grapes, and by a modern statue of Venus by *Willy Kreitz*. The goddess of love has taken the place once occupied by Ceres, the goddess of fertility. Above, in a niche, is Honour with a cornucopia.

An oval monument commemorates Rubens' brother and son, both named Philip. The tombstone of the former, brought here from the abbey of Sint Michiel which was destroyed in 1830, rests against the wall.

G. Museum voor Schone Kunsten

The ****Museum voor Schone Kunsten**, the **Fine Arts Gallery**, is in the Leopold de Waelplaats. It was constructed between 1878 and 1890 to the designs of J.J. Winders and F. van Dyck. The chariots, which surmount the building, are the work of the Belgian sculptor Thomas Vinçotte, 1850–1925.

The nucleus of the collection was formed by the Burgomaster Florent van Ertborn in the mid-19C. Many additions have been made since that time. Today more than 1000 works from the 14C to the 17C are exhibited on the top floor. The Flemish Primitives are represented by Jan van Eyck, Roger van der Weyden, Hans Memling, Joachim Patinir and Quinten Metsys. There are also paintings by foreign artists like Jean Fouquet, Simone Martini and Lucas Cranach. A large section is devoted to Rubens, van Dyck, Jordaens and other artists of the Antwerp school.

On the ground floor there are about 1500 paintings by 19C and 20C Belgian and foreign artists, including works by de Braekeleer, Ensor, Evenepoel, Permeke and Wouters.

The paintings are hung in large, well-lit galleries. From time to time there are temporary exhibitions of works from churches closed for restoration or of pictures sent to the museum for restoration.

It is possible to list only some of the most important paintings in such a large and rich collection. They may not always be in the rooms indicated below. Paintings are moved for various reasons to new locations, removed for cleaning and restoration, and occasionally lent to other galleries. Enquiries about particular works should be addressed to the museum's excellent information and education service.

The musem is open daily from 10.00 to 17.00, except Monday, 1 January, 1 May, Ascension Day, 1 November and 25 December.

We begin our visit in the ENTRANCE HALL. Here there are busts of two governors of the Spanish Netherlands by *Artus Quellin the Elder* and *Willem Kerrickx*. The murals by *Nicaise de Keyser* illustrate the history of the Flemish school. Small key pictures are hung beside the stairway.

Upper Floor: Old Masters

The rooms are lettered A to T. The Primitives are in S, Q, N and O. These rooms face the landing at the top of the stairs. The Rubens' rooms, J and I, are straight ahead. We start with the Primitives, continue with the paintings by Rubens, and then visit the remaining rooms in clockwise order.

PRIMITIVES, ROOMS S, Q, N, O.

Gerard David: the side panels of a triptych of 1480–85. These show the Holy Women and the Jewish Judges and Roman Soldiers. The central section, which depicts Christ being nailed to the Cross, is No. 3067 in the National Gallery in London.

Hans Memling: Portrait of c 1478, generally accepted to be of Giovanni de Candida, a courtier to Mary of Burgundy. Christ with Angels singing and playing Instruments.

Jean Fouquet: Madonna and Child surrounded by Angels. There is an interesting affinity between the unnaturally pale and bare-breasted Madonna and the equally unnatural, strangely coloured angels. This is part of a diptych painted for Etienne Chevalier.

Simone Martini: panels of uncertain date showing the Annunciation, the Crucifixion and the Descent from the Cross.

Master of St Veronica: The Man of Sorrows between Our Lady and St Catherine. The wheel and sword were the instruments of the saint's martyrdom.

Anonymous. Possibly form the studio of Roger van der Weyden: portrait of Jan Zonder Vrees, John the Fearless, the son of Philip the Bold. John was murdered in 1419, so this picture of c 1450 is perhaps a copy of an earlier portrait.

Jan van Eyck: St Barbara, 1437. According to a 10C legend the saint's father, a wealthy pagan of Nicomedia, imprisoned his beautiful daughter in a tower to protect her from importunate suitors. While in the tower she was converted to Christianity. When she refused to renounce her faith, her enraged father had her tortured and then beheaded. van Eyck shows the saint with a prayer-book and palm, symbols of her belief and suffering. On the tower is the triple-lancet window which Barbara had installed as a symbol of the Trinity and which first aroused the suspicions of her father; Madonna at the Fountain, of 1439.

Roger van der Weyden: Triptych of the Seven Sacraments; Portrait of Philippe de Croy, a nobleman at the time of Philip the Good and Charles the Bold. The panel is thought to be the right side of a diptych. The left side, the Madonna and Child, is in the Huntington Collection in New York.

Antonello da Messina: Crucifixion with the Virgin Mary and St John the Evangelist, 1475. The artist is known to have admired Flemish painting and this work is important, as it shows a happy marriage between Flemish detail and Italian scope; *Albert Bouts*: Adoration of the Shepherds; *Master of the St Magdalene Legend*: The Holy Family, a charming, entirely natural domestic scene.

PIETER PAUL RUBENS ROOMS I, J. These paintings are, for the most part, altarpieces commissioned for various Antwerp churches.

1. Triptych of the Incredulity of St Thomas, 1613–15. Commissioned by Rubens' patron Nicolaas Rockox, he and his wife are depicted on the side panels. 2. Triptych, Christ on the Straw, 1618. 3. The Prodigal Son, 1618. The animals arouse more interest than the humans in this picture. 4. The Last Communion of St Francis, 1619.

5. Christ Crucified between the two Thieves; also known as The Lance. Commissioned in 1619 by Nicolaas Rockox, this painting shows the artist's masterly portrayal of anatomy.

6. The Education of Mary, c 1625. A very unconventional portrayal of Mary as a young girl with her parents.

7. Portrait of Gaspard Gevartius, 1593–1666, municipal official, poet and historian. Gevartius is shown beside a bust of Marcus Aurelius about whom he had written a commentary.

8. St Theresa of Avila obtaining the delivery of Bernardino de Mendoza from Purgatory, c 1634. Bernardino was a wealthy nobleman who donated a property to the saint for a new convent. He died suddenly, unshriven. St Theresa then interceded on his behalf to Christ, who is shown in this picture instructing an angel to help Bernardino from the flames of purgatory.

9. Virgin with a Parrot, c 1614.

10. The Triumphal car of Kallo. In 1638 the Infante Ferdinand defeated the United Provinces at Kallo, just across the river from Antwerp. The authorities commissioned Rubens to produce a design for the consequent celebrations. The artist's feeling for symbolism and allegory is well illustrated in this sketch.

We continue our visit in a clockwise direction through the OTHER ROOMS in the museum.

ROOM T. *Jan Brueghel*: Visit to the Farm, probably a copy of a grisaille by his father, which has disappeared. Riverside Landscape. *Pieter Brueghel the Younger*: several works. *Pieter Brueghel the Third*: Slaughter of the Innocents. *Jacob Grimmer*: View of the Kiel, an interesting picture with its animated foreground and view of fortified Antwerp in the right distance, 1578. View of the Scheldt. *Abel Grimmer*: The Four Seasons.

ROOM R. *Quinten Metsys*: Triptych, Lamentation. On the left wing Herod, Salome and John the Baptist and on the right the Death of John the Evangelist. Dated to 1511 this triptych was commissioned for an altar in the cathedral. St Mary Magdalene. Diptych, Saviour of the World and Mary at Prayer, c 1505. *Portrait of Pieter Gilles. *Joachim Patinir*: Flight into Egypt. The strange pastoral landscape with stylised rocks, farm, sea or lake tends to overshadow the picture's protagonists. This is the only signed painting by Patinir. *Master of the Antwerp Adoration*: The Adoration of the Magi, early 16C. *Anonymous*: Sculpture of Christ Crucified, c 1500. *Lucas van Valkenborgh*: View of Huy, c 1570.

ROOM L. *Lucas Cranach the Elder*: Caritas. Adam and Eve. Eve. *Lucas Cranach the Younger*: Portrait of a Man. *Jean Clouet*: portrait of the Dauphin, son of François I. Clouet became court painter to François in 1518. *Jan Metsys*: Judith, a favourite subject with this artist. *Pieter Pourbus*: several portraits, including one of Olivier van Nieulant, alderman and recorder of Bruges. *Anonymous*, mid 16C: Portrait of a Young Man. *Bernard van Orley*: Head of a Woman. *Corneille de Lyon*: Portraits of a Young Nobleman and of a Young Man.

ROOM K. *Titian*: Jacopo Pesaro introduced to St Peter by Pope Alexander VI. Pesaro was commander of the papal fleet which defeated the Turks in 1502 and the picture c 1502–10 is clearly associated with this event. *Frans Francken the Younger*: The Gallery of Sebastian Leerse. A wealthy Antwerp merchant, Leerse is shown with his second wife and his son. Among the pictures in the gallery are a Susanna and the Elders by (?) Jan Metsys, a Mountain Landscape by Joos de Momper, and a Marine Scene by Bonaventure Peeters. Also in this room are several works by *Antoon van Dyck* and *Jordaens*.

ROOM M. *Cornelis de Vos*: several portraits of families and individuals. *Jan Brueghel*: Flowers in a Vase. Travellers attacked by robbers. *Sebastian Vranckx*: Plundering of a Hamlet and another picture of an Attack on Travellers.

ROOM G is devoted to paintings of animals, still life and landscapes. *Paul de Vos*: Partridge shooting. *Jan Fyt* and *Frans Snyders*: several works. *Jan Siberechts*: an attractive series of four pictures showing peasants and carts crossing water.

ROOM GA. *Abraham Janssens*: Peace. *Theodoor Rombouts*: Lute Player. The Game of Cards. *David Teniers the Younger*: View of Valenciennes.

ROOM F is mainly devoted to the work of *Jacob Jordaens* . Note particularly an Adoration of the Shepherds of c 1650 and Nuns of the Antwerp Gasthuis, a striking portrayal of charity and poverty.

ROOM H. There are several works by *Jordaens*, including Day and Night, with a remarkable candlelight effect, and As the Old sing the Young play Pipes, of 1638, a genre piece of a family concert. The old man in the picture is Jordaens' teacher and father-in-law Adam van Noort. *Van Dyck* is represented by a number of portraits, a Descent from the Cross and an Entombment.

ROOM E. *Frans Hals*: Fisher boy. Portrait, 1650–52, of Stephanus Geraerdts, an alderman of Haarlem. *Rembrandt*: Portrait of Eleazor Swalmus, *Meindert Hobbema, Jan van Goyen, Salomon van Ruysdael* and *Jacob van Ruisdael*: various Landscapes. *Jan Steen*: Howelijksfeest. *Adriaen van Ostade*: The Smokers.

ROOM D. *Lucas van Uden*: Landscape with a Rainbow. *Otto Venius*: St Luke and St Paul before the governor of Caesarea. *Jacob de Backer*: Last Judgement.

ROOM B. *Joachim Beuckelaer*: The Fish Market. The Vegetable Market, 1567. *Marinus van Reymerswael*: several works.

ROOM C. *Adriaen Brouwer*: Card Players. Kermesse; *David Teniers the Younger*: several works including an unusual Temptation of St Anthony. *Joos van Craesbeeck*: several works, notably At 't Wapen van Antwerp; *Roelant Savery*: Paradise of the Birds. *Gonzales Coques*: Five delightful pictures of Five Senses.

ROOM A. *Frans Pourbus the Elder*: Portrait of a Woman. *Frans Pourbus the Younger*: Portrait of Nicolaas van Hellincx: *Lambert van Noort*: Adoration of the Shepherds.

ROOM P. *Frans Floris*: several works including the Fall of the Rebel Angels, of 1554. This is the central section of a triptych commissioned for an altar in the cathedral. The panel, badly damaged by the Calvinist iconoclasts in 1566, lost its wings at that time. *Paul Bril*: Landscape. *Tobias Verhaecht*: Tower of Babel.

The intrigue by James Ensor, 1860–1949, Museum voor Schone Kunsten, Antwerp

Ground Floor: Modern Art

The catalogue of the museum's 19C and 20C paintings runs to more than 500 pages, an indication of the size of the collection. Only a relatively small number of the paintings can be shown at one time.

The rooms are numbered 1 to 29. Temporary exhibitions are usually mounted in Rooms 16–18, but not infrequently spread out into other parts of the ground floor. For this reason and because pictures are rotated at intervals, the arrangement of the rooms can vary considerably. Only a few representative artists are mentioned below.

ROOMS 29 to 24, on the S side of the building, are devoted to 19C and early 20C Romanticism, Realism and Impressionism. These range from *Alfred Stevens'* portrayals of apparently innocent young women, through the carnival world of *James Ensor* to the scenes of hardship and poverty recorded so movingly by *Charles de Groux* . Among the many artists whose works hang in these rooms are *George Hendrik Breitner*, *Henri de Braekeleer*, *Hendrik Leys*, note the striking self-portrait and the portrait of his wife, *Leon Frederic*, Two Peasant Children, *Louis Artan*, several marine scenes and *Emile Claus*, Flax Field in Flanders.

The central section is arranged as two halls, N and S, each with three divisions.

In the NORTH HALL, Rooms 13, 14, 15, there are paintings by *Gustave de Smet*, *Edgard Tytgat*, *Jean Brusselmans*, *Albert Servaes*, *Gustave van Woestyne*, *F. van den Burghe* and *Constant Permeke*.

In the SOUTH HALL, Rooms 19, 20, 21, works by *Rik Wouters*, pictures and sculpture, *Jacob Smits* and *James Ensor*.

ROOMS 4 to 10, on the N side of the building, bring an abrupt change of mood. They are devoted to Abstract Art and Surrealism. This challenging group is epitomised by the works of *Karel Appel* in Room 9, Man Flying and Animal and Child against a Blue Background, in Room 10, by *Paul Delvaux's* strange, ghostly ladies in De Roze Strikken, and by *René*

Magritte's The Storm Cape, The Wreck, and that particularly macabre, theatrical assemblage, Madame Recamier.

17

North between Antwerp and Holland

In addition to the A1/E19 motorway there are three main roads N from Antwerp to Holland. All cross the woods and heath which mark the western edge of the KEMPEN (p 119). See also 'Blue Guide Holland'.

ANTWERP TO WUUSTWEZEL, for **Breda**; 29km to the border.

At *10km* is **Brasschaat** (population 31,500), known for its sports and recreational park. *14km* **Wuustwezel** (population 9000) is a the centre of a district popular with walkers. At *Brecht*, 5km SE of the motorway, there is a Kempen museum. 2km farther E at *Sint Lenaarts*, the three statues above the porch of the 15–16C church are by Cornelis Floris, 1514–75. The frontier is *5km* N of Wuustwezel.

ANTWERP TO ESSEN, for **Roosendaal**; 30km to the border.

Follow the Wuustwezel road as far as 13km Maria ter Heide. There take a NW fork to *7km* **Kalmthout**, population 15,000. The *Kalmthoutse Heide* is a large nature reserve of dunes, heath, marsh and pine woods with many miles of signposted walking, cycling and riding tracks. The Arboretum is open from March to mid November from Monday to Friday between 09.00 and 17.00, Saturday, Sunday, public holidays, from 10.00 to 17.00. There is also the Apicultura Bee Museum at 51A Heikantstraat. This is open daily in July and August from 14.00 to 17.00 and at the same times on Sunday from early April to mid October.

10km **Essen** (population 12,000), the border town, boasts four small museums. In the Gemeentehuis there is the Museum Gerard Meeusen, open on request during normal working hours. This preserves material from the area. At Kiekenhoeve, 54 Moerkantsebaan, until 1767 a chicken farm belonging to the abbey of Tongerlo, there is an exhibition of agricultural vehicles. This is open daily, except Monday, from April to June and September and October, and Monday and Tuesday from November to March. In the park of Wildertse Duintjes there is a forest museum with exhibits on the flora and fauna of the Kempen, and in Sint Janstraat there is a bakery museum in a windmill.

ANTWERP TO PUTTE, for **Bergen op Zoom**; 17km to the border.

At *17km* **Putte** is made up of two villages, one each side of the border. The grave of the painter Jacob Jordaens, who as a Protestant could not be buried in Antwerp, is in the Dutch village. *Stabroek*, 3km to the SW and still a polder village, was the home of the Plantin-Moretus family.

18

Antwerp to Turnhout and Maaseik

Total distance 122km.—*26km* **Oostmalle**—*14km* **Turnhout**—*12km* **Retie**—
19km **Mol**—*13km* **Leopoldsburg**—*7km* **Hechtel**—*16km* **Bree**—*15km*
Maaseik.

This Route traverses the northern part of the KEMPEN (p 119). For places
lying between this Route and Route 20, see Route 19.

Leave **Antwerp**, (Route 16), through the suburb of **Deurne**. The road,
Turnhoutsebaan, N12, skirts the N side of the large recreational park of
Rivierenhof. Near the SW corner of the park, at 160 Hoofdvunderlei, is the
Museum Het Sterckshof in the château of the same name. 14C in origin,
the château was rebuilt in 1525 and further restored in 1934. In the period
rooms there are displays of silver, copper, pewter, iron and glassware, calico
prints, coins, medals and weights and measures. The museum is open daily,
except Monday and Friday, from Palm Sunday to October from 10.00 to
17.00.

We continue across the Albert Canal and through the residential district
of Schilde. Just before *Westmalle* is a Trappist abbey founded in 1791. The
church dates from 1836.

At *26km* **Oostmalle**, by the road junction, the modern *Sint Laurentiuskerk*
stands beneath the tower of its predecessor of 1683. In the interestingly
shaped interior of the church hangs a striking ironwork representation of
Christ Crowned.

For Sint Lenaarts and Brecht, 6km and 9km NW, see Route 17.

DIVERSION TO HOOGSTRATEN AND MEERLE, N 20km.

At *11km* **Hoogstraten** is the *Sint Katharinakerk*, built between 1524 and
1546 to plans by Rombout Keldermans. The lofty tower of 105m, with much
of the rest of the church, was rebuilt after suffering considerable damage
during the Second World War. It was blown up by the retreating Germans
on 23 October 1944. Inside the church the handsome marble and alabaster
tomb of the founders, Count Antoine de Lalaing, died 1540, and of his wife
Elisabeth of Culemborg, died 1555, is probably the work of Jean Mone,
1529. The 16C stained-glass windows show, amongst others, Charles V,
Margaret of Austria and members of the Lalaing line. The pulpit is by
Theodoor Verhaeghen.

The *Stadhuis*, adjoining the church, is a rebuilding of a 16C structure by
Rombout Keldermans. The *Begijnhof*, a short way N of the church and
founded in the 14C, was largely destroyed by fire in 1506. The present
buildings are of the 17C and 18C. The baroque-style church dates from
1687.

At *Minderhout*, just N of Hoogstraten, the road crosses the little river
Mark and virtually touches the Dutch border to the E.

At *9km Meerle* a part of the tower and central nave of the church dates
back to the 13C. The Dutch border is 3km to the N and 3km to the SE. A
minor road will take you the 10km to the curious Belgian enclave of *Baarle-
Hertog* (see below), from where you can rejoin the main Route 18 by taking
the road S to Turnhout.

Beyond Oostmalle the N12 continues through *Vlimmeren*, where the church, but not the tower, dates from the 14C. At *Vosselaar* there is a 13C wooden figure of Our Lady Comforter of the Afflicted in the church.

14km **Turnhout** (population 38,000. Tourist Information Office at 1 Grote Markt), is a lively industrial town best known for the manufacture of playing cards.

From the 14C to the 16C Turnhout belonged to Brabant. Then Charles V gave the town to his sister Mary of Hungary. After the Treaty of Münster in 1648 it was for a time an appanage of the House of Orange and then until 1753 of Brandenburg. At Turnhout in 1789, during the Brabançon Revolt, the Belgians defeated the Austrians, so paving the way for the brief United States of Belgium.

In the GROTE MARKT stands the *Sint Pieterskerk*, the 12C successor of wooden chapels dating back to the 8C. Of the 12C structure all that survives is the lower part of the tower. The apse was built in 1486 and further additions and alterations were made through to the 18C. There are some fine baroque stalls. The confessionals are by J.P. Baurscheit the Younger. The 19C pulpit by H. Peeters has a striking depiction of the Miraculous Draught of Fishes.

The road N from the Grote Markt leads to the *Kasteel*. First built c 1110, it was the residence of the dukes of Brabant and of Mary of Hungary. It was rebuilt during the 17C for Amalia von Solms, wife of Prince Frederick Henry of Orange-Nassau.

The Museum Taxandria, the local archaeological, historical and industrial museum, will reopen towards the end of 1992 at 28 Begijnenstraat, a 16C house. It may be visited on Wednesday, Friday and Saturday from 14.00 to 17.00, on Sunday from 10.00 to 12.00 and 14.00 to 17.00, and in June, July and August also on Tuesday and Thursday from 14.00 to 17.00.

A short way farther on, to the W of the road, is the *Begijnhof*. First mentioned in 1372, it was completely rebuilt during the 17C. The church dates from 1665. One of the houses has been converted into a museum. Visiting hours: Sunday from 15.00 to 17.00, Wednesday and Friday, 14.00 to 17.00.

Herentalsstraat leads S out of the Grote Markt. After some 500m, at 18 Druivenstraat the *Museum van de Speelkaart*, the Playing Cards Museum, is housed in a former factory hall. It is open on Wednesday, Friday and Saturday from 14.00 to 17.00, on Sunday from 10.00 to 12.00 and 14.00 to 17.00 and in June, July and August also on Tuesday and Thursday from 14.00 to 17.00.

From Turnhout a visit may be made to **Baarle-Hertog**, 12km to the N. This is a geo-political curiosity where the Belgian enclaves of Baaarle-Hertog are mixed up with the Dutch village of Baarle-Nassau. In 1479 the village of Baarle was divided into two parts for inheritance reasons. Eventually, one part was absorbed by North Brabant, which is Dutch, and the other by South Brabant, which is Belgian. As a result of the division some strange situations have arisen. The market square is Dutch territory, except for one tavern. The old church is Belgian. There are two town halls, police stations, schools and post offices.

This odd state of affairs saved Baarle-Hertog from German occupation during the First World War. In October 1915 the Belgians established a radio station there and, in spite of a barbed-wire fence built around the commune by the neutral Dutch, the village became an important centre of Allied espionage.

Beyond Turnhout the main road, the N18, bears SE. In the church of *Oud-Turnhout* there is a Last Supper, of 1698, by Jan Erasmus Quellin.

Crossing the A21/E34 motorway, we continue to *12km* **Retie**, with its Tree of Justice in front of the church. This is the centre of a pleasant district of woods, heath and dunes. Part of a large estate sold by the Crown in 1950 has been turned into the *Prinsenpark*. This nature reserve of 165 ha. with walks and picnic areas is some 5km along the road to Geel.

The Premonstratensian abbey of **Postel** is in wooded and marshy country c 7km NE of Retie. Founded in 1140 by monks from Floreffe as a hospice for pilgrims, it became an abbey in 1621. Suppressed in 1797 during the period of religious strife, it was restored to the monks in 1847.

The modern Contact Centre beyond the 17C gateway is considered by some visitors to have spoiled the appearance of the courtyard. The Romanesque church, dating from c 1190 and built of tufa from the Eifel in Germany, was much altered in the 16C and 17C. A beautifully decorated 13C doorway by the side of the cloister survives. The domestic buildings date from 1631, with additions of 1713 and 1743. The library has a rich collection of incunabula, 16C books, etchings and old atlases. The belfry of 1610 has a carillon of 40 bells which was placed there in 1947.

Beyond *4km Dessel* the road crosses the Kempisch Kanaal which was excavated in 1845. 3km W there is a research complex for the peaceful use of nuclear power. Part of this is used by Euratom.

At *5km* is **Mol** (population 29,500. Tourist Information Office at 22 Markt), a straggling town set in a typical Kempen landscape. The *Sint Pieter en Pauwelkerk*, rebuilt in 1852, has a tower of 1492 with a carillon of 49 bells. A museum of religious art is open from April to September on Tuesday at 11.00, Saturday, 15.00, in July and August also Sunday at 15.00. Enshrined in the church is a thorn from Christ's crown. There are two statues on the transept pillars attributed to Artus Quellin the Elder, and a painting by G.J. Herreyns. A monument nearby commemorates the Peasants' Revolt of 1798. In the square there is part of an old pillory.

Achterbos-Sluis, just N of Mol, was a place much favoured by the Kempen painter Jacob Smits, who died in 1928. There is a small museum at Sluis (Oude Pastorie) dedicated to him. This is open on Saturday and Sunday and daily, except Monday, during school holiday periods from 14.00 to 18.00.

At *Zilvermeer*, 5km NE of Mol, there is a provincial park with two large lakes, facilities for camping, swimming and boating, and a natural history museum.

Continue to *4km Balen*. Circa 3km NE is *Keiheuvel*, an area of dunes and scrub used for many recreational purposes including gliding. The hamlet of *Scheps*, 2km S, was the birthplace in the 8C of St Odrade, who performed many miracles and who is invoked to bring fine weather.

At *9km* is **Leopoldsburg**, population 10,000. This is just in the province of Limburg. It is a garrison town for the military establishments at *Beverlo*, 4km to the S, founded in 1850 by Leopold I. There is a museum in the former military hospital in Hechtelsesteenweg.

In *Oostham*, 6km W, the church tower was rebuilt after war damaged its 11C predecessor. Note the masonry in herringbone pattern.

Continue for *7km* to **Hechtel** where the N73 and N715 meet. Hechtel is the centre of a large district of dunes, heath and woodland. To the NW at *In de Brand* and SE at *Begijnenvijver* there are two nature areas. At *Eksel*, 3km to the NE, there is a museum concerned with the flora and fauna of the Kempen. It is open from June to August on Wednesday, Saturday and Sunday from 13.30 to 14.30 and 16.30 to 17.30.

Follow the N715 in a northerly direction from Hechtel to the *Park der Lage Kempen*. With signposted walks and picnic areas, this lies slightly to the W. Just W of the junction, at 10km, of the N715 and the N71, there is a Polish war cemetery. At 4km farther to the W is **Lommel**. This small town, with lead and zinc industries, is set in typical Kempen surroundings. The tower of its *Sint Pieterskerk* dates from 1388. The town has two museums, the Streek museum at 14 Markt, which is concerned with the area, and the Eymardininstituut, at *Kattenbos* to the S, which has a collection of prehistoric finds. The Kattenbos woods and heath form a popular nature reserve. There is a restored windmill of 1805 and a large German war cemetery.

To the E of the crossroads are *Overpelt* and *Neerpelt*, towns in a rapidly expanding industrial zone. **Achel**, 5km NE of Neerpelt, is a pleasanter place, with a 15C church. At 2km to the NE is a 13–14C tower known as *De Tomp*.

For N715 S from Hechtel, see Route 19.

6km Peer has a town hall of 1637. At *10km* **Bree** (population 8000. Tourist Information Office 3 Cobbestraat), there are two museums. One, concerned with the local area, is in the Oud Gemeentehuis. It has a model of the town as it was in 1700. The other, a war museum, is at 85 Kanaallaan. The Gothic *Sint Michielskerk*, dating from 1452, was enlarged in 1901. It replaced a Romanesque church, which in turn had replaced a 7C chapel.

Bree was the principal town of a district which from the 14C to the 16C grew prosperous from the wool trade. Its church and many of those in the surrounding villages are reminders of that prosperity. They are built in a style known as Limburg Gothic. Generally the walls are of local marl, as is also the vaulting, which has diagonal ribbing. Other parts are in bluestone. Many contain ancient statues of the saints. The best of the Limburg Gothic churches is at *Neeroeteren*, 9km to the SE (see below). Others near Bree are at *Gerdingen*, 1km to the NW, *Beek* 2km to the N, *Opitter*, 4km to the SE, *Gruitrode* and *Neerglabbeek* 5.5km to the S, and *Opglabbeek* 11km to the S.

Beyond Bree the N73 continues E to the frontier with Holland and to Roermond beyond. This Route bears SE on N721 through *Opitter* (see above) to *9km* **Neeroeteren**. The *Limburg Gothic church at Neeroeteren was built in the 15C. Apart from the addition of the tower in 1719, few alterations have been made to it. It has an outstanding collection of early 16C statues. These include images of St Lambert, the patron, St James and St Christopher. The Marianum, a representation in wrought and painted iron of Our Lady in a garland of roses, is one of only two in Belgium. The other is at Zoutleeuw, near Sint Truiden.

6km **Maaseik** (population 21,000. Tourist Information Office at 45 Markt), is a pleasant small town on the Maas. Here the river forms the border with Holland. The Markt, with its lime trees and scattering of 17C and 18C houses, is particularly attractive. Note the monument of 1864 to Jan and Hubert van Eyck. Reputedly the van Eyck brothers were born at Maaseik, Jan c 1390 and Hubert, if he existed, some 20 years earlier. Also in the Markt is an 18C pharmacy with furniture and equipment of the period. This now serves as a museum with exhibits from the pharmacy and concerning local archaeology and baking. It is open daily, except Monday, from 09.00 to 12.00 and 14.00 to 17.00. In the 19C *Stadhuis* there is a copy of the van Eycks' Mystic Lamb (see Route 13).

The streets off the Markt, notably Bosstraat, have some 17C and 18C façades. In the *Katharinakerk* there is an important treasury which is usually opened on request. It possesses an evangelistery of the early 8C, the Codex Eyckensis. This is the oldest book in Belgium. It is believed to have once belonged to SS Relindis and Herlindis, who founded a Benedictine convent at nearby *Aldeneik*, c 750.

At Aldeneik a stone church built in 870 was restored in the 11C. Additions were made in the 13C, by which time the nuns had been replaced by a community of monks. More restoration and alterations followed during the

19C. Of the present church the central part of the Romanesque nave, with
its 13C frescoes, dates from the 11C or 12C. The W part is early 13C and
the choir late 13C. The neo-Romanesque aisles and the tower are 19C.

19

Antwerp to Genk

Motorway distance 81km.—*20km* **Grobbendonk** and **Herentals**—*14km*
Geel (also **Tongerlo** and **Westerlo**)—*14km* **Tessenderlo**—*7km Paal*—*17km*
Houthalen—*9km* **Genk**.

This Route follows the A13/E313 and A2/E314 motorways. Crossing the
central and southern part of KEMPEN, it is a convenient way of reaching a
number of places of interest situated between Routes 18 and 20. The main
distances are those between the points at which the motorway is left.

Antwerp, see Route 16. At *7km* the motorway A21/E34 bears NE for
Eindhoven in Holland.
   At *13km* is **Grobbendonk**, just to the N of the motorway. This large village
has a *Diamond Museum* with exhibits covering the mining, cutting and
polishing of diamonds, and their industrial and decorative use. It is open
from Monday to Friday from 09.00 to 16.30, on Saturday from 10.00 to 13.30,
on Sunday from 10.00 to 12.00 and 14.00 to 16.00. It is closed on 1 January,
30 and 31 December.
   At *Vorselaar*, 2.5km to the NE, there is a pillory dating from 1759. A fine
avenue of limes leads to an imposing moated château, which in the 13C
belonged to the van Rotselaar family, the chief stewards of the dukes of
Brabant. It was rebuilt in the neo-Gothic style during the 19C. There is no
admission to the château, but the attractive exterior is worth a detour.
   Herentals (population 24,000) is *6km* to the E of Grobbendonk. Since the
14C it has been the chief town of the Kempen. From here fresh water was
sent by barge to Antwerp for use by the city's breweries. The *Sint Walde-
trudiskerk*, dating in part from the 14C, contains an early 16C retable by
Pasquier Borremans and paintings by Frans Francken the Elder. The
Stadhuis, once the cloth hall, has a belfry of 1590. Built c 1400, it was
destroyed by fire in 1512. Rebuilt two years later it suffered major restoration in 1880. The Stadhuis houses an interesting collection of casts and
sculptures by Charles Fraikin who was born in Herentals in 1817. At the
time of writing the collection is closed.
   The *Begijnhof* in the northern part of the town dates from the 17–18C. It
replaced one founded c 1266 on a different site which was destroyed by
the Calvinists in 1578. The church dates from 1595–1614. The horizontal
courses of white stone were brought from the previous begijnhof.
   Two of the town's old gates survive, the 14C *Zandpoort* on the road to
Lier, and the *Bovenpoort* of 1402 on the road to Geel.
   14km **Geel** (population 31,000. Tourist Information Office in the Stadhuis)
is 5km N of the motorway. It is known worldwide for its system of treating
the insane. Patients are boarded out among the townspeople. They enjoy
domestic comforts, a measure of freedom, personal care, and opportunities
to follow a useful occupation. This humane and successful method, under

official and medical supervision since about 1850, originated in the 13C from a pilgrimage made to the shrine of St Dympna, the patron of the insane. She was an Irish princess who fled to Geel to escape from the unwelcome attentions of her crazed and incestuous father. Unfortunately, Dympna and her confessor, St Gerebernus, were caught and executed, reputedly on the site of the *Sint Dimpnakerk*.

Built between 1344 and 1492, the church contains the reliquaries of the two saints as well as other treasures. The tower dates from the 16C. The *mausoleum of Jean III, Count of Mérode, and of his wife Anne de Ghistelles, of 1554, is by Cornelis Floris. There are several superb *retables. One, of the Passion, is attributed to Goswin van der Weyden, c 1490. Another dated to 1513 tells the story of St Dympna. This is by Jan van Waver. A third, depicting the Apostles, is a sandstone carving of 1350. The 'Sieckencamere', sick room, is where the mentally afflicted pilgrims made their novenas.

Close to the church, in a 15C chapel at 1 Gasthuisstraat, the *Sint Dimpna en Gasthuismuseum* has a special section on the saint. It is open mid May to September on Sunday, Wednesday and Thursday from 14.00 to 17.30.

Sint Amandskerk, near the Markt, was built between 1490 and 1531. It has one of the best baroque interiors in Belgium. The high altar is by Pieter Verhaghen. Pieter Valckx and W. Kerrickx did much of the carved work.

From Geel follow the N19 in a southerly direction, across the motorway, for 9km to the walled and moated Premonstratensian ***Tongerlo Abbey**. Founded in 1130 in the desolate and barren Kempen, the area around the abbey was soon transformed by the agricultural skills of the monks. Dissolved in 1796, the abbey was restored to the monks in 1840 and is once again flourishing.

The approach is along a stately drive lined with 300-year-old lime trees. At the end, two Romanesque arches, 12–14C, admit us to the large inner court. On the walls of the buildings around the court are their names, dates of construction and some other information. To the right is the Prelaatshuis, by Willem Ignatius Kerrickx, 1726, with an interesting façade.

The *Da Vinci Museum*, open daily, except Friday, May to September between 14.00 and 17.00, is reached by crossing a garden. Note the Guest House of 1547, with its elegant turret of 1479, on the left. The museum, opened in 1956, occupies a small theatre. In it hangs a copy of Leonardo Da Vinci's Last Supper. This was painted between 1506 and 1507 by the artist's pupil Andrea del Solario, apparently by order of Pope Clement VII for Henry VIII of England. Bought by the abbey in 1545, the painting aroused the admiration of Rubens and van Dyck. It is well lit and admirably positioned for study. There is a commentary on the painting in English.

Westerlo (population 20,000), 2km S of the abbey is pleasantly situated on the Grote Nete. This is a popular area for walkers and cyclists. There are two châteaux. The *Kasteel van Gravin J. de Mérode*, a neo-Gothic building of 1911, serves as a municipal and cultural centre. The *Kasteel de Mérode* exhibits a mélange of styles from the 14C to the 19C.

At *14km* is **Tessenderlo**. This town of 14,000 inhabitants is 3km S of the motorway and just in the province of Limburg. Its 14–15C *Sint Martinuskerk* has a fine rood-screen of c 1500 depicting the life of Christ.

7km Paal stands at the crossing of the motorway and the N29 from Diest (Route 20) to Leopoldsburg (Route 18). **Beringen**, 2km E, is a small, former colliery town, where it is possible to visit a mine. The tower of the *Sint Theodardskerk*, the 'Miners' Cathedral' 1939–43, is detached because of the danger of subsidence. St Theodard was a 7C bishop of Liège.

We continue along the motorway in a SE direction for *5km* to a road junction. There we bear due E along the A2/E314. Immediately to the S, though not visible from the motorway, is the motor trials and race track of *Terlaemen-Zolder*.

Near *12km* **Houthalen**, 2km N of the motorway, there are three recreation areas: the holiday and bungalow park of *Molenheide*, 5km N, with walks and an animal enclosure, *Hengelhoef*, 5km NE with accommodation, aviary, animal enclosure and many sports facilities, and *Domein Kelchterhoef*, 6km E, with similar attractions.

To the S of the motorway, at c 8km, is the large *Bokrijk Provinciaal Domein*, a 550 ha. open air museum with Flemish farmhouses. See Route 20 for further information.

9km **Genk** (population 61,000) is 3km S of the motorway. An expanding industrial town, it is surrounded, especially on the S and E, by typical Kempen country of wood and heathland. Many parts of this are designated nature reserves. The *Villa van Doren*, at 21 H. Decleenestraat, houses a local museum and also works by Emile van Doren, the 19C landscape artist who lived here. It is open on Wednesday, Saturday and Sunday from 10.00 to 12.00 and 15.00 to 18.00.

The *Zwartberg Limburg Zoo*, 3km N of the motorway and due N of Genk, was formed in 1970. It has a good collection of animals in a pleasant parkland setting. The zoo is open daily from Easter to mid November between 09.00 and 19.00.

The motorway, continuing E through the Kempen country, reaches the Dutch border and the Maas at 19km.

20

Antwerp to Hasselt and Maastricht (Holland)

Total distance 100km.—*14km* **Lier**—*12km* **Heist-op-den-Berg**—*14km* **Aarschot**—*10km* **Scherpenheuvel**—*5km* **Diest**—*21km* **Hasselt**—*13km* **Bilzen**—*11km* **Maastricht** (Holland).

Leave **Antwerp** (see Route 16) by the Grote Steenweg. After the southern suburb of *Berchem*, the road, the Liersesteenweg/N10, bears E past Mortsel to *Boechout*, birthplace of J.F. Willems who began the Flemish nationalist movement.

At *14km* is **Lier** (population 31,000. Tourist Information Office in the Stadhuis). At the confluence of the Grote and Kleine Nete, it is a delightful town with much to interest the visitor. Sections of the 14C ramparts have been laid out as walks.

Founded during the 8C, Lier became the refuge of St Gummarus, 717–74. A nobleman at the court of King Pepin, after many years of patient endurance Gummarus fled to Lier to escape from his spendthrift and nagging wife.

Lier received town status from Duke Henry of Brabant in 1212. Philip the Handsome and Joanna of Castile were married here in 1496. In 1523 Christian II of Denmark and his queen, Isabel of Austria, sister of Charles V, came to live in Lier after their flight from Denmark.

It was the home of L. van Boeckel, 1857–1944, who produced artistic works in iron, of the writer Felix Timmermans, 1886–1947, of the painter Baron Isidore Opsomer, 1878–1967, and of the clockmaker L. Zimmer, 1888–1970.

The GROTE MARKT is a mixture of modern, rather undistinguished architecture and older façades. The *Vleeshuis* dates from 1418. The *Stadhuis* of 1740 replaced a medieval cloth hall. The preliminary plans for this rococo style building were drawn by J.P. Baurscheit the Younger. It has more than 3500 small, bottle-green window panes. Inside there are an elaborate staircase of 1775 and a clock by Zimmer. The attached belfry of 1369 formed part of the medieval cloth hall and town meeting-place.

The *Museum Wuyts van Campen-Baron Caroly* is just W of the Grote Markt at 14 Florent van Cauwenberghstraat. It houses important collections bequeathed in 1886 by the family which owned the house at that time, and by Baron G. Caroly in 1935. Works usually on show include: *Bernard van Orley*: Madonna with Child and Angel. *David Teniers the Elder*: the Seven Works of Mercy, The Alchemist. *Pieter Brueghel the Younger*: St John, Flemish Proverbs. *Jan Brueghel*: Madonna and Child. *Frans Floris*: The van Berchem Family. *Antoon van Dyck*: St Sebastian, Portrait of a Nobleman. *Pieter Paul Rubens*: St Theresa. *David Teniers the Younger*: Jealous Wife, The Village of Perk. *Jan Steen*: Brawling Peasants. *Murillo*: Bacchus.

The museum is open daily, except Wednesday and Friday, from Easter to October from 10.00 to 12.00 and 13.30 to 17.30. Other times of the year: Sunday, from 10.00 to 12.00 and 13.30 to 16.30.

Eikelstraat leads SW out of the Grote Markt through the *Eikelpoort*, a part of the ancient defences, which dates from c 1375, but was altered in 1727. For a number of years it was used as a prison and, consequently, is sometimes called the Prisoners' Gate.

The Eikelpoort occupies the NW end of ZIMMERPLEIN, which was under water until the end of the 19C. At the opposite end stands the *Zimmertoren* in another section of the ramparts. This has two unusual clocks and the Astronomic Studio, the work of Louis Zimmer. Visiting hours: daily from 09.00 to 12.00, 14.00 to 19.00 or to 16.00 in winter.

The *Centenary Clock*, 1930–31, on the Zimmertoren has a central dial surrounded by 12 smaller dials. Complicated mechanism shows the phases of the moon, the 19-year metonic cycle covering the changes of the moon, Greenwich Mean Time, the signs of the zodiac, the solar cycle of 28 years, the dominical letter, the days of the week, the globe, the months with their various distinguishing features—Ice, Duck, Fish, Fool, Flower, Shearing, Hay, Harvest, Fruit, Wine, Butchering, Rest—the calendar, the seasons, the tides at Lier and the ages of the moon.

At noon figures representing the first century of Belgian independence—the national arms, three kings, the arms of Lier, the burgomasters—appear.

In the *Astronomic Studio* on the first floor of the tower 57 dials record, by groups, the subdivisions of time, the tides, the planetary system, astronomical calculations, rotation of the sun and planets, the phases of the moon and the tides, astronomical phenomena and the constellations of the northern hemisphere.

The combined mechanism of the Centenary Clock and the Astronomic Studio may be seen on the second floor.

Nearby is the astronomical *Wonder Clock*, which was a feature of the Brussels World Fair of 1935 and New York World Fair of 1939. It has 14 automata and three large dials, each surmounting a panel of 30 smaller dials.

In the small garden there is an exhibition of artistic ironwork by van Boeckel.

The *Begijnhof*, one of the largest in Belgium, is located to the SW of Zimmerplein. Although founded c 1200 on its present site, the existing buildings date mainly from the late 17C. In the baroque chapel, completed between 1664 and 1767, there is an antependium whose design is attributed to Rubens and the embroidery to his daughter. There is also a tabernacle by Willem Ignatius Kerrickx and sculpture by Artus Quellin the Younger.

Near the Zimmertoren cross the Kleine Nete by a small bridge. Just beyond is the *Timmermans-Opsomerhuis*. In addition to exhibits relating to Timmermans and Opsomer, it contains van Boeckel's forge together with examples of his work. From Easter to October the house is open daily, except Wednesday and Friday, 10.00 to 12.00 and 13.30 to 17.30; otherwise Sunday 10.00 to 12.00 and 13.30 to 16.30.

The Werft, once the waterside commercial quarter, follows the river northwards. Across the water is the *Fortuin*, a medieval granary. This has been converted into a restaurant.

At the next bridge follow the Rechtestraat in an easterly direction to the *Sint Gummaruskerk*. This church, in the Flamboyant style, was built between 1425 and 1540. The base of the tower is 14C, but the octagonal upper part is an 18C replacement. The interior merits a visit for its many art treasures. The *stained-glass, which was restored after war damage in 1914, includes some of the oldest and best in Belgium. It dates from the 15C to modern times. Of especial interest are the 15C Crowning of the Virgin in the S aisle, a window of 1475 by Rombout Keldermans in the choir, left first row, and a group of five windows above the high altar. Three of these were presented by the Emperor Maximilian when he visited Lier in 1516. The rood-loft, with the Way of the Cross, is of 1534. The pulpit and altar are by Artus Quellin the Elder. Note the triptych in the first ambulatory chapel on the left. The wings, which depict St Clare and St Francis, are by Rubens. In the fourth chapel another triptych of c 1516 is attributed to Goswin van der Weyden. The chapels also contain works by Otto Venius, Martin de Vos, Michiel Coxie and Frans Francken the Elder.

Immediately N of the church is the *Sint Pieterskapel*. Founded in 1225, it was largely rebuilt after war damage in 1914. The *Jesuitenkerk*, a short way SE in Berlaarsestraat, has a fine baroque façade. It was built between 1749 and 1754.

12km **Heist-op-den-Berg** is built on a hill 45m above sea-level, the highest natural point in the province of Antwerp. In the *Sint Lambertuskerk* of 1587 there is a marble Madonna by Artus Quellin the Younger. A house called *Die Zwaene* in the pleasant close houses the collection of the local museum. It is open from Easter to September on Saturday from 14.00 to 18.00 and on Sunday from 10.00 to 12.00 and 14.00 to 18.00. Nearby there is an observation tower.

14km **Aarschot**, population 13,000, is in the province of Brabant. Standing on the Demer at an important crossroads, it is a centre for agricultural products and light industry.

The town is of ancient origin. One tradition states that its name derives from the fact that the Romans kept their eagles, i.e. their standards, here. According to another legend Julius Caesar shot an eagle in the neighbourhood.

Prosperity came to the town with the cloth trade in the 13C. Later Aarschot lived through violent times. In 1489 it was sacked by Maximilian of Austria. It suffered during the wars of Charles the Bold and in the 16C was pillaged several times and burnt by the Spanish. In 1782 Joseph II razed the town's fortifications. This encouraged many of the inhabitants to support the Brabançon Revolt a few years later. In 1914 Aarschot experienced German brutality. Four hundred houses were burnt and 149 citizens, including the burgomaster, murdered.

There is a good view from the *Orleanstoren*, a relic of the 13C walls, on the hill above the town.

Near the river is the Gothic *Onze Lieve Vrouwekerk*. This has a 13–14C choir, a 15C nave and a tower 85m high. There are paintings by de Crayer and Verhaghen, a chandelier by Quinten Metsys and lively *misericords on the choir stalls by Jan Borchman, 1500. Do not miss the naive and unusual painting, the *Mystic Winepress, by an unknown Flemish artist of c 1525.

On the lower part of the painting the Seven Sacraments are depicted. On the upper part the Holy Blood, which Christ on the 'press' of the Cross sheds for our redemption, is likened to wine. The simile is continued on the left, where Peter and the other Apostles press the grapes. The Four Evangelists take the grape juice to the church. There the barrels are closed by the Pope, Emperor, Cardinals and Bishops and then placed in the cellars. Priests offer the wine of Christ to the faithful who make their confessions and hear Mass.

Immediately W of the church there is a large Renaissance mansion. This was once the house of a burgomaster. Beyond is the *Begijnhof*, founded in the 13C but largely destroyed during the two World Wars and by later town extensions. A part, restored in 17–18C style, houses municipal offices, old people's homes and the town's *Museum*. This is open from Monday to Saturday, except Tuesday afternoon, from 08.30 to 12.00 and 14.00 to 17.00; on Sunday from 10.00 to 12.00.

Opposite the museum entrance a small monument, the Lacemaker, recalls a local skill, now lost. Beyond and straddling the river are's *Hertogenmolens,* the 13–16C ducal mills.

At Sint Pieters-Rode, 6km S of Aarschot, is the attractive château of **Horst**. Of the early medieval, 13–15C castle only the tower and keep remain. The rest of the building, which dates from the 15–17C, has remained unaltered since it was last occupied in the 17C. Thus, Horst, surrounded by water, stands as an unspoilt example of a seigneurial home of the period. Despite being unoccupied, the château has been well maintained. The most interesting feature of the interior is the late 17C decoration by Jan Hansche of the ceiling of the great hall with scenes from Ovid's 'Metamorphoses'.

To the W and SW of Aarschot are 7km **Tremelo** and 10km **Rotselaar**. Father Damien, the saintly missionary priest, was born in Tremelo in 1840. He devoted his life to the leper outcasts on the Hawaiian island of Molokai and died of the disease there in 1889. In 1936 his body was brought to the chapel of St Antonius in Louvain. The house in which he was born is now a museum. It is open daily, except Sunday morning and Monday, from 10.00 to 12.00 and 14.00 to 18.00.

At Rotselaar there is a high fortified tower. Of unknown date, it is thought to have been rebuilt during the 15C.

10km **Scherpenheuvel** (population 20,500), is the scene of Belgium's most important annual pilgrimage. This is held on the Sunday after All Saints.

About the year 1514 a shepherd found a statue of Our Lady and the Child Jesus attached to an oak near Scherpenheuvel. He tried to remove it, but became fixed to the ground. His pious master, who had come to look for his missing servant, took this to mean that Our Lady wished to be honoured in this place and he built a chapel to house the statue. In 1578 the Duke of Parma prayed here before laying siege to Zichem, 3km to the N. Two years later the statue was destroyed by the iconoclasts. In 1601 Albert and Isabella vowed to make a pilgrimage to Scherpenheuvel, if their commander Spinola forced the United Provinces forces to retreat. Spinola took Ostend and in 1607 Archduke Albert had the town built in the shape of a seven-pointed star.

The circular *Basilica* was completed by Wenceslaus Coeberger, the court architect, in 1627. It is based on the design of St Peter's in Rome. The seven windows in the lantern turret symbolise the seven Sacraments. There is a copy of the original miraculous statue above the tabernacle on the high altar. Among the many gifts made by pilgrims are a brass font of 1610 and a head of Christ by Duquesnoy from Albert and Isabella, six paintings by Theodoor van Loon from Isabella, and an Assumption attributed to Martin de Vos.

The old town of **Zichem** is 3km to the N. In the church of c 1300 there is some stained-glass dating from 1387. By the river the Maagdentoren marks the site of the 14C ramparts. There is a museum containing memorabilia of the writer Ernest Claes, who was born here in 1885.

The Premonstratensian **Averbode Abbey**, 4km farther N, stands on the watershed between the valleys of the Demer and the Nete at a point where the provinces of Antwerp, Brabant and Limburg meet. Founded in 1134, the abbey was closed down and sold at the time of the French Revolution. It was reopened in 1833. Access to the inner court is by a 14C gatehouse. In the court there are the vaulted 17C cloisters and the 18C abbot's house, which was rebuilt. Most of the domestic buildings were restored after a fire in 1942. The large baroque church, by D. van der Ende, 1664–72, has a choir which is longer than its nave.

5km **Diest** (population 21,000) is an ancient, attractive walled town has many picturesque corners. The irregular shaped GROTE MARKT is surrounded by 17C and 18C buildings. One of these is the *Stadhuis* of 1735 by Willem Ignatius Kerrickx. This replaced a group of much earlier buildings. The Gothic cellar of the former aldermen's house of c 1320 and the 13C Romanesque cellar, with its original well, of the house of the lords of Diest, are all that remain of the earlier structures. They now house the *Stedelijk Museum*. This museum has a fine collection of silver dating from c 1600; a small frame-reliquary full of meticulously labelled sacred relics; a marble statue of the Virgin of 1345, a replica of an original in the Metropolitan Museum of Art, New York; pictures by Theodoor van Loon; and a dramatic *Last Judgement by an unknown artist of c 1420–50.

Nearby is the *Sint Sulpitiuskerk*. Under construction from 1321–1534, the colours of the stone record the successive stages of building. Excavations have revealed the remains of two earlier churches. The older dates from the 11C. There is a tradition that a wooden chapel stood here as early as the 7C. This may also have been dedicated to St Sulpitius, Bishop of Bourges until his death in 647.

The choir stalls of Sint Sulpitiuskerk date from 1491. Note the lively misericords. There is an interesting treasury, some fine 15–16C stained-glass, a 13C Sedes Sapientiae and the tomb of Philip of Nassau, who died in 1618. The son of William the Silent, Philip was lord of Diest.

Just W of the church, at the roadside, is 'Holle Griet', dating from the 15C. The best view of the nearby *Halle*, the 14C Cloth Hall, is from its E end. The oldest part of Diest is to the E of this area. There are interesting views from the corner of Ketelstraat and Guido Gezellestraat. Note the fine 17C baroque façade of the *Sint Barbarakerk* in Guido Gezellestraat.

WARANDE STADSPARK in the E part of the town was once a hunting ground of the princes of Orange. In the cemetery at the SE corner of the park there are the ruins of a 14C church.

The abbeys of Tongerlo and Averbode had refuges inside the walls of Diest in the area to the N of the Grote Markt. The 16C refuge of Tongerlo is E off Demerstraat. The 15C refuge of Averbode is in the N part of

Refugiestraat, near the point where it joins Demerstraat.

Koning Albertstraat leads NE out of the Grote Markt to reach at 500m Begijnenstraat. Here is the *Onze Lieve Vrouwekerk*, which dates from the 13C. This replaced an earlier chapel. Towards the far end of the Begijnenstraat a baroque portal of 1671 marks the entrance to the *Begijnhof*. Founded in 1252, much reconstruction was undertaken between 1538 and 1575 by its chaplain, Nicolaas van Esch. The present houses, which occupy four streets, are mainly of this period and later. The interior of the 14C Gothic church was restored in the rococo style.

A short walk from the Onze Lieve Vrouwekerk by way of Schaffensestraat will bring you to the N edge of the town. Here is the *Schaffensepoort*, a narrow fortified way over two arms of the river Demer and successive lines of ramparts.

You leave Diest by the Hasseltsestraat (N2) and after 2km cross the border into the province of Limburg.

At 5km is **Halen**, with its pleasant square of 18C and 19C houses. A monument commemorates a victorious charge by the Belgian cavalry in August 1914. Note the attractive old mansion and bridge to the right of the E exit from the village.

In the church of the adjoining village of *Donk* there is a 16C recumbent statue of the Virgin. Prayers to cure sterility are said before this statue.

4km **Herk-de-Stad** was the birthplace in 1872 of Pauline Jeuris, a missionary martyred in China in 1900. Beatified in 1946 as the Blessed Amandina, her life and work are remembered in a small museum.

At *4km* **Spalbeek** Hendrik van Veldeke, the first Netherlands troubadour, was born in the 12C. To the N of the road by the railway crossing there is an old chapel with a 12C choir of unusual horseshoe shape and 14C murals.

6km **Kuringen** was the site of the abbey of Herkenrode. Founded in 1182 it was served by Cistercian nuns until its suppression in 1797 by the French invaders. At that time its treasures were dispersed widely. Some of the beautiful stained-glass from the abbey is now in Lichfield Cathedral. Other precious possessions, including a monstrance in which a Miraculous Host was displayed, are at Hasselt (see below). The buildings visible today date from the 16C to the 18C.

At *2km* is **Hasselt**. With a population of 64,000, Hasselt is the administrative and commercial capital of the province of Limburg. The Tourist Information Office is in the Stadhuis, 3 Lombaardstraat.

In the 8C and 9C Hasselt was just one of a group of villages. It received its charter as a town in 1200. In 1798 the capture at Hasselt of the guerrilla leader Emmanuel Rollier put an end to the Peasants' Revolt. In 1831 the Belgians were defeated here by the Dutch, although this proved to be only a temporary setback in the fight for independence. The town was made a bishopric in 1967.

In the GROTE MARKT a house bearing the sign Het Sweert, which means 'the sword', is a good example of 17C Mosan architecture. It is now a chemist shop.

The *Sint Quintinus Kathedraal* has a 13C tower standing on an 11C base and an 18C spire. In 1292 work started on the nave, transepts and choir. Some chapels were built in the 14C and 15C, the ambulatory and its chapels were constructed during the 16C and various neo-Gothic features added during the 19C. For some time the monstrance of 1297, in which the Miraculous Host of Herkenrode (see above) was exposed for veneration, was kept in the cathdral. It is now in the Museum Stellingwerff-Waerdenhof (see below). The cathedral is dedicated to St Quentin or Quintin, variously described as a bishop or Roman soldier, who evangelised the area around Amiens. He was martyred c 287 at the town on the Somme which bears his name.

Onze Lieve Vrouwekerk, just W of the Grote Markt, was rebuilt in the style of 1728 after suffering bomb damage in 1944. It also has some of the treasures which once belonged to the abbey of Herkenrode. These include the high altar by Jean del Cour and a miraculous 14C statue of the Virgin, the 'Virga Jesse'. There are other sculptures by del Cour and monuments to two abbesses of Herkenrode: that of Anne-Catherine de Lamboy, who died in 1675, is by Artus Quellin the Younger and that of Barbara de Rivière, who died in 1714, by Laurent Delvaux.

The *Begijnhof*, 250m NE of the Grote Markt by Zuivelmarkt, dates from 1707.

The *Museum Stellingwerff-Waerdenhof* at 85 Maastrichterstraat is housed in a building which has been restored with taste and care. It has an interesting collection of artefacts connected with the history of Hasselt and the province of Limburg. There are also some fine 19C and 20C paintings, art nouveau ceramics and historic signboards. Among the church plate on display is the Monstrance of Herkenrode (see above). The museum is open from Tuesday to Friday between 10.00 and 1700 and on Saturday, Sunday and public holidays from 14.00 to 18.00. It is closed on Monday, 1, 2 and 11 November and from 24 December to 31 January.

Hasselt has been associated with the jenever industry since the 17C. At the *Nationaal Jenevermuseum*, 19 Witte Nonnenstraat, there is a step-by-step display of the manufacturing process of this popular drink, from grain to bottle. Visitors may sample the product in the museum's bar at the end of their visit. The Jenevermuseum is open at the same times as the Museum Stellingwerff-Waerdenhof.

The Provincial Estate of *Bokrijk, 7km NE of Hasselt, may be reached from the Hasselt to Genk road, the N75. It is open every day throughout the year. The word, Bokrijk, is of medieval origin and means Beech Estate. Until 1797 Bokrijk belonged to the abbey of Herkenrode. After over a century of private ownership, the estate was acquired in 1938 by the Province of Limburg. Since then it has become one of Belgium's most popular recreation centres. In addition to a large park, it has a rose garden, extensive children's play area, an arboretum with some 5000 species, a deer reserve and an excellent open air museum.

This museum, the *Openlucht Museum*, was established in 1958 and has been expanding ever since. It has a large display of buildings: farmhouses, mills, cottages, chapels, tall town houses and village inns dating from the 15C to the end of the 19C. Every part of Flemish Belgium is represented. The houses are usually arranged by district and generally have appropriate, contemporary interiors.

Frequent tours, duration 30 minutes, by 'motor-train' take visitors around the estate. Cafés and restaurants offer regional dishes and beers. There is an excellent, illustrated guidebook in English with more than 100 entries. The Openlucht Museum is open daily from 30 March to 3 November between 10.00 and 18.00.

There is a similar museum devoted to Walloon Belgium near St Hubert. See Route 36, Musée de la Vie Rurale en Wallonie.

There are references as early as 741 to *Kortessem*, which is 9km SE of Hasselt on the Tongeren road. Its Sint Pieterskerk dates in part from 1040.

13km **Bilzen** has a town hall dating from 1685. The attractive château of

Oude Biezen, 3km to the S, was founded in 1220 as a commandery of the Order of the Teutonic Knights. The Order continued in Belgium until 1798. The present building, which dates from the 16C and 17C, was badly damaged by fire in 1971. Later restored, it now serves as a Flemish cultural centre.

11km **Maastricht** is beyond the Albert Canal which marks the border with Holland. Built along the Maas, it is one of the oldest fortified towns in Holland. An attractive, lively, interesting place with picturesque streets and small, quaint squares, it has two magnificent churches. Extensive stretches of the town wall remain. Deep in the nearby Sint Pietersberg there are some caves, which merit a visit. For further information about Maastricht and its environs see 'Blue Guide Holland'.

21

Brussels to Liège

There are three routes from Brussels to Liege. One, by way of the N2, N3, N79 and N20, takes us through Louvain (Leuven in Flemish), Tienen, Zoutleeuw, Sint Truiden and Tongeren. Another, with many changes of road number, follows a more southerly course across a mainly French-speaking area. The A3/E40 motorway runs between these two routes, enabling the traveller to visit places on either.

A.   Via Louvain (Leuven), Tienen, Sint Truiden and Tongeren

Total distance 100km.—*23km* **Louvain (Leuven)**—*18km* **Tienen**—*14km* **Zoutleeuw**—*8km* **Sint Truiden**—*11km* **Borgloon**—*9km* **Tongeren**—*17km* **Liège (Luik)**.

In addition to the motorway, the A3, there are two roads from Brussels to Louvain. The N2 leaves **Brussels** by the Chaussée de Louvain and passes to the S of the national airport. A description of places near the airport—*Evere, Diegem, Zaventem* and *Steenokkerseel*—will be found in Routes 1F and 15B. Note that hothouse grapes from the district to the S around Duisburg are often on sale beside this road.

The other road takes us via **Tervuren**, which is described in Route 1G. About 6km from Tervuren and on the outskirts of Louvain is *Leefdaal*. Its château, rebuilt after 1626, retains the two pepperpot towers which flanked the drawbridge of its predecessor.

At *Vrone*, 1.5km NE of Leefdaal, there is a Romanesque chapel which probably dates in the main from the 12C. The choir and tower may be as old as 1000. At *Bertem*, a short distance farther on, there is an 11C church with a fortified tower.

At *23km* is **LOUVAIN**, population 85,000. The Tourist Information Office is in the Stadhuis.

Louvain is the English and French name for the ancient Flemish town of **Leuven**. Famous for its history, its architecture, especially the Sint Pieters-kerk and the Stadhuis, and its university, Louvain has long been a bastion of Flemish Catholicism.

History. According to a popular local tradition Louvain was founded on a camp established by Julius Caesar. However, the first written reference to the place is in a 9C chronicle. At that time the area was occupied by Norsemen. They were defeated at the end of the 9C by Arnold of Carinthia. He built a castle around which a town began to grow. The site of his building, with traces of its successors, is on the Keizersberg on the N edge of the town.

The first Count of Louvain was named Lambert. About the year 1000 he built a church on the site now occupied by Sint Pieterskerk. Count Henry II annexed the county of Brussels and in 1190 assumed the title of Duke of Brabant. Louvain then became the capital of this county. In the 13C, like other Flemish towns, it prospered through the growth of the cloth trade and the population increased to more than 50,000. The 14C, marked by conflicts between the nobles and the citizens, was a key period in Louvain's history. In 1338 Edward III of England, the ally of Jacob van Artevelde of Ghent, wintered in the castle outside the Mechelen gate. In 1356, when Wenceslas of Luxembourg acquired Brabant through marriage, he was obliged to sign the 'Joyeuse Entrée' declaration. Almost immediately this produced increasing bitterness between the citizens, who were favoured by the declaration, and the nobles. In 1360 the tribune Pieter Courtercel was master of the town for a short period. In 1379 the citizens threw seventeen nobles from the windows of the Stadhuis on to the guildsmen's pikes below. This savage act brought an equally savage response from Wenceslas, who favoured the nobles' cause. In 1383 the citizens were finally obliged to submit. As a result thousands of weavers emigrated to England, the prosperity of Louvain declined rapidly and, when the ducal residence was removed to Vilvoorde, Brussels became the principal town of Brabant.

Distinction returned in the next century with the foundation in 1425 of the university. This became a famous seat of learning, its theological faculty acquiring a particular distinction. During the following centuries the history of Louvain is largely the history of its university (see below).

In 1466 Quinten Metsys was born in Louvain. The young Charles V lived in the castle c 1507 where he was educated by Adrian Florisz, later Pope Adrian VI.

The Germans occupied Louvain on 19 August 1914. A Belgian counter-attack six days later reached Herent, 3km north-west. The Germans panicked and an outburst of firing degenerated into arson and massacre during which the famous university library and the Sint Pieterskerk were gutted. Two days later the civilian population was evacuated. When they returned, they found the town had been sacked and more than 1500 houses burnt down. There was similar destruction in the suburbs. During the Second World War the university library and the church were again damaged.

The **University** of Louvain was founded in 1425 by Pope Martin V and Duke John IV of Brabant. By the early 16C it had become one of the leading universities of Europe boasting more than 6000 students and 52 colleges.

With the help of a bequest from H. van Busleyden, Erasmus founded his 'Collegium Trilingue' here in 1517 for the study of Hebrew, Greek and Latin. However, his dream of offering a liberal Catholic education was shattered by the actions of Luther in Germany. The authorities took fright and strict orthodoxy was enforced. Erasmus went to Switzerland in 1521 and never returned to his native land.

Mercator learned his geography here, founding and running an institute of carto-graphy until hounded out of the country in 1544. The university was suppressed by the French in 1797. The foundation in its place of the 'Collège Philosophique' by William I of Holland in 1817 was bitterly resented by the Belgian clergy. In 1833 they established a Catholic university at Mechelen. Two years later this was transferred to Louvain.

Controversy has raged, particularly during the present century, about language, whether teaching should be in both Flemish and French. This was silenced briefly in 1962 by a statement from the Primate which affirmed again that Louvain would remain a Catholic university and that teaching would continue in both languages. However,

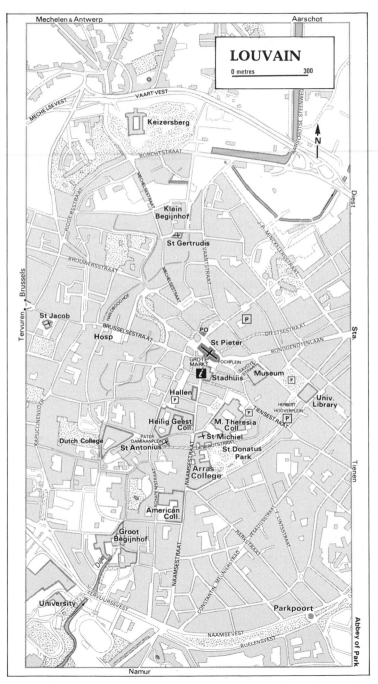

dispute and violence persisted and in 1970 the decision was taken to form a French-speaking university at Louvain-la-Neuve, 28km to the S (see Route 27).

Adrian Florisz, who became Pope Adrian VI, Bishop Jansenius and Justus Lipsius all taught here. Among the students during the 19C and 20C were Father Damien, Cardinal Mercier and Emile Verhaeren.

All the main roads into Louvain converge at the GROTE MARKT where the Sint Pieterskerk and the Stadhuis are located.

Before the present *Sint Pieterskerk there were two earlier Romanesque churches on this site. One built c 1000 was destroyed by lightning in 1176. The other was burned to the ground in 1373. The ancient crypt, filled in during the 15C, was revealed by bomb damage in 1944. The present late Gothic building was begun c 1425 by Sulpicius van der Vorst of Diest. After his death in 1439 it was continued by Jan Keldermans of Mechelen who completed the S aisle and part of the nave. In 1445 Mathys de Layens is believed to have built the central nave and N aisle. When the church was completed c 1497, the towers of the W façade were those of the earlier Romanesque church. These were pulled down and in 1507 work started on new Gothic towers to a grandiose design by Joos Metsys, the brother of Quinten. Sadly the foundations proved too weak and between 1612 and 1630 the unfinished towers were reduced to the level of the roof.

In 1914 most of the nave was burnt out, and in 1944 the choir suffered the bomb damage which exposed the ancient crypt.

The church may be visited daily from Tuesday to Saturday between 10.00 and 12.00 and 14.00 and 17.00, and on Sunday and holidays from Easter to September between 14.00 and 17.00.

The interior is lit by 90 windows with elaborate Flamboyant-style tracery. Perhaps the most striking feature in the nave is the elaborate *pulpit of 1742. The work of Jacques Bergé, it was originally at Ninove. Its subject is St Norbert falling from his horse after being struck by lightning. Note the intricate carving with representations of beavers, birds, a frog and a crowing rooster.

Also worthy of note are: the rood-loft of 1490; in the first S chapel the tomb of an Irish rector of the university, Dr Thomas Stapleton of Fethard, who died in 1694; in the S transept Joos Metsys' stone model for his ambitious W tower; and, in the baptistry, the crane of the font cover which is attributed to Quinten Metsys. In the choir there are a tall Gothic stone *tabernacle of 1450 by Mathys de Layens and a Renaissance screen of 1568 by Jan Veldener.

Many of the church's treasures have been placed in and near the ambulatory, which has been arranged as a museum of religious art. It should be noted that the position of objects in the museum may differ from that given below. From time to time some are removed for conservation or for inclusion in temporary exhibitions. Proceeding in an anticlockwise direction, we come first to:

First Chapel, dedicated to St Anthony. The *funerary monument of Duke Henry I of Brabant, Count of Louvain, is preserved here. Dated 1235, it is the oldest monument of its kind in Belgium. The laudatory inscription describes Duke Henry as an 'example of good morals, mirror of justice, avenger of the wicked, flower of our country, peace of the Church, shield of widows, hope of remission, crucible of fine mannners (and) protector of the poor.' His two wives Matilda, who bore him seven children, and Maria, who gave him two, are also commemorated. Matilda's tomb is in the Chapel of St Andrew, no. 15.

Second Chapel, dedicated to St Augustine. This once belonged to the

Guild of St Sebastian, the guild of archers. Note the 12C head of Christ.

Third Chapel, dedicated to St Aubert. It housed at one time a famous picture of the Descent from the Cross by Roger van der Weyden. This is now in the Escorial in Spain, but an old copy may be seen in Chapel 12. On the altar there is an Ecce Homo by Gerard Seghers.

Fifth Chapel, of the Virgin of Seven Sorrows. The triptych of 1593 of the Martyrdom of St Dorothea is by Joost van den Baeren.

Sixth Chapel, of the Holy Trinity. The funerary monument of the Crucifixion dates from 1520. This shows St Luke and St James with the donor, Jacques Bogaerts, professor of medicine, kneeling below.

Seventh Chapel, dedicated to St Ann. A triptych by Joost van den Baeren shows St Ivo, defender of the poor against unjust judges.

Eighth Chapel, is the Chapel of St Margaret or Blessed Margaret of Louvain. Sometimes called Proud Margaret, she was killed in 1225. A servant at an inn, Margaret witnessed the murder of her master and mistress by robbers, who abducted her. When she refused to marry one of her captors, she was slain and her body was thrown into the river. Much of her story is depicted on the shrine.

Ninth Chapel, of the Last Judgement, has a series of paintings by Pieter Verhagen, 1728–1811, about St Margaret. These show the murder; her body floating upstream in the river Dijle; her body recovered from the river; her remains being carried to St Pieterskerk; the faithful praying at her grave.

Tenth Chapel, dedicated to the Blessed Sacrament. Two paintings: Christ and the Disciples at Emmaus by Erasmus Quellin and the Martyrdom of St Ursula by Theodoor van Thulden, a pupil of Rubens.

Eleventh Chapel, of St Erasmus. A *triptych by Dirk Bouts, the Martyrdom of St Erasmus, an early bishop of Antioch and patron saint of mariners.

Twelth Chapel, of St Julian. A copy of 1463 of Roger van der Weyden's painting of the Descent from the Cross, now in the Escorial in Spain.

Thirteenth Chapel, dedicated to St Agatha. A *triptych of c 1464 of the Last Supper by Dirk Bouts. The Last Supper is depicted as taking place in a Gothic hall. The view through the window on the left may be of Louvain's Grote Markt in the 15C, with the Stadhuis under construction.

Fifteenth Chapel, of St Andrew. The tombs of Matilda of Flanders, wife of Duke Henry I of Brabant, and of their daughter Mary, wife of Emperor Otto IV of Germany are here.

The crypt, which may have been the burial place of the 12C Counts of Louvain, was an eastern extension of the early Romanesque churches. Filled in when the Gothic church was built in the 15C, it remained hidden until the bombing of 1944 revealed it. Vestments, reliquaries, church plate and religious sculpture are now displayed here. On the pillars there are some graffiti which may date from the 11C.

The ***Stadhuis**, a highly decorated Flamboyant Gothic structure by Mathys de Layens, was built between 1448 and 1463. It is one of Belgium's most important buildings from this period. The façade is almost as high as it is long. Three storeys of Gothic windows are surmounted by a steep roof of dormers and six graceful turrets. The bases of the niches between the windows are carved with biblical subjects of medieval grotesqueness and freedom. The 230 large and 52 small niches remained empty until the exterior of the building was restored between 1828 and 1850. Then 236 statues representing eminent citizens, artists, savants, royalty, nobility, religious personalities, municipal institutions, municipal privileges, virtues and vices were placed in them.

In the imposing and richly decorated interior there are sculptures and paintings by artists such as Constantin Meunier, Jef Lambeaux, P.J. Ver-haghen, Gaspard de Crayer and Antoon Sallaert .

Guided tours of the Stadhuis take place at the following times: Easter to September from Monday to Saturday between 11.00 and 15.00, on Sunday and public holidays at 15.00; October to Easter from Monday to Friday between 11.00 and 15.00.

A separate entrance leads to the cellars where there is a **Brewery Museum.** This is open from Tuesday to Saturday between 10.00 and 12.00 and from 14.00 to 17.00.

EAST OF THE GROTE MARKT. The fountain in the Fochplein to the E of the Sint Pieterskerk was given by the university to the town to commemorate 550 years of association, from 1425 to 1975, between town and gown. On the S a bank occupies a 1921 reconstruction of the **Tafelronde**, or Round Table, the 15C house of the guilds. A little farther to the E in Savoyestraat is the *****Museum Vanderkelen-Mertens**. This was built on the site of the Savoy College, founded in 1545 to house indigent students from Savoy in SE France. The portal dates from 1650, but the building is mainly an enlargement and restoration of the 17C and 18C. After the French Revolu-tion it became the mansion of the Vanderkelen-Mertens family. In 1918 they gave it to the town for use as a municipal museum. It has an interesting collection of paintings, sculpture in wood and stone, Gothic and Renais-sance furniture, metalwork, porcelain and tapestry.

Note that objects in the museum are moved to new positions from time to time.

Treasures not to be missed are a Descent from the Cross with Donors by an unknown artist of c 1567, a superb Mosan Sedes Sapientiae of the 11C or 12C, the Childhood and Passion of Christ by a painter of the Antwerp School of c 1520, the Holy Trinity by *Roger van der Weyden*, a Mourning over the Body of Christ by *Quinten Metsys*, a Madonna and Child by *van Cleef* and a Temptation of St Antony, reminiscent of Bosch, by *Jan Mandyn*.

The Ground Floor is taken up mainly by 15C and 16C religious works. Many of these, paintings and sculptures, are by unknown masters. Among the named artists are *Jan Rombouts*: the wing of a diptych, *Pieter Coecke, Jan van Rillaer, Michiel Coxie*: a triptych, and *Pieter Aertsen*: The Samari-tan Woman. Do not miss the circular calendar full of fascinating detail, the work of an unknown artist of c 1500.

Most of the Upper Floor is devoted to pictures of the 17C. They include *Michiel Mierevelt*: several portraits; *Frans Francken the Elder*: Ulysses and Achilles, *Frans Francken the Younger*: four versions of the Crucifixion; *David Vinckeboons*: Landscapes, an Allegorical Fight. *Benjamin Cuyp*: Riders resting; *Wolfgang de Smet*: Interior of the Sint Pieterskerk. *Cornelis de Vos*: Two side panels of a triptych. *P.J. Verhaghen*: several works including an Adoration of the Magi.

The museum is open from Tuesday to Saturday between 10.00 and 12.00 and from 14.00 to 17.00, also on Sunday and public holidays between Easter and September from 14.00 to 17.00.

From the museum we follow Tiensestraat in a SE direction to Herbert Hooverplein. At the farther end of the square is the **University Library**. This replaces the building destroyed by the Germans in 1914. In Flemish Renaissance style with a high, graceful belfry, it was designed by Whitney Warren, built largely with American aid and opened in July 1928. The tower is 85m high and the carillon commemorates American engineers who lost their lives in the First World War.

The former library, which was in the Hallen in Naamsestraat, had 500 manuscripts, 1000 incunabula, many of them produced at Louvain, and over 250,000 printed books. Theology figured prominently in the collection. A feature of the library was its collection of Irish MSS and literature. The Treaty of Versailles required Germany to make reparation by furnishing material of equal value to that destroyed. On the initiative of the John Rylands Library in Manchester large contributions of books were made by Britain. The United States also contributed handsomely. The names of institutions that helped are inscribed on the walls of the new library.

SOUTH OF THE GROTE MARKT. From the Grote Markt we follow Naamsestraat in a S direction, passing the Stadhuis on the left and a little farther on the *Hallen* on the right. The Hallen is a Gothic style building erected by the Clothworkers' Guild between 1317 and 1345. In 1619 it was given to the **University** which added a baroque upper storey to house its library.

Interior of Sint Michielskerk, 1650–66, Louvain

Largely destroyed in 1914, the Hallen was rebuilt and it now serves as the administrative centre of the university. The rear façade dates from 1723.

Farther along Naamsestraat is *Heilig Geest College* for diocesan clergy on the right. This was rebuilt after being damaged in an air raid in 1944. Almost opposite on the left is the **Sint Michielskerk**. This handsome Jesuit church was built by Father Willem Hessius between 1650 and 1666. Badly damaged in 1944 it was rebuilt between 1947 and 1950. Sint Michielskerk retains its splendid baroque façade and it has some outstanding 17–18C woodwork.

Behind the church, in Sint Michielsstraat, is the 18C *Maria Theresia College*, with the university assembly hall. Nearby is the *Pope's College* which takes its name from its founder, Pope Adrian VI.

S of Sint Michielskerk, we take De Beriotstraat E to *Sint Donatus Park*, where there are remains of the 12C to 15C ramparts. At the N corner of De Beriotstraat and Naamsestraat is *King's College*. Founded in 1579 by Philip II, the present buildings date from the 18C. On the S corner is the 18C building of the *Premonstratensian College* which was founded in the 16C by the abbeys of Parc, Ninove, Grimbergen and Averbode. Next to this is the 18C *Arras College*, which was founded in 1508 by a bishop of Arras. Note also the nearby 15C *Van 't Sestich Huis*. Opposite is the 16C *van Dale College*, now a school. On the W side of Naamsestraat at the corner of Karmelietenberg, is the *American College* of 1857. This occupies the site of the mid 16C refuge of the abbey of Aulne.

We descend Karmelietenberg to the **Groot Begijnhof*, which is sited beside the river Dijle. Founded in the 13C, it soon became one of the largest beguinages in Belgium. The present buildings were erected between the 14C and 18C. In 1961 the Groot Begijnhof was acquired by the university authorities. Beautifully restored, the greater part has been converted into a residential quarter for the university. The church was constructed in 1305, but the side aisles flanking the nave are of more recent date.

From the Begijnhof we take the Schapenstraat in a N direction to the Pater Damiaanplein. In the *Sint Antonius Kapel* is the grave of the missionary priest Joseph de Veuster better known as Father Damien, his name in religion. After years of caring for the outcast lepers of Molokai, Hawaii, Damian finally contracted leprosy and died from the disease in 1889. His body was brought here in 1936. The chapel is served by the community of Irish Franciscans in nearby St Anthony's College.

A short distance to the W is the 18C *Dutch College*. This is now a school. Bishop Jansenius was master here from 1618 to 1636. A tower dating from 1616 in the college garden was used by him as a retreat. It rests on remains of the 12C town walls.

WEST OF THE GROTE MARKT. From the Grote Markt take Brusselsestraat, where there are several interesting old houses, and cross over one of the arms of the river. No. 65, on the left, leads to a court and the brick buildings of the former Augustinian convent. The modern hospital next door preserves the 13C doorway of its ancient chapel and, alongside, a Renaissance portal. Opposite the hospital in the *Handbooghof*, a garden beside the Dijle, there are vestiges of the 12C town walls. Farther on, c 700m from the Grote Markt, is the *Sint Jacobskerk*. This church was erected between the 13C and 15C. The choir dates from the 18C. Outside the church stands a statue of Father Damien, by Constantin Meunier.

NORTH OF THE GROTE MARKT is the post office and the telephone building.

A short distance farther on join Mechelsestraat and continue in a N direction over the Dijle. Beyond the river, c 600m from the Grote Markt, is the **Sint Gertrudiskerk**. This was the church of an abbey, which was suppressed at the time of the French Revolution. The choir was built between 1298 and 1310, the nave between 1327 and 1380. Sint Gertrudiskerk was largely complete in 1453, when the 71m high spire, by Jan van Ruysbroeck, was erected. His work remained in place until the mid 19C, when because of structural weakness the spire had to be rebuilt. The 16C choir stalls, badly damaged in an air raid in 1944, were skilfully restored by Jan van Uitvanck. Note the interesting *misericords and the high reliefs of scenes from the Passion. The Sint Gertrudiskerk may be visited from June to September on Thursday, between 10.00 and 12.00 and from 14.00 to 17.00.

The **Klein Begijnhof** is a short distance N of the church. Originating as an infirmary c 1275, it continued to flourish until its suppression in 1796. Now it consists of a single street of 17C and 18C houses.

On the **Keizersberg**, which rises above the N end of Mechelsestraat, are the ruins of the castle of the dukes of Brabant and a modern Benedictine abbey.

At 108 Mechelsevest is the **Museum Humbeeck-Piron**. This is devoted mainly to the paintings of Pierre van Humbeeck and his wife Marie Piron. There are also displays of furniture, porcelain and pictures collected by the couple and of objects connected with various religious orders. The museum is open daily, except Tuesday, from 10.00 to 18.00.

ENVIRONS OF LOUVAIN. About 2km from the Grote Markt, beyond the Parkpoort to the SE of the town, is the Premonstratensian abbey of **Park**. Established in 1129 by Godefroy I of Brabant, it was closed by the French in 1797 when the Church was greatly oppressed by the invaders. In 1836, after Belgium had obtained its freedom, the monks returned to the abbey. It has flourished ever since.

The existing abbey buildings date mainly from the 17C and 18C. We enter through a gateway of 1722 and cross the farm court, a scene of rustic calm and order. The farm buildings were constructed in the late 17C. The church, which is basically 13C Romanesque, was refaced in the baroque style in 1729. It has some good paintings by Erasmus Quellin and Pierre Joseph Verhaghen. The E side of the cloister is 16C, the rest 17C. The ceilings of the baroque style library and refectory (usually open on Sundays at 16.00) were decorated by Jan Hansche between 1672 and 1679.

The château of **Arenberg** is S of the town in Heverlee, c 1.5km from the Grote Markt. Built in 1511 by Guillaume de Croy on the W bank of the Dijle, it has been much restored. The château and park were presented in 1921 by the Duke of Arenberg to the university. There are several scientific institutes in the park.

At Kessel-Lo, 3km to the NE of the Grote Markt, are the remains of the once-famous Benedictine abbey of Vlierbeek which was founded in 1125 and suppressed by the French in 1796. The abbot's lodging dates from 1675. The former abbey church now serves the parish. Designed by Laurent Dewez, it was erected between 1776 and 1783.

In the provincial demesne of Kessel-Lo there are pleasant walks and facilities for a variety of sporting activities.

At 18km is **Tienen**, in French **Tirlemont**, with a population of 33,000. The Tourist Information Office is at 4 Grote Markt.

Today this ancient town at the centre of a beet-growing district is, perhaps, best known for its production of sugar. The wrapped cubes produced in Tienen will be familiar to most travellers in Belgium. The sugar refinery, which was established in the 19C, is on the outskirts of the town to the right of the road to Liège.

The earliest evidence of human occupation dates from the late neolithic period, i.e. c 2500 BC. A decorated vase of the La Tène period, c 250 BC and many Gallo-Roman remains attest to the presence of later peoples. Tienen was awarded town status in 1194. In 1635 it was sacked by a joint French and Dutch force. The pillage, murder and rape continued for three days. More than 600 houses, the convents of the Carmelites and other religious orders, the town hall and the hospital were destroyed.

The ring road around the N of the town follows the course of the fourth and last fortifications, which were erected in the 16C and 17C.

The town's huge GROTE MARKT is second in size to that of Sint Niklaas in Waasland, the largest in Belgium. On the E side stands the *Onze Lieve Vrouw ten Poel Kerk*, Our Lady of the Pool. Built between 1345 and 1460, but with later additions, this church replaced a 13C chapel which was a famous place of pilgrimage. Many cures were claimed for a nearby miraculous spring. This dried up in the 18C. Among the architects connected with the construction of the church, which does not have a nave, were Sulpicius van der Vorst, Jan Keldermans and Mathys de Layens. The W portal of 1360, with small figures on the pedestals of the statueless niches, opens on to the transepts. The statue of Our Lady above the main door is a copy of the 1365 original by Walter Paris, which is now over the high altar.

On the S side of the Grote Markt is the *Stadhuis* of 1836. A stone star opposite marks the position of the pillory and guillotine. The *Gerechtshof* of 1846, on the N side of the square, occupies the site of the medieval cloth hall. In the NE corner there are two memorials. One, by Jef Lambeaux, is to the volunteers of 1830; the other commemorates those who lost their lives in Belgium's struggle for independence from the Dutch in 1830 and 1831 and during the two World Wars.

The *Museum Het Torentje* is also on the Grote Markt. Reached through the courtyard of the Gerechtshof, it has an interesting collection of Gallo-Roman coins, Romanesque fonts and medieval sculptures, one of which, a St Martin, may be from the studio of Jan Borman (fl. 1479 to 1520). It is open from Monday to Friday between 08.30 and 12.30 and from 13.30 to 17.00, also between Easter and Christmas on Saturday, Sunday and public holidays from 14.00 to 18.00.

Two streets, Peperstraat and the Wolmarkt, lead up the hill, the Celtic 'dunen', which some believe give Tienen its name. In the Wolmarkt there are several 17C houses which were built to replace those burned down in 1635. The *Sint Germanuskerk*, of 9C origin, was rebuilt several times. Parts of the choir, the W façade and the main tower date from the 12C. Further reconstruction was undertaken c 1535 by P. van Wijenhoven, architect to Charles V, and again a century later after the sack of the town by the French and Dutch. Note the 15C copper pelican lectern and some rather theatrical 16C and 17C sculptures in the SE chapel.

From the Wolmarkt we descend by the Grote Bergstraat to the site of the Begijnhof, most of which was destroyed by air raids in 1944. Only a few of the old houses remain.

At **Opheylissem**, 7km SE of Tienen on the Hannut road, the 18C buildings by Laurent Dewez of a Premonstratensian abbey are now used by the provincial government.

In the 14C to 16C church at **Oplinter**, 4km NE of Tienen, there is a polychrome statue of Christ which once belonged to a nearby Cistercian abbey. In the 19C the abbey was converted into a farm. Some of the original buildings survive.

We leave Tienen by the N3 and, continuing in an E direction, pass the sugar refinery on the right. Opposite, the Pastoriestraat leads to the cemetery chapel of *Sint Pieter, Grimde*, with its 11C tower and nave. This has been made into a mausoleum for 140 Belgian soldiers who fell near here on 18 August 1914.

About 800m along the N3 from the refinery, a short path on the right leads to three large c 2C *Gallo-Roman tumuli*.

At *3km* from Tienen is **Hakendover**. In the 13C to 16C church, with its Romanesque tower, there is an oak *retable of 1430. On this is depicted a legend about the building of the church. Some pious virgins attempted to raise a church near Tienen. However, they were dismayed to find that each day's work was pulled down during the night. Finally, angels told them in a vision to build the church near a hawthorn, a 'hagedoorn'. At this site the virgins were successful. They employed twelve workmen. The Saviour Himself helped as a thirteenth. Hence the dedication of the church is to the Salvator.

At *11km* a turning on the left leads to **Zoutleeuw** (French **Léau**). This small town with a population of 8000 is 4km N of the main road. At its most prosperous in the 13C and 14C, it later suffered a slow decline. Its economic eclipse came in the 18C, when it was bypassed by the main Brussels to Liège road.

Today Zoutleeuw is visited mainly for the sake of the wonderful **collection of religious art** in the **Sint Leonarduskerk** (mid April–October: daily except Tuesday, 14.00 to 17.00; apply 2 Markt). This was the only important Belgian church to escape the fury of the Calvinist iconoclasts of the 16C and the destruction and pillage of the French after the Revolution in the 18C. The tower, W front and apse date from the 13C, the nave from the 14C. During the 16C extensions were made to the chapels. The church's treasures—retables, triptychs, furniture and vestments—are all clearly described in English. Some of the vestments in the chapels are protected by curtains.

High up in the NAVE hangs a *Marianum, a representation of the Blessed Virgin in a garland of roses. Probably a Rhenish work, this is made of wrought and painted iron and dates from 1533. The only other other Marianum in Belgium is at Neeroeteren, near Maaseik.

In the CHOIR with its fine triforium there is a magnificent six-branched *candelabrum of 1483 by Renier van Thienen. It is surmounted by a Crucifix and statuettes of the Blessed Virgin, St John and St Mary Magdalene, remarkable for drapery, attitude and expression. The huge wooden cross of 1483 which hangs in the choir arch is by Willem van Goelen.

In the AMBULATORY there is a series of statuettes dating from the 12C to the 18C. These include a 12C Sedes Sapientiae and a 16C St Mary Magdalene. A Sedes Sapientiae is a statue of Our Lady, seated, and with the Child Jesus on her left knee. In her right hand she sometimes holds a staff. Usually made of wood, the statues were often clothed in richly embroidered garments or covered with silver or gold plates. Many date from 1000 or earlier.

NORTH TRANSEPT. The stone **tabernacle in the chapel of the Blessed Sacrament was made by Cornelis Floris between 1550 and 1552 for Marten van Wilre, lord of Oplinter. The spire, 18m high, is in seven tiers and has several groups of figures. Facing it is the tomb of van Wilre, who died in 1558, and of his wife, who died in 1554. This is also the work of Cornelis Floris. To the left of the altar the triptych, the Baptism of Christ, is probably by Frans Floris , the brother of Cornelis.

SOUTH TRANSEPT. The chapel, with murals of 1490 of the Last Judgement, is dedicated to St Leonard. It contains an altarpiece of 1478 by Arnold de Maeler depicting the life of the saint. A statue of St Leonard, painted and studded with precious stones, dates from c 1300.

The *Stadhuis* of 1539, built to plans by Rombout Keldermans, and the *Hallen* next door, built between 1316 and 1320, recall the town's early prosperity.

Neerwinden, 4km S of the N3, was the scene of two important battles. In 1693 the army of the Grand Alliance under William III of England was defeated here by Marshal Luxembourg. Patrick Sarsfield, Earl of Lucan, Jacobite and romantic Irish patriot, was mortally wounded at this battle. In 1793 the Austrians overcame the French under Dumouriez here.

Landen (population 14,000) is 3km to the SE of Neerwinden. Pepin the founder of the Carolingian dynasty died here in 640. Before being removed to Nivelles his body lay beneath a hill which still bears his name.

At 8km is **Sint Truiden** in French **Saint Trond**, with a population of 36,000. The Tourist Information Office is in the Stadhuis. This ancient town just in the province of Limburg is named after the Benedictine abbot St Trudo. Ordained by St Clodulphus of Metz, he founded and ruled an abbey c 660 on his father's estate. Sint Truiden is the principal town of the Haspengouw, in French the Hesbaye, district. The Pepin family, rulers of the Franks, from which the Carolingian dynasty sprang, originated here.

From the S side of the large GROTE MARKT there is a fine view of the towers of Sint Truiden's three principal buildings. From W to E they are the former Abbey, the Stadhuis and the Onze Lieve Vrouwekerk. The *Stadhuis* dates from the 18C, but the attached Spanish-style *Belfry* was erected in 1606, when its predecessor was blown down. It stands on a concealed 12C or 13C base. The *Perron*, at the foot of the belfry, dates from 1361. As Sint Truiden once belonged to the prince-bishops of Liège, it has the Flemish belfry and the Walloon perron, both symbols of liberty.

The first church on the site of the *Onze Lieve Vrouwekerk* was consecrated in 1058. This was destroyed by fire in 1186. The present church is a Gothic style building erected between the 14C and the 16C. The tower, which was repaired many times, collapsed in 1668. It was last rebuilt in 1854 by Louis Roelandt. In the church there is a reliquary of St Trudo.

The story of the *Abbey* is told in a delightful carving above its main entrance. Every time St Trudo built something it was pulled down by an interfering woman. In desperation the saint prayed for help. His prayer was answered. The woman was struck with paralysis. The abbey became one of the great houses of the Benedictine order. It suffered much at the time of the French Revolution, when its buildings were greatly damaged by the atheistic invaders. The 11C tower was given a new spire in the 18C. At its base is a gateway of 1655. The main gatehouse of 1779 provides access to the principal courtyard. The abbey is now a seminary.

Off the S side of the Grote Markt at 5 Naamsestraat is the *Museum Hedendaagse Kantwerken*; where modern lacework by the Ursuline Sisters is exhibited. The museum is open from Easter to September on Sunday and holidays between 10.00 and 12.00 and from 14.00 to 18.00. To the SE of the square is the neo-classical *Minderbroederskerk*, the Franciscan church. Built in 1731, the only support for its lofty roof is provided by 50 pillars. The *Sint Franciscusmuseum*, at 5 Minderbroedersstraat, contains collections of medieval statuary and a number of pictures. There is an etching by Rembrandt and paintings attributed to Rubens and Cranach. The museum is open from April to October on Tuesday and Wednesday from 14.00 to 18.00. It is advisable to make an appointment.

To the SE, by the junction of the roads to Tongeren and Liège, is the *Brustempoort*, the undercroft of a gateway of the 15C ramparts. This may be visited from Easter to September on Sunday and holidays from 13.30 to 17.30. Farther S, on Naamsesteenweg, is the *Sint Pieterskerk*. In this notable Romanesque building of the late 12C there is the tomb of Wirik, an abbot of c 1180.

The *Begijnhof* is on the NE edge of the town, beyond the large cattle market on the road to Hasselt. Founded in 1258, it remains a peaceful enclosure surrounded today by small houses of the 17C and 18C. In the centre there is a 13C church with murals dating from the 13C to the 17C. Visits may be made from April to October from Tuesday to Friday between 10.00 and 12.00 and from 13.30 to 17.00, and on Saturday and Sunday from 13.30 to 17.00.

In the *Festraets Studio* nearby there is a remarkable astronomical clock, the achievement of Kamile Festraets, 1904–1974. The studio may be visited between Easter and June, September and October on Sunday and holidays from 09.45 to 11.45 and 13.45 to 16.45. During July and August it is open daily at 10.45 and at 15.45.

At **Kortenbos**, 5km NE of Sint Truiden, the baroque style *Onze Lieve Vrouwebasiliek* is said to owe its origin to the plight of a wealthy widow. She owned some land which was being menaced constantly by a band of brigands. In 1636, as a deterrent, she placed a figure of the Blessed Virgin in a hollow oak that grew on her property. This act of faith seems to have been successful. By 1641 plans had been agreed to erect a church to take the place of the chapel which at that time sheltered the statue of Our Lady. Later additions have been made to this church, which was built between 1641 and c 1665. Inside there are some fine baroque furnishings and a number of paintings by Gaspard de Crayer and A. van Diepenbeek.

TO LIEGE DIRECT. At *2km Brustem* there is a large military airfield. In 1467 it was the scene of a victory by Charles the Bold during his campaign to suppress Liège.

At *10km* the border with the province of Liège is reached. Note that the town of *Waremme*, at 5km SW, is signposted Borgworm in Flemish. *Oreye* is the first French-speaking town. About 4km farther we cross the road from Tongeren to the river Meuse (the Maas in Flemish). This was an important Roman trade and military road. At *Othée*, 3km NE, John the Fearless crushed the citizens of Liège in 1408. On the N side of the road 13km farther on, just before the motorway crossing, are the ruins of **Fort Loncin**. A memorial commemorates a Belgian force under General Leman which made a brave stand here against the Germans in August 1914. General Leman was found unconscious beneath the ruins. In a chivalrous gesture his sword was returned to him by the commander of the German forces. Across the road a memorial commemorates a Royal Air Force crew who died here in July 1943. For *6km* **Liège**, see Route 34.

TO LIEGE VIA TONGEREN. This route is only 6km longer than the direct road. At *3km* **Zepperen** is the 15C *Sint Genovevakerk*. The tower is

Romanesque. The interior is decorated with some fascinating 15C *murals of the Last Supper and the lives of St Christopher and St Genevieve.

A mansion of 1655 near the church belonged to the provost of Sint Servaas at Maastricht in Holland, to whom this village was formerly subject.

At *2km Rijkel* there is a large château. This dates from c 1600 with some later additions.

6km **Borgloon**, Looz in French, is the centre of a fruit-growing area. It was the chief town of the county of Looz in the 11C, hence its French name. The old stocks, in which malefactors were punished, are kept at the entrance to the *Stadhuis* of 1680. The *Sint Odulfuskerk*, which dates in part from the 11C, has some interesting 15C murals. The tower is of 1406 and some neo-Romanesque additions were made to the nave in 1900. St Odulfus was a native of Brabant, who helped St Frederick with the evangelisation of Frisia. He died c 855. It is said that the relics of St Odulfus were stolen in 1034 and taken first to London and then to Evesham abbey.

In *Klooster Marienlof*, the Cistercian convent of *Kolen (Kerniel)*, 2km to the N, there is a reliquary of St Odile. According to an ancient tradition she was one of St Ursula's 11,000 virgins. Dating from 1292, it is among the oldest examples in Belgium of painting on wood. The reliquary was seriously damaged during the 19C by a carpenter who tried to force it into a niche. There are also a 12C Romanesque choir stall, some paintings by the 18C artist M. Aubé and 18C church furnishings. The convent may be visited from Monday to Friday between 10.00 and 11.30 and from 15.00 to 18.00.

At *9km* is **Tongeren** (French **Tongres**) with a population of 29,500. The Tourist Information Office is in the Stadhuis. Tracing its history back to pre-Roman times, Tongeren is the oldest town in Belgium. It preserves important remains from its past, particularly from the Roman period.

History. Tongeren, the capital of the Eburones and the Tungri, has been identified with the Atuatuca Tungrorum mentioned by Caesar. Ambiorix, a leader of the Eburones, defeated the Romans here in 54 BC. Circa AD 70 it was a walled Roman settlement on the road from Bavai to Cologne. Protected by fortifications 4.5km in length, parts of which survive, the settlement was larger in area than the modern town. After its destruction by the Franks c 300, a less extensive wall, 2.7km in length, was built. Of this only the foundations of a tower remain. Tongeren was the site of the first bishopric to be established in Belgium. It was set up by St Maternus of Cologne. However the first bishop, St Servatius, moved to Maastricht in 382. Servatius gave refuge to St Athanasius when the latter was an exile in the West. In 720 St Hubert moved the see to Liège. Tongeren was ravaged by the Norsemen in the 9C, but became a prosperous dependency of the prince-bishops of Liège during the Middle Ages. A third protective wall was constructed during the 13C and 14C. In 1486, moved by the eloquent pleading of the Sire de Humbercourt, the town was spared by Charles the Bold. Two centuries later it was not so fortunate. In 1677 the greater part of Tongeren was burned to the ground by the soldiers of Louis XIV. It did not begin to recover until after the establishment of Belgium as a separate state in 1831.

On the SE side of the GROTE MARKT is the *Stadhuis*, which was built between 1737 and 1754. In addition to the Tourist Information Office this houses the *Stedelijk Museum*. The museum has a large collection of old prints, paintings, statuary and documents about the history of Tongeren. There is a fine 14C Pietà. A multivision display is included in the entrance fee. The museum is open from 10.00 to 12.00 and from 14.00 to 16.00.

Just to the E of the Stadhuis are the foundations and lower courses of a 4C *Roman rampart tower*, all that is left of the second, shorter wall. Enquire at the Tourist Information Office about entry to the excavation.

Also in the square is an 18C statue of Ambiorix, the Eburones leader, who defeated the Romans in 54 BC.

The *Onze Lieve Vrouwebasiliek*, founded c 350, claims to be the first church N of the Alps to be dedicated to Our Lady. A little of the 11C and 12C building survives, but the nave and S transept of the present Gothic style church date from 1240 and the remainder was constructed between the 14C and 16C. In the N portal of 1532 there are a few traces of the 13C building.

In the choir there are four stained-glass windows of 1550 and a 16C elaborately carved retable, with scenes from the life of Our Lady. Note also a paschal candlestick of 1372, a lectern of 1375 and four candelabra of 1392. All are the work of Jehans Josès of Dinant.

In the N transept there is a walnut statue of Our Lady of Tongeren dated 1479. In the first chapel in the N aisle there is a 15C Man of Sorrows and in the last a Pietà of 1400. Do not miss the curious antique alms box made from a tree stump and the Madonna and Child of 1280 in the NW porch. The organ dates from 1753. Below the loft there is a brass gate of 1711 by Christian Schwertfeger. In the W chapel of the S aisle there is a 16C altar. The fifth chapel is dedicated to St Lutgart. A pious lady born in Tongeren in 1182, she was a Black Bendictine nun for a number of years. As she did not wish to be appointed abbess, she moved to a Cistercian convent. Outstanding among the women mystics of the Middle Ages, St Lutgart was blind for the last eleven years of her life.

At the E end of the S aisle, in a vestibule, there is a *Crucifix which is believed to date from the 11C. The vestibule provides access to the treasury and the *cloister. In the cloister there are three walks. One is surrounded by small columns each crowned with a different capital. This dates from the 12C. The other two were added during the 13C and 14C. The lintel of the garden doorway is late 11C. The two Gothic chapels date from the 15C.

The **treasury is one of the richest in Belgium. It has a number of reliquaries dating from the 10C to the 13C. Do not miss the following: a mid 12C *triptych-reliquary of the Holy Cross; a *10C evangelistary with a 14C cover embodying an 11C ivory plaque; a 14C monstrance-reliquary of St Ursula; a 12C or 13C portable altar of porphyry; an 11C Head of Christ.

The treasury may be visited daily between May and September from 09.00 to 12.00 and from 14.00 to 17.00.

The *Gallo-Roman Museum*, to the E of the basilica, is closed. It is due to reopen in 1993. In the museum there is an interesting collection of artefacts, most of which come from Tongres and the surrounding area. They date from the neolithic period to the centuries of Roman occupation. There are fine displays of Roman coins and glass and a copy of the Tabula Peutingeriana. This road map of the Roman world from Britain to India in the second half of the 4C was copied in the 13C.

In the SE of the town, 500m from the Grote Markt, is the *Moerenpoort* of 1379, one of the medieval gates. The small museum of local military history in the gate is open from May to September on Saturday, Sunday and public holidays from 10.00 to 16.00. On either side of the gate there are stretches of the 13C ramparts. The section to the N along Leopoldwal is on a 2C Roman base. There is another length of the medieval wall on the N edge of the town. In the *Begijnhof*, to W of the Moerenpoort, there are some small 17C and 18C houses. There is also a church of 1294 which was altered during the 16C.

On the NW outskirts of the town beyond the ring road, a section of 1C and 2C Roman wall crosses the Hasseltsesteenweg along the line of

Legionenlaan. There is another section farther to the SW on the approach to the *Beukenberg*, a raised walk between beech trees. Nearby is the 17C château of *Betho*. This has a 13C keep. To the NW of the château is the *Pliniusbron*, a medicinal spring known to Pliny.

For *17km* **Liège**, see Route 34.

B.   Via Louvain, Jodoigne and Hannut

Total distance 105km.—*23km* **Louvain** (**Leuven**)—*26km* **Jodoigne**—*8km* **Jauche**—*10km* **Hannut**—*38km* **Liège**.

For **Brussels**, Route 1, to *23km* **Louvain** (**Leuven**) see above.

We leave Louvain by the N25, the Namur road. This crosses the motorway before traversing the forest of Meerdaal. At *12km* Hamme-Mille is in French-speaking Brabant. After skirting the S side of the airfield of Beauvechain, the N91 continues S to Namur. Our Route takes us E along the N240. *Gobertange*, just N of the road, gives its name to the white stone used in many local buildings and in the town halls of Brussels and Louvain and the cathedral in Brussels.

At *14km* is **Jodoigne** (Flemish **Geldenaken**). This was an important trading centre in Roman times, when it was known as Geldonia. In the Middle Ages it was a fortress which controlled the road to Louvain and consequently was attacked frequently. The funnel-shaped Grand-Place was deliberately designed for defensive purposes. The *Hôtel de Ville*, on the site of the 13C cornmarket, dates from 1733. The *Chapelle Notre-Dame du Marché* is from the 14C.

The mixed Romanesque and Gothic *Eglise Saint Médard* is dedicated to a Frankish nobleman who lived between c 470 and c 568 and was Bishop of Tournai. Like St Swithin his name was connected with the weather. He was also invoked by sufferers from toothache in search of relief from their pain. The church of St Médard is the oldest building in Jodoigne. It was built in the 12C on the site of a 7C chapel. Burned down in 1568 and 1578 by the soldiers of William of Orange, it was restored in 1606. It was converted into a Temple of Reason at the time of the French Revolution, but was returned to the church authorities in 1802. It has a chalice, part of which is attributed to Hugo d'Oignies, a painting of the Virgin and Child by Cornelis Schut and a triptych ascribed to Otto Venius.

Just S of *Glimes*, 6km from Jodoigne, is one of the largest tumuli in Belgium. This is 12m high and 50m in diameter.

At *8km* is Jauche. In the village of **Orp-le-Grand**, c 4km to the NE, there is a Romanesque church which dates mainly from the end of the 12C. This was much damaged by fires in 1356, 1485 and 1637. Damage resulting from a German attack in 1940 revealed the foundations of two older churches and a large crypt. The earliest church on the site has been dated to the 8C or 9C. At Orp-le-Grand there is also a small museum in the Maison Communale. This has a collection of jewellery and weapons from the neolithic period to Merovingian times. It is open on Monday, Tuesday, Thursday and Friday from 13.00 to 1700, and on Wednesday until 16.00.

At *Folx-les-Caves*, 3km S of Jauche, there are underground quarries which may date back to Roman or even earlier times. Some may be visited. A number are used for growing mushrooms.

At the village of **Ramillies**, 3km farther S, the allies under Marlborough defeated a French army commanded by Villeroi on Whitsunday 1706.

The forces were evenly matched. The French, facing NE, occupied a line through Autréglise-Offus-Ramillies-Francqnée-Taviers. Their flanks were protected by small, marshy streams. Marlborough made a feint against the French left, then concentrated his attack against Ramillies, while his Dutch troops attacked Francqnée and Taviers. Both attacks were successful, though Marlborough himself was unhorsed. The French retired in disorder on Louvain. The Allied casualties, mainly Dutch, were some 5000 while the French lost 15,000.

At *10km* is **Hannut**, population 11,000, in the province of Liège. The church has a large, very striking 14C statue of St Christopher.

14km Waremme (Flemish *Borgworm*) is the centre of a sugar-beet district. The road crosses the old Roman way from Tongeren to the Meuse, now the N614. Having skirted the N side of Liège's airfield of *Bierset*, which offers air tours of Liège and Walloon Brabant, it passes over the E42 motorway.

For *24km* **Liège**, see Route 34.

SOUTH BELGIUM

Provinces of Hainaut, southern Brabant, Namur, Liège and Luxembourg

Apart from the small German-speaking district of the Cantons de l'Est, South Belgium is French or Walloon Belgium. The language of the people, whose origins go back to the Wala, the Romanised Celts, is French. Although it may have fewer fine buildings than the North, South Belgium is not without its interesting towns and fine landscapes. Visitors go there to explore the forests and heathland of the Ardennes and to visit the picturesque castles and great abbeys, both ruined and flourishing, which abound.

South Belgium may be divided roughly into two parts: the provinces of Hainaut and S Brabant in the NW, and the Ardennes, which spread across the other three provinces, in the S and E.

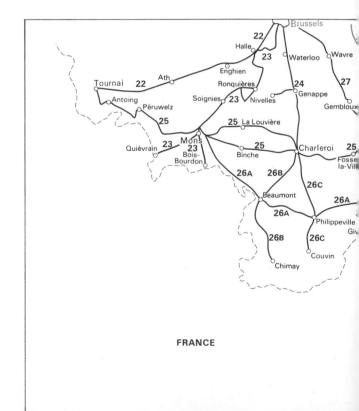

Hainaut and southern Brabant

A large part of the provinces of Hainaut and S Brabant is taken up by a rolling, placid, fertile landscape which is devoted to agriculture. Around Mons and Charleroi there are mining and industrial districts. The BOTTE DU HAINAUT, to the S of Chimay, is a sparsely populated, wooded enclave of great charm.

One of the most interesting towns in **Hainaut** is *Tournai*, a Roman staging post and later capital of the Franks. Its magnificent Romanesque and early Gothic cathedral is one of the finest in Belgium. *Mons* and *Soignies* have many reminders of the First World War. In *Charleroi*, a centre of mining and industry, there is an unusual and beautiful museum of glass and an outstanding municipal art gallery. Hainaut is crossed by an important canal system which links Charleroi and Brussels. The great Sloping Lock at *Ronquières*, to the NW of Nivelles, attracts many visitors.

The province of **Brabant** is made up of Flemish N Brabant, the city of Brussels and S Brabant. With *Nivelles* as its principal town, S Brabant is sometimes known as the 'Roman Pays'. The main objective for many visitors to the province will be the battlefield of *Waterloo* and places such as *Quatre-Bras* and *Ligny*, which is just in Namur, where some of the preliminary fighting took place. Waterloo is described at the end of Route 1; the preliminary battles in Route 24.

The Ardennes

The **Ardennes**, known to the Romans as Arduenna Silva, are still called the Forest of the Ardennes. Covering much of the provinces of Namur, Liège, and Luxembourg, they stretch S from the Meuse between Namur and Liège and E of that city and extend into Germany, the Grand-Duchy of Luxembourg and France.

Apart from the German-speaking Cantons de l'Est, the region is inhabited by the true Walloons who have given their name to the whole of French-speaking Belgium. The area is made up of forest, heath and cultivated, wooded upland divided by steep, winding and generally narrow valleys. Apart from the extensive forests, it is these valleys that provide most of the scenic attractions. Those who confine their visits to the upland areas may well be disappointed. Walking is a popular activity in the Ardennes. Most towns provide special guidebooks and maps which describe signposted tracks to local places of interest.

Several touring areas are suggested below. These have been selected largely, though not entirely, on scenic grounds.

The best part of the MEUSE VALLEY is between *Namur, Dinant* and the French frontier. In summer it is possible to travel the whole of this stretch by boat. There are also boat excursions down the Lesse from Dinant.

Between Namur and Liège the valley is partly industrialised and the scenery is not particularly outstanding. However, *Liège*, a historic and lively city with interesting museums and art galleries, merits a visit. *Namur* and *Huy* are also attractive towns.

The German-speaking CANTONS DE L'EST, *Eupen, Malmédy*, and *St Vith*, are mainly a region of high forests, moors, lakes and reservoirs above large dams. In the Hautes Fagnes the *Signal de Botrange* at 694m is the highest place in Belgium.

The winding OURTHE VALLEY can be followed from Liège to *La Roche*, a beautifully situated small town in the heart of the Ardennes. From here Route 36A, after traversing an area of forest, descends from *Bertrix* to the Semois.

The deep, wooded SEMOIS VALLEY follows a sinuous course along the French frontier. There are particularly beautiful stretches on either side of the historic fortress of *Bouillon* and farther E near *Florenville*.

Another popular centre is HAN-SUR-LESSE, surrounded by forests and famous for its grottoes.

Grottoes. There are many grottoes in the Ardennes. Evidence of occupation in prehistoric times has been found in several. A number may be visited. The largest and most popular is at *Han-sur-Lesse*. *Remouchamps* also attracts many visitors. Underground boat trips may be made in both of these grottoes.

There are other grottoes at *Goyet*, where an attempt has been made to illustrate, with imaginative displays, the life of prehistoric man, and at *Rochefort* and *Dinant*.

Legends. The legendary **Quatre Fils Aymon** were associated with several Ardennes castles. Renaud, Guichard, Alard and Richard were the sons of Aymon of Dordogne, a vassal of Charlemagne. The emperor knighted the brothers and gave them the fabulous horse Bayard. On his back all four could ride at the same time. Later they lost the emperor's favour and were outlawed. The romantic adventures and perilous feats of the subsequent pursuit by the emperor are chronicled in a 13C poem, one of the most popular romances of the Charlemagne cycle. William Caxton printed 'The Foure Sonnes of Aymon' and Renaud, as Rinaldo, and the others figure also in the poems of Tasso, Boiardo and Ariosto.

The **Wild Boar of the Ardennes**. This was the name given to the nobleman William de la Marck, who lived from 1446 to 1485. Banished from Liège for murdering the bishop's secretary, he became a robber baron and established strongholds at a number of places including Amblève, Franchimont, Aigremont and Logne. In 1482 he captured Liège and murdered the bishop. That led to his undoing. The new bishop invited him to a feast, seized him and had him executed.

The **Battle of the Ardennes**, popularly known as the Battle of the Bulge, took place at the end of 1944 and the beginning of 1945. This counter-offensive, Hitler's last fling, was commanded by von Rundstedt. It was aimed at the weak Allied centre, which had resulted from the decision to strike at Germany from Aachen in the N and Alsace in the S. In this central area, which ran along the German border from Monschau to Wasserbillig, the American 8th Corps was holding a front of 120km. Hitler planned to break through here, split the Allied front, and seize Antwerp. The Germans attacked on 16 December. By 25 December the 'bulge' had been formed. Isolated within it was the important crossroads of *Bastogne*, to which the 101st Airborne Division had been sent. However American and British reinforcements soon reached the Ardennes. On 23 December there was a major Allied air offensive against the German lines of supply and during the last week of the month, in snow and bitter weather, Patton's counter-attack, launched from Arlon, was approaching Bastogne. On 3 January Montgomery started his offensive from the N. The two counter-attacks met at *Houffalize* on 16 January and by the end of January the Germans were back behind the frontier, having lost 120,000 men.

22

Tournai to Brussels

Total distance 75km.—**Tournai**—*16km Leuze* (for **Beloeil**)—*12km* **Ath** (for **Chièvres** and **Cambron-Casteau**)—*7km Ghislenghien* (for **Lessines**)—*12km* **Enghien**—*14km* **Halle**—*14km* **Brussels**.

TOURNAI (Flemish name **Doornik**) has a population of 67,000. The Tourist Information Office is at 14 Vieux Marché aux Poteries near the Belfry.

This ancient town on the Escaut, the Scheldt, has a long and colourful history. Its cathedral is generally regarded as being the finest in Belgium. It has many interesting monuments, several museums and an excellent gallery of paintings. The main part of the town is on the W bank of the river. This is encircled by boulevards constructed in the mid 19C, which follow the line of the 13C ramparts. Sections of these fortifications are still visible. Tournai has long been known for the quality of its sculptures, tapestries, gilt bronzes and porcelain.

History. The Roman settlement of Tornacum was a staging post on the road from Boulogne to Cologne. Its inhabitants were converted to Christianity by St Piat or Piaton of Benevento in S Italy, who was sent by the pope to evangelise the areas around Tournai and Chartres. It is believed that Piat was martyred c 286 at Tournai during the persecutions of Maximian.

By the end of the 4C Tournai had become a Frankish royal city. Clovis may have been born here in 465 and Childeric I almost certainly died here in 481. About 486 St Eleutherius, who was from Tournai, was appointed bishop. He built the town's first church c 501. In 532 Eleutherius was beaten to death in front of this church by a local mob of fanatical Arian heretics.

After belonging in turn to the counts of Flanders and Hainaut, Tournai came into the hands of the French kings in 1187. It remained faithful to them during the Hundred Years War. In 1340 the town withstood a siege by Edward III of England. This was raised after a treaty between Edward and Philip VI of France was signed at Esplechin,

6km to the SW. In 1513 Henry VIII of England captured Tournai during his war against France. He gave the bishopric to Cardinal Wolsey. However, it was sold back to the French five years later, largely at the instigation of Wolsey, who hoped to gain favour with the French through this action. In 1521, after a siege lasting a month, the town was taken by the army of Charles V and became a part of the Spanish Netherlands.

In 1581, in an effort to throw off the Spanish yoke, Tournai was bravely, but unsuccessfully, defended against the Duke of Parma by the wife of the governor, Christine de Lalaing, Princess of Epinoy. It was captured in 1667 by Louis XIV and fortified by Vauban. During the War of the Spanish Succession it was retaken by allied forces under the command of Marlborough in 1709. In 1713 under the terms of the Treaty of Utrecht Tournai was ceded to Austria. Apart for three years after the defeat of the English at the Battle of Fontenoy in 1745, it remained under Austrian rule until the French conquests of 1792 to 1794.

During the First World War Tournai suffered some damage. In November 1918 the retreating Germans blew up the bridges. In May 1940, the town while crowded with refugees, was subjected to vicious air bombardment by the Germans. Most of the old houses in the Grand-Place were destroyed. In September 1944 Tournai was liberated by British troops. It was the first Belgian town to be freed.

The painters Robert Campin, sometimes known as the Master of Flémalle, and Roger van der Weyden were natives of Tournai as were Piat Sauvage and Louis Gallait in more recent times.

Perkin Warbeck was born here c 1474. The son of a Tournai official, he was persuaded by the Yorkist faction to impersonate Richard, Duke of York, the son of Edward IV and the younger of the two princes murdered in the Tower. Landing in Cornwall in 1497, he was proclaimed king and called himself Richard IV. However, the rebellion fizzled out and this youthful pretender to the English throne surrendered to Henry VII on promise of a royal pardon. He was imprisoned. Later charged with attempting to escape, he was executed in the Tower in 1499.

Gabrielle Petit, the First World War heroine, was born in Tournai in 1893.

The slate-coloured **Tournai marble** has been used since Roman times for both building and carving. In the 14C and 15C the sculptors of Tournai were widely celebrated. Fonts of Tournai marble are to be found in many English churches. The cathedral of Pamplona in Spain possesses a fine monument by a Tournai artist. In Tournai itself much of the work of its sculptors was mutilated by Calvinist fanatics in the 16C and by the irreligious French revolutionaries of the late 18C. However, there are some examples in the cathedral.

The ****Cathédrale de Notre-Dame** is open daily between Easter and the end of October from 10.00 to 13.00 and from 14.00 to 18.00; between November and Easter it closes at 16.30.

Adjudged by many to be the finest cathedral in Belgium, it is a notable example of the development of Romanesque and Early Gothic architecture. Probably the best view of the exterior is from the small square below the N transept, the Place Paul Emile Janson, named after a Tournai deputy who perished in Buchenwald in 1944. In the square there is a sculpture group of 1908, 'The Blind', by G. Charlier.

The church built here c 501 by St Eleutherius was replaced during the 9C by a Carolingian basilica. This was badly damaged by Norse raiders in 881. The present building was consecrated in 1175. The oldest part is the great Romanesque nave. This was probably completed by 1150. The apsed and aisled transepts, the most original feature of the cathedral, were constructed mainly between 1150 and 1171. Apparently they were not completed until 1200, when the vault was built by Bishop Etienne. Between 1245 and 1255 Bishop Walter de Marvis, a great church-builder, reconstructed the choir in a purely N French style. Much damage was done to the interior by bands of Protestant iconoclasts in 1566 and by French revolutionaries in 1797. The upper part of the Gothic W front was made 'Romanesque' in the 19C.

The cathedral's most distinctive external feature is its five towers, 'les chongs clotiers' in the local patois. The oldest, 80m high, is in the centre. The two on the E are 12C Romanesque, the NW tower, which housed the chapter prison, is 12C to 13C Transitional and the SW tower is 13C Gothic. The great bell of the bishop, the Marie-Gasparine sometimes called the Marie-Pontoise, which weighs 8000 kilos and was cast in 1842, is housed in the SE tower. Of the other four bells, the oldest is called Marc. This was cast in 1617 and weighs 250 kilos. The pyramidal spires were added during the 16C.

The N door, the Porte Mantile, is named after one Mantilius who was cured of blindness by St Eleutherius. The *carvings around the door depict the Virtues and the Vices. While Virtue struggles with Vice, Avarice, weighed down by his purse, is carried off by the Devil. Though badly mutilated, these are the most important 12C Romanesque decorative sculptures in Belgium.

The W façade, which was rebuilt in the 13C, is preceded by a 14C portico. In the upper part a fake Romanesque rose window was altered in the 19C. The sculptures are of considerable interest. In the lowest row, which dates from the 14C, there are figures of Adam and Eve, the prophets and the early fathers of the church. Above them are 16C reliefs showing the history of the see of Tournai. At the top, 17C figures of apostles and saints flank a 14C statue of Notre-Dame des Malades. The head of Our Lady and of the Child were restored in 1609.

By the W façade the cathedral is connected with the *Evèché*, the Bishop's Palace, by an archway called the *Fausse Porte*. Its vaulting dates from 1189. This is some of the earliest Gothic style work in Belgium. It houses a small chapel dedicated to St Vincent. The palace, rebuilt after being destroyed by fire in 1940, has Romanesque cellars and a slender turret of 1643. It occupies the site of the Merovingian royal residence.

The cathedral is 134m long and 66m wide. It occupies an area of 5120 sq m. The length of the NAVE is the same as that of the choir. The height of the nave, vaulted with brick of 1774, is 22m. The triforium is almost equal in height to the main arcade. Above are a smaller gallery and a plain clerestory.

The intricately carved capitals, which were once painted in glowing colours, deserve close scrutiny. The sculptors drew their inspiration from illuminated manuscripts, local flora, oriental tapestries, Byzantine ivories and pictures of fabulous beasts.

The pulpit of 1740 is ornamented with statues of Faith, Hope and Charity by François Gillis, founder of Tournai's academy of design.

Off the S aisle is the Chapelle Saint Louis of 1299, which was built to commemorate a visit to Tournai in 1257 by St Louis IX, king of France. In it there are restored stained-glass windows containing 14C and 15C fragments, and a Crucifixion by Jordaens. Off the S triforium, which is sometimes used for special exhibitions, there is a chapel with 13C wallpaintings depicting the Legend of St Catherine and the Crucifixion.

The TRANSEPTS. The 16C stained glass in the principal window of the S transept is by Arnoult de Nimègue. This depicts a number of events which had a considerable effect on the history of Tournai. The lower panels record the shadowy period between c 570 and 615. This was the unsettled, anxious time, which followed the death of Clotaire, the successor of Clovis. The Frankish realm was divided between Clotaire's sons. Sigebert received Austrasia in the E, Chilpéric got Neustria, which had its capital at Soissons. Tournai belonged to Neustria. The brothers married Brunehaut and Galswinthe, the daughters of the king of the Visigoths. Shortly after her arrival at court Galswinthe was murdered by Chilpéric's mistress, Frédégonde. Determined to avenge her sister, Brunehaut urged her husband Sigebert to go to war (first panel). He won (second panel). Chilpéric fled to Tournai (third panel). But Frédégonde would not accept defeat and armed his soldiers with poisoned daggers (fourth panel). With this they murdered Sigebert, (fifth panel). The victor, Chilpéric, conferred temporal powers, symbolised by a key, on the bishops of Tournai (sixth panel). As a result the magistracy had to swear loyalty annually (seventh panel).

The upper part of the window continues the story by illustrating how the bishops made use of their newly acquired powers. One panel makes it clear that a tax was levied on every head of cattle which crossed the river. Taxes on wine and beer, weights and measures are shown on other panels.

In the N transept the late 12C or early 13C *murals are generally accepted as being the most important Romanesque wallpaintings still existing in Belgium. They tell the story of St Margaret, a shepherdess of Antioch in Pisidia, who was martyred under Diocletian. On confessing her faith to the local governor, she was whipped. Refusing to sacrifice to the gods, she was tortured and beheaded. An angel then carried her head away. Note the glorious blue used in some of the paintings. The red Lancastrian rose in the fourth picture was inserted by order of Henry VIII of England c 1513. A Calvary takes the place of the throne, which Henry had placed in this transept for his personal use while hearing Mass.

The great rood-screen of 1572 in front of the CHOIR is a Renaissance work by Cornelis Floris. The daringly slender piers in the choir, which took their inspiration from Soissons, have had to be doubled in thickness, except in the apse. The high altar of 1727 was brought from the abbey church of St Martin at Tournai in 1804.

AMBULATORY. The ambulatory chapels on the N side contain a number of 15C Tournai memorial sculptures. Some of these were brought from other churches. Many were mutilated by the French at the time of the Revolution. Behind the high altar there is a composite monument to the bishops of Tournai. This bears the effigy of Bishop Villain de Gand, who died in 1644, and attractive sculptures from other 17C tombs. Note the painted walls, pillars and roof in this part of the ambulatory.

In the S ambulatory are a Raising of Lazarus by Pieter Pourbus and Our Lady of the Seven Sorrows by Wenceslas Coeberger. In a chapel of c 1300 hangs a picture of the Souls in Purgatory by Rubens. The stained-glass here dates from 1526 and was originally in the great W window.

In the *TREASURY there are many objects of interest. These include an 9C ivory diptych of St Nicasius, a 13C ivory Madonna, a 6C or 7C Byzantine cross-reliquary lavishly decorated with gems and pearls, a mid 13C reliquary of St Eleutherius, an Arras tapestry of 1402 depicting the stories of St Eleutherius and St Piat, 16C Brussels and Tournai tapestries, 12C, 13C and 14C psalters, a 13C missal, a chasuble worn by St Thomas à Becket shortly before his martyrdom, and a cope made from a mantle worn by Charles V at the 20th chapter of the Order of the Golden Fleece.

In the GRAND-PLACE there is a statue of 1863 of the heroic Christine de Lalaing. The **Halle aux Draps**, on the S side of the square, was originally a Renaissance building of 1611 by Quentin Rate. This was rebuilt after its destruction in 1940.

At the SE end of the square is the oldest **Belfry** in Belgium. A detached tower 72m high, it was constructed between 1200 and 1294. The carillon

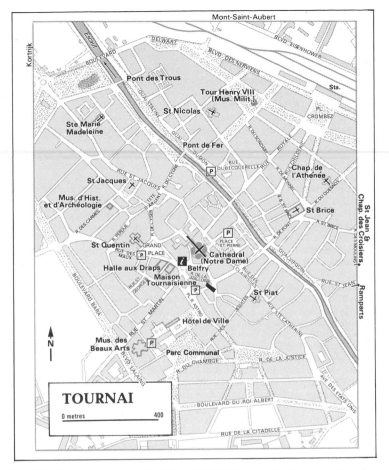

TOURNAI

0 metres   400

has 43 bells, cast between the 16C and 19C. It is open daily, except Tuesday, 10.00 to 12.00 and 14.00 to 17.30; closed 11 November, 25 December and 1 January.

The **Eglise Saint Quentin**, on the W side of the Grand-Place, dates from c 1200. The choir was extended in 1464. There were churches on this site as far back as the 7C. The interior is unusual as it has a transept composed of two round chapels. It houses the tomb of Jacques Kastangnes, a provost of Tournai who died in 1327. Just S of the church, 10 Rue des Maux, which dates from 1633, was the tithe barn of the abbey, a part of whose site is now occupied by the Hôtel de Ville (see below).

Follow the Reduit des Sions along the side of the Halle aux Draps to the Maison Tournaisienne with its fine façade of 1677. This is now the home of the **Musée de Folklore**, which has an interesting collection illustrating old Tournai trades and typical interiors. There is also some good 18C and 19C porcelain from the area. It is open daily, except Tuesday, 10.00 to 12.00 and 14.00 to 17.30; closed 11 November, 25 December and 1 January.

Close to the Grand-Place there are four towers which formed part of the first defensive walls erected in the 11C and 12C. These are in a cul-de-sac off the Rue du Cygne, in the Rue Perdue to the NW, in the Rue Saint Georges to the SW and off the Place Reine Astrid to the SE. The towers in the Rue Perdue and the Rue Saint Georges are the nearest to the Grand-Place.

NORTH AND WEST OF THE GRAND-PLACE. Leave the Grand-Place at its N corner and take the Rue de l'Yser, Rue Tête d'Argent and the Rue du Cygne down to the river. Note the defensive tower on the right which is referred to above. About 400m downstream is the **Pont des Trous**, a 13C bridge of three arches guarded by towers. This formed part of the 13C ramparts. River trips leave from the nearby jetty.

From the Pont des Trous take the Rue des Foulons to the *Eglise Sainte Marie Madeleine*, which was built by Bishop Marvis in 1252. This has a sculptured Annunciation of 1482 by Jean de la Mer with polychrome painting by Robert Campin.

About 300m farther to the SE is the *Eglise Saint Jacques*. This has a 12C tower, a 13C nave and a 14C choir. In the SE chapel there is a monument to Colart d'Avesnes, who died in 1404. This is a bas-relief with faint traces of colour. The lectern dates from 1411.

A short distance to the SW of this church at 8 Rue des Carmes is the **Musée d'Histoire et d'Archéologie**, easily recognised by its striking tall slender turret. It occupies the former Mont de Piété, a pawnshop of 1622 erected by Wenceslas Coeberger. In the museum there are artefacts from the Gallo-Roman period—local and imported pottery, jewellery and a number of reconstructed graves. From the Middle Ages and later there are stelae of Tournai marble from the 12C, sculptures, decorated capitals and documents, manuscripts and books on trade and the administration of the town. There is also a fine collection of gold, silver and bronze coins from Tournai together with dies and casts of ancient seals. The display of local chinaware includes many beautiful pieces decorated 'aux oiseaux de Buffon' and 'du Duc d'Orlèans'. The museum is open daily, except Tuesday, from 10.00 to 12.00 and from 14.00 to 17.30. It is closed on 11 November, 25 December and 1 January.

About 200m farther to the SW is the *Eglise Sainte Marguerite* of 1363, which was rebuilt in 1760. Another 600m, by Avenue de Gaulle, is the pretty *Chapelle de la Ladrerie du Val d'Orcq* of 1163.

SOUTH OF THE GRAND-PLACE. By following the Rue Saint Martin for c 250m we reach the Hôtel de Ville, the Parc Communal and the Musée des Beaux Arts. All of these formed part of the Cluniac abbey of St Martin which was founded in 1095. By the 13C this had become one of the wealthiest abbeys in western Europe. It was disestablished at the time of the French Revolution. There is a plan of the abbey on the wall of a building to the left of the entrance to the Musée des Beaux Arts. The **Hôtel de Ville** by L. Dewez, 1763, together with an annexe housing a small natural history museum, occupies the site of the abbot's palace. Some Romanesque cellars survive. Demolished by German bombing in 1940, the building was restored after the war. What remained of the 15C abbey cloister was incorporated in the new structure.

The ***Musée des Beaux Arts** occupies a light, spacious building of 1928 by the Belgian Art Nouveau architect Victor Horta. Its wide-ranging collection includes pictures from early Flemish artists to those of the present century. It is strong on French and Belgian artists, including natives of

Tournai such as Roger van der Weyden and from more recent times Piat Sauvage and Louis Gallait. There are also works by Campin, Gossaert, Snyders, Rubens, Jordaens, Watteau, Manet, Monet, Seurat, Van Gogh and Ensor. The museum is open daily, except Tuesday, from 10.00 to 12.00 and from 14.00 to 17.30. It is closed on 11 November, 25 December and 1 January.

The entrance hall is given over to sculpture, including some admirable pieces by *Guillaume Charlier*. Terraces and rooms open off this hall. Frequent rearrangement of the pictures for temporary exhibitions and a rather haphazard room numbering system make it difficult to give precise directions about the location of individual works. However, the Old Masters will probably be in the far left corner and the well-known *Piat Sauvage* trompe l'oeil paintings are usually in an adjoining room. *Louis Gallait* monopolises a large room to the left of the entrance.

The following works are usually in the Old Masters room or on the nearby terrace: *Jan Brueghel*: two small landscapes. Note the exquisite detail. *Pieter Brueghel the Younger*: The Fowler. *Gaspard de Crayer: Adoration of the Shepherds. Frans Francken the Younger*: Concert of the Muses. *Abel Grimmer*: The Good Shepherd. *Jacob Jordaens*: The King Drinks. Jesus with Martha and Mary. Jesus teaching Nicodemus. Until recently the latter painting was attributed to Rubens. *Jan Fyt*: A Dog guarding Game. *Adriaen Key*: Portrait of a Gentleman. *Joos de Momper*: Mountain scenes. *Pieter Paul Rubens*: A small sketch. *Roger van der Weyden*: a Triptych.

A room to the left of the entrance is devoted to the works of *Louis Gallait*. It is dominated by two huge historical canvases, *Plague in Tournai in 1092 and the Abdication of Charles Quint. Note also the very moving *Last Rites over the bodies of Counts Egmont and Horn.

The display of modern works in other rooms is frequently changed. Paintings usually on show include: *Edouard Agneessens*: *Female portraits. *Hippolyte Boulenger*: various works. *Henri de Braekeleer*: The Laundry. The Studio. *Emile Claus*: Lady at a Table. *James Ensor*: Still life. *Fantin-Latour*: A Girl Reading. Study of a female artist. *Charles de Groux*: Pilgrimage at Diegem. The Lost Harvest. The Drunkard and in a different mood, Study for the Head of a Religious Man. *Edouard Manet*: Argenteuil. At the Père Lathuille. Moorland. *Claude Monet*: Marine scene. *Théo Rysselberghe*: A Nude. *Guillanne van Strydonck*: several works. *Jan Toorop*: Studies of a male head. *Theodoor Verstraete*: Departing Fishermen, Funeral in Kempen.

The upper floor is reserved for contemporary art and temporary exhibitions.

In the Parc Communal there are two figures by Charlier. One a bronze of 1891 is of the painter Louis Gallait. The tower on the far side of the Place Reine Astrid is part of the 11C and 12C fortifications. To the E, in the Rue des Jésuites are the former Jesuit church of 1603 on the right and a house belonging to the order, which was erected between 1619 and 1672. In the same street is the **Eglise Saint Piat**. This occupies a site on which a 6C church once stood. Traces of this were discovered during restoration work in 1971. See the plaque and model inside the NW door. The tower of the present church dates from the 12C, the choir from the 13C and the apse from the 14C. There is a lectern of 1403 and, above the high altar, a Crucifixion attributed to J. van Oost the Elder.

EAST OF THE RIVER. From the Belfry take the Rue de la Wallonie and continue in a NE direction to the river. On the other side the Rue de Pont leads to the **Eglise Saint Brice**, which is dedicated to the disciple and successor of St Martin of Tours. Forced to flee after 20 years in office because of his arrogance and licentiousness, Brice went to Rome. There he repented, returned to Tours and was reinstated in his see. Such was the change in his life and manner that he was proclaimed a saint after his death. The nave of the church dates from the 12C, the choir was extended eastwards in 1405. There is a 12C crypt, which was discovered in 1941. A silver-gilt fibula from the tomb of Childeric (see below) is kept in the sacristy.

Immediately to the W of the church there are two very interesting old houses. The façades of 12 and 14 Rue Barre-Saint-Brice date from between 1175 and 1200. They are among the oldest private houses extant in Western Europe.

A plaque on 8 Place Clovis, just to the N of the church, records the discovery here in 1653 of the tomb of the Frankish king Childeric, who died in 481. The tomb contained Childeric's sword and other relics including the so-called golden bees which are believed to have been used to ornament the royal robes. Adopted as a symbol by Napoleon, in preference to the fleur-de-lys, they are now in the Bibliothèque Nationale, Paris.

To the E of the church there is a memorial to the First World War heroine Gabrielle Petit. She was a native of Tournai. In the Rue du Quesnoy to the NE, the *Chapelle de l'Athénée* has a façade of 1612. About 350m to the SE of the church, reached by Rue Saint Brice and the Rue des Moulins is the *Eglise Saint Jean*. Rebuilt in 1780, this retains its graceful tower of 1367. Nearby in the Rue des Croisiers is the *Chapelle des Croisiers*, the Crutched Friars, which dates from 1466. The Rue des Croisiers ends at the ring boulevard. About 350m to the S by way of the Avenue de Craene, there are well-preserved sections of the 13C ramparts. Surmounted by two towers, *Marvis* and *Saint Jean*, the fortifications extend down to the river.

NW from the Eglise Saint Brice follow the Rue de Monnel and the Rue du Sondart for c 450m to the PLACE VERTE. Here in 1513–18 Henry VIII of England established a citadel for his garrison. This was demolished by Louis XIV except for the massive **Tour Henri VIII**, a cylindrical keep with walls 7m thick at their base and a conical, brick-vaulted roof. The *Musée d'Armes* in the tower has an interesting collection of weapons, munitions and uniforms. The oldest object on show is a late 14C bombard. There is a section devoted to the Resistance movement in Tournai during the last war. The museum is open daily, except Tuesday, from 10.00 to 12.00 and 14.00 to 17.30. It is closed on 11 November, 25 December and 1 January. The *Eglise Saint Nicolas*, to the NW of the Place Verte, at one time inside the citadel, was completed in 1213.

ENVIRONS OF TOURNAI. The *Mont Saint Aubert*, 5km to the N, is an isolated hill of 147m, which has a commanding view of the Scheldt valley. Its name recalls a 7C bishop of Cambrai-Arras, who had a great enthusiasm for the monastic life. Under his influence a large number of monasteries were established in Hainaut and Flanders. There is a modern leisure centre with swimming pool, facilities, a restaurant, bars and accommodation on Mont Saint Aubert; and a large campsite of more than 20 hectares.

On the Courtrai road *Esquelmes* at 6km has a little Romanesque church. At *Pecq*, 3km farther on, there are the ruins of a castle and a 13C church.

The road to 14km Roubaix in France passes through *Templeuve* at 8km. It is believed that St Eleutherius (see above) was born here. At *Royère*, 4km to the N, there are ruins of a 13C castle.

The French city of **Lille** is 20km to the W of Tournai. At 7km *Hertain*, just before the border, a memorial commemorates the entry into Belgium on 3 September 1944 of British liberating troops.

At *Rumes*, 8km S of Tournai, there is a small Gallo-Roman museum.
For Tournai to *Mons*, see Route 25.

At *16km Leuze* is the 13C Collegiate Church of Peter, which was rebuilt in 1745 in Louis XV style. About 10km to the N of Leuze is the 16C château of *Anvaing* where the Belgian capitulation of 27 May 1940 was signed.

Beloeil, 10km to the SE of Leuze, has an imposing château which traces its origins back to the 12C. This has been in the possession of the princes of Ligne since the 14C. The wings of the present building were constructed between 1682 and 1695, but the central portion was completely rebuilt after a fire in 1900. It has an important art collection, with works dating from the 15C to the 19C, many fine tapestries, Louis XVI furniture, a valuable library of 25,000 volumes and the family archives from the 12C. In the **gardens, laid out after 1711 in the style of Le Nôtre, stretches of greensward alternate with large lakes surrounded by formally clipped hedges.

The Orangery, arranged as a recreation area, has a restaurant. There is also a camping and caravan site. The château is open daily between April and September from 10.00 to 18.00. The Park is open all the year round from 09.00 to 20.00 or until dusk.

Ligne, Arenberg and Croy are three linked families, whose members have played a not unimportant part in the history of Belgium. They are the owners of large estates in various parts of the country. In the 12C Arenberg was a duchy to the W of Cologne. In 1547 the lordship of Arenberg passed to Jean de Brabançon, of the house of Ligne, through his marriage to the sister of the childless Robert d'Arenberg. Jean's son Charles was created Prince de Ligne in 1576. He was married to Anne de Croy, the heiress of Croy and Chimay. This alliance greatly increased the wealth and extended the estates of the family.

To Prince Charles Joseph, 1735 to 1814, a distinguished soldier and author, is attributed a famous cynical observation on the Congress of Vienna, 'Le Congrès danse mais ne marche pas'.

At *Moulbaix 7km* from Leuze and c 2km S of the main road there is a windmill of 1624, one of the last in Belgium still in use. Visitors are welcome.

From Moulbaix return to the main road and continue for *5km* to the busy little town of **Ath** (population 24,000). The *Tour de Burbant*, all that remains of a castle dating from c 1150, is the oldest surviving example of military architecture in Hainaut. The tower, c 100m from the Grand-Place down the narrow Rue du Gouvernement, is surrounded by an attractive group of 15C buildings.

In the Grand-Place the *Hôtel de Ville* constructed between 1614 and 1624 is by Coeberger. The *Eglise Saint Julien*, founded in 1393, was struck by lightning in 1817. Only the E end and the tower escaped damage.

There are several places worthy of a detour on the N56 road from Ath to Mons.

WEST OF THE ROAD. In **Chièvres**, which traces its history back to the 9C, there is the 16C late Gothic *Eglise Saint Martin* with a chapel of the 12C. Against the churchyard wall is the 15C *Tour de Gavre*. This is flanked by two lengths of the ancient ramparts, which date from the same period. The *Chapelle de la Ladrerie*, the lazar house (for the poor and diseased), dates from 1112. A military airfield near the town was used by German bombers during the Second World War.

Pilgrimages are made in September and February to a miraculous 11C statute of the Virgin, which is kept in the 1777 basilica of **Tongre Notre-Dame**, 2km W of Chièvres. Mary is honoured here as patroness of universities, poets and writers.

At **Herchies**, 6km S of Chièvres, is the small red-brick 14C keep of the lords of Egmont. This is surrounded by pleasant, well-kept gardens. The château nearby, which dates from 1511, was built by Charles de Berlaymont.

EAST OF THE ROAD. The **Château d'Attre**, 5km from Ath, was built in 1752 near the site of a medieval structure erected by the Count de Gomegnies. Retaining its original decoration and furnishings, it has some fine silver, ivory and porcelain as well as paintings by Watteau, Snyders and others. In the park there are the remains of a 10C tower, which is known as the Tour de Vignon. According to a popular local legend this was the lair of a brigand named Vignon who, masquerading as a hermit, robbed and murdered his visitors. There are also the former village pillory, a 17C dovecot, a 19C man-made hill with a Swiss chalet, and a strange artificial rock. This was constructed by de Gomegnies as a pavilion for the Archduchess Marie-Christine of Saxe-Teschen, who was Marie Theresa's governor in the southern Netherlands. Visiting times are: from April to June and in September and October on Saturday, Sunday and public holidays from 10.00 to 12.00 and from 14.00 to 18.00; daily, except Wednesday, in July and August.

In **Cambron Casteau**, 4km SE of Attre, are the ruins of a Cistercian abbey which was founded in 1148 and suppressed in 1797 by the French Revolutionaries. Beyond the entrance gate of 1722 are the 18C farm buildings and an octagonal dovecot. In the ruined church, which was erected between 1190 and 1240, there are sections of the ancient columns, parts of a 14C cloister and a number of recumbent effigies of the Tournai school in niches in the cloister wall. The tower, which is 56m high, was built in 1774. The undercroft dates from the 12C. In the park, crossed by the Dendre, there is a balustraded stairway and bridge of 1776.

An interesting diversion may be made from *7km Ghislenghien* to **Lessines** (population 16,000), which is 6km to the NW. This has important porphyry quarries which were first exploited in 1707. The *Hôpital Notre-Dame à la Rose* was founded in 1242 by Alix du Rosoit, widow of one of the lords of Lessines. It was restored in the early 17C. The present buildings date mainly from that time. They may be visited from April to September on Sunday and public holidays at 15.00. The *Eglise Saint Pierre* was badly damaged in 1940 and largely rebuilt. A part of the central nave dates from the late 12C and much of the choir from the 14C. Near the town centre there is a small medicinal herb garden.

At *Bois de Lessines*, 4km to the SE, a tree by the church was planted in 1793 as a symbol of liberty.

Deux-Acren, 2km to the N of Lessines is in a district famous for its herbal gardens. The church has a 12C tower. The baptismal font is a fine example of 12C Tournai stonework.

The town of *12km* **Enghien** (population 10,000), is just S of the language frontier with Flemish-speaking Brabant. Its Flemish name is **Edingen**. Long an appanage of the Bourbon family, Henry IV of France sold it to the Count of Arenberg in 1607. In the 17C *Chapelle des Capucins* is the alabaster tomb by Jean Mone, of Guillaume de Croy Archbishop of Toledo who died in 1521. The archives of the Arenberg family are also kept here. The Arenberg château, apart from the 15C chapel and the stables, was destroyed by the French at the time of the Revolution.

At *9km* is **Saintes** (Flemish **Sint Renelde**), in Brabant. Here St Renelde, the sister of St Gudule, her priest Grimoald and their servant were martyred in 680. The saint and the priest were beheaded. The servant had nails driven into his skull. In the church of 1553 are a wooden figure of St Renelde of c 1500 which may be by Jan Borman, her silver shrine and a curious painting on wood depicting her family tree.

At **Rebecq-Rognon**, 5km SW of Saintes, a small steam train operates in summer over 6km of line. The local museum is concerned with the history of the area and of porphyry. It is housed in an old mill which straddles the Senne. The mill was rebuilt after a fire in 1858.

5km **Halle**. Halle, Halle to Mons, and Halle to *14km* **Brussels** are described in Route 23 below. For Brussels, see Route 1.

23

Brussels to Mons

The distance by the direct road, the N6, is 50km. This Route is 23km longer. Between Brussels and Halle and again between Tubize and Braine-le-Comte it follows minor, but more interesting, roads to the east.

Total distance 73km.—*10km* **Beersel**—*9km* **Halle**—*4km* **Tubize**—*5km* **Braine-le-Château**—*12km* **Ronquières**—*6km* **Ecaussinnes**—*6km* **Braine-le-Comte**—*6km* **Soignies**—*15km* **Mons**.

Brussels is described in Route 1. From the Porte de Hal take the Chaussée d'Alsemberg to *10km* **Beersel**, where there is a large ruined castle.

Dating from the 14C, the castle of Beersel was much damaged in 1489, when the owners, the Wittem family, supported Maximilian in his struggle against the towns. Rebuilt soon afterwards, it was not occupied after 1544 and suffered much from neglect. In 1932 it came into the care of the Association Royale des Demeures Historiques. Since then it has been carefully and sympathetically restored. The castle retains its medieval aspect. Surrounded by a moat, its three towers, linked by massy walls, look down on a circular courtyard. The moat is crossed by a small drawbridge. For defence purposes the towers are rounded on the outside, but have a typical Flemish stepped construction above the courtyard.

Visiting hours are: March to mid November daily from 10.00 to 12.00 and 14.00 to 18.00; other months: Saturday, Sunday, from 14.00 to 17.00.

At *3km* **Alsemberg** the 15C church contains some interesting murals and a pulpit of 1837 by van Geel and van Hool. This is decorated with carvings of Christ teaching the people. The figures are natural and well observed. Note the homely touch of a woman with two children, one of whom is pulling away from her to catch a tortoise. There are also a 12C font, a Descent from the Cross by Theodoor Rombouts and a 13C figure of the Virgin.

Between Alsemberg and Halle is the provincial recreational estate of *Huizingen*. There are gardens, deer enclosures, and a château converted into a restaurant.

At *6km* is **Halle**, French name **Hal**. This town of 32,000 inhabitants owes its fame to the huge Gothic-style *Onze Lieve Vrouwebasiliek*, which was built between 1341 and 1409. This has long been a place of pilgrimage because of its famous 13C 'black' Virgin which was originally venerated in a chapel on this site. Note the heavy 18C tower, the curious 'balloon' above the octagonal baptistry and, over the S portal, the 15C group of the Virgin and musician angels.

In a recess to the right of the porch there are 33 cannon balls, which were aimed at the church during a siege of the town in 1580. According to a pious local tradition these were caught by the Blessed Virgin in her robe. Another tradition asserts that the black colour of the famous statue is due to gunpowder. However it is probable that the darkening of the statue was caused by centuries of candle smoke and the oxydisation of the silver which once covered it.

In the chapel off the N aisle, built by Gilles de Trazegnies c 1647, there is an alabaster reredos of 1533 in the best Renaissance style by a local sculptor, Jehan Mone. The carvings show St Martin dividing his cloak, the evangelists Mark and Luke and a representation of the Seven Sacraments. The statues of the Apostles in the choir date from 1410. In a niche in the Lady Chapel, which is to the left of the choir, there is a tiny black marble effigy of 1460 of Joachim, the Dauphin of France and son of Louis XI. Nearby is a picture in the naive style showing a dramatic rescue, which was attributed to the intervention of the Blessed Virgin. The octagonal baptistry, with stained-glass of 1408, contains a brass font of 1446 by Jean de Febvre of Tournai. The crypt, which is supported by a single column, houses the Treasury. Among the many precious objects kept there is a silver monstrance presented by Henry VIII of England after the capture of Tournai by his army in 1513.

For Halle to Tournai, see Route 22.

In *4km* **Tubize** (Flemish name **Tubeke**), just across the language frontier, the *Musée de la Porte* has an interesting display of Gallo-Roman artefacts, religious art, fossils and coins. It is open on Saturday and Sunday from 10.00 to 12.00 and 14.00 to 18.00, on Tuesday from 09.30 to 11.30, on Thursday from 18.30 to 20.00, and on Wednesday and Friday from 15.00 to 17.00.

Tubize merges with *Clabecq*, where steelworks lining the river Sennette and the Charleroi canal were founded in 1828 by Edouard Goffin. His statue stands in the Grand-Place.

From Tubize the N6 continues S to 10km Braine-le-Comte, but this route turns E to *5km* **Braine-le-Château**. This small town preserves the pillory erected in 1521 by Maximilian de Hornes, chamberlain to Charles V. His tomb is in the church. The entrance to the château of the Counts Horn is across the road from the pillory. An old water mill at 4 Rue des Comtes de Robiano has been restored and reopened as a museum. Visiting times are: April to September on Saturday and Sunday from 14.00 to 18.00.

We now bear S for *4km Ittre*, a secluded village with a forge which dates from 1701. This is open from Easter to October on Sunday 14.00 to 18.00.

8km •**Ronquières**, with its interesting Sloping Lock, is in the province of Hainaut. The lock, completed in 1963, is on the Charleroi to Brussels canal. It has two large tanks which can carry barges up to a total of 1350 tonnes up or down a change of level of 68m over a distance of 1432m. Each tank has 236 rollers, runs on rails and is 91m long, 12m broad and has a water depth of between 3m and 4m. At the upper end of the slope there is a bridge dock, 300m long, 60m broad, standing on 70 pillars, each nearly 20m high and 2m in diameter. This lock has reduced the average time for journeys by barge between Charleroi and Brussels from 25 hours to 18. Roads and paths line the impressive complex. At the top soars a tower 150m high. Here visitors may see an explanatory film and an audio-visual presentation on the province of Hainaut, look into the winch room and visit an exhibition whose theme changes every year. There is also a fine view of the surrounding countryside. The lock may be visited daily between May and August from 10.00 to 18.00. Around one hour should be allowed for the visit to the tower. The last admission is 45 minutes before closing time. Boat excursions to the lock at Ittre and back are also possible. They last about an hour and are run daily, except Wednesday and Saturday unless those days are public holidays, between May and August at 12.00, 15.00 and 17.00.

6km **Ecaussinnes** (population 20,000), is divided in two. Ecaussinnes-

Lalaing is on one side of the valley, Ecaussinnes d'Enghien on the other. Each takes the name of its former overlord. Ecaussinnes d'Enghien is mainly given over to industry. In **Ecaussinnes-Lalaing** there is a large *castle*. This dates from the 12C, but was altered continually up to the 18C. It has had a number of owners—the Roeulx family in the 12C, the Lalaings in the 14C and 15C and the Croys in the 16C. Its 15C kitchen is almost unchanged. In its chapel of the same period there is a 14C statue of the Madonna ascribed to the school of André Beauneveu. In the hall and armoury there are two early 16C chimneypieces, some fine furniture and displays of glass and Tournai porcelain. Visiting times are as follows: daily between April and October, except Tuesday and Wednesday unless they are public holidays, from 10.00 to 12.00 and 14.00 to 18.00,

The 15C *Eglise Sainte Aldegonde*, dedicated to the sister of St Waudru of Mons, contains the tomb of Blandine Rubens, the sister of the painter. There is also an Assumption by de Crayer. The *Château de la Folie* on the N edge of the town derives its name from 'feuillie', meaning leafy. Built between the 16C and 18C, it replaced a 14C castle of the lords of Enghien. The attractive 16C court may be seen from the road.

At *Arquennes*, 6km to the E, there is a Renaissance chapel of 1622. At *Feluy*, 2km S of Arquennes, a moated château beside the road has the remains of its medieval predecessor beside it. **Seneffe**, 4km farther S, has given its name to two battles: Condé's victory over William of Orange in 1674, and the French defeat of the Austrians in 1794. The 18C château at Seneffe by L. Dewez is under restoration. In its grounds are an orangery and a small, attractive Palladian theatre.

'Petit Granit'. A feature of the Ecaussinnes district, extending W to Soignies, are the quarries of 'little granite' or 'bluestone'. Since at least the 8C they have produced this stone which has been used in the construction of many Belgian buildings and monuments, e.g. the Collégiale Sainte Waudru at Mons and several of the houses in the Grand-Place in Brussels.

6km along the N6 from Tubize is **Braine-le-Comte**, population 16,500. At the N entrance to this town, whose Flemish name is **'s Gravenbrakel**, is the mainly 16C *Eglise Saint Géry*. Named after one of the earliest inhabitants of Brussels, the church has a Renaissance high altar of 1577 and a 3.40m tall, 15C statue of St Christopher. Carved from a single piece of walnut, this stands on an octagonal base of 'petit granit'. Across the road from the church a small structure marks the site of a section of the town's 12C fortifications. Ruined ramparts of the same period may be seen in the Ruelle Larcée behind the 17C Hôtel de Ville.

6km farther S along the N6 is **Soignies** (population 23,000; Flemish name **Zinnik**). Its venerable Romanesque *Collégiale Saint Vincent* is dedicated to St Vincent Madelgar, governor of Hainaut and husband of St Waudru of Mons. After the birth of his fourth child, he became a monk and founded a Benedictine abbey here. He died in Soignies in 677.

In the 9C the abbey was destroyed by the Norsemen, but it was rebuilt soon afterwards. The choir and a section of the cloister are the oldest parts of the church. They date from c 960. The transepts, with 17C vaulting, and the central tower were built in the 11C. The nave with its plain arcades was added a century later. The narthex and W tower are a 13C rebuilding. The main portal was added to them c 1620.

The 60 superb Renaissance *choir stalls of 1576 are by Jacques Laurent and David Mulpas. On the S side of the choir is a 15C *Entombment with terracotta figures. Immediately below the rood-loft there is a French 14C polychrome statue of the *Blessed Virgin. The Shrine of St Vincent, a reconstruction of 1803, is above the high altar. The original 13C shrine was buried for safekeeping in a nearby garden at the time of the French Revolution. A plaque with a Latin inscription commemorating this event may be seen on a wall in the Rue de la Régence beside the church. When recovered in 1799, the shrine was so damaged that it had to be remade. The Chapel of St Vincent houses the Treasury. In it are the crozier of St Landry, the son and successor here of St Vincent Madelgar, and a reliquary of St Vincent. Both date from the 13C. The E walk of the 10C cloister may be reached either from the church or from the Rue de la Régence.

A short distance to the N of the church is the ancient chapel, dating in part from the 9C or 10C, of the old cemetery. In this there is a small archaeological museum.

Between the 15C and 18C Soignies was famous for its Song School. This was served by a number of noted musicians. They included an Englishman, Peter Philipps, born in 1560, who was a canon here in 1610. The musical tradition is continued by a modern school.

8km Casteau-Maisières has its place in the history of the First World War. A memorial by the W side of the road, shortly before the SHAPE headquarters (see below), commemorates the first shot fired by a British soldier in Belgium since Waterloo and the first British mounted action against the Germans. The shot was fired at daybreak on 22 August 1914 by Corporal Thomas of the 4th Royal Irish Dragoon Guards. His target was the outpost of the German 4th Cuirassiers. A little over four years later, at the time of the cease-fire at 11.00 on 11 November 1918, Canadian troops halted on this same spot.

SHAPE, Supreme Headquarters Allied Powers in Europe, is the overall military headquarters within NATO. Previously in France, near Versailles, SHAPE and NATO were forced to leave in 1967 on French insistence.

A further *7km* brings us to **MONS** or **Bergen** in Flemish. This town of 90,000 inhabitants is the capital of the province of Hainaut. Sprawling over the hill which gives it its name, Mons is encircled by the boulevards which have replaced the ancient ramparts. Visitors are drawn to the town mainly because of its great church, the Collégiale Sainte Waudru, and its associations with both World Wars.

There are two **Tourist Information Offices**: for *Mons* at 22 Grand-Place and for the *Province of Hainaut* at 31 Rue des Clercs.

History. It is probable that Mons began as a Roman military post on a hill just E of the road from Bavai to Utrecht. During the 7C a settlement grew up around the hermitage founded by Waudru, the daughter of Count Walbert of Hainaut and wife of St Vincent Madelgar of Soignies (see above). There is a tradition that men from Mons fought on the English side at the battle of Crécy in 1346. In 1433 the luckless Jacqueline of Hainaut surrendered to Philip the Good at Mons. A century later, under Charles V, the town enjoyed a period of great commercial prosperity. It was famous for the quality of its cloth. In 1572 Mons was taken by Louis of Nassau, but soon after was recaptured by the duke of Alva. Subsequent conquerors included Louis XIV in 1691, Marlborough, after Malplaquet, in 1709, the Prince de Conti, after Fontenoy, in 1746 and Dumouriez in 1792.

Among famous natives of Mons are Philippa of Hainaut, c 1314 to 1369, the wife of Edward III of England, Orlando di Lasso sometimes known as Roland de Lassus, 1532 to 1594, the rival of the great Palestrina, and Louise de Stolberg, Countess of Albany, 1752 to 1824, the wife of the Young Pretender.

Vincent van Gogh lived at Pâturages and Wasmes 7km to the SW between 1878 and 1879, during his evangelising mission among the miners of the nearby Borinage. The following year he moved to Cuesmes just S of Mons, where he had his first studio.

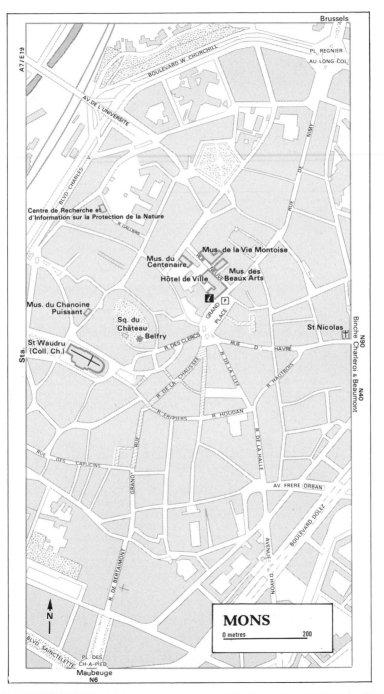

Brussels

PL. REGNIER-AU-LONG-COL

A7/E19

BOULEVARD W. CHURCHILL

AV. DE L'UNIVERSITE

BLVD - CHARLES -

RUE DE NIMY

Centre de Recherche et
d'Information sur la Protection de la Nature

R GALLIERS

Mus. de la Vie Montoise

Mus. du
Centenaire

RUE NEUVE

Mus. des
Beaux Arts

Hôtel de Ville

GRAND PLACE

P

Mus. du Chanoine
Puissant

Sq. du
Château

Belfry

St Nicolas

St Waudru
(Coll. Ch.)

Sta.

R. DES CLERCS

RUE D HAVRÉ

N90 Binche Charleroi à Beaumont

N40

R. DE LA CHAUSSEE

R. DE LA CLEF

R. HAUTBOIS

R. "ERIPIERS

R. HOUDAN

R. DE LA HALLE

RUE DES CAPUCINS

GRAND' RUE

AV. FRERE (ORBAN)

BOULEVARD DOLEZ

R. DE BERTAIMONT

AVENUE D'HYON

N

MONS

0 metres   200

BLVD. SAINCTELETTE

PL. DES
CH-A-PIED

Maubeuge
N6

Mons during the World Wars

At the opening of the **First World War** the British army, in support of the general French offensive, moved to Mons. By the morning of 23 August 1914 it was in position. One flank faced NE between the town and the river Sambre, the other faced N along the line of the Canal du Centre, which runs W from Mons. In spite of much gallantry—the first two Victoria Crosses of the war were won here by Lieutenant Dease and Private Godley—this long front of some 45km proved impossible to hold against a German superiority of twenty to one, particularly after a French withdrawal on the right flank. The First Battle of Mons opened at 09.00. By early afternoon the town had to be evacuated, and on the following morning the historic retreat to Le Cateau and the Marne was under way. The story of the 'Angels of Mons' belongs to this battle..It is said that at a critical point in the struggle angels appeared in the sky, whereupon the British returned to the attack and for a time the Germans retreated. The legend is depicted in a painting in the Hôtel de Ville.

Mons remained in German hands until freed by the Canadians on 11 November 1918 at the conclusion of the Second Battle of Mons.

In the **Second World War** French troops entered Mons on 10 May 1940. The Germans subjected the town to several air attacks during the following week. Two bombs hit the Collégiale Sainte Waudru. The French then withdrew. The inhabitants fled and on 19 May the Germans took over what was a virtually empty town.

In 1944 Mons came under severe air attack again, this time by the Allies. The town was freed on 2 September by American forces which had driven straight through from Meaux near Paris. There followed two days of fierce fighting to the S as large German rearguard elements attempted to isolate the Americans. This fighting ended with the destruction of the German attackers and the taking of 27,000 prisoners.

In the GRAND-PLACE is the **Hôtel de Ville**. Built by De Layens in 1458, but since much altered it has a tower of 1718. On the front is the 15C 'Grande Garde', an iron monkey. Perhaps once part of a children's pillory, the monkey is believed to bring good luck to those who stroke its head. The elaborate lock on the door represents the town's demolished castle. It is a copy of the original which is kept inside the building. Beneath the porch there are several memorials. These include one to the 5th Royal Irish Lancers, one commemorating the Canadian liberation of Mons in 1918 and a plaque expressing gratitude for food sent to Belgium by America during the First World War.

There are some early chimneypieces in the Hôtel de Ville, also a number of 17th and 18C tapestries. A painting of 1934 by Marcel Gillis depicting the legend of the Angels of Mons is in the mayor's office, which is not open to visitors. Visits are permitted to other parts of the Hôtel de Ville during working hours, if there is no civic function.

A former 16C pawnshop occupies a corner of the pleasant JARDIN DU MAYEUR. This now houses the **Musées du Centenaire**. In front of the building stands a prehistoric menhir. The four museums in the building are open daily, except Monday, from 10.00 to 12.30 and 14.00 to 18.00. Between October and April they close on Sunday at 17.00, and between May and September on Friday at 17.00.

The *War Museum* occupies the ground and third floors. The ground floor is devoted almost entirely to Mons during the First World War. It has five national sections—British, French, Canadian, Belgian and German. There are also displays on life during the years of occupation, the story of the Mons civic guard from 1830 to 1914, and the Italian front. The third floor is concerned with the Second World War. The emphasis here is on the liberation of the town in September 1944.

The *Ceramic Museum* on the first floor owes its origin to a bequest by Henri Glépin, a wealthy citizen of Mons who died in 1898. Since then many additions have been made to the collection. This now occupies four rooms. In the first, objects later than 1850 are displayed, special attention being given to Belgian products. The second room has older porcelain from Mons, Tournai and Brussels as well as from a number of European countries. The principal feature of the third room is a fine display of over 500 pieces of Delftware. The fourth room is devoted to French faience; more than 30 factories are represented.

The *Numismatic Museum* on the second floor also owes its origin to the generosity of Henri Glépin. It has some 13,000 coins and medals of wide provenance and a large and interesting collection of engravings of historical personages and events.

On the same floor is the *Museum of Prehistory*. This has an interesting display of palaeolithic, mesolithic and neolithic objects found locally. Despite its name, it also has Gallo-Roman bronzes and ceramics, artefacts from the Frankish period and objects found in France, Switzerland, Denmark and Egypt.

Access to the *Conciergerie*, an underground prison of 1512, is from the Rue d'Enghien. This may be visited between April and September. Apply to the Musées du Centenaire.

To reach the **Musée des Beaux Arts** take the Rue Neuve at the N corner of the Grand-Place. This museum owes its foundation to a bequest by Henri Glépin (see above). Opened in 1913, it was enlarged considerably and modernised in 1970. The museum mounts frequent temporary exhibitions, so part or all of the permanent collection may not always be on show. Works in the permanent collection, which are displayed in rotation, are arranged in the following groups:

Primitives and 16C Flemish. Includes paintings by Cornelis de Vos, Jan Gossaert, Jan Metsys, Paul Bril, Antoino Moro and Otto Venius.

French, 17C and 18C; Dutch, 17C and 18C; Italian, 18C; late 19C with works by Louis Gallait, F.J. Navez , Jan Portaels, H. Boulenger and T. Baron.

Early 20C and Contemporary. Paintings by Paul Delvaux, Edgard Tytgat, Léon Frederic and others. Also artists of the Nervia and Maka groups.

Modern Sculpture.

The museum is open daily, except Monday, from 10.00 to 12.30 and 14.00 to 18.00. Between October and April it closes on Sunday at 17.00; between May and September it closes on Friday at 17.00.

Just beyond the Musée des Beaux Arts is the **Musée de la Vie Montoise**. Occupying a 17C former convent, this has displays on the life and customs of Mons and the surrounding district.

From the S corner of the Grand-Place take the the Rue d' Havré to the 17C *Eglise Saint Nicolas*. This has some notable 18C woodcarvings in the choir. The street ends at the Place de Flandres where there is an equestrian statue of Count Baldwin of Flanders, 1171–1205. One of the leaders of the Fourth Crusade, Baldwin was elected Emperor of Constantinople in 1204. The following year he was taken in battle by the Bulgarians and died in captivity.

From the W corner of the Grand-Place the Rue des Clercs climbs to the SQUARE DU CHATEAU. This occupies the site of the castle of the counts of Hainaut, which was pulled down in 1866. In the baroque style **Belfry**, built between 1662 and 1672 by local architect Louis Ledoux, there is a carillon of 47 bells. The belfry is 87m high. From the top, where there are panoramas of the Battles of Mons, there is an excellent view of the town. At a ceremony in 1935 earth from the graves of every British and Canadian soldier killed locally during the two World Wars was buried at the foot of the belfry.

The *British and Canadian War Memorial* stands on the edge of the park. Designed by Lutyens, the monument was unveiled in 1952 by Field Marshal Lord Alexander who fought here in 1914. Also in the park are a small tower, a relic of the 11C ramparts, and the 12C basement of the castle.

Nearby is the much altered *Chapelle Saint Calixte*. This was built in 1051 by Richilde, Countess of Hainaut to house the relics of St Calixtus which had been given to her by her aunt, abbess of a convent near Cologne. St Calixtus was a Christian slave who became pope in 217. Famed for his lenient attitude to repentant sinners, he was probably martyred c 222. The chapel is, at least in part, the oldest building in Mons. In it are murals recreated in 1951 from records and drawings of the 11C or 12C originals (now destroyed), which were discovered in 1872. There are also three effigies dating from the 12C to the 14C which were transferred here from Saint Ghislain and Cambron-Casteau. The much damaged 12C figure is of Gilles de Chin, a famous knight and Grand Chamberlain of Hainaut. The large collection of flagstones, from the 11C to 17C, once formed part of the flooring of the castle.

To the left of the chapel is the *Iconographical Museum*. In it are pictures of churches, chapels, castles, towers, ruins, church furniture and plate, which were built or made between the 9C and 1436 in Hainaut.

From below the Square du Château take the the the Rue des Clercs and, passing the Province of Hainaut **Tourist Information Office**, continue to the *Collégiale Sainte Waudru**. Though lacking a tower, this is one of the finest examples of the late Gothic style in Belgium.

St Waudru founded her hermitage and built her primitive chapel on this site during the latter part of the 7C. Of this building and of the three that followed it over a period of some 800 years there is no trace. It is known that a Romanesque church stood here in 1450, the year in which work on the present building began. The early architects were Jean Spiskin and Mathys de Layens. The choir was completed in 1502, the transepts by 1527, and the nave by about the end of the 16C. In 1547 the decision was taken to build a tower and the plans, which are held in the town archives, were for a structure similar to but even higher than that at Mechelen. It was to be 190m high. However, work stopped on the death of the architect, Jean de Thuin, c 1570, and it was decided in 1686 that the tower should remain in an unfinished state.

The vast interior, 115m long, 32m wide, 24m high, is notable for its structural simplicity and unity of style. Of particular interest are the *sculptures by the local artist Jacques du Broeucq, who lived between c 1505 and 1584. His work is to be found in many parts of the church. Note especially the fragments of his masterpiece the great rood-loft made between 1535 and 1539 which was broken up in 1797. These include the reliefs of the Resurrection, Ascension and Descent of the Holy Ghost in the N transept. There is a rare sculptor's signature near the right foot of Christ on the Resurrection relief. In the S transept there are reliefs of the Flagellation of Christ and of the Bearing of the Cross. Other works by this artist include the statues surrounding the choir and the reliefs on the high altar and in the chapels. Do not miss the unusual and effective rendering of the Last Supper in the fourth ambulatory chapel on the N side of the church. The sculptor's memorial in the S transept has three medallions on the themes of the Creation, the Triumph of the Church and the Last Judgement.

In three adjoining chapels off the N aisle there are some beautifully preserved 15C funerary reliefs. In the E chapel of the S aisle a heraldic painting of 1577 sets out the genealogy of St Waudru. The choir stalls of 1707 from the church of St Germain, now demolished, are surmounted by medallion-heads from the abbey of Cambron-Casteau. The *Car d'Or* of

1780 is used to carry the shrine of the saint in solemn procession through the town on Trinity Sunday.

The Treasury, in the former chapter house, has the Ring, Cross and Brooch of St Waudru, also a 13C reliquary of St Vincent attributed to Hugo d'Oignies. It may be visited every day, except Monday, during July and August between 14.00 and 17.00.

The entrance to the **Musées du Chanoine Puissant** is at 22 Rue Notre-Dame Debonnaire. They occupy a 16C house, Le Vieux Logis, once a refuge of the abbey of Ghislenghien, and the 13C Chapelle Sainte Marguerite. The collections were made by Canon Edmond Puissant (1880 to 1934), who, by special dispensation, was buried in the chapel. In Le Vieux Logis there are 16C chimneypieces, furniture, weapons and ironwork. In the chapel there are 15C to 17C wooden statues, church furnishings and plate, vestments, books, MSS, textiles and lace. Visiting hours: daily except Monday from 10.00 to 12.30 and 14.00 to 18.00, 17.00 on Sunday.

The **Centre de Recherche et d'Information sur la Protection de la Nature** is some 200m farther N in the Rue Galliers. A curiosity of the collection is the skeleton of Julius Koch, who died in 1902 aged 30. Known as Giant Constantin he measured 2.59m and may well have been the world's tallest man. Visiting hours: Monday to Friday, 08.30 to 12.00, 13.00 to 17.00, Saturday, 10.00 to 12.00, 14.00 to 18.00. Closed on Sunday and public holidays.

It was to *Cuesmes*, 3km SW of the Grand-Place, that van Gogh came in August 1879. He stayed there over a year practicing the basic principles of art. The small house in which he lived is beautifully set in a wood on the northern edge of Cuesmes, slightly less than 2km from Mons station. It is open daily, except Monday, from 10.00 to 18.00.

Mont Panisel and *Bois de Mons* are two hillocks on the SE outskirts of Mons. Throughout the afternoon of 23 August 1914 three British battalions held a whole German corps here. This made possible the withdrawal of the main British force. There is a memorial at La Bascule, the junction of N90 and N40. On 9 and 10 November 1918 German rearguards on these hillocks stubbornly held out against the attacking Canadians.

Between Mons and France

FROM MONS TO QUIEVRAIN is a distance of 18km. For much of the way this road crosses the Borinage, a thickly populated district where coal has been won since the 13C, but which is now being forced to embark on major industrial diversification.

At *3km Jemappes* a memorial commemorates the victory of the French under Dumouriez over the Austrians in 1792. Here on 23 August 1914 the German crossing of the canal was fiercely contested by the British 9th Brigade.

Continue to *5km* **Hornu**. Here there is a specially built 'miners' township', Grand Hornu. The concept of Bruno Renard and Henri de Gorge, this was established between 1820 and 1832. It has been restored and listed as an industrial archaeological site. Information is available from the Hôtel de Ville.

Saint Ghislain, 2km N of Hornu, was another place where in 1914 the canal crossing was gallantly defended. The town, largely rebuilt after the First World War, owes its name to St Gislenus, who died in 680. He was a Frankish recluse who attracted a large number of followers. To house them he founded the Benedictine abbey of SS Peter and Paul here.

In the towns of *Pâturages* and *Wasmes*, just S of Hornu, van Gogh lived between 1878 and 1879 as missionary and pastor to the Borinage miners.

After some time at Pâturages as an independent pastor, he was given an official appointment to Wasmes. He lived in poverty, gave away his clothes, preached, taught and nursed the victims of typhus. However, he was dismissed for being over-zealous. In particular his action in pestering the authorities and the mine owners to improve the lot of the miners was resented. Van Gogh's missionary and philanthropic endeavours are commemorated by a monument at Wasmes by Zadkine.

The techniques of mining are explained in the Musée des Mines, 14 Rue du Pont d'Arcole, by the use of galleries specially built in 1932 for mining instruction. The museum is open from Monday to Friday between 09.00 and 15.00.

2km Boussu was the lordship of Maximilien de Hennin, who lived between 1542 and 1579. Known in Dutch history as 'Bossu', the Hunchback, he served the States General between 1576 and 1577 in their struggle against the forces of Don John of Austria.

8km **Quiévrain** is the last Belgian town before the frontier with France. In 1914 at *Audregnies*, 4km to the SE, the 9th Lancers made a gallant charge and the Victoria Cross was won by Captain Grenfell.

Roisin, on the border 6km farther S, was the home of the poet Emile Verhaeren, 1855 to 1916. His house, burnt in 1914, was restored and is open to visitors daily, except Friday, from 10.00 to 12.00 and 14.00 to 18.00.

MONS TO BOIS-BOURDON is a distance of 10km. For *Cuesmes*, see above. To the E of the road c 2km from the Mons ring boulevard are the ruins of the abbey of *Bélian*, headquarters of Louis XIV in 1691 and of Marlborough in 1709.

At the *Cheval Blanc* crossroads *6km* from Mons and at *Bois-Bourdon 4km* farther on there was heavy fighting in September 1944, when the Germans tried to cut off the Americans who had reached Mons. The Château de Warelles, to the W of the road about halfway between Cheval Blanc and Bois-Bourdon, was the American headquarters. Almost surrounded here, the American commander's call for help brought massive air support. As a result the short stretch of Roman road, which runs W from Bois-Bourdon to the village of Goegnies-Chaussée, was blocked by over a thousand destroyed German vehicles. A memorial to the American 1st Infantry Division stands by the road at Bois-Bourdon.

Château de la Haie at *Sars-la-Bruyère*, 7km to the NW of Bois-Bourdon, was the British headquarters before the first Battle of Mons.

Malplaquet, where Marlborough and Prince Eugene defeated the French marshals Villars and Boufflers on 11 September 1709, is just in France, 8km S of Sars-la-Bruyère.

For Mons to *Tournai*, and Mons to *Charleroi*, see Route 25.

24

Brussels to Charleroi

Total distance 45km.—*14km* **Waterloo**—*2km Mont Saint Jean*—*9km*
Genappe—*4km* **Quatre-Bras** (with **Ligny**)—*16km* **Charleroi**.

This road, which crosses the battlefield of Waterloo, is redolent of history.
Between 15 and 19 June 1815 it saw Wellington lead his troops S to
Quatre-Bras and then withdraw them to Waterloo. It witnessed Napoleon's
confident advance before the battle and frantic flight to Paris afterwards.
Finally, it was along this road that Blücher's Prussians chased the beaten
French on the evening of the fateful day.

An alternative road branches SW at Mont St Jean to reach Charleroi via
Nivelles. However, as Nivelles is the only place of interest along this road,
it is included below as one of two diversions from Genappe.

Brussels, see Route 1. *14km* **Waterloo** and *2km Mont St Jean*. See Route
1G for Brussels to Waterloo, for the battlefield and for the Charleroi road
as far as *Belle Alliance* and *Ferme du Caillou*.

9km **Genappe** was the home between 1456 and 1461 of the future
Louis XI of France. He found refuge here during his struggle with his father,
Charles VII.

The small town was the scene of a fierce skirmish on 17 June 1815. During
a violent thunderstorm, Wellington's cavalry, closely pursued by French
lancers, tried to retire through the narrow street. Napoleon was seen among
the French. The following night he was here again, this time fleeing from
the battlefield. Hurriedly changing from his carriage to horseback, he
narrowly avoided capture by the Prussians. Wellington spent a part of the
night of 16 to 17 June at the Auberge du Roi d'Espagne. On 20 June General
Duhesme, commander of Napoleon's Young Guard, died here. See commemorative plaque.

DIVERSIONS FROM GENAPPE. Two places of interest, which are easily
reached from Genappe, are Villers-la-Ville and Nivelles. The description
of the main Route S to Charleroi on the N5 continues on p 326.

At **Villers-la-Ville** (population 7300), 5km to the SE, there are the ruins
of a great *Cistercian Abbey*. Established in 1146 on a small hill, it was
moved a short distance the following year to its present site beside the river.
Reputedly this was done on the advice of St Bernard who was visiting the
new foundation. The abbey was sacked by French revolutionaries in 1794
and formally suppressed two years later. Then followed a long period of
neglect, during which time the central nave of the church collapsed. The
site was acquired by the Belgian government in 1893 and is now managed
by the French Community of Belgium. The abbey is open daily from mid
March to October between 10.00 and 18.00, in July and August on public
holidays from 10.00 to 19.00.

The impressive ruins in their charming, undulating, wooded setting fall
into two main parts. The older spans the period from the 12C to the 14C,
the newer the 17C and 18C. While many visitors may wish to wander at
will, the following suggested route, starting with the older parts of the
abbey, may commend itself to those who wish to see all the principal areas
of interest. Most buildings carry identification signs with dates.

The entrance is at the S of the site. From here a track leads in a NW direction to a group of domestic buildings which include the 14C Romanesque warming room, the Transitional period refectory and the kitchen, which was built during the 12C and 13C.

To the N are the cloisters, originally Romanesque, but later rebuilt in Gothic style. Today they are almost wholly in ruins. Of the Romanesque period all that survives are twin 12C windows in the E walk. In the S walk there is a collection of gravestones. Opening off the E walk are, from S to N, the stairway to the dormitory, the parlour, the chapter house and the mortuary. The tomb in the NE corner is of Gobert d'Aspremont, a crusader knight. He became a monk here and died in 1263. In the NW corner are the crypt, which is dark and often flooded, and a Transitional period doorway with a three-cusped arch.

The huge ruined church adjoins the N walk of the cloisters. Despite neglect, spoliation and the collapse of the nave in 1884, this remains impressive. The large 13C brewhouse is to the NW of the church. The area immediately to the E of the apse was the burial ground. Now unrecognisable as such, it is divided by the railway line.

The 17C and 18C part of the complex lies to the SE of the church and cloisters. It contains the ruins of the Abbot's Palace and, to the E, what was the kitchen garden, but is now given over to flowers and ornamental shrubs. Beyond the garden, steps lead over the railway line to a chapel of 1615.

A restaurant opposite the entrance to the abbey occupies the former abbatial mill. In the parish church there are two *retables, one dating from the early 15C, the other from the late 16C. Both are from the abbey. Note their exquisitely detailed carving.

In *Tilly*, 3km S of Villers-la-Ville, there is a 12C keep. It was the birthplace of Jean 't Serclaes, Comte de Tilly, 1559 to 1632, the ascetic commander of the Catholic League, which opposed Gustavus Adolphus during the Thirty Years War.

For *Gentinnes*, 5km to the E, see Route 27.

7km to the W of Genappe is **Nivelles** (Flemish **Nijvel**), a town of 22,000 inhabitants. The Tourist Information Office is in the Waux-Hall, Place Albert I.

Nivelles is the chief town of the 'Roman Pays', the French-speaking part of the province of Brabant. Although much of its centre was destroyed by fire during bombing in May 1940, the town retains much of its character. It still has a number of dignified buildings dating from the 17C to the 19C. The origins of Nivelles are closely linked with its great church, the *Collégiale Sainte Gertrude*. This is open daily from 09.00 to 17.00.

A convent was founded here c 650 by Blessed Itte, the widow of Pepin of Landen. She brought her husband's remains to the convent and appointed her daughter, St Gertrude, as the first abbess. The convent church, which was originally dedicated to St Peter, gradually changed its name after Gertrude was buried there. Building of the present church began at the end of the 10C, but later centuries brought much alteration and addition. This was due largely to the fact that the building was burnt some 19 times. The last occasion was during the bombing of May 1940. Restoration of the church, including the reconstruction of the upper part of the Romanesque tower, was completed in the mid 1980s.

The church is a notable example of a double-ended Rhenish-Roman structure, i.e. with transepts and choirs at opposite ends. A 12C addition on the W side had an apse until this was demolished in 1619. It was given a somewhat incongruous baroque portal in 1664. The W tower is flanked by two 12C turrets. On the S turret there is the tall figure of an armed knight

Nivelles, the Collégiale Sainte Gertrude

known as Jean de Nivelles. This was a 15C jacquemart, a figure used to strike the hours. Originally it graced the former town hall which was demolished in the 18C. It was placed on the church in the early 17C. The other turret is called La Tour Madame, because it was near the palace of the abbess.

Entry to the church is normally at the W end through one of two aisle doors. These have finely carved lintels. The Portail de Samson on the N is the more elaborate. In the nave there is a fine rococo pulpit of 1772 by Laurent Delvaux. In the E choir is the magnificent 13C shrine of St Gertrude. This has been meticulously restored after almost melting away in the fire of 1940. Both nave and choir are pleasing in their simplicity and fine proportions.

There are guided visits daily, except Saturday and Sunday mornings, at 10.00, 11.00, 14.00, 15.00 and 16.00. They include the large crypt of c 1100, with its three aisles and six vaulted bays, and the even more ancient Sous-sol Archéologique where traces have been identified of no fewer than five earlier churches. These are the 7C funerary chapel, the first church, which dates from the late 7C, with the tomb of St Gertrude, the first Carolingian church built in the late 9C, the 10C second Carolingian church and the third Carolingian church, also 10C.

There is a fascinating mystery concerning some ancient material found here. This has established shadowy links with a 7C Irish saint. Accompanied by his brothers SS Fursey and Ultan, St Foillan left his native Ireland to labour for souls in East Anglia. In time he became abbot of Burghcastle near Great Yarmouth. When this abbey was destroyed by the Mercians, he crossed over to Belgium and c 650 established the abbey of Fósses-la-Ville on land given to him by Blessed Itte. She was the widow of Pepin of Landen who founded this convent at Nivelles (see above). St Foillan and three companions were murdered by robbers near Le Roeulx c 665.

A stone found in the Sous-sol Archéologique bears the inscription 'Hic +Re/Quiescunt Mem/Bra Inlata Bea/Ta Memoria/ Sin/ E (or Q) Vvaloni Qui Fu/ (I)t Interfec(tus) No(nis) IV(niis or liis)'. This is sometimes translated as: Here lie the remains of Sinewalon or Sinqualon of blessed memory. He was murdered on the ninth of June (or July). However if an alternative reading of S(ancti) M(artyri) Fvvaloni is substituted for Sine(q)vvaloni, a connection, tenuous perhaps, is made with St Foillan. This was strengthened by the discovery near the inscription of a sarcophagus, dated to the 7C, which contained the bones of four people.

The cloister is entered from the N aisle of the church. The NE corner dates from the 11C or 12C and the N walk from the 13C. The remainder is a poor rebuilding of 1846.

The *Musée d'Archéologie* in the Rue de Bruxelles immediately to the NE of the church, occupies the 18C refuge of the abbey of Orval. Its collection, which comes in part from the Collégiale Sainte Gertrude, includes artefacts from the prehistoric to Merovingian times and statues from the 15C to the 18C. There are works by the 18C sculptor Laurent Delvaux, Flemish paintings including a number attributed to Rubens, furniture, Brussels tapestries, ancient locks and keys, weapons of various kinds and musical instruments.

The museum is open daily, except Tuesday, from 09.30 to 12.00 and from 14.00 to 17.00. On Wednesday it is open from 09.30 to 17.00.

On the wall of a house opposite the museum entrance a plaque reminds us that the Gestapo was active in Nivelles during the war. In the Rue Seutin, which runs W from the church, No. 38 is the *Tour Simonne*, the only survivor of the 11 towers which formed part of the 12C ramparts of the town. *La Tourette* in the Avenue de la Tour de Guet in the SW part of the town is a tower of 1620 which was used as a country retreat by the Jesuits.

The motor-racing circuit of *Nivelles-Baulers* is 2km N of Nivelles. At *Bois-Seigneur-Isaac*, 2km farther N, there is a Premonstratensian abbey, rebuilt in 1903 on old foundations. The entrance dates from 1764. The richly decorated chapel, built betwen 1550 and 1580, is beside the road.

Baisy-Thy 2km S of Genappe was the birthplace of Godfrey de Bouillon, 1060 to 1100. A leading figure in the First Crusade, he distinguished himself at the siege of Jerusalem and after its capture was chosen to be ruler of the city. Famed for his pious and simple life Godfrey generated many legends and Chansons de Geste. He is commemorated by a monument erected in 1855 in the church.

At *2km* **Quatre-Bras** and **Ligny**, which is 9km to the SE in the province of Namur, there were important battles on 16 June 1815 which set the stage for Waterloo.

On learning that the French were approaching Quatre-Bras, Wellington left the Duchess of Richmond's ball in Brussels in the early hours of 16 June. He ordered his army to concentrate at Quatre-Bras, where he arrived at 10.00. At this moment, though neither side was aware of it, Marshal Ney's force before Frasnes, 3km to the S, had a vast superiority in both men and guns. Around noon Wellington rode to Ligny to confer with Blücher, who was there with his Prussian army. Across the small river Wellington and Blücher had a clear view of Napoleon and his massed troops. Wellington observed that Blücher would be 'damnably mauled', with his men drawn up as they were on an exposed forward slope. By 14.30 Wellington was back at Quatre-Bras, only to find that battle had not only been joined but almost lost. At the same time he heard the cannon which signalled the start of the fighting at Ligny. At Quatre-Bras Allied reinforcements were now arriving and Wellington was able to hold Ney. By 21.00 the battle had petered out. Early next morning, 17 June, Wellington sent his aide-de-camp, Alexander Gordon, to find out what had happened at Ligny. Gordon returned with the grim news that the Prussians had been defeated and had fallen back on Wavre. Wellington then had no choice but to order a retreat to the position he had already selected S of Waterloo.

At Quatre-Bras, where the fighting was in open country, the Duke of Brunswick was killed. There is a monument to his memory. Wellington narrowly escaped capture, jumping his horse clear over the Gordon Highlanders lining a bank. At Ligny the battle raged for five hours in narrow village streets. The Ferme d'en Haut, marked by a plaque, in the village was a typical defensive point. Blücher, too, narrowly avoided capture. Leading a dashing but useless final cavalry charge, he fell and was twice ridden over. He was probably saved by the action of his aide-de-camp who covered the field marshal's medals to hide his identity. Blücher was carried to *Mellery*, 7km to the N, where for several vital hours he lay in a parlous condition on the edge of consciousness.

Fleurus, 2km S of Ligny—or perhaps Presles, see Route 25, may have been the place where Caesar inflicted a crushing defeat on the Nervii in 57 BC. Fleurus has given its name to other battles. In 1690 the French under Marshal Luxembourg defeated the Germans and Dutch here. More memorable, perhaps, was the victory of the French revolutionary army under Marshal Jourdan on 26 June 1794 over the Austrians, who were indifferently led by the Prince of Coburg.

At *4km Frasnes-lez-Gosselies*, the first village in Hainaut, there is an interesting church built between the 13C and 17C.

6km Gosselies is an industrial extension of Charleroi with an airfield by the roadside.

6km **CHARLEROI** (population 212,000) is the centre of the principal industrial zone of Belgium. The Tourist Information Office is in the Square de la Gare du Sud.

Built partly on a hill and partly in the valley of the Sambre, it is visited mainly for the sake of two outstanding museums, the Musée des Beaux Arts and the Musée du Verre, the Glass Museum.

Charleroi grew out of a colliery village which the Spaniards developed into a fortress in 1666. They changed its name in honour of their king, Charles II. Louis XIV captured it nine months later and Vauban built ramparts which remained in place until 1868, when they were replaced by boulevards. It was besieged four times by the French in

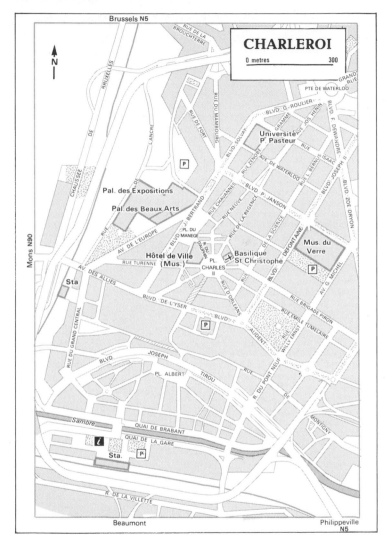

1794. Napoleon crossed the Sambre at Charleroi in 1815, driving out the Prussians and advancing up the roads to Quatre-Bras and Ligny. In August 1914 French troops vainly attempted to defend the Sambre bridgehead against overwhelming German strength. The town was captured by the Germans in May 1940 and remained under occupation until liberated by the Americans on 3 September 1944.

The town centre is the PLACE CHARLES II on the hilltop. Here are the *Basilique Saint Christophe* and the *Hôtel de Ville*, which was built in 1936. The basilica has a front dating from 1667. It was extended considerably in 1968. The Hôtel de Ville occupies a triangular area between Place

Charles II and the large PLACE DU MANEGE. It has a tall belfry and houses the Musée des Beaux Art and a concert hall.

The ***Musée des Beaux Arts**, opened in 1980, is on an upper floor of the Hôtel de Ville. It exhibits works by native Hainaut artists, and by others who worked in or were inspired by the province and in particular by the district around Charleroi. The paintings fall into three main divisions: portraits and other subjects by the Charleroi artist *François Joseph Navez*, 1787 to 1869, and his pupils; the realistic portrayal of Hainaut mining and industrial life as recorded by several 19C artists; and, in total contrast, the colourful works of artists like Paul Delvaux and René Margritte. There are several paintings by members of Nervia. This was not so much a school or movement as a loose association formed between 1928 and 1938 to encourage the development of Walloon art.

We begin our visit with two rooms in which there are displays of Walloon ceramics, stonework, furniture and pewter. Next comes the *Galerie Navez* where there is a fine selection of works by Charleroi's own painter including his picture of two girls with a bird's nest. There are also works by Navez's pupils and other 19C artists. They include the Portrait of a North African Girl by the widely travelled *Jan Portaels* who was Navez's son-in-law. This is typical of a theme which this artist made popular. In complete contrast are the works which portray the world of the Pays Noir, the black country around Charleroi. Outstanding in this part of the museum are the paintings and figures of manual workers by *Constantin Meunier*. Among other artists who deal with the same themes is *Marius Carion*. He was an orphan who has left a moving record of the Borinage of his impoverished childhood. Note also *Xavier Mellery*'s Scene in a Mine and the works of *Maximilien Luce*. He was a neo-Impressionist who specialised in paintings of mines and factories and of those who worked in them. Alex-Louis Martin was a miner's son whose early deprivation is reflected in his pictures. *P.P. de Chatelet*, who came from a comfortable artistic background, was fired by a visit in 1909 to record the harsh reality of life in the Pays Noir.

We leave these sombre themes and move to 'Le Monde de l'Irrationel', a fantasy world far removed from the toil and poverty of the Pays Noir. Here are *Paul Delvaux*'s cynical, bright blue Annunication; *René Magritte*'s La Liberté de l'Esprit and *Jean Ransy*'s amusing, if somewhat confused, La Maison d'Ange.

Lastly there are the works of Nervia (see above), where such contrasting styles as those of *Louis Buisseret*, *Anto Carte* and *Rodolphe Strebelle* are represented.

The museum is open from Tuesday to Saturday between 09.00 and 17.00. It is closed on Sunday, Monday and public holidays.

To the W of the Place du Manège are the *Palais des Beaux Arts* and the *Palais des Expositions*. The former is used for cultural purposes, the latter for technical, commercial and industrial exhibitions. A short distance to the N is the *Université Paul Pasteur*, which is devoted to technology.

The ***Musée du Verre** occupies a modern building in the Boulevard Defontaine, some 200m to the E of Place Charles II. In the collection there are examples of many types of glass, ancient and modern. Of particular interest are the fine pieces of Roman, Chinese, Islamic, Byzantine, Venetian and Bohemian glass on display. There are also illustrative exhibits on the manufacture, shaping and decoration of glass.

The museum is open from Tuesday to Saturday, 09.00 to 17.00. It is closed on Sunday, Monday and public holidays.

For Charleroi to *Mons*, and Charleroi to *Namur*, see Route 25. For Charleroi to *Chimay*, the Botte du Hainaut, and Charleroi to *Couvin*, see Route 26B and C.

25

Tournai to Mons, Charleroi and Namur

Total Distance 123km.—*6km* **Antoing**—*13km* **Péruwelz-Bon-Secours**—
30km **Mons**—*15km* **Binche** (or *17km* **La Louvière**)—*21km* (from Binche) or
19km (from La Louvière) **Charleroi**—*9km* **Châtelet**—*13km*
Fosses-la-Ville—*7km* **Floreffe**—*9km* **Namur**.

For a description of **Tournai**, see Route 22. The best route from Tournai to Mons is by minor roads through Péruwelz, 19km to the S, and then by the motorway. The alternatives are the N7 and N50 through Barry and Basècles, which pass through an area of little interest, and the motorway, which is fast, featureless and rather dull. The route via Péruwelz is described below.

From Tournai take the road which runs along the S bank of the Escaut, the Scheldt, in a SE direction. This soon reaches the dusty PAYS BLANC, so named because of the limestone which has been quarried there since Roman times or perhaps earlier. At *4km Calonne* there is the château in which Louis XV lodged at the time of the Battle of Fontenoy.

After 2km cross the river to **Antoing**, population 8000. Its *Hôtel de Ville* dates from 1565. Although the imposing *Château* is largely a late 19C reconstruction, it has managed to retain its 12C walls, 15C keep and a 16C tower. There are some fine gravestones of the Melun and Ligne families in a corner tower. A number of these monuments are Tournai work dating from the 11C to the 16C.

The château is open from mid May to September on Sunday and public holidays. There are guided tours at 15.00, 16.00 and 17.00.

Long the home of the Melun family, princes of Epinoy, in the course of time the château passed by marriage to the princes of Ligne. In 1565 the wedding ceremonies of Floris de Montmorency, which were held here, were used to initiate the first moves in the nobles' rebellion against Spain. Counts Egmont and Horn, the latter the brother of the bridegroom, and Jean de Glymes were present. All three, and Floris, were dead by 1568—executed or assassinated.

Fontenoy, 2km E of Antoing, has given its name to an important battle which was fought nearby in May 1745. With the able assistance of the Irish Brigade, a French army led by an ailing Marshal Saxe defeated a British, Hanoverian, Austrian and Dutch force under the command of the Duke of Cumberland.

The main French line faced S between Antoing and Fontenoy, with an important fortified redoubt to the rear. After early attacks failed to turn the French position, Cumberland decided to make an assault between Fontenoy and the redoubt. He led. His army followed with drums beating and colours unfurled. As the combatants met, Captain Lord Charles Hay of the Grenadier Guards ran forward, drank to the French and called for three cheers. Astonished, the French soldiers cheered in reply and, according to some reports, invited the English to 'tirez les premiers'. This 'messieurs les anglais' did. They advanced and were soon deep in the French lines, apparently the victors. However, although deserted by his courtiers, Louis XV stood firm. Marshal Saxe rallied and brought his artillery into action. This shattered the allied square which, still fighting, was forced to fall back on Vezon.

A Celtic cross, erected in 1907, commemorates the part played by the Irish Brigade in this battle.

Near Hollain, 2km to the S of Antoing on the W side of the river, is the *Pierre Brunehault*, a large menhir 4.40m high.

From Antoing the Mons road meanders across country for *13km* to **Péruwelz-Bon-Secours** (population 17,000), centre of a marble quarrying industry. In the S part of the town, astride the frontier, is the Château de L'Hermitage. This was built by Marshal de Croy in 1749.

There is also a large *Basilica* which was erected between 1885 and 1892. A pious legend relates that in the 16C a young girl was accustomed to pray here before a figure of the Virgin Mary, which she had placed on an oak tree. In 1636, threatened by the plague, the people of Péruwelz pleaded with the Virgin to save them. Their prayers were answered and in gratitude they built a chapel. This was enlarged in 1642 and replaced in 1885 by the present building. It is said that the high altar stands on the site of the oak. The statue of Our Lady is carried in procession through the town on the first Sunday in July in fulfilment of a vow made by the townspeople in 1648. This event attracts many pilgrims.

Bernissart is 4km to the SE. In 1878 fossil iguanodons 250 million years old were found here. They are now in the Institut des Sciences Naturelles at Brussels. There is a local museum which is open between April and October on Sunday from 15.30 to 17.30. At *Blaton*, 2km to the N of Bernissart, there is a Romanesque church which dates from c 1183. Since 1470 this has been dedicated to All the Saints, the only such dedication in Belgium.

From here continue by motorway to *30km* **Mons**. For a description of Mons, see Route 23.

There is a choice of two roads, described below, between Mons and Charleroi. Both are c 36km. The N90 will take you through the pleasant town of Binche. The northerly road through La Louvière, with the fine park and museum of Mariemont, passes through some industrial areas, but includes the great hydraulic lift-locks on the Canal du Centre.

Mons to Charleroi via Binche

6km Villers-Saint Ghislain was the headquarters in August 1914 of General Allenby, commander of the British cavalry. Péronnes is 7km to the E. The first important cavalry action of the war was fought on 22 August on the rise to the W of this place.

At *9km* is **Binche**, population 35,000. The Tourist Information Office is in the Hôtel de Ville. This ancient, fortified hill town is, perhaps, best known for its exuberant annual carnival.

The first fortifications of Binche seem to have been built c 1150 by Count Baldwin IV of Hainaut. These were enlarged and strengthened later, notably in 1491 by Margaret of York, widow of Charles the Bold. In 1545 Mary of Hungary, regent of the Netherlands and sister of Charles V, demolished a part of the defences to make room for a palace which she wished to construct in the town. In 1549, in the presence of Charles V, she organised a great festival in Binche to celebrate the Spanish conquest of Peru. Five years later Henry II of France, at war with Charles V, destroyed the palace of Mary of Hungary and most of the town. Louis XIV razed a large part of the ramparts in 1675.

The origins of the **Carnival** have been traced back to the 14C, but it seems to take much of its present form from Mary of Hungary's festival of 1549. The important days are Shrove Tuesday and the preceding Sunday and Monday. However, preparations begin in January and there are masked and fancy dress balls during the month before the carnival. On Shrove Tuesday there is the dance of the 'Gilles', a clown found only in Binche. It is said that their costumes are based on those worn by the nobles at Mary's festival, who were dressed as Peruvian Incas.

The southern part of Binche has some of the oldest and the most interesting buildings. Work on the *Hôtel de Ville* in the Grand-Place was started by Jacques du Broeucq in 1555. This replaced the building destroyed by the French the year before. Further alterations, including the stucco façade, were carried out by Laurent Dewez in 1735. The *Collégiale Saint Ursmer*, to the S of the Grand-Place, is dedicated to the 8C builder of the Benedictine abbey at Aulne. First built in the 12C, only the base of the tower and the Romanesque main portal survive from that church. By the church is a figure of a 'Gille', erected in 1952. Nearby is the *Musée International Carnaval et Masque*. Occupying the 18C Collège des Augustins, the museum has a wonderful collection of masks from four continents. In the permanent section there are didactic displays on the carnivals and winterfeasts of Europe. The museum is open on weekdays, except Friday, from 15 January to 15 November between 09.00 and 12.00 and 14.00 to 17.00; on Saturday, Sunday and public holidays from 14.00 to 18.00.

In a park to the E end of the church there are a few fragmentary ruins of the palace of Mary of Hungary. This was partly rebuilt by du Broeucq after its destruction in 1544. It was used for municipal purposes until the 18C, when it was neglected and allowed to decay. The park ends at a stretch of the ancient ramparts which are perched high above the river. To the W of the Collégiale is the little 16C mortuary *Chapelle Saint André*. In this there are some finely carved stalls and interesting sculptures. Behind the chapel is the town's ancient cemetery, which was in use from the 14C to the 19C, and another section of the ramparts.

The former abbey of *Bonne Espérance*, now a seminary, is 3km to the S of Binche. The buildings date mainly from the 17C and 18C, but the church by Dewez of 1770 to 1776 incorporates a 15C tower and a cloister in which there is some 13C work.

At *Carnières*, 5km to the NE of Binche, there are some works in the town hall by the painter A.L. Martin, 1887 to 1954. These may be seen on Monday, Wednesday and Thursday between 08.00 and 11.30 and 13.00 and 16.00.

At *11km* is **Fontaine-l'Evêque**, population 19,000. The *Hôtel de Ville* is in a former château of 1558, with a chapel and towers of the 13C and 14C. During the summer there are exhibitions by local artists in the chapel. The towers are linked by an underground gallery which has been converted into an imaginatively arranged *Musée de la Mine*. This shows an extensive section of a coal-mine complete with working machinery. The museum is open between 15 March and 31 October on Tuesday, Thursday, Saturday and Sunday, 10.00 to 12.00 and 14.00 to 18.00.

10km **Charleroi**, see Route 24.

Mons to Charleroi via La Louvière

At *5km* **Havré** the ruins of a château of 1603 stand on 12C foundations. Jean Dunois, the 'Bastard of Orleans' and companion of Joan of Arc, was lord of Havré between 1452 and 1468. Later the estate belonged to the family of Croy-Havré who entertained Marlborough and Prince Eugene here in 1709.

The Canal du Centre between *Thieu*, which is *2km* beyond Havré, and *7km Houdeng-Goegnies* has been served for many years by four unusual and impressive lift-locks. These are at Thieu, where the road crosses the canal at the lock, and at Bracquegnies, Houdeng-Aimeries and Houdeng-Goegnies. Built between 1885 and 1919, they have a daily limit of 12 barges of 380 tonnes. These locks are being replaced by a single giant lock, the world's largest, which will have a capacity of 1350 tonnes. This is at *Strépy-Thieu*, signposted at exit 21 from the motorway. There is a Visitors' Centre which is open daily from 10.00 to 18.00.

The château of *Le Roeulx* is 4km to the NW of Houdeng-Goegnies. Built during the 14C and 15C, it was given a new façade and had other alterations made between 1713 and 1760. It has belonged to the Croy family since the 15C and contains many of the possessions which they acquired in five centuries. There is a tradition that the 7C St Foillan and his companions were murdered in this park (see Nivelles, Route 24). The park has a fine rose garden and magnificent trees.

At *3km* is **La Louvière** (population 78,000), a busy industrial centre.

The *Museum of Mariemont*, set in a fine park of 50 ha. 3km to the SE of the town, merits a visit. It takes its name from Mary of Hungary, sister of Charles V and regent of the Netherlands, who built a palace here in 1546. This was destroyed by Henry II of France in 1554 and the site was abandoned until Charles de Lorraine built here again in 1756. This château also only lasted a short time. It was burnt by French revolutionaries in 1794. The ruins are in the park. The third château of 1831 was owned by the Warocqué family. In 1917 it was bequeathed to the nation by the latter-day Maecenas and art lover of catholic taste Raoul Warocqué, together with a vast collection of precious objects. Unfortunately, this building was badly damaged by fire in 1960 and some of the porcelain destroyed. A fine new museum was constructed to house the collections and this opened its doors to the public in October 1975.

The museum has two main departments. On the first floor there are displays of European, Asiatic and Oriental antiquities. The lower ground floor is devoted to the archaeology of Hainaut and the history of Mariemont. It also has the finest collection of Tournai porcelain in Belgium. Do not miss the service 'aux oiseaux de Buffon' made for the Duke of Orleans in Tournai in 1787.

Among Mariemont's many treasures are Greek classical funerary monuments, statues, black and red-figure vases; Hellenistic statuettes, jewellery and other material from Greece, Italy, Anatolia, Syria, Egypt, Cyprus and Russia; Egyptian statuary; wallpaintings from Pompeii; Han and Tang ceramics, Ming porcelain, jade, lacquer, furniture and a 16C commemorative stele from Peking. There are displays of artefacts from Coptic Egypt, Syria and Palestine. In the Merovingian section there is a magnificent lead sarcophagus and a variety of finds from sites in Belgium and Germany. The museum also has more than 12,000 books and ancient MSS.

After visiting the museum it is worthwhile spending some time in the park where there are the ruins of Charles de Lorraine's building and the rose garden. There are also open air displays of 19C and modern sculpture. Among the delightful Asiatic pieces is a serene Buddha, seated cross-legged on a lotus blossom and surrounded by flowering shrubs and trees.

The museum is open daily, except Monday, from 10.00 to 18.00. It is closed on 1 January and 25 December. The park is open from 09.00 to 16.00, 17.00 or 18.00 depending on the time of year.

At *10km Trazegnies* there is a small château. First built in the 12C, it was rebuilt in the 16C and 17C and enlarged in 1854. In the 13C church there are the tombs of the lords of Trazegnies. One is by Luc Fayd'herbe.

For 9km **Charleroi**, see Route 24.

9km **Châtelet** occupies the SE corner of the industrial complex around Charleroi. *4km Presles* claims, as does Fleurus (Route 24), to be the place where Caesar defeated the Nervii in 57 BC.

At *9km* is **Fosses-la-Ville** (population 7000), in the province of Namur. This ancient town traces its origins back to Celtic times when the place was called Biberona, the valley of the beavers. During the Gallo-Roman period the Latin name Fossa, which presumably referred to its fortifications, replaced Biberona. Circa 650 the widow of Pepin of Landen gave land to the Irish monk St Foillan or Feuillen (see also Nivelles) for the foundation of an abbey here. This was later sacked by the Norsemen. About 974 Bishop Notger of Liège built fortifications around a new abbey church. The present *Collégiale Saint Feuillen* is the successor of these earlier churches. This dates mainly from the 18C, but parts of the foundations are of the 9C and 10C and it has a slightly later Romanesque tower and crypt. The stalls and pulpit are early 16C and the marble choir screen has brass gates of 1756 by the Nalinnes of Dinant. In the pleasant Place du Chapitre beside the church are some of the canons' houses. The largely 16C Maison du Doyen du Chapitre incorporates part of the ramparts.

Tamines, an industrial centre 7km to the NW, was the scene of one of the worst German massacres of the First World War. On 20 August 1914 384 civilians were mowed down by machine gun and rifle fire in front of the church. A monument records this tragic event. The victims rest beside the church where they died.

The famous medieval goldsmith, Brother Hugo d'Oignies, was a member of the community of the abbey of *Oignies* which is on the other side of the river from Tamines. The abbey is now a glassworks.

The *Lac du Bambois*, 2km to the S of Fosses-la-Ville, is a popular recreation area. *Mettet*, 5km farther S, is a centre for motor-cycle sport.

Vistors come to *7km* **Floreffe**, a small town on the Sambre, to explore its grottoes and visit its great abbey. A slim 16C tower marks the position of the *grottoes* which are beside the main road. They are the only dolomitic caverns in Belgium. Human bones and those of bears, as well as other evidence of occupation during prehistoric times, have been discovered in them. Some of the finds are on display. The grottoes are open daily between Easter and mid October from 09.00 to 19.00.

The imposing buildings of the *Abbey of Floreffe* overlook the green water meadows of the Sambre. Below the main complex, in the Moulin-Brasserie, bread, beer and cheese made in the abbey are served to visitors. The brasserie claims to be the oldest commercial establishment in Belgium.

Now a school, the abbey may be visited daily between March and November from 11.00 to 19.00 or 20.00 at weekends. There are frequent presentations of an audio-visual description of its buildings and history.

In 1120 St Norbert, the founder of the Premonstratensian Order, passed through Namur on his way back from Cologne. During his stay he was invited by a local nobleman to found an abbey here. In the centuries that followed, the abbey of Floreffe suffered grievously. It was sacked in 1188 by the Count of Hainaut, in 1232 and 1237 by the Counts of Flanders, in 1683 by the soldiers of Louis XIV and finally suppressed by the invading French at the time of the revolution.

The existing domestic buildings date mainly from the 18C. By the church entrance is the small vaulted Salle des Frères Convers of c 1150, the oldest surviving part of the abbey. This has some 12C murals. The church is a complex mixture. The choir, transepts and nave are 12C or 13C, the tower is 16C, the eastern extension of the choir dates from 1638 and the baroque W front was added during the 18C. During the same century Laurent Dewez converted the interior, facing the walls with stucco. The baroque *stalls of 1632 to 1648 are by Peter Enderlin, a German who lived in Namur. Note his carved signature. A leaflet detailing the subjects of the carvings is available.

At *3km* is *Malonne*, a small place straggling up a steep-sided, wooded valley. The mainly 17C church replaced an abbey church founded here before 698 by the Anglo-Saxon monk and missionary St Bertuin.

For a description of *6km* **Namur** see Route 28.

26

Between the Sambre and the Meuse

This Route is divided into three sections. It deals with places in an area which is bounded, roughly, on the N by the Mons, Charleroi and Namur road, on the S by the French border and on the W and E by the Sambre and Meuse rivers. Note that the E–W Route 26A, Mons to Dinant, is crossed by the N–S Routes 26B and 26C at Beaumont and Philippeville respectively.

Once past the largely industrial area around Charleroi, the countryside, which can be regarded as a westwards extension of the Ardennes, is open, agricultural upland with wide vistas and, towards the S, forests.

A. Mons to Dinant

Total distance 79km.—*21km Solre-sur-Sambre*—*10km* **Beaumont**—*12km Silenrieux* (for **Walcourt**)—*10km* **Philippeville**—*26km* **Dinant**.

For a description of **Mons** see Route 23. Leave the town and, at La Bascule where Route 25 runs E to Binche, take the right fork on to the N40.

An area of open fields to the W just beyond *5km Spiennes* known as Camp à Cailloux is the site of neolithic flint mines (no admission at present). Immediately after (*5km*) Givry this route crosses the Roman road from Bavai to Binche.

At *11km Solre-sur-Sambre* there is a moated castle, one of the finest feudal strongholds in Hainaut. It has a 12C keep, which was the original fortified house, and a square court enclosed by walls with 14C cylindrical towers at the corners.

In a quiet setting a short way S of the main road at *4km Montignies-Saint-Christophe*, just on the border with France, an attractive Roman bridge spans the little river Hantes. This is about the last trace of the ancient road from Bavai to Trier.

At *6km* **Beaumont** (population 5800) an ancient town sited picturesquely on a hill, there are still some sections of the 11C and 12C fortifications. The

Tour Salamandre, a short walk from the Grand-Place, is all that is left of the castle of the Counts of Hainaut. This was built c 1051 and demolished in 1691. The tower with its small museum is open daily between May and September from 09.00 to 12.00 and 14.00 to 19.00; in October on Sunday from 10.00 to 12.00 and 14.00 to 17.00.

For places N and S of Beaumont, see Route 26B.

10km Boussu-lez-Walcourt is just short of the border with the province of Namur. Between here and *Cerfontaine*, 6km to the S, stretches the attractive area of the **Barrages de l'Eau d'Heure**. In this system of dams and reservoirs there are paths for ramblers, picnic sites, view-points, recreational and water sports facilities and 70km of roads. An Information Centre near the Plate Taille dam is open daily between Easter and September from 09.00 to 18.00. A belvedere overlooks the dam at Eau d'Heure. The old station at Cerfontaine has been turned into a museum. This is open on Sunday from 15.00 to 18.00 between Easter and mid-September.

The scheme, which has a capacity of 47 million cubic metres of water, has three main purposes: to feed the Brussels to Charleroi canal; to dilute urban and industrial pollution; and to maintain the flow of the Meuse. The principal dams are *Eau d'Heure* in the N and *Plate Taille*, where there is a power generating station, in the S. To ensure a constant water level there are three pre-dams. These are *Feronval*, close to Eau d'Heure, and *Ry Jaune* and *Falemprise*, to the E.

At *2km* Silenrieux, in the province of Namur, take a left turning to 3km **Walcourt**. The Place de la Poste of this pleasant little town was once occupied by a Gallo-Roman camp. Later a medieval castle stood here. According to a local tradition the 4C St Maternus of Tongeren, incensed at finding a pagan altar, built the first Christian church. This was a predecessor of the present *Basilique Saint Materne*. The choir and the transepts of the basilica are 13C, the rest was completed by 1477. The base of the tower and the narthex belong to an earlier church which was constructed between 990 and 1026. The upper part of the tower, with its strange 17C steeple, dates from c 1200. The marble *rood-loft of 1531, an elaborate piece in the Flamboyant style, was presented by Charles V when he made a pilgrimage to the miraculous Virgin of Walcourt. It is believed that this wooden figure dates from the 11C. However, the local people insist that it is much older, even claiming that it may have been made by Maternus. The silver plating on the image dates from 1626. In the Treasury there are some pieces attributed to the medieval goldsmith Hugo d'Oignies who was a native of Walcourt. (see also Oignies, Route 25).

For *Thy-le-Château*, 4km to the N, see Route 26C.

10km **Philippeville** (population 7000) was built as a fortress in 1555 by Charles V to replace Mariembourg, 12km to the S, which the French had captured the previous year. He named it after his son Philip II. (See the commemorative stone on the first pillar on the left in the church.) Civilians were not allowed to live here until 1620. The town retains its star-shaped fortress plan and defensive galleries, the 'souterrains', which are open to visitors every day in July and August from 13.00 to 18.00. The former powder magazine is now the Chapelle des Remparts.

For places N and S of Philippeville, see Route 26C.

Florennes, 8km to the NE, claims to be the birthplace of Arletta. The daughter of a tanner, she was mother of William the Conqueror of England. The 18C Eglise Saint Gangulphe rests on foundations laid down in 1001. It is dedicated to a Burgundian nobleman who became a recluse. His isolation did not protect him. He was murdered c 760 by his wife's lover.

At *Senzeille*, 8km to the SW of Philippeville, there is a remarkable astronomical clock. This was built by a local craftsman at the beginning of the century.

In the church at *20km Onhaye* is the tomb of St Walhere. A priest here, he reproached another ecclesiastic for his dissolute life and was murdered for his pains.

For *6km* **Dinant**, see Route 29.

B.   Charleroi to Chimay

Total distance 47km.—*12km Gozée* (for W **Aulne**, **Thuin** and **Lobbes**; and E **Ham-sur-Heure**)—*13km* **Beaumont**—*12km Rance*—*10km* **Chimay**.

South of Beaumont this Route passes through the centre of the wooded **Botte Du Hainaut**, a narrow parcel of land bounded by France to the W and S, and by the province of Namur to the E.

The direct road to Beaumont is the N53 through Gozée and Strée. This was a Roman road and Strée's name, which is derived from the Latin 'strata', recalls that fact. The principal places of interest, the abbeys of Aulne and Lobbes and the town of Thuin, are to the W along the Sambre. As they are close to each other, they are easily reached from Gozée or by minor roads along the Sambre valley from Charleroi.

Gozé is 12km to the S of Charleroi. 3km to the E is **Ham-sur-Heure** with its imposing castle. Dating from the 11C, this was virtually rebuilt in the 18C and 19C. It now belongs to the municipality. Visits may be possible. In the *Eglise Saint Martin* there is a 12C font, a 15C retable and, in the porch, the 15C 'poutre aux apôtres', a carved 'Apostles beam'.

The ruins of the abbey of **Aulne**, 3km to the NW of Gozée, are in a delightful sylvan setting beside the Sambre. The abbey's name is derived from the alder (aune) grove in which it was founded in 657 by monks from Lobbes, led by St Ursmer and possibly St Landelin. It adopted the Cistercian rule in 1144 and prospered sufficiently under the protection of the prince-bishops of Liège to be called 'Aulne-la-Riche'. It was sacked in the 15C and 16C and almost completely burned down by French revolutionaries in 1794. However, some of the domestic buildings, mainly those dating from the 18C, were saved. These have been restored and with a chapel of 1837 are used as a home for the aged. The great abbey church, now in ruins, was built between 1214 and 1250. The most conspicuous remains are of some of the later additions, the 16C apse, parts of the transepts and something of the W front of 1728.

The abbey may be visited daily, except Monday, at the following times: between April and October from 09.30 to 12.00 and 13.30 to 18.30; on Sunday and public holidays from 10.00 to 12.00 and 13.00 to 20.00; out of season from 13.00 to 16.00.

Thuin (population 13,000) is 6km to the S of Aulne. Occupying the high ground above the Sambre, it was an outpost of the bishops of Liège and a strongly fortified place. The town's walls were razed to the ground in 1408 on the orders of John the Fearless of Flanders and Luxembourg after he had crushed the Liègeois at the battle of Othée. The Place du Chapitre is the town centre. Here is the tower of the *Belfry* of 1638, all that remains of the former collegiate church. The base of the *Tour Notger* across the road is a relic of the fortifications erected c 1000 by Bishop Notger of Liège. A short distance up the main street the post office occupies the early 16C refuge of the abbey of Lobbes. On the opposite side of the street is the refuge of the abbey of Aulne. This is also a 16C building.

A striking modern addition to the landscape is the S-shaped, 300m-long viaduct over the Sambre.

Lobbes (population 5000) is 2km to the NW of Thuin on the opposite bank of the Sambre. Its Benedictine abbey was founded c 654 by St Landelin, a repentant brigand of noble birth, who was also associated with Aulne. Destroyed by the French in 1794, all that survives of the mainly 18C domestic quarters are a gateway and part of a farm building near the railway station. On the hilltop is the Romanesque *Abbey Church of St Ursmer*. Dedicated to the builder of Aulne who was a monk here, it dates in part from c 825 and is an outstanding example of pre-Romanesque and Romanesque building. The E crypt, chancel and W tower are all 11C, but the central tower and the roof of the W tower are rather unfortunate additions of 1865.

Immediately to the S of Gozée, to the E of the road, is the menhir known as the *Pierre de Zeupire*.

At *13km* from Gozée is **Beaumont**. For a description see Route 26A.

Continue to *8km Sautin*. About 1km to the SW there are two menhirs called *Les Pierres-qui-tournent*. In the church of 1572 at *Renlies*, 3km to the NE of Sautin, there is a particularly fine retable of 1530. At *Sivry*, 3km to the W of Sautin, a local museum dedicated to Natural History and Toys is open on weekdays, except from 15 December to 15 January, between 10.00 and 17.00; at weekends and on public holidays from Easter to September between 14.00 and 18.00. There is also a Centre for the Study of Nature. This is open daily, except Monday, in July and August from 14.00 to 18.00.

Continue to *4km Rance* which is famous for the red marble quarried here. The chimneypieces at Versailles and some of the columns in St Peter's at Rome are made from this marble. There is a museum which is open every day, except Monday if it is not a public holiday, from 09.30 to 18.00; on Sunday from 14.00 and 18.00 between April and October.

Continue for a further *10km* to **Chimay** (population 9000). Chimay's Tourist Information Office is in the Vielle Tour, Rue de Noailles. In this pleasant town above the Eau Blanche the chronicler Froissart, canon and treasurer of the collegiate church, died in 1410. He is commemorated by a statue in the Place Froissart. In the Grand-Place there is a monument to the princes of Chimay.

Also in the square is the *Collégiale Saints Pierre et Paul*. The three E bays of the choir date from the 13C, the remainder of the church is largely 16C with a tower of 1732. Inside are the tomb of Charles de Croy, first Prince of Chimay, who died in 1525, and the grave-stone of Mme Tallien (see below). A stone arch in the Grand-Place marks the entrance to an attractive, short, narrow street. This leads to the *château* which is perched high above the river. Dating from the 15C, the château was much modified in 1607, badly damaged by fire in 1935, and later rebuilt on the original lines.

It is open daily from Easter to all Saints' Day 10.00 to 12.00, 14.00 to 18.00.

The property passed to the de Croy family at the start of the 15C and in 1486 Charles de Croy was created Prince de Chimay by the emperor Maximilian. In 1835 the lady usually known as Madame Tallien died here. Born Jeanne Marie Ignace Thérèse Cabarrus in 1773, she played a not unimportant part in the French Revolution. Daughter of a Spanish banker, she married and was divorced from the Marquis de

Fontenay. In 1793, while a prisoner at Bordeaux awaiting execution, she met the revolutionary Jean Tallien. He had suppressed all opposition by his ruthless use of the guillotine. Tallien fell in love with her and they were soon married. She became involved in revolutionary affairs and helped him in his Thermidor coup against Robespierre, whom she hated. Notorious for her harsh and dissolute conduct, Madame Tallien was dubbed 'Notre-Dame de Thermidor' and became a leading figure in the revolutionary salons. In 1802 Tallien divorced her and three years later she married the Prince de Chimay.

Most of the valuable objects in the château were saved from the fire of 1935. There are some interesting family portraits, including one of Madame Tallien, furniture and bric à brac of the 18C and 19C. The small rococo theatre, used now during Chimay's summer festival, was built for Madame Tallien by her son Prince Joseph. There are some Louis XI banners in the chapel.

The *Etang de Virelles*, 3km to the NE, an important venue for water sports and a popular recreation area, has an area of 125 ha. It is the largest lake in Belgium.

C. Charleroi to Couvin

Total distance 38km.—*10km Somzée—12km* **Philippeville**—*12km* **Mariembourg**—*4km* **Couvin**.

10km Somzée is in the province of Namur. At *Thy-le-Château*, 3km to the W, the castle of 1188 has a fine hall which was drastically restored between 1920 and 1939. It houses an important collection of paintings by the 20C artist Charles Delporte. The castle is open from May to mid September on Saturday, Sunday and public holidays from 14.00 to 18.00.

A further *12km* brings us to **Philippeville**, described in Route 26A.

About halfway between Philippeville and Mariembourg, to the E of the road, is the village of *Roly*. Here there is a fortified farm which dates in part from the 12C. There is a small museum and the estate has been converted into a nature reserve with signposted walks and drives.

12km **Mariembourg** was built as a fortress in 1542 by Charles V and named after his sister Mary of Hungary. Believed to be impregnable, it was taken by the French in 1554, a loss which led to the construction of Philippeville. Little trace now remains of the town's military past. The *Chapelle Notre-Dame de la Brouffe* is a survival from a priory of 1134.

A steam train, which runs between Mariembourg and Treignes in the valley of the Viroin, is a popular holiday attraction. The round trip takes two hours. There are three or more trains every day between April and September.

A further *4km* brings us to **Couvin**. This pleasant, small town of 5000 inhabitants on the Eau Noire is a popular centre with visitors who enjoy walking and driving in the surrounding forests and along the rocky, wooded hillsides. The nearby *Cavernes de l'Abîme* are a popular attraction. Since prehistoric times these caves have been a home and refuge to man. In 1940 the inhabitants of Couvin sheltered from the dangers of war in them. The caves may be visited every day in June, July and August from 10.00 to 12.00 and 14.00 to 18.00; in April, May and September on Sunday at the same times. The visit takes 45 minutes. There is an exhibition on prehistory and an audio-visual show.

To the E of Couvin along the valley of the Viroin, whose waters combine the Eau Noire and Eau Blanche, there are several places of interest. At **Pétigny** is the *Grotte de Neptune* which was discovered at the end of the 19C. This is open daily from Easter to September from 09.30 to 12.00 and 13.30 to 18.00; also on Sunday in October. The visit, which lasts 45 minutes, includes a boat ride on the underground Eau Noire and a Son et Lumière performance near a waterfall. The *Barrage du Ry de Rome*, 3km to the S of Petigny, is a large reservoir of 24 ha. in a forest setting.

Farther along the valley are *Nismes, Olloy* and *Dourbes*, small resorts with ruined castles, unusual rock formations and geological features like the Fondry des Chiens and signposted walks.

The forest extends to the S of Couvin. *Brûly-de-Pesche* , 6km to the SW, was the site of Hitler's headquarters in 1940. It may be visited from Easter to September: daily from 09.00 to 12.00. 13.00 to 18.30; on Sunday in October.

The N5 continues S from Couvin and reaches the French border after 10km.

27

Brussels to Namur

Total distance 53km.—*13km* **Overijse**—*8km* **Wavre**—*16km* **Gembloux**—*16km* **Namur**.
This Route runs roughly parallel to the motorway A4/E411.

For **Brussels**, see Route 1. Leave the city by the Chaussée de Wavre. This road crosses a corner of the Forêt de Soignes. See Route 1F.

At *13km* is **Overijse** (population 12,000) on the southern edge of a grape growing district. This town covers a steep hillside in the valley of the Ijse. The centre is the Justus Lipsiusplein, named after the distinguished scholar and classical historian who was born at 10 Isidoor Taymansstraat behind the Stadhuis, in 1547. Lipsius taught at Louvain, Jena, Cologne, Antwerp and Leiden and died in 1606. The 16C *Stadhuis* may be from a design by Antoon Keldermans. The *château*, now a school, dates mainly from the 17C. Of the *Begijnhof*, which was founded before 1267, only the restored 15C chapel survives. This is in the W part of the town near a sports complex.

In **Huldenberg**, 3km to the NE, the church was built between the 11C and 14C. It has statues dating from c 1400 of the Virgin, St Catherine and St Barbara and also an Assumption attributed to de Crayer. The château, which has been much altered, was built in 1514.

DIVERSION TO LA HULPE, GENVAL AND RIXENSART. As, apart from Tombeek (see below), there is little of interest along the main road to Wavre a short detour of c 8km through wooded country to La Hulpe, Genval and Rixensart is suggested. These lie to the W and may be reached by following the N253 across the motorway. **La Hulpe** (Flemish **Terhulpen**) has a church which dates partly from the 13C. In this is the gravestone of Charles Baillie, 1542 to 1625, a secretary of Mary Queen of Scots.

Genval with its lake is to the SE of La Hulpe. It is a popular holiday and recreation centre and has a spring which is the source of Schweppes mineral water.

In nearby **Rixensart** is the *Château de Merode*. Built between 1631 and 1662, it has belonged to the de Merode family since 1787. The attractive court is laid out in the form of a cloister with galleries of flattened arches. Inside the château there are tapestries, family portraits and a collection of Arabic weapons brought from Egypt by Gaspard Monge. He had directed archaeological and scientific studies during Napoleon's campaign in that country. There is also the lance-pennon of Frédéric de Merode, who was killed during the 1830 revolution. His memorial is in the Place des Martyrs in Brussels. The château is open on Sunday and public holidays from Easter to October between 14.00 and 18.00.

Continue to Wavre through Bierges. Wavre is described below.

2km from Overijse is *Tombeek*. Just beyond the village is Belgium's principal broadcasting transmitter. Opposite is the Ferme des Templiers, an estate given to the Templars c 1180 by Godfrey III of Brabant. After the suppression of the Order in 1312 the property passed to the Knights of Malta in whose hands it remained until the French Revolution. Except for a chapel of 1643 the present buildings, which are private, date from the 18C and 19C. Just beyond Tombeek is the language boundary.

At *6km* is **Wavre** (Flemish **Waver**), with a population of 26,000. The Tourist Information Office is in the Hôtel de Ville. This old and pleasant town on the Dyle suffered much bomb damage in 1940 but has been rebuilt in part in the old style.

On a site known to have been occupied since prehistoric times, the present town traces its origins to the 11C when a trading centre developed at this important crossroads and river crossing. It was granted a charter in 1222. During the centuries that followed Wavre suffered much from marauding armies. In 1489, after rebelling against Maximilian, the town was pillaged and burnt. It suffered again in the late 16C and early 17C, this time at the hands of the Spanish. In 1647 it was sacked by the Dutch. In 1815, on the day of Waterloo, it was the scene of a battle between the French under Grouchy and the Prussians.

Marshal the Marquis de Grouchy, in command of Napoleon's right flank, pursued Blücher's Prussians as they retreated from Ligny to Wavre. Adhering rigidly to ill-drafted and contradictory orders he pressed on to Wavre instead of turning W towards Waterloo, a manoeuvre which would have allowed him to cut off the Prussians and bring Napoleon badly needed support. Later he was held partly responsible for the French defeat at Waterloo. He was court-martialled and exiled for a time. See also Walhain, below. In May 1940 150 houses and the Hôtel de Ville were destroyed by bombing.

The *Hôtel de Ville* at Wavre is unusual in so far as it occupies the buildings of a former Carmelite friary. Built between 1715 and 1726, the friary was appropriated in 1797 by the invading French revolutionaries. Soon after the town acquired its buildings. The friary church continued to be used until 1856. Later it served as a public hall. Largely destroyed in 1940, the building was carefully restored and officially reopened in 1961. The window on the soaring façade pictures the lords of Wavre handing over the keys of the town. The *Eglise Saint Jean-Baptiste*, down the Rue Haute opposite the Hôtel de Ville, dates from c 1476. It was damaged by fire three times: in 1489 during the uprising against Maximilian, in 1582 during the wars of religion and in 1604 by mutinous Spanish soldiers. The tower, striped in white stone, grew in stages between the 15C and 17C. Inside, a French bullet of 1815 remains lodged in one of the pillars.

The *Musée Historique et Archéologique* at 23 Rue de l'Ermitage has material from a Roman villa excavated near Basse Wavre in 1904. (NB: there is nothing visible at the site.) The museum is open on Wednesday and Saturday from 14.00 to 16.00.

Bierges, 2km to the W, saw heavy fighting on the afternoon of 18 June 1815 as the French tried to cross the river. A memorial by the mill records that the French General Gérard was wounded here. *Walibi*, nearby, is a popular recreation park with many attractions for children.

In the 18C church at *Basse Wavre*, 2km to the NE, there is a copper-gilt reliquary. This was given by the Archbishop of Mechelen in 1628 to replace one destroyed by religious fanatics in 1580. It contains the relics of several saints and martyrs. The high ground to the NW of the railway was the site of a Roman settlement. The villa referred to above occupied a position on the slope.

Visitors not pressed for time may like to make a diversion to the area to the SE of Wavre and N of the motorway. To the NW of the village of *Chaumont-Gistoux*, 9km from Wavre, there are tumuli and traces of earthworks which belonged to a prehistoric settlement, the Bois de Chaumont. There are more tumuli between this site and *Bonlez* farther to the NW, a village whose château dates in part from 1230. The hamlet of *Dion Valmont*, to the W of Bonlez, is mentioned in a document of 987.

5km **•Louvain-la-Neuve** is a new and fast growing university campus and town. This was created for French-speaking students after the language-split at Louvain University in 1970. Stretching westward towards Ottignies, it covers a hilly area that offers scope for daringly imaginative planning and architecture. The buildings, of pleasing light brickwork, are in a variety of modern designs which provide some interesting architectural vistas. There is an upper level town for pedestrians and cyclists and a lower level for service roads and car parks.

2km Corbais. In the village there are the remains of a 12C or 13C defensive keep, the Tour Griffon. A better preserved keep of 1324, which once formed part of a manor house, is on an islet at *Alvaux*. This is reached by continuing along the N4 for 1km and then following a narrow road W for 1.5km.

4km Walhain, 1.5km E of the main road, has associations with Marshal Grouchy (see also Wavre above). On 18 June 1815 he arrived here in time for a late breakfast which was disturbed by the sound of the opening cannonade at Waterloo. Although urged by his staff to 'march to the guns', Grouchy refused, obstinately sticking to Napoleon's woolly instruction that he should 'head for Wavre'.

The Rue du Château leads out of the village in a S direction to the overgrown ruins of a castle believed to date from the 13C. *Baudeset*, just beyond, is thought to cover the site of a Roman fort.

Gentinnes is 7km to the SW of the Walhain crossroads. The château here was given in 1903 to the Order of Saint Esprit and used to train missionaries for the Congo. It still belongs to the Order. In front of the building there is a striking sculpture by Raf Mailleux. This and the austerely beautiful chapel of 1967 by Charles Jeandrain commemorate those missionaries who lost their lives during the troubles which marred the granting of independence to the Congo in 1962. On the façade are the names of 181 Catholic missionaries and of 30 Protestant victims. Inside the chapel the altar is of Congo granite and the benches of Congo wood.

At *5km* is **Gembloux** (population 17,500), in the province of Namur. This is an agricultural and sugar-refining centre of some importance. It is also known for the manufacture of cutlery. The Tourist Information Office is in the Ancien Hôtel de Ville.

The once powerful and learned *Benedictine Abbey* is now an agricultural college. The abbey was founded in 940 by St Guibert, a Lotharingian military leader who became a hermit on his estate here. It was last rebuilt by Dewez between 1760 and 1779. Beside the main entrance stands a substantial section of the old wall. The parish church, by Dewez, 1779, was formerly the abbey church. It has an 11C crypt. In the Rue de Mazy in the S of the town a restored 17C chapel commemorates a victory of Don John of Austria in 1577 over the 'Les Gueux'.

Work on the great castle of *Corroy-le-Château*, 3km to the SW of Gembloux, started c 1270. This has seven solid round towers linked by massive walls. Formerly topped by crenellations, they are now roofed. Built as part of the defensive system for S Brabant, the castle saw little fighting and thus has scarcely changed in outward appearance. There are some interesting portraits, good furniture, a painting by van Dyck and a collection of dolls. The castle is the residence of the Marquis de Trazegnies. Visiting times: May to September: Saturday, Sunday and public holidays, 10.00 to 12.00, 14.00 to 18.00.

The village church dates from the early 12C. It also has changed little. St Norbert, the founder of the Premonstratensians, preached here in 1119.

The Château of *Mielmont* is 5km to the S of Corroy-le-Château and immediately N of the E42 motorway. Dating from 1160, it has been much rebuilt. Its collection of paintings is mainly concerned with the history of Belgium. Visiting times: Easter to September: Saturday, Sunday and public holidays, 14.00 to 18.00.

For *16km* **Namur**, see Route 28.

28

Namur

NAMUR (Flemish **Namen**; population 102,000) is the capital of the province of the same name. A town of great character and interest, it lies mainly to the N of the confluence of the Meuse and the Sambre, a point dominated by the fortifications of the citadel. The town's strategic and defensive position ensured a violent history which has obliterated most buildings from the medieval and earlier periods. Much, however, survives from the 17C and 18C, thanks in part to the edicts of 1687 and 1708 which prohibited the construction of timbered and thatched houses.

Tourist Information Offices. *Namur Town*: Square Léopold, close to the station. *Province of Namur*: 3 Rue Notre-Dame, across the Sambre beyond the Pont du Musée.

There is a **teleferic** to the Citadel from S end of Pont du Musée. This operates daily from April to mid September from 10.00 to 18.00, but on Sunday only from mid September to mid November.

Boats. *Local* Sambre et Meuse cruise. Mid April to mid September: five times daily between 10.00 and 17.00; afternoon only in early April and late September. Duration 45 minutes. To *Dinant*. July and August: Sunday at 10.00. Duration 9 hours. It is advisable to check on round-trip timings as these are liable to change. To *Wépion*, Daily in July and August at 14.00. Duration 3 hours.

History. Namur has been identified, on rather tenuous grounds, with the stronghold of the Aduatuci mentioned by Caesar. It enters documented history in the Merovingian period as *Namurcum Castrum*. At that time it consisted simply of the citadel and the spit of land below which lies between the rivers. Soon an important commercial centre, Namur developed into a feudal holding by the 10C. Its rulers styled themselves counts. In 1421 Count Jean III de Dampierre sold the County of Namur to Philip the Good of Burgundy. The town was besieged many times. In 1577 it fell to Don John of Austria. In 1692 it was taken by Vauban for Louis XIV, an event celebrated by Boileau and Racine. In 1695 it was recaptured by William of Orange, when it inspired the martial spirit of 'Tristram Shandy'. Seized by the French revolutionaries in 1792 and 1794, it was, until 1814, the capital of the French department of Sambre-et-Meuse. In 1815 there was a gallant stand here by Grouchy's rearguard.

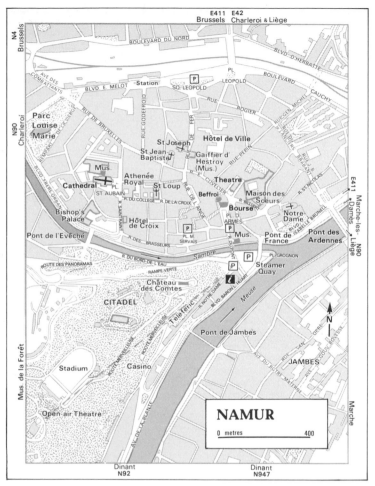

E411 E42
Brussels Charleroi & Liège

NAMUR

0 metres 400

The fortifications, dismantled by Joseph II between 1782 and 1784, were rebuilt by the Dutch United Kingdom of the Netherlands in 1816. They were razed to the ground between 1862 and 1865 and replaced by boulevards and gardens. In 1887 the construction of an outer ring of nine forts made Namur once more an important fortress. However, its supposed impregnability was disproved in August 1914 when the Germans overran the forts in three days. Afterwards they burned and looted parts of the town. Namur suffered more damage, particularly to its bridges, during the Second World War. In April 1975, after about 2000 years of military occupation, the last army unit left the citadel and its keys were handed over to the town.

Charles de Berlaymont, 1510–78, councillor to Margaret of Parma, was a native of Namur. He was the first to call the Netherlands League of Nobility 'ces gueux', those beggars. The painter and engraver Félicien Rops, 1833–98, was also born here.

The town's main artery, c 1km long, is the Rue de Fer and its continuation the Rue de l'Ange. These streets link the Square Léopold near the station with the Place d'Armes close to the confluence of the rivers. The route described below, which includes the cathedral and other important buildings to the W and E of the main axis, is rather more than 2km in length.

In the Rue de Fer there are several 18C mansions, including the *Hôtel de Ville* on the left. This is best seen from the garden. At No. 24, also on the left, the *Hôtel Gaiffier d'Hestroy* houses two museums.

The *Musée Félicien Rops* has many examples of the work of this versatile artist—paintings, drawings, engravings, lithographs, small sculpture, and book illustrations including those made for Charles de Coster's 'Ulenspiegel'. It is open daily, except Tuesday, from 3 January to 23 December, 10.00 to 17.00. It closes at 18.00 from Easter onwards and is open on Tuesday during July and August.

The *Musée des Arts Anciens du Namurois* has exhibits of local painting, sculpture and metalwork. Most of these date from the 14C to the 17C. It is open on Monday, Wednesday, Thursday and Friday from 10.00 to 12.00, 14.00 to 17.00; on Saturday from 14.00 to 17.00; and on Sunday from 10.00 to 12.00. It is closed from 23 December to 3 January and on Tuesday.

The *Eglise Saint Joseph* opposite dates from 1650. At the next intersection, the Rue de l'Ange leads to the Place de l'Ange, where there is a fountain of 1791.

To the right, a little farther on, in the tranquil Marché aux Légumes is the *Eglise Saint Jean Baptiste*. A part dates from the 13C, but the present building is mainly 16C with restoration and additions of 1616 and 1890. Of the early furnishing only the font remains.

From here take the Rue de la Croix to the baroque **Eglise Saint Loup**. This was built for the Jesuits between 1621 and 1645. Note the extensive use of different coloured marbles inside and the carved sandstone vaulting. The altar is made of wood painted to look like marble. This curious situation arose, because the ship bringing the marble altar from Italy for Saint Loup was wrecked at Calais. There the altar was seized and placed in one of that town's churches.

Farther on, in the Rue du Collège, is the *Athénée Royal* of 1614, the former Jesuit college. The Rue du Collège ends at the PLACE SAINT AUBAIN. In this square the offices of the *Provincial Government* occupy the former episcopal palace which was built between 1726 and 1740. Opposite is the **Cathédrale Saint Aubain**. This neo-classical building by Gaetano Pizzoni, with stucco by the Moretti brothers, was completed between 1751 and 1767. There were several earlier churches here. The first was consecrated in the 3C. Behind the apse is a tower of 1388 which was heightened in 1648. This is all that is left of the church pulled down in 1751. In the cathedral there are pictures by pupils of Rubens—the Jesuit priest J. Nicolai and Nicolas Roose—a Calvary attributed to van Dyck; works by Jacques Baudin; and others attributed to Gaspard de Crayer. Behind the high altar a tablet marks the place where the heart of Don John of Austria is buried. He died in his camp at Bouge, to the NE of Namur, soon after his successful assault on the town in 1577.

Among the many treasures in the **Musée Diocésain** is a magnificent 13C golden crown-reliquary containing two thorns from the Crown of Thorns. There is also a 14C silver-gilt statuette of St Blaise who died c 316. He was a physician who became bishop of Sebaste in Armenia. Devotion to St Blaise was spread throughout Europe by returning crusaders. He saved the life of a boy who had choked on a fish bone. This started the custom of the Blessing of St Blaise against infections in the throat. Usually portrayed with the wool-comb with which he was martyred, he is honoured by the Eastern and Western Churches.

Note also a 12C portable altar with 11C ivory panels; a silver-gilt reliquary arm attributed to Hugo d'Oignies; a pax dating from the 14C or 15C; and a 9C reliquary from Andenne.

Visiting times: from Easter to October daily, except Monday, from 10.00 to 12.00, 14.30 to 18.00; November to Easter from 14.30 to 16.30. The museum is closed on Sunday morning and Monday.

From the cathedral take the Rue Saintraint to the 18C **Hôtel de Croix**. This replaced a building of 1605 which was a refuge of the abbey of Villers. It is now a museum illustrating the arts and crafts of the Namur region during the 18C. The exhibits include furniture, portraits, paintings of the sieges of Namur, flower paintings by Joseph Redouté, sculpture and porcelain by Jacques Richardot, Vonèche glass, Namur clocks including a grandfather of 1759 in marble, silver, sculpture by Laurent Delvaux, porcelain largely from Saint Servais and Andenne and an 18C game of Lotto with delightful cards illustrating trades of the period. Part of the fireplace in the kitchen is from the original refuge.

The museum is open daily, except Tuesday. There are guided tours at 10.00, 11.00, 14.00, 15.00, 16.00. It is closed between 23 December and 3 January.

To the S of the Hôtel de Croix is the Rue des Brasseurs. Among several 17C to 19C houses in this street is No. 168, the home of Félicien Rops. Cross the Place Maurice Servais, where there are more period houses, and continue to the Rue du Pont.

A few paces to the left is the PLACE D'ARMES. Here the *Bourse* has replaced the 19C Hôtel de Ville which was burnt down in 1914. Behind the Bourse is the *Tour Saint Jacques* or *Beffroi.* This surviving tower of the late 14C walls was provided with a bell chamber in 1746. Immediately to the NE of the Bourse is the PLACE DU THEATRE. In the Rue de la Tour to the S of the square there is a small ramparts-tower known as the *Tour Spillar.* In the Rue Julie Billiart to the SE is the **Maison des Soeurs de Notre-Dame**. Here is kept the **Treasury of the Priory of Oignies.* This was hidden from the marauding French revolutionaries when they sacked the priory in 1794. There are some superb examples of early 13C work by Hugo d'Oignies, including an evangelistery cover, a silver-gilt chalice, a reliquary for St Peter's rib, two magnificent double-crosses, one with enamel portraits and several phylacteries. It is open daily (ring bell for admittance), except Sunday morning and Tuesday, from 10.00 to 12.00, 14.00 to 17.00. It is closed on public holidays and from 11 November to 25 December.

A short way beyond to the right is the 17C portal of the former refuge of the abbey of Floreffe. About 100m to the E (in a rather seedy area), reached by the Rue de Gravière, is the 1775 **Eglise Notre-Dame** which was built by Franciscan Recollects. There were several earlier churches on the site. Although at present closed, inside there is a figure of St Anthony by Laurent Delvaux. The high altar is the work of Denis Bayart. An inscription to the left of the altar records the burial here of two Counts of Namur, William I who died in 1391, and William II who died in 1418. Near the entrance to the church is the old façade of the *Hospice d'Harscamp*, the former Franciscan convent, with the modern hospital buildings behind.

The hospital faces the Boulevard Isabelle Brunell. Its name commemorates the hospital's 19C founder. Her statue by Willem Geefs, 1872, stands in the quayside garden. To the E, by the Pont des Ardennes of 1957, there is a striking modern sculpture, by Olivier Strebelle, of the Quatre Fils Aymon and their horse Bayard.

The old town of Namur from the citadel

From the Place d'Armes the Rue du Pont leads to the Sambre. On the left just before the bridge is the **Ancienne Maison des Bouchers** of 1590, the former meat hall. Now used for municipal purposes, it houses the *Musée Archéologique*. In the museum there are displays of objects found in prehistoric graves, Roman villas, Gallo-Roman burial grounds and Merovingian sites. They include superb pottery, amphorae, bronze tools, seals, statuettes, jewellery, coins, a rare glass oil lamp, fibulae and buckles. There are also reconstructions of a Frankish tomb and of a 2C Roman tomb complete with cinerary urn and grave goods. All were found in the town or province of Namur.

The museum is open daily from 10.00 to 17.00, but closed on Friday between Easter and 1 November and on Tuesday between 1 November and Easter; on Saturday, Sunday and public holidays it opens at 11.00.

The glass-walled building behind the Ancienne Maison des Bouchers is the *Palais de la Culture* of 1961. This is used for exhibitions. On the river bank below stands the *Porte de Sambre-et-Meuse* by Bayart of Namur, 1728.

Between the Rivers

To the S of the Place d'Armes two bridges cross the Sambre, the Pont du Musée (Rue du Pont) and the Pont de France. An open space, gardens and some very busy roads fill the pointed spit at the confluence of the rivers. In the Place Grognon, at the tip, there is an equestrian statue of King Albert. Two figures and some Walloon verses symbolise the union of the Sambre and Meuse. Excursion boats leave from a quay a short way to the S on the Meuse.

The Boulevard Baron L. Huart passes the Pont de Jambes, also known as the Pont de Meuse. The first bridge was built here in the 11C. The present structure replaces one blown up in 1944. A short distance farther on is the *Casino*. This is open daily from 14.00, 13.00 on Sunday. Behind the Casino is the Route Merveilleuse, one of the approach roads to the citadel.

At 3 Rue Notre-Dame, opposite the teleferic terminus, is the Tourist Information Office of the Province of Namur. The building between the Boulevard Baron L. Huart and the Rue Notre-Dame is the 17C *Hospice Saint Gilles*.

The N side of the citadel hill is skirted by the Rue du Bord-de-l'Eau. On the left is the *Rampe Verte*, a footpath to the citadel. A little farther on is the *Porte Bordiale* of 1766, the only surviving town gate. Just beyond, the Route des Panoramas ascends to the citadel.

The Pont de l'Evêché crosses the Sambre here to the *Evêché*, the Bishop's Palace. This occupies the former refuge of the abbey of Malonnes.

The CITADEL may be divided broadly into two areas. The Mediane to the E includes the ancient stronghold of the Counts of Namur and the fortifications of the 15C and 16C. In the Terra Nova to the W are the later defences.

The citadel can be reached by either the Route Merveilleuse or the Route des Panoramas, on foot by the Rampe Verte, by the teleferic, or in summer by a bus service which leaves from the station at roughly hourly intervals. There is also a 'Tourist Train' which during the season covers much of the area.

The Route des Panoramas winds upwards to the Terra Nova, skirting on the left near the top the area of the *Fort d'Orange*. Constructed in 1690, this was largely demolished by the Dutch in 1816 when they rebuilt the whole citadel, preserving only the older foundations. On the E is the *Centre Attractif Reine Fabiola*, a children's recreation area. At this point the road becomes the Route Merveilleuse. It passes the **Musée de la Forêt**. This occupies a building of 1910 in hunting-lodge style which stands on the site of a former fort. The displays include some fine dioramas and a vivarium and cover most aspects of Belgium's forests. The museum is open daily, except Friday, between April and October from 09.00 to 12.00, 14.00 to 17.00. It is open every day at Easter and from mid June to mid September.

Beyond the museum the road circles the sports stadium and passes an open air theatre and the upper station of the teleferic. It then drops to the Mediane area, the historic fortified part of the Citadel. Here is the *Château des Comtes*, now simply two towers. Only their foundations are original. During the holiday season visits by the light of flares may be made to the casemates and lower fortifications. There is a wonderful view of the town and of the two rivers from the battlements.

Here also is the **Parfumerie Guy Delforge**. Delicate perfumes are made and allowed to mature in the ancient vaults. Visitors are able to see the whole production process and purchase, if they wish, some of the perfumes.

In the citadel's Taverne they may sample local dishes and drink a specially brewed beer, Blanche de Namur. This is named after the daughter of Marie d'Artois and Jean I, Count of Namur. Blanche became Queen of Sweden in the 14C. In the adjoining Vielle Forge a wide range of quality food products, all locally produced, is sold.

The road now twists under itself. It offers wonderful views of the rivers before reaching the bank of the Meuse near the Casino.

For the suburb of **Jambes**, on the right bank of the Meuse, see Route 31.

For Namur to *Brussels*, see Route 27; to *Charleroi*, see Route 25; to *Dinant*, see Route 29; to *Bastogne, Arlon* and *Luxembourg*, see Route 33; to *Liège*, see Route 31.

29

Namur to Dinant continuing to Givet, and to Rochefort and Han

As far as 24km Dinant this Route is in two parts: the main road up the left bank of the Meuse is described in section A, the narrower and rather winding road up the right bank in section B. Both roads are scenic, keeping close to the river which flows between steep, rocky, wooded hills. There are road bridges to the N and S of Profondeville, at Annevoie and at Yvoir and a footbridge beside the railway 1km to the S of the Yvoir road bridge. For information about boat travel, see Route 28 and under Dinant below.

South of Dinant this Route continues to 21km Givet in France, and to Rochefort and 37km Han-sur-Lesse.

A. Left Bank of the Meuse

Total distance 24km.—*5km Wépion*—*5km Profondeville*—*4km* **Annevoie**—*4km Anhée*, for **Molignée Valley**—*4km* **Bouvignes**—*2km* **Dinant**.

Namur is described in Route 28. Leave the town by the Boulevard Baron L. Huart. *5km Wépion* is a popular riverside village. It has acquired a reputation, locally, for the quality of its strawberries. There is a small museum. *5km* farther on *Profondeville* is another pleasant holiday resort. Facing some picturesque and rocky cliffs, the town traces its origins to Roman times. Its inhabitants claim that the monks of Fosses-la-Ville hid the relics of St Foillan here when their abbey was sacked by the Norsemen.

The château at *4km* **Annevoie** is best known for its beautiful gardens. Laid out in 1775, with lakes and fountains, the gardens are in French, Italian and English styles. There are special floral displays which vary according to the season. The château is 18C but with a 17C tower. It has interesting stucco work by the Moretti brothers. Visiting times: Gardens: April to October, daily, 09.00 to 19.00; Château: Easter to June and September, Saturday, Sunday, public holidays, July and August daily: 09.30 to 13.00, 14.00 to 18.30.

4km Anhée is an attractive small resort at the foot of the picturesque Molignée valley.

MOLIGNEE VALLEY. The unhurried visitor may like to spend a little time exploring this narrow, winding, wooded valley. Just under 2km, on the left, is a large farm. This was formerly an abbey. At *6km* from Anhée to the left of the road the ruined castle of *Montaigle* clings precariously to a spur of rock. Built in the 13C by Guy de Dampierre, it belonged to the Counts of Namur. The French blew it up in 1554. During the holiday season the work of local artists is displayed in an interesting fortified farm of 1670 at *4km Falaën*.

4km. The imposing neo-Gothic buildings of the Benedictine abbey of **Maredsous**, founded in 1872, stand high above the valley. The large, austere monastic church is very impressive. In the Centre Grégoire Fournier there is an audio-visual presentation on monastic life. Exhibitions are also held there from time to time. Light refreshments are available. Visitors are welcome to attend the sung Offices: Sunday Mass is at 10.00,

Vespers at 16.00. Weekday Mass is at 12.00, Vespers at 18.30. Visiting times: Abbey: every day throughout the year from 09.00 to 18.00; Centre Grégoire Fournier: weekdays from May to August and weekends in May, June and September from 10.00 to 12.30, 13.30 to 18.00; Sunday, 11.00 to 13.00, 14.00 to 19.00.

The Benedictine convent at *Maredret*, built 1891, is a short distance to the W. It produces liturgical prints, miniatures, ceramics and embroidery. It also offers traditional hospitality. For information about accommodation telephone (082) 69 91 34/69 91 45 and ask for the sister in charge of guest quarters. Visitors may attend certain services and Mass which is said daily at 11.45 and on Sunday at 11.30. Craft exhibitions are held in the village. There is also a Musée du Bois with exhibits of 18C to 20C woodwork. This is open daily, except Wednesday, from 09.30 to 12.30, 14.00 to 18.00. It is open also on Wednesday in July and August.

4km **Bouvignes**. Turn off the main road to visit this interesting town. Although now something of a backwater, it has a long history. First mentioned in 882, a fortress built here in the 11C by the Count of Namur was strengthened by town walls in 1176. In 1320 the castle of *Crèvecoeur*, now no more than a ruin, was built above the town. This obsession with fortifications was due largely to a deep enmity and commercial rivalry between Bouvignes, which belonged to Namur, and Dinant, which belonged to Liège. The rivalry, accentuated by the grant of a charter to Bouvignes in 1213, was not finally 'resolved' until 1964 when Dinant officially absorbed Bouvignes. However, an indication of local feeling is made clear by an inscription above the entrance to the Musée de l'Eclairage, '1213 Bouvignons nous étions. 1964 Bouvignons nous resterons.'

Ironically, both towns were sacked and burnt by the French in 1554. From that horrendous event comes the story of the three ladies of Crèvecoeur. Widows of the castle's defenders, heroically they took up arms and fought until they were without ammunition. Then, preferring death to dishonour, they leapt hand-in-hand from the battlements.

In the square stands the 16C *Hôtel de Ville* which houses the Musée de l'Eclairage. Unique in Belgium, this museum traces lighting techniques and methods from prehistoric times to the present day. More than 300 exhibits—lamps, accessories and documents—are displayed and categorised according to theme. The museum is open daily, except Monday, from 11 May to 29 September between 13.00 and 18.00. Guided visits on request.

The *Eglise Saint Lambert* dates from c 1200 but was altered in the 15C, again after the French siege of 1554 and yet again during the 18C. After war damage in 1914 the restorers aimed at giving the church its pre-1554 appearance. Among its treasures are an early 16C polychrome Antwerp *retable, a lively representation of the Passion with more than 50 figures clad in costumes that are a curious mixture of East and West, and an early 16C, poignant wooden *Bon Dieu de Pitié. On the N side of the church is the main town gate flanked by two small fortified towers. Bouvignes may have been the birthplace of St Walhere, who was murdered by a dissolute ecclesiastic whom he had reproached for his scandalous life. The artist Herri met de Bles, who painted in the style of Joachim Patinir, was born here in 1480.

At *2km* is **Dinant**. This is described in section B. below.

B. Right Bank of the Meuse

Total distance 24km.—*11km Lustin Station—6km* **Yvoir**—*7km* **Dinant**.

Leave **Namur** through the suburb of *Jambes* which is described in Route 31. After *11km* you arrive at *Lustin Station*. Here a road climbs the Rochers de Frênes to a café-belvedere which offers a splendid view of the Meuse. There is a small grotto nearby. Lustin village is just beyond.

6km **Yvoir**, a small riverside resort, stands at the foot of the winding Bocq valley. *Crupet*, 6km to the NE, and *Spontin*, 10km to the E, are described at the beginning of Route 33. A diversion of 4km from Yvoir will bring you to the ruins of the castle of *Poilvache*. This may also be reached by footpath from Houx which is on the river 2km to the S of Yvoir. The castle, which is 125m above the Meuse, offers some fine views. In its extensive ruins there are oubliettes and a rock-well. Tradition claims that it was built by the Quatre Fils Aymon. It certainly existed in the 10C and served as a stronghold of the Counts of Namur and of John the Blind of Luxembourg until destroyed by the Liègeois in 1430. Its name, Poilvache which means 'cow's skin', comes from a successful assault by besiegers who disguised themselves in skins and hid among the cattle.

Between Yvoir and Houx is the *Musée Vivant de la Forêt* or *Oasis Nature*, an educational centre and park devoted to the fauna of Belgium. Visiting times: April to October and on Sunday in November from 10.00 to 18.00, 19.00 from June to August. Sometimes open only to groups. To the S of Houx there is a good view across the river to the ruins of the castle of Crèvecoeur above Bouvignes.

At *6km* from Yvoir is *Leffe*. Here there is a much restored Premonstratensian abbey. This was founded in 1152, dissolved in 1794 and restored to the Church in 1902. The buildings extant date from the 17C to the 20C.

Dinant at *1km* is described below.

DINANT (population 12,000) is picturesquely sited on the Meuse. Its buildings huddle under a steep cliff which is crowned by a 19C citadel. After centuries of violence and strife, Dinant is now a popular holiday resort. It is a good centre for exploring the W part of the Ardennes and for making leisurely excursions on the river.

The **Tourist Information Office** at 37 Rue Grande adjoins the Casino and is some 300m to the S of the bridge.

There are **boat excursions** to Namur, to Anseremme at the confluence of the Meuse and Lesse, farther S to Waulsort, Hastière and Heer-Agimont on the French border and sometimes to Givet in France. Timings are usually as given below, but there may be additional services on some public holidays. It is advisable to check departure and return times and to obtain tickets in advance.

To *Namur*: June to August, Saturday depart Dinant at 15.00, arrive Namur at 18.30. Namur to Dinant: June to August, Sunday depart Namur at 10.00 or 11.00.

To *Anseremme*: Easter to mid October: daily every 30 minutes from 10.00 to 11.30 and every 20 minutes from 13.00 to 18.00. Return trip, 45 minutes.

To *Waulsort, Hastière* and *Heer-Agimont*: Sunday in June and daily in July and August. Leave Dinant at 14.00, return by 19.00. One hour stop at Heer-Agimont. Passengers may disembark at Waulsort or Hastière and then catch the return boat. This allows about 2½ hours at Waulsort or about 1½ hours at Hastière.

Descent of the Lesse. For the popular boat descent of the Lesse (Houyet to Anseremme), see Route 30.

History. There is a tradition that Dinant owes its name to Diana, the Roman goddess

Dinant

of the hunt. This may be true as the place was inhabited in Roman times. In the Middle Ages it was a prosperous town which produced 'dinanderie'—articles for domestic or church use made of copper, brass or bronze. By the 14C, when the population numbered some 50,000, perhaps 7500 persons were engaged in the manufacture or sale of dinanderie. The industry began to decline in the 19C and efforts are now being made to revive it.

The first fortress on the cliff top was built c 1050. From that time onwards Dinant was frequently at war. Often its quarrels were with its neighbours, particularly with Bouvignes (see Route 29A). In 1466 the town was pillaged and burnt by Charles the Bold for having revolted against Burgundian rule. Charles brought his aged father, Philip the Good, to see the punishment which he inflicted on the inhabitants. More than 800 of them were bound back to back in couples and thrown into the Meuse. In 1554 Dinant was sacked again, this time by the French during the war between Charles V and Henry II. In 1675 the French returned once more, when Louis XIV attempted to bring the Spanish Netherlands under his control.

In August 1914 the French came as allies. On the 15th they fought valiantly to defend the citadel, but on the 23rd the Germans occupied the town. Alleging that their troops had been fired on by *franc-tireurs*, they executed 674 citizens, deported 400 more to Germany and sacked and burned Dinant to the ground. During the Second World War Dinant saw bitter fighting in May 1940, and in September 1944 the town was the target of American artillery during the three days it took to dislodge the Germans from the Citadel.

The painters Joachim Patinir, c 1475–1524, and Antoine Wiertz, 1806–65, were natives of Dinant, as was Adolphe Sax, 1814–94, who in 1846 patented the saxophone.

The main part of the town is on the right bank below the Citadel. The Meuse is crossed here by a bridge first built by monks from Waulsort in 1080. This was blown up in 1914, rebuilt and destroyed again in 1944. Some of the original piers are kept in the Citadel.

The Gothic **Eglise Notre-Dame** was consecrated in 1240, but was destroyed several times and rebuilt, always to the original plan. According to tradition it stands on the site of a chapel established by St Maternus in 320. The last of these chapels was destroyed by a rock fall in 1227. Some parts of it can still be seen in the present structure, e.g. a sandstone arch on the N exterior and a porch of three carved Romanesque arches in the baptistry to the right of the entrance. In the S transept there are two pictures by Antoine Wiertz; also a fine modern window by Perot. In the N transept is the tomb of Gérard de Blancmoustier, who died in 1306.

The station of the teleferic to the Citadel is beside the church. A little way upstream from the bridge are the embarkation quays for river excursions. The narrow Rue Grande, which runs S from the church, leads to the 17C *Hôtel de Ville*. This was rebuilt after 1918. On the left in a small garden is an allegorical group called La Triomphe de la Lumière by Antoine Wiertz. In the hill-side is the *Grotte de Montfort*, a Stone Age cave. This may be visited between Easter and October from 10.00 to about 18.30. Here there is a chair-lift, which operates between Easter and October, to the *Tour de Montfort*. Erected in the 14C, the tower was restored in 1910. A garden and recreation area have been added to its attractions. From the Tourist Information Office continue in a southerly direction via the Rue Léopold to the Rue Daoust where an inscription marks the *Mur des Fusillés* commemorating those massacred in August 1914.

Across the river from the Eglise Notre-Dame are the railway station and, some 500m from the bridge, the **Grotte la Merveilleuse** which is noted for the whiteness of its stalactites. This is open daily between April and mid October from 11.00 to 16.00 or 10.00 to 17.00 from May to August.

The **Citadel**, perched more than 100m above the Meuse, offers magnificent views of the town and the surrounding countryside. It can be reached by teleferic, by 408 steps cut by the French in 1577 or by a road journey of 3km. Visitors who walk up the steps or come by road pay a lower entrance fee. The main area may be seen only by taking a conducted tour which lasts 30 minutes. Be prepared for large crowds during the holiday season. Visiting hours are as follows: between 11 January and 31 December daily from 09.30 to 18.30, out of season 10.00 to 16.00; closed on Friday from November to March.

It is thought that there was some kind of fortification here as early as the 4C. This was destroyed during the raids by the Norsemen in the 9C. New fortifications were built by the Bishop of Liège in 1051. These were followed by a succession of fortresses, which were destroyed and rebuilt, until the last major dismantlement of the fort by the French in 1707. The present buildings were, in all essentials, built by the Dutch between 1818 and 1821.

The guided tour includes a part of the casemates, the gallery in which trapped French soldiers held out against the Germans for five hours in 1914, a memorial commemorating the French and German dead of 1914, prison cells from the period of Dutch occupation which now house a guillotine and instruments of torture, the Dutch forge, kitchen and bakery, the piers of the 11C Meuse bridge built by the monks of Waulsort and taken from the river in 1952, the carriage of Mme de Maintenon who stayed at Dinant in 1692 while Louis XIV was besieging Namur, historical dioramas including one of the visit by Mme de Maintenon and a small museum of arms from the 17C to the 19C.

Dinant from the Meuse, with the Rocher Bayard in the background

Dinant to Givet in France

Total distance 21km.—*6km Freyr—4km Waulsort—3km* **Hastière**—*5km Heer-Agimont* (frontier)—*3km* **Givet** (France).

This Route follows the beautiful left bank of the Meuse. The sector to Heer-Agimont, and sometimes the complete journey to Givet, may be made by boat.

Across the river are first the Rocher Bayard (see below) and then Anseremme which is described in Route 30. *6km Freyr* has a château mainly of the 18C with fine gardens in the French style. At *4km Waulsort* a 17C château occupies the site of the abbey established c 962 by the Irish missionary bishop St Forannan. The monks from here built the first bridge at Dinant in 1080 (see above).

3km **Hastière** is divided in two. At *Hastière-Lavaux* on the left bank are the Grottes du Pont d'Arcole. These are open daily between April and September from 10.00 to 16.00; July and August from 09.00 to 18.00. Across the bridge in *Hastière-par-delà* is a mixed Romanesque and Gothic church. This once belonged to a priory which was subordinate to Waulsort. The present church, much restored, was built between c 1033 and 1260. The crypt is the oldest part of the building. Some of the misericords of the stalls in the apse date from the 13C and are, with those at Celles, the oldest in Belgium. Note the tomb of 13C Abbot Allard who was responsible for much of the later construction work. There is a striking triptych of 1914 by Auguste Donnay depicting the martyrdom of St Walhere and an interesting Vietnamese Stations of the Cross.

5km Heer-Agimont is at the frontier. *3km* farther S **Givet** in France lies on both sides of the Meuse.

Dinant to Rochefort and Han-sur-Lesse

Total distance 37km.—*7km* **Furfooz Park**—*4km Vêves*—*2km* **Celles**—
18km **Rochefort**—*6km* **Han-sur-Lesse**.
This Route crosses the FAMENNE a western extension of the Ardennes.

Leave Dinant by the right bank of the Meuse and continue southwards to
the *Rocher Bayard*. This detached rock pinnacle, 60m high, is named after
the horse of the Quatre Fils Aymon. He dislodged it with his hoof when
leaping the river. The road beside the rock was cut by Louis XIV when on
his way to seize Dinant in 1675. A plaque records King Albert's climb of the
Rocher Bayard in 1933.

While Route 30 through Anseremme continues in a southerly direction,
this Route bears E taking minor roads through Furfooz and Vêves before
returning to the main road at Celles.

At *7km* from Dinant is **Furfooz National Park**. This covers a steep, rocky
promontory within a loop of the Lesse, one of whose streams flows underground at this point. Cars must be left outside the park. Signposted paths
lead to lofty view-points, Roman baths reconstructed on the original foundations, earthworks and other remains of a Roman camp. There are also
several 'trous'. These deep holes are of considerable geological and archaeological interest. In one, the Trou du Frontal, bones of mesolithic man were
found.

The park is open daily between mid March and mid November from 10.00
to two hours before sunset. Allow 1½ hours for the visit.

Follow minor roads from here to the *4km* castle of *Vêves* which stands
dramatically on a ridge above its village. It would appear that the site was
fortified from c 640, but the present building dates from the 15C or 16C and
has been much restored. The 17C half-timbered balconies around the court
are perhaps its most interesting feature. It is open daily between Easter and
end of October from 11.00 to 12.00, 13.00 to 18.30.

About 1770 the owner of the castle at that time, the Comte de Beaufort,
moved to his small manor house of Noisy. However his grandson, the Comte
de Liedekerke Beaufort, 1816–90, found this to be too modest and built the
huge *Château de Noisy* in the Scottish-Baronial style. Its turrets can be
glimpsed across the valley.

Celles is *2km* farther on. At the crossroads here von Rundstedt was forced
to halt his advance in December 1944. In the village is the partly fortified
Romanesque *Eglise Saint Hadelin*, which was built c 1035. This is an
outstanding example of Mosan construction. St Hadelin was a Merovingian
courtier who c 670 decided to withdraw from the world. He established a
hermitage here which grew into a monastery. Four centuries later the
monks built the present church out of local stone. St Hadelin's reliquary is
in the Eglise St Martin at Visé (see Route 39). The 13C stalls are, with those
at Hastière, the oldest in Belgium. There are also the splendid 16C tombstone of Louis de Beaufort and his wife and a 13C stone lectern. The church
has two crypts. One dates from the 11C, the other smaller crypt below the
tower possibly from the 8C.

The village of *Foy Notre-Dame*, 2km NW of Celles, is entered through an
arch formed by old houses. Behind the church and a short way down the
Ciney road a stone marks the limit of the German advance here in December 1944. The church of 1623 owes its construction to the Virgin of Foy, a
small figure carved in local stone. This was found in 1609 by a woodman
inside an oak which he had felled here. Several miracles occurred and in

1619 the Archdukes Albert and Isabella, the rulers of the Spanish Netherlands, made a pilgrimage to Foy. As a direct result of this visit the church
was built. The lime in front of the building is said to have been planted on
the site of the oak. The original 14C or 15C statute of the Virgin is now
rarely seen. Since its theft and recovery in 1974 a copy has generally been
displayed. The church has a superb and unusual panelled *ceiling with 147
individual portraits. This is the work of the 17C Dinant artist Michel
Stilmant, a pupil of Rubens, who was also responsible for the design of the
building and much of its woodcarving.

At *4km* S of Celles a road forks W and drops for 5km through woods to
Houyet on the Lesse. This is the starting place for boat trips down the river
(see Route 30).

At *14km* is **Rochefort** (population 10,700) on the river Lomme. In this
popular holiday town there is a *Grotto* of wild and menacing aspect.
Discovered in 1865, it has marble as well as limestone formations. In the
huge Salle du Sabbat, 125m by 65m by 85m high, a Son et Lumière display
is given. During this a fire-balloon is released to show the vastness of the
cavern. The grotto is open daily between Easter and September from 09.30
to 17.15. There are guided tours at roughly hourly intervals.

Opposite the entrance road to the grotto, beside a 19C mansion, are the
ruins of a feudal castle. A monument at the roadside commemorates the
arrest here in 1792 of La Fayette by the Austrians. He had commanded one
of the three French revolutionary armies formed to attack Austria. However,
his intention was to use this force to restore the French monarchy. Declared
a traitor, he had to flee France.

For Rochefort N to *Liège* and S to *Bouillon*, see Route 35.

6km **Han-sur-Lesse** is a small Ardennes town which depends almost
entirely on tourism. Its famous grottoes and safari park, for which there is
a combined ticket at a reduced price, attract many visitors. A visit to both
the grottoes and the safari park takes about four hours.

The *Musée du Monde Souterrain* is by the main car park. Devoted to the
geology of the local caves and to archaeological objects found in or near
them, it is open daily between Easter and mid October from 10.00 to 12.30,
13.30 to 18.00.

**The *Grottoes* are open daily between March and December: from 10.00
to 16.00 in March, November and December, 16.30 in April, September and
October; 09.30 to 17.00 in May and June, 18.00 in July and August. They
are closed in January and February. Tickets may be bought at the office in
the town.

The caves are reached by a special tram which leaves from the car park.
The visit requires about two hours. The complex, a series of caverns in
Devonian limestone below carboniferous rock, was first explored in 1814.
It is some 8km in length, but only a part is visited. The Salle du Trophée,
20m high, has the largest stalagmite. The Galerie Lannoy, 250m long, leads
to the Mystérieuses, four small caves particularly rich in limestone formations. The Salle d'Armes, where there are refreshments, is a circular cave
50m across. The lower part of the vast Salle du Dôme, 129m high, is filled
by a small lake. From here visitors leave the caves by boat and proceed
along the Lesse. The exit is near the town.

The *Safari Park* is open daily between March and December: 10.00 to
16.00 in March, November and December; 10.00 to 16.30 in April, September and October; 09.30 to 17.00 in May and June, 18.00 in July and August.

Covering some 250 ha. of beautiful countryside, it has many specimens of the fauna of the Ardennes forests. These include bison, tarpan, wild ox and the brown bears which once lived in the region. The visit, by safari car, requires about 1½ hours.

In the Belgian Space Communications Centre at *Lessive*, 4km to the NW of Han-sur-Lesse, there is a full-scale model of a communications satellite. The Centre is open daily between 11 April and 11 October 09.30 to 17.00, 17.30 in July and August. In addition to an interesting exhibition there is a children's play area. Refreshments are available in a self-service restaurant.

The château of *Lavaux-Sainte-Anne* is 7km to the W of Han-sur-Lesse. With massive squat round towers and surrounded by a moat, the château was constructed between the 14C and 17C. It houses the Hunting and Nature Museum and the Museum of the Countryside and Peasant Wisdom. An audio-visual display, 'La Seigneurie de Lavaux', is given in French and Dutch. The castle is open daily between 2 January and 31 December: 09.00 to 12.00, 13.00 to 18.00 between April and October, and 08.30 to 12.00, 12.30 to 17.00 between November and March.

30

Dinant to Bouillon via the Valley of the Semois

Total distance 81km.—*4km* **Anseremme**—*15km* **Beauraing**—*15km Gribelle*—*18km Bohan*—*15km Rochehaut*—*14km* **Bouillon**.

Leave **Dinant** by the right bank of the Meuse. Proceeding southwards the road soon passes the *Rocher Bayard* (see Route 29). **Anseremme**, at *4km*, is a small resort at the mouth of the Lesse, which is crossed here by a 16C bridge. There is a railway bridge, with footpath, over the Meuse.

DESCENT OF THE LESSE. The Lesse is a beautiful river. For much of its lower course, the 21km between Houyet and Anseremme, it flows below steep, wooded hills. The descent of the river by kayak or crewed larger boat is a popular excursion and attracts many visitors. It is offered by three firms: Lesse-Kayaks M.M. Pitance, 2 Place de l'Eglise, Anseremme; Meuse et Lesse Libert Frères, 13–15 Rue Coussin, Dinant; and Kayaks Ansiaux, 15 rue du Velodrome, Anseremme. As a rule the boats operate between May and September. It is advisable to book in advance. Trains leave Anseremme between c 08.00 and 10.45 for *Houyet*, the starting point for the descent. The journey takes about 5 hours. There are several stops en route. Scenically, the best stretch is below *Gendron*, where the river passes beneath the rocky slopes of Furfooz National Park and the 13C castle of Walzin which was rebuilt in 1581. Gendron is also the starting point for a shorter trip.

12km **Beauraing** (population 7500), has been an important pilgrimage centre since 1932–33 when the Blessed Virgin Mary appeared several times to five children. In a corner of the *Sanctuaire Marial* is the Jardin de l'Aubépine, the Hawthorn Garden, where the apparitions took place. Around this a complex, which includes a large crypt, an upper church and a museum, has developed. The castle, which dates from the 12C, has 16C towers. It is reserved for the use of pilgrims.

At *15km* is Gribelle. The direct road to 25km Bouillon is the N95 through Bièvre. This Route bears SW for the *VALLEY OF THE SEMOIS. After c 12km, not far from the border with France, a right fork leads down a wooded valley to *Bohan, 18km* from Gribelle. Just below, the river flows into France and changes its name to the Semoy. The road to the SE now climbs and descends, generally following the beautiful, winding valley through pleasant villages like *Membre, Vresse* and *Alle.* These, though decreasingly, are concerned with the tobacco industry. There are drying houses and a tobacco museum at Vresse. In the museum there is a collection of pipes, tobacco jars, snuffboxes, old tools used in the tobacco industry, a typical Ardennes kitchen, paintings by Marie Howet and Albert Raty and the vintage locomotive 'Le Belge'. Between April and October there are descents by kayak from Vresse to Bohan and Alle to Vresse. Mountain bikes may be hired at Vresse. Just beyond Alle is the border with the province of Luxembourg.

At *15km* from Bohan is *Rochehaut.* Here a road side view-point offers a magnificent view of the village of Frahan far below and of a great loop in the river. At *4km* is Poupehan where the river is crossed. For a description of *10km* **Bouillon** see Route 35.

31

Namur to Liège

Total distance (S bank) 61km.—*9km Namèche—9km* **Andenne**—*12km* **Huy**—*16km Grottes de Ramioul—5km Val Saint Lambert—3km* **Seraing**— *7km* **Liège**.

Below **Namur**, which is described in Route 28, there are good roads along both banks of the Meuse as far as 9km Namèche, where there is a bridge. The main road is on the S bank.

NORTH BANK. Between *Beez* and *Marche-les-Dames,* 7km from Namur, the road runs below the Rocher du Roi where Albert I fell to his death in 1934 while undertaking a solitary rock-climb. This event is commemorated by a cross. There is also a museum. According to tradition the straggling village of Marche-les-Dames owes the second part of its name to the crusaders' wives who settled here in the 11C and who may have been the founders of the abbey. This, a short way along the Gelbressée road, is now a school. Its buildings date largely from the 18C, although the church, which has a 13C figure of Our Lady, is from about the 14C. The nearby château of Arenberg, a rebuilding of 1917, is military property.

The Gelbressée valley was the scene of heavy fighting in 1914. At 3km *Gelbressée* there is a Romanesque church. Beyond is the attractive moated château of *Franc-Waret.* Rebuilt in 1748, but retaining its early 17C tower, the château has period furniture, Brussels tapestries from designs by Bernard van Orley, and Flemish paintings. It is open between June and September on Saturday, Sunday and public holidays from 14.00 to 17.30.

Namèche, with a bridge across the Meuse, is 2km beyond Marche-les-Dames. From Namèche onwards minor roads serve the N bank. In places these are rough and cobbled and lead through unattractive industrial districts.

SOUTH BANK. Leave Namur through *Jambes*. At the eastern edge of this suburb, on the right at the rear of a supermarket car park, is the small keep of the Château d'Enhaive. In 1283 Jean of Flanders, Bishop of Liège, lived here. After his death in 1291 the château became a fortified farm. The ruins of this, with a 16C round tower, are nearby.

The village of *Samson*, on the S bank roughly opposite Namèche, lies below a group of rocks crowned by fragments of a 13C ruin. This was once the residence of Sibylle de Lusignan, the mother of Baldwin V, King of Jerusalem.

A pleasant road ascends the VALLEY OF THE SAMSON. About 2km beyond an animal park, where there are beavers, it reaches the *Grotte de Goyet*. More than 100 years of excavation here have brought to light many traces of human occupation and the fossilised remains of countless animals. The presence of prehistoric man is recalled by reconstructed scenes of his life and activities. There are guided tours in English, French, Dutch and German.

At *Faulx-les-Tombes*, 3km above Goyet, the road runs below an extraordinary turreted folly of 1870 which stands on 10C foundations. About 1km farther on are the remains of the Cistercian abbey of *Grand-Pré*, now part of a large farm.

9km **Andenne**, population 22,000, owes its origin to a convent founded here c 690 by St Begga, who died in 698. The daughter of Blessed Pepin of Landen and St Ida, she married Angisilus, the son of St Arnulf of Metz. Her son Pepin of Heristal was the founder of the Carolingian dynasty. One day, while hunting, he found a hen protecting her seven chicks from his hounds. Regarding this as a sign from Heaven, Begga built her convent and seven churches. Of this ancient foundation nothing survives in this largely industrial town. The 18C *Collégiale Sainte Begge* by Dewez, in the S of the town against the hill, houses the saint's tomb and a bust-reliquary.

At 29 Rue Charles Lapierre, near the church, the *Musée de la Céramique* has some interesting material dating from the Gallo-Roman period. It is open between May and September on Tuesday, Saturday and Sunday from 14.30 to 17.30. On the eastern outskirts of the town, in the suburb of Andenelle, is the Romanesque *Eglise Saint Pierre*. This dates from 1100.

Beyond Andenne we enter the province of Liège.

At *12km* is **Huy**, population 18,000. The Tourist Information Office is at 1 Quai de Namur, near the S end of the bridge. This town, which stands on both banks of the Meuse, is dominated by its citadel. This was the site in the 11C, or perhaps earlier, of the first bishops' castle around which the town grew. The bridge replaces one blown up in 1944. There are local river excursions during the holiday season.

SOUTH BANK. The *Collégiale Notre-Dame*, begun in 1311 was completed in 1536. The third church to occupy this site, it is an outstanding Gothic building with a magnificent •rose window and tall, slender, lancet windows in the apse. There are some good statues inside. These include a 15C St Christopher and the 14C Notre Dame de Huy in the N transept.

In the Treasury there are four exquisite shrines: The Châsse de la Vierge of 1240; the Châsse de St Marc of c 1200; and the shrines of St Domitian of 1173 and St Mengold of 1175, both by Godefroid de Huy. There is also a small silver chalice of c 1100 from the grave of Bishop Dietwin of Liège.

St Domitian, who died c 560, evangelised the peoples living along the Meuse. He became Bishop of Tongeren. St Mengold, fl. 892, may have been a nobleman of Huy, said to have been of English origin. He spent seven years doing penance for all the blood he had shed. However, there was also a hermit here of similar name and date, and it may well be that the two have become confused.

The Treasury is open daily except Friday and during services from 09.00 to 12.00, 14.00 to 17.00.

A lane, lined with old gravestones, runs along the S wall of the church to the former canons' entrance, the restored *Porte de Bethléem* which bears 14C reliefs of the Nativity.

Cross the Avenue des Ardennes to the Grand-Place where there is a fountain with a bronze basin of 1406 and figures of SS Mengold, Domitian and Catherine, also of Ansfrid, the last Count of Huy. In 985 Ansfrid gave the town to Bishop Notger of Liège. Behind the Hôtel de Ville of 1766 is the 14C *Eglise Saint Mengold* which houses the tomb of its patron saint.

A high-walled lane behind the church leads to the *Justice de la Paix* which preserves the charming cloister, built between 1664 and 1687, of a former Franciscan friary. This now houses the *Musée Communal*. The collection includes objects connected with wine-making; artefacts from the neolithic, Gallo-Roman and Frankish periods; engravings; coins of the prince-bishopric of Liège minted at Huy; an oak figure of 1240 Le Beau Dieu de Huy, a 16C statue of the Virgin and Child, a Christ in ivory; The Judgement of Solomon by an unknown artist of c 1570, The Presentation in the Temple by Frans Badeloz, a local artist; ceramics; toys and glasswork. The museum is open between April and mid October: Monday to Saturday from 14.00 to 18.00, Sunday and public holidays from 10.00 to 12.00, 14.00 to 18.00.

In a park to the right of the main Liège road, the Quai d'Arona, are the scanty remains of the abbey of *Neufmoustier*, founded by Peter the Hermit. Peter preached the First Crusade and led an army which was defeated by the Turks at Nicaea. Later he fought at the siege of Antioch. He died here in 1115.

The CITADEL may be reached by a steep path from the waterfront. There is also a teleferic from the N river bank which operates between Easter and September on Sunday and daily in July and August from 10.00 to 19.00. About 1400m in length, it offers a fine view of the town and surrounding countryside. It continues to La Sarte where there is a recreation area.

The present citadel was built by the Dutch between 1818 and 1823. During the Second World War it was used by the Germans as an internment camp. Visitors can see the camp cells and photographs of the period. There is also a small military museum. The citadel may be visited at Easter and from May to September: daily 10.00 to 18.00, 19.00 in July and August.

NORTH BANK. There are two old buildings of particular interest on the quay. Downstream, the *Hôtel de la Poste* was once the staging post for the 'river-coaches' to Liège. Upstream the *Maison Batta* of 1575 was formerly the refuge of the abbey of Val Saint Lambert. From the bridge follow the Rue Neuve in a NW direction for 150m to the Rue Saint Pierre on the right. Here, in the church of the same name, there is a Romanesque font.

Between Huy and Liège you have a choice. Either bank of the Meuse may be followed. There is more of interest along the N bank, but the S bank road is less industrialised. Crossovers are easy as there are several bridges.

HUY TO LIEGE BY THE NORTH BANK. The abbey of *Val Notre-Dame*, 3km to the N of Huy and to the W of the N64, was founded c 1210 by Count Albert of Moha, the last of his line. Apparently his two sons ran each other through during a friendly joust. Suppressed in 1796, the abbey has been occupied since 1901 by nuns of the Order of the Assumption. The entrance, flanked by towers, and the attractive dovecot just inside date from 1629. The farm buildings are mainly 16C. The rest, apart from the church which was rebuilt after a fire in 1932, was constructed between 1741 and 1745. The ruins of the 11C castle of the Counts of Moha are just to the N of *Moha*, 3km to the W of the abbey.

At **Amay**, *7km* from Huy, the Romanesque *Collégiale Sainte Ode* occupies a site which has revealed evidence of prehistoric and Roman occupation. It is dedicated to a French princess who was married to a Duke of Aquitaine. After his death St Ode devoted her time and wealth to the care of the sick and needy. She died in 723. The nave of the church dates from 1098, the towers from 1525. Other parts were built in the 17C and 18C. Among its treasures is a reliquary of c 1230 of St Ode and St George. This is a decorated work in gilt and enamelled copper with reliefs of the Apostles and silver plaques depicting scenes from the lives of the two saints.

Clearly visible from the road is the château of *Jehay-Bodegnée*. This moated, turreted building with curiously chequered walls, 4km to the N of Amay, dates mainly from the 16C. Excavations have produced mesolithic remains and evidence that the château stands on the site of a Castrum Romanum. It has some fine tapestries which date from the 15C to the 17C. These include Brussels, Aubusson and Gobelins after designs by Teniers. There are paintings by A. van Ostade, Frans Snyders, Murillo, Luca Giordano, the school of Rubens, Dominichino, Peter Lely (a portrait of Nell Gwynn) and Cornelis de Vos. The furniture is of many periods and styles—Louis XIII, XIV, XV, XVI, Queen Anne. There are collections of lace, including pieces which belonged to the Prince-Bishops of Liège, porcelain, Celtic gold ornaments from Ireland, Gothic statues of the Virgin, a 15C St Anne, and bronzes by Guy van den Steen. Note especially a unique piece by that artist, Marsyas tortured by the Nymphs. In a room devoted to the Duke of Marlborough, there are manuscript maps, orders of battle and other militaria. The cellars house an archaeological museum which has a large collection of objects found locally. The château is open Easter Saturday to mid September on Saturday, Sunday and public holidays 14.00 to 18.00.

There is a monument in *Jehay* village to Zénobe Gramme, 1826–1901, the physicist and inventor of the dynamo who was born here.

High above *8km Engis* is the château of *Aigremont*. The present building, which dates mainly from the early 18C, replaced a fortress of William de la Marck, the Wild Boar of the Ardennes. It is furnished in the style of the 18C. In the entrance hall and by the staircase there are striking wall and ceiling paintings by the Huy artist Jean Delloye. The château is open daily, except Monday, at Easter, Whitsun and in July and August from about 10.00 to 12.00, 14.00 to 18.00. However, it is frequently used for exhibitions and receptions and these may sometimes restrict access.

The 18C château, above *3km Chokier*, preserves one medieval tower.

For a description of *13km* **Liège**, see Route 34.

HUY TO LIEGE BY THE SOUTH BANK. This road traverses districts which become increasingly industrial and are of little interest to the visitor.

At *16km* the *Grottes de Ramioul*, which were discovered in 1911, are on two levels. They have a small museum on prehistory and speleology. The grottoes are open between May and September on Sunday and public holidays from 14.00 to 18.00.

5km farther on the cristallerie, glassworks, of *Val Saint Lambert* occupy a former Cistercian abbey. Founded in 1202, the abbey was suppressed in

1796. The glassworks were set up in the mainly 18C buildings in 1826. The younger brothers of Louis XVI, the Count of Provence later Louis XVIII, and the Count of Artois later Charles X, were given shelter at Val Saint Lambert when they fled from France at the time of the Revolution.

3km **Seraing** is the home of the huge Société Cockerill which was founded here in 1817 by John Cockerill as an extension to the works his father William, a mechanic from Lancashire, had started at Liège in 1807. These Seraing works were the first on the Continent to build locomotives, in 1835, and the first to use the Bessemer process in the production of steel, in 1863.

At *7km* is **Liège**. For a description, see Route 34.

32

Dinant to Liège

Total distance 69km.—*6km Sorinnes—9km* **Ciney**—*4km Emptinne—11km Havelange—8km Pont de Bonne—8km Scry* (**Villers-le-Temple**)—*5km Saint Séverin—4km Neuville-en-Condroz—14km* **Liège**.

For **Dinant**, see Route 29.

Some of the furnishings of the church at *6km Sorinnes* come from the abbey of Leffe near Dinant. The building was restored in 1777 and enlarged in 1890. *Foy-Notre-Dame*, 2km to the S, is described in Route 29. The church at *Thynes*, 2km to the N, has an 11C Romanesque crypt.

9km **Ciney**, population 13,000, is the capital of the CONDROZ, the pastoral NW part of the Ardennes which lies between the Ourthe and the Meuse. Its church, which is said to have replaced one founded by the 4C St Maternus, was badly damaged in a storm in 1618. The Romanesque tower and crypt survive.

At *Chevetogne*, 8km to the S, there is an Orthodox monastery whose monks follow the Benedictine rule. Established in 1925, it is dedicated to the promotion of Christian unity. Its Eastern-style church of 1957 has some modern frescoes of the Cretan and Macedonian schools.

At *4km Emptinne* you cross Route 33. *11km Havelange* is just before the border with the province of Liège.

Here you may make a pleasant detour which will add only 7km to your journey. This will take you W through *Evelette*, then down to the valley of the Vyle. You rejoin the main road at Pont de Bonne. This wooded country road passes attractive fortified farms at *Libois* and *Tahier*.

At *8km* is *Pont de Bonne*. The château of *Modave* is 1km to the SE. Its approach and situation are dramatic. A long avenue of trees leads to the château which is perched precariously on a cliff 80m above the little Hoyoux river. The walls of the keep are 12C but the remainder of the building dates largely from c 1649. The richly decorated interior is mainly the work of J.C. Hansche. An ingenious 17C wooden device, which brought river water up to the château, is demonstrated daily at 14.00. The château is open every day between April and mid November from 09.00 to 12.00, 14.00 to 18.00.

Continue to *8km Scry*. Just to the N of Scry is **Villers-le-Temple**. Here the 13C church contains the tomb of a Templar, Gerard de Villiers, who died in 1273. He was the founder of the local commandery. The church was much altered in the 18C when it was given its baroque style apse. There are the ruins of the fortified house of the Knights Hospitallers who took over the Templars' properties when the latter were suppressed for heresy in 1312.

At *Quatre-Bras*, just beyond Scry, this Route joins Route 35, Liège to Bouillon.

The church at *5km Saint Séverin*, attractively set above the village green beside old farm buildings, was once part of an abbey. Built c 1140, the church has a font of the same date. This is of an unusual design; it has multiple supports.

In the village of *Neuville-en-Condroz, 4km* farther on, there is a 16C manor house. The American Ardennes Cemetery here contains over 5000 Second World War graves and a monument to the Supply Services. Wall maps in marble illustrate the campaign.

At *10km Sart-Tilman* the road passes the interesting modern buildings of the University of Liège. On the campus there are some good sculpture and the university's botanic gardens.

At *4km* is **Liège**. For a description of the city see Route 34.

33

Namur to Luxembourg via La Roche-en-Ardenne and Arlon

Total distance 149km.—*43km* **Marche-en-Famenne**—*20km* **La Roche-en-Ardenne**—*25km* **Bastogne**—*37km* **Arlon**—*24km* **Luxembourg**.

This is the principal W to E Route across the ARDENNES. Between Marche-en-Famenne and Bastogne it leaves the main N4 and takes the road N888 through La Roche-en-Ardenne. It crosses the following N to S Ardennes Routes which start from Liège—Route 35 at Marche-en-Famenne; Route 36A at La Roche-en-Ardenne, and Route 36B at Bastogne.

For **Namur**, see Route 28. Leave the town by the suburb of *Jambes* which is described in Route 31. At *8km Wierde* there is an 11C Romanesque church. Note the unusual loopholes in the tower. Continue to *2km Sart-Bernard*. Just beyond a diversion southwards through Crupet and Spontin is recommended.

At **Crupet** there is a very attractive manor house, built between the 14C and 16C. The tower, standing on its own, is surrounded by water. Its only link to the house is a small bridge. In the 14C church there are some interesting funerary monuments. A tomb immediately to the left of the entrance depicts the formal dress of the period.

Spontin is 5km to the SE of Crupet. Its *château*, which claims to be the oldest feudal residence in Belgium, belonged to the Beaufort-Spontin family from the 13C to the 19C. Beyond a reconstructed farm courtyard, the building is an interesting example of a feudal stronghold combined with a manorial home. The lower keep was built in the 11C. However, the building was largely destroyed in 1466 and again in 1555. Rebuilt after that, though still fortified in appearance, it served only as a manor house. It is open daily from 09.00 to 18.00.

We rejoin the main road at *Emptinne*, *14km* from Sart-Bernard, and cross Route 32. At *8km* is the château of *Jannée*. Occupying the site of a 12C keep and surrounded by a fine park, it was built in an unusual horseshoe shape between the 17C and 19C. It has some good furniture, interesting pictures, porcelain and hunting trophies. The château is open daily between Easter and September from 09.30 to 18.30. *Hogne, 6km* farther on, is on the border with the province of Luxembourg.

5km **Marche-en-Famenne** (population 15,000) owes its name to its position on the march, or border, of Luxembourg and Liège. In 1577 Don John of Austria signed the Perpetual Edict with the States General here. To mark the event, the town was honoured with the Order of the Golden Fleece.

The Perpetual Edict, which accepted many of the demands of the Dutch, was soon placed at one side. The Catholic nobles, alarmed by the spread of Calvinism, regrouped and in 1579 signed the Union of Arras. This was followed by a similar declaration, the Union of Utrecht, by the Protestant provinces and all possibility of a *rapprochement* between the two religious factions vanished.

There is a museum in a tower called the *Rempart des Jésuites*, the only surviving part of the town's fortifications. Here archaeological and historical artefacts and examples of local crafts are displayed. The museum is open daily in July and August; during other months from Tuesday to Saturday, 09.00 to 12.00, 14.00 to 17.00.

The village of *Waha*, 2km to the S, merits a visit for the sake of its 11C Romanesque church which is interesting in its simplicity. It was built by village masons. Note the consecration stone of 1050. Inside there are some curious 11C wooden figures. The commemorative stone of the Perpetual Edict, which bears the arms of Philip II, the blazons of Luxembourg and of Marche, is kept in the church.

For places N and S of Marche, see Route 35 which we cross here.

The direct road to 38km Bastogne, the N4, traverses forests and crosses open uplands. We continue E along the N888.

At *20km* is **La Roche-en-Ardenne**, population 1814. The town's Tourist Information Office is in the Place du Marché; the Office for the Province of Luxembourg is at 9 Quai de l'Ourthe. At the foot of steep, wooded hills, the town nestles comfortably within a wide loop of the Ourthe. In the centre of the Ardennes, La Roche is the region's most popular summer resort.

Above the town the road divides, offering a choice of descents. Here a belvedere with adequate parking provides visitors with their first view of the place. In the 11C the lowering *castle*, now in ruins, was the seat of Henri, Count de la Roche. Earlier structures on this site probably dated back to the 9C. Later the castle was held by the Dukes of Burgundy. Louis XIV rebuilt its defences, but surrendered it after the Peace of Utrecht was concluded. It was dismantled on the orders of Joseph II in the 18C. The ruins are haunted by the ghost of Countess Berthe.

The castle may be visited in April, May, June and September daily from 10.00 to 12.00 and from 14.00 to 17.00; in July and August from 10.00 to 19.00; from October to March from 10.00 to 12.00 and 14.00 to 16.00. It is closed on Tuesday and when there is snow or black ice.

The crafts centre, Les Grès de la Roche, welcomes visitors. There they can see the complete manufacturing process of the coarse blue-grey pottery, Grès, for which La Roche is famous. Examples may be purchased and there are opportunities to try the local food specialities and sample the beers. The centre is open on weekdays between March and December from 10.00 to 12.00 and 14.00 to 16.00. It is open every day during July and August and in the week between Christmas and New Year.

La Roche is an excellent centre for walkers. Several routes are numbered and signposted. Recommended are: Nos 9 and 10 which take in the view-point of the *Croix de Beausaint*, 4km from the town; No. 5, a circuit of 5.5km, which passes the 17C *Chapelle Sainte Marguerite*, the *Parc à Gibier*, where there are deer, boar and other animals, and the *Diable-Château*, rocks that resemble a ruined castle.

Some of the finest scenery in the VALLEY OF THE OURTHE is close to La Roche. The following circuit of some 23km is recommended. Take the N834 in a SE direction and, after 5km, bear left for the *Belvédère de Nisramont* where there is a fine view of the Ourthe and its dam. Just above this point the river divides into its E and W streams. The road crosses the river, then climbs to *Nadrin* on the N860. About 2km to the W is the tower of the *Belvédère des Six Ourthe*. This crowns a rocky ridge high above the river which here makes six wide curves. From Nadrin return to 12km La Roche. Alternatively, follow the N860 in an easterly direction E to join Route 36B at Houffalize.

The *Tramway Touristique de l'Aisne*, an old country tram, runs through some 10km of typical scenery between Erezée, which is 14km N of La Roche, and Lamorménil, just N of Dochamps. It operates from Easter to September and in October on Saturday, Sunday and public holidays and daily in July and August from 10.30 to 17.00.

For La Roche N to *Liège* and S to *Florenville*, see Route 36A.

At *25km* is **Bastogne**, population 11,950. The Tourist Information Office is at 24 Place MacAuliffe. Though an ancient foundation, few reminders of Bastogne's past remain. The most interesting are the 13C *Porte de Trèves* and the *Eglise Saint Pierre*. The church has a 12C tower and a 15C Gothic Mosan style nave with elaborate and colourful vaulting. Since at least the 15C Bastogne has been famous for its smoked hams. In modern times it is known for the heroic American stand here during the Battle of the Ardennes in December 1944.

The earliest mention of Bastogne dates from 634. Many times besieged, it was sacked in 1236 by the Ligeois. In 1318 the attacks of Louis of Nassau were repulsed by the inhabitants. In 1688 Louis XIV razed the ramparts to the ground. Bastogne's latest trial was in December 1944, when the Germans encircled the town which was defended by the American 101st Airborne Division commanded by General MacAuliffe . To the German commander's summons to surrender, MacAuliffe's laconic reply was 'Nuts'. Despite heavy bombardment and much destruction, Bastogne held out until Allied pressure on both flanks forced the Germans to withdraw.

In the main square, the Place MacAuliffe, are a tank and a bust of the general. The *American Memorial*, by Georges Dedoyard, 1950, stands on the hill of Mardasson 2km to the NE of the town. It takes the form of a five-pointed star, with colonnades and an upper gallery surrounding a central opening. The story of the battle is told in gold letters on the memorial's pillars. Nearby is another star-shaped building, the *Bastogne Historical Centre*, of 1975. Here the Battle of the Ardennes is explained on film and by other presentations. The Centre is open in March, April and from October to 15 November between 10.00 and 16.00; in May, June and September between 09.30 and 17.00; in July and August from 09.00 and 18.00; during the winter only to groups on written request.

For Bastogne N to *Liège* and S to *Florenville*, see Route 36B. For *Wiltz* and *Esch-sur-Sûre*, to the E in the Grand-Duchy of Luxembourg, see Route 44B.

At *19km* is *Martelange*, population 1500. Here the border between Belgium and the Grand-Duchy of Luxembourg runs along the E side of the road. As petrol is generally cheaper in the Grand-Duchy, this road is lined with petrol stations. In the small Musée de l'Haute Sûre there is a reconstruction of the interior of a house of a slate worker.

A further *18km* to the S is **Arlon**, population 23,000. The Tourist Information Office is in the Parc Léopold. Arlon is the capital of the province of Luxembourg and one of the oldest towns in Belgium. An important administrative, business, military and educational centre, it has a number of Roman remains and a particularly good archaeological museum. 'Maitrank', an aperitif made from very dry white wine and woodruff, *Asperula odorantis*, is a popular summer drink in Arlon.

In the 2C Orolaunum Vicus was a trading post on the Roman road from Rheims to Trèves, Trier. Walled in the 4C against attacks from the E, it stood at the edge of the area where the invading Franks were not absorbed by the Gallo-Romans. A Germanic dialect still survives in the surrounding villages. In 1226 the Marquessate of Arlon was attached to the County, later the Duchy, of Luxembourg by the marriage of Marquess Waleran IV with Ermesinda of Luxembourg. The town suffered much from invasions by the French between 1552 and 1554 and again in 1558. In 1671 the ramparts were torn down, but the French refortified the place during their occupation from 1681 to 1697. In 1785 much of the town was destroyed by a fire. It was from Arlon at the end of 1944 that the American General Patton launched the counter-offensive that relieved Bastogne.

The centre of the modern town is not, as might be expected, the Grand-Place, but PLACE LEOPOLD. Here are the post office, and a tank memorial to the Americans who liberated Arlon on 10 September 1944. There is also a plaque honouring victims of the concentration camps and members of the Resistance.

The archaeological museum is 200m to the NW of here and the Grand-Place 150m to the NE, higher up the hill. Here, successively, were a castle of the marquesses, a Capuchin convent of 1626 and a citadel built for Louis XIV.

The hill is now crowned by the *Eglise Saint Donat*. Once the 17C chapel of the Capuchins, it became the parish church in 1825. It was altered considerably in 1858 and 1900. Inside, frescoes of the 17C or 18C in the chapel of St Blaise tell the story of a Roman legion commanded by Donat. This was saved from thirst when the prayers for rain of its Christian members were answered. There is a fine view of the town and the surrounding area from the tower. An orientation table points to places in Belgium, France and Luxembourg.

Outside the church, to the SE, there are some relics of the medieval parish church which stood in the Grande Rue until 1935, when it was demolished. Below there is a doorway of 1634. The gate of 1700 from the convent of Clairefontaine, 4km to the SE of Arlon, has been placed at the NE outside corner of the church.

At 18 Grand-Place are the remains of a 4C *Roman wall and tower*. Tombstones were used at the base of these defences which seem to have been erected in haste to protect the townspeople from Germanic invaders. Visiting times: daily, except Sunday morning and Monday, 09.00 to 18.30. In the Grande Rue, just to the S, a 16C vaulted passage and some cellars below are the sole relics of medieval Arlon. A tablet in the passage records a visit by Goethe in 1792.

The remains of the 1C *Roman Baths* are in the grounds of an archaeological park off the Rue des Thermes, some 400m to the SE of the Grand-Place.

Athough the greater part of the complex was destroyed at the beginning of the century, it is possible to see the outline of the caldarium and of the urinals. Nearby is the site of the *Roman Basilica*. Used by the Christians during the 5C and 6C, its ruins mark the position of the oldest church in Belgium. It was 25m long and 12m wide. During the 6C and 7C the Franks buried their dead here. Objects found in the baths and basilica are displayed in the Musée Luxembourgeois. Visiting times: May to September 09.00 to 12.00, 14.00 to 17.00.

The *Musée Luxembourgeois*, Arlon's archaeological museum, is 200m to the NW of Place Léopold at 13 Rue des Martyrs. Its outstanding collection of Gallo-Roman sculpture and stone monuments is imaginatively arranged and displayed. Most of the material in the museum comes from Arlon and the surrounding area. Supplemented by models and drawings, it provides a clear and detailed picture of the life and customs of the people in this part of NW Europe during the first centuries of the Christian Era.

Not to be missed are the sculptures relating to the period of the Roman conquest which show cavalry, an officer making a sacrifice, and the late 2C column of a Celtic cavalry deity with its representation on the capital of the four seasons. Note also the touching memorial to the children Vervicius Modestinus and Vervicia Modestina which has a sculptured frieze of scenes from the Iliad, the Odyssey and the Aeneid. The inscription reads: To the shades of the departed Sextus Vervicius Modestinus and Vervicia Modestina, their parents have erected this monument.

Among other funerary monuments of interest are the late 2C pillar of Attianus and the striking stele which shows a nude female dancer. Graceful and voluptuous, her head is slightly inclined, her eyes modestly cast down. She raises her right arm above her head, bending the elbow and wrist, and turns slowly and languidly for ever.

There is a large and representative collection of ceramics, statues, coins, seals and objects concerned with daily life. Among the latter is a relief showing one of the first agricultural machines ever made, the harvester of Trévires. The subject of this relief remained a puzzle until the discovery of a similar carved stone at Montauban in 1958 (see Route 36B). There are two reconstructed tombs. One is of a 1C cremation, the other of a 4C inhumation. Near the stairs is a large, vibrant stone thyrsus, a phallic symbol greatly beloved by maenads, satyrs and other followers of Dionysus.

The rooms upstairs have displays of prehistoric and Frankish artefacts. There is also an instructive section on Roman building methods. In addition, the museum has a collection of religious art which includes a good 16C retable of the Antwerp school.

It is open from Monday to Saturday between 09.00 and 12.00, 14.00 to 17.00; on Sunday and public holidays from mid June to mid September between 10.00 and 12.00, 14.00 to 16.30.

For *Virton*, 28km to the SW, and the surrounding district of *Gaume*, see Route 36B.

On the outskirts of the town the road to Luxembourg passes, on the left, the *Source of the Semois*. This is clearly signposted. Beside the spring there is a replica of a Roman statue in the archaeological museum.

After *8km* you cross the border into the Grand-Duchy of Luxembourg. To the N is the scenic and interesting district of the valleys of the Eisch and Mamer (see Route 44A).

At *10km* is **Mamer**, the Roman Mambra. On the E outskirts of the town, road CR101 for Mersch branches N. On the left c 300m along this road are the remains of 1C *Roman Baths*. These were much damaged by the Franks in 275. In a nearby tomb two skeletons dating from the Middle Ages were found. This interesting site, explained by diagrams and pictures, is well worth the short diversion.

After a further *6km* you come to **Luxembourg City**, see Route 40.

34

Liège

LIEGE, Flemish **Luik**, German *Lüttich*, is the ancient and historic capital of the province of the same name. The city is spread along the valley of the Meuse, just below its confluence with the Ourthe. With a population of 202,000, Liège is one of Europe's major industrial centres. However, industry is largely confined to the perimeter, leaving the elegant inner city undisturbed. The area of greatest interest to the visitor is on the left bank of the Meuse. The Place Saint Lambert can be regarded as the city centre.

Tourist Information Offices. *City* 92 En Féronstrée, 500m NE of Place Saint Lambert and at the Gare des Guillemins; *Province of Liège* 77 Boulevard de la Sauvenière. Helpfully, many street-name plaques carry an explanatory note.

Main Railway Station. Gare des Guillemins, c 2km to the S of the Place Saint Lambert.

Boats. Operator: Tel: 04187-4332. Embarkation City Centre, right bank. To Visé and Maastricht, 10 hours, with 2½ hours in Maastricht. July and August on Friday.

Also via Visé to the Li Trembleur complex at Blégny (see Route 39). 10 hours. July and August: daily.

History. Liège probably derives its name from the Légie brook, a tributary of the Meuse now long hidden underground. It dates its beginning to the building of a chapel here in 558 by St Monulphus, Bishop of Maastricht. In 705 St Lambert, also Bishop of Maastricht, was murdered in this area, traditionally because he had accused Pepin of Herstal of incest. His successor, St Hubert, at once erected a basilica in his memory and shortly afterwards, in 720, moved his see to Liège. For more than 1000 years afterwards Liège was a centre of ecclesiastical power, occupying a commanding political and geographical position between the spheres of influence of France, the Netherlands and the Holy Roman Empire.

Already in the 9C a centre of learning, Liège reached real eminence under the vigorous Bishop Notger, who was appointed in 972. By his acquisitive policy he raised the see to a position of real territorial power and, as a result, was nominated Prince-Bishop by Otto I. This title and authority were the prerogatives of his successors for almost 800 years. Bishop Notger fortified his city and encouraged trade. Soon after his death in 1008 the first bridge across the Meuse was built. Its seventh successor is the present Pont des Arches. Quarrels between the prince-bishops, the municipal authorities, the wealthy merchants, the landed gentry and the tradespeople were continuous, except when Liège was threatened from outside. Such occasions were in 1213, when the Liègeois defeated Duke Henry II of Brabant and in 1343 when the people supported Bishop Adolphe de la Marck against Brabant. In return they demanded and were granted the representative council of XXII.

The coal mines were already being exploited in the 12C and a metallurgical industry developed. Social conditions improved, but the rise to power of the dukes of Burgundy was for a time fatal to the development of civil liberty. John the Fearless crushed Liège at Othée in 1408. Philip the Good defeated the Liègeois at Montenaken in 1465. In 1468 Charles the Bold won the battle of Brustem, sacked the city, annulled civil liberties, and carried off the Perron to Bruges. Nine years later Mary of Burgundy restored the city's privileges and for three centuries the principality preserved a neutral stance in the wars between France and the Empire. In 1482 William de la Marck, the 'Wild Boar of the Ardennes', captured and killed Bishop Louis de Bourbon. His successor, Bishop Jean de Hornes, invited William to a feast, seized him and sent him to Maastricht for execution. The story is told in Walter Scott's 'Quentin Durward'.

During the religious wars Liège maintained its neutrality. In 1702 the citadel was stormed by Marlborough and in 1794 Dumouriez captured Liège for revolutionary France, expelling the last prince-bishop, Antoine de Mèan.

At the outbreak of the First World War Liège under the command of General Leman (see p 295), guarding the gap between Holland and the Ardennes, put up a stubborn resistance from 5 to 14 August. Throughout the war the men working in the small-arms factories refused to make weapons. At the end of the Second World War the bridges were blown up by the retreating Germans and the city was hit by more than 1500 flying-bombs and rockets.

Industry. Liège is the centre of a mining district rich in coal, lead, zinc and iron. This forms the basis of a vast metallurgical industry whose origins can be traced back to the 12C. The 19C saw great expansion and the firm establishment of heavy industry. Among the most important factories were the Cockerill works in Liège and at *Seraing*, the blast furnaces at *Ougrée*, the ironworks at *Sclessin* and the Usines de la Vieille-Montagne at *Angleur*. Other industries in the area are armaments, glass, electronics and petro-chemicals.

Port. Largely due to the completion in 1939 of the Albert Canal, linking Liège and the Meuse to Antwerp and the Scheldt, the city has the third largest inland port in western Europe. Only Paris and Duisberg are bigger. Installations stretch from about *Herstal* downstream, through the length of the city to *Chokier* upstream. The main area is downstream at *Monsin*. Here the beginning of the Albert Canal is marked by a memorial to King Albert. This incorporates a tower 45m high and a 14m high figure of the king.

Art. In medieval times Liège was known for its fine metalwork and ivories and later, from the 16C to the 18C, for architecture and carpentry, particularly cabinet-making. In the 14C it was famous for its Song School which supplied most of the singers for the refounded Sistine Chapel. Musicians native to Liège include André Grétry, César Franck and the violinist Eugène Ysaye.

In 1753 Charlotte, the only daughter of Prince Charles Stewart, the Young Pretender, was born in Liège.

The feast of Corpus Christi was instituted in the diocese of Liège in 1246 at the instance of Blessed Juliana of Cornillon, 1192–1258, the prioress of Mount Cornillon.

The busy PLACE SAINT LAMBERT with its constant streams of traffic has been subjected to some bold and imaginative planning. Excavations have shown that mesolithic people of six or more millennia ago lived here, as did also their neolithic successors. A Gallo-Roman family has left traces of its villa. After the adoption of Christianity a chapel was built here, perhaps by St Lambert. There followed the sanctuary constructed by St Hubert to shelter St Lambert's relics. In the 10C came Bishop Notger's cathedral which was burned down in 1185. From the 13C to the 18C the great Gothic Cathedral of St Lambert covered most of the area in front of the palace of the prince-bishops. Destroyed in 1794 as an unacceptable symbol of the power of the expelled prince-bishops, the ruins served as a useful quarry for 30 years. Then slowly the Place began to assume its present shape and purpose.

On the N side stands the huge **Palais des Princes-Evêques**, the Palace of the Prince-Bishops. This now houses the law courts. Bishop Notger's original building was burned in 1505. The palace was rebuilt between 1526 and 1533 by Bishop Erard de la Marck. This new building, however, was damaged by another serious fire and the façade giving on to Place Saint Lambert was reconstructed in 1737. The whole building was restored between 1848 and 1883 and a W wing was added for the provincial

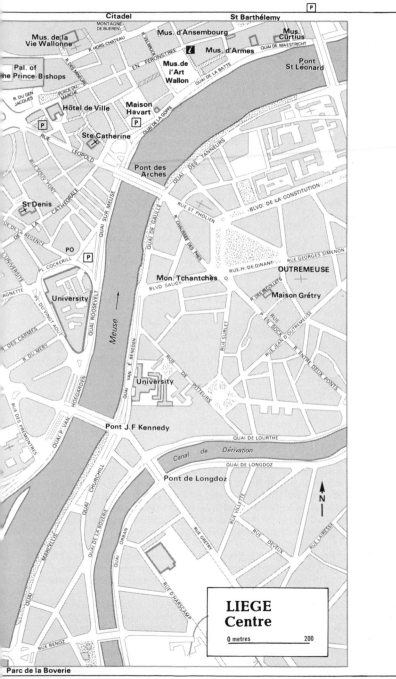

Citadel
St Barthélemy
MONTAGNE
DE BUEREN

Mus. de la
Vie Wallonne

Mus. d'Ansembourg

Mus.
Curtius

R. HORS-CHATEAU

R. VERLBOIS

QUAI DE MAESTRICHT

EN FERONSTREE

i Mus. d'Armes

Pal. of
he Prince-Bishops

R. DES MINEURS

Mus. de
l'Art
Wallon

Pont
St Léonard

QUAI DE LA BATTE

R. DU GEN
JACQUES

PLACE DU
MARCHE

Hôtel de Ville

Maison
Havart

QUAI DE LA GOFFE

P

P

RUE

Ste Catherine

LEOPOLD

Pont des
Arches

QUAI DES TANNEURS

RUE SOUS-PONT

St Denis

CATHEDRALE

RUE ST PHOLIEN

BLVD. DE LA CONSTITUTION

QUAI SUR MEUSE

QUAI DE GAULLE

R. CHAUSSEE DES PRES

DE LA REGENCE

L'UNIVERSITE

AGNETTE

PO

PL COCKERILL

P

Mon. Tchantchès

RUE GEORGES SIMENON

RUE H. DE DINANT

OUTREMEUSE

BLVD SAUCY

University

Meuse

QUAI ROOSEVELT

QUAI VAN E BENEDEN

R. DES RECOLLETS

Maison Grétry

RUE

PL DU VINGT AOUT

RUE SURLET

R. EN SOCX D'OUTREMEUSE

DES CARMES

RUE DE PITTEURS

RUE JEAN D'OUTREMEUSE

R. DU MERY

University

R. ENTRE DEUX PONTS

HOEGARDEN

RUE DES PREMONTRES

QUAI P. VAN

Pont J F Kennedy

QUAI DE LOURTHE

Canal de Dérivation

QUAI DE LONGDOZ

QUAI CHURCHILL

Pont de Longdoz

N

QUAI DE LA BOVERIE

RUE VILLETTE

RUE GRETRY

RUE DEVEUX

RU LAIRESSE

QUAI MARCELLIS

QUAI ORBAN

RUE RENOZ

RUE D'HARSCAMP

LIEGE
Centre

0 metres _____ 200

Parc de la Boverie

government. The two 16C courtyards are open to visitors. Each of the columns in the first is carved with different grotesques. The second courtyard is reached by a passage off the SE corner of the first. Though smaller, it is more pleasant, with grass, a fountain and a collection of old stonework, the Galerie Lapidaire.

West of Place Saint Lambert

Three churches in this part of the town merit mention. The **Eglise Saint Servais** or **Servatius**, the second church on this site, is a short way to the NW of Place Saint Lambert. Basically a 13C building which was much altered in the 16C, it has some good Renaissance stained-glass, a 13C figure of the saint who was Bishop of Tongeren and Maastricht in the 4C, and a 14C Visitation.

The composer César Franck was born in 13 Rue Saint Pierre in 1822. About 150m farther on is the **Eglise Sainte-Croix**. This is the only church in Belgium whose nave and aisles are of equal height. The tower and baptistry are late 12C, the remainder 14C, although traces of a wall from 979 survive. In the baptistry, which forms a kind of W apse, is a 15C polyptych, and in the Treasury there is a symbolical key which was given by Pope Gregory II to St Hubert in 722. Only two of these keys survive in Europe. The other is at Maastricht. They were given by the Pope to distinguished visitors to Rome as a symbol of their right of entry to the crypt of St Peter.

The **Eglise Saint Martin**, 500m to the W of Sainte Croix, stands on the Publémont, the hill where coal was first won in the Liège district. The church was founded in 965 by Bishop Eracle as the result of a vow. After praying at the tomb of St Martin, he was cured of a serious illness. There are pictures in the choir of this miracle. This early building was burned down in 1312. Apart from its 15C tower, the present church dates from the 16C.

In the church of St Martin the feast of Corpus Christi was first observed. It was instituted by Bishop Robert de Torote in 1246 at the request of Blessed Juliana, the prioress of a nearby convent who had a vision while venerating the Blessed Sacrament.

North East of Place Saint Lambert

The short Rue du Bex leads to the PLACE DU MARCHE. In the centre of this square stands the *Perron*, symbol of the liberty of Liége. Erected in 1697 this perron, which incorporates a fountain, replaced one destroyed in a storm. The group of the Three Graces is by del Cour. On the S side of the square is the **Hôtel de Ville** (1718). This is often referred to as 'La Violette' because in the 13C the municipal authorities met here in a house bearing that name. In the present building there are statues by del Cour and a rich 18C decor.

The domed *Bourse* on the N side of the Place was formerly a church of 1722 dedicated to St Andrew. At the E end of the square the *Fontaine de la Tradition* of 1719 has an armorial door of the same date and bronze reliefs of 1930 depicting some Liège folklore characters.

Beyond the NE end of the Place du Marché, the Rue des Mineurs ends at the Cour des Mineurs. As its name suggests, this was once the site of a Franciscan friary. The buildings, destroyed by a flying bomb in 1945, have been reconstructed and now house the **Musée de la Vie Wallonne**. Its extensive collection illustrates many aspects of Walloon life, past and present. The museum is open from Tuesday to Saturday between 10.00 and 17.00; on Sunday and public holidays, 10.00 to 16.00. It is closed on 1 January, 1 May, 1 November, 25 December.

Nearby in the Rue Mère-Dieu is the **Musée d'Art Religieux et Mosan**. This has a wide-ranging collection of religious and Mosan art. Note particularly a painting of about 1475, Notre Dame 'a la Donatrice'. Attributed to the Master of St Gudule, this is one of the museum's treasures. There is also a sensitively carved oak statue of Christ Enthroned of c 1240. The museum is open daily, except Monday, from 13.00 to 18.00; on Sunday from 11.00 to 16.00. It is closed on 1 January, 1 May, 1 November, 25 December.

The narrow Rue Hors-Château, running in a NE direction below the citadel slopes, has kept a number of old alleys and courts. Off this road the 407 steps of the *Montagne de Bueren*, named after a hero of the city's defence of 1468 against Charles the Bold, lead to the CITADEL. No longer fortified, this now has a hospital, public park and war memorials. The citadel can also be reached by road.

EN FERONSTREE, i.e. Rue des Ferroniers, The Street of the Ironworkers, runs NE out of the Place du Marché. The city *Tourist Information Office* is on the right at No. 92. At No. 86 is the striking modern building of the **Musée de L'Art Wallon**. This presents, in an austere setting, works by Walloon artists from the 16C to the present day. These include Lambert Lombard, Joachim Patinir, Gérard Douffet, Bertholet Flémalle, Jean Latour, Léonard Defrance, Antoine Wiertz, Constantin Meunier, Alfred Stevens, Pierre Paulus and Paul Delvaux. Do not miss the striking painting of St Denis and St Paul before the Altar of the Unknown God by Lambert Lombard, the same artist's self-portrait made familiar by its reproduction on the Belgian 100 franc note; the huge canvas by Antoine Wiertz of The Greeks and the Trojans quarrelling over the Body of Patroclus; La Mise au Tombeau and L'Homme de la Rue by Paul Delvaux; and Le Forêt by René Magritte. Special exhibitions are held in the museum from time to time and the paintings on show are rotated regularly, as works are brought out from the reserve collection. Visiting times: weekdays from 13.00 to 18.00; Sunday and public holidays 11.00 to 16.30. Closed 1 January, 1 to 8 May, 1, 2 and 5 November, 24, 25, 26 and 31 December.

114 En Féronstrée, a fine patrician mansion built between 1735 and 1741, houses the **Musée d'Ansembourg** which is dedicated to the decorative arts. In sumptuously appointed rooms, which retain much of their original décor, fine furniture, glittering chandeliers, delicate porcelain, glowing tapestries, Mechelen leather, Delft and Liège tiles testify to the taste and wealth of the 18C *haute bourgeoisie*. The museum is open daily, except Monday, from 13.00 to 17.00; Sunday, public holidays from 10.00 to 13.00; Thursday also from 19.00 to 21.00. It is closed on the same days as the Musée de L'Art Wallon.

Almost opposite is the **Eglise Saint Barthélemy** which dates from the end of the 12C. While externally it retains its Romanesque appearance, the interior, apart from the narthex, was completely changed at the beginning of the 18C. The church has a splendid bronze *font, of 1118. This is almost certainly the work of Renier de Huy and was made at the request of Hellin, the abbot of Notre Dame at Liège from 1107 to 1118. At that time baptisms could be performed in only one Liège church, Notre Dame aux Fonts, and it was for this church that the font was commissioned. Notre Dame aux Fonts was demolished by the French revolutionaries, but the font was hidden from them and so escaped destruction. After the conclusion of the concordat of 1804 between the Vatican and France it was placed in its present position. Resting on ten half-figures of oxen, the font is decorated in high relief with baptismal groups. Visiting times: Monday to Saturday, 10.00 to 12.30, 14.00 to 17.00; Sunday and public holidays 10.00 to 16.00).

We return to Place Saint Lambert along the quays, starting at the Quai de Maestricht by the Pont Saint Léonard.

The ***Musée Curtius** occupies a splendid mansion with a very distinctive high-pitched roof and tower. This was built c 1600 for a wealthy merchant Jean de Corte, or Curtius in the more familiar Latin version of his name.

The museum, which was opened in 1909, contains more than 110,000 objects. These cover a wide variety of subjects: regional archaeology; prehistory; Belgo-Roman and Frankish eras; numismatics; Mosan art from the 11C to the beginning of the 13C; decorative art of the Middle Ages in Western Europe; furniture from the 16C to the 18C; tapestries; miniatures; European ceramics from the 16C to the 19C; and a collection of funerary monuments from the Middle Ages to the end of the 18C.

The museum is open on Monday, Thursday and Saturday from 14.00 to 17.00; Wednesday and Friday 10.00 to 13.00; on the second and fourth Sundays of the month from 10.00 to 13.00; on the first and third Sundays guided visits only at 10.00 and 11.30. It is closed 1 January, 1 to 8 May, 1, 2 and 11 to 15 November, 24, 25, 26 and 31 December.

In the archaeological section there are several small objects which were found in the Place Saint Lambert; Roman glass, pottery, bronze and terracotta figurines; enamelled fibulae; Roman and Frankish ornaments from tombs in the Hesbaye district; and Gallo-Roman bronzes from the Liège suburb of Angleur. From the Middle Ages there is an English alabaster statue of the Virgin of c 1400; a 16C Pietà from Eben-Emael; 15C German carved wooden groups of the Death of the Virgin and the Last Supper; Byzantine ivories and icons; the 11C or 12C Arenberg Evangelistery; statues of St Anne and the Virgin and Child; sculpture from the destroyed cathedral of St Lambert; a Sedes Sapientiae from Xhoris; *Bishop Notger's Evangelistery, a 10C manuscript with a binding of ivory; Mosan enamels of c 1170; the Virgin of Dom Rupert; and an unusual profane work, the Mystery of Apollo.

Other exhibits of interest are 17C and 18C Liège woodwork and tapestries; the Moxhon Collection of miniatures, paintings and 18C silver; an astonishing late 18C six-face clock by Hubert Sarton of Liège; weapons, coins, medals and seals from the Gallo-Roman period up to the mid 19C; and a series of old plans of Liège which show the Maison Curtius prominently. Do not miss the Renaissance chimneypieces bearing the arms of Bishop Erard de la Marck. In the courtyard there are reliefs showing three earlier versions of the Pont des Arches.

The Musée de Verre is at the rear of the courtyard. Of international repute, it tells the story of glass from earliest times to the present day. There are more than 9000 examples of ancient European, Byzantine, Islamic, Venetian and modern glass.

A short distance along the quay is the **Musée d'Armes**. This occupies a mansion of c 1775 which served as the French prefecture of the Ourthe between 1800 and 1814 and as the seat of the Dutch governor from 1815 to 1830. Napoleon stayed here twice—in 1803 and 1811. His visits are commemorated by a portrait by Ingres. Blücher was also a guest here.

The museum, founded in 1885, has the most complete collection of small-arms in Europe. It contains more than 12,000 pieces. Only a small proportion of these is exhibited. Those made for the nobility or the rich are beautifully made and decorated.

Visiting times: Monday, Thursday and Saturday, 10.00 to 13.00; Wednesday and Thursday 14.00 to 17.00; on the first and third Sunday of the month 10.00 to 13.00; on the second and fourth Sunday only guided visits at 10.00 and 11.30. It is closed on the same days as the Musée Curtius.

On a wall just beyond the museum an attractive tile-plaque recalls that the diligence, the stage coach, left here for Brussels, Antwerp, Verviers, Germany, Switzerland and Italy in 1750.

The Quai de Maestricht becomes first the Quai de la Batte and then the Quai de la Goffe. On these quays there is a lively general market on Sunday morning, the Marché Dominical de la Batte. 'Batte' is old Walloon for 'quay'.

18C coach station, Liège

As early as the 12C or 13C this area was the home of cloth workers and other artisans associated with this trade. However, even at the beginning of the 16C the waterfront here was little more than a frequently flooded meadow. Change started in the mid 16C when a trading quay was built. Commercial activity then expanded quickly. The cattle market, arriving first, was soon followed by other commercial ventures, including a horse market in 1663. At this time all three quays were known as the 'Batte', the division dates only from 1863.

On the Quai de la Goffe the 16C *Maison Havart* is largely made of wood. The *Vieille Boucherie* is the old meat market of 1545. The present **Pont des Arches**, which was inaugurated in 1947, is seventh in a line reaching back to 1026, when the first bridge was put across the river. The name recalls the seven arches of the early bridges. It is thought that one of these appears in a painting of the Virgin with Chancellor Rolin by Jan van Eyck which is now in the Louvre in Paris. Reliefs showing the earlier bridges can be seen at the Musée Curtius. The statues on the present bridge represent the following themes: resistance to invaders, upstream, right bank; Liège's

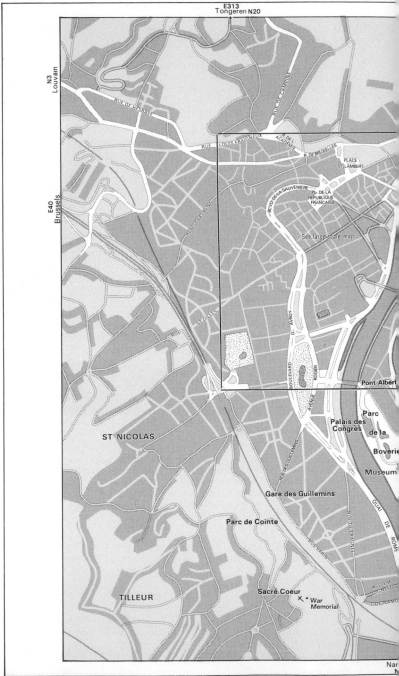

E313
Tongeren N20

N3
Louvain

E40
Brussels

RUE DE HESBAYE

RUE DE CAMPINE

RUE LOUIS FRAIGNEUX

R. DE L. ACADEMIE

R. DE BRUXELLES

PLACE ST LAMBERT

BVD DE LA SAUVENIÈRE

PL. DE LA
REPUBLIQUE
FRANCAISE

RUE ST GILLES

See large-scale map.

D. AVROY

BOULEVARD

ROGIER

AVENUE

Pont Albert

ST NICOLAS

RUE DES GUILLEMINS

Palais des
Congrès

Parc
de la

Boverie

Museum

Gare des Guillemins

QUAI DE ROME

Parc de Cointe

RUE VARIN

RUE D'HARSCAMP

TILLEUR

Sacré Coeur
✕ War
Memorial

AVE EM
D'OINEVEUX

RUE DE NAMUR

Nam

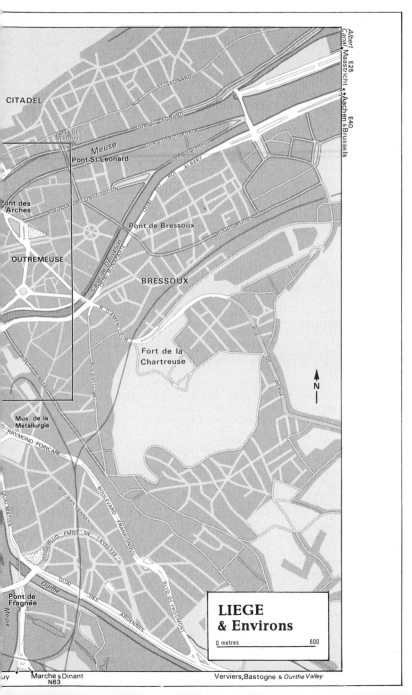

CITADEL

PL. DES
DÉPORTES

Meuse
Pont St-Léonard

Pont des
Arches

OUTREMEUSE

Pont de Bressoux

BRESSOUX

Fort de la
Chartreuse

N

Mus. de la
Metallurgie

Pont de
Fragnée

Meuse

**LIEGE
& Environs**

0 metres   600

RUE ST-LÉONARD

QUAI ST-LÉONARD

QUAI GOFFIN DE TURPS

QUAI DU ROI ALBERT

BLVD. DE LA CONSTITUTION

Canal de Dérivation
QUAI BONAPARTE

R. D'AMERCŒUR

RUE BASSE-WEZ

RUE DE HERVE

RUE DE MUGEN

D. RAYMOND-POINCARE

RUE CRETRY

QUAI MATIVA

RUE DES VENNES

BOULEVARD FRANNINOUL

BLVD. EMILE DE LAVELEYE

QUAI DES ARDENNES

BLVD. DE FROIDMONT

Ourthe

Albert
Canal Maastricht
E25
E40
Aachen & Brussels

Marche & Dinant
N63

Verviers, Bastogne & *Ourthe Valley*

struggle against the Burgundians, upstream, left bank; the revolutionary spirit of 1789 and 1830, downstream, right bank; and the emergence of Liège as a regional power at the time of Bishop Notger, downstream, left bank.

From the Pont des Arches take the Rue Léopold back to Place Saint Lambert. To the right is the domed *Eglise Sainte Catherine*, a rebuilding of 1691.

South of the Place Saint Lambert

In the district to the south of Place Saint Lambert most places of interest to visitors lie within an area enclosed by the Meuse and, to the W, by the loop formed by the boulevards de la Sauvenière and d'Avroy. These wide roads follow the course of a former branch of the river. See old plans of the city in the Musée Curtius.

A good place to start your visit is the PLACE DE LA REPUBLIQUE FRANCAISE, 250m to the SW of the Place Saint Lambert. From here the Place du Roi Albert, the Rue Pont d'Avroy, a main shopping street, and the cathedral are some 350m to the S. The Parc d'Avroy, with its sculpture and terraces, is about 700m S of the cathedral, while the Gare des Guillemins is nearly 1km farther S again.

The **Théâtre Royal**, on the Place de la République Française, stands on the site of a Dominican convent. It was built in 1818 with material from the convent and two demolished churches. Eight marble columns, which now decorate the façade of the theatre, came from one of these, the church of the Carthusians. In front there is a statue by Willem Geefs of André Grétry, 1741–1813. The heart of the composer lies within the plinth.

About 250m to the SE is the **Eglise Saint Denis**. Dedicated to the first bishop of Paris, it was the second church founded in Liège by Bishop Notger in the 10C. The nave, aisles and tower base date from 987, the rest of the structure was altered between the 14C and 18C. The church may be entered from the Rue de la Cathédrale by way of an 18C cloister or from the small Place Saint Denis. In the S transept there is a good early 16C Brabant retable.

To the SE of the church is the *Post Office*, a curious building of 1901 constructed in 16C Gothic style. Farther to the S is the **University** which was established in 1817 by William I. Built between 1820 and 1824, it incorporates part of the former Jesuit church. Since its foundation it has been much enlarged. It has some buildings on the other side of the river. The library and various scientific collections are open to the public on application. The most popular are the *Musée de la Préhistoire* open on Wednesday and Friday from 10.00 to 17.30, and across the river on the Quai E. van Beneden, the *Musée de Zoologie*, the aquarium, open daily from 10.30 to 12.30, 14.00 to 18.00.

From Place de la République Française take the Rue Hamal and Place Xavier-Neujean to the **Eglise Saint Jean**. Founded c 997 by Bishop Notger, it was built on the plan of the Carolingian basilica in Aachen. The tower, which was not finished until 1200, is all that survives of the early church although the 18C nave and choir rest on 10C foundations. There is a good view of the tower from the 16C and 17C cloister on the W. In the entrance porch there are two 13C polychrome wood figures of the Virgin and St John. Inside is a Sedes Sapientiae of c 1200. The doors of the treasury date from the 14C.

The Boulevard de la Sauvenière runs SE to reach, on the left, Rue Pont d'Avroy. To the N of this busy shopping street is a *quartier populaire* of narrow lanes. Continue to the PLACE DU ROI ALBERT. On the N side of this square, by the entrance to the pedestrian precinct Vinave d'Ile, is the *Fontaine de la Vierge* of 1695 by Jean del Cour.

In 1801 the **Cathédrale Saint Paul** replaced the Cathédrale Saint Lambert which was destroyed by French revolutionaries in 1794. The first church on this site, founded in 971, was demolished in the 13C. The present structure was built between the 13C and the 19C. The apse, the lower part of the tower and the aisleless choir are 14C, the 13C nave and 15C aisles were rebuilt at the beginning of the 16C. The upper part of the tower was completed with materials taken from the ruins of St Lambert's in the 19C. The cathedral has several sculptures by del Cour. Inside, the roof is painted with arabesques of 1570, all that the 19C restorers left of the original decoration.

The treasury in the 15C cloisters is entered from the S transept. It has a doorway incorporating early 13C wrought iron. Among its treasures are a silver-gilt reliquary of 1505 containing the skull of St Lambert, a 10C Byzantine painting of the Blessed Virgin and a 9C book of the Gospels bound with an ivory plaque in high relief. The treasury is closed from 12.00 to 14.00 and at 17.00.

In the pleasant little Place Saint Paul, immediately to the SW of the cathedral, is the *Monument Jean del Cour* of 1911. This honours the sculptor who produced such fine works as the memorial to Bishop Allamont in Ghent cathedral and the Fontaine de la Vièrge in Liège. He died here in 1707.

From the Place Saint Paul take the Rue Saint Rémy to the **Eglise Saint Jacques**. This was the church of a Benedictine abbey. Because it was independent of the bishops' jurisdiction, the abbey was charged with guarding the town's charters and it was here that the burgomasters took their oath of office. The abbey was closed c 1750 at the request of its own monks. Architecturally, the church combines several styles. It has a Romanesque façade of 1170. This has lost its towers. One was struck by lightning, the other was demolished. The main part of the structure, begun in the 15C, reached window-level by 1421, work then stopped. It was continued between 1518 and 1538 in the Flamboyant style. Note the change in the colour of the stone. The Renaissance N portal of 1558 leads into a Gothic vestibule. At the end of this, above the entrance, there is a Coronation of the Virgin of 1380. Inside, the gallery around the nave, the niches, cresting and vault ribs are very elaborate. The rood-screen dates from 1600. There are interesting grotesques on the 14C stalls. A stair provides access to the Burgomasters' Gallery where the oath of office was administered. The church is open daily from 08.00 to 12.00, but sometimes longer in July and August.

Rue Eugène Ysaye, to the S of the church of St Jacques, leads to the Boulevard Piercot. Here, beyond a garden containing busts of musicians, is the *Conservatoire de Musique* of 1881. Inside the Conservatoire there is a monument of 1922 to César Franck.

An equestrian statue of Charlemagne of 1868 by Louis Jehotte stands just beyond the W end of Boulevard Piercot at the N limit of the PARC D'AVROY. In this park there are some fine reproductions in bronze of antique sculptures. These include the Borghese Gladiator, in the Louvre; the Wrestlers, in Florence; the death of Laocoön and his Children, in the Vatican; the Faun and the Child, in the Louvre; and Perseus holding up the head of Medusa, in Florence.

On the E side of the park the Avenue Rogier leads to the *Monument National à la Résistance*. The work of P. Etienne and L. Dupont, this was inaugurated in 1955. The figures on the left represent armed resistance, those on the right intellectual resistance. Engraved on the sides of the gilded bronze shrine are representations of the clandestine press, and of the information and active service units.

Opposite are the *Terraces*, gardens containing a very popular sculpture, the *Bull Tamer* by Léon Mignon. A huge, nude male figure is shown bringing a struggling bull to its knees. The Liègois call the group *Li Tôore*, the bull, and generations of students have turned their appreciation of its rampant virility into a slightly bawdy cult. The traditional call '*Av vèyou l'Tôre'*? (Have you seen the bull?) has long been a familiar rallying cry in the city.

Here the Meuse is crossed by the Pont Albert I which leads to the Parc de la Boverie. From the Resistance monument, the Avenue Rogier continues S to a crossroads where there is a memorial to Charles Rogier, 1800–50. Rogier was a leading figure in the revolution of 1830. Later he was largely responsible for developing Belgium's a railway system. From here Rue des Guillemins leads to the *Gare des Guillemins* which is c 600m to the S.

Outer Liège

The PARC DE COINTE with its sports grounds and recreation facilities, sprawls over a hillside to the S of the Gare des Guillemins. From here there is one of best views of Liège and its suburbs. There is a useful orientation table beside the road to the N of the sports grounds. In the eastern part of the park are the *Basilique du Sacré-Coeur* and the 83m high *Allied War Memorial* of 1936. To the S of the park the *Pont de Fragnée*, at the junction of the Meuse and the Ourthe, has four piers which survived the destruction of 1944. It is the only Liège bridge to have been rebuilt to its pre-war design. In the little garden on the point between the two rivers there is a monument of 1905 by Vinçotte to Zénobe Gramme, the inventor of the dynamo. Gramme worked in Liège between 1849 and 1855.

The PARC DE LA BOVERIE is on the right bank of the Meuse immediately across the Pont Albert I. To the NE is the large *Palais des Congrès* of 1958. The Canal de Dérivation marks the eastern boundary of the park.

On the E side of the canal at 17 Boulevard R. Poincaré is the unusual **Musée de la Métallerguie** which is devoted to the iron and coal industries. On the ground floor there is a largely authentic Walloon forge of the 17C and 18C, complete with a huge bellows turned by a waterwheel. The waterwheel, alas, is not now working. The museum also has a magnificent display of ironwork, including some elaborately patterned and illustrated firebacks. One of these dates from 1584. There are models; locks and keys, including some from the Roman, Merovingian and Carolingian periods; and several interesting pictures of different kinds of industrial activity. A taped commentary in English will be played on request. The museum is open from Monday to Friday between 09.00 and 17.00.

OUTREMEUSE is the name given to the *quartier populaire* on the right bank of the Meuse across from the Pont des Arches. The Rue Chaussée-des-Prés leads to the Place Saint Nicholas. Here stands the *Monument Tchantchès*, a folklore figure representative of the real Liègois. In the streets around there are several *potales*, niches with a statue of the Blessed Virgin or of a saint. Some of these street shrines date from the 17C. Interested visitors may make a tour of the potales with the aid of a detailed guide obtainable from the Tourist Information Office.

The *Maison Grétry* at 34 Rue des Récollets 100m SE of the Monument Tchantchès, is the house where the composer lived as a young man. It is open on Monday, Wednesday and Friday from 14.00 to 16.00, on Saturday from 14.00 to 17.00 and by appointment.

Farther S, at 56 Rue Surlet, the *Musée Tchantchès* is devoted to Liège folklore. This is open on Wednesday and Thursday from 14.30 to 16.00.

For the CITADEL, see p 374. For the PORT, see p 370.

From Liège to *Brussels*, see Route 21; to *Namur*, see Route 31; to *Dinant*, see Route 32; to *Rochefort* and *Bouillon*, see Route 35; to *Florenville*, see Route 36; to *Luxembourg*, see Route 37; to the *Cantons de l'Est*, see Route 38; for between Liège, *Maastricht* and *Aachen*, see Route 39.

35

Liège to Rochefort and Bouillon

Total distance 106km.—*20km Quatre-Bras*—33km **Marche-en-Famenne**—*11km* **Rochefort**—*18km Transinne*—*21km Noirefontaine*—*3km* **Bouillon**.

Leave **Liège** (see Route 34) by the right bank of the Meuse. Then, after passing the railway bridge, follow the winding Route du Condroz which ascends through a pleasantly wooded landscape. Continue on Route 32 past Sart-Tilman, Neuville-en-Condroz and Saint Séverin to the road fork at *Quatre-Bras*.

At *12km Bois-et-Borsu* there is a late 9C church containing 14C carvings and frescoes. The frescoes, which are in the nave, tell the stories of St Lambert and St Hubert. The Romanesque church at *Ocquier*, 2km to the E, dates from 1017 and stands on the foundations of perhaps three earlier churches.

4km Méan is in the province of Namur. We enter the province of Luxembourg 4km before *17km* **Marche-en-Famenne** (see Route 33, which is crossed here, for a description of Marche-en-Famenne and nearby Waha).

At *4km* is the castle of *Jemeppe*. This dates in part from the 12C. We re-enter the province of Namur at *4km Jemelle*. There are bus services from Jemelle's railway station to Rochefort and Han-sur-Lesse.

For a description of *3km* **Rochefort**, see Route 29. Here you have a choice. The direct road S through *Tellin* in Luxembourg, or a road slightly to the W which will enable you to visit *Lessive, Han-sur-Lesse* and *Lavaux-Sainte-Anne*. These places are described in Route 29. Both roads meet at *Transinne* which is *18km* from Rochefort. From here on much of the way is through forests, but there are stretches of open country with some fine vistas.

After *4km* is *Maissin*. To the NW, a 16C Breton Calvary adjoining a war cemetery commemorates 3000 Bretons and over 200 Germans who fell here on 22 and 23 August 1914. At *7km* is *Paliseul*, the childhood home of the poet Verlaine. In earlier times, as 'Palatidum', it was a hunting-seat of the first Merovingian kings. After a further *10km* you arrive at *Noirefontaine*.

From here a diversion can be made W to 4km *Botassart*. Just S of here there is an excellent view across the Semois to the *Tombeau du Géant*, a large natural mound enclosed by a sharp bend in the river.

To visit the villages of the upper Semois turn E from Noirefontaine. Then continue to *Herbeumont* on Route 36A or return, part of the way S of the river, to your starting point.

At *3km* is **Bouillon**, population 5600. The Tourist Information Office is at Porte de France. Dominated by its ancient castle, which is perched high above the town, Bouillon is sited near some of the most scenic stretches of the Semois river. It is a very popular tourist centre.

From the 8C a castle was held here by the Counts, later the Dukes, of Lower Lorraine. Godfrey, the fifth duke, was one of the leaders of the First Crusade in 1096. After the capture of Jerusalem by the Crusaders in 1099 he was elected king of a Christian state based on the newly liberated Holy City. Modestly, Godfrey preferred to be called 'Advocate of the Holy Sepulchre' rather than King of Jerusalem. He reigned for one year only, dying probably from a disease caught during his campaigns in Palestine. However, the chronicler Matthew of Edessa ascribed his demise to a more sinister cause. According to him Godfrey was poisoned by his Muslim adversaries during a visit to Caesarea of Philippi. 'Godfrey accepted (the supplies brought by the Muslims) and unsuspectingly ate the dishes they prepared, which were poisoned. He died several days later…and was buried in Jerusalem…on the hill which is called Golgotha.'

Before leaving for the Holy Land, Godfrey sold or mortgaged his ancestral lands to the prince-bishop of Liège to pay for his own equipment and that of some of the poorer Crusaders. The prince-bishops were only able to rule the duchy through lords, who were virtually independent and who later styled themselves princes. They were the family of La Marck and later of La Tour d'Auvergne. In 1678 Bouillon was granted to Louis XIV under the terms of the Peace of Nijmegen. The last of the direct line of the princes of Bouillon adopted Philippe d'Auvergne, 1754–1816, who came from Jersey in the Channel Islands. He reigned at Bouillon from 1814 until the duchy was ceded to the Netherlands by the Treaty of Vienna.

Prince Charles Edward, the Young Pretender, lived here with Clementina Walkinshaw from 1755 to about 1760. In 1870 Napoleon III spent the night of 3 September at the Hôtel de la Poste in Bouillon as a prisoner of the Prussians.

The origins of the *Castle of Bouillon go back to the remote past, but the present building dates mainly from the 15C and later. It was altered considerably by the French military engineer Vauban after Bouillon was ceded to France in 1678.

During January and February the castle is open on Saturday and Sunday from 10.00 to 17.00; between March and December daily from 10.00 to 17.00, 18.00 or 19.00. It is closed on Monday and Tuesday in December. In July and August there are nightly visits by torchlight at 22.00.

The various parts of the castle are marked by numbers which refer to the explanations given in the official guide. An English version of this is available. The parts likely to be of greatest interest to visitors are described below.

No. 1 is the second of three bridged ditches which protected the castle. The last, No. 3, was paved in 1686 and provided with a moat that could be filled when necessary. No. 5, which is hewn out of the rock, is the so-called Room of Godfrey de Bouillon. The age of the ancient wooden cross on the floor, which was was discovered in 1962, is not known. Also in the room are a statue of Godfrey, armour and medieval weapons. No. 6 is the main courtyard where the duke's residence once stood. Note the bell of 1563 and the twin-level triple-slitted loopholes. These were probably the work of Vauban as is certainly No. 10, the present rampart walk and No. 11, the semicircular tower. The clock-tower at the end of the rampart walk is a rebuilding by Vauban of an earlier watch-tower. The present clock dates from 1810, but the hour bell belongs to a clock of 1606. The Tower of Austria, to the right of the clock-tower, is named after George of Austria, Prince-Bishop of Liège, who converted it into a caponier c 1551. In its earlier form the tower was designed to protect this part of the castle. No. 12 has been given the name Godfrey de Bouillon's Chair. This is a double lookout hewn from the rock. It is one of the oldest parts of the castle since it could only have fulfilled its function before the building of the clock-tower and the construction to the S. No. 13, the top of the Tower of Austria, affords a view of both the castle and of much of the town below. (For the dam across the river, see No. 24.) No. 14, the basement of the Tower of Austria, was once a guard-room. Medieval weapons are exhibited here. In No. 20, popularly known as the Torture Room, instruments of torture are exhibited. It was probably the armourer's workshop. Nos 21 and 22 were dungeons. No. 24 is a doorway (entry prohibited). This leads to a stairway of 396 steps which descends to the site of a 15C water mill. The last remains of the mill disappeared during the Second World War but its dam across the Semois survives. No. 25, with a large cistern at one end, is a gallery some 90m in length. The castle's main corridor, it was lined with storerooms. No. 27 is the well, much widened and deepened by Vauban.

The *Musée Ducal* is in an 18C house on the road up to the castle. Explanations of the exhibits are in English and a taped commentary in English will be played on request. The history of the duchy is set out in some detail. A reconstruction of a small living-room and adjoining kitchen illustrate life in the 16C. There is a model of Bouillon in 1690 and rooms devoted to hunting, clogmaking, carding, lacemaking and weaving.

The adjoining *Musée Godefroid de Bouillon* occupies a 19C mansion. Here there are exhibits concerning the Crusades, objets d'art of the High Middle Ages from Europe and the Near East, arms of the period and furniture. There are several interesting models of war engines and weapons, medieval ecclesiastical objects, notably Limoges work of the 13C, ivories of the 13C and 14C, a remarkably well-preserved 14C belt and a 14C Shrine of the Virgin.

The museums are open at the following times: between April and June and in September and October daily from 09.30 to 17.30; in July and August daily from 09.00 to 19.30.

For Bouillon via the VALLEY OF THE SEMOIS to *Dinant*, see Route 30.

36

Liège to Florenville continuing to Virton and the district of the Gaume

Two routes are described below. The first, Route 36A, generally follows the winding VALLEY OF THE OURTHE as far as La Roche-en-Ardenne. The valley has some splendid scenery; many stretches are flanked by steep wooded hills or cliffs. A favourite holiday area, it attracts many walkers.

The other road, Route 36B, through Bastogne is rather shorter and faster, but does not compare scenically with 36A and it passes fewer places of interest.

Beyond La Roche-en-Ardenne on Route 36A and Neufchâteau on Route 36B both roads climb to the higher levels of the Ardennes, running through forests broken by open upland permitting wide vistas.

A. Via the Ourthe Valley
and La Roche-en-Ardenne

Total distance 148km.—*13km* **Esneux**—*9km* **Comblain-au-Pont**—*8km* *Hamoir*—*15km Barvaux*—*6km* **Durbuy**—*10km* **Hotton**—*15km* **La Roche-en-Ardenne**—*23km* **Saint Hubert**—*13km Recogne*—*12km Bertrix*—*10km Herbeumont*—*14km* **Florenville**.

Leave **Liège** (Route 34) by the right bank of the Ourthe. This is crossed in the suburb of *Angleur* and again just before *8km Tilff* where there is a museum of bee-keeping in the château. This is open in April, May and September on Saturday, Sunday and public holidays from 10.00 to 12.00, 14.00 to 18.00; daily in June and August.

5km **Esneux**, set below steep wooded hills, has a large and pleasant riverside area with cafés and parking space, while in the Parc du Mary there is a visitor complex with picnic sites, walks, view-points and an arboretum. For the next 17km, as far as Hamoir, the road keeps to the left bank of the Ourthe in a narrow, wooded and winding valley.

9km **Comblain-au-Pont** is a small town just above the confluence of the Ourthe with the Amblève. The stump of an old tower stands above the town. From Comblain-au-Pont a diversion may be made 5km to the W to *Anthisnes* where the 'Avouerie', with its 12C keep and residential additions of 1648, is used for receptions and exhibitions. It also houses a beer museum. Avouerie is open at weekends between April and October from 10.00 to 12.00, 14.00 to 19.00. At *Comblain-la-Tour*, across the river and to the S of Comblain-au-Pont, there is a 14C tower. Continue to *8km Hamoir* where there is a monument to the sculptor Jean Del Cour, who was born here in 1627.

This Route now turns eastwards, generally following the Ourthe and rejoining the main road at Durbuy.

At *Tohogne* on the main road there is an 11C Romanesque church.

From Hamoir follow the N66 E to *3km* Filot and continue on the N86 S to *5km* **Vieuxville**. At *La Bouverie*, just to the W, an attractive farm built in 1570 by the monks of Stavelot-Malmédy now houses a local museum, information office and crafts shop. This is open daily, except Wednesday, in July and August from 10.00 to 17.00. Nearby is the ruined castle of *Logne*. This occupies a site used by prehistoric peoples and by the Romans. Later it was a stronghold of that 15C picaresque figure William de la Marck, the Wild Boar of the Ardennes. It was destroyed in 1521 by Henry of Nassau in the service of Charles V. The ruins may be visited in May, June, September and October at weekends from 13.00 to 18.00; in July and August daily from 10.00 to 19.00; on public holidays from 13.00 to 18.00. The guided visit takes one hour.

A road NW out of Vieuxville leads to 4km *Sy* which is at the head of one of the most picturesque ravines on the Ourthe.

The N86 winds above the castle of Logne, crosses into the province of Luxembourg and reaches *3km Bomal*. This small town of 7500 inhabitants is linked with Beaujolais in France. Appropriately it offers wine-tasting. Continue to *4km Barvaux*. This is a popular holiday resort which is near three districts with contrasting scenery: Condroz which is devoted to farming, Famenne which is pastoral and the forested uplands of the Ardennes. Here too there is wine-tasting. From Barvaux walkers may follow a path along one of the loveliest stretches of the river to 7km Durbuy.

Visitors interested in prehistory will want to make a short diversion of 4km to *Wéris* which lies to the SE of Barvaux. To the NW of Wéris, beside the road, there is a dolmen with a massive roof slab. Among the other stones and tombs in the district is a menhir just to the SW of the village. The church at Wéris dates in part from the 11C. It has a 13C stone tabernacle.

From Barvaux you reach Durbuy by a winding road known as the Route Touristique. This will take you through *Bohon*.

6km **Durbuy** (population 7600) is a most attractive small town close to where the Ourthe flows through a wild ravine whose rocks have been tortured into bizarre shapes by some primeval cataclysm.

Standing on Roman foundations, Durbuy was made a town in 1331. Though popular with visitors, it has managed to retain much of its ancient character. Wandering through the cobbled lanes of the old quarter, it is easy to return in spirit to the past. Here is the 16C *Halle aux Blés*, the former corn market. A few paces away in a quiet street is the delightful Hôtel Clos des Récollets. Comfortable, friendly, its rooms redolent of the past, this is an excellent base for exploring the town and the surrounding countryside. The turrets and steep roof of the *Château des Comtes d'Ursel* are mirrored in the waters of the Ourthe. Of 9C origin, the castle had a stormy history. It was frequently besieged. The present building dates almost entirely from the 19C, but one 11C turret survives.

10km **Hotton** (population 3500) lies below an escarpment which was occupied by prehistoric man. It also served as a Roman strongpoint. The *Grottes de Hotton*, known as the 'Thousand and One Nights' because of their wildly exotic formations, were discovered in 1958. They are open daily between April and October from 09.00 to 18.00. Visitors may go as far as the so-called balcony. From here the river, some 30m below, can be heard roaring away into the Stygian darkness.

The *Château of Deulin*, 5km to the NW, dates from 1760. It is used for concerts, exhibitions and other cultural activities.

For the *Tramway de l'Aisne*, see Route 33 after the description of La Roche-en-Ardenne.

8km Marcourt was until the 11C the seat of the Counts of Montaigu. On the site of their stronghold above the village stands a chapel of 1637.

Marcourt was the birthplace of Anne-Josèphe Terwagne, 1762–1817, the Amazon of the French Revolution. She was better known under her assumed name of Théroigne de Méricourt.

At 7km is **La Roche-en-Ardenne**. See Route 33 which is crossed here. The road ascends through forests, reaching eventually the important crossroads of *Barrière de Champlon* and continuing across the marshy Forêt de Freyr.

At *23km* is **Saint Hubert**, population 5500. The Tourist Information Office is in the Place de l'Abbaye. Traditionally St Hubert underwent his conversion in the forest near here. The spot is marked by a chapel c 8km to the NE of the town.

Saint Hubert was also the birthplace in 1759 of the flower painter Joseph Redouté.

Hubert was born of a noble family c 656. On Good Friday 683, when out hunting, his hounds cornered a stag. At bay, the animal turned and Hubert saw that between its antlers it bore the Cross. At the same time a voice reproached him for his impiety in hunting on such a solemn day. He at once renounced the world and entered the abbey of Stavelot. In 705, when in Rome, he learnt of the murder at Liège of Bishop Lambert of Maastricht and Tongeren. The Pope then offered Hubert the bishopric. At first he refused on grounds of unworthiness but later accepted when an angel appeared to him in a dream and draped a white episcopal stole around his neck.

St Hubert died in 727 and in 823 his remains were brought from Liège to the 7C abbey which stood near the site of his conversion. He acquired such a reputation for sanctity that it was believed a shred of his mantle could cure madness and hydrophobia. From the 9C onwards the abbey and the town, which grew around it, became known as Saint Hubert. In later times he became the patron of hunters and hunting dogs are still brought to the church on his feast day, 3 November, to be blessed. His remains disappeared a long time ago, but the abbey remains a place of pilgrimage.

The abbey, which was rebuilt in 1729, survived until the French Revolution. Its domestic buildings on the main square are now a cultural centre. The abbey church, the *Basilique Saint Hubert*, in Flamboyant style of 1526 to 1560, has an Italianate W façade of 1702. Between the towers there is a relief of St Hubert. The lofty brick vaulting of 1683 inside replaced the shingle vaulting destroyed by Protestant fanatics in 1568. The crypt below the choir is in part of the 11C. The stalls, Liège work of 1733, are carved with the stories of St Hubert and St Benedict. In the S ambulatory there is a *retable with Limoges enamels of 1560, after Dürer's Small Passion. This is one the few furnishings to have survived, albeit damaged, the destructive fury of the Protestants. The saint's tomb of 1847 by W. Geefs was a gift from King Leopold I who was a lover of the hunt.

There is a *Parc à Gibier*, with game animals, off the N849 2km to the NW of the town. In the forest beyond and signposted on the road a squat pyramid in a lonely clearing recalls that King Albert often visited this spot. The last occasion was shortly before his death in 1934.

Continue on the N849 to *Fourneau Saint Michel* which is 8km from Saint Hubert. This has been arranged as an ironwork complex of the 18C. Beside the road are an 18C forge built by the last abbot of Saint Hubert and a barn where a fine collection of firebacks is exhibited. Tools and other equipment are on display in a museum. This is open from March to June and September to December daily from 09.00 to 17.00 or 18.00 on Sunday; in July and August daily from 09.00 to 19.00.

The *Musée de la Vie Rurale en Wallonie*, a short distance farther N, is an open air museum illustrating Walloon rural life from the 16C to the 18C through preserved and re-erected buildings—schools, chapels, cottages, tobacco halls and wash-houses. These are generally arranged topographically and by themes. The museum is open from a week before Easter to mid September daily from 09.00 to 17.00 or 18.00 in July and August.

From Saint Hubert the N89 continues S through forest. At *13km Recogne* Napoleon III stayed in 1870 after his defeat at Sedan. The poet Verlaine claimed descent from the lords of Verlaine, which is 3km to the SE. Near *12km Bertrix* this Route leaves the main N89, which continues to Bouillon, and makes a lovely wooded, winding descent to the valley of the Semois. On the left, about halfway between Bertrix and Mortehan, the so-called Château des Fées is a defensive work which seems to have been in use from the 4C until perhaps the 11C.

Continue to *6km* Mortehan. Near *Cugnon*, which is just to the NW, there are traces of a Gallic camp of the 1C BC and grottoes by tradition associated with St Remaclus. It is said that he was offered land here for a monastery and that he dug the grottoes to serve as a chapel.

At *4km Herbeumont* the ruins of the 12C castle of the local counts are perched high above the river. The castle was destroyed by Louis XIV in 1658. The view from the crumbling ramparts amply repays the effort of the climb up from the village. S of Herbeumont the road crosses the river. On the other side a hotel occupies the site of the 18C abbey of Conques.

At *10km Chassepierre*, which is off the main N83, there is a view-point greatly favoured by artists. It is claimed that the village existed in prehistoric times and that primitive fishermen used its grotto. During the period of the Roman occupation it was known as 'Casa Petra'. At *Azy*, 3km to the N within a loop of the Semois, there is a dolmen. For a description of *4km* **Florenville**, see Route 36B below.

B. Via Bastogne

Total distance 127km.—*10km Beaufays*—*11km* **Aywaille**—*28km Baraque de Fraiture*—*15km* **Houffalize**—*15km* **Bastogne**—*27km Neufchâteau*— *21km* **Florenville**.

Leave **Liège** (see Route 34) by the right bank of the Ourthe and continue to the suburb of *Chênée*. Here Route 38B branches E for Chaudfontaine and the Cantons de l'Est. We take the road S to *10km Beaufays*, where Route 37 to the Grand-Duchy of Luxembourg diverges to the SE. At *7km Sprimont* the Musée Régional de la Pierre, housed in the former generator house of the local quarries, is concerned with stones from their mining to their use for industrial or decorative purposes. The museum is open during the week between Easter and All Saints Day from 09.00 to 17.00; on Sunday from 14.00 to 17.00. After Sprimont the road descends to the Amblève valley at *4km* **Aywaille**. The ruins of the *Château d'Amblève* are on the N cliff 2km downstream. Traditionally this was once a stronghold of Les Quatre Fils Aymon. Later, it belonged to William de la Marck, the Wild Boar of the Ardennes. It was demolished by the Duke of Parma in 1587. For *Remouchamps*, 3km to the E of Aywaille, see Route 37.

At *4km Harzé* the road curves round the restored 12C to 17C château. At present this is closed for further conservation. Just beyond *7km Werbomont* we enter the province of Luxembourg. *17km Baraque de Fraiture* in a bleak heathland is, at 636m, the second highest place in Belgium.

At *15km* is **Houffalize** (population 4000) whose name is derived from 'haute falaise', high cliff. The town sprawls over both sides of the steep valley of the eastern arm of the upper Ourthe. It was largely destroyed during the Battle of the Ardennes, as it was the place where Patton's and Montgomery's counter-offensives met. The *Eglise Sainte Catherine* has a 13C tower. It was formerly the church of a priory founded in 1248 by Thierry, Lord of Houffalize. His tomb is in the church. There is also a fine brass lectern of 1372 by Jehans Josès of Dinant.

At *Tavigny*, 4km to the SE, there is a particularly interesting fortified-farm. For *Hachiville*, 6km farther to the E in the Grand-Duchy of Luxembourg, see Route 44B.

For the next 42km the road traverses open, rather dull country. It passes through *15km* **Bastogne**, on Route 33, on the way to *27km Neufchâteau*. The Tour Griffon here is a relic of a castle destroyed in 1555.

The countryside now becomes more interesting as the road begins to pass through forests. At *14km Epioux* the château of 1650 was the home between 1862 and 1871 of Pierre Bonaparte, nephew of Napoleon. *4km* **Lacuisine** is a summer resort nestling in a loop of the Semois. The wonderful scenery here is best appreciated by making a boat descent, Le Défile du Paradis, from *Chiny* which is 4km to the N. This may be done every day between April and September from 09.00 to 18.00.The time required is c 1½ hours.

Continue for a further *3km* to **Florenville**, population 5500. The Tourist Information Office is at Place Albert I. Florenville is a small frontier town on a hill which commands a wide view across the valley of the Semois. This is best enjoyed from a terrace behind the church which has an orientation table and multi-language taped commentary or from the top of the church tower. The church, rebuilt in 1950 after the destruction of half the town in 1940, has a modern carillon of 48 bells. One of these was presented by No. 1 Fighter Wing, Royal Canadian Air Force, in thanks for hospitality received from the people of Florenville.

The Gaume

The GAUME, also known as Belgian Lorraine, is the southernmost corner of the country. Scenically one third forest, it is geographically an extension of the Ardennes. Ethnically it is a melting pot in which Walloon, Lorraine and Luxembourg dialects and customs mingle. The language of the inhabitants closely resembles that of Lorraine. The name of the area is believed to come from the 'Gaumains', the porters who carried iron products produced here to Liège and other towns. Ironworking, long the principal industrial activity of the area, has left its mark in the form of many abandoned forges. Some excellent examples of the ironwork of long-dead craftsmen can be seen in the Musée Gaumais at Virton.

There are also many caves, large and small in the Gaume. These are known locally as Trous des Nutons or des Fées. They are the homes of gnomes and fairies who never show themselves, but are famed for their hard work and kind hearts. It is said that clothes which require washing or mending are often meticulously washed and mended by these accommodating little people if left near the caves.

The principal town of the Gaume is *Virton*. Two places of particular interest to visitors to the area are the abbey of *Orval* and the archaeological site of *Montauban*.

The circuit described below starts at Florenville and follows an anticlockwise route through Orval, Virton and Montauban to 44km Etalle on the Florenville to Arlon road. Arlon is 16km to the E of Etalle and Florenville 23km to the W.

8km the **Abbey of Orval**, pleasantly set in a green and wooded valley, is composed of the ruins of the ancient foundation and the buildings, completed in 1948, of the new abbey. Visitors are admitted to the ruins and to the museum in the 18C cellars of the modern abbey. There are guided tours daily from the Sunday before Easter to the end of September from 09.00 to 12.00, 13.30 to 18.00; at other times daily from 10.00 to 12.00, 13.30 to 17.00.

According to an ancient story Matilda of Lorraine, who lived from 1046 to 1115, was sitting beside a spring in this place one day. By a mischance she lost her gold ring in the water. After praying at a nearby oratory, she returned to the spring and a fish swam up with her ring in its mouth. This gave the place its name, which is an inversion of Val d'Or.

What is not a legend is that Benedictine monks founded an abbey here in 1020 and that, when they abandoned it, Cistercians took it over c 1132. Orval soon became one of the richest Cistercian houses in Europe. It was famed for the quality of its ironwork. In the 18C the abbey was largely rebuilt by Dewez, only to be virtually destroyed by French revolutionaries in 1794. In 1926 the estate was acquired by Trappists, a reformed branch of the Cistercian order. The new buildings were consecrated in 1948.

A detailed plan and guide in English are included in the price of the entrance ticket. The 12C and 13C ruined church is part Romanesque and part Gothic. Note the splendid rose window and the pillars with Romanesque capitals. Near the ambulatory are the foundations of two very early buildings: a late 11C church and an earlier oratory, perhaps the place where Matilda prayed. A 20 minute audio-visual explanation of modern monastic life is given in the former guest-house which preserves a 13C gable. Do not miss Matilda's Fountain, the remains of the cloisters, the museum, the modern church and the garden of medicinal plants which are used by the monks. On sale are the abbey's excellent brown bread, cheese and dark beer, one of only six real Trappist beers brewed anywhere in the world. Visitors are welcome to attend the services held in the abbey church.

At *17km* is **Virton** (population 3700) the chief town of the Gaume. There is an active and helpful Tourist Information Office in Virton which produces a detailed guide in English to the town and its environs. A very useful pamphlet, with map, which describes 18 signposted walks around Virton is available from the same source. The hotel Le Cheval Blanc, Rue du Moulin, offers a quiet and comfortable base to those visitors who wish to spend some time exploring the area.

In Roman times the settlement, on which the modern town stands, was known as Vertunum. About 1060 a stronghold was built here by one of the Counts of Chiny. The oldest known document which mentions Virton is a bull of Pope Lucius II of 1133. In 1340 the County of Chiny was sold to John the Blind, King of Bohemia and Count of Luxembourg. This change of suzerainty brought four centuries of misery and unrest to the area. Virton was captured, sacked and burned several times. It suffered at the hands of brutish mercenaries employed by its powerful neighbours and during the French Revolution it was raided frequently by the sans-culottes.

The Indian totem pole at the entrance to the municipal park is a symbol of happier international relations. This was a gift from Canadian forces stationed at a nearby NATO base.

The *Musée Gaumais* in the Rue D'Arlon occupies a former Franciscan Récollet convent which was built at the end of the 17C. A reminder of that time is provided by a jacquemart dressed as a Récollet friar which strikes the hours. Opposite the entrance there is a reconstruction of a Gallo-Roman pottery. The museum's collection has a strong regional bias. The principal subjects represented are: local archaeology, with many objects from the prehistoric and the Gallo-Roman periods; the arts with religious and secular sculptures and paintings by Brother Abraham of Orval, Camille Barthélemy, Nestor Outer and others; 15C to 19C work from the Gaume founderies including firebacks with many varied designs; customs and crafts of the Gaume; and period furniture. Do not miss the diorama which shows the adventures of the fiddler Djan d'Mady. A local hero, he met a wolf in the woods and killed it with a blow of his umbrella.

The museum is open from April to end of October from 09.30 to 12.00 and 14.00 to 18.00. It is closed on Tuesday during April, May, September and October.

To the S of Virton there are two places which no traveller should miss, Torgny and Avioth. *Torgny* with its low, tiled houses, is the most southern village in Belgium. Protected by a ridge, la Montagne, from the cold N winds, it has a mild, sunny climate. Flora and fauna not found in any other part of the country are not uncommon here. The small cicada, *Cicadetta montana*, the praying mantis, eight different orchids, the rare *Iberis amara*, all have been found in this area. In 1951 a vineyard was created with 2000 Riesling vines. Since then other varieties, including the Müller Turgau, the

Pinot Noir and Pinot Gris producing vines, have been added. At present six vineyards cover 3 ha. of land, the largest vine growing area in Belgium. Wines from Torgny, accompanied by good local dishes, can be sampled in the village. It is an experience to be savoured and enjoyed.

In the tiny village of *Avioth* there is a huge basilica dedicated to Our Lady. During the course of centuries the documents concerning the construction of this church have disappeared and have been replaced in the popular imagination by fanciful legends involving, among others, the devil. This enormous church, which towers over the quiet village square, houses a miraculous image of the Blessed Virgin. The statue shows some Byzantine influence which suggests that it may have come to Avioth at the time of the Crusades. In past centuries pilgrims flocked to Avioth and placed their offerings in the *recevresse*. Perhaps this money was used to finance the construction of the building. The mystery is unlikely to be solved now.

For the modern visitor it is enough to be able to see this wonderful building whose stones have been shaped and burnished by the weather of centuries. The opportunity to examine the intricate carving of long-dead craftsmen, to walk on flagstones worn by the feet of countless pilgrims, to pray in the church's dim, mysterious nave is sufficient reward for the detour.

At *Montquintin*, 6km to the SW, an 18C farm has been turned into a museum of country life. This farm was built by Monseigneur de Hontheim, bishop, author and one of the last squires of Montquintin, in 1765. The kitchen and the pèle or best room have 18C furnishings. There are exhibitions of photographs from the turn of the century and of 18C and 19C head-dresses. In the barn are displays of tools connected with all aspects of farming in the Gaume. The museum is open from Easter until 15 September on Sunday from 14.00 to 18.00; in July and August daily during the same hours.

At *Latour*, 4km to the SE, there is a museum of local history, with particular reference to a Walloon regiment, the Latour Dragoons. There are also documents concerning the noble family of Baillet-Latour and the two World Wars in the Gaume. The museum is open from Easter to October every Sunday from 15.00 to 18.00; during July and August daily from 14.00 to 18.00. At *Gomery*, 5km to the E, there is a dolmen.

Croix-Rouge, with a Trou des Fées, is a crossroads in the forest *10km* to the N of Virton. Circa 1.5km to the N is the little Huombois Potter Museum where there is a 1C undamaged Gallo-Roman pottery kiln. This is open on request to groups.

The *4km* **Archaeological Park of Montauban** may be reached by continuing N through *Buzenol* or by bearing E at Croix-Rouge and then after 3km turning N towards Buzenol. A 10 minute climb will bring you to the quiet, wooded spur occupied by this extensive site. As the remains are rather scanty, some effort of the imagination is needed to get the most from a visit to Montauban. An Iron Age earth rampart of c 500 BC was replaced in the 2C BC by a stone wall. A part of this, together with the outline of some huts, survives. In the 4C a Gallo-Roman wall was built as a defence against the Franks. In the Middle Ages there was a castle here which had associations with Les Quatre Fils Aymon. A section of the keep of this building can be seen.

From the archaeological point of view the Gallo-Roman wall is the most important feature of the site. This was strengthened at some time with carved Roman funerary stones and stelae which, the archaeologists believe, may have been hurriedly collected from abandoned settlements in the neighbourhood. Most of the blocks have been replaced by replicas. The originals, with other Gallo-Roman stonework, are on display in the site's purpose-built museum.

Of the carved blocks the most interesting is the incomplete representation of a Roman harvesting appliance. Discovered in 1958 this depicts an agricultural machine which is described by Pliny the Elder in his 'Historia Naturalis'. Another damaged stone block found in Arlon in 1854 and now in the Musée Luxembourgeois, which shows the same device, was not identified until the Montauban discovery. The machine was operated by a donkey which pushed a wheeled container, edged with teeth. These teeth tore off the ears of corn and dropped them into the container. A wooden reconstruction of the device stands near the museum. The Park is open throughout the year. Visitors wishing to see the exhibits in the museum should make prior arrangements through the Musée Gaumais at Virton.

Across the road from the car park are the remains of ironworks which flourished here between the 16C and 19C.

From Montauban the main Florenville to Arlon road is reached at *5km Etalle*.

37

Liége via the Valleys of the Amblève and the Salm to the Grand-Duchy of Luxembourg

Total distance 81km.—*10km Beaufays—6km Louveigné* (for **Banneux-Notre-Dame**)*—6km* **Remouchamps**—*19km* **La Gleize**—*6km Coo—3km* **Trois-Ponts**—*13km* **Vielsalm**—*18km Frontier of Grand-Duchy*.

For **Liège** to *10km Beaufays*, see Route 36B. At *6km* is *Louveigné*. About 2km to the NE is **Banneux-Notre-Dame**. In 1933 the Blessed Virgin appeared here eight times to a girl aged 12. Since then a pilgrimage complex with a hospital and chapels has been established. The Chapel of the Appearances is immediately to the left of the entrance. Set back from the other side of the road is the Magnificat Altar. The Source, a spring, is a short distance farther along the road. A fragment of stone from the grotto at Lourdes has been built into it.

After Louveigné this Route turns S along N666, the Vallon des Chantoirs which gets its name from the many *chantoirs* or holes in the limestone. It descends to the valley of the Amblève at *6km* **Remouchamps**, a pleasant riverside resort in a wooded valley. The *grotto* here has been carved out by the Rubicon, a minor tributary of the Amblève. It was inhabited by prehistoric man. The visit, which requires about an hour, takes you to the Salle de la Cathédrale and for a 1km-long subterranean boat ride. The grotto is open daily May to August 09.00 to 18.00; March, April, September and October daily 09.30 to 16.30; the last departure is one hour before closing.

Sougné, just below Remouchamps, is a village at the foot of a rock-rampart called the Heid des Gattes from which the French dislodged the Austrians in 1794.

The road, the N633, follows the winding valley of the Amblève. *19km* **La Gleize** is a bleak, mountain village. A German Tiger tank and militaria in the local museum recall that the infamous Kampfgruppe Peiper (see also Route 38B, Baugnez) made its last stand here during the Battle of the

Ardennes. At *Cheneux*, 3km to the SW, there is a memorial to the American 509th parachute Infantry Regiment of 82nd Division which stormed and retook La Gleize.

At *6km Coo* the river flows in a loop of c 4km. The narrow, rocky neck was sundered by the monks of Stavelot in the 18C to form a cascade of about 17m. This has helped to turn the place into a popular tourist attraction with cafés, go-karts and souvenir shops. A chair-lift ascends to the top of the 450m high *Montagne de Lancre* from where there is an extensive view. The lift operates daily from mid March to mid November 09.00 to 20.00.

From *3km* **Trois-Ponts** (population 2000) it is possible to follow two sectors of the signposted *Circuit des Panoramas* which promises ever-changing views in a picturesque, wooded countryside. The W sector, which goes through Haute-Badeux, Reharmont and Bergeval, is 21km; the E sector through Wanne is 15km. *Stavelot*, 5km to the NE, is described in Route 38B.

During the Battle of the Ardennes, Trois Ponts witnessed one of the most gallant and decisive actions taken against the advancing Kampfgruppe Peiper (see also La Gleize above). Just before midday on 18 December the German battle-group's advance guard tanks, which had come from Stavelot, clattered under the railway viaduct to swing left for the vital Amblève bridge. There they were faced by a lone American anti-tank gun which immediately destroyed the lead tank. There followed a brief, uneven contest which ended inevitably with the destruction of the gun and the death of its crew of four. However, the gallant stand of these American soldiers gave sufficient time for the demolition of the bridge and the destruction of Peiper's hopes of a dash to the Meuse. Instead he had to turn N for La Gleize and defeat.

The road now winds past wooded cliffs in the valley of the Salm. After 5km you enter the province of Luxembourg. *6km* from Trois-Ponts is *Grand Halleux*. To the S is the *Parc du Monti*, a game park in which forest animals enjoy a degree of freedom.

7km farther on is **Vielsalm**, population 7000. It was an American head-quarters during the Battle of the Ardennes. A memorial immediately below a church on the road from Trois Ponts commemorates the members of the Ardennes Secret Army. At a road junction in the S part of the town a small fountain and a rough, dark stone remember the American 7th Armoured Division. Nearby a tablet reminds us that this square is named after General Bruce C. Clarke, a combat commander within that division. By way of contrast another memorial on the left of the road from Vielsalm to *2km Salmchâteau*, recalls the many people of this region who fought against slavery in the Congo.

In Salmchâteau are the ruins of the castle of the counts of Salm which was first built in the 9C. Visitors interested in geology may like to visit the Musée de Coticule. Hone stone or razor stone from quarries in this district was much in demand during the 19C and early 20C. As markets declined quarrying diminished and ceased altogether by 1980. The museum is open between April and October from Tuesday to Sunday, 13.00 to 17.00; in July and August on the same days but also from 10.00 to 12.00.

11km Beho, at an altitude of 500m on the Ardennes plateau, is where the British vanguard crossed the then German frontier on 1 December 1918. The church at Beho has a 12C tower. The rest is a rebuilding of 1712. It has some good baroque furnishings. At *5km* is the frontier with the Grand-Duchy of Luxembourg. For *75km* **Luxembourg City** see Route 44.

38

Liège to the Cantons de L'Est

The largely German-speaking CANTONS DE L'EST are **Eupen**, **Malmédy** and **Sankt Vith**. They are bounded on the E by Germany and on the W by a line running roughly from Eupen through Baraque Michel and Malmédy to the border of the Grand-Duchy of Luxembourg near Beho. Before the French Revolution these lands belonged to a number of rulers. Eupen was a district of the duchy of Limburg. Malmédy belonged in part to the ecclesiastical principality of Stavelot-Malmédy and in part to the duchy of Luxembourg. Sankt Vith was also divided, a part was in the duchy of Luxembourg, but the communes of Schönberg and Manderfeld were ruled by the prince-bishop of Trèves or Trier. This ended when Belgium was absorbed into republican France. In 1815 the Congress of Vienna gave the Cantons, less the district of Moresnet and the town of Stavelot, to Prussia. A vigorous Germanisation policy was pursued until the First World War. In 1920 the League of Nations awarded the Cantons to Belgium, where they have since remained, apart from 1940 to 1945 when Hitler declared them reunited to Germany. Today the Cantons have no administrative significance as such and all form a part of the province of Liège.

The pleasant small towns and villages of the Cantons, many very German in atmosphere, are scattered through an area of upland forest interspersed with lakes and reservoirs. Between Eupen and Malmédy the Hautes Fagnes, where Belgium's highest point, the Signal de Botrange , 694m, is located, are an area largely of peat bogs and sphagnum moss which hold reserves of very pure water. The plants are of low Alpine and Nordic type and the indigenous trees are beech, oak, birch and alder. Spruce has been introduced for environmental purposes. The pillars and crosses seen here were guides along ancient trails and pathways.

A. Liège to Verviers and Eupen

Total distance 43km.—*30km* **Verviers**—*7km* **Limbourg**—*6km* **Eupen**.

For a description of **Liège**, see Route 34. *30km* **Verviers** (population 54,000) is most easily reached by motorway, the A25/E25 down the right bank of the Meuse, followed by the A3/E40 and A27/E42. A more interesting, if slower, alternative is to follow Route 38B as far as Pepinster.

The Tourist Information Office is at 11 Rue Vielle Xhavée.

Still an important textiles centre, Verviers was granted the right as early as 1480 to sell cloth in Liège. Curiously, it was not given official town status until 1651. It has three good museums.

The town centre is formed by the PLACE VERTE and the adjacent PLACE DU MARTYR. From Place Verte the Rue Crapaurue, a main shopping street, leads to the neo-classical *Hôtel de Ville*, by J.B. Renoz, 1780. Dr Grégoire Chapuis is commemorated by a memorial in the Place du Martyr which is named after him. A doctor who served the poor and was later attached to the magistrature, he was executed in 1794 because he solemnised a civil marriage according to French Revolutionary law. This was construed by the Prince-Bishop of Liège, briefly back in power after the Austrian defeat of Dumouriez at Neerwinden, as a seditious act. At the NW corner of this square the *Eglise Notre-Dame* dates from 1647.

From the E end of the square the Rue du Collège leads to the Rue des Raines where there are some 17C and 18C houses. No. 42 is the *Musée d'Archéologie et Folklore*. The ground and first floors are devoted to 17C and 18C furniture, pictures, largely by local artists, and objets d'art. There are also the memorabilia of the violinist Henri Vieuxtemps (1821–81), who was born in Verviers. He has given his name to the Place Vieuxtemps in the S part of the town. On the second floor there are weapons and a small collection of archaeological material found locally. This includes Roman coins found near the museum. There is also a room devoted to lace. The museum is open as follows: Tuesday, Thursday, 14.00 to 17.00; Saturday, 09.00 to 12.00; Sunday, 10.00 to 13.00.

The *Musée des Beaux-Arts et de la Céramique* is a short distance to the NW in the Rue Renier beside the river Vesdre. Occupying a late 17C former almshouse, it has an important collection of ceramics and paintings from the 16C to the 20C. These include works by Joachim Patinir, Landscape and St Christopher; Pieter Pourbus the Elder, Punishment of Annanias; Jan van Goyen, A Landscape; Nicolas de Largillière, two portraits; Roelant Savery, Landscape with a white Horse and Animals in a Landscape; Cornelis de Vos, Portrait of a Child; Gerrit Dou, Adoration of the Magi; Daniel Seghers, The Virgin among Flowers; Jan Weenix, Portrait of Admiral van Heemskerk; Gerard de Lairesse, The Council of the Gods; Joshua Reynolds, Head of a Child; Marie Louise Vigée-Lebrun, A Self-portrait; Henri de Braekeleer, Inn by a Lake; Johann Barthold Jongkind, Skaters and A Canal Bridge.

On the first floor there are carved and sculpted 15C and 16C religious figures. The collection of modern paintings is also on this floor. Among the artists represented are Gustave Courbet, Jacob Smits, Constantin Meunier, Hippolyte Boulenger, René Magritte, Paul Delvaux, Edgard Tytgat and Emile Claus. Note that pictures are sometimes removed temporarily to make room for special exhibitions. In the passage leading to the basement architectural fragments and gravestones are exhibited.

The Museum is open on Monday, Wednesday and Saturday from 14.00 to 17.00; on Sunday from 15.00 to 18.00.

Vervier's third museum is the *Musée de Laine* at 8 Rue de Séroule in the SW part of the town. This is concerned with the history of the local textile industry, mainly before 1800. This is told through an interesting display of pictures, written records, textiles and costumes, and tools. It is open from Monday to Saturday between 14.00 and 17.00 or 18.00 on Wednesday.

7km **Limbourg** (population 3700) stands on a ridge 275m above the Vesdre. A former fortress, it was the capital of the duchy of Limburg from feudal times until 1648.

Limbourg's present air of provincial tranquillity belies its history which was often savage and bloody. The town was besieged many times and frequently sacked. The perceptive visitor will sense something of these traumatic events, while clambering over the town's ruined defences or while wandering through its picturesque, cobbled streets.

The church, which dates mainly from the 15C and 16C, has a tower of 1300.

The *Barrage de la Gileppe*, 4km to the SE, is a peaceful lake enclosed by wooded hillsides. There is a good view from the Belvédére of the lake and its surroundings. A Sentier Touristique, a tourist path, descends to the dam which was built to form a reservoir for Verviers between 1869 and 1878. Further work to increase its height was undertaken between 1967 and 1971.

At *2km Baelen* look out for the curious spiral steeple of 1773 on the village church.

Continue for a further *4km* to **Eupen** (population 17,000) a mainly German-speaking town. The Tourist Information Office is at 6 Bergstrasze. Largely because of the availability of water from the Vesdre, Eupen has been concerned with textiles since the 14C. The industry received a substantial boost in the 17C and 18C when a number of French Calvinists settled here.

The baroque *Eglise Saint Nicolas*, built between 1721 and 1726, has a striking interior. The altar of 1744 is astounding.

The *Barrage de la Vesdre*, 5km to the E, was completed in 1950. It is the largest dam in Belgium. There is a Panoramic Tower with lift, and from the top there is a superb view of the reservoir and the great forest of the Hertogenwald which surrounds it.

The N67 cuts through the Hertogenwald and crosses the border to the small German town of *Monschau*.

Raeren, 8km to the NE of Eupen, was from the 15C to the 19C a thriving pottery centre. Its products were known both locally and as far away as Ireland and Sweden. The castle, 14C in origin, houses a museum of pottery which spans the period from the 12C to the 19C. It is open daily, except Monday, from 14.00 to 16.45.

For the HAUTES FAGNES to the S of Eupen, see the introduction to this Route, also Route 38B, Malmédy to the Hautes Fagnes and Eupen.

B. Liège to Spa, Stavelot, Malmédy, the Hautes Fagnes and the Canton of Sankt Vith

Total distance 61km.—*10km* **Chaudfontaine**—*15km Pepinster*—*5km* **Theux**—*7km* **Spa**—*8km Francorchamps*—*8km* **Stavelot**—*8km* **Malmédy**.

Leave **Liège** by the right bank of the Ourthe and continue to the suburb of *Chênée* where you cross the Vesdre. The road then follows the narrow, winding valley of the river. The hill of *Chèvremont* on the N bank is crowned by a pilgrimage-church of 1697.

At *10km* is **Chaudfontaine**, population 19,500, a pleasant little spa which was much admired by Victor Hugo. The Tourist Information Office is in Maison Sauveur, Parc des Sources. Visitors may sample the water from the spring which is just behind the large car park. Reaching a temperature of 36.5°C, this water rich in minerals has been used since 1676 for the treatment of rheumatism. There is an audio-visual presentation about the spa and its healing waters in the Maison Sauveur, site of the town's first thermal baths.

15km Pepinster is 4km to the SW of *Verviers* which is described in Route 39A. At *Tancrémont*, 4km to the SW of Pepinster, a chapel houses a striking and unusual 11C robed figure of Christ.

5km **Theux** traces its origin to a Roman settlement. Later it was owned in turn by the Carolingian kings and the prince-bishops of Liège. It received town status in 1456. The walls and nave of the church, which has a fortified tower, date from 1000 or earlier. It has an interesting 12C font whose middle section may be Roman. In the pleasant town square there are several 17C and 18C houses. Theux's *Hôtel de Ville* dates from 1770. The *perron* is of 1769. Its predecessor of 1456 was destroyed by Charles the Bold in 1468. The town's early history is linked closely with that of the castle of *Franchimont*, whose ruins are on the hill above. A pentagonal fortress with corner towers, it dates for the most part from the 14C. It was from this castle that a heroic band of 600 men sallied out one day in 1468 to make a vain attack on the army of Charles the Bold after he had defeated Liège at Brustem. In revenge Charles sacked Theux and destroyed its perron. Later the castle was a stronghold of William de la Marck, the Wild Boar of the Ardennes. After William's execution his brothers held the castle successfully against a siege mounted by the Bishop of Liège.

The castle is open daily from 09.00 to 19.00 or dusk if earlier. It is closed on Tuesday from October to March. The principal features are numbered and a key in English is provided with the entry ticket. This also admits to the adjoining museum where local history is explained by means of maps and some interesting illustrations.

At *7km* is the town of **Spa**, population 9700. The Tourist Information Office is at 43 Place Royale, by the casino.

The oldest of Europe's spas, its name has been borrowed by many other health resorts. Today there are only faded reminders of the elegance which led Joseph II to describe it as the 'Café of Europe'. An echo of past glories is provided by the fascinating list of distinguished visitors from the 16C to the 19C which is inscribed on the semicircular monument just S of the Pouhon Pierre-le-Grand.

Lying in a valley beneath wooded hills and moors, it is still visited for its mineral springs and its recreation facilities which include a casino. Spa is also a convenient centre for exploring this part of Belgium.

History. The first foreign visitor of note was Augustino, the Venetian physician of Henry VIII of England. Later came Henry III of France, Marguerite de Valois, Charles II of England, Christina of Sweden and Peter the Great of Russia. By the 18C the gaming tables had become as much a fashionable draw as a gambling attraction.

In 1918 Spa witnessed many of the last moves of the Germans as the First World War drew to a close. In March the German General Headquarters was established here in the Hôtel Britannique. This is now a school. On 26 October Ludendorff's dismissal was agreed by the Kaiser who was living at the Château de Neubois, 2km to the E of Spa. Later the Kaiser moved to La Fraineuse. It was here during the afternoon of 9 November that he learned of the action in Berlin of the chancellor Prince Max von Baden, who had on his own initiative announced the abdication of his sovereign. Early the next morning the Kaiser left for Holland from Spa station. After the Armistice a German military mission remained in Spa for a few months in conference with the Allies.

Baladeuses are road-trains with open carriages which provide a pleasant method of seeing the town and its environs. Starting from the Place Royale and the Jardin du Casino, they offer a choice of routes. They operate daily in July and August from 09.00 to 19.00; also in May, June, September and October on weekends in fine weather.

The *Pouhon Pierre-le-Grand* at the town centre is, after Sauvenière, the oldest spring. It has been known since at least the 16C. For long no more than an open niche, the spring was given a colonnaded shelter in 1822 and then its present building in 1880. The medallion inside, which bears the arms of Russia, was given by Peter the Great to express his thanks for a successful cure here in 1717. The Livre d'Or, a work of 1894 by the local artist Antoine Fontaine, portrays 93 of Spa's best known visitors of earlier centuries.

A memorial on the outside wall of the building records the gratitude of the people of Spa to the US 1st Army which liberated the town on 10 September 1944. Near this stands the semicircular monument listing distinguished visitors which is mentioned above.

The *Hôtel de Ville* of 1768 by J.B. Renoz is 200m to the N. This has been in turn the Grand Hotel, a factory, three different schools and the municipal library. In the Rue de la Sauvenière, which runs in a SE direction from the Pouhon Pierre-le-Grand, is the *Hôtel Britannique* (see above).

The *Casino*, immediately to the W of the Pouhon Pierre-le-Grand, was founded in 1763 and rebuilt in 1919. In addition to gaming tables, it has gardens, a restaurant, theatre, reception and exhibition rooms. The *Etablissement des Bains*, which was built between 1862 and 1868, is next door.

The waters of Spa are cold and aerated, contain iron and bicarbonate of soda and are mainly used for drinking. They are prescribed for a number of complaints including heart and respiratory problems and rheumatism. The chief springs are Pouhon Pierre-le-Grand in the town centre, and the Tonnelet, Sauvenière, Groesbeek, Géonstère and Barisart to the S (see Tour des Fontaines, below). The bottling works of Spa Monopole are near the station. Visitors are welcome.

Off the NW corner of the PLACE ROYALE, the open area roughly opposite the Etablissement des Bains, is the *Parc de Sept Heures*. Originally laid out in 1758 by the Archbishop of Augsburg, this became an elegant evening rendezvous of the bobelins, the foreign visitors. It has a number of memorials and is now, in part, used for recreational purposes. Farther to the W along Avenue Reine Astrid c 400m from Place Royale is the *Villa Royale*, once a favourite residence of Queen Marie-Henriette who died in 1902. A part is now occupied by the *Musée de la Ville d'Eau*. This has an interesting collection of articles made by Spa craftsmen, notably 'jolités', little boxes and other objets d'art of lacquered and painted wood dating from the late 16C. On request the attendant will loan a description in English of Spa work, its origins and purposes. The museum also has a section on equestrianism. It is open daily between mid June and mid September from 14.30 to 17.30; from mid March to mid June and from September to December on Saturday, Sunday and public holidays. The station is 400m to the SW of the museum. Above it are the bottling works of Spa Monopole.

The TOUR DES FONTAINES, the Circuit of the Springs, is normally made by baladeuse. It takes about one hour. The *Tonnelet*, which became popular in the early 17C, is so named because the water was once piped into a small barrel. The *Sauvenière* is the oldest spring. Traditionally said to have been known to St Remaclus, it was believed as early as 1300 to provide a cure for sterility. Nearby there is an arboretum. The *Groesbeek* is named after Baron Groesbeek who paid for the marble niche in 1651. The *Géronstère*, with rather sulphurous water, was patronised by Peter the Great to alleviate his indigestion. The *Barisart*, although known since at least 1559, was not in popular use until 1850.

The *Lac de Warfaaz*, 2km to the NE of the town, may be reached by car or baladeuse. The road names en route, Boulevard des Anglais, Route de Balmoral and others of the same genre, recall the popularity of Spa with 19C British visitors. On the road to the lake you pass the estate of *Fraineuse* (see the entry under History, above). This is now a large sports complex. The lake, in a hilly and wooded setting, was formed by a dam built in 1890. It offers boating and fishing.

At *La Reid*, 6km to the W of Spa, there is a game park where deer and wild boar are kept. It is open daily from 09.00 to dusk.

8km Francorchamps derives its name from Francorum Campus. A battle was won here by Charles Martel, the grandfather of Charlemagne. Today it is best known for its 14km-long motor-racing circuit. (See also the description of the Musée Circuit de Spa-Francorchamp in Stavelot, below.)

Stavelot and Malmédy share a common history.

Both places owe their origins to abbeys founded in 650 and 648 respectively by St Remaclus, a nobleman born in Aquitaine who became a Benedictine monk. The twin abbeys remained up to the French Revolution the centre of a principality ruled by a succession of powerful prince-abbots. Politically these prince-abbots owed allegiance to the Holy Roman Empire. Ecclesiastically, there was a division. Malmédy came under jurisdiction of Cologne, Stavelot of Liège. Later this division had an important result. When the Congress of Vienna awarded the Cantons de l'Est to Prussia in 1815, Stavelot was excluded and, with Belgium, became a part of the United Kingdom of the Netherlands.

8km **Stavelot** has a population of 5500. The Tourist Information Office is in the Ancienne Abbaye. It is a charming little town in whose narrow, winding streets there are some fine 18C houses.

Stavelot was fought over viciously and badly damaged during the Battle of the Ardennes. On 18 December 1944 the Allies failed to demolish the Amblève bridge below the abbey, possibly because of sabotage by German commando groups wearing American uniforms. This enabled the spearhead of the German attack, the Kampfgruppe Peiper (see also Baugnez below), to cross the river. Despite American success in holding the Place Saint Remacle for about two hours, the Germans were able to swing to the SW and head for Trois Ponts. It was in Stavelot and Trois Ponts, and at hamlets and farms in between like Ster, Renardmont, Parfondruy and Hurlet that the worst of the atrocities against civilians were committed. These were largely the crimes of SS youths who were enraged by their inability to advance in the face of American artillery and hysterically convinced that every house sheltered Belgian and American snipers.

Of the abbey buildings there survive two 18C quadrangles approached through a huge 16C archway. This is in fact the lower part of the tower-arch of the now demolished church. From the garden beyond the archway, steps descend to the main quadrangle with the Hôtel de Ville and three museums.

The *Musée Regional d'Art Religieux et de l'Ancienne Abbaye* is in four main sections: religious art from the 14C to the 19C including church plate, statues, vestments and liturgical books; the story of the abbey and its excavations; tanning which was an important local industry until 1939; and contemporary Belgian ceramics. It is open daily between Easter and 4 November from 10.00 to 12.30, 14.30 to 17.30.

The Romanesque cellars of the abbey house the *Musée Circuit de Spa-Francorchamps*. This has cars, posters and other material concerning the history of the Francorchamps circuit since 1907. It is open daily from Easter to 3 November from 10.00 to 12.30, 14.30 to 17.30; from 4 November to Easter daily 10.00 to 12.00, 14.00 to 16.30.

Finally, in the Hôtel de Ville, there is the *Musée Guillaume Apollinaire*, with memorabilia of this Franco-Polish poet who lived from 1880 to 1918. Credited with introducing Cubism to literature, his poems are a mixture of traditional and modern techniques. Apollinaire's sojourn in Stavelot in 1899 is commemorated by a plaque on the wall of the Hôtel de Luxembourg. He decamped without paying his bills.

The museum is open daily in July and August from 10.30 to 12.00, 14.30 to 17.30.

The sloping Place Saint Remacle, the 18C market-square, above the abbey has a perron of 1769. There is also a stone commemorating the halting of von Rundstedt's offensive in December 1944. The *Eglise Saint Sébastien* of 1751 has a pulpit and medallions from the abbey. In the Treasury there are several richly decorated shrines and reliquaries. These include the *Shrine of St Remaclus of 1263 in gilt and enamelled copper; a reliquary bust by Jean Gossin of 1626 of St Poppo the abbot of Stavelot-Malmédy who died in 1048; a reliquary holding a part of the skull of St Poppo; and a 19C reliquary with the skull of St Remaclus.

On the left of the road to Malmédy stands the national monument to Bomb Disposal Units.

8km **Malmédy**, with a population of 10,000, is sited at the confluence of two small rivers, the Warche and the Warchenne. The Tourist Information Office is at 11 Place de Rome. The town suffered considerable damage from Allied bombing in December 1944. Apart from the cathedral little of interest has survived. Encircled by wooded hills, it is a good centre for walks and excursions into the surrounding countryside. The *Cathedral*, dedicated to St Peter, St Paul and St Quirinus, was constructed between 1775 and 1784. The latest in a line reaching back to the abbey church of St Remaclus, it has a somewhat austere interior with a lofty domed crossing and half-domed transepts. Note the exceptionally elegant Louis XVI pulpit and the fine carved stalls and cathedra. On the altar there are four silver busts of Roman soldiers. They are the reliquaries of martyred members of the Theban Legion.

According to early chroniclers the Theban Legion formed part of the army of Maximinian Herculeus. The soldiers were Christians recruited in Upper Egypt. Commanded by the *primicerius* Maurice, who was later canonised, the legion was sent to northern Italy and then to Switzerland c 287. Ordered to offer sacrifice to pagan deities before battle, the soldiers refused and were slaughtered at Agaunum, now St Maurice-en-Valais, in Switzerland. A basilica was erected there to enshrine their relics c 369. A company, detached to Cologne, suffered the same fate. Presumably the relics in Malmédy are of these martyrs.

The domestic buildings of the abbey of c 1701 are now a school and offices. Just to the W, off Place Albert I in Chemin-Rue, the *Maison Villers* of 1724 survived the bombing of 1944.

MALMEDY TO THE HAUTES FAGNES AND EUPEN. N 32km. The direct road, the N68, follows a zigzag course above the valley of the Warche. A more interesting road leads upwards to *9km* **Robertville**, population 5600. This is close to the beautifully situated reservoir formed by the *Barrage de la Warche*. Below this there is a very deep valley. Take a path of c 800m from the dam or a road from the village to the castle of *Rénastène* or Reinhardstein. Dating from 1354, this was largely in ruins until restored and furnished in 1969. It is normally open only to groups. Beyond Robertville the road ascends to the **Hautes Fagnes** which are described in the introduction to this Route. At *7km* is the *Signal de Botrange* on a forest plateau. The highest point in Belgium, it is 694m above sea level. There is a tower with an orientation table. A further *3km* is *Baraque Michel*, a bleak spot at the heart of the Hautes Fagnes. Here there is a statue to Albert Bonjean, 1858–1939, who wrote about this district. The road now drops through the Hertogenwald to *13km* **Eupen**.

MALMEDY TO BUTGENBACH AND BULLINGEN. E 19km. Follow road N62 for *4km* to the hamlet of **Baugnez**. Here there is a crossroads. The N62 turns S and the N632 leads away in a NE direction to Waismes. At this road junction, sometimes known as the *Croix des Américains*, stands a memorial. It recalls one of the worst atrocities, at any rate in terms of the number of prisoners murdered, of the Second World War. This was perpetrated by Kampfgruppe Peiper which spearheaded the German counter attack in the Battle of the Ardennes. The group was led by the ruthless SS Lieutenant Colonel Joachim (Jochen) Peiper.

Although there have been some changes in the landscape, it is not difficult to picture the dreadful events which took place here in the snow just one week before Christmas Day 1944.

Soon after noon on 17 December the German combat group was advancing N along the minor road from Thirimont which is 2km to the SE of Baugnez. At the same time B Battery of 285th Field Artillery Observation Battalion, having just left Malmédy, reached Baugnez. Here they were directed S along what is now the N62. Almost at once, and taken wholly by surprise, the Americans came under tank fire from the German column. The German infantry stormed across the open fields between the two roads, which are more or less parallel, while their tanks swung the short distance W and then S through Baugnez. It was obvious very quickly that the American situation was hopeless. Their only protection was the roadside ditch. Still there, its inadequacy is obvious. Their rifles useless against tanks and machine guns, the Americans surrendered. Marched back the few yards to the road fork, they were lined up in rows in the open field, now partly built over, immediately to the S of the café. Soon afterwards they were mown down by fire from two tanks. Miraculously 43 survived out of a total of some 150.

After the war a temporary memorial was erected in what is now the car park of the café. The present monument, a wall along the length of a stretch of green, is on the other side of the road. Individual plaques bear the names of the victims and, at one end, there is a chapel shrine.

At *10km* is *Bütgenbach* (population 5000) a scattered township with an attractive fortified farm. To the E is the Barrage de la Warche. The reservoir, which offers boating and fishing, is less wooded and steep-sided than others in the area. Scenically it is not very interesting.

The N632 continues in a SE direction, passing a memorial to the America 1st Infantry Division, to reach at *5km Büllingen* (French Bullange, population 5000). A place of ancient origin, it stood at the crossing of the Roman roads from Maastricht to Trier, the Via Mansuerisca, and from Rheims to Cologne. It was also the site of a Carolingian royal villa.

MALMEDY TO SANKT VITH, REULAND AND OUREN. S 42km. The sector to *4km* the *Croix des Américains* is described above. Continue for a further *4km* to *Ligneuville*, where you cross the Amblève. This place is mentioned in documents of the 9C and 10C. There is a memorial by the Moulin hotel to American soldiers shot while prisoners of war.

12km **Sankt Vith**, population 8300, derives its name from the fact that c 836 the remains of St Vitus, who died 500 years earlier, rested near here while being carried from Paris to Corvey in Westphalia. A settlement grew up around a chapel built to commemorate this event.

Sankt Vith was virtually obliterated by bombing in 1944. The *Büchelturm*, rebuilt in 1961 on a base dating in part from 1350, is as a reminder of the medieval fortifications of the town. There is a small regional museum, 'Zwischen Venn und Schneifel', at 7 Heckingstrasse. This has reconstructions of typical local interiors, some sculpture and a number of exhibits about the history of the town and surrounding area. The museum is open on Sunday from 09.00 to 12.00.

At *12km Reuland* there are the ruins of an 11C castle, successor to a stronghold first mentioned in 963. From here a minor road winds along the valley of the Our into a narrow pocket of Belgium which lies between the Grand-Duchy of Luxembourg and Germany. *10km Ouren* is a village with some scant remains of its medieval castle. Just beyond, where the little river is crossed, the three frontiers meet. From here the Grand-Duchy's main N to S road, the N7, is reached after 6km. For further information on this area see Route 44. A footpath descends the valley of the Our for 14km to *Dasburg*; see Route 44D.

39

Between Liège, Maastricht and Aachen

The little-visited triangle of Belgium, which lies between Liège, Maastricht in Holland, and Aachen or Aix-la-Chapelle in Germany, has some quiet upland scenery, a number of small places worth visiting, and an interesting mix of Walloon, Flemish and German customs and languages. The route described below goes N from Liège to Visé, then E towards Aachen. The total distance is 50km.

From **Liège** follow either bank of the Meuse. The W side is more interesting. On the edge of the city it passes the port area and the start of the Albert Canal with its huge statue of the king. *6km* **Herstal**, the birthplace of Pepin of Herstal, is a large industrial extension of Liège. It is the home of the Fabrique Nationale which manufactures small-arms. Beyond Herstal the road passes below the A3/E40 motorway. From here onwards there are fewer signs of industry.

At (*4km*) *Oupeye* there is a château which dates from the 17C or 18C. It was originally built by the Jean de Corte who owned the mansion in Liège now occupied by the Musée Curtius. The château houses a museum of local archaeology. Around the churchyard at *4km Haccourt* there is a good but much restored medieval wall. This was probably built with stones first used by the Romans.

Eben-Emael, 7km to the N, had a supposedly impregnable casemated fort. Despite a gallant defence, this was taken by German paratroops during the invasion of 1940. The fort may be glimpsed from the memorial just to the E of the village. Note: visitors are not admitted.

2km **Visé**, on the E bank of the Meuse, traces its origin to a bridge built here during the 8C. This town has had a stormy history. It changed hands many times and was repeatedly sacked. In 1914 it was burnt down by the invading Germans. In the 16C *Eglise Saint Martin* there is the *Châsse Saint Hadelin, a silver and gold coffin-reliquary of the 11C or 12C with scenes from the life of the saint. St Hadelin was born in Gascony. He accompanied St Remaclus to Maastricht and Stavelot and founded a Benedictine monastery at Celles. The shrine came from Celles where

Hadelin died in 690. It contains not only the saint's remains but also some of his vestments. The adjacent silver bust dates from 1650. The *Hôtel de Ville*, rebuilt in the original style of 1612, houses a local museum. This is open on Thursday from 10.00 to 12.00.

From the frontier, 2km to the N, a narrow tongue of the province of Limburg extends E for 15km. Known as the VOERSTREEK or Région des Fourons, this quiet, pastoral almost hidden district has six pleasant villages along the little rivers Berwijn, Voer and Gulp. The area was the subject of bitter dispute during the language-frontier negotiations of 1962. In *Sint Martens-Voeren* and *Sint Pieters-Voeren* there are 11C churches.

At *5km Warsage* the church has a Romanesque tower. Continue a further *8km* to the **Abbaye Val Dieu**. The Cistercians usually built their abbeys in quiet, often remote, places. Here in Val Dieu they found a delightful setting. The abbey, founded c 1216, was closed in 1798 during the French occupation. The Cistercians returned in 1844 and there is now a flourishing community here. The choir of the abbatial church, the fourth on this site, may date from the 13C. Parts of the nave and transepts are 14C and 15C, the remainder is a rebuilding of 1870. It possesses a fine 12C statue of St Bernard. The 18C domestic buildings, reached through the archway beside the church, merit a visit.

A diversion may be made to **Blégny**, 7km to the SW of the abbey, where there is a tourist complex. Here it is possible to visit a disused coal mine and its associated museum. They are open daily from April to mid October. The visit takes about 2½ hours. At Mortroux there are museums about cheese, rural life and transport. There is also a boat cruise link with Liège.

Continue to *4km Aubel*. About 3km to the E there is a large Second World War cemetery where both American and German soldiers are buried. Most of these were killed in the attack on Aachen in September and October 1944. The American colonnade-memorial, by Holabind, Root and Burgee, has a chapel at one end. At the other end maps and a four-language text tell the story of the campaign which preceded the final drive into Germany. At *8km* is *Moresnet* and a further *2km Neu-Moresnet*.

The tiny district of MORESNET, with important zinc calamine mines, was at the northern tip of the Cantons de l'Est. Unlike most of the rest of the Cantons territory it was not awarded to Prussia in 1815 but instead was left under the joint administration of Prussia and the United Kingdom of the Netherlands, Belgium took the place of the Netherlands after the revolution of 1830. The district became fully Belgian in 1920.

The *Drielandenbos*, N of Neu-Moresnet and spreading into Germany and Holland, was once a Carolingian hunting forest. It is now a popular walking area with signposted paths. The frontiers of the three countries meet at the 322m high *Drielandenpunkt*.

The German border is *2km* beyond Neu-Moresnet. **Aachen** is *5km* farther on.

The river Sûre in Luxembourg

GRAND-DUCHY OF LUXEMBOURG

Introduction to the Grand-Duchy

The Grand-Duchy of Luxembourg, an independent country with a population of about 400,000 and an area of 2586 sq km, measures some 80km from N to S and some 55km across its central and broadest part. The capital, Luxembourg City, is in the southern part of the country. Bounded by Belgium, France and Germany, and with a history which has brought not infrequent change of rule by all three, the country is a mingling of cultures and languages. Nevertheless it has managed to keep a very distinct ethnic and cultural identity.

The main attractions of the Grand-Duchy for the visitor are its dramatically situated capital, the vine clothed valley of the Moselle, and its attractive, often rugged, scenery.

In the N the Sûre river cuts across Luxembourg from W to E, from Belgium to the German border. Its sinuous course and those of its tributaries, notably the Wiltz, the Clerve and the Our, are marked by wooded, cliff-lined valleys. Romantic castles perch picturesquely on rocky crags. Neat, well-kept villages and hamlets are set comfortably in fertile valleys. A high, windswept plateau offers extensive vistas. Luxembourg is a country of scenic contrasts.

Two places which merit a special mention are *Esch-sur-Sûre* at the end of its long lake and, on the E frontier, the valley of the Our with its fairy-tale castle of *Vianden*. To the S of the Sûre the country is undulating and devoted to agriculture. Between Luxembourg City and the border with France lies the *Bassin Minier*, a mining and heavy industry region which is not without its own charm.

Aspects of the Grand-Duchy

Constitution. Luxembourg is a constitutional monarchy, under a Grand-Duke. Executive power rests with the Cabinet, legislative power with the Chamber of Deputies. There is an independent judiciary. The Chamber of Deputies is elected by universal franchise. Persons over the age of 18 have the right to vote. One deputy represents 5500 electors.

The **Grand-Ducal Family** originated from the House of Nassau. The Luxembourg Dynasty was founded by Grand Duke Adolphe in 1890. Since 1964 the throne has been occupied by Grand-Duke Jean. His consort is Grand-Duchess Joséphine Charlotte, daughter of King Leopold III and Queen Astrid of Belgium. They have five children. Prince Henri, born in 1955, is the heir to the throne. He married Miss Maria Teresa Mestre in 1981. They have five children, the Princes Guillaume, Félix, Louis and Sebastien, and Princess Alexandra.

Language. Three languages, Letzeburgesch, French and German, are used throughout the country. Letzeburgesch, a Germanic dialect, is the normal spoken language. It is also written and has a literature of its own. French

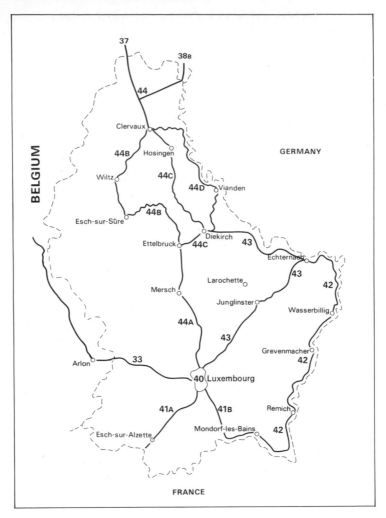

is the official language of the civil service, the law and the government, but this does not preclude the use of the others in, for example, legal proceedings. German is more often the language of the press. Education is in both German and French, the former is used mainly at primary level, the latter at secondary level.

English is taught as the first foreign language and is widely understood.

Industry. The principal industries are banking, iron and steel, agriculture, the media, tourism and wine.

Wine. Luxembourg's vineyards are concentrated in the Moselle valley, where still and sparkling white wines are made. Many of the *caves* are open to visitors for *dégustation* and purchase. For further information see Route 42. The authenticity and quality of Luxembourg's wines are guaranteed by the State Viticulture Institute which is located at Remich.

Walking is a very popular activity in Luxembourg. Many of the most interesting paths are signposted. Those that have been established, and are maintained, by the State have yellow signs. Others have been planned and set up on a local basis. Walkers have a good choice of maps. The 'Circuits Auto-Pédestres', published by the Ministry of Tourism and obtainable at bookshops, are quite popular. A number of towns also provide maps of walks in their localities.

Archaeological Sites. Although they are of relatively minor importance and are little known outside the country, the archaeological sites in Luxembourg merit a visit. Most are of the Gallo-Roman and earlier periods. Almost all may be reached by car.

Notable are the Gallo-Roman baths near Mamer, Route 33; the Titelberg Gallic and later remains, Route 41A; the Gallo-Roman complex at Echternach, Route 43; and four sites, Goeblange, Steinsel, Mersch and Bill, all on Route 44A.

Inspection of the sites should be complemented by a visit to the archaeological department of the Musée National in Luxembourg City, where there are some excellent models and explanations of the excavations and where many of the artefacts found in them are displayed.

History of the Grand-Duchy

Note: Up to 1839 the term 'Luxembourg' can generally be taken to cover both the territory of the present Grand-Duchy and that of the Belgian province of Luxembourg. The historical outline below should be read in conjunction with that of Belgium.

The Roman roads from Paris to Trèves or Trier and from Metz to Liège crossed at a point in the centre of the present Luxembourg City. The station of Andethannale Vicus, now Niederanven between the city and the Moselle, is recorded in the *Itinerarium Antoninianum*, a late AD 3C collection of routes which may have been used for the movement of troops. The iron ore of the Alzette valley was already being worked in Roman times. In the 3C a tower, later known as *Lucilinburh*, is said to have been built under Gallienus where Luxembourg City now stands. The Frankish invasions of the 3C to 5C, and the evangelisation of the 6C and 7C, followed the same pattern as in eastern Belgium.

963. Sigefroi of the Ardennes built the first castle on the Rocher du Bock in Luxembourg City. He and his successors held it and the surrounding lands as a fief of the Holy Roman Empire. William, who died in 1129, was the first ruler to assume the title of Count of Luxembourg. That honour is sometimes claimed for a predecessor, Conrad who died in 1086.

1136. Henry IV of Namur, surnamed the Blind, succeeded to the county. He ruled over Namur, La Roche, Durbuy and Luxembourg.

1196 to 1247. Countess Ermesinda gained the marquessate of Arlon, but only retained that part of Namur E of the Meuse, with headquarters at Poilvache. She granted charters to the more important towns, including Luxembourg in 1244 and Echternach in 1236.

1288 to 1310. The reign of Henry VII. Elected emperor in 1308, he was famed for his strong administration and acute sense of justice.

1310. Bohemia was added to the possessions of the House of Luxembourg. The county was ceded to Henry's son, John the Blind.

1346 to 1354. John's eldest son, Charles IV, was elected emperor. John was killed at Crécy and was succeeded by his son Wenceslas. However, Charles IV usurped the government. In 1354 he returned the heavily mortgaged county to Wenceslas, at the same time making it a dukedom.

1353 to 1383. Wenceslas I acquired Brabant, Limburg and Chiny. At this period Luxembourg extended almost to Malmédy in the N, to Metz in the S, to the Saar in the E, and to around Sedan in the W, an area about four times greater than the present Grand-Duchy.

1383. Wenceslas II, Emperor and Duke of Luxembourg, brother-in-law to Richard II of England, used the duchy simply as a means of raising money.

1411 to 1443. Civil war between the legal sovereigns and the *engagistes*, to whom the duchy had been pledged by Wenceslas II. Emperor Sigismund, last male of the House of Luxembourg, died in 1437.

1441. The *engagiste*, Elizabeth of Goerlitz, ceded her rights in Luxembourg to Philip the Good of Burgundy.

1443 to 1506. Luxembourg ruled by the House of Burgundy.

15C to the 18C. Luxembourg's history was much the same as that of the Spanish and Austrian Netherlands. During the Revolt of the Netherlands Luxembourg remained loyal to the Catholic faith and to Spain. In the 17C the duchy suffered appallingly during the Thirty Years War, especially from the excesses of the Croat and Polack mercenaries of Ottavio Piccolomini, Duke of Amalfi.

In 1684 Louis XIV captured the city and held it until 1697, when it was returned to Spain. During the period of French occupation Vauban fortified the city.

In 1714, at the close of the War of the Spanish Succession, the Treaty of Rastatt awarded Luxembourg to Austria. Its rule lasted until 1795, when the duchy was incorporated in the French republic and renamed the Départment des Forêts.

After the fall of Napoleon the Congress of Vienna agreed that Luxembourg should become an independent **Grand-Duchy**, with William I of the Netherlands as first grand-duke. This was in exchange for the German possessions of the House of Orange-Nassau, confiscated by Napoleon in 1806, which the powers gave to Prussia. At the same time all territory E of the Moselle and Our was joined to Prussia, while in compensation the new Grand-Duchy received the greater part of the duchy of Bouillon and part also of the territory of the former prince-bishopric of Liège. Although sharing the same sovereign, there was no political link between the United Kingdom of the Netherlands and Luxembourg. The powers decided that Luxembourg should be a member of the Germanic Confederation and that the city of Luxembourg should be a Confederation fortress manned by Prussians.

The construction of the high road between Luxembourg and Marche-en-Fammene, 1817 to 1827, greatly facilitated communications between the Grand-Duchy and Belgium

Major change came in 1830 with the Belgian revolution and secession from the United Kingdom of the Netherlands. The Grand-Duchy revolted also and placed itself under Belgian authority. Luxembourg City, controlled by its Prussian garrison, could not join in the revolt and remained under William I. In 1839, under the Treaty of London, the Grand-Duchy was divided into two. The larger, French-speaking, western part went to Belgium to become the province of Luxembourg, the smaller eastern part was retained by William I. This gave the Grand-Duchy its present frontiers.

In 1842 Luxembourg was incorporated into the German Zollverein, Customs Union. In 1867, with the dissolution of the Germanic Confederation, the Prussian garrison was withdrawn from Luxembourg City. The fortifications were dismantled and the Great Powers guaranteed the Grand-Duchy's neutrality.

When William III died without a male heir in 1890, there was a succession problem. His daughter Wilhelmina could succeed to the throne of the Netherlands, but the Orange-Nassau family pact of 1783 barred her from the throne of Luxembourg. The pact provided for transmission of the Crown in direct line of primogeniture in the male descent. The throne went therefore to Duke Adolf of Nassau.

In 1914, despite the guarantee of neutrality given by all the Great Powers including Prussia, Germany occupied Luxembourg. After the war Grand-Duchess Marie-Adelaide abdicated in favour of her sister, Charlotte. All the economic rights that Germany had enjoyed in the Grand-Duchy were revoked and Luxembourg joined in an economic union with Belgium.

In 1939 Luxembourg proclaimed her neutrality, but was invaded by the Germans in 1940. A general strike in 1942 was an effective protest against military conscription. On 10 September 1944 the country was liberated by the Americans.

1950 to date. Luxembourg with Belgium and Holland formed the Benelux customs union, and later joined NATO and the European Economic Community. Several community institutions have been established here. It is the seat of the European Court of Justice, the European Investment Bank, and the Monetry Fund, the European Parliament has offices in Luxembourg City, the Council of Ministers of the Community regularly holds discussions here and, with Strasbourg and Brussels, it is one of the meeting places of the European Parliament.

Relations with Belgium were strengthened in 1953 when Prince Jean married Princess Joséphine-Charlotte, the sister of King Baudouin. He succeeded his mother the Grand-Duchess Charlotte, when she abdicated in his favour in 1964.

See also the entry on the Grand-Ducal Family, above.

Practical Information

Note: only matters particular to the Grand-Duchy are dealt with below. Much of the practical information given on Belgium applies to Luxembourg also.

Office National du Tourisme. *Grand-Duchy*. Enquiries by post to: PO Box 1001, Luxembourg, L 1010. Enquiries in person: air-terminus building, Place de la Gare, Luxembourg City, tel: 400808. Open daily 09.00 to 12.00, 14.00 to 18.00; from July to mid September, 09.00 to 19.30. Closed Sunday from December to March.

There are local tourist offices in all the principal towns.

United Kingdom: 122 Regent St, London W1R 5SE, tel: 071–434 2800, fax: 071–734 1205. *United States*: 801 2nd Avenue, New York, NY 10017, tel: 212–370–9850, moving in July 1993 to 17 Beekman Place, New York, NY10022.

Motoring. Generally the points listed under Motoring in Belgium apply. The *Automobile Club du Grand-Duché de Luxembourg* offers assistance to members of affiliated clubs. Their breakdown service is at 54 Route de Longwy, 8007-Bertrange, tel: 450045. The club operates a round-the-clock assistance service throughout the country with yellow vehicles marked 'Automobile Club, Service Routier, tel: 311031.

Speed limits are 50kph in built-up areas; 90kph elsewhere; 120km/h when so indicated. Note, however, that lower speed limits are frequently imposed.

Railway and Bus. A combined train and bus network operated by Luxembourg National Railways covers some 1500km. Several reduced-fare plans are offered. These include a reduction of 50 per cent for persons over the age of 65, but there are restrictions on the use of frontier stations. A network ticket, valid from the time of purchase until 8am the next day, can be used on all trains and buses. Coach tours operate during the season from Luxembourg City, Echternach and Mondorf-les-Bains.

Accommodation and Restaurants. A guide to hotels, pensions and restaurants in the Grand-Duchy is published annually by the Office National du Tourisme; see also their brochures 'Luxembourg at Bargain Rates' and 'Rural Holidays'. The Office also publishes a yearly guide to camp sites.

Food in Luxembourg tends to be rich. It is similar to that of the Belgian Ardennes but with some German influence. Specialities include black pudding (treipen); smoked pork with beans; Ardennes ham; jellied sucking pig (gras-double); and calf's liver dumplings (quenelles).

Public Holidays. 1 January, Easter Monday, 1 May, Ascension Day, Whit Monday, 23 June (National Day), 15 August (Assumption Day), 1 November (All Saints Day), 25 December, 26 December. When a public holiday falls on a Sunday, the following day is usually declared to be a holiday. Carnival Monday in February and All Souls Day in November are also treated as holidays.

Currency and Banking. The unit of currency is the Luxembourg franc, which closely resembles and is tied to the Belgian franc. While the latter is accepted in both countries, the reverse may not apply. Normal banking hours are Monday to Friday, 08.30 or 09.00 to 12.00, 13.30 or 14.00 to 16.30 or 17.00.

40

Luxembourg City

LUXEMBOURG CITY (population 120,000), the capital of the Grand-Duchy, occupies a dramatic and commanding site on a high bluff above the narrow valleys of the Alzette and the Pétrusse. Because of its strategic location it was for many centuries one of the strongest fortresses in Europe, with ramparts and casemates lining the rim of the precipitous cliffs. Demolished in 1867, the remains of this defensive system offer some fine views over the city. New areas have been developed beyond the bluff, notably towards the railway station on the S side of the Pétrusse ravine and in the N on the Plateau de Kirchberg, which since 1952 has welcomed several European institutions.

Tourist Information Offices. *City*: Place d'Armes, tel: 222809; *Grand-Duchy*: air terminus building, Place de la Gare, tel: 400808/481199.

City Tours. In summer from the bus station which is next to the railway station, platform 5.

Railway Station. In the S of the city, c 1.5km from the Place d'Armes. There are frequent bus services.

Airport. Findel, 10km to the E on the road to Trier. The town terminal is at the railway station.

Embassies. *United Kingdom*: 14 Boulevard Franklin Roosevelt, tel: 229864; *Ireland*: 28 Route d'Arlon, tel: 450610; *USA*: 22 Boulevard Emmanuel-Servais, tel: 460123.

History. The city's history is substantially the same as that of the lands which now make up the Grand-Duchy. Luxembourg may have obtained its name from a 3C tower, later known as *Lucilinburh*, which, it is said, was built during the reign of the emperor Gallienus.

Although there is evidence of earlier settlement in the Alzette valley, it was around the fortress built on the Rocher du Bock by Count Sigefroi c 963 that a walled town began to grow. Some 300 years later, in 1244, it received its charter from Countess Ermesinda.

During the centuries that followed, as the fortress was extended and strengthened by successive rulers, the town spread out. By the end of the 15C it covered practically the whole area now occupied by the older quarters. The present upper town was largely rebuilt under Philip II in the second half of the 16C. Taken by the French in 1684, the fortifications were remodelled and reinforced by Vauban.

In 1815 Luxembourg City became the capital of the new Grand-Duchy under the sovereignty of William I of the Netherlands. However, as the capital of a country linked to the Germanic Confederation, it had a Prussian garrison. When Belgium broke away from Holland in 1830, the Grand-Duchy allied itself with Belgium, but the Prussian garrison ensured that the town remained under the rule of William I. Only in 1839, under the terms of the Treaty of London, was the town able to rejoin the Grand-Duchy. After the dissolution of the Germanic Confederation in 1866, the Prussians left and work was started on dismantling the fortifications. The conversion of the defences into boulevards was completed in 1870.

Since the Second World War, Luxembourg City has become home to many international bodies. These include the European Court of Justice, the Investment Bank, the Monetary Fund, the European Parliament (shared with Strasbourg) and some parts of the European Community.

The part of the city of greatest interest to visitors is not large and can be visited without difficulty on foot. Our visit starts in the PLACE D'ARMES, where there are cafés, restaurants and the city's *Tourist Information Office*. This is a favourite meeting-place and on summer evenings the animated conversation from the café terraces makes the music of the military band almost inaudible. Here also is the *Cercle*. Completed in 1909 and much used for municipal and private functions, this building has a frieze which shows Countess Ermesinda granting the city its first charter in 1244. Just to the N of the Place d'Armes is the Grand-Rue. In origin a Roman road, it is one of the city's principal shopping streets.

S of the Place d'Armes a passage from the Rue du Curé leads into the PLACE GUILLAUME. The Franciscans had a friary here until the time of the French Revolution, so Luxembourgers call this square *Knuedler* after the knotted cords which the friars tie about their habits. Knued means knot in Letzeburgesch. In the square there is an equestrian statue of William II. There is also an amusing memorial to the poet Michel Rodange (1827–76).

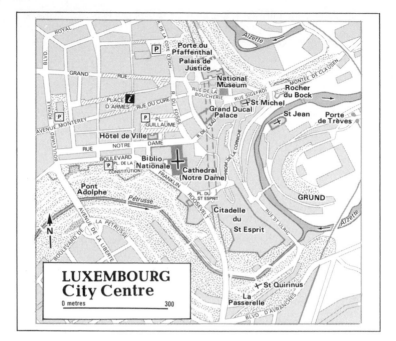

**LUXEMBOURG
City Centre**
0 metres   300

The figure of a little fox recalls Rodange's version in the local dialect of 'Reynard the Fox'. From the E side of the square take the Rue de la Reine to the **Palais Grand-Ducal**. Originally the town hall, this was constructed in 1554 and enlarged in 1741. In 1795 it became the seat of government. Towards the end of the 19C the building was enlarged and the Grand-Duke and his family took up residence there. It has a Renaissance façade with strapwork decoration, but is closed for restoration until 1995.

Immediately to the S is the *Chamber of Deputies* building of 1859. From here follow the Rue de l'Eau in a SW direction to Rue Notre-Dame below Place Guillaume. Here is the *Hôtel de Ville* which was built between 1830 and 1838. Opposite the Hôtel de Ville and flanking the cathedral there are two interesting buildings. On the E are government offices of 1751. These were previously the refuge of the abbey of St Maximinus at Trèves. On the W is the *Bibliothèque Nationale* of 1611, a former Jesuit College.

The **Cathédrale Notre-Dame** was built for the Jesuits between 1613 and 1618 by Jean du Blocq. With twin towers, it is in the Gothic manner but has a Renaissance portal. Note the massive pillars in the nave with their curious strapwork decoration and, in the unusually broad choir, the arms of the principal cities of the Grand-Duchy when its boundaries were at their widest. In the crypt are buried members of the grand-ducal family and the bishops of Luxembourg. Also there is the tomb of John the Blind, king of Bohemia, who was killed at Crécy in 1346. John's motto, *Ich Dien*, I Serve, was adopted by the Black Prince out of respect for his father, Edward III, who led the English troops at that battle.

The S side of the cathedral is skirted by the Boulevard Franklin Roosevelt. To the W is the PLACE DE LA CONSTITUTION, where there is a monument

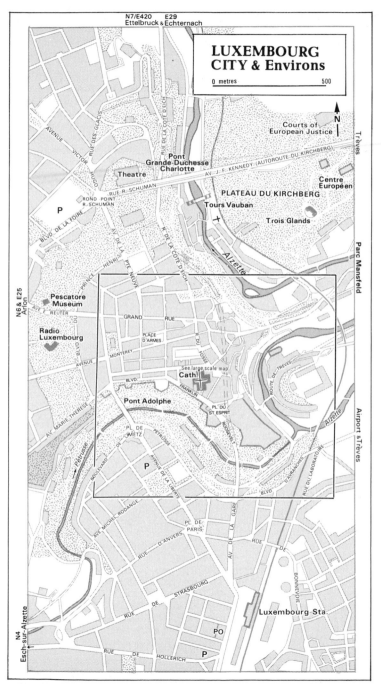

LUXEMBOURG CITY & Environs

0 metres   500

N7/E420   E29
Ettelbruck & Echternach

N

Courts of
European Justice

Trèves

AVENUE — VICTOR — HUGO

RUE-DES-GLACIS

RUE DE LA CÔTE D'EICH

Pont
Grande-Duchesse
Charlotte

Theatre

AV. J. F. KENNEDY (AUTOROUTE DU KIRCHBERG)

Centre
Européen

RUE R. SCHUMAN

ROND POINT
R. SCHUMAN

RUE
R. SCHUMAN

P

PLATEAU DU KIRCHBERG

BLVD DE LA FOIRE

Tours Vauban

Trois Glands

AV DE LA PTE NEUVE

R. DE LA CÔTE D'EICH

Alzette

AV. DU — PRINCE — HENRI

Parc Mansfeld

N6 & E25
Arlon

AV.E. REUTER

Pescatore
Museum

GRAND

RUE

R. DU FOSSÉ

BLVD DU

Radio
Luxembourg

MONTEREY

PLACE
D'ARMES

AVENUE

BLVD

ROUTE DE TRÈVES

AV. MARIE-THÉRÈSE

See large scale map.
Cath.

FRANKLIN

Pont Adolphe

PL DU
ST ESPRIT

ROOSEVELT

Pétrusse

PL DE
METZ

PÉTRUSSE

Alzette

Airport & Trèves

BOULEVARD

DE

AVENUE DE LA LIBERTÉ

P

BLVD

D'AVRANCHES

RUE DU LABORATOIRE

AV. MICHEL-RODANGE

PL DE
PARIS

AV. DE LA GARE

RUE

DE

N4
Esch-sur-Alzette

RUE

D'ANVERS

BONNEVOIE

RUE

DE

STRASBOURG

Luxembourg Sta.

PO

RUE

DE

HOLLERICH

P

to the fallen of the two World Wars and also the entrance to the *Casemates de la Pétrusse* dug by the Spanish in 1674. The corridors and chambers are 24km in length. They may be visited between July and September at the times stated at the entrance. From here there is a splendid view across the valley of the Pétrusse. To the right is the Pont Adolphe of 1903.

To the E Boulevard Franklin Roosevelt leads to the PLACE DU SAINT ESPRIT and to the *Citadelle du Saint Esprit* which was built by Vauban on the site of a convent. Here stands the very moving *Monument de la Solidarité Nationale* of 1971. This commemorates the dead of the Second World War and the resistance of the people of Luxembourg to the German invaders. The design conveys something of the concentration camps and barracks to which so many citizens were consigned. In the chapel, which has stained-glass walls, a rock symbolises the tomb of the victims.

Ahead the valley is crossed by La Passerelle, a viaduct built between 1859 and 1861 to link the town to the railway station. Below is the 14C *Chapelle Saint Quirinus* which is partly hollowed out of the rock.

From the Place du Saint Esprit the *Promenade de la Corniche*, which is for pedestrians only, follows the course of the 17C ramparts northward to the ***Rocher du Bock**. Crowned with a ruined tower of the ancient castle of the counts, this juts out high above a loop of the Alzette. Here Sigefroi built his fortress in 963. A plan describes the various fortifications. In addition to the ruins of the castle these include some of Vauban's fortifications of 1685 and the *Casemates du Bock* of 1737 to 1746. Visiting times: from March to October, daily between 10.00 and 17.00. A monument recalls Goethe's visit to Luxembourg in 1792.

There is a splendid view from the Rocher du Bock. Ahead is the *Plateau Altmunster*, named after an abbey destroyed in 1544. To the E can be seen the *Tour Jacob* and the *Porte de Trèves*. Barely visible on the skyline are the three so-called *Spanish Towers* of the ramparts of c 1400 which protected the Plateau du Rham. Below, in the district of GRUND, are the mainly 17C buildings of the former abbey of Neumunster, which was founded in 1083, and of the former Hospice Saint Jean, founded in 1309. To the N is the *Plateau de Kirchberg* (see below).

From the Rocher du Bock take the Rue Sigefroi to the *Eglise Saint Michel*. Founded as the castle chapel in 987 but many times destroyed and rebuilt, the present building dates from the 17C. Some Romanesque windows have survived on the N side.

The MARCHE AUX POISSONS occupies the site of the Roman crossroads. Later this was the centre of the little town which grew up around the castle. The old houses around the square have been restored and, as part of the Musée National, show typical 18C and 19C interiors and local industrial and popular art. They are open from Tuesday to Friday between 14.00 and 16.45; Saturday and Sunday, 14.00 and 17.45. They are closed on Monday.

The **Musée National** in the former governor's house has a large and varied collection of artefacts which span the ages from prehistoric to modern times. The Gallo-Roman material is outstanding. There are some excellent models and illustrations of the archaeological sites in the Grand-Duchy. These include the baths at Mamer and the palace at Echternach. There are interesting displays of coins in the Trésor. Note the small book of 1546 which illustrates the legal tender of the day, a kind of 16C traveller's vade-mecum (handbook). Among other exhibits are some fine medieval sculpture, a replica of the Hachiville retable (see Route 44A), well-displayed ceramics, arms and armour and objects illustrative of the geology and natural history of Luxembourg.

The museum is open from Tuesday to Friday between 10.00 and 16.45; Saturday, 14.00 to 17.45; Sunday, 10.00 to 11.45, 14.00 to 17.45. It is closed on Monday.

There is also a small but excellent art gallery. Among the artists represented are Pieter Brueghel the Younger, a Calvary; Pieter Brueghel the Third, a Village Wedding; Lucas Cranach the Elder, Caritas; Gerard David, Group around the dead Christ; Antoon van Dyck, Portrait of a Man; Jacob Jordaens, St Simon; Cornelis Metsys, St Jerome; Joachim Patinir, Descent from the Cross; David Teniers the Younger, After the Meal.

The 16C *Palais de Justice* is immediately to the N of the museum. Here a lane descends to the *Porte du Pfaffenthal* which was built in 1685 on the site of a 10C gate. The lane, once a Roman road, continues to a second gateway, the *Trois Tours*. Constructed in the 11C, this gate was altered between the 14C and 16C. From this point there is a splendid view across the Alzette.

To the left of the road there are the ruins of two old gateways. To the N is the *Pont Grande-Duchesse Charlotte* of 1966 which carries the city's ring road across the valley. Below and to the S of this is a fortified footbridge, across the river, the *Tours Vauban*. To the NE is the *Plateau de Kirchberg* (see below). The *Hospice Civil* of 1684 near the river was formerly the convent of Saint Esprit. This was built here at the command of Louis XIV when Vauban converted the convent's original site into the Citadelle du Saint Esprit.

Now we come to the areas on the outskirts of the city.

On the W side there is an extensive wooded park, laid out on part of Vauban's fortifications. In the centre, *Radio Luxembourg* is built on the site of Fort Louvigny. To the N of Avenue E. Reuter is the *Musée J.P. Pescatore*. Occupying a 19C mansion, this has a collection of Dutch and French paintings from the 17C to the 19C. It is closed to the public until 1995 because it serves as the offical residence of the Grand-Duke while the Palais Grand-Ducal is undergoing restoration.

The ROND-POINT ROBERT SCHUMAN, to the N, is an important traffic roundabout. It is named after the man who promoted in 1951 the plan for pooling Europe's steel and coal resources, the precursor of the Common Market. The *Théâtre Municipal* of 1963 is a striking modern building by Alain Bourbonnais. To the E rises the striking monument to Robert Schuman. Its six points represent the founder members of the Coal and Steel Community.

Beyond the memorial, the Pont Grande-Duchesse Charlotte crosses the valley of the Alzette at a height of 85m. On the PLATEAU DE KIRCHBERG there are several European institutions. To the N of the road are the Investment Bank, the Court of Justice, and the Jean Monnet building housing various departments of the European Community. To the S are the Robert Schuman building, which houses the parliamentary secretariat, and the European Centre. The latter is in two parts, an administrative sky-scraper and a conference and parliament complex.

Also S of the road are the *Trois Glands*, three redoubts of an Austrian fortification of 1732, to be converted into a Museum of Contemporary Art by the architect I.M. Pei and due for opening to the public in 1995 or 1996.

At *Hamm*, off the road to the airport, there is an American military cemetery in which General George Patton, 1885–1945, commander of the American 3rd Army, is buried.

For Luxembourg to *Esch-sur-Alzette* and *Mondorf-les-Bains*, see Route 41; to *Echternach*, see Route 43; to *Ettelbruck* and the N of the country, see Route 44. For Luxembourg to *Arlon* and *Namur*, see Route 33; to *Liège*, see Routes 37 and 44.

41

South from Luxembourg

A. South-West

The roads SW of Luxembourg City lead to the BASSIN MINIER, sometimes known as the 'red earth' district. This stretches for over 20km along the French border from Dudelange in the E to Pétange in the W with Esch-sur-Alzette as its principal town. Towards the end of the last century *minette*, the red, iron-bearing rock was rediscovered here. Extracted by the *Minettsdäpp*, as the miners of this area were called, the phosphorus-rich ore was used to develop an important steel industry. Repeated crises since 1970 in the Bassin Minier have brought about many industrial and social changes with losses in the production of steel, unemployment and reduced incomes. However, the Minettsdäpp are a resourceful people and have adapted well to changed conditions. The landscape, so long exploited for commercial purposes, is changing also. As nature regains the upper hand the ugly traces of an industrial past are being softened and blurred. New vegetation covers abandoned, rusting machinery. Tangled vines hang like curtains over the entrances to the closed mines. The woods return to their old glory. This is a country with a strange and different kind of beauty. It is well worth a visit.

The round journey described below is about 50km.

At 18km is **Esch-sur-Alzette**, population 25,000. The Tourist Information Office is in the Hôtel de Ville. This town claims to be of ancient origin, as its name is derived from the Celtic 'esk', meaning a stream. Rue de l'Alzette is the country's longest shopping street and a pedestrian-only zone. The impressive Town Hall of the 1930s has been restored, and next to it is the Old Town, 'Aal Esch', which is being restored and is a pleasant square with pubs, a hotel and shops. In the Place du Bril there is a combined War and Resistance shrine and museum.

At *Rumelange*, 6km to the SE, is the Musée National des Mines. Housed in a disused mine called 'Waalert', it illustrates mining techniques of the 19C and 20C. A train carries visitors for 500m to the underground galleries where the extraction of ore is demonstrated. There is also an exhibition of the tools used in mining. The guides are all former miners. The museum is open from Easter to October daily, 14.00 to 18.00. The last guided visit begins at 17.00. Other months: every second Saturday and Sunday at the same hours.

12km to the NW of Esch-sur-Alzette **Pétange**, with *Rodange* and *Lamadeleine*, forms an industrial community of some 12,000 people. Nearby is the 410m high *Titelberg* where there are traces of 1C BC Gallic presence and of a later Gallo-Roman occupation which lasted until the beginning of the 5C. A geological hike, marked by a 'G', can be followed through a former open-air mine. From Bois de Rodange you can make an interesting excursion to Lasauvage on the small steam 'Train 1900'. This runs from May to September on Sunday and public holidays at 15.00, 16.20 and 17.40. *3km* to the NE of Pétange is *Bascharage*, a brewing town. Here also is the country's only gem factory, Taillerie de Pierres Précieuses. From here return to *16km* **Luxembourg**.

B.   South-East

Total distance 19km.—*5km Hespérange—10km Aspelt* (for *Dalheim*)—*4km* **Mondorf-les-Bains**.

At *5km Hespérange* (population 2600) are the ruins of an 11C castle. Enlarged in the 14C, destroyed in 1483 by Maximilian, it was rebuilt only to be pulled down again by the French in 1679. Continue to *7km Frisange*. About 5km to the W is the *Parc Merveilleux de Bettembourg*, a large, popular recreational complex. Among its many attractions are a miniature train, miniature cars and boats, a Lunapark, playground facilities and a botanical garden. There is a restaurant with a covered terrace. The park is open from Easter to October, Monday to Saturday, 09.30 to 18.00; Sunday, 09.30 to 19.00. Château Collart has been restored and houses the Town Hall. There is an attractive park next to the parish church. Frisange is on the French border and here this Route bears E.

At *3km Aspelt* a short diversion of 2km to the NE is recommended. Just before *Dalheim* a pillar crowned with an eagle was erected in 1855 to commemorate five centuries of Gallo-Roman civilisation in this area. Demolished by the Germans in 1940, the pillar was restored in 1957. A notice nearby records that it is the site of a Gallo-Roman town of the 1C which stood on a crossroads along the great highway between Metz and Trier. First discovered during road construction in the 19C, later aerial reconnaissance revealed a street system and both public and domestic buildings. Excavation was started in 1977. At present visitors are not admitted to this site, where there is little to interest non specialists.

From Aspelt it is *4km* to **Mondorf-les-Bains** (population 2000), the Grand-Duchy's thermal spa. In a beautiful, landscaped setting, two springs are used for the alleviation of rheumatism and of liver and similar complaints. In addition to the usual thermal therapy a wide range of health regimes is offered. Luxembourg's only gaming casino is at Mondorf-les-Bains. It is open daily from 16.00 to 03.00; 18.00 to 03.00 on Sunday and public holidays. Persons under 18 are not admitted, and a passport is required.

From Mondorf-les-Bains the Moselle (Route 42) may be reached at *Schengen* 8km to the SE or at *Remich* 8km to the NE.

42

The Moselle and Lower Sûre Valleys: Schengen to Wasserbillig and Echternach

Total distance 57km.—*10km* **Remich**—*21km* **Grevenmacher**—*6km* **Wasserbillig**—*20km* **Echternach**.

This scenic Route ascends the length of the Luxembourg Moselle from Schengen to Wasserbillig. The river forms the boundary with Germany. Here in Luxembourg's wine country the Moselle flows slowly past vine-clad hillsides where the grapes hang heavy at the time of the *vendange*. There are many *caves* by the roadside some of which may be visited. The small entrance fee charged will usually allow you to taste the wines which may also be purchased. Off the main road many of the smaller towns have retained something of their late medieval character and are well worth a detour.

As a rule the river boat 'Princesse Marie-Astrid' operates from May to September between Schengen and Wasserbillig with many stops en route. On some days it continues to Trier (Trèves) and Bernkastel in Germany.

Schengen, with nearby *Remerschen* and *Wintrange*, form an important viticulture centre close to the borders with France and Germany. There is a bridge across the Moselle to Perl in Germany. 8km *Schwebsange, Wellenstein*, which are off the main road, and *Bech-Kleinmacher* make up one of the most important wine growing areas. The Caves Cooperatives at Wellenstein can be visited daily from May to August, 09.00 to 17.00. At Bech-Kleinmacher there is a wine and folklore museum in a 17C wine grower's house, 'A Possen'. This is open from 15 March to 31 October on Friday, Saturday and Sunday, 10.00 to 11.30 and 14.00 to 19.00.

At *2km* is **Remich**, population 3000. The Tourist Information Office is on the Esplanade. The State Viticulture Institute which guarantees the quality and authenticity of Luxembourg's wines is located here. The area's famous sparkling wine can be tasted at the Caves Saint Martin. The entrance charge includes a free glass of wine or grape juice. The caves are open daily from April to October, 09.00 to 11.30, 13.30 to 17.30. A bridge across the river leads to the German village of Nennig (3km) where there is a Roman pavement.

10km Ehnen is a particularly attractive village with old, narrow cobbled streets behind a wide, verdant river front. It has the only round church in the Grand-Duchy. A wine museum in the village is open daily, except Monday, between April and October, 09.30 to 11.30, 14.00 to 17.00.

2km Wormeldange (population 1100), with Ehnen, Ahn and Machtum, forms another wine producing group. Wormeldange styles itself the 'Capital of the Riesling'. There are visits to the Caves Cooperatives daily from April to October between 09.00 to 17.00.

At *9km* is **Grevenmacher**, population 3000. The Tourist Information Office is at 32 Route de Thionville. The chief town of the Luxembourg Moselle district, Grevenmache produces sparkling wine. The Caves Bernard-Massard offer tastings. They are open daily from April to October, 09.00 to 11.30,

14.00 to 17.30. The Caves Cooperatives are also open to visitors from April to October every day, 09.00 to 11.30, 14.00 to 17.30. A Tropical Butterfly Garden can also be visited, open April to mid October, 09.30 to 17.30.

There is a dolmen 2km to the N of Grevenmacher on the minor road CR137 to Manternach. The road from Grevenmacher to Luxembourg follows the course of the old Roman road from Trier to Arlon. *Niederanven*, 10km before Luxembourg, is probably the site of the Roman halfway station Andethana.

6km from Grevenmacher is **Wasserbillig**, population 2000. This is a frontier town at the mouth of the Sûre. Here the Moselle curves away E into Germany. The Roman funerary column of *Igel*, which is believed to date from the 3C, is 4km to the E over the border. Trier is 9km farther on.

This Route now ascends the winding valley of the Sûre. At first the sides are covered with vines. Later where the valley narrows they are densely wooded. Germany is on the other side of the river. At *15km Rosport* there is a hydro-electric dam forming a reservoir which is popular with water sports enthusiasts. For *5km* **Echternach**, see Route 43.

43

Luxembourg to Echternach continuing to Diekirch

Total distance 35km.—*15km Junglinster* (for **Larochette**)—*10km Consdorf* (for **Suisse Luxembourgeoise**)—*10km* **Echternach**.

Leave Luxembourg City by the E29 and continue to 13km *Bourglinster* where there is an attractive turreted château. At *2km Junglinster* farther on are the masts of Radio Luxembourg's transmitters.

About 12km to the N of Junglinster is **Larochette**, population 1200. The Tourist Information Office is at 4 Rue de Medernach. This attractive small town is set in the narrow, rocky valley of the Ernz Blanche at a point where this valley is joined by two others. On a crag overlooking the town is a double castle. The first was constructed in the 11C, the second in the 14C. Both were destroyed by the French in 1683, but have been restored and are once again occupied. Larochette's beautiful, rustic square, the *Bleiche,* is greatly cherished by the villagers who will not allow cars to park there.

10km Consdorf is a village at the S end of the SUISSE LUXEMBOURGEOISE, an area of thick woods, narrow valleys and deep ravines. This stretches N almost to the valley of the Sûre. It is well served by a network of minor roads and the motorist can see the most interesting parts by driving from Consdorf up the Müllerthal to the Sûre or to the village of *Berdorf.* The church in Berdorf has an unusual feature. The altar table rests on a large Roman stone bearing reliefs of Hercules, Apollo, Minerva and Juno. Most of the houses in Consdorf and Berdorf were destroyed in December 1944 during the Battle of the Ardennes. They were rebuilt after the war.

The Suisse Luxembourgeoise is especially popular with walkers. There are numerous signposted paths to its ravines, caverns, rocks, view-points and other natural features. Some visitors find the area rather gloomy and forbidding and are content with a rather brief *coup d'oeil.*

Continue for *10km* to **Echternach**, population 4500. The Tourist Information Office is at the Parvis de la Basilique. This ancient town on the Sûre
with a splendid abbey, a substantial section of its medieval ramparts and
some Roman remains, is one of Luxembourg's principal tourist attractions.
In summer it is crowded with visitors. Many come from Germany which is
just across the river. Cars, buses and coaches take up every parking place;
restaurants and cafés overflow. Collectors of odd items of information may
like to know that Echternach was the first place in the Grand-Duchy to be
lit by electricity. A plaque on the abbey wall records this fact for posterity.

There was a settlement here in Gallo-Roman times, but the town grew up around the
abbey. This was founded by the Northumbrian monk St Willibrord on land gifted by
St Irmina of Ouren. A great benefactress of Irish and British missionaries, she was the
daughter of the Frankish king Dagobert II. Irmina died c 710.
   Willibrord was educated at Ripon and trained for the missionary life in Ireland. With
11 companions he went to Friesland c 690. Consecrated bishop by Pope Sergius, he
established his see at Utrecht. After converting many thousands in Friesland and
Denmark, he founded the abbey of Echternach in 698. Here he died in 739. His relics,
which still rest in the abbey, have always been greatly venerated.
   From the time of its foundation the abbey exercised great influence spiritually,
culturally and politically over a wide area. During the 11C, under the guidance of
Abbot Humbert, beautiful manuscripts were produced here. Seven magnificent copies
of the bible made at that time still exist. One of these, the so-called 'Golden Gospel',
is now in Nuremberg. It got its name from the gold coloured ink used by the scribe.
   The abbey and the town also saw difficult times. In 1444 the town was destroyed by
fire. The abbey was spared on that occasion. In 1552 they were both sacked by roving
bands of vagabonds and at the time of the French Revolution the monks were
dispossessed by the atheistic invaders. In 1944 the Germans reduced the abbey to a
heap of rubble. The buildings were reconstructed after the war in the Austrian and
German baroque style of the last great rebuilding in the 18C. Fortunately, the 8C crypt
and the tomb of St Willibrord were undamaged.
   Echternach's Dancing Procession, which is held on Whit Tuesday, attracts many
thousands of pilgrims. Dating from the 13C, this celebrates St Willibrord's many cures
of epilepsy and murrain, a plague affecting cattle.

In the Place du Marché is the 15C *Old Town Hall*. This has an arcaded porch
dating from 1520 to 1530 where justice was once administered. An inscription records the granting of town status to Echternach in 1236 by Countess
Ermesinda of Luxembourg. The present town hall, which dates from the
18C, is next door.
   Off the Place du Marché are the *Abbey buildings*. The extensive domestic
quarters are now occupied by municipal offices and schools. Apart from its
8C crypt, the Romanesque *Basilique Saint Willibrord* dates from the 11C.
It has Gothic additions of the 13C and was extensively restored between
1862 and 1868 and again after the war damage of 1944. The crypt, with its
five aisles and plain Romanesque vaulting, is architecturally the most
interesting part of the building. Here there are 11C or 12C murals and the
white marble tomb of 1906 of the saint. In front of the basilica the *Porte
Saint Willibrord* leads to the Orangery of 1761, which is ornamented with
statues of the four seasons.
   To the SE of the abbey complex the *Eglise Saint Pierre et Saint Paul*, with
Romanesque towers, stands on a hillock occupied in turn by a Roman camp
and then a 7C chapel and hospice. The foundations rest on a part of the
monastery given by Irmina to Willibrord. Near the church is the *Musée de
Préhistoire* which is housed in a building of 11C origin. Inside, note the
immense beams and splendid roof. The museum is open from April to
September, Tuesday to Sunday, 10.00 to 12.00, 14.00 to 17.00. The Musée

de l'Abbaye provides information on the Echternach school of illumination, which produced its most celebrated works in the 11C. There is a facsimile of the Codex Aureus. The museum is open daily, 10.00 to 12.00 and 14.00 to 18.00 from Whitsun to September, otherwise on Saturdays and Sundays from 14.00 to 17.00;

The four-arched bridge over the Sûre rests on Roman foundations. At the S of the town a good length of the medieval ramparts has been preserved. The wall between the bridge and the abbey is a later defence erected to protect abbey territory.

Just to the SW of the town centre at 1km from the Luxembourg road a large recreation area has been created around an artificial lake. During the summer months this is very popular with aquatic sports enthusiasts. By the side of the approach road there are the extensive remains of a Gallo-Roman property which developed between c AD 50 and c 400 into a large complex or palace. The outline of this structure is shown largely by the reconstructed lower courses. Some of the original stonework is also visible.

For Echternach to *Wasserbillig* and *Schengen*, see Route 42.

For the SUISSE LUXEMBOURGEOISE, a popular excursion from Echternach, see the description above. 8km *Berdorf* can be reached on foot by a path which passes some interesting rock formations and the 10m wide and 150m long *Gorge du Loup*.

ECHTERNACH TO DIEKIRCH. 30km. This winding road with many fine views ascends the valley of the Sûre. *10km Grundhof* is at the mouth of the Ernz Noire, the valley which leads into the Suisse Luxembourgeoise.

Continue to *3km Dillingen* where a road climbs to the ruined castle of **Beaufort**. Beautifully sited on a steep, wooded slope, this is open daily from April to mid October, 09.00 to 18.00. Its foundations rest on the site of a Roman camp, the *Castellum Belfurti*. The castle has known many owners. It came into the hands of Pierre, Duc de Mansfeld in 1593. (His bastard, Count Ernest Mansfeld, was one of the Protestant leaders in the Thirty Years War.) The oldest part of the building dates from 1150. There followed in 1380 an extension on the valley side and c 1500 the wing with High Renaissance windows was added. After 1646 the castle was abandoned. The owner at that time, Baron de Beck, was the defender of Luxembourg during the Thirty Years War. He built the adjacent Renaissance château but never lived in it. He was killed in battle before he could do so. Apparently the castle was untouched by war until 1944, when it was hit by shells during von Rundstedt's offensive.

The tour of the ruins is by a numbered route. Illustrations, captioned in English, identify the various parts. Do not miss sampling the blackcurrant wine, a delicious local speciality.

5km Wallendorf-Pont is at the confluence of the Ernz Blanche, Our and Sûre. Here the Sûre turns to the W and ceases to be the frontier with Germany. Roads ascend the Our to 10km *Vianden*, see Route 44D, and the Ernz Blanche to *Larochette*, see the description above. For *12km* **Diekirch**, see Route 44C.

44

North from Luxembourg

A.   Luxembourg to Ettelbruck

Total distance 28km.—*7km Steinsel*—*9km* **Mersch**—*12km* **Ettelbruck**.

Apart from Steinsel there is little of interest to the visitor on the main road, the N7, to Mersch.

An alternative route to the W will take you to Mersch through the little visited wooded valleys of the Mamer and Eisch with their pleasant upland views, quiet roads and isolated villages. Gallo-Roman remains and medieval castles are some of the attractions to be seen en route. This rewarding diversion will add no more than 50km to your journey.

VALLEYS OF THE MAMER AND EISCH. Leave Luxembourg by the N12. This road passes through woodland on the way to *Kopstal* on the Mamer. The Roman baths at Mamer, 4km to the S, are described at the end of Route 33. About 2km beyond Kopstal, just before the crossroads of Quatre-Vents, a left turn leads to a chapel and cemetery at *Schoenberg-Kehlen*. Inside the cemetery many of the old crosses, mainly of the 17C, have been placed around the wall. Outside is a replica of a Roman stone with four divinities. The original, now in Luxembourg City's Musée de l'Etat, probably stood on this spot at one time. Two of the gods were removed, perhaps when the stone became a Christian altar. Hercules and Apollo remain. The former, judging by the inscription, doubled for St Anthony in Christian times. In *Kehlen* village there is an attractive little tower of 1576.

Nospelt, 2km to the W, has long been known for the quality of its pottery. Each year on Easter Monday the Emaischen is celebrated here in honour of the patron saint of potters. Then pottery of all kinds and whistles in the form of little birds, *Péckvillchen* , are on sale. The small pottery museum in the village is open daily, except Monday, at Easter and in July and August, 14.00 to 18.00. Continue in a W direction from here to Goeblange. On the edge of the village, a road on the right leads through the woods to the ruins of two Gallo-Roman villas. Part of an agricultural settlement, they date from the 1C to the 4C. The foundations, wells, traces of a stair and, in the eastern villa, something of the heating system remain. At *Koerich*, 1km to the W of Goeblange, there is a ruined castle. Parts of this date from the 14C to the 18C. The village church of 1750 has a magnificent baroque altar.

From Koerich the road descends in a NW direction to the wooded valley of the Eisch, the Valley of the Seven Castles. Continue to *Septfontaines* where, appropriately, there is a seven-mouthed fountain. The castle above the village was founded in the 13C. Facing the door of the 14C parish church are two unusually well preserved and detailed gravestones of 1540. Inside are a painted sculpture group, with vibrant animated faces, of Christ Ascended and a wooden Pietà.

The road now bears E to 7km *Ansembourg* where a 12C to 16C ruined castle perches high above the thickly wooded valley. Beyond the village an ornate baroque gateway leads to the large 17C château which the lords of Ansembourg occupied after they had abandoned the old castle. In *Mariental*, just E of Ansembourg, the convent in the valley was founded in 1232. At the time of the French Revolution the nuns were forced to flee and the building was partly destroyed. For a period in the 19C it was occupied by the White Fathers. Now owned by the government, it is used as a holiday centre for young people. From here a road rises steeply to *Hollenfels*. The defences of this castle, which was constructed in 1380, are formidable. The Great Hall and the Chapel, which has an unusual choir on four levels, are particularly striking and should not be missed. An 18C addition now houses a youth hostel. The church at *Tuntange* has a moving Pietà and some fine modern stained-glass. At *Saeul*, 2km to the NW, there is a 12C church. From here continue to 10km *Mersch*.

Tombstone in the parish church of Septfontaines

7km from the centre of Luxembourg City is *Steinsel* where there is a small Gallo-Roman site. Not easy to find, this is likely to be of interest mainly to enthusiastic and agile lovers of the antique. A minor road climbs steeply at an angle up the wooded hill to the W of the town. Near the top it curves to the right and, leaving the wood, passes a large private property on the right. After c 200m the wood starts again. Leave your car here and follow the signposted track on the right for 300m to the site. Here are the lower-course remains of a once important woodland sanctuary. This was made up of a 1C to 4C temple and several attendant buildings.

At *9km* is **Mersch**, population 4000. The Tourist Information Office is in the Mairie. Mersch, at the confluence of the Eisch and the Mamer with the Alzette, is the Grand-Duchy's most important agricultural centre. Located in the heart of the Gutland, it stores and redistributes most of the cereals and other foodstuffs needed by the Luxembourgers. Now, skills acquired during centuries of prosperous trading are being turned to the development of tourism.

The *Tour Saint Michel*, with its bulbous top, is all that remains of the old church which was demolished in 1851. The castle, opposite, in origin 12C and 13C is largely a rebuilding of the 16C.

There is a *Gallo-Roman villa* some 500m to the SW of the Tour Saint Michel. It may be reached by rounding the N side of the 19C church with its twin bulb-towers and then continuing along the Rue des Romains. The villa is housed in a building on an isolated green plot c 200m beyond 1A Rue des Romains, where the key is kept. (A key is also held in the Mairie.) Much of the area originally occupied by the villa is now covered by housing. The furnace chamber and a heated room, which was supported on *pilae*, have been preserved and a part of the hypocaust reconstructed. The villa may be visited all the year round.

From Mersch a diversion of 8km may be made NW through Fensterdall to *Bill* on CR115. In woods just to the S of this hamlet there is a large 3C Gallo-Roman tumulus. Signposted on the W side of the road, this is 24m in diameter, was originally 6m to 7m high, and is surrounded by a low stone wall which has been largely reconstructed. At *Useldange*, on the river Attert 5km to the NW of Fensterdall, there is a ruined 11C castle.

For *Larochette*, 10km to the NE of Mersch, see Route 43.

At *8km* is the château of *Berg*, the residence of the Grand-Duke. Dating from the 11C and 12C, the castle was acquired by William II of Holland in 1845 and rebuilt by his son in a medieval style. It is not open to the public.

Continue for *4km* to **Ettelbruck**, population 6500. The Tourist Information Office is at 1 Place de la Gare. At the meeting-place of three valleys, this is a major road and rail junction. It has an agricultural training college and is an important business and trading centre for the farmers of the Ösling area.

Ettelbruck was much damaged in 1944. A statue to General Patton on the Sûre bridge to the E of the town marks the point where the German southward advance was checked by the Americans. The Patton Museum is open daily from 10 July to 1 September, 10.00 to 12.00 and 13.00 to 18.00.

B. Ettelbruck to Clervaux via Esch-sur-Sûre and Wiltz

Total distance (direct) 53km.—*17km* **Esch-sur-Sûre**—*10km* **Wiltz**—*26km* **Clervaux**.

The distances given above are for the direct road, N15, between Ettelbruck and Esch-sur-Sûre. However, apart from an unusual small octagonal church at *Heiderscheidergrund* c 3km before Esch-sur-Sûre, there is little of interest on this road.

It is suggested that you use one of the alternatives described below. The road through Bourscheid traverses some of the finest scenery in the Grand-Duchy, while the other road will take you to Rindschleiden where there are some outstanding 15C frescoes.

ESCH-SUR-SURE VIA BOURSCHEID. 34km. Follow the scenic wooded valley of the Sûre through Michelau to *Bourscheid-Moulin*. Here take a minor road up to the magnificent *Castle of Bourscheid* which occupies a commanding site 155m above the valley. The oldest part of the castle, in the centre, dates from the 11C. In the 14C this was surrounded by a high wall protected by seven towers. Roughly triangular in shape, the castle is entered through a 16C barbican. This provides access to the upper area. In the lower part, the so-called Maison des Stolzembourg which was built in 1384, there is a museum. The castle fell into decay at the beginning of the last century and much damage was caused by neglect and the elements. Repairs carried out during the last 30 years have restored it to its former glory. The castle is open daily from March to September, 10.00 to 19.00.

Beyond the village of Bourscheid, the road descends to the Sûre at *Göbelsmühle*. From here continue to Esch-sur-Sûre.

ESCH-SUR-SURE VIA RINDSCHLEIDEN. 30km. Take the main N15 for 5km to *Feulen*. From here minor roads lead westward through the villages of Mertzig and Grosbous to the isolated hamlet of **Rindschleiden**. This is the smallest local government community in the Grand-Duchy. Its modest Romanesque church was built between the 12C and 15C on the foundations of a 10C chapel. In 1952 the 15C **frescoes, which cover the vaulting and much of the walls of the interior, were discovered. The work of unknown artists, they depict various scenes from the Old and New Testaments. A coin-operated light illuminates the frescoes. A booklet in German about the paintings may be purchased from the sacristan. Note also the small sculpted Pietà which forms the central vault boss and the ancient font. It is thought that the font dates from c 900 and that it belonged to the earlier chapel. It was discovered in 1954 during roadworks near the church. Inverted, it was being used as the base of a wayside shrine. The church is open from Monday to Saturday, 08.00 to 18.00.

From Rindschleiden, Esch-sur-Sûre may be reached either by taking the road NE to join the N15, or by following minor roads N to Insenborn on the Lac de la Haute-Sûre.

The direct route to *17km* **Esch-sur-Sûre** passes through a short tunnel constructed in 1850. Esch is a small fortified town built in a loop formed by the Sûre. It was never a place of great importance; a record from the beginning of the 10C gives it a population of less than 150. After its traditional industries of weaving and tanning disappeared, Esch went into an economic decline. Happily, this charming place now prospers. Tourism is the main source of income.

On a steep crag above the town stands the romantic ruin of a 10C castle which once belonged to the dukes of Lorraine. The detached round tower, which is separated from the keep by a deep ravine, served as an outpost. Much of the castle was demolished at the time of the French Revolution and its stones were carted away to be reused in other buildings.

Immediately above Esch the Sûre was dammed in 1937 for a hydro-electric scheme. The **Lac de la Haute-Sûre**, which was formed then, extends for some 10km up the valley. A visit to this area is recommended. From the dam a road, with many attractively sited parking and picnic areas, skirts the S side of the winding lake and leads to 5km *Insenborn*. Another road crosses the dam and climbs to a large parking area which has splendid views over the lake and its surroundings.

Continue on the N84 and N12 to *10km* **Wiltz**, population 4100. The Tourist Information Office is in the château. Built on a steep hillside, Wiltz is divided into a lower and an upper town. It has had close associations with the Boy Scout movement for many years and has many chalets and camping grounds. There are opportunities for canoeing, hiking and other sports.

The town holds an international open air festival of music and theatre in the gardens of the château during July and August. More than 30,000 Portuguese live in the Grand-Duchy and many of these make a pilgrimage twice each year to a Shrine of Our Lady of Fatima which has been erected in Wiltz. On Whit Monday the *Genzefest* is held. Gaily decked floats carry folklore groups through streets hung with yellow decorations, the colour of Ösling's broom which at that time of the year is in flower.

Two castles protected Wiltz during the Middle Ages, when it was an important trading centre. In the 19C its tanneries and weaving mills flourished. In 1942 the people of Wiltz lead the resistance of the Luxembourg people against an attempt by the Nazi invaders to introduce conscription. This resulted in a national strike. The Nazis reacted savagely. Many people were imprisoned or sent to concentration camps. Six were executed.

In the upper town the *château*, which stands on 12C foundations, was built between 1631 and 1727. Today it houses the Tourist Information Office, a home for the aged and two museums. The Museum of the Battle of the Bulge is open daily at Whitsun and from 1 June to 15 September, 10.00 to 12.00, 13.00 to 17.00. The Museum of Art and Handicrafts is open daily from Whitsun to 15 September, 10.00 to 12.00, 13.00 to 17.00. In summer an international music and theatre festival is held in the gardens.

Near the entrance to the château is the *Cross of Justice* of 1502. The statues are of later date. Beside the main road there is a memorial to the American 28th Infantry Division which liberated Wiltz on 10 September 1944. Between the upper and lower towns a memorial incorporating an observation tower commemorates the strike of 1942 against conscription (see above). The church in the lower town dates from 1510 but the tower is much older. It may have been part of a castle. In the church are the tombs of the lords of Wiltz. There are also heraldic decorations on the vault.

17km Antonuishaff is a hamlet at a road fork. Here a short diversion to two beautiful churches is strongly recommended. First follow minor roads to 5km *Hachiville*. In the village church there is a fine coloured *retable which is believed to date from the 16C. Its panels are filled with small, exquisitely carved figures which enact various biblical events including the Nativity and the Crucifixion. The retable, which was stolen in 1976 and later recovered, is now protected by a strong metal grill.

At *Troisvierges*, 5km farther to the NE, the church of 1630 is an artistic treasure house. It has an elaborately decorated baroque screen, paintings from the school of Rubens and the three statues of maidens which give the village its name. They represent the theological virtues of Faith, Hope and Charity. Note the fine wood panelling and the intricate carving on the confessionals and around the doors. The church belonged to the Franciscans up to the time of the French Revolution, when they were violently dispossessed. Adjoining the church is the cloister. A part of this has been lovingly restored.

The Belgian frontier is 5km to the north. For a description, see Route 37.

At Antoniushaff this Route turns to the E for *9km* **Clervaux** which is described in Route 44C.

C. Ettelbruck to Clervaux via Diekirch and Hosingen

Total distance 36km.—*5km* **Diekirch**—*20km Hosingen*—*11km* **Clervaux**.

From Ettelbruck to **Diekirch** (population 5600) is *5km*. The Tourist Information Office is in Place Guillaume.

Evidence of a pre-Roman settlement in Diekirch has been found. From the Gallo-Roman period there are foundations, walls, the outline of a temple and three fine 3C floor mosaics. The mosaics came from a villa which was probably destroyed by the Franks. Somewhat provincial in style and execution, one shows a lion head, another a double-faced Gorgon. Two were discovered in 1926 under the Esplanade, the main road just to the E of Place Guillaume, the third was found nearby in 1950. With some portrait heads and other artefacts of the same period they are kept in the Municipal Museum in the Place Guillaume. Diekirch has also a museum devoted to the 1944 Battle of the Bulge. Both museums are open daily from Easter to the end of October, 10.00 to 12.00, 14.00 to 18.00.

A short distance to the E of Place Guillaume is the *Eglise Saint Laurent*. The first church on this site was built in the 5C on the remains of a Roman structure. A Romanesque style church replaced this building in the 11C. In the 15C the style was changed once again, this time to Gothic. The 11C turret was restored in 1913. Inside the church there are the remains of 15C and 16C frescoes, the work of unknown artists. In an ancient crypt more than 20 Merovingian tombs of the 8C and 9C were found. Some of these can be seen through an opening in the floor of the nave. The church may be visited daily from Easter to mid October, 10.00 to 12.00, 15.00 to 17.00.

In a pedestrian precinct in the centre of the town there is an unusual fountain. This takes the form of a protesting donkey, with legs braced and ears raised, which is carrying a large sack. It commemorates the poor beasts which were used formerly to carry heavy loads up the nearby Härebierg.

About 1km to the S of the town on the Larochette road look out for a sign to the *Deiwelselter*, the Devil's Altar. A 10 to 15 minute walk will take you to a dolmen which was subjected to a rather fanciful reconstruction at the end of the 19C.

At *5km* from Diekirch take a turning off the N7 to the *2km Castle of Brandenbourg* which once dominated the valley of the Blees. This dramatic ruin standing alone on a rocky outcrop surrounded by trees is now silent and deserted. The keep, the oldest part of the castle, dates from the 12C. The other buildings were added during the next three centuries. In 1668 the castle was abandoned and partly destroyed. Those unafraid of the dark will enjoy exploring the eerie cellars and musty underground rooms. Take a flashlight.

From *7km Hoscheid* follow minor roads in an easterly direction for c 8km to the upper reservoir of the Our hydro-electric complex. The **Centrale-Hydro-Electrique de Pompage** is an international undertaking which was completed during the 1960s. It uses a lower and an upper reservoir connected by pipes through the mountain. The lower reservoir, which is 8km long, was formed by damming the Our just above Vianden at the *Barrage de Lohmühle*. The road N from the town skirts and then crosses the lower lake. There are several parking places and view-points. After *4km* it reaches the *Caverne*, the pumping station in the mountain. Here there is a Visitors' Gallery with models and pictures which explain the operation of the complex. Farther into the tunnel the turbines and control room can be seen through observation windows. The Caverne may be visited daily from Monday to Friday at 09.00, 10.00, 11.00, 13.00, 14.00 and 15.00.

2km from the Caverne is *Stolzembourg*. Here there is a château of 1898 which has been grafted on to a medieval predecessor. Continue to *15km Dasburg*. In the narrowing valley of the Our between here and 14km *Ouren* there is no road, only a footpath. See Route 38B.

The *Bassin Supérieure* is a large reservoir on 330m Mont Saint Nicolas.

From the approach roads there are extensive views over both Luxembourg and Germany.

5km to the N of Hoscheid, the N7 is joined by the minor road CR322. For c 21km this delightful, curving road follows the course of the river Wiltz through a wooded valley to the town of the same name. International canoe competitions are held at *Kautenbach*, a picturesque village in a beautiful mountain and forest setting.

Continue on the N7 to *8km Hosingen*. The parish church formerly belonged to an Augustinian friary founded in the 12C. The present building dates mainly from the 17C.

At *11km* is **Clervaux**, population 1000. The Tourist Information Office is in the Castle.

The town of Clervaux lies within a wide bend of the Clerve. Its romantic valley setting is dominated by a large neo-Romanesque church of 1910 and the *Castle*. The oldest parts of the original castle dated from the 12C. It was rebuilt in the 17C. When it was turned into a residence at the end of the 19C the outlying buildings and the defensive walls were pulled down. During the Battle of the Ardennes German phosphorous bombs burned it to the ground.

This castle had a chequered history and has known many owners. It was built in the 12C by Gerhard von Sponheim, the first lord of Clervaux. During the reign of John the Blind it was occupied by the Meysenbourgs. The three tomtits on Clervaux's coat of arms remind us of their name. Later owned by the Brandenbourgs and other lordlings, it was attacked by the Burgundians and sacked by Dutch freebooters. In the mid 17C it came into the hands of the de Lannoy family. They managed to hold it through the difficult days of the French Revolution, when it was known as the *Ferme du Citoyen Lannoy*. Finally, it became the property of the de Berlaymont family.

Completely restored after its war damage in 1944, it is now the permanent home of a notable exhibition of photographs known as 'The Family of Man'. The work of Edward Steichen, an American photographer with Luxembourg connections, this exhibition was shown all over the world before coming to Clervaux. There is also an exhibition about the Battle of the Ardennes.

The castle is open daily in June, 13.00 to 17.00; 1 July to 15 September, 10.00 to 17.00; 16 September to 31 May on Sundays and public holidays, 13.00 to 17.00. It is closed in January and February.

Above the station a chapel of 1786 contains the tombs of the lords of Clervaux.

The Benedictine *Abbey of Saint Maurice and Saint Maur* stands high above the town. It may be reached by road or by way of a pleasant path through the woods. Established here in 1890, the buildings in the warm local stone were constructed in 1910 after the monks were forced to leave France by anti-religious legislation. Visitors are welcome to attend services in the abbey church. There is an exhibition on monastic life in the 20C.

The hamlet of *Lausdorn* is 13km to the N of Clervaux on the N7. From here a minor road descends into the valley of the Our at a place where the frontiers of Luxembourg, Belgium and Germany meet (see Route 38B). There is a new Golf Glub at Eselborn.

For Clervaux to *Wiltz*, see Route 44B and to *Vianden*, Route 44D.

D. Ettelbruck to Clervaux via Diekirch and Vianden

Total distance 48km.—*5km* **Diekirch**—*11km* **Vianden**—*21km Dasburg*—
11km **Clervaux**.

For *5km* **Diekirch**, see Route 44C. After *2km* the N19 turns E for Echternach
which is described in Route 43. We continue N on the N17, climbing out of
the Sûre valley to reach *6km* Fouhren. Here the steep, winding descent to
the valley of the Our begins. Immediately before Vianden a road to the left
leads to a parking area which offers one of the best views of the castle.

From here continue to *3km* **Vianden**, population 1600. The Tourist Information Office is in the Musée Victor Hugo.

After Luxembourg City, Vianden undoubtedly occupies the most spectacular site in the Grand-Duchy. Under the shadow of its great medieval
castle the streets of this litle town cluster round the river crossing and climb
the steep, wooded sides of the valley. Although for most of its course the
Our forms the border between the Grand-Duchy and Germany, at Vianden
there is a Luxembourg enclave on the E bank. Signposted walks lead to
view-points and sections of the ancient ramparts. These are shown on a
wall map near the bridge.

On its sinuous way down to the town the Route de Diekirch becomes the
Grande Rue. It passes the *Croix de Justice* of 1902, a copy of its 14C
predecessor. The *Eglise des Trinitaires* of 1250 has an exuberant rococo
altar of 1758. Now the parish church, this formerly belonged to a Trinitarian
abbey. On the S side is the restored 14C cloister of the abbey. Here are the
tombs of, among others, Maria of Vianden who died in 1400 and Henry of
Nassau who died in 1589. There is also a stone carving which shows the
sin of St Hubert. He went hunting on Good Friday. A lane leads to the
Hockelstour, a relic of the town's ramparts. The *Hôtel de Ville* is a patrician
mansion of 1579 once owned by the Veyder family.

On the bridge there is a statue of St John Nepomuk. He was martyred by
being thrown into the river Moldau, so bridges and those who use them
come under his protection. There is also a bust by Rodin of Victor Hugo on
the bridge. He stayed in Vianden five times between 1862 and 1871. The
house which he occupied is now the *Musée Victor Hugo*. Reconstructed
after war damage in 1944, it is open daily from April to October, 09.30 to
12.00, 14.00 to 18.00. Out of high season it is closed on Wednesday. There
are also a *Folklore Museum* with furniture and household objects from past
times, and a *Toy and Doll Museum* which has a good collection of dolls from
1860 to 1900. These museums are open daily from Easter to mid October,
10.00 to 12.00, 14.30 to 18.00. Out of season they close on Monday. On the
E side of the river a chairlift ascends to a belvedere and café 200m above
the town. This operates daily from Easter to September, 09.30 to 19.00;
11.00 to 18.00 out of season. Vianden's *Nössmaart*, Nut Market, is held on
the second Sunday in October.

Traces of a Roman fort of the late 4C and early 5C have been found on
the lowering crag now occupied by Vianden's ***Castle**. The foundations of
the oldest parts of the existing building have been dated to the Carolingian
period. At the beginning of the 13C it belonged to Count Henry I. A local
ruler of some importance, he was married to Marguerite de Courtenay, the
daughter of Peter de Courtenay who was crowned Latin Emperor of
Constantinople by the Pope in 1217. Some time later the castle passed into

The castle at Vianden

the hands of the Counts of Luxembourg. From them it went to the Orange-Nassau dynasty. In 1820 it was sold by William I to a merchant who gutted it. He removed the roof, doors, windows, anything that could be sold. In 1827 William bought it back. It remained in a dilapidated condition until 1978, when the Grand Duke gave it to the state. Repairs were soon in hand and the castle has been fully restored.

It is open from January to March on Saturday, Sunday and public holidays, 10.00 to 12.00, 13.00 to 16.00; April daily, 10.00 to 17.00; May to September daily, 09.00 to 19.00 or 18.00 in September; October daily, 10.00 to 16.00.

Above and to the left of the gateway there is a balcony from which official proclamations were made. Also above the gateway are the chutes through which boiling oil was poured down to discourage attackers. Inside the complex do not miss the following places: the wine cellar, a large store with two aisles and Romanesque arches; an oubliette; the principal watch-tower; and the 13C great hall of the Count. Above there is another hall and above that a granary. The Romanesque chapel is particularly interesting because of its decagonal shape and because of the opening to a lower chapel which, it is believed, was for the use of prisoners and servants. Note the narrow terrace which surrounds and lights the principal chapel. The Byzantine Room is so called because of its large trefoil windows. Beyond, and now forming a single unit with Gothic vaulting, are a reception room, an armoury, and the private room of the Count. There are magnificent views over the town and surrounding country from the castle's many terraces.

'Before long the whole of Europe will visit Vianden, this jewel set in its splendid scenery...', Victor Hugo wrote in 1871. While his prophecy has not been fulfilled so far, Vianden has become one of the most popular places to visit in the Grand Duchy of Luxembourg.

Alternative Place Names
(Flemish, French and Other)

Selected names below are listed alphabetically under North (Flemish) Belgium, South (Walloon) Belgium, and Cantons de l'Est and Various.
Belgium = België or La Belgique
Brussels = Brussel or Bruxelles

North (Flemish) Belgium

Flemish	French	Other
Aalst	Alost	
Albert Strand	Albert Plage	
Antwerpen	Anvers	Eng: Antwerp
Baarle-Hertog	Baarle-Duc	
Brugge	Bruges	
Borgloon	Looz	
De Haan	Le Coq	
De Panne	La Panne	
Diksmuide	Dixsmude	
Gent	Gand	Eng: Ghent
Geraardsbergen	Grammont	
Halle	Hal	
Haspengouw	Hesbaye	
Ieper	Ypres	
Ijzer	Yser	
Kempen	Campine	
Koksijde	Coxyde	
Kortrijk	Courtrai	
Leie	Lys	
Leuven	Louvain	
Lier	Lierre	
Maas	Meuse	
Mechelen	Malines	
Meen	Menin	
Mensen	Messines	
Neerheylissem	Hélécine	
Oostende	Ostende	Eng: Ostend
Oudenaarde	Audenarde	
Roselare	Roulers	
Ronse	Renaix	
Schelde	Escaut	Eng: Scheldt
Scherpenheuvel	Montaigu	
Sint Truiden	Saint Trond	
Temse	Tamise	
Tienen	Tirlemont	
Tongeren	Tongres	
Torhout	Thourout	
Veurne	Furnes	
Vlaanderen	La Flandre	Eng: Flanders
-Voeren	Fourons-	
Zeebrugge	Zeebruges	
Zoutleeuw	Léau	

South (Walloon) Belgium

French	Flemish	Other
Ath	Aat	
Braine-le-Château	Kasteelbrakel	
Braine-le-Comte	's Gravenbrakel	
Clabecq	Klabbeek	
Comines	Komen	
Enghien	Edingen	
Escaut	Schelde	Eng: Scheldt
Hainaut	Henegouwen	
Jodoigne	Geldenaken	
La Hulpe	Ter Hulpen	
Lessines	Lessen	
Liège	Luik	Ger: Lüttich
Lys	Leie	
Meuse	Maas	
Mons	Bergen	
Mouscron	Moeskroen	
Namur	Namen	
Nivelles	Nijvel	
Oreye	Oerle	
Othée	Elch	
Saintes	Sint Renelde	
Soignies	Zinnik	
Tournai	Doornik	
Tubize	Tubeke	
Waremme	Borgworm	
Wavre	Waver	

Cantons de l'Est and Various

German	French	Flemish
Aachen	Aix-la-Chapelle	Aken
Büllingen	Bullange	
	Dunkerque	Duinkerke
	Lille	Rijsel
Monschau	Montjoie	
Mosel	Moselle	
Reinhardstein	Rénastène	
Sankt-Vith	Saint-Vith	
Trier	Trèves	
Weismes	Waimes	

INDEX TO ARTISTS

INDEX

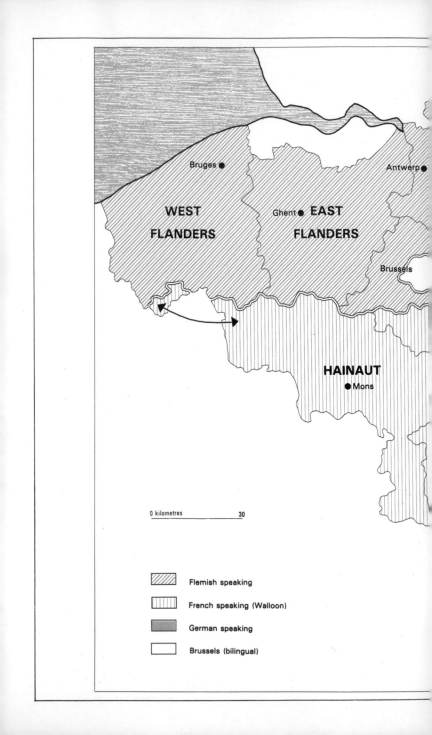

WEST
FLANDERS

EAST
FLANDERS

Bruges ●

Ghent ●

Antwerp ●

Brussels

HAINAUT

● Mons

0 kilometres   30

Flemish speaking

French speaking (Walloon)

German speaking

Brussels (bilingual)

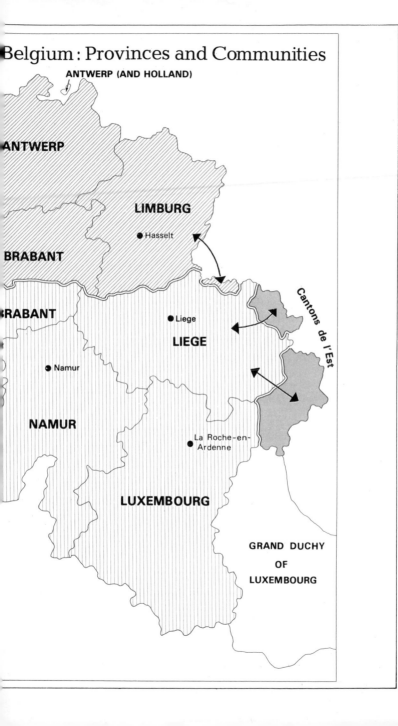

Belgium: Provinces and Communities

ANTWERP (AND HOLLAND)

ANTWERP

LIMBURG

● Hasselt

BRABANT

BRABANT

● Liege

LIEGE

● Namur

NAMUR

Cantons de l'Est

● La Roche-en-
Ardenne

LUXEMBOURG

GRAND DUCHY

OF

LUXEMBOURG

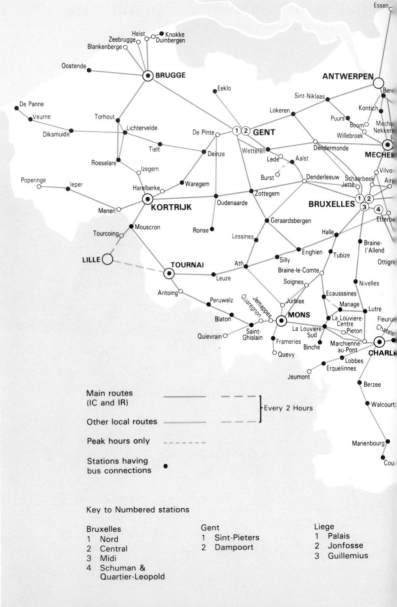

Main routes
(IC and IR)

Other local routes

Peak hours only

Stations having
bus connections

} Every 2 Hours

Key to Numbered stations

Bruxelles
1 Nord
2 Central
3 Midi
4 Schuman &
   Quartier-Leopold

Gent
1 Sint-Pieters
2 Dampoort

Liege
1 Palais
2 Jonfosse
3 Guillemius

Belgian National Railways

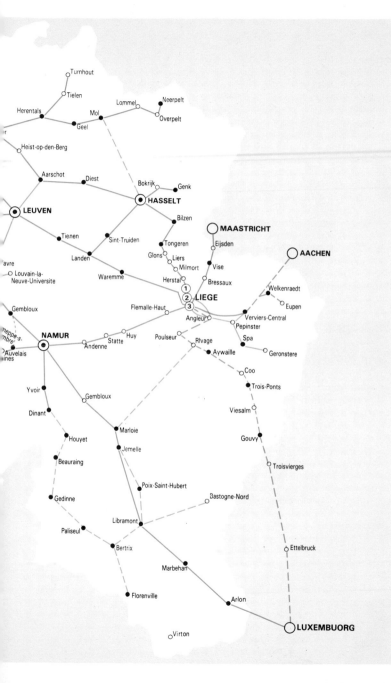

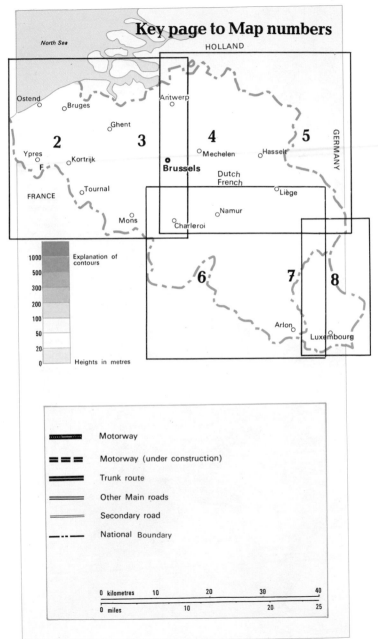

Key page to Map numbers

North Sea

HOLLAND

Ostend

Bruges

Antwerp

Ghent

2

3

4

5

GERMANY

Ypres

F.

Kortrijk

Mechelen

Hasselt

Brussels

Dutch

French

FRANCE

Tournai

Liège

Namur

Mons

Charleroi

| 1000 |
| 500 |
| 300 |
| 200 |
| 100 |
| 50 |
| 20 |
| 0 |

Explanation of contours

6

7

8

Heights in metres

Arlon

Luxembourg

| Motorway |
| Motorway (under construction) |
| Trunk route |
| Other Main roads |
| Secondary road |
| National Boundary |

| 0 kilometres | 10 | 20 | 30 | 40 |
| 0 miles | | 10 | 20 | 25 |

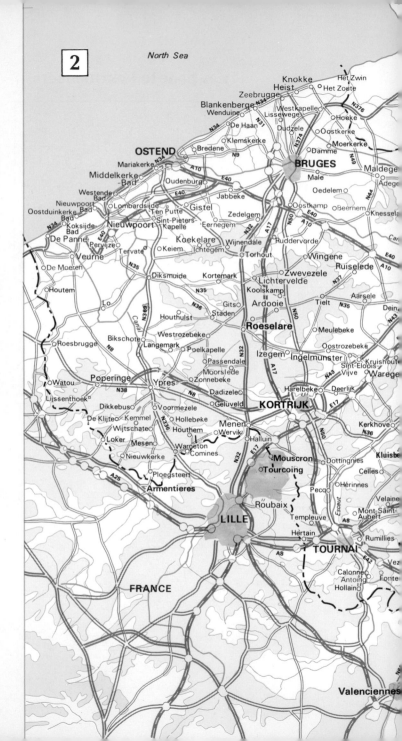

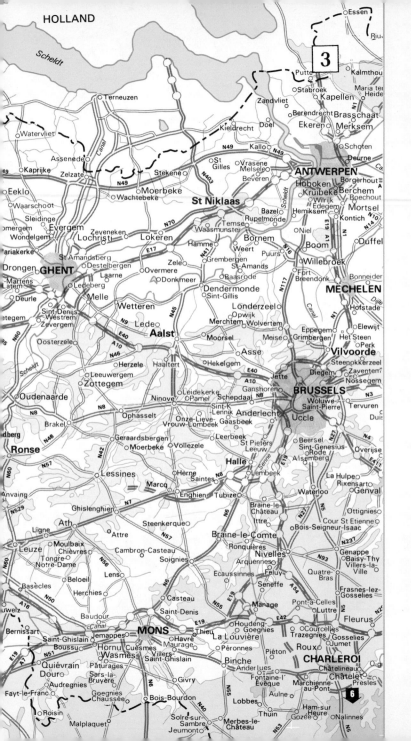

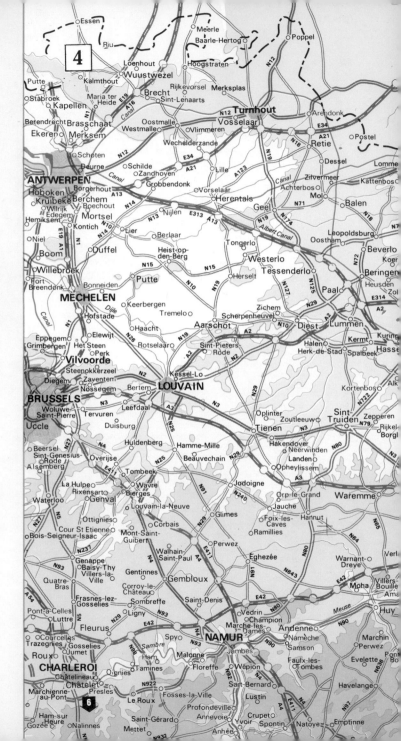

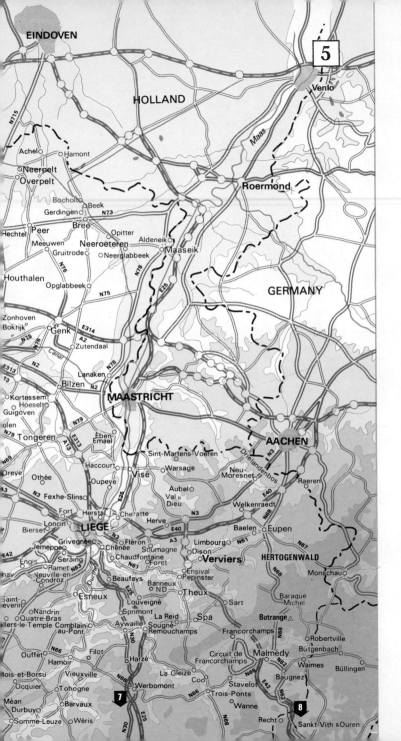

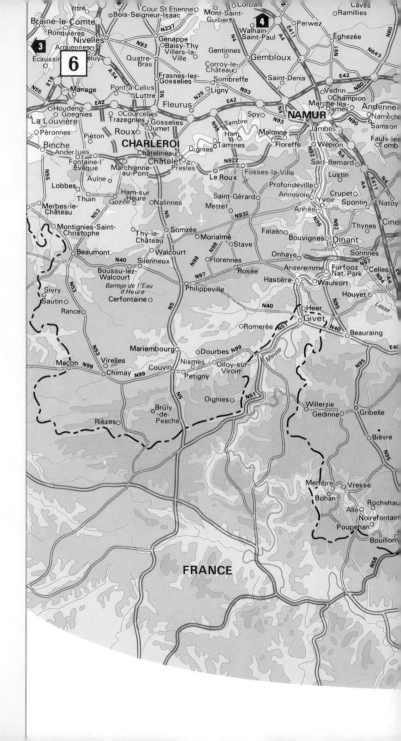

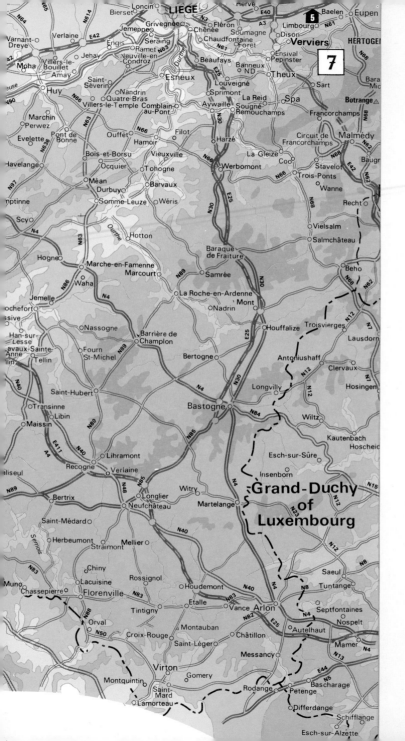

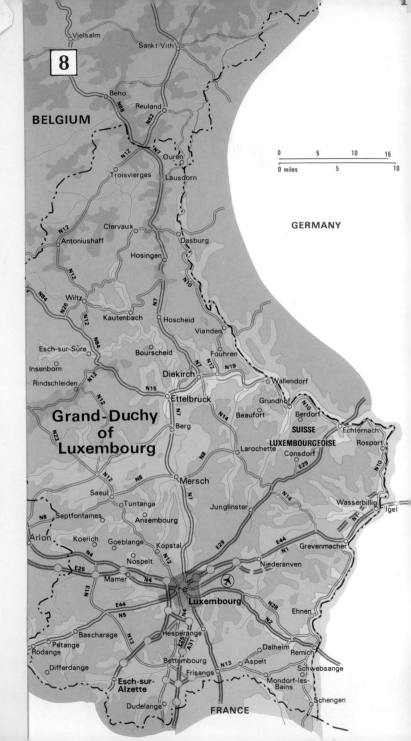